OXFORD WORLD'

TALES OF GLASS T
AND GO[

CHARLOTTE (1816–55), BRANWELL (1817–48), EMILY (1818–48), and ANNE BRONTË (1820–49) were born in Thornton, West Yorkshire, and moved to Haworth in 1820 where their clergyman father Patrick was perpetual curate. Their mother died in 1821 and her sister took care of the five daughters and one son. In 1824 the girls, except Anne, were sent to a boarding school where the eldest, Maria and Elizabeth, became ill, returning home to die in 1825; Charlotte and Emily were brought home soon after. For the next six years, the young Brontës were educated at home and developed a rich fantasy life amongst themselves, inspired by Branwell's twelve soldiers and the 'plays' they wove around their imaginary characters. They wrote dozens of poems, tales, dramas, and magazines that developed into the Glass Town, Angrian, and Gondal sagas.

The Brontës all pursued careers in teaching but aspired to be famous writers and artists. Charlotte attended school at Roe Head, Mirfield (1831–3), and returned to teach (1835–8), when Emily briefly and then Anne became pupils. Charlotte, Emily, and Anne held various teaching posts, and Emily and Charlotte attended the Héger Pensionnnat in Brussels in 1842–3. Branwell tried various occupations in addition to teaching but lost his positions and took to alcohol and opium. Yet he was the first of the Brontës to achieve publication, signing his poems 'Northangerland', the Angrian character with whom he was still obsessed. In 1846 the sisters published *Poems by Currer, Ellis, and Acton Bell*, the pseudonyms they used for all their published writings. *Jane Eyre* was published in 1847 and achieved immediate success. Emily's only novel *Wuthering Heights* (1847) received savage reviews and few sales, but is now acknowledged as one of the greatest books in English literature. Anne's *Agnes Grey* was published at the same time, and her second novel, *The Tenant of Wildfell Hall*, appeared in 1848. Both Branwell and Emily died later that year, and Anne died in 1849. Charlotte struggled on alone, publishing *Shirley* in 1849 and *Villette* in 1853. She died in March 1855, a few months after marrying the Revd A. B. Nicholls, her father's curate. Her first novel *The Professor* was published posthumously.

CHRISTINE ALEXANDER is a Scientia Professor of English at the University of New South Wales, and a Fellow of the Australian Academy of the Humanities. She has written extensively on the Brontës, including *The Oxford Companion to the Brontës* (2003, co-authored with Margaret Smith).

OXFORD WORLD'S CLASSICS

*For over 100 years Oxford World's Classics have brought
readers closer to the world's great literature. Now with over 700
titles—from the 4,000-year-old myths of Mesopotamia to the
twentieth century's greatest novels—the series makes available
lesser-known as well as celebrated writing.*

*The pocket-sized hardbacks of the early years contained
introductions by Virginia Woolf, T. S. Eliot, Graham Greene,
and other literary figures which enriched the experience of reading.
Today the series is recognized for its fine scholarship and
reliability in texts that span world literature, drama and poetry,
religion, philosophy, and politics. Each edition includes perceptive
commentary and essential background information to meet the
changing needs of readers.*

OXFORD WORLD'S CLASSICS

THE BRONTËS

Tales of Glass Town, Angria, and Gondal
Selected Writings

Edited with Introduction and Notes by
CHRISTINE ALEXANDER

OXFORD
UNIVERSITY PRESS

OXFORD

UNIVERSITY PRESS

Great Clarendon Street, Oxford ox2 6DP
Oxford University Press is a department of the University of Oxford.
It furthers the University's objective of excellence in research, scholarship,
and education by publishing worldwide in

Oxford New York

Auckland Cape Town Dar es Salaam Hong Kong Karachi
Kuala Lumpur Madrid Melbourne Mexico City Nairobi
New Delhi Shanghai Taipei Toronto

With offices in

Argentina Austria Brazil Chile Czech Republic France Greece
Guatemala Hungary Italy Japan Poland Portugal Singapore
South Korea Switzerland Thailand Turkey Ukraine Vietnam

Oxford is a registered trade mark of Oxford University Press
in the UK and in certain other countries

Published in the United States
by Oxford University Press Inc., New York

British Library Cataloguing in Publication Data

Data available

Library of Congress Cataloging in Publication Data

Data available

Typeset by Glyph International, Bangalore, India
Printed in Great Britain
on acid-free paper by Clays Ltd., Elcograf S.p.A.

ISBN 978-0-19-282763-0

ACKNOWLEDGEMENTS

This edition has been many years in the making and many people have contributed to supporting and encouraging its outcome. Preeminent among these is Judith Luna, my commissioning editor at Oxford University Press: a special debt of gratitude goes to her for her patience during a time of personal difficulty and for her support and advice for this project that showcases the writing of the imaginary worlds of all four Brontës. I am also grateful to the librarians where the Brontë manuscripts are located, in particular to Ann Dinsdale and Sarah Laycock at the Brontë Parsonage Museum Library in Haworth, Yorkshire, and to Christine Nelson at the Pierpont Morgan Library in New York. Other libraries that have generously made their collections available to me include: the British Library; the Harry Ransom Center, University of Texas at Austin; the Houghton Library and Widener Library at Harvard University; the Huntington Library; the New York Public Library (Berg Collection); Princeton University Libraries (Robert H. Taylor Collection); and the Wellesley College Library. The librarians at the University of New South Wales Library have provided valuable assistance, especially Julie Nolan and Interlibrary Loans. I also owe a debt to previous Brontë scholars referred to in the Explanatory Notes, especially editors who, like myself, have transcribed the minuscule Brontë script and wrestled with difficult editorial decisions.

I am indebted to the Australian Research Council that has supported my research over many years, and to the Faculty of Arts at the University of New South Wales that enabled me to check the manuscripts in the UK and USA. Princeton University Library generously awarded me the Firestone Library Fellowship.

I would like to thank Judy McKenzie, Richard Frith, and Donna Couto, who have all been excellent research assistants at different times during the project; and Rowena Anketell for her efficient copy editing. My special thanks go as always to my husband, Professor Peter Alexander, for his unfailing support 'in sickness and in health'.

Dedicated to the memory of my daughter

Rebecca Mary Alexander

20 October 1981–7 October 1999

who shared my enthusiasm for the Brontës and
illustrated the characters in their early writings

CONTENTS

BRANWELL BRONTË

EMILY BRONTË

LIST OF ILLUSTRATIONS

INTRODUCTION

While researching her *Life of Charlotte Brontë* (1857), Elizabeth Gaskell was lent a 'most extraordinary' packet of papers containing much of the Brontë juvenilia. She found them 'curious' but important enough to necessitate the hasty rewriting of some forty pages to make way for a new chapter on Charlotte's early writings. She speaks of the 'immense amount of manuscript, in an inconceivably small space; tales, dramas, poems, romances, written principally by Charlotte, in a hand which it is almost impossible to decipher without the aid of a magnifying glass'.[1] Unaware of the encompassing sagas of Glass Town, Angria, and Gondal, and quoting fragments from only the earliest manuscripts at the top of the packet, she appears to calmly dismiss the juvenilia as comprehensible only to 'the bright little minds for whom it was intended'. Her subdued tone in the biography, however, is in stark contrast to the excited letter she wrote to her publisher George Smith after securing these manuscripts: 'they are the wildest & most incoherent things, . . . *all* purporting to be written, or addressed to some member of the Wellesley family. They give one the idea of creative power carried to the verge of insanity.'[2] She thought them similar to some manuscripts of William Blake she had recently seen, yet she gave no hint to the public of the imaginative excess she detected in this 'wild weird writing'. The Brontë children's early addiction to a fantasy world and the later sexually charged adolescent writing, that she undoubtedly noticed[3] and that Charlotte herself referred to as her 'world below', would not square with Gaskell's mission to present her subject in a heroic light, as a misjudged rational and suffering heroine.[4]

[1] Elizabeth Gaskell, *The Life of Charlotte Brontë* (1857), ed. Angus Easson (Oxford: Oxford University Press, 1996), 64.

[2] J. A. V. Chapple and Arthur Pollard (eds.), *The Letters of Mrs Gaskell* (Manchester: Manchester University Press, Mandolin: 1997), 398.

[3] It is significant that although Gaskell includes a facsimile page of the opening of Brontë's story 'The Secret', she says nothing at all about the content of this manuscript, a tale of blackmail, jealousy, and murder, demonstrating the sadistic power of men over women, and suggestions of infanticide—themes inappropriate for the adolescent Victorian girl, and certainly not in keeping with Gaskell's representation of Brontë as a friend to be vindicated from the charges of coarseness and immorality that reviewers found in *Jane Eyre*.

[4] I have explored Gaskell's practice and motivation for her handling of Charlotte's juvenilia in 'Elizabeth Gaskell and Victorian Juvenilia', *Gaskell Society Journal*, 18 (2004), 1–15.

We are now free to discover and appreciate what Gaskell felt she was obliged to conceal: a fictional world of stories, plays, and poems that document the unfettered imaginations of four aspiring young writers—Charlotte, Branwell, Emily, and Anne—as they explore their intellectual and physical surroundings. The Brontë juvenilia are rich in allusion to other books and writers, to art and artistic techniques, to history, geography, current events, and social attitudes. Through writing the young authors create and experience vicariously a world of sexual passion and political intrigue beyond the range of their years or parsonage upbringing. Their juvenilia represent the apprentice works of writers who produced such renowned novels as *Jane Eyre*, *Wuthering Heights*, and *The Tenant of Wildfell Hall*; but they are also important documents in themselves: evidence of the making of literary minds, the collaboration and particularly the rivalry of writers—that 'intelligent partisanship'[5] with which the Brontës imitated and 'played at' the lively publishing scene of the early nineteenth century. The Brontë juvenilia provide the richest record we have of youthful literary activity:[6] a fascinating uncensored world where the young writer can create a parallel political and social space, experiment with adult relationships, test genre and technique, and experience the power of the author and editor.

The Brontës' Collaboration and Literary Play

Two of the early manuscripts that captured Gaskell's attention were 'History of the Year' (1829) and 'Tales of the Islanders'. Together they tell and retell the genesis of the Brontë 'plays'—the now-famous story of the Reverend Patrick Brontë's birthday gift to his 12-year-old son Branwell of a box of twelve wooden toy soldiers, in June 1829. Charlotte, a year older than her brother, and Emily and Anne, several years younger, each excitedly claimed ownership of a soldier who became their special character. 'The Twelves', or Young Men, as the soldiers were called—all veterans of the Duke of Wellington's army in the Peninsular War (1808–14)—provided the catalyst for the imaginary play that grew into the Glass Town and Angrian saga. There had been earlier 'plays' but the Young Men, together with 'Tales of the Islanders', captured the children's imaginations and provided a source of literary inspiration for the next twenty years.

[5] Gaskell, *Life of Charlotte Brontë*, 54.

[6] Only Jane Austen's brilliantly ironic juvenilia rivals that of the Brontës, but it is neither as voluminous nor as revealing of the inner life of its author.

A striking feature of this early imaginative play is the confidence and bravado of the players that belies the usual story of the Brontës' desolate childhood, derived from Gaskell's account of the four motherless children huddled together against a hostile environment, living with their morose father in an isolated village on the edge of the Yorkshire Moors. It is true that they were constantly reminded of death and in need of emotional security: the parsonage was surrounded on two sides by the graveyard and by the time the Young Men's Play began the family had lost three of its eight members. Their mother had died in 1821 when Charlotte was 5 and Anne only 1 year old; and their two older sisters, Maria and Elizabeth, had both died of consumption in 1825. But they were not isolated. They were cared for by the good-natured servant Tabitha Aykroyd and their aunt Elizabeth Branwell—practical, stern, and religious—who lived with them and helped to provide stability and order in their chaotic early lives. Their parsonage home was a centre of social life, close to the church, the Sunday school, and public houses; and Haworth itself was actually a busy manufacturing community important to the wool trade of the district.[7] As parsonage children they would have been relatively isolated from the village children, but they had little need to look beyond their family circle for friendship and entertainment. Close in age, intelligent and active, they naturally formed what their father called 'a little society amongst themselves'.[8]

It was their father, however, who was central to the happiness of the four surviving children. Patrick Brontë's unusually liberal views meant that his children had an unconventional Victorian childhood. Strongly influenced by Wordsworth's attitudes to education, he encouraged them to roam freely on the moors, at first in the care of a servant, and allowed them to read whatever they liked from his bookshelves. He gave them basic lessons in literacy, geography, history, and mathematics, and even managed despite his poor clergy salary to pay for art and music lessons by the best teachers in the district. He taught Branwell the classics and their aunt endeavoured to train the girls in the female accomplishment of sewing. But it was their father's passion for poetry and the classics, his own early 'indescribable pleasure' in writing, his enthusiasm for military and literary heroes of the day, for politics and military campaigns, and his love of nature, that provided the Brontës with a rich, if eclectic, imaginative life.

[7] C. Alexander and M. Smith, *The Oxford Companion to the Brontës* (Oxford: Oxford University Press), 235–7. Even by 1820 when the Brontës arrived in Haworth, there were eighteen small textile mills, and by 1850 over 2,000 people were employed in the spinning and weaving industry.

[8] *Brontë Society Transactions* (1933), 8(43), 92.

'This is the Duke of Wellington! It shall be mine!' shouted Charlotte as she snatched up her toy soldier and named it after her father's revered hero. The real Duke, his family and friends, became her fictional equivalents in the children's plays, and when his character proved too restricting Charlotte replaced her chief hero by imaginary recreations of his two sons: Arthur, Marquis of Douro, and his younger brother Charles Wellesley. Their names and early characters, especially that of the mischievous Charles, are transferred to the Duke's fictitious sons: Arthur, Marquis of Douro (later Duke of Zamorna and King of Angria), and Lord Charles Wellesley (later Charles Townshend). Branwell chose Wellington's adversary Napoleon, before creating his hero Alexander Percy ('Rogue', later Lord Ellrington and Earl of Northangerland); and Emily and Anne nominated soldiers who later grew into Parry and Ross, the venerated kings of the Glass Town saga, named after famous explorers. The sheer delight and authority of Charlotte's claim of the Duke of Wellington characterizes the enthusiastic naming and recording of characters, institutions, and landscape in imitation of the adult world. As if sensing its significance, Charlotte and Branwell immediately documented the event as 'History' in language charged with excitement, drew up maps and tables, and over the following year reworked the advent of their Glass Town saga in fictional form. 'A Romantic Tale' (also called 'The Twelve Adventurers') tells, in the form of a popular travel narrative, the story of the Young Men's voyage to the west coast of Africa, their settlement after warfare and negotiation with the indigenous Ashantee tribes, their election of Arthur Wellesley, Duke of Wellington, as their leader, and the founding of Great Glass Town at the delta of the River Niger. Branwell's 'History of the Young Men', written two years later in 1831, documents the same events in exhaustive detail and provides a map of the new kingdoms. Like their models from the real world, the Brontës were colonizers—both literally and imaginatively—imitating and reconfiguring the political and social world of nineteenth-century England that they encountered in their extensive reading.

The juvenilia tell us much about the reading of the young Brontës. Soon after the death of their mother, Maria, the eldest of what were then five siblings, would gather the children together in their tiny nursery that doubled as a bedroom and read newspapers to them, a practice Charlotte continued after Maria's death. As the earliest manuscripts demonstrate, the children were passionate little Tories, mimicking their father's views and absorbing the attitude and tone of *Blackwood's Edinburgh Magazine*, whose back-issues were lent to the family by a parishioner. Here we find, together with *Fraser's Magazine* to which the Brontës subscribed in 1832, the largely masculine culture of individual genius and military heroism that was to fuel the young Brontës' imaginations. The advent of each instalment was as exciting as a new video game nowadays, revealing adventures well beyond their reach: the explorations of Parry and Ross in the Arctic, campaigns of the British Army in America, political news from Paris, stories of mysterious occurrences, and poems on the death of Napoleon. It was not by chance that their imaginary kingdoms were established through the auspices of the four Chief Genii and located in Africa. *The Arabian Nights*, that favourite book of the child Jane Eyre, was—together with *Tales of the Genii* and the Book of Revelation—instrumental in infusing the early stories with magic and the supernatural. Throughout the 1820s and 1830s, *Blackwood's* carried articles on British exploration and emigration in Africa, on the Ashantee Wars and customs. The actual site of the Great Glass Town can be traced to the June 1826 issue of *Blackwood's* (vol. 19, p. 705), which contained an article by James McQueen (who would also become a character in the saga) and an accompanying map based on Denham and Clapperton's explorations in northern and central Africa from 1822 to 1824.[9] Not only did Branwell copy this map for his own illustration of Glass Town locations (see map, p. xxix), but he and his sisters also followed the author's advice on the most favourable site for a new colony—one that 'would COMMAND the trade, the improvement, and the civilization of all North Central Africa'.

British attitudes to Africa reflected in the juvenilia can also be found in the Brontës' old geography books (especially their well-used *A Grammar of General Geography* by Revd J. Goldsmith); and elements of classics such as *The Pilgrim's Progress* and *Gulliver's Travels* are woven into early tales. Traces of Gothic and historical romance (from their literary heroes Sir Walter Scott and Lord Byron in particular), and quotations from Shakespeare, Milton, and the Bible abound. Scott's *Life of Napoleon* (1827) was as familiar to all the children as was his poetry, and *Tales of a Grandfather*, given to them by their aunt for Christmas 1828, helped to stress the importance of historical models like Mary, Queen of Scots who appears in various guises in both the Glass Town and Gondal sagas. Romantic poetry by Wordsworth, Coleridge, Southey, and Byron was plundered for its exotic settings, sensational plots, and intense emotions. Paintings too form the intertext of the sagas, with verbal references to visual works by contemporary artists like Thomas Bewick, John Martin,

---

[9] Reprod. in Alexander (ed.), *An Edition of the Early Writings of Charlotte Brontë* (hereafter Alexander *EEW*) (Oxford: Basil Blackwell, 1987–91), 2(2), frontispiece.

and Edward Finden, whose prints the children saw on the walls of the parsonage, in books and in engravings they copied in drawing lessons.

It was not simply knowledge and quotation they appropriated from their reading: the example of authorship and publication, particularly the magazine culture gleaned from *Blackwood's*, helped to determine the Brontës' writing practice and attitudes towards authorship. The early volumes of juvenilia were imitations of adult publications in all except size: they were initially designed the size of large postage stamps for the 12-inch toy soldiers and written in minuscule script to represent print. The tiny size of the print, which was used by all four Brontës almost uniformly throughout their juvenilia, had the added advantage of rendering the contents of the manuscripts illegible to adult eyes, helping to maintain the secrecy of their shared imaginary world. The pages were bound and carefully sewn into brown paper wrappers, and the layout of title pages and contents were modelled on *Blackwood's*, the Annuals, and other books owned by the Brontës. Publication conventions were taken seriously by the young writers but they were also open to parody, as we see when Charlotte ironically notes the fictive nature of their enterprise in one of her title pages: 'The Search after Happiness A Tale by Charlotte Bronte Printed By Herself And Sold By Nobody.'

Almost as soon as the Glass Town was established, Branwell began a monthly journal for the Young Men in imitation of *Blackwood's*. Here the children could practise their 'scriblomania'—Charlotte's pet word for their obsessive literary pursuits. 'Branwell's Blackwood's Magazine' was begun in January 1829, but soon taken over by Charlotte when Branwell lost interest and began a newspaper instead. She changed the name first to 'Blackwood's Young Men's Magazine' and then to 'Young Men's Magazine' in August 1830 when she began a 'second series', clearly relishing the authority of the editor as much as her brother had done. Branwell had announced his resignation with characteristic pomposity:

We have hitherto conducted this Magazine & we hope to the satisfaction of most. (No one can please all.) But as we are conducting a Newspaper which requires all the time and attention we can spare from ot[h]er employments we hav[e] found it expedient to relinquish the editorship of this Magazine but we recommend our readers to be to the new Editor as they were to me. The new one is the Cheif Genius Charlotte. She will conduct it in future tho' I shall write now and then for it. ΔΘΗ July 1829 P B Brontë.[10]

[10] C. Alexander and V. Benson (eds.), *Branwell's Blackwood's Magazine* (Edmonton: Juvenilia Press, 1995), 34. The Greek letters preceding the date and Branwell's signature do not spell any particular word; they simply show his knowledge of the letters delta, theta, and eta.

Charlotte also assumes a proprietorial tone: 'This second series of magazines is conducted on like principles with the first. The same eminent authors are also engaged to contribute for it'; and stamps her own mark on the content, replacing drinking songs and tales of violent murders with stories of magic, mysterious occurrences, and romance, much to Branwell's consternation. He complains to the new editor in a series of poems, but he no longer has the controlling voice and Charlotte's rule prevails. It is not clear what role Emily and Anne played in relation to the magazine: their chief characters are present in stories which make it clear that they had their own more realistic preferences for Yorkshire models of setting and character. Perhaps they were simply too young at this stage for their exacting older siblings to accept their literary contributions, or perhaps their prose pieces were destroyed at the same time as their prose juvenilia of Gondal?

The title page for the 'Young Men's Magazine' for October 1830 (included in this edition) announces that it is 'Edited by Charlotte Brontë' and 'SOLD BY SERGEANT TREE AND ALL OTHER Booksellers' in the various 'Glass Town' capitals of the Glass Town Federation. Distribution and editorial policy are as carefully planned as the elaborate contents and advertisement pages. Like the original *Blackwood's*, the magazines include a variety of genres: stories, articles, poems, reviews of paintings and books, letters to the editor, and 'Conversations', the latter based on the renowned discussions of literary and current affairs known as 'Noctes Ambrosianae' (1822–35). The 'Nights', as the Brontës also called them, were evening affairs held in the convivial masculine atmosphere of Ambrose's Tavern in which *Blackwood's* fictitious and opinionated personalities—'Christopher North' (John Wilson), 'The Ettrick Shepherd' (James Hogg), 'The Opium Eater' (De Quincey), 'Timothy Tickler' (John Lockhart or Robert Sym), and their company—displayed their rhetorical skills, trying to outdo each other's eloquence, so that their good-humoured debate becomes a type of verbal pugilism that underlined the Brontës' early view of journalism as competitive literary play.

The same kind of rivalry is evident in the Brontës' earliest articles and reviews. Under the guise of fictitious poets, historians, and politicians, they jockey for the Glass Town public's attention by writing slanderous reviews on each other's work. In the process the young writers are not only playing with their material but with the process of narration itself. In one article the lawyer and bookseller Sergeant Bud (Branwell's voice) scorns Charlotte's degenerate editorial policy;[11] in the next, Lord Charles Wellesley (Charlotte's voice) satirizes Emily's 'Parry's land' with its Yorkshire puddings and dull landscapes.[12] The young writers carry on a continual verbal battle in editorial notes, prefaces, afterwords, and the actual texts of their stories. Lockhart, one of the leading lights of *Blackwood's*, had characterized himself as 'the scorpion, which delighteth to sting the faces of men'.[13] Likewise, Charlotte's Captain Tree aims to scotch 'one small reptile',[14] namely, his literary rival Lord Charles Wellesley (another of Charlotte's own pseudonyms). In the preface to his next work, however, Lord Charles assures 'the reading publick' that he has not been 'expiflicated by the literary Captain's lash'.[15]

One of the most remarkable features of the Brontë juvenilia is their robust dialectic nature. The Glass Town writings constitute a literary marketplace where various roles and ideas can be explored and questioned. There is a cacophony of voices as narrators of disparate texts challenge each other for the 'Truth' of their story, appealing to their Glass Town audiences through the authority of their genre (the history writer Captain Bud carries more weight than his annoying young nemesis Lord Charles Wellesley who specializes in romance, Gothic tales, and scandal). Historians, poets, and novelists jostle with each other for their readers' attention. Editors and critics reinterpret and cast doubt on their rival's productions. The Glass Town writers are all male like their *Blackwood's* originals, but they are hardly all-powerful. Incompetent poets are mocked (in 'The Poetaster' the extravagant 'Rhymer'—a parody of Branwell's poetic persona 'Young Soult'—narrowly escapes beheading!) and scandalmongers like Lord Charles (Charlotte) are barred from the inner circles of political power (as we see in 'The Spell'). Through their narrative personae, Charlotte and Branwell constantly satirize and rewrite each other's versions of events. They analyse, admire, or scorn each other's characters. Their personae act as 'masks', allowing them to identify and 'play' with opposing points of view. Branwell and Emily are critical of Charlotte's penchant for romance; they prefer the cut and thrust of politics and war, and the mundane Yorkshire landscape of moorland, factories, and canals

---

[11] 'Lines spoken by a lawyer on the occasion of the transfer of this magazine', in Victor Neufeldt (ed.), *The Works of Patrick Branwell Brontë: An Edition*, 1 (New York: Garland, 1997), 73.

[12] 'A Day at Parry's Palace', in Alexander *EEW* 1. 229–33.

[13] Ian Jack, *English Literature 1815–1832*, The Oxford History of English Literature (Oxford: Clarendon Press, 1963), 19.

[14] Alexander *EEW* 2(1). 44.

[15] Ibid. 128.

rather than love affairs, palaces, and exotic settings. But Charlotte is not unaware of her own desires. Her assumption of various masks allows her to argue as much with her own polyphonic voices as with those of Branwell. Under cover of 'Lord Charles' (later Charles Townshend) she can analyse (and ironize) her indulgence in romantic fiction while still exploring the passionate relationships of her central characters. Her adoption of a male pseudonym—not unlike Charles Townshend—for her first novel *The Professor* was not only to mask the woman writer but was a continuation of the assumption of literary authority practised since childhood.

The whole notion of fiction is explored in levels of narrative reality. The four Brontës were both creators of and characters in their 'plays', and these characters in turn created both 'true' and fictitious tales about other characters and themselves. In 'Tales of the Islanders' they control the course of events and participate in the action as 'Little King and Queens', appearing and disappearing at crucial moments in the plot, conveying vital messages and raising characters from the dead. Part of the literary fun is the 'making alive' of characters that have been killed off in a previous story. In early Glass Town stories the children appear as the omnipotent Chief Genii, each responsible for their particular soldiers and kingdoms. The Genii dwell in Mt. Aornos, which (like Mt. Olympus) is the home of the 'gods', and also inhabit the Jibble Kumri (or Mountains of the Moon) and the great Sahara Desert to the north of the Glass Town Federation. Branwell plays with their association of godlike power and with his identity as Chief Genius 'Banni Lightening', derived from the relationship of the Greek god Zeus with lightning and thunder (*bronte* means thunder in Greek, and in Italian *brontolare* means to grumble or rumble, specifically with reference to thunder). He makes it clear to his sisters and to their characters that, as in 'A Romantic Tale', they hold absolute power of life and death, a despotism instituted and liberally used by Branwell, though railed against by Charlotte's Young Men not simply because she resents Branwell's self-appointed leadership but because she knows that narration is by its nature disparate and unstable. Lucy Snowe, in Charlotte's final novel *Villette*, presents a duplicitous narrator who plays with the reader and dupes even herself. The juvenilia demonstrate that even at an early age, Charlotte's grasp of narrative process and its implications was surprisingly sophisticated.

In 'Albion and Marina', written at 14 years old, Charlotte's sharp observation of her own creative process is clearly evident, and in an article in the 'Young Men's Magazine' she imagines this process from the viewpoint of her creature. When the cynical disaffected Lord Charles is musing in the Glass Town Public Library, he finds his identity as a writer becoming increasingly insubstantial and his narrative voice alarmingly precarious:

Whilst I was listlessly turning over the huge leaves of that most ponderous volume, I fell into the strangest train of thought that ever visited even my mind, eccentric and unstable as it is said by some insolent puppies to be.

It seemed as if I was a non-existent shadow, that I neither spoke, eat, imagined or lived of myself, but I was the mere idea of some other creatures brain. The Glass Town seemed so likewise. My father, Arthur and everyone with whom I am acquainted, passed into a state of annihilation: but suddenly I thought again that I and my relatives did exist, and yet not us but our minds and our bodies without ourselves. Then this supposition—the oddest of any—followed the former quickly, namely, that WE without US were shadows; also, but at the end of a long vista, as it were, appeared dimly and indistinctly, beings that really lived in a tangible shape, that were called by our names and were US from whom WE had been copied by something—I could not tell what.[16]

As Lord Charles senses his fictionality his confidence wanes and he begins to disintegrate, his self splits between subject ('WE') and object ('US') whose identification depends on point of view. He returns to his senses (the narrative 'I') only when the 'other creature' (Charlotte) whose idea he is comes into view and he finds himself, Gulliver-like, in the hands of his author. In this clever parody of the insubstantiality of the imaginative world the Brontës had made so pivotal to their lives, we sense Charlotte's (probably unconscious but prescient) adolescent anxiety about the lack of real control she actually has as both child and female over her life.[17]

The reality of her position and that of her sisters was all too clear during their brief periods of schooling at Roe Head, Mirfield. Charlotte attended Miss Wooler's small private school from 17 January 1831 until mid-June 1832, returning as a teacher in July 1835 and remaining until December 1838. Emily attended for only three months in 1835, when Anne replaced her as a pupil, both sisters' fees being paid for by

[16] Ibid. 257.

[17] Heather Glen takes this interpretation further in her perceptive analysis of 'Strange Events' in relation to 'A History of the Year', where the presence of 'papa' frames and limits the children's power to create. Thus 'Strange Events' speaks not only of power but, more crucially, of 'the imagination of powerlessness'. At 14, Brontë was beginning 'to explore the intuition that "reality" might be less simply that which is than that which is constructed by the powerful' ('Configuring a World', in Mary Hilton et al. (eds.), *Opening the Nursery Door* (London and New York: Routledge, 1997), 229–31).

Charlotte's teaching. All three sisters suffered illness and depression in varying degrees away from home and in the presence of strangers. Despite several lasting friendships for Charlotte and Anne, they were acutely conscious of their difference, intellectually and materially, from the other girls of the new manufacturing families of the district. More significantly, at school they were separated from the writing partnerships that had by then developed between Charlotte and Branwell and Emily and Anne. Without the freedom to indulge in their shared imaginary worlds they could not express themselves; they became physically sick. Emily became so ill at Roe Head that Charlotte feared for her life. When she again attempted to live away from home as a teacher at Law Hill, near Halifax, Emily survived a mere six months. Home represented the space where her creativity could have free reign, where she might experience the passionate elemental world of Gondal amidst the mundane regularity of routine life at Haworth. Anne and Charlotte, despite their sustaining sense of duty and Christian faith, also eventually succumbed to the strain and suffered severe religious crises that necessitated a return to the nurturing atmosphere of 'Haworth and home [that] wakes sensations which lie dormant elsewhere'. Charlotte's *Roe Head Journal*, part autobiographical and part Angrian, documents her frustration as a young woman needing to make her own way in life yet longing for the fictional world that brought release for her creative energy.

At home the collaborative writing immediately resumed, but the relationships changed. Charlotte and Branwell were both strong-willed and enthusiastic, and Emily and Anne had followed their lead. In 1831, however, while Charlotte was at school, the younger siblings had taken the opportunity to form their own Pacific kingdom of Gondal, although they still remained privy to Glass Town and Angrian events, as Emily's 1837 Diary Paper attests. Modelled on themes in their early collaborative play, the Gondal saga was also concerned with love and war, played out against a dramatic background drawn from the writings of Shakespeare, Scott, and Byron. As with Glass Town writings, their poems explore different modes of identity through the voices of various personae—issues of class and gender, rebellion and incarceration, sexual desire and power.

After her first eighteen months away at school, Charlotte also had new ideas to pursue. The soldiers had belonged to Branwell; he assumed leadership of the 'play' and established the plot lines, and Charlotte—sharing his interests—had been happy to follow in her own style, reacting to his constant innovations and puncturing the pomposity of his extravagant creations. But Scott's novels and ballads began to take priority, mixing with Byron's Gothic tales as the source of invention. On her return home, she launched into long Gothic romances like 'The Spell' (1843) that obsessively explore the motivations of characters, especially her own fascination for the Byronic Duke of Zamorna and his increasingly complicated love affairs. Branwell was still focused on military and political adventures but he too became progressively obsessed by his persona 'Northangerland' and the possibilities of the dark side of the Byronic character. In 'The Politics of Verdopolis', he takes account of Charlotte's new tales, provides a more sophisticated lineage for his hero as a descendant of the Northumberland Percys, lays the foundations for Mary Percy's future role as wife of Zamorna and Queen of Angria, and introduces the Ashantee leader Quashia Quamina as an accomplice who will aid Northangerland in his future insurrection in Angria.

From the outset the two older siblings had had a stimulating effect on each other's development; now in their teens, Branwell reacted to Charlotte's new dimension to their saga: the creation of Angria, a kingdom to accommodate Zamorna's increasing tyranny and his new social and political coteries. The old world of Glass Town (now 'Verdopolis') could be seen as historical background, against which Angria defines itself as a more sophisticated and 'modern' space where a new generation of characters can be made to explore their authors' pubescent desires and anxieties. 'Mina Laury' (1838) and 'Caroline Vernon' (1839) represent Charlotte's later novelettes in this edition, revealing not only the increasing sophistication of her writing and deep commitment to the now-Angrian saga, but also her increasing unease with her own emotions and position as a young woman. Her poem 'We wove a web in childhood' acknowledges her acute awareness of the importance of her rich imaginative life—that 'web of sunny air' that constitutes the Glass Town and Angrian saga—to her ability to express herself and to provide her with some agency in the real world over which she now has little control. If she is to maintain that agency she must bridge the imaginative divide between her 'bright darling dream' and the real world: her 'Farewell to Angria' maps out the route she will take towards the more sober world of *The Professor*. Yet although Charlotte came to see her early writing as sinful fantasy and characterized it as 'lurid'—a hothouse of 'ornamented and redundant composition' (preface to *The Professor*) from which she must withdraw for a time—she also acknowledged the value of her 'practice of some years', the formative experiences without which a novel like *Jane Eyre* could not have been written.

Branwell, too, increasingly questioned his sense of identity and agency as a writer with ambitions to join the ranks of his revered *Blackwood's*. From the age of 18, he wrote repeatedly to the editor requesting a place on his staff, but the many unanswered letters and final rebuff simply confirmed this talented young man's early sense of insecurity. *Blackwood's* had long fed his image of a man of letters as a purveyor of power: through the Glass Town and Angrian saga he had cultivated this ambition. As the privileged only son in a Victorian household, he was expected to pursue a respectable if not illustrious career; but the unrealistic confidence placed in him and his haphazard home education did little to curb his ebullient nature or provide guidance in self-control. At 16, Branwell laughs at his own pretensions to art, his physical inadequacies, and—despite his age and fluency in writing—his inability to respond appropriately or even articulately in social situations, when he creates his self-important alter ego Patrick Benjamin Wiggins. Charlotte joins in the joke: 'as musician he was greater than Bach; as a Poet he surpassed Byron; as a painter, Claude Lorrain yielded to him'.[18] Her mockery of his 'almost insane devotion to all celebrated characters in Verdopolis' and reference to his three sisters as 'miserable silly creatures not worth talking about', is as much comic self-deprecation as criticism of her brother.

As Charlotte asserted herself in the partnership and Branwell became less sure of himself in the real world, this note of insecurity—comic but ominous—began to creep into his other literary personae. Robert Patrick S'Death (derived from the oath 'God's Death') is Wiggins's uncle and reincarnation of Chief Genius Bannii: he is cast as former servant and sinister mentor of the young Alexander Percy (then 'Rogue' and later 'Northangerland'), who appears in 'The Pirate' as captain of the pirate ship *The Rover*. A Mephistophelean figure that mockingly quotes Scripture and orchestrates evil, he is impervious to any attempts to destroy him. His evil relationship with the young Percy owes much to James Hogg's study of evil possession and double personality in *The Private Memoirs and Confessions of a Justified Sinner* (1824). 'The Pirate' marks the beginning of Northangerland's career and 'The Politics of Verdopolis' illustrates his increasingly duplicitous personality and the split between public and private life that was later to haunt Branwell himself. Gradually Percy/Northangerland morphs into the sinister, atheistic personality we see represented by Charlotte in 'Caroline Vernon'—anarchic, powerful, but damned—the Byronic figure Branwell admires but also fears. Northangerland and his cronies

[18] 'My Angria and the Angrians', Alexander *EEW* 2(2). 245–53.

become increasingly inebriated (Branwell himself was drinking at this time) and treacherous in their dealings with both Angria and the Verdopolitan Union. At the same time Branwell's manuscripts degenerate into formless chronicles of political and military skirmishes, with detailed accounts of speeches, manoeuvres, and casualty lists. His production had always been prodigious: through poems, travel books, verse dramas, magazines, historical novelettes, translations of Horace and Virgil, he cultivated his image as man of letters; but now the very form and style of his writing expressed its decline. The exploration of self afforded by literary play is no child's game: long after Charlotte bade farewell to Angria, Branwell continued to explore his deepest desires and fears through Northangerland. Unknown to his sisters, eighteen of his poems were published in local newspapers under 'Northangerland', the pseudonym that continued to frame his identity; but he never obtained a secure job or became the successful writer or artist his early talents and ambition promised.

Like Branwell, Emily continued to play the Gondal game until the year of her death. There is no evidence that Emily's imaginative world had anything but a constructive effect on her mature writing. It appears to have provided sustenance, security, and inspiration for her intensely secretive and self-contained personality. She moves seamlessly in her poetry between Gondal and the real world: both are portrayed as intensely abstract and personal; and although the Gothic power of Gondal may have combined with Scott and Shakespeare to provide the inspiration for *Wuthering Heights*, the novel is solidly structured within the domestic world of a middle-class Victorian narrator. Anne also made the adjustment to Victorian domestic fiction without trauma, taking with her her early lessons in writing. The development of her moral sense led her increasingly away from Emily's often anarchic world and it is significant that she was not always party to innovations in Emily's Gondal plot, as the Diary Papers indicate.

Glass Town and Angrian Saga: Charlotte and Branwell

Poised on the Great Bay at the confluence of rivers, Glass Town—capital of the Glass Town Federation—is a city of reflections: 'the Queen of the Earth, who looks down on her majestic face mirrored in the noble Niger . . . [and] the glass that her harbour gives her'.[19] As the saga became more sophisticated, and its creators acquired more knowledge,

[19] Ibid. 241.

the title 'Glass Town' was changed first to 'Verreopolis' ('Glass Town' in Latin) then corrupted to 'Verdopolis'. The name, like that of the saga itself, was clearly significant for the Brontës, suggesting the paradoxical nature of their imaginative world, a fantasy that was founded on and became an alternative reality.

The Glass Town and Angrian saga centred first on the Glass Town Federation and its principal city Verdopolis (initially called the Great Glass Town), and then moved to Angria, a new kingdom created in 1834 to the west of the Federation. It is most commonly referred to as the 'Glass Town Saga'; the titles 'Angrian Saga' or 'Angrian Legend' are used by writers to refer to later stories centred on the kingdom of Angria, but no separate saga is involved. This fictitious world established in Africa bears little resemblance to Africa itself apart from occasional place names, incursions by Ashantee tribes, and exotic scenery that owes as much to fairy tale and the *Arabian Nights* as it does to geographical descriptions of what was known as 'the dark continent'. The Brontës filled this imaginative space with their own version of early nineteenth-century society with its international relations and domestic affairs. Here they reconfigured European colonial aspirations, republican uprisings, military and administrative organization, buildings and landscapes, social ideology and cultural institutions. Struggles of the Peninsular Wars, together with the names and battles associated with Wellington and Napoleon, were mapped on to the African colony. Even Quashia, the only indigenous African to be fully charactized in the saga, is associated with Wellington. Just as the historic Duke adopted the son of a chief in the Indian wars, so Charlotte's Wellington adopts Quashia Quamina, who later rebels, aligns his warriors with the republican rebellion of Northangerland (formerly Branwell's Napoleon), and lusts after the Queen of Angria (daughter of Northangerland and wife of Wellington's son Zamorna, King of Angria). This single example demonstrates the intricate association between fictional and historical characters, constitutional and republican rivalries, and the authors themselves.

Much of the saga was formulated only in discussion amongst the creators; knowledge was assumed between the collaborators, who had no need to explain circumstances or background in individual stories. Some tales, like 'An Adventure in Ireland', appear to bear no relation to the saga at all but were often written as independent contributions to the 'Young Men's Magazine'. Other stories from the saga can be bewildering, since the Brontës were continually rewriting events and reinventing the personalities of their characters.

HISTORY, GEOGRAPHY, AND EVENTS[20]

The history of the Young Men became the history of the Glass Town and Angrian saga; and the geography of the four kingdoms ruled by the original heroes of the Young Men's Play constituted the Glass Town Federation in the new saga, becoming increasingly associated with the geographical regions of Britain: Wellington's Land (Ireland, birthplace of the historical Wellington), Sneaky's Land (Scotland), Parry's Land, and Ross's Land (both roughly equivalent to Yorkshire and lowland Scotland), each of which has its own provincial 'Glass Town' capital (such as 'Wellington's Glass Town').

The great capital Glass Town, founded by the Twelves, is not simply a dream world but a working city, where 'lofty mills and warehouses piled up storey above storey to the very clouds, surmounted by high tower-like chimneys vomiting forth the huge columns of thick black smoke, while from their walls the clanking, mighty din of machinery sounded and resounded till all that quarter of the city rang again with the tumult'.[21] Beneath the symmetry and elegance of the brilliant white marble buildings lies a subterranean Gothic world of labyrinthine caves that reach, like those below the palace of Kubla Khan in Coleridge's famous poem, down to the sea. But the young Brontës put them to good use: it is here that the labourers, the artisans, the prisoners and the underworld of Glass Town live. Branwell and Emily were determined to create prisons, and factories, despite Charlotte's preference for palaces and country estates. Below the illustrious Tower of All Nations (modelled on the Tower of Babel) lie the state dungeons[22] that, together with the dungeons in the Palace School in the Islanders' Play, prefigure the Gothic prisons of Gondal.

Wars and political upheavals dominate the events of the saga throughout its history. They are chronicled in obsessive detail by Branwell and form the background to many of Charlotte's stories. In March 1831 there is insurrection in Verdopolis, the Great Rebellion, in which Rogue sets up a provisional government on the French model of 1789. Order is restored miraculously, but a year later Rogue again leads a rebellion in the north which is eventually defeated at the battle of Fidena by Alexander Sneaky, King of Sneaky's Land, and his son John, Duke of Fidena, assisted by forces from the other kingdoms.

---

[20] Much of the material in the following sections is drawn from my essays 'Glass Town and Angrian saga' and 'Gondal saga' in Alexander and Smith, *Oxford Companion to the Brontës*.

[21] Alexander *EEW* 1. 139.

[22] Ibid. 2(1). 194.

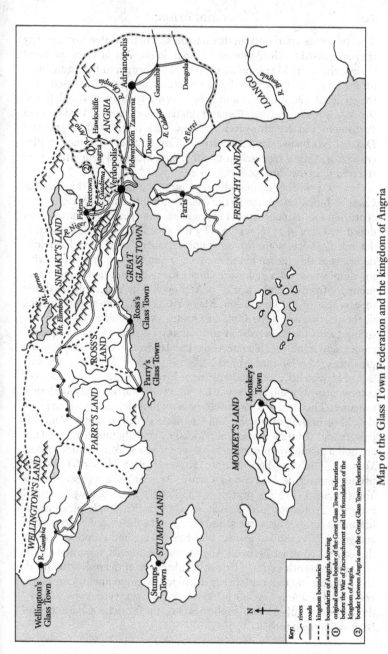

Map of the Glass Town Federation and the kingdom of Angria

(Based on Branwell Brontë's frontispiece to 'The History of the Young Men' (1831), with Angria added by Christine Alexander.)

The Ashantees are a constant threat to the east of the Federation. In 1833 they are joined by the Arabs and French in the War of Encroachment against the united Verdopolitan forces. This proves to be a watershed for the Federation in which the new kingdom of Angria is created from the spoils of war. Zamorna and Percy (formerly Rogue), who defeated the Ashantees in the east, demand the territory from the Verdopolitan Parliament and are also given the new titles of King of Angria and Duke of Northangerland respectively. Constant parliamentary battles ensue to win equal representation for Angria in the old Federation, now referred to as the Verdopolitan Union.

Angria, probably named after the pirate kingdom on the Malabar Coast of India, celebrated in the late seventeenth and early eighteenth centuries for its successful repulsion of European powers until its defeat by Clive in 1756, was won by the sword and must be constantly defended. It has some of the same legendary wealth and dubious notoriety as this Indian kingdom: its new capital is an opulent 'marble toy shop' whose inhabitants are chiefly the nouveaux riches and entre-preneurs from the 'old world' of Verdopolis. Its geography basically repeats that of the Federation. Major rivers flow from the mountains in the north-east to the Gulf of Guinea, with prosperous manufac-turing towns like Edwardston and Zamorna on their banks. Repeated names and phrases characterizing the landscape of Angria's seven provinces ('the Howard Moors', 'the savannah of Arundel', 'the for-ests of Hawkscliff', 'the sandy plains of Etrei'), governed by Zamorna's coterie, provide a solid reference for Branwell's warfare and Charlotte's romance. The action of Branwell's stories remains chiefly on the bat-tlefield or in the parliament, and Charlotte's tales continue to inhabit palaces and country houses; but Yorkshire and the north of England are now a distinctive presence, as we see in 'Mina Laury' and 'Caroline Vernon'. The new hero Warner Howard (after Haworth) Warner, prime minister of Angria and a native Angrian, is quintessentially a Yorkshireman (like his prototype Sir Robert Peel), a tough-minded earnestly Protestant businessman who values the simple pleasures of life and is scrupulously moral and loyal, unlike the ruler he serves. The antagonistic yet mutual respect between Warner and Zamorna reflects the central contrast between Angria and Verdopolis, a contrast built on the nineteenth-century British divide between the industrial north and London and the south (a rift examined by contemporary novelists, not least Elizabeth Gaskell in *North and South*). Verdopolis remains the centre of culture and sophistication, the London Charlotte and Branwell longed to visit.

With the advent of Angria, Glass Town political alliances are cemented into distinct factions and leaders. Zamorna, as King of Angria, appoints Northangerland (now his father-in-law) as prime minister, but Northangerland remains in league with his old republican associates and leads a rebellion against Zamorna. The ensuing Angrian Wars ravage the country, and Zamorna is repeatedly deposed and reinstated.

GLASS TOWN AND ANGRIAN SOCIETY

Glass Town's social history is equally developed and becomes extraordinarily complex. The royal families of each of the kingdoms have an entourage of friends, associates, servants, and retainers who follow them between their palaces in Verdopolis and their country houses. In the capital itself there are lower-class groups of 'rare lads', body-snatchers, vagabond Frenchmen, servants, and pugilists (Branwell's favourite sport was boxing) who interact with the 'High Life' in various ways. The professionals and the military mix freely with the aristocracy, united by political alliances and by a common enthusiasm for literature in which many of them take an active part. The Twelves are venerated as the elders of society, but considered too authoritative and serious by the younger generation of gallants. Stumps and Monkey (original Twelves) are retired to islands off the Glass Town coast, whose inhabitants are mocked by Verdopolitans for their bizarre dialect and old-fashioned manners and dress (a parody of provincial Yorkshire compared to London). Branwell's original Frenchyland continues to exercise a political presence through the machinations of Northangerland and Montmorency. Several Glass Town institutions, such as Bravey's Inn, the Great African Games (modelled on the Olympic Games), the Elysium (a type of Masonic society), and the university on Philosopher's Island, have a significant impact on the lives of the inhabitants and events in the saga.

Social life focuses on a group of characters: the Duke of Wellington and his two sons, their friends and admirers, and their enemies. As Wellington becomes an elder statesman, Zamorna moves into centre stage, accompanied by his older sometime friend and enemy Northangerland. The cynical young Lord Charles records Zamorna's marriages (to Helen Gordon, Marian Hume, and Mary Percy), his mistresses (chiefly Mina Laury, Sofala, Rosamond Wellesley, and potentially Caroline Vernon), his children (who are destined to repeat their father's disastrous relationships), friends, and political associates. Zamorna also surrounds himself with artists and writers (based on British cultural society), all of whom record their own versions of his life and character.

Northangerland has an equally colourful coterie, ranging from former pirates, cattle thieves, and revolutionaries (for example Naughty, Caversham, Simpson, and O'Connor) to French noblemen (like Montmorency) and the Ashantee leader Quashia. As with Zamorna, Glass Town's authors constantly analyse Northangerland's character as it develops from the early pirate and republican revolutionary 'Rogue' ('Rougue' to Branwell) into a sinister and embittered aristocrat on his marriage to Zenobia Ellrington ('Elrington' to Branwell), and finally evolves into the Luciferian villain-hero of Romantic literature. His marriages (to Maria di Segovia, Maria Henrietta Wharton, and Zenobia Ellrington) and mistresses (especially Harriet O'Connor and Louisa Vernon) are as confusing and difficult to reconstruct from individual stories as those of Zamorna. His pathological hatred for his sons, however, contrasts with Zamorna's love for his children. Despite their cruel abandonment as babies, Edward and William Percy work their way back into aristocratic society and continue the theme of rivalry between two brothers, begun by Wellington's two sons—a theme that continues to play itself out in *The Professor* and *Shirley*.[23]

The driving force of the Glass Town and Angrian saga is the complex love-hate relationship between Northangerland and Zamorna. Zamorna's early conflicting attitudes to the 'vile demagogue' are complicated by his marriage to Northangerland's beloved daughter Mary. She becomes a pawn in their political rivalry during the Angrian Wars, for which Northangerland is basically responsible. The wars originate in the republican Northangerland's inability to work for long with any constitutional leader, even his own son-in-law. Their struggle is that of two gigantic personalities fascinated by each other but both lusting for the same power. Resolution of their relationship is impossible and only old age finally subdues their fiery antagonism. Branwell traces Northangerland's career relentlessly to the doors of Pandemonium, in a series of unstructured chronicles. Charlotte at first moves her ideal hero (the early Arthur Wellesley) closer to Northangerland's ruthlessness, indulging in the Byronic personality she now creates for Zamorna (Arthur's new name not only reflects his new title but also his modified personality); but she maintains a realistic attitude towards her egotistical hero through her cynical narrator Lord Charles. In 'Caroline Vernon', her final Angrian tale, Zamorna is viewed as a comic figure, a spent

---

[23] See 'Two Rival Brothers', in Alexander, *The Early Writings of Charlotte Brontë* (Oxford: Basil Blackwell, 1983), 219–33.

womanizer and despotic ruler; and Charlotte's conventional heroines are beginning to be superseded by the independent Elizabeth Hastings, a prototype of Jane Eyre. Yet it is the flamboyant Zenobia Ellrington, the devoted mistress Mina Laury, and the adolescent Caroline Vernon struggling with her emotions that characterize the heroines of the juvenilia. It is through such women and their relationships with Zamorna that Charlotte can test various responses to men well beyond her likely range of experience, just as 'Northangerland' enabled Branwell to test boundaries.

Charlotte made a formal repudiation of her Angrian writings at the age of 23 and, although she struggled against its influence for several more years and continued to draw on elements of her early creative life in her later writing, her first novel *The Professor* represents a distinct break with her juvenilia. Branwell never made this break: until his death at the age of 31, his poetry and prose remained within the sphere of Angria, his mind imprisoned in and his behaviour largely circumscribed by his early fictional world. Although he published a review of the artist Thomas Bewick and translated at least six Odes of Horace, his final poems, published in local newspapers, were all signed 'Northangerland', the character that had fascinated and obsessed him since the age of 12.

The Gondal Saga: Emily and Anne

Unlike the Glass Town and Angrian saga, the Gondal saga cannot be easily reconstructed. The prose chronicles have disappeared and all that survives to indicate their former existence is a few passing references in Emily and Anne's Diary Papers and fragmentary lists of characters (see Appendices A and B). The Diary Papers were designed to take stock of life and contemplate the future: the sisters agreed to write a paper every three or four years, usually on Emily's birthday, to lock it away in a tin box (rather like a time capsule) and then open it only before writing the next one to assess what changes had taken place in their lives. The papers are particularly significant in revealing the way the imaginative world of Gondal formed an integral part of the sisters' everyday existence. They also indicate, as do the poems, that the plot and characters of Gondal owed much to Glass Town and Angria.

These few brief manuscripts, together with the poetry, are the only evidence we have by which to trace the events and nature of Gondal. Several attempts have been made to detail Gondal's history (these are discussed below); but without the prose manuscripts we can only glimpse the broad outlines. Even names remain confused and uncertain: the same Gondal character may be referred to in different ways, by initials, titles, Christian or full name, or the same initials may stand for more than one person. There are few narrative clues since the poems represent moments in the Gondal epic, points of intensity or crisis that lend themselves to expression in poetry rather than prose. Only the barest framework can be safely pieced together from available evidence, but it is arguable that this is all that is needed for an appreciation of Emily and Anne's Gondal poetry.

ORIGINS AND NATURE OF GONDAL

We know from Charlotte and Branwell's manuscripts that Emily and Anne were not always happy with their secondary role in the Glass Town saga. Their characters and tastes were different: their heroes Parry and Ross were a blunt, unpolished Yorkshireman and a sour Scot, and their palaces were square stone buildings with slate roofs. The younger sisters preferred the cold-climate northern hemisphere they knew so well to the balmy African landscape and the high life of the Verdopolitan nobility. Charlotte told her publisher that she had 'always liked Scotland as an idea';[24] and for Emily, in particular, the northern landscape of lakes and mountains—filtered through the pages of Sir Walter Scott's highland romances and James Hogg's writings on Scottish folklore in *Blackwood's*—had a special appeal. The Yorkshire beginnings of Parry's and Ross's Lands were gradually transformed first into the Scottish northern provinces of Glass Town and then into the setting so often evoked in the Gondal poems. Even the names of Gondal heroes were predominantly Scots (see Appendix B), although the influence of the oriental tales of Thomas Moore and Lord Byron are also evident in the poems (see, for example, Emily's 'And now the housedog stretched once more', and Anne's 'Verses by Lady Geralda' and 'Alexander and Zenobia', where the more exotic landscape may reflect the warmer climate of southern Galdine in the Gondal saga). The supreme importance of nature, whether Scottish or Yorkshire, in the Gondal poems, however, owes as much to Emily and Anne's close affinities to Wordsworth as to their own childhood experience of the moors.

From the beginning of the four children's collaborative plays, Emily appears to have asserted her independence. Charlotte's 'History of the Year' records 'Emily's and my bed plays', a secret collaborative

[24] Charlotte Brontë to W. S. Williams, 20 July 1850: M. Smith (ed), *The Letters of Charlotte Brontë* (Oxford: Clarendon Press, 1995–2004), 2. 427.

venture that was probably the origin of much of the Islanders' Play in which Emily seems to have assumed a major role, again in league with Charlotte. Anne performs a role as one of the 'Little Queens' but is not mentioned by name in any of the tales. In 'Tales of the Islanders', the young authors enter their own dramas, interacting with the characters and experiencing their adventures. One of these escapades involves Charlotte and Emily alone, amid the landscape so often evoked in Emily's poems, where 'the wind sweeps with more fearful blast over this wild bleak moor', where mountain sheep graze on the heath and find shelter among the rocks, where the lark springs from his mossy bed as the authors approach. Further, when Charlotte had grown tired of the Islanders' Play (recorded by her in volume 2, October 1829), it was Emily who took the lead, initiating the School Rebellion that looks forward to a central theme of Gondal. There is mutiny at the Palace School and the ringleaders are her characters, 'little Johnny Lockhart' and the Princess Victoria.

The concept of a female authority figure seems to have been peculiar to Emily. Her early fascination with the Princess Victoria, only ten months younger than herself, informs the Gondal saga, setting it apart from the male-dominated power structures of Glass Town. Suddenly thrust into the limelight in 1830 as heir to the British throne, Princess Victoria was adopted as a central player by Emily and her character and fortune reconfigured with that of another Brontë heroine, Mary, Queen of Scots, whose tragic life of suspicion, murder, lovers, imprisonment, and death permeates the Gondal saga.[25] Seven years later Emily's interest in Victoria had not abated: she recorded the young queen's imminent ascension to the throne in her Diary Paper of 26 June 1837, and transposed the event into her Gondal setting (Appendix A).

When Emily and Anne established their own imaginary world in 1831, after Charlotte's departure for Roe Head, they took with them much of the Glass Town formula: the concept of islands, the wild moorland scenery, a powerful princess, the struggles of a predominantly royalist world, and even some names. The name 'Almeida', for example, reappears in Gondal as 'Almeda' (sometimes even spelt 'Almeida'), and 'Augusta' suggests not only Byron's half-sister 'Augusta' but Augusta di Segovia, Branwell's wicked femme fatale in the Glass Town saga. Much of Zamorna's early 'Scottish' past, derived from Byron's Gordon relations, is replayed in Gondal. The Gondalian 'Unique Society', wrecked on a desert island, recalls the secret society of Glass Town

---

[25] For Mary, Queen of Scots as a Brontë heroine, see Alexander and Smith, *Oxford Companion to the Brontës*, 322.

nobles on Philosopher's Island. As in the Islanders' Play, the 'Princes & Princesses' of Gondal are besieged within the Palace of Instruction, some kept as prisoners in vaulted dungeons. In the Islanders' Play, it was Emily who kept the key to the cells for 'naughty school children': 'These cells are dark, vaulted, arched and so far down in the earth that the loudest shriek could not be heard by any inhabitant of the upper world, and in these, as well as the dungeons, the most unjust torturing might go on without any fear of detection.'[26] Dungeons proliferate in Gondal. Savage passion, imprisonment, murder, and rebellion were to be the hallmarks of the new saga.

Other habits from the early plays also influenced Gondal. The methods of acting out events and of writing episodes in random order are particular features of Gondal. Even at the age of 27, during a train journey to York, Emily persuaded Anne to join her in playing at being a variety of characters 'escaping from the palaces of instruction to join the Royalists who are hard driven at present by the victorious Republicans' (Diary Paper, 30 July 1845). In the same Diary Paper, Emily mentions that she is writing the First War that took place at the beginning of the saga dated elsewhere in the 1820s. There was once a detailed chronology of Gondal, as the dating on the various poems confirms, but they are not written in the saga's chronological order. As in the Gondal and Angrian saga, the same events could be recalled and rewritten at different times. They function as a storehouse for the young authors to plunder as the occasion arises.

THE KINGDOM OF GONDAL AND ITS RECONSTRUCTION

The central focus of the saga is the island of Gondal in the North Pacific, divided into four kingdoms and ruled by rival families, suggestive of the Shakespearean rivalries in *Romeo and Juliet*. In a landscape of wild moorland, harsh winter winds and snows, a drama of rebellion and betrayal in love and war is played out, as the enmity between the central characters is explored. The poems focus especially on the violent passions of the strong-willed heroine Augusta Geraldine Almeda (A.G.A.) and on the power struggle of Julius Brenzaida, who at one time was either her husband or lover.[27] The action moves between Gondal,

---

[26] Alexander *EEW* i. 24.

[27] Lara Hinkley adds a third and less plausible possibility, suggesting two generations of Gondal history (see Derek Roper, *The Poems of Emily Brontë* (Oxford: Clarendon Press, 1995), App. 7): the first dominated by Julius Brenzaida and the second by his daughter, whom she identifies as A.G.A.; a reading endorsed by Robert and Louise Barnard in *A Brontë Encyclopedia* (Oxford: Blackwell, 2007), 126–7.

whose capital is Regina, and the recently discovered Gaaldine, an island in the South Pacific, also divided into kingdoms but with a contrasting tropical climate and verdant landscape. After friction between the Royalists, civil war breaks out and the Republicans gain the upper hand. A.G.A. becomes Queen of Gondal, but is murdered during the civil war, the topic of Emily's final poem.

The heroine A.G.A. is the subject and speaker of many of Emily's poems. She is a passionate dark beauty, ruthless in both political and personal relationships, a female alternative to the Byronic heroes of Glass Town and Angria. When she tires of Amedeus, the lover of her childhood friend Angelica, she sends them both into exile. After an affair and marriage with Alfred Sidonia of Aspin Castle, she abandons him to die of a broken heart. Her relationship with Alexander, Lord of Elbë, also ends in his violent death by Lake Elnor. Fernando De Samara meets a similar fate: A.G.A. loves, imprisons, then drives him into exile and suicide. And when her 'passionate youth was nearly past', she is murdered by the outlaw Douglas at the instigation of Angelica, while alone on Elmor Hill. The faithful Lord Eldred contemplates her tempestuous life that inspired both hate and devotion but never fulfilled its promise.

Julius Brenzaida, Prince of Angora, is equally ambitious and ruthless. He is educated with Gondal's other nobles, but imprisoned in 1825 (Gondal chronology) for his involvement with the ambitious Rosina Alcona, whom he probably married. Other lovers include Geraldine Sidonia, whom he left grieving over their child in Zedora. He conquers Almedore in Gaaldine and, as King, he breaks his promise of union with Gerald Exina, warring against him for the throne of Gondal. Eventually Julius is made emperor, but soon assassinated (possibly by Amedeus) in his palace, where Rosina lies ill. Fifteen years later, Rosina laments his loss over his grave 'on Angora's shore', probably on his estate ('Cold in the earth').

This brief structure of events, woven around two central characters, can be gleaned from available evidence; other attempts to provide a detailed chronology are more speculative. Some critics have seen all of Emily's poems as part of a single epic, arranging them in a sequence to show Gondal representing 'Wuthering Heights in the making'.[28] Others

---

[28] Fannie Ratchford, Gondal's Queen (Austin: University of Texas Press, 1955), 27. C. W. Hatfield (Complete Poems of Emily Jane Brontë) endorsed Ratchford's influential reconstruction, much of which has proved correct; but problems remain with her identification of three characters as the single heroine A.G.A. and the grouping of all Emily's poems to fit this pattern.

focused on the imaginative transformation of Gondal characters into Catherine, Heathcliff, and Edgar.[29] Yet other critics maintained a rigid separation between Gondal and non-Gondal poetry, reducing the importance of Gondal and arguing its regressive influence on the quality of both Emily and Anne's work. They condemned Gondal verse as 'Byronic melodrama' and 'pseudo-martial rubbish'.[30]

Emily herself appears to give support to the idea of separation since she copied her work into two notebooks in February 1844, one initialled 'E.J.B.' (E.J.B. Notebook; also referred to as the Honresfeld manuscript) and the other headed 'Gondal Poems' ('Gondal Poems' Notebook). In the 'Gondal Poems' Notebook the verse appears to follow a chronology and to be grouped around certain characters, whereas the E.J.B. Notebook includes essentially personal lyrics with no specific Gondal references. From 1844 on, Emily added new poems to each notebook, ostensibly making a distinction between Gondal and non-Gondal verse. However, a third notebook she copied poems from, known as the Ashley MS, made no distinction between 'personal' and Gondal poetry. One poem in particular ('O Dream, where art thou now?') was transcribed without change into the E.J.B. Notebook and four others were copied into the 'Gondal Poems' Notebook.[31] The fact that not all the poems were copied suggests that Emily was selecting the best, perhaps for future anonymous publication[32] and that she was selecting from poetry that in her mind had a unified vision but that needed to be 'deGondalized' for other readers. The distinction between Gondal and non-Gondal, then, may not be so clear-cut as is generally believed, and its persistent use seems designed to discourage biographical readings.[33]

More recent critics, while often acknowledging an ostensible Gondal and non-Gondal division, prefer to see Emily's work as a whole. They argue that the same preoccupations occur in all her poetry, the same

[29] See esp. Mary Visick, *The Genesis of Wuthering Heights* (Hong Kong: Hong Kong University Press, 1958). Further summaries of Gondal reconstructions can be found in Derek Roper, *The Poems of Emily Brontë* (Harmondsworth: Penguin, 1992), App. 7, and in Janet Gezari; *Emily Jane Brontë: The Complete Poems*, xxix–xxxii.

[30] Derek Stanford, in Muriel Spark and Derek Stanford, *Emily Brontë: Her Life and Work* (London: Peter Owen), 143–4.

[31] 'Lord of Elbë, on Elbë hill', 'O wander not so far away!', 'To the bluebell', and 'From our evening fireside now'.

[32] Fannie Ratchford first put forward the view that Emily probably thought of publication before Charlotte suggested it to her (*Gondal's Queen*, 31–2).

[33] See e.g. Lucasta Miller, *The Brontë Myth* (New York: Alfred A. Knopf, 2003), 252, where Virginia Moore's 'sensationalist' 1936 personal reading of 'The Prisoner' is countered by the narrative Gondal context; although Miller concedes that the poem 'does have a penumbra of metaphorical meaning'.

exploration of the constraint and limitation of human existence, and the same element of dramatization.[34] Seemingly personal poems, like 'Well some may hate and some may scorn', need not refer specifically to a dead person in Emily's experience. It is not hard to imagine that many of the poems classified as 'personal' might have originally been spoken by Gondal characters, whose views reflect those of their creator ('Shall Earth no more inspire thee', for example); certainly a number of these personal poems either discuss the source of Emily's imaginative experience ('Alone I sat' and 'I'll come when thou art saddest') or directly address her 'God of Visions' (as in 'To Imagination'). Her poems are chiefly dramatic lyrics, spoken by imagined characters at particular moments in time. Gondal allows Emily a lyric impersonality: she can participate in different scenarios, write with abandon and yet write intensely out of her own experience.

Thus when Emily came to select poems for the sisters' joint publication of *Poems* in 1846, after Charlotte's dramatic discovery of one of her manuscript notebooks, she needed to alter only the occasional Gondal word to make her poems appear personal (see the Explanatory Notes to Emily's poems). Even the simple removal of the Gondal speaker's initials might suggest the poem is personal, as in 'Song' (beginning 'The linnet in the rocky dells'). And even after the publication of *Wuthering Heights*, Emily still found in her epic world a source of inspiration for her personal concerns. As late as May 1848, seven months before her death, she was working on a Gondal civil war poem: she never abandoned her imaginary world. As she stated in her Diary Paper of 1845: 'We intend sticking firm by the rascals as long as they delight us.'

In Emily's case, then, it is more constructive to see her poetic vision whole. Although her poems selected for this edition are generally her more obvious Gondal ones, other important poems (such as 'To Imagination') are included because they express the same concerns as those of the Gondal saga or have been inspired by similar powerfully imagined situations.

There is no such problem with Anne's Gondal poems; they can be clearly distinguished. Comparatively few poems by Anne exist, approximately fifty-three compared to some two hundred by Emily, and of these just under half were composed within a Gondal context. Anne's Gondal poems can be divided into two groups, based on periods when she was at home: her earliest extant poems written

---

[34] See e.g. Lyn Pykett, *Emily Brontë*, (London: Macmillan, 1989), 69. Louise and Robert Barnard point out that 'the personal or confessional note is comparatively rare' in the so-called 'personal' poems (*Brontë Encyclopedia*, 272).

between 1836 and 1838, when she was aged 16–18, and those written between late 1845 (after she left Thorp Green) and 1846. This does not appear to have been accidental. From the beginning she seems to have followed Emily's lead, writing about Gondal almost entirely under her influence (with the sole exception of her 30 July 1841 Diary Paper). Like Emily, Anne continued to exploit the Gondal context throughout her life, but her involvement with the saga was never as intense or as committed as that of her sister.

As Anne matured and gained a greater experience of the outside world than Emily, she seems to have deliberately distinguished, in a way that Emily never did, between the fantasy she wished to retain for Emily's sake and her own increasingly personal concerns about her role in life and her relationship with God. Comparisons between her few letters and her personal poetry reveal that her practice was that of her heroine Agnes Grey, who considered her poems as 'relics of past sufferings and experience, like pillars of witness set up in travelling through the vale of life, to mark particular occurrences' (*Agnes Grey*, ch. 17). The heroine of Anne's earliest poem ('Verses by Lady Geralda', 1836) reflects keenly her author's endurance and determination: despite a profound sense of loss and sadness, this Gondal heroine leaves home, as Anne herself did two months before, happy in the prospect of activity. Even in her Gondal poetry, Anne was already articulating the personal concerns that were to become the hallmark of her philosophical and religious poems.

Ellen Nussey noted that Emily and Anne were 'like twins' during their early years, but as they grew older Emily's obsessive desire for privacy, particularly from her family whom she felt might misunderstand her, meant that even Anne was increasingly excluded from a knowledge of what she had written. Emily's pen-and-ink sketch that fills approximately a third of the Diary Paper manuscript of 26 June 1837 shows the sisters in a collaborative venture. Anne is seated at the top left of a table, leaning on her elbows thinking. Emily is facing Anne with her back to the viewer and on the table are books, papers, and 'The Tin Box', in which the papers were kept. Yet the accompanying text makes clear that despite this proximity, the two writers were not fully aware of the content of each other's work. Anne knows that Emily is writing 'the Emperor Julius's life', since she has heard some of it and wants 'very much to hear the rest', but Emily is silent about the poetry she is writing and Anne is left to record 'I wonder what it is about?' Furthermore, only a few character names were used by both sisters, suggesting they were responsible for different characters and kingdoms in the saga.

Although Emily and Anne both used the same memorandums and chronologies, drawn up in the early stages of Gondal, their compositions appear to have been independently conceived.

THE SIGNIFICANCE OF GONDAL

The importance of collaboration in the early writing lives of the Brontës cannot be underestimated in its contribution to their literary development.[35] Anne's first novel *Agnes Grey* follows a straightforward linear structure strongly suggestive of the autobiographical Gondal chronicles she and Emily were writing: 'Augustus-Almedas life 1st v.', 'the Emperor Julius's life', 'the 4th volume of Sofala Vernon's life', and 'the third volume of passages in the life of an Individual' (Appendix A). Although preceded and followed by references to Gondal, it is thought that the latter may refer to an early draft of *Agnes Grey*.

Gondal is of particular importance, however, in relation to Emily Brontë's only novel, *Wuthering Heights*. The relationship between the two is inescapable: not only do we find similar themes, associations, and images which strongly suggest that the novel grew out of the saga,[36] but Emily continued writing about Gondal after her novel was completed. Numerous parallels have been detected, such as a dark, inscrutable Gondal child similar to Heathcliff, and a theme of childhood contrast, recorded in the Explanatory Notes to this edition. More significant than detailed parallels, however, Emily's poetry can be seen as providing 'the emotional and spiritual context' for *Wuthering Heights*.[37]

For Emily, both poetry and novel were clearly 'hewn' in the same 'wild workshop'.[38] As in *Wuthering Heights*, the Gondal poetry is dominated by situations of isolation, exile, revenge, and death. Characters lament their separation and imprisonment, often from a loved one as a result of death. Like the relationship between Heathcliff and Catherine,

[35] In *The Birth of Wuthering Heights* (London: Macmillan, 1998), Edward Chitham extrapolates from Gondal poems Emily's working techniques in *Wuthering Heights* and supports his detailed chronology for the composition of the novel by showing how Gondal was transposed into *Wuthering Heights*.

[36] Mary Visick's *Genesis of Wuthering Heights* provides a useful list of 'possible parallels' between Gondal and the novel.

[37] Janet Gezari, *Last Things: Emily Brontë's Poems* (Oxford: Oxford University Press, 2007), 4. Gezari's fascinating study examines Emily's poetry in relation to her overwhelming preoccupation with Death and its relation to the joy of life and to eternity; she makes no distinction between Gondal and non-Gondal poems, focusing instead on the way the poetry works as Romantic lyric and philosophical statement. Her notion of 'intentional dreaming' (p. 7) is helpful in understanding the personal nature of the 'Gondal' poems.

[38] Charlotte Brontë, Preface to 1850 edition of *Wuthering Heights*.

their loyalties are strong and their emotions violent. The beauties of nature, especially the wind and the moors, console and bring spiritual release to Gondal's prisoners. Life in Gondal is dominated by a pervading sense of confinement, sometimes physical and sometimes spiritual, where the speaker is chained by powerful emotions, memories, and the consequences of action. In such a world, death becomes a liberating alternative. Unlike the Glass Town and Angrian saga, where relationships can be redeemed and lives remade, events in Gondal are final and players in 'Earth's dungeon tomb' must reconcile themselves to a life of 'change and suffering' ('Cold in the earth').

In 'Julian M. and A.G. Rochelle', vision and imagination offer the captive a means of transcending the 'living grave' of prison bondage. Paradoxically, A.G. Rochelle is rescued from her dungeon existence by a nightly 'messenger of Hope', who presages a visionary experience that raises her to a reality beyond her physical restriction. Immured instead within this recurring vision that is 'divine', she is reconciled to the 'unapproved' sentence of this world's 'gloom and desolate despair'. Again, in the more simple lyric 'I'm happiest when most away', the speaker rejoices in the soul's transcendence of mortal limits. The sense of liberty expressed in this poem represents the same need that Charlotte documented so urgently in her *Roe Head Journal*; and the wind brings the same small voice that would herald relief from 'this world's desolate and boundless deluge'. Emily's visionary world became habitual and sustaining, a form of practised meditation that could free the poetic mind from the confines of a circumscribed and bigoted world.

Anne, too, found relief in Gondal from the limitations imposed on the lives of young Victorian women. Like Emily she came to see her own condition as a kind of imprisonment, with few alternatives of escape. Her prisoners glimpse in dreams the consolation of love—a physical love grounded in reality, unlike Emily's visionary consolation—but, denied such human joys, they resign themselves to the permanence of captivity. Their loved ones are equally constrained, denied the emotional sustenance of their relationship. In 'Weep not too much, my darling', acceptance of this 'dungeon gloom' and possible delivery from 'fruitless yearnings' comes in an imaginative identification with the loved one's experience of nature, drawn as it is from the memories of past pleasures of 'Nature's bounties'. For Anne, the natural world does not alter; it is the speaker's perception that changes and that can be changed again by memory and (particularly in her later and more personal poems) by belief in an all-loving God, author of the natural landscape that provides so much consolation. Even within the world of

Gondal, Anne's faith and hope in life contrasts with Emily's dogged stoicism and points towards the high ideals expressed in *Agnes Grey* and in Anne's last brave poem where she still desires to do good in the world despite the news of devastating illness.[39]

Gondal has been called 'the secret room in Emily Brontë's imagination'.[40] The poetry allows us only glimpses of a creative space occupied by stories of personal resilience, powerful love, and tragedy that would find their ultimate expression in Emily's great novel *Wuthering Heights*. Yet Gondal, like Glass Town and Angria, was not so much an alternative to the actual world as 'a way to write about that world';[41] it provided 'occasions for powerful poems'. Through Gondal both sisters discovered the resources of poetry for spiritual and emotional expression. As the sisters grew older, Anne—once as close as a twin—gradually ceased to share Emily's personal vision of the saga, just as the partnership between Charlotte and Branwell slowly disintegrated as their interests and aesthetic vision changed with maturity. There can be no doubt, however, that their early collaboration provided a unique imaginary world that was both workshop and playground. Using the biblical images of the mustard seed and almond rod, both planted in youth, Charlotte describes the momentous effect Glass Town, Angria, and Gondal had on the lives of herself and her siblings:

> The mustard-seed on distant land
> Bends down a mighty tree,
> The dry unbudding almond-wand
> Has touched eternity.

The young Brontës nourished each other's imaginations and developed in their youthful writings the independent styles and themes that can be seen fully developed in their mature poetry and famous novels.

---

[39] 'A dreadful darkness closes in' (Chitham (ed.), *Poems of Anne Brontë* (London: Macmillan, 1979, repr. 1987), 163–4), written after news of her incurable tuberculosis.

[40] Nina Auerbach, 'This Changeful Life: Emily Brontë's Anti-Romance', in Sandra Gilbert and Susan Gubar (eds.), *Shakespeare's Sisters: Feminist Essays on Women Poets* (Bloomington: Indiana University Press, 1970), 49.

[41] Gezari, *Last Things*, 59.

NOTE ON THE TEXT

This selection from the Brontës' writings is designed to illustrate the collaborative nature of their early creative life, and the progression of their youthful plays into the elaborate sagas of Glass Town and Angria, and Gondal. The Brontës continued to write poems and stories associated with their childhood creations well into their twenties and even beyond, making subject matter rather than the authors' ages the most useful basis for selection from their so-called juvenilia.[1] I have therefore chosen material that is clearly related to their imaginary worlds. In Emily's case the choice is nuanced: because it is important to view all Emily's poetry as the product of a single imaginative source, several of her most significant poems that are often considered 'personal' are also included, since they too can be seen as articulating both her Gondal characters' and her own concerns. The volume of Charlotte's early writings is greater than all her novels, and Branwell's juvenilia are equally voluminous. In the case of Emily and Anne, only six early Diary Papers with brief references to Gondal and a few notes survive in prose (see Appendices A and B), and selection must be made from their body of surviving poetry. I have tried to keep in check the temptation to include more of the larger sample of Charlotte's and Branwell's juvenilia, and to concentrate on texts that are most representative of their shared nature and intertextuality. Above all this edition seeks to convey the frenetic family activity, the sheer mass and literary allusiveness of the young Brontës' all-encompassing imaginative world.

The text of this edition has been prepared from the surviving holograph manuscripts, with the exceptions of the 'E.J.B.' Notebook poems (also known as the Honresfeld Manuscript and available only in facsimile) and 'Two Romantic Tales' (available in an early transcription). All sources and manuscript details, including significant variants in early drafts, are recorded in the Explanatory Notes. Although eight of Emily's and four of Anne's poems in this edition were published in the 1846 edition of *Poems* arranged by the Brontë sisters themselves, I have chosen to include the manuscript versions that were composed as part of the Gondal saga rather than the published versions where all Gondal references were removed for a general audience; the changes made on

---

[1] In the case of the Brontës, the term 'juvenilia' is generally extended beyond its common meaning of works produced in an author's youth.

publication are listed in the Explanatory Notes.[2] The text follows the manuscripts closely (including the layout of headings and signatures), while recognizing that a printed transcription must diverge from a handwritten source in certain ways and that the aim of this edition is to produce an accessible version of the Brontës' early writings for general readers and students.

The Brontës' original grammar (including errors) and their often idiosyncratic word division have been retained; for example *up-stairs*, *upstairs*, and *up stairs*, which the *OED* notes were all in common usage in the nineteenth century. Other idiosyncrasies and inconsistencies, which form part of the texture of the writing, such as capitals in display print and abbreviations (for example, the use of initial letters for names, *&c* for *etc*, and ampersand—except where it begins a sentence) have also been preserved. Archaisms, which often reflect the Brontës' sources, are preserved in the texts (for example, *devine* for *divine*); all four Brontës were inclined to use both modern and obsolete spellings of the same word indiscriminately. They also frequently used alternative spellings of the same word (for example, *inquire* and *enquire*); both spellings for such words can be found in this edition, often in the same story. It may be surprising to discover that apparently incorrect words like *cheif*, *accuratly*, *deafning*, and *untill* are used in the King James Version of the Bible and in editions of Shakespeare, Milton, and other writers read by the Brontës; and the past tense of common verbs like *to eat* could still be rendered alternatively *ate* or *eat* in the nineteenth century. However, spelling errors (including the common confusion of *their* for *there*, *were* for *where*, *whos* for *whose*, *you're* for *your*) have been corrected, and occasional letters left off the beginning or end of a word owing to speed of writing have been replaced as in a spelling correction (for example, where *the* should be *they*, *of* should be *off*, *as* should be *has*). Less perfunctory omissions of words and parts of words have been inserted and signalled by square brackets (for example, proceed[ed]). French accents and spelling errors have been corrected or noted. The occasional repeated or redundant word mistakenly left in the text when an authorial change was made has been omitted. The spelling of historical names and places has been corrected; but the variant spellings

---

[2] In most cases these variants illustrate the removal of Gondal references for publication, often altering the context to such an extent that it could be argued that several manuscript poems revised for the 1846 edition represent different versions rather than early drafts of the same poem (as in the case of Emily's 'Julian M. and A.G. Rochelle').

of names and places in the sagas have been preserved, except for inconsistent hyphenation and where spellings are inconsistent in the same manuscript. The variant spellings of names and places reflect different usage by the authors. For example, the spellings *Ellrington*, *Wellesley*, *Rogue*, *Sdeath*, *Jibbel Kumri* generally identify Charlotte's manuscripts, whereas Branwell often uses the spellings *Elrington*, *Wellesly*, *Rougue* or *Rouge*, *Sdeath*, and *Jibbel Kumrii*. And Charlotte's spelling of *Free-Town* in 'The Spell' indicates an earlier manuscript than 'Caroline Vernon' where her predominant spelling is *Freetown*, as in the capital of Sierra Leone (then a British Colony) on which the imaginary town is based.

A distinction has been made between prose (including poems occurring in a prose text) and poetry texts in the treatment of punctuation. In the prose the erratic manuscript punctuation has been altered and missing punctuation supplied while still preserving much of the original, including some idiosyncratic punctuation in display headings. In Charlotte's manuscripts, for example, her habit of indicating punctuation with dashes has been retained where possible but dashes that simply fill the end of a line have been omitted. Generally her dashes are used indiscriminately but occasionally they represent her headlong style, as when she is keen to reflect her narrator's excitement or a character's thoughts, rather like Jane Austen's indirect narrative style. Paragraphs have been introduced where necessary (including a new line for a new speaker) in what would otherwise frequently be pages of unbroken prose text. In the poetry, where the layout is clearer for the reader and the rhythm and syntax more idiosyncratic, manuscript punctuation has been preserved even where ambiguities exist since they may indicate meaning. The sole exceptions are where I have felt it necessary to complete quotation marks, remove or add very occasional punctuation (recorded in notes), and regularize apostrophes for possessives, contractions, and elisions (as, for example, in Emily's use of *o'er* and *'twas*). In line with this policy, capitalization has been regularized in the prose manuscripts since it appears not to show nineteenth-century practice but to have been used indiscriminately, making the preservation of irregular capitals meaningless. In poetry manuscripts, however, decisions about capitalization are less clear-cut and may indicate emphasis. I have therefore preserved the idiosyncratic capitalization within poems since it is less frequent and again may carry meaning; but I have added capitals in a few titles and at the beginning of lines where necessary. Nevertheless, because of the minuscule scripts, distinguishing in transcription between some capital and lower-case letters (such as *s*, *f*, *m*, and *w*) remains problematic.

Despite the use of a magnifying glass to assist in deciphering the minuscule script of the Brontës' early writings, some readings must remain conjectural; all such readings are noted in square brackets with a question mark. Editorial insertions are made in square brackets, as indicated above, and have been kept to a minimum; these are used chiefly in Branwell's stories to replace parts of words that have been torn or crumbled away at the edge of a manuscript where the paper has deteriorated. In several of Charlotte's early manuscripts, too, parts of words are obliterated by ink blots and the ends of words are missing at the edges of the page because of the way the little booklets have been divided and the pages mounted by early book collectors. Branwell's relatively neat but minute hand is difficult to decipher (letters like *t* and *l*, *r* and *v* can be easily confused); and his rapid composition resulted in little or no punctuation, random pen marks and dashes that are easily confused with possible punctuation, and sporadic paragraphing.

Sample facsimile pages from Charlotte and Branwell's earliest works have been included (p. 2) to illustrate the editorial problems and the difficulty of transcription and also to demonstrate the highly developed sense of design and 'publication' implicit in their attitudes towards their writing. Their concern for the layout of their text was developed in imitation of adult magazines and books, and this has been reproduced in headings, signatures, and general format in this edition, with only occasional minor alterations. For example, I have used italics to represent Charlotte's longhand script where she has deliberately distinguished her own signature and date of composition from the minuscule printed script of her pseudonymous signature 'Charles Wellesley'. In her later novelettes where she was less concerned with layout, I have introduced the headings 'Part 1' and 'Part 2' to clarify the divisions she indicates by her chapter headings. Most of Anne's poems are fair copies, written in a neat, clear longhand, unlike her siblings who were less amenable to Mr Brontë's admonitions to write 'in a good, plain, and legible hand'.[3] She used minuscule script only for drafts and for occasional signatures, dates, and line numbers (represented in the text in italics); her manuscripts exhibit few of the problems encountered in the transcription of Emily's untidy minuscule script. A facsimile page is included to represent Emily and

---

[3] Comment by Mr Brontë at the top of the first page of one of Anne Brontë's notebooks, Princeton University Library.

Anne's collaborative Diary Papers (p. 486); this particular manuscript, written by Emily, demonstrates her lack of concern for mechanics that is perhaps as significant as her siblings' concern for neatness and design, suggesting her lack of interest in public performance and the more private nature of her imaginary world. The first page of her 'Gondal Poems' Notebook, with its decorated heading (illustrated on p. 392), however, is an exception that recalls the pride in book-making she shared with her siblings.

SELECT BIBLIOGRAPHY

There is a mass of published material on the Brontës and yet surprisingly little has been written on their early writings, apart from chapters in biographies or critical volumes. In the following list I have tried to indicate the most useful titles, arranged chronologically within each category.

Readers are also advised to consult Christine Alexander and Margaret Smith, *The Oxford Companion to the Brontës* (2003), which contains feature articles on juvenilia, Glass Town and Angrian saga, Gondal saga, Diary Papers, devoirs, and poetry; detailed entries on characters and places in the sagas; and further guidance to other sources.

The Oxford World's Classics editions of the Brontë novels are also recommended; they include the text of the authoritative Clarendon Edition produced under the general editorship of Ian Jack.

EDITIONS OF THE JUVENILIA

Alexander, Christine (ed.), *An Edition of the Early Writings of Charlotte Brontë*, vol. 1. *The Glass Town Saga 1826–1832* (Oxford: Basil Blackwell, 1987); vol. 2. *The Rise of Angria 1833–1835*: part 1, *1833–1834*, part 2, *1834–1835* (Oxford: Basil Blackwell, 1991); vol. 3 (forthcoming).

Barker, Juliet (ed.), *Charlotte Brontë: Juvenilia 1829–1835* (London: Penguin, 1996).

Gérin, Winifred (ed.), *Five Novelettes* (London: Folio Press, 1971).

Glen, Heather (ed.), *Charlotte Brontë: Tales of Angria* (London: Penguin, 2006).

Neufeldt, Victor (ed.), *The Works of Patrick Branwell Brontë: An Edition*, vol. 1 (New York: Garland, 1997), vols. 2 and 3 (1999).

Shorter, Clement, and Hatfield, C. W. (eds.), *The Twelve Adventurers and Other Stories* (London: Hodder and Stoughton, 1925).

Wise, Thomas James, and Symington, John Alexander (eds.), *The Miscellaneous and Unpublished Writings of Charlotte and Patrick Branwell Brontë* (The Shakespeare Head Brontë), 2 vols.: 1 (1936) and 2 (1938).

EDITIONS OF THE POETRY

Barker, Juliet R. V. (ed.), *The Brontës: Selected Poems* (London: Dent, 1985).

Bell, Currer (ed.), *Wuthering Heights and Agnes Grey* (London: Smith, Elder & Co., 1850).

[Brontë], *Poems by Currer, Ellis, and Acton Bell* (London: Aylott & Jones, 1846).

Chitham, Edward (ed.), *The Poems of Anne Brontë: A New Text and Commentary* (London: Macmillan, 1979; repr. 1987).

Gezari, Janet (ed.), *Emily Jane Brontë: The Complete Poems* (Harmondsworth: Penguin, 1992).

Hatfield, C. W. (ed.), *The Complete Poems of Emily Jane Brontë* (New York: Columbia University Press, 1941).

Neufeldt, Victor (ed.), *The Poems of Patrick Branwell Brontë: A New Text and Commentary* (New York: Garland, 1990).

Roper, Derek (ed.), with Edward Chitham, *The Poems of Emily Brontë* (Oxford: Oxford University Press, 1995).

BIBLIOGRAPHY

Alexander, Christine, *A Bibliography of the Manuscripts of Charlotte Brontë* (The Brontë Society in association with Meckler Publishing: Howarth and New York, 1982).

—— and Rosengarten, Herbert J., 'The Brontës', in Joanne Shattock (ed.), *The Cambridge Bibliography of English Literature*, vol. 4 (3rd edn., 1999).

Neufeldt, Victor, *A Bibliography of the Manuscripts of Patrick Branwell Brontë* (New York: Garland, 1983).

BIOGRAPHY, LETTERS, AND ESSAYS

Barker, Juliet, *The Brontës* (London: Weidenfeld and Nicholson, 1994).

Barnard, Robert, *Emily Brontë* (London: British Library, 2000).

Chitham, Edward, *A Life of Emily Brontë* (Oxford: Basil Blackwell, 1987).

—— *A Life of Anne Brontë* (Oxford: Basil Blackwell, 1991).

Du Maurier, Daphne, *The Infernal World of Branwell Brontë* (1960; repr. Harmondsworth: Penguin, 1972, 1974).

Fraser, Rebecca, *Charlotte Brontë* (London: Methuen, 1988).

Gaskell, Elizabeth C., *The Life of Charlotte Brontë* (1857), ed. Angus Easson (Oxford: Oxford University Press, 1996).

Gérin, Winifred, *Branwell Brontë* (London: Thomas Nelson, 1961; repr. Hutchinson, 1972).

—— *Charlotte Brontë: The Evolution of Genius* (Oxford: Clarendon Press, 1967; repr. with corrections 1968).

—— *Emily Brontë* (Oxford: Oxford University Press, 1971).

Leyland, F. A., *The Brontë Family, with Special Reference to Patrick Branwell Brontë*, 2 vols. (London: Hurst and Blackett, 1886).

Lonoff, Sue (ed. & trans.), *The Belgium Essays: Charlotte Brontë and Emily Brontë* (New Haven and London: Yale University Press, 1996).

Smith, Margaret (ed.), *The Letters of Charlotte Brontë with a Selection of Letters by Family and Friends*, vol. 1. *1829–1847* (Oxford: Clarendon Press, 1995), vol. 2. *1848–1851* (2000), vol. 3. *1852–1855* (2004).

BACKGROUND AND CRITICISM

Alexander, Christine, *The Early Writings of Charlotte Brontë* (Oxford: Basil Blackwell, 1983).

—— and Sellars, Jane, *The Art of the Brontës* (Cambridge: Cambridge University Press, 1995).

Allott, Miriam, *The Brontës: The Critical Heritage* (London: Routledge and Kegan Paul, 1974).

Barnard, Robert and Louise, *A Brontë Encyclopedia* (Oxford: Blackwell, 2007).

Blom, Margaret Howard, *Charlotte Brontë* (London: George Prior and Boston: Twayne, 1977).

Bock, Carol, *Charlotte Brontë and the Storyteller's Audience* (Iowa City: University of Iowa Press, 1992).

Gezari, Janet, *Last Things: Emily Brontë's Poems* (Oxford: Oxford University Press, 2007).

Glen, Heather, *Charlotte Brontë: The Imagination in History* (Oxford: Oxford University Press, 2002).

Homans, Margaret, *Women Writers and Poetic Identity: Dorothy Wordsworth, Emily Brontë, and Emily Dickinson* (Princeton: Princeton University Press, 1980).

Langland, Elizabeth, *Anne Brontë: The Other One* (London: Macmillan, 1989).

Lloyd Evans, Barbara and Gareth, *Everyman's Companion to the Brontës* (London: Dent, 1982).

McNees, Eleanor (ed.), *The Brontë Sisters: Critical Assessments*, vol. 1 (Mountfield: Helm Information, 1996).

Maynard, John, *Charlotte Brontë and Sexuality* (Cambridge: Cambridge University Press, 1984).

Paden, W. D., *An Investigation of Gondal* (New York: Bookman Associates, 1965).

Pinion, F. B., *A Brontë Companion: Literary Assessment, Background and Reference* (London: Macmillan, 1975).

Pykett, Lyn, *Emily Brontë* (London: Macmillan, 1989).

Ratchford, Fannie Elizabeth, *The Brontës' Web of Childhood* (New York: Columbia University Press, 1941).

—— *Gondal's Queen: A Novel in Verse by Emily Jane Brontë* (Austin: University of Texas Press, 1955).

Shuttleworth, Sally, *Charlotte Brontë and Victorian Psychology* (Cambridge: Cambridge University Press, 1996).

Smith, Anne (ed.), *The Art of Emily Brontë* (London: Vision Press, 1976).

Visick, Mary, *The Genesis of Wuthering Heights* (Hong Kong: Hong Kong University Press, 1958).

Wordsworth, Jonathan, 'Wordsworth and the Poetry of Emily Brontë', *Brontë Society Transactions* 16: 82 (1972), 85.

PERIODICAL ARTICLES AND CHAPTERS IN BOOKS

Alexander, Christine, 'Angria Revalued: Charlotte Brontë's Efforts to Free Herself from her Juvenilia', *AUMLA*, 53 (May 1980), 54–63.

—— 'Art and Artists in Charlotte Brontë's Juvenilia', *Brontë Society Transactions*, 20: 4 (1991), 177–204.

—— '"That kingdom of gloom": Charlotte Brontë, the Annuals and the Gothic', *Nineteenth-Century Literature* (formerly *Nineteenth Century Fiction*), 47 (1993) 409–36.

—— 'Readers and Writers: *Blackwood's* and the Brontës', *Gaskell Society Journal*, 8 (1994), 54–69.

—— '"The Burning Clime": Charlotte Brontë and John Martin', *Nineteenth-Century Literature*, 50 (Dec. 1995), 285–316.

—— 'Imagining Africa: The Brontës' Creations of Glass Town and Angria', in P. Alexander, R. Hutchinson, and D. Schreuder (eds.), *Africa Today: A Multi-Disciplinary Snapshot of the Continent* (Canberra: Humanities Research Centre, ANU, 1996), 201–19.

—— 'Elizabeth Gaskell and Victorian Juvenilia', *Gaskell Society Journal*, 18 (2004), 1–15.

—— 'Charlotte Brontë and the Duke of Wellington: Further Evidence of Hero-Worship', *Notes and Queries*, NS 54 (June 2007), 142–5.

Blom, M. A., '"Apprenticeship in the world below": Charlotte Brontë's Juvenilia', *ESC* 1 (1975), 290–303.

Bock, Carol, '"Our plays": the Brontë Juvenilia', in Heather Glen (ed.), *The Cambridge Companion to the Brontës* (Cambridge: Cambridge University Press, 2002), 34–52.

Brown, Helen, 'The Influence of Byron on Emily Brontë', *Modern Language Review*, 34 (1930), 374–81.

Chitham, Edward, 'Emily Brontë and Shelley', in Edward Chitham and Tom Winnifrith (eds.), *Brontë Facts and Brontë Problems* (London: Macmillan, 1983), 58–76.

Concover, Robin St John, 'Creating Angria: Charlotte and Branwell Brontë's Collaboration', *Brontë Society Transactions*, 24: 1 (1999), 16–32.

Glen, Heather, 'Configuring a World: Some Childhood Writings of Charlotte Brontë', in Mary Hilton, Morag Styles, and Victor Watson (eds.), *Opening the Nursery Door: Reading, Writing and Childhood 1600–1900* (London and New York: Routledge, 1997).

Miles, Rosalind, 'A Baby God: The Creative Dynamism of Emily Brontë's Poetry', in Anne Smith (ed.), *Art of Emily Brontë*, 68–93.

Neufeldt, Victor A., 'The Writings of Patrick Branwell Brontë', *Brontë Society Transactions*, 24: 2 (Oct. 1999), 146–60.

Ratchford, Fannie E., 'Charlotte Brontë's Angrian Cycle of Stories', *PMLA* 43 (1928), 494–501.

—— 'The Brontës' Web of Dreams', *Yale Review*, 20 (1931), 139–57.

Stephens, Fran Carlock, 'Hartley Coleridge and the Brontës', *TLS*, 14 May 1970, 544.

Williams, Meg Harris, 'Book Magic: Aesthetic Conflicts in Charlotte Brontë's Juvenilia', *Nineteenth Century Literature*, 42: 1 (1987), 29–45.

CHRONOLOGY

1812   Marriage of Patrick Brontë (b. 17 Apr. 1777) to Maria Branwell (b. 15 Apr. 1783) at Guisely, near Leeds, Yorkshire (29 Dec.).

1814–20 Children born in quick succession: Maria (baptized (23 Apr.); birth date unknown), Elizabeth (8 Feb. 1815), Charlotte (21 Apr. 1816), Patrick Branwell (26 June 1817), Emily Jane (30 July 1818), Anne (17 Jan. 1820). Brontë family goes to live in the Parsonage, Haworth, where Patrick is perpetual curate (Apr. 1820).

1821   Aunt Elizabeth Branwell comes to live with the family (May). Mrs Brontë dies (15 Sept.).

1824   Maria and Elizabeth go to Clergy Daughters' School at Cowan Bridge (21 July); followed by Charlotte (10 Aug.) and Emily (25 Nov.).

1825   Maria dies of tuberculosis (6 May), as does Elizabeth (15 June). Charlotte and Emily removed from school (1 June). Brontë children taught at home by their father and aunt (1825–30).

1826   Branwell receives box of toy soldiers from his father (5 June) inspiring the Young Men's Play which leads to Brontë children's imaginary sagas of Glass Town and Angria, and Gondal.

1827   Branwell's earliest extant manuscript, 'Battell Book', illustrated with pencil and watercolour (12 Mar.).

1828   Charlotte's earliest extant manuscript, 'There was once a little girl and her name was Ane', illustrated with tiny watercolours (Jan.).

1829   First indication of the influence of *Blackwood's Edinburgh Magazine* in 'Branwell's Blackwood's Magazine' (Jan.). Charlotte writes 'The History of the Year' (12 Mar.). Brontë children stay with their Uncle Fennell, Parsonage House, Crosstone; Charlotte's earliest surviving letter with the first written reference to drawing (23 Sept.).

1831   Charlotte goes to Margaret Wooler's school at Roe Head, Mirfield (17 Jan.), makes lifelong friends with fellow pupils Ellen Nussey and Mary Taylor. Aunt Branwell acquires *Fraser's Magazine* for the Brontës (May).

1832   Charlotte leaves Roe Head (mid-June) and teaches her sisters at home.

1833   Patrick Brontë joins Keighley Mechanics' Institute gaining access to library, reading room, and lectures. Branwell writes 'The Politics of Verdopolis' (23 Oct.–15 Nov.).

1834   Charlotte and Branwell create Angria, a new kingdom in the Glass Town saga; Emily and Anne break away to create Gondal. Charlotte

exhibits two pencil drawings at summer exhibition of the Royal
Northern Society for the Encouragement of the Fine Arts, Leeds
(June); she writes 'The Spell' (21 June–21 July). Emily and Anne
write their first extant diary paper, including earliest mention of
Gondal (24 Nov.).

1835   Branwell visits Liverpool, purchases Byron's *Childe Harold's
Pilgrimage* (30 May); drafts letter to Royal Academy of Arts
requesting permission to present his drawings (June–July).
Charlotte accompanied by Emily returns to Roe Head as teacher
(29 July). Branwell's course of art lessons with William Robinson
completed; he writes to Robinson to arrange further lessons to
prepare for entry as a student to the Royal Academy Schools
(16 Nov.). Anne replaces Emily at Roe Head (late Oct.). Branwell
asks the editor of *Blackwood's Magazine* to employ him to replace
James Hogg; he receives no reply to this or later letters (7 Dec.).

1836   Branwell now a member of Freemason's Lodge, Haworth; acts
as secretary for Masonic meetings (Apr.). Emily writes her
first extant poem, a fragment from the Gondal saga (*c.*12 July).
Charlotte sends specimens of her poetry to Robert Southey
telling him of her ambition to be 'for ever known' as a poet
(29 Dec.). Anne writes her first extant poem 'Verses by Lady Geralda'
(Dec.).

1837   Branwell sends a poem to Wordsworth advising of his ambition
to be a poet (10 Jan.). Wordsworth fails to reply. Southey's reply to
Charlotte acknowledges her 'faculty of verse' but advises her
to 'write poetry for its own sake . . . not with a view to celebrity'
(12 Mar.). Charlotte's *Roe Head Journal* reveals conflict between her
imaginary world and duty to teach 'dolts' in the classroom. Anne
leaves Roe Head ill and depressed, a state exacerbated by religious
crisis (Dec.).

1838   Branwell sets up as a portrait painter in Bradford (May). Margaret
Wooler's school moves from Roe Head to Heald's House, Dewsbury
Moor (?Feb./Mar.); Charlotte leaves the school suffering from nervous
depression (23 May); returns to school (late June/Aug.). Emily takes
up teaching post at Miss Patchett's school at Law Hill, near Halifax
(end Sept.). Charlotte leaves Margaret Wooler's school for the last
time (Dec.).

1839   Emily returns to Haworth from Law Hill (Mar.). Anne goes as
governess to the Inghams at Blake Hall, Mirfield (8 Apr.). Branwell
abandons career as professional artist and returns to Haworth (mid-
May). Charlotte goes for three months as governess to Sidgwicks
at Stonegappe, near Skipton (May); returns to Haworth (19 July).
Branwell visits Liverpool (July). Charlotte writes her last novelette
'Caroline Vernon' (July–Dec.), 'Farewell to Angria' (late Sept.).
Anne leaves the Inghams (Dec.).

1840   Branwell becomes tutor to Postlethwaites at Boughton-in-Furness (1 Jan.); writes to Hartley Coleridge, asking him for his opinion on his poem 'At dead of midnight' and his translations of two of Horace's Odes (20 Apr.); is encouraged by Hartley when he visits him at Rydal Water. Anne goes as governess to Robinson family of Thorp Green, near York (?8 May). Branwell sends Horace translation to Hartley Coleridge (27 June); returns to Haworth after dismissal by Postlethwaites (June); engaged as Assistant Clerk at Sowerby Bridge Railway Station (31 Aug.). Charlotte sends the opening chapters of a MS novel (*Ashworth*) to Hartley Coleridge (?Nov.); acknowledges his candid opinion that her novel unlikely to be accepted for publication (10 Dec.).

1841   Charlotte goes as governess to White Family of Upperwood House, near Bradford (end Feb.–Mar.). Branwell moves to Luddenden Foot as Clerk in Charge of the station (1 Apr.); becomes first of Brontë children to be published author with appearance of his poems in *Halifax Guardian* (5 June). Charlotte, Anne, and Emily plan to start school of their own (July); Charlotte declines invitation to take over Margaret Wooler's school (Oct.).

1842   Patrick Brontë escorts Charlotte and Emily to the Pensionnat Heger in Brussels where they enrol as pupils to improve their languages (Feb.). Branwell held responsible for discrepancy in accounts and dismissed by Leeds and Manchester Railway (31 Mar.). Aunt Elizabeth Branwell dies (29 Oct.), leaving a legacy of £350 for each of her nieces. Anne returns to Haworth for the funeral (3 Nov.). Charlotte and Emily arrive too late (8 Nov.).

1843   Branwell joins Anne at Thorp Green as tutor to young Edmund Robinson (?21 Jan.). Charlotte returns to Brussels (27 Jan.); gives English lessons to M. Heger and his brother-in-law; becomes increasingly lonely and obsessed with her love for M. Heger. Emily remains at Haworth as housekeeper.

1844   Charlotte leaves Brussels to return to Haworth (1 Jan.); discovers her father's eyesight failing which inhibits her plans for starting a school; she abandons the idea after unsuccessfully advertising for students (Nov.). Emily begins to transcribe her poems into two notebooks, one titled 'Gondal Poems', the other untitled (Feb.).

1845   Anne resigns a month before Branwell dismissed from Thorp Green following suspicions of an affair with Mrs Robinson; he drinks to drown his distress. Anne and Emily make their 'first long journey' together to York (30 June to 2 July). Charlotte discovers one of Emily's notebooks of poetry and persuades her sisters to prepare a selection for joint publication (Sept.); they also begin writing their first novels for publication. Branwell's poem 'Penmaenmawr', published in *Halifax Guardian*, contains covert references to Mrs Robinson as his 'Angel' (20 Dec.).

1846   *Poems* by Currer, Ellis, and Acton Bell published by Aylott
        & Jones (May), only two copies sold. Charlotte offers 'three
        tales' (*The Professor*, *Wuthering Heights*, and *Agnes Grey*) to
        Aylott & Jones for publication; they decline but offer advice
        (6 Apr.). During the next year the MSS are rejected by five more
        publishers. Patrick Brontë's sight restored by cataract operation
        and, while nursing him in Manchester, Charlotte begins *Jane Eyre*.
        Anne writes her final Gondal poem 'Gloomily the clouds are sailing'
        (Oct.).

1847   Thomas Cautley Newby accepts Emily's *Wuthering Heights* and
        Anne's *Agnes Grey* for publication but not Charlotte's *The Professor*;
        Smith, Elder and Co. also reject it but accept *Jane Eyre* which is
        published to immediate acclaim (19 Oct.). Newby hastily publishes
        Wuthering Heights and *Agnes Grey* together in 3 vols., confusing the
        Bell authorship (beg. Dec.).

1848   Emily writes her final poem 'Why ask to know' (13 May). Anne's
        second novel *The Tenant of Wildfell Hall* by Acton Bell, published
        in three volumes by Newby (*c.*June). Charlotte and Anne travel
        to London to prove there is more than one author named 'Bell'
        and are entertained by publisher George Smith (7–11 July).
        Branwell dies of chronic bronchitis and marasmus (24 Sept.)
        aged 31. Emily dies of pulmonary tuberculosis (19 Dec.) aged 30.

1849   Anne dies of pulmonary tuberculosis at Scarborough (28 May),
        aged 29. Charlotte's novel *Shirley* published by Smith, Elder
        (26 Oct.).

1850   Charlotte's 'edited' edition of *Wuthering Heights* and *Agnes Grey*,
        published with 'Notice' about her sisters and a selection of their
        poems (10 Dec.).

1853   *Villette*, Charlotte's final novel, published by Smith, Elder
        (28 Jan.).

1854   Charlotte marries Revd Arthur Bell Nicholls, her father's curate (29
        Jan.).

1855   Charlotte dies in early stages of pregnancy (31 Mar.); outlived by her
        father (d. 1861) and husband (d. 1906).

1857   Elizabeth Gaskell's *Life of Charlotte Brontë* published in two volumes
        (25 Mar.). *The Professor, A Tale* by Currer Bell, published in two
        volumes by Smith, Elder and Co., with a preface by Nicholls (6
        June).

CHARLOTTE BRONTË

Plate 1: (a) The *Young Men's Magazine* for October 1830, 'edited' by Charlotte Brontë; and (b) the final pages of Branwell Brontë's *The Pirate* (courtesy of the Brontë Parsonage Museum).

The History of the Year

Once Papa lent my sister Maria* a book. It was an old geography and she wrote on its blank leaf, 'Papa lent me this book'. The book is an hundred and twenty years old. It is at this moment lying before me while I write this. I am in the kitchen of the parsonage house, Haworth. Tabby the servant* is washing up after breakfast and Anne, my youngest sister (Maria was my eldest), is kneeling on a chair looking at some cakes which Tabby has been baking for us. Emily is in the parlour brushing it. Papa and Branwell are gone* to Keighley. Aunt* is up stairs in her room and I am sitting by the table writing this in the kitchin.

Keighley is a small town four miles from here. Papa and Branwell are gone for the newspaper, the Leeds Intelligencer, a most excellent Tory news paper edited by M^r [Edwa]rd Wood [for] the proprietor Mr Hernaman.* We take 2 and see three newspapers a week. We take the Leeds Intelligencer, party Tory, and the Leeds Mercury,* Whig, edited by Mr Baines and his brother, son in law and his 2 sons, Edward and Talbot. We see the John Bull; it is a High Tory, very violent. Mr Driver* lends us it, as likewise Blackwood's Magazine, the most able periodical there is. The editor is Mr Christopher North,* an old man, 74 years of age. The 1st of April is his birthday. His company are Timothy Tickler, Morgan O'Doherty, Macrabin, Mordecai Mullion, Warrell, and James Hogg,* a man of most extraordinary genius, a Scottish shepherd.

Our plays were established: Young Men, June 1826; Our Fellows, July 1827; Islanders, December 1827. Those are our three great plays that are not kept secret. Emily's and my bed plays were established the 1st December 1827, the others March 1828. Bed plays mean secret plays. They are very nice ones. All our plays are very strange ones. Their nature I need not write on paper, for I think I shall always remember them. The Young Men play took its rise from some wooden soldiers Branwell had, Our Fellows from Aesop's Fables,* and the Islanders from several events which happened. I will sketch out the origin of our plays more explicitly if I can.

Young Men's*

Papa bought Branwell some soldiers at Leeds.* When Papa came home it was night and we were in bed, so next morning Branwell came to our door with a box of soldiers. Emily and I jumped out of bed and I snatched up one and exclaimed, 'This is the Duke of Wellington! It shall be mine!'* When I said this, Emily likewise took one and said it should be hers. When Anne came down she took one also. Mine was the prettiest of the whole and perfect in every part. Emily's was a grave-looking fellow. We called him Gravey. Anne's was a queer little thing, very much like herself. He was called Waiting Boy. Branwell chose Bonaparte.*

March 12 1829

'The origin of the O'Dears'*

The origin of the O'Dears was as follows. We pretended we had each a large island inhabited by people 6 miles high. The people we took out of Aesop's Fables. Hay Man was my cheif man, Boaster Branwell's, Hunter Anne's, and Clown* Emily's. Our cheif men were 10 miles high excep[t] Emily's, who was only 4.   March 12, 1829

'The origin of the Islanders'

The origin of the Islanders was as follows. It was one wet night in December. We were all sitting round the fire and had been silent some time, and at last I said, 'Supose we had each an Island of our own.' Branwell chose the Isle of Man, Emily Isle of Arran and Bute Isle, Anne, Jersey, and I chose the Isle of Wight.* We then chose who should live in our islands. The cheif of Branwell's were John Bull, Astley Cooper, Leigh Hunt, &c, &c. Emily's Walter Scott, Mr Lockhart, Johnny Lockhart &c, &c. Anne's Michael Sadler, Lord Bentinck, Henry Halford, &c, &c. And I chose Duke of Wellington & son, North & Co., 30 officers, Mr Abernethy, &c, &c.* March 12, 1829.

TWO ROMANTIC TALES
by Charlotte Bronte
April 28, 1829

THE TWELVE ADVENTURERS*
Written April 15 1829

CHAPTER I
The Country of the Genii

There is a tradition that some thousands of years ago twelve men from Britain, of a most gigantic size, and twelve men from Gaul* came over to the country of the Genii,* and while there were continually at war with each other and, after remaining many years, returned again to Britain and Gaul. And in the inhabited [parts] of the Genii country there are now no vestiges of them, though it is said there have been found some colossal skeletons in that wild, barren land,* the evil desert.

But I have read a book called 'The Travels of Captain Parnell', out of which the following is an extract.*

'About four in the afternoon I saw a dark red cloud arise in the east, which gradually grew larger till it covered the whole sky. As the cloud spread the wind rose and blew a tremendous hurricane. The sand of the desert began to move and rolled like the waves of the sea. As soon as I saw this I threw myself on my face and stopped my breath, for I knew that this was the tornado or whirlwind. I remained in this situation for three minutes, for at the end of that time I ventured to look up. The whirlwind had passed over and had not hurt me, but close by lay my poor camel quite dead. At this sight I could not forbear weeping, but my attention was soon diverted by another object. About one hundred yards further off lay an immense skeleton. I immediately ran up to it and examined it closely. While I was gazing at the long, ghastly figure which lay stretched upon the sand before me the thought came into my mind that it might be the skeleton of one of those ancient Britons who, tradition tells us, came from their own country to this evil land and here miserably perished. While I was pursuing this train of meditation, I observed that it was bound with a long chain of rusty iron. Suddenly the iron clanked and the bones strove to rise, but a huge mountain of sand overwhelmed the skeleton with a tremendous crash, and when the dust which had hid the sun and enveloped every[thing] in darkness cleared away, not a mark could be distinguished to show the future traveller where the bones had lain.'*

Now, if this account be true—and I see no reason why we should suppose it not—I think [we] may fairly conclude that these skeletons are evil genii chained in these deserts by the fairy Maimoune.*

There are several other traditions, but they are all so obscure that no reliance is to be placed on them.

CHAPTER II

The Voyage of Discovery

In the year 1793 the Invincible, 74 guns, set sail with a fair wind from England. Her crew—twelve men, every one healthy and stout and in the best temper—their names as follows: Marcus O'Donell, Ferdinand Cortez, Felix de Rothsay, Eugene Cameron, Harold FitzGeorge, Henry Clinton, Francis Stewart, Ronald Traquair, Ernest Fortescue, Gustavus Dunally, Frederick Brunswick, and Arthur Wellesley.*

Well, as I said before, we set sail with a fair wind from England on the 1st of March 1793. On the 15th we came in sight of Spain. On the 16th we landed, bought a supply of provisions, &c. and set sail again on the 20th. On the 25th, about noon, Henry Clinton,* who was in the shrouds, cried out that he saw the Oxeye.* In a minute we were all on deck and all eyes gazing eagerly and fearfully towards the mountain over which we saw hanging in the sky the ominous speck. Instantly the sails were furled, the ship tacked about, and the boat was made ready for launching in our last extremity.

Thus having made everything ready we retired to the cabin, and everyone looked as sheepish as possible and noway inclined to meet our fate like men. Some of us began to cry, but we waited a long time and heard no sound of the wind, and the cloud did not increase in size.

At last Marcus O'Donell exclaimed, 'I wish it would either go backward or forward.'

At this Stewart reproved him, and Ferdinand gave him a box on the ear. O'Donell returned the compliment. But just then we heard the sound of the wind, and Ronald bawled* out, 'The cloud is as big as me!'

Brunswick pulled Ronald away from the window and ordered him to hold his tongue. Ronald said he would not and began to sing. Felix de Rothsay put his hand over Ronald's mouth. H. FitzGeorge got Rothsay behind by the throat. E. Fortescue held his fist in O'Donell's face, and Marcus floored Ernest. Cameron kicked Clinton to the other end of the cabin, and Stewart shouted so loud for them to be quiet that he made the greatest noise of any.

But suddenly they were all silenced by a fierce flash of lightning and a loud peal of thunder. The wind rose and the planks of our ship creaked. Another flash of lightning, brighter and more terrible than the first, split our mainmast and carried away our foretop-sail. And now the flashes of lightning grew terrific, and the thunder roared tremendously. The rain poured down in torrents, and the gusts of wind were most loud and terrible. The hearts of the stoutest men in our company now quailed, and even the chief doctor was afraid.*

At last the storm ceased, but we found it had driven us quite out of our course and we knew not where we were.

On the 30th, G. Dunally, who was on deck cried out, 'Land!'

At this we were all extremely rejoiced. On the 31st we reached it, and found it was the island of Trinidad. We refitted our ship and got in a store of provisions and water, and set sail once more on the 5th of May.

It would be endless to describe all our adventures in the South Atlantic Ocean. Suffice it to say that after many storms, in which we were driven quite out of our course and knew not in what part of the world we were, we at last discovered land. We sailed along the coast for some time to find a good landing-place. We at last found one.

We landed on the 2nd of June 1793.* We moored our battered ship in a small harbour and advanced up into the country. To our great surprise we found it cultivated. Grain of a peculiar sort grew in great abundance, and there were large plantations of palm-trees,* and likewise an immense number of almond-trees. There were also many olives and large enclosures of rice. We were greatly surprised at these marks of the land being inhabited. It seemed to be part of an immense continent.

After we had travelled about two miles we saw at a distance twenty men well armed. We immediately prepared for battle, having each of us a pistol, sword and bayonet. We stood still and they came near.

When they had come close up to us they likewise stopped. They seemed greatly surprised at us, and we heard one of them say, 'What strange people!'

The Chief then said, 'Who are you?'

Wellesley answered, 'We were cast up on your shores by a storm and request shelter.'

They said, 'You shall not have any.'

W[ellesley]: 'We will take it then!'

We prepared for battle; they did the same.

It was a very fierce encounter, but we conquered: killed ten, took the Chief prisoner, wounded five, and the remaining four retreated. The Chief was quite black [and] very tall. He had a fierce* countenance and the finest eyes I ever saw. We asked him what his name was, but he would not speak. We asked him the name of his country, and he said, 'Ashantee.'*

Next morning a party of twelve men came to our tents bringing with them a ransom for their Chief, and likewise a proposition of peace from their King. This we accepted, as it was on terms the most advantageous to ourselves.

Immediately after the treaty of peace was concluded we set about building a city. The situation was in the middle of a large plain, bounded on the north by high mountains, on the south by the sea, on the east by gloomy forests, and on the west by evil deserts.*

About a month after we had begun our city the following adventure happened to us.

One evening when all were assembled in the great tent, and most of us sitting round the fire which blazed in the middle of the pavilion, listening to the storm which raged without our camp, a dead silence prevailed. None of us felt inclined to speak, still less to laugh, and the wine-cups stood upon the round table filled to the brim. In the midst of this silence we heard the sound of a trumpet, which seemed to come from the desert. The next moment a peal of thunder rolled through the sky, which seemed to shake the earth to its centre.

By this time we were all on our legs and filled with terror, which was changed to desperation by another blast of the terrible trumpet. We all rushed out of the tent with a shout, not of courage, but fear, and then we saw a sight so terribly grand that even now when I think of it, at the distance of forty years from that dismal night when I saw it, my limbs tremble and my blood is chilled with fear. High in the clouds was a tall and terrible giant. In his right hand he held a trumpet, in his left, two darts pointed with fire. On a thunder cloud which rolled before him his shield rested. On his forehead was written 'The Genius of the Storm'.* On he strode over the black clouds which rolled beneath his feet and regardless of the fierce lightning which flashed around him. But soon the thunder ceased and the lightning no longer glared so terribly.

The hoarse voice of the storm was hushed, and a gentler light than the fire of the elements spread itself over the face of the now cloudless sky. The calm moon shone forth in the midst of the firmament, and the little stars seemed rejoicing in their brightness. The giant had descended to the earth, and, approaching the place where we stood trembling, he made three circles in the air with his flaming scimitar, then lifted his hand to strike. Just then we heard a loud voice saying, 'Genius, I command thee to forbear!'

We looked round and saw a figure* so tall that the Genius seemed to it but a diminutive dwarf. It cast one joyful glance on us and disappeared.

CHAPTER III

The Desert

The building of our city went on prosperously. The Hall of Justice was finished; the fortifications were completed; the Grand Inn was begun; the Great Tower* was ended.

One night when we were assembled in the Hall of Justice, Arthur Wellesley, at that time a common trumpeter, suddenly exclaimed, while we were talking of our happiness, 'Does not the King of the Blacks view our prosperity with other eyes than ours? Would not the best way be to send immediately to England, tell them of the new world we have discovered and of the riches that are in it, and do you not think they would send us an army?'

Francis Stewart immediately rose and said, 'Young man, think before you speak! How could we send to England? Who could be found hardy enough to traverse again the Atlantic? Do you not remember the storm which drove us on the shores of Trinidad?'

A[rthur] W[ellesley] answered, 'It is with all due deference that I ventured to contradict the opinions of older and more experienced men than I am, and it is after much consideration that I ventured to say what I have said. Well do I remember that storm which forced us to seek refuge among foreigners. I am not so rash as to suppose we of ourselves could cross the ocean in the damaged and leaky vessel we possess, or that we could build another [in] time enough to avert the danger which I fear is coming. But in what a short time have we built [the city] we now are in! How long has it taken to rear the Grand Hall where we now are? Have not those marble pillars and that solemn dome been built by supernatural power? If you view the city from this Gothic window and see the beams of the morn gilding the battlements of the mighty towers, and the pillars of the splendid palaces which have been reared in a few months, can you doubt that magic has been used in their construction?'

Here he paused. We were all convinced that the Genii had helped us to build our town. He went on, 'Now, if the Genii have built us our city, will they not likewise help us to call our countrymen to defend what they have built against the assaults of the enemy?'

He stopped again, for the roof shook and the hall was filled with smoke. The ground opened, and we heard a voice saying, 'When the sun appears above the forests of the east be ye all on the border of the evil desert. If ye fail I will crush you to atoms.'

The voice ceased, the ground closed, and the smoke cleared away. There was no time for us to consult. The desert lay ten miles off, and it was now midnight. We immediately set off with the Duke of York at our head. We reached the desert about 4 a.m.; there we stopped. Far off to the east the long black line of gloomy forests skirted the horizon. To the north the Jibbel Kumri, or Mountains of the Moon, seemed a misty girdle to the plain of Dahomey. To the south the ocean guarded the coasts of Africa. Before us to the west lay the desert.

In a few minutes we saw a dense vapour arise from the sands, which gradually collecting took the form of a Genius larger than any of the giants. It advanced towards us and cried with a loud voice, 'Follow me!'

We obeyed and entered the desert. After we had travelled a long time, about noon the Genius told us to look around. We were now about the middle of the desert. Nothing was to be seen far or near but vast plains of sand under a burning sun and cloudless sky. We were dreadfully fatigued and begged the Genius to allow us to stop a little, but he immediately ordered us to proceed. We therefore began our march again and travelled a long way, till the sun went down and the pale moon was rising in the east. Also a few stars might now be dimly seen, but still the sands were burning hot and our feet were very much swollen.

At last the Genius ordered us to halt and lie down. We soon fell asleep. We had slept about an hour when the Genius awoke us and ordered us to proceed.

The moon had now risen and shone brightly in the midst of the sky—brighter far than it ever does in our country. The night-wind had somewhat cooled the sands of the desert, so that we walked with more ease than before, but soon a mist arose which covered the whole plain. Through it we thought we could discern a dim light. We now likewise heard sounds of music at a great distance.

As the mist* cleared away the light grew more distinct till it burst upon us in almost insufferable splendour. Out of the barren desert arose a palace of diamond, the pillars of which were ruby and emerald, illuminated with lamps too bright to look upon.* The Genius led us into a hall of sapphire in which were thrones of gold. On the thrones sat the Princes of the Genii. In the midst of the hall hung a lamp like the sun. Around it stood genii, and fairies without, whose robes were of beaten gold sparkling with diamonds. As soon as their chiefs saw us they sprang up from their thrones, and one of them seizing A W and exclaimed, 'This is the Duke of Wellington!'

A W asked her why she called him D of W.

The Genius answered, 'A prince will arise who shall be as a thorn in the side of England, and the desolator of Europe. Terrible shall be the struggle between that chieftain and you! It will last many years, and the conqueror shall gain eternal honour and glory. So likewise shall the vanquished, and though he shall die in exile his name shall never be remembered by his countrymen but with feelings of enthusiasm. The renown of the victor shall reach to the ends of the earth. Kings and Emperors shall honour him, and Europe shall rejoice in its deliverer. Though in his lifetime fools will envy him, he shall overcome. At his death renown shall cover him, and his name shall be everlasting!'

When the Genius finished speaking we heard the sound of music far off, which drew nearer and nearer till it seemed within the hall. Then all the fairies and genii joined in one grand chorus, which rose rolling to the mighty dome and stately pillars of the Genii Palace, and reached among the vaults and dungeons beneath, then gradually dying away it at last ceased entirely.

As the music went off the palace slowly disappeared, till it vanished* and we found ourselves alone in the midst of the desert. The sun had just begun to enlighten the world and the moon might be dimly seen, but all below them was sand as far as our eyes could reach. We knew not which way to go, and we were ready to faint with hunger, but on once more looking round we saw lying on the sands some dates and palm-wine. Of this we made our breakfast and then began again to think of our journey, when suddenly there appeared a beaten track in the desert, which we followed.

About noon, when the sun was at its meridian, and we felt weary and faint with the heat, a grove of palm-trees appeared in sight towards which we ran. And after we had reposed awhile under its shade and refreshed ourselves with its fruit, we resumed our march, and that same night, to our inexpressible joy, we entered the gates of our beautiful city and slept beneath the shadow of its roofs.

CHAPTER IV

News from Home

The next morning we were awoke by the sound of trumpets and great war-drums, and on looking towards the mountains we saw descending on the plain an immense army of Ashantees. We were all thrown into the utmost consternation except A W, who advised us to look to the great guns and to man the walls, never doubting that the Genii would come to our help if we of ourselves could not beat them off by the help of the cannon and rockets. This advice we immediately followed, while the Ashantees came on like a torrent, sweeping everything, burning the palm-trees, and laying waste the rice-fields.

When they came up to the walls of our city they set up a terrible yell, the meaning of which was that we should be consumed from the face of the earth, and that our city should vanish away, for as it came by magic it should go by the same. Our answer to this insolent speech was a peal of thunder from the mouths of our cannon. Two fell dead, and the rest gave us leg bail* setting off towards the mountains with inconceivable* swiftness, followed by a triumphant shout from their conquerors.

They come back in the afternoon and in the most submissive terms asked for their dead. We granted their request, and in return they allowed us to witness the funeral.

A few days after, on the 21st of Sept., Ronald came running into the Hall of Justice, where we all were, shouting out that there was a ship from England. The Duke of York immediately sent A W to ascertain the truth of this.

When he arrived at the seashore he found all the crew, consisting of fifty men, had landed. He then examined the state of the ship and found it was almost a complete wreck. He asked the men a few questions and they seemed greatly surprised to find him here, and asked him how he contrived to live in such a country. He told them to follow him.

When he brought them to the Hall of Justice, the Duke of Y ordered* them to relate their story.

They cried, 'We were driven on your shore by a storm and request shelter.'

The Duke of York answered, 'Fellow-English,* we rejoice that you were driven on our part of the coast, and you shall have shelter if we can give it.'

Accordingly they remained with us about a fortnight, for at the end of that time the Genii had fitted out their ship again, when they set sail for England accompanied by A W.

For about ten years after this we continued at war with the blacks, and then made peace, after which, for about ten years more, nothing happened worth mentioning.

On the 16th of May 1816 a voice passed through the city saying, 'Set a watch on the tower which looks towards the south, for tomorrow a conqueror shall enter your gates!'

The Duke of York immediately despatched Henry Clinton to the highest tower in the city. About noon Clinton cried out, 'I see something at a great distance upon the Atlantic.'

We all of us ran to the watch-tower, and on looking toward the ocean we could discern a dark object upon the verge of the horizon which, as it neared the shore, we saw plainly was a fleet. At last it anchored and the crew began to land. First came 12 regiments of horsemen, next, three of infantry, then several high officers who* seemed to be the staff of some great general. And last of all came the general himself, whom several of us asserted had the bearing of Arthur Wellesley.

After he had marshalled the regiments he ordered them to march, and we saw them enter the gates of the city. When they arrived at the tower they stopped, and we heard the general in the tone of W say, 'Hill,* you may stop here with the army while I go to the Palace of Justice, as I suppose they are all there if they be yet in the land of the living. And Beresford,* you must come with me.'

'No, no, we are here, Arthur, almost terrified out of our wits for fear you shall burn the tower and sack the city!' exclaimed the Duke of York, as we descend[ed] from our hiding-place.

'What! Are you all here, and not one of you slain in battle or dead in the hospital?' said His Grace, as he sprang from his war-horse and we shook hands with him one at a time. 'But come, my brave fellows, let

us go to the Grand Inn, and in Ferdinando Hall we will talk of what we
have done and suffered since we last met.'

'Please, Your Grace, in what part of the town are the army to be quar-
tered?' said one of the staff.

'Oh, never you fear for the army, Murray,* we are not among
Spaniards. Let them follow me.'

'The army are to follow His Grace the Duke of Wellington,' said
Murray.

'His Grace the Duke of Wellington!' we all exclaimed at once in
surprise.

'Yes—His Grace the Duke of Wellington,' said another of the staff.
'I don't know who you are, but our most noble general is* the conqueror of Bonaparte and the deliverer of Europe.'

'Then the Genii don't always tell lies,' said Marcus O'Donell, 'and
I am very glad of it, for I always thought, Duke, you would return to us
with more glory than you had [when you] went away from us.'

'Indeed!' said Murray with a sneer.

'Murray,' said His Grace sternly, 'I shall call you to account for this
insolence and punish by martial law if you don't make a handsome
apology to this Gentleman.'

Murray immediately advanced to O'Donell and said, 'Sir, I am very
sorry for my foolish insolence, and I promise you I will never offend
you so again.'

'Very well, Murray, very well indeed,' said the Duke. 'Now shake
hands and be friends. I hate civil war.'

By this time we had arrived at the Grand Inn, which was a most
superior* building and large enough to accommodate 20,000 men. We
were soon seated in the hall and listening to Beresford as he related to
us how Europe had been set free from the iron chain of a despot,* and
how the mighty victory had been achieved with which all the civilised
world had rung; of the splendid triumphs which had taken place on
that glorious occasion; and how all the high sovereigns of Europe had
honoured England with their presence on that grand occasion. Longer
could we have listened and more could he have told had we not heard
the sound of the midnight bell which reminded us that it was time to
retire to rest.

Some days after this the Duke of York expressed a wish to return
to his own country, and one of the ships with about twenty men were
appointed to convey him there.

There were now in the city fifteen thousand men, and we determined to elect a King. Accordingly a council of the whole nation was

summoned for the 14th of June 1827. On that day they all assembled
in the Palace of Justice. Around the throne sat Marcus O'Donell,
F Cortez, H Clinton, G Dunally, Harold FitzGeorge, and the Duke
of Wellington and his staff. An intense anxiety pervaded the council
to know who would be proposed as King, for not a man of us knew
and no hints had been thrown out. At length the great entrance was
closed, and Cortez proclaimed the whole nation to be present. Stewart
then rose and said, 'I propose the most noble Field-Marshall Arthur,
Duke of Wellington, as a fit and proper person to sit on the throne of
the realms.'

Immediately a loud shout burst forth from the multitude, and the
hall rang, 'Long live our most noble Duke!'

Wellington now rose. Immediately* a profound silence pervaded*
the house.

He said as follows, 'Soldiers,* I will defend what you have committed
to my care.' Then, bowing to the council, he retired amidst thundering
sounds of enthusiastic joy.

C. BRONTË

AN ADVENTURE IN IRELAND

During my travels in the south of Ireland the following adventure
happened to me. One evening in the month of August, after a
long walk, as I was ascending the mountain which overlooks the
village of Cahir,* I suddenly came in sight of a fine old castle. It was
built upon a rock, and behind it was a large wood and before it was a
river. Over the river there was a bridge, which formed the approach to
the castle.

When I arrived at the bridge I stood still awhile to enjoy the prospect
around me. Far below was the wide sheet of still water in which the
reflection of the pale moon was not disturbed by the smallest wave.
In the valley was the cluster of cabins which is known by the appellation
of Cahir, and beyond these were the mountains of Killala. Over all the
grey robe of twilight was now stealing with silent and scarcely perceptible advances. No sound except the hum of the distant village and the
sweet song of the nightingale in the wood behind me broke upon the
stillness of the scene.

While I was contemplating this beautiful prospect, a gentleman,
whom I had not before observed, accosted me with 'Good evening, sir.
Are you a stranger in these parts?'

I replied that I was. He then asked me where I was going to stop for the night. I answered that I intended to sleep somewhere in the village.

'I am afraid you will find very bad accommodation there,' said the gentleman. 'But if you will take up your quarters with me at the castle, you are welcome.'

I thanked him for his kind offer and accepted it.

When we arrived at the castle I was shown into a large parlour, in which was an old lady sitting in an armchair by the fireside, knitting. On the rug lay a very pretty tortoise-shell cat. As soon as we entered the old lady rose, and when Mr O'Callaghan (for that, I learned, was his name) told her who I was, she said in the most cordial tone that I was welcome, and asked me to sit down.

In the course of conversation I learned that she was Mr O'Callaghan's mother, and that his father had been dead about a year.

We had sat about an hour when supper was announced, and after supper Mr O'Callaghan asked me if I should like to retire for the night. I answered in the affirmative, and a little boy was commissioned to show me to my apartment. It was a snug, clean, and comfortable little old-fashioned room at the top of the castle. As soon as we had entered, the boy, who appeared to be a shrewd, good-tempered little fellow, said with a shrug of the shoulder, 'If it was going to bed I was, it shouldn't be here that you'd catch me.'

'Why?' said I.

'Because,' replied the boy, 'they say that the ould masther's ghost has been seen sitting on that there chair.'

'And have you seen him?'

'No, but I've heard him washing his hands in that basin often and often.'

'What is your name, my little fellow?'

'Dennis Mulready, please your honour.'

'Well, good-night to you.'

'Good night, masther, and may the saints keep you from all fairies and brownies,' said Dennis as he left the room.

As soon as I had laid down I began to think of what the boy had been telling me, and I confess I felt a strange kind of fear, and once or twice I even thought I could discern something white through the darkness which surrounded me. At length, by the help of reason, I succeeded in mastering these, what some would call idle fancies, and fell asleep.

I had slept about an hour when a strange sound awoke me, and I saw looking through my curtains a skeleton wrapped in a white sheet. I was overcome with terror and tried to scream, but my tongue was paralysed and my whole frame shook with fear. In a deep hollow voice it said to me, 'Arise, that I may show thee this world's wonders,' and in an instant I found myself encompassed with clouds and darkness. But soon the roar of mighty waters fell upon my ear, and I saw some clouds of spray arising from high falls that rolled in awful majesty down tremendous precipices, and then foamed and thundered in the gulf beneath as if they had taken up their unquiet abode in some giant's cauldron.*

But soon the scene changed, and I found myself in the mines of Cracone. Here were high pillars and stately arches, whose glittering splendour was never excelled by the brightest fairy palaces. There were not many lamps, only those of a few poor miners, whose* homely figures and rough visages formed a striking contrast to the dazzling grandeur which surrounded them. But in the midst of all this magnificence I felt an indescribable sense of fear and terror, for the sea raged above us, and by the awful and tumultuous noises of roaring winds and dashing waves it seemed as if the storm was violent. And now the mossy pillars groaned beneath the pressure of the ocean, and the glittering arches seemed about to be overwhelmed. When I heard the rushing waters and saw a mighty flood rolling towards me, I gave a loud shriek of terror.

The scene vanished and I found myself in a wide desert full of barren rocks and high mountains. As I was approaching one of the rocks, in which there was a large cave, my foot stumbled and I fell. Just then I heard a deep growl and saw by the unearthly light of his own fiery eyes a royal lion rousing himself from his kingly slumbers. His terrible eye was fixed upon me, and the desert rang and the rocks echoed with the tremendous roar of fierce delight which he uttered as he sprang towards me.

'Well, masther, it's been a windy night, though it's fine now,' said Dennis, as he drew the window-curtain and let the bright rays of the morning sun into the little old-fashioned room at the top of O'Callaghan Castle.

C. BRONTË,
April 28th, 1829

SECOND VOL OF TALES OF THE ISLANDERS

TALES of the ISLANDERS
VOLUME II

CHAP. I
The School Rebellion*

I have before put forth a volume of these tales, in which the subject of the school was mentioned. In that volume, I laid down the rules by which the school was governed & likewise the names of the governors with their several characters, &c.* I shall now proceed with this subject.

For some time after it was established, the institution went on very well. All the rules were observed with scrupulous exactness. The governors attended admirably to their duty. The children were absolutely becoming something like civilized beings, to all outward appearance at least: gambling was less frequent among them; their quarrels with each other were less savage; & some little attention was paid by themselves to order & cleanliness. At this time we constantly resided in the magnificent palace of the school, as did all the governors, so that nothing was left entirely to the care of servants & underlings. The great room had become the resort of all the great ministers in their hours of leisure (that is in the evenings) and they, seeing how well it* were conducted, resolved to uphold the institution with all their might.

This prosperous state of affairs continued for about six months, & then Parliament was opened & the great Catholic Question* was brought forward & the Duke's measures were disclosed, and all was slander, violence, party spirit & confusion. O those 3 months, from the time of the King's speech to the end! Nobody could think, speak or write on anything but the Catholic Question and the Duke of Wellington or Mr Peel.* I remember the day when the Intelligence Extraordinary came with Mr Peel's speech in it, containing the terms on which the Catholics were to be let in. With what eagerness Papa tore off the cover, & how we all gathered rou[nd h]im, & with what breathless anxiety we listened, a[s o]ne by one they were disclosed & explained & argued upon so ably & so well, & then, when it was all out, how Aunt said she thought it was excellent & that the Catholics [could] do no harm with such good security.* I remember also the doubts as to whether it would pass into the House of Lord[s] & the prophecies that it would not. Wh[en] the paper came which was to decide the question, the anxiety was almost dreadful with which we listen[ed] to the whole affair: the opening of the doors, the hus[h], the royal dukes in their robes & the great Duke in green sash & waistcoat, the rising of all the peeresses when he rose, the reading of his speec[h], Papa saying that his words were like precious gold &, lastly, the majority one to 4 in favour of the bill. But this is a digression & I must beg my readers to excuse it. To proceed with my subject then.

In consequence of this Catholic Question, the Duke & Mr Peel were of course obliged to be constantly in London & we soon took ourselves off to the same place. O'S[haughnesy] and his nephew* were away shooting somewhere & the whole management of the school was left to the Marquis of D[ouro] and Lord Charles W[ellesley]. The upshot will be seen in the next chap[ter].

CHAPTER II

For sometime we heard not a word about the school & never took the trouble to inquire, until at length, one morning as we were sitting at breakfast, in came a letter, the which when we had opened we perceived was from my Lord W[ellesley]. The purport was as follow[s]:

June 8. Vision Island

Little Kings & Queens,

I write this letter to inform you of a rebellion, which has broken out in the school, the particulars of which I have not time to relate. All I can say is that I am at present in a little hut built in the open air and—. But they are coming & I can say no more—.

I remain yours &c—

Charles W

PS Since I wrote the above we have had a battle in which our bloodhounds fought bravely & we have conquered. We are, however, reduced to a great extremity for want of food, & if you don't make haste & come to our help, we must surrender. Bring my father's great bloodhound with you & Doctor Hume* & the gamekeeper likewise——— —

As soon as we had read this letter, we ordered a balloon, the which when it was brought we got into & then steered our way through the air towards Strathfieldsay. When we had there arrived, we took up 'Blood an 'ounds'* & the gamekeeper & then went quick-way to the island.

We alighted in the grounds about the school and, on casting our eyes towards the myrtle grove, we saw the stately palace rising in its magnificence from the green trees which grew thickly around & towering in silent grandeur over that isle, which [was] rightly named a dream, for never but in the visions of the night has the eye of man beheld such gorgeous beauty, such wild magnificence, as is in this fairy land, & never, but in the imaginings of his heart, has his ear heard such musick as that which proceeds from the giant's harp, hid from sight amid those trees. Listen! There is a faint sound, like the voice of a dying swan, but now a stronger breeze sweeps through the strin[gs] and the music is rising. Hark how it swells! What grand[eur] was in that wild note! But the wind roars louder. I now heard the muttering of distant thunder: it is drawing nearer & nearer, & the tunes of the harp & swelling till all at once, amidst the roaring of thunder & the howling of the wind, it peals out with such awful wildness, such unearthly grandeur, that you are tempted to believe it is the voice of spirits speak[ing], 'This [is] the storm.'

But to proceed with my subject. After we had been in the island about half an hour, we saw Lord W[ellesley] approaching at a distance. When he came near he accosted us with, 'Well, Little Queens, I am glad you are come. Make haste & follow me, for there is not a mome[nt] to be lost.'

As we went along, he, at our request, gave us the following narrative as to the origin of the school rebellion.

'For about 3 days after you were gone, things went on very well, but at the end of that time symptoms of insubordination began to manifest themselves. These we strove to check, but in vain, &, instead of growing better, they grew worse. The school now was divided into 4 parties, each of whom was headed by a cheiftain, namely, P[rince] Polignac, P[rince] George & Johnny Lockhart & the Princess Vittoria.* These 4 were constantly quarrelling & fighting with each other in a most outrageous maner, &, after strugglin[g] a few weeks with them to no purpose, they all ran off & are now encamped in a very wild part of the island which we shall presently come to. They are well provided with 2 cannons each party & a quantity of powder & shot. Sometimes they all unite agains[t] us & then we have a bad chance, I assure you, but now you are come to our assistance, we shall soon do for them.'

As soon as he had ended, we emerged from the forest in which we had till then been travellin[g] & entred a deep glen, through which rushed an impetuous, brawling river, roaring & foaming amongst the large stones which impeded its cours[e], & [?then], as its channel deepened & widened, it became calm & smooth, flowing silently through the wide, green plain on the right hand, fertilizing & refreshing it as it went. On our left arose rocks, frowning darkly over the glen & blackning it with their mighty shadow. In some parts they were covered with tall pine trees, through which the wind moaned sadly as it swept among their scathed branches. In other parts, immense fragments of rock looked out from their shaggy covering & hung their grey summits awfully over the vale. No sound but the echo of a distant cann[on], which was discharged as we entered the glen, & the scream of the eagle startled from her aerie* disturbed the deathlike silence.

In a short time we came to the place where the children were encamped. The tents of the Vittorians wer[e] pitched on the summit of a rock; those of the Polignac[s], in a deep ravine; & the Georgians had taken up their abode in a open spot of ground & the Lockhartians had entrenched themselves among some trees. The hut of the Marquis of Douro & Lord Wellesley was built beneath the shade of a spreading oak. A tremendous rock rose above it. On one side was a gently swelling hill, on the other, a grove of tall trees & before it ran a clear, rippling stream.

When we had entered the humble abode, we beheld the Marquis of D[ouro] lying on a bed of leaves. His face was very pale. His fine features seemed as fixed as a marble statue. His eyes were closed & his glossy, curling hair was in some parts stiffened with blood. As soon as we beheld this sight, Charles rushed forward &, falling on the bed beside his brother, he fainted away. The usual remedies were then applied to him by Doctor Hume, & after a long time he recovered. All this while Arthur had neither spoke nor stirred, & we thought he was dead. The game-keeper was raving, & even the hardihearted* H[ume] shed some tears, & Charles seemed like one demented.

In this emergency, we thought it advisabl[e] to send quick-way for the Duke of Wellington. This we accordingly did &, as soon as we saw him coming, one of us went out to meet him. When we had informed him of what had happened, he became as pale as death. His lips quivered

& his whole frame shook with agitation. In a short time he arrived at the hut & then, going up to the bedside, he took hold of one lifeless hand & said in a tremulous & scarcely audible voice, 'Arthur, my son, speak to me.'

Just then, at the sound of his father's words, Arthur slowly opened his eyes & looked up. When he saw the Duke he tried to speak, but could not. We then, in the plenitude of our goodness & kindness of heart, cured him instantaneousl[y] by the application of some fairy remedie, for as soon as we had done so the Duke drew from his finger a diamond ring & presented it to us. This we accepted & thanked him for it.

After these transactions, we informed His Grace of the school rebellion. He immediately went out, without speaking a word, & we followed him. He proceeded up to the place where they were encamped & called out in a loud tone of voice that if they did not surrender they were all dead men, as he had brought several thousand blood hounds with him, who would tear them to peices in a moment. This they dreaded more than any thing & therefore agreed to surrender, which they did immediately. And for a short time thereafter the school prospered as before, but we, becoming tired of it, sent the children off to their own homes & now only fairies dwell in the Island of a Dream.

C. Bronte October 6, 1829

CHAPTER the THIRD

A Strange Incident in the Duke of Wellington's Life

About a year after the school rebellion, the following wonderful thing happened in the family of the Duke of Wellington. One pleasant morning in the month of September 1828, the Marquis of D[ouro] and Lord Charles W[ellesley] went out to follow the sport of shooting. They had promised to return before 8 o'clock but, however, 10 o'clock came & they had not returned; 12 [o'clock] & still no signs of them. Old Man Cockney* then ordered the servants to bed & when they had retired & [?all] was quietness, he went into the great hall & sat down by the fire, determined not to go to bed till they came back.

He had sat about half an hour listening anxiously for their arrival whe[n] the inner door gently opened & Lady W[ellesley] appeared. O[ld] M[an] [?Cockney] could see by the light of the fire, for he ha[d] put out the candle, that she was very pale & much agitated.

'What is the matter, madam?' said he.

L[ady] W[ellesley]: 'I was sitting down working when suddenly I saw th[e] light cast on my work by the taper turn blue & death-like, burning phosphorus or asphalt, as I looked up & saw the figures of my sons all bloody & distorted. I gazed on them till they vanished, unable to speak or stir, & then I came down here.'

She had scarcely finished the recital of this strange vision when the great door was heard to open with a loud, creaking noise, & the Duke of W[ellington] entered. He stood still for a moment earnestly looking at L[ady] W[ellesley] & the old man & then said, in a distinctly audible but hollow tone of voice, 'Catherine, where are my sons, for I heard while sitting in my study their voices moaning and wailing around me & supplicating me to deliver them from the death they were abou[t] to die. Even now, I feel a dreadful foreboding concernin[g] them which I cannot shake off. Catherine, where are th[ey?]'

Before Lady W[ellesley] could answer, the door again opened & we appeared. He immediately addressed us & begged of us to tell him what had become of them. We replied that we did not know, but that, if he liked, we would go in search of them. He thanked us gratefully, adding that he would go with us, & then, after he had taken leave of Lady W[ellesley], we immediately set off.

We had gone as near as we could, [?about] 4 miles, when we entred a very wild, barren plain, which none of us had ever seen before. We continued on this plain till we lost sight of everything else & then suddenly perceived the whole aspect of the [?sky] to be changed. It assumed the appearance of large, rolling waves, created with white foam. Also we could hear a thundering sound, like the roaring of the sea at a distance, & the moon seemed a great globe of [?many] miles in diameter.

We were gazing in silent astonishment at this glorious sight, which every minute was growing grander & grander & the noise of thunder was increasing, when suddenly the huge waves parted asunder & a giant clothed in the sun with a crown of 12 stars on his head* descended on the plain. For a moment our sight was destroyed by the glory of his apparel, & when it was restored to us we found ourselves in a world the beauty of which exceeds [?beyond] my powers of description. There were trees & bowers of light, waters of liquid crystal flowing over sands of gold with a sound the melody of which far exceeds music of the finest toned harps or the song of the sweet voiced nightingales. There were palaces of emerald & ruby, of diamond, of amethyst and pearl, arches like the rainbow of jasper, agate & sapphire spanning wide seas whose mighty voices were now hushed into a gentle murmur & sang in sweet unison with the silver streams which flowed through this radiant land, while their glorious song was echoed & reechoed by high mountains, which rose in the distance & which shone in the glowing light like fine opals set in gold.

We had been here for a short time when the sky blackned; the winds rose; the waves of the ocean began to roar. All beautiful things vanished & were succeded by tall, dark cypress & fir trees, which swayed to & fro in the wind with a mournful sound like the moans of dying mortals. A huge black rock appeared before us. A wide & dark cavern opened in it, in which we saw A[rthur] & C[harles] W[ellesley]. The giant then came again &, taking them & us in his arms, flew swiftly through the air & landed us all in the great hall of Strathfieldsay.

CHAPTER the IV

The Duke of Wellington's Tale to his Sons

It was a beautiful evening in the month of August when the Duke of Wellington & his sons were seated in a small private parlour at the top of the great round tower at Strathfieldsay. The sun was just setting & its beams shone through the gothic window, half veiled by a green, velvet curtain which had fallen from the golden supports & hung in rich festoons with a glowing brillia[nce] equal to the crimson light which streams from the oriental ruby, but unlike to that beautiful gem, it was every moment decreasing in splendou[r], till at length only a faint rose tint remained on the marble pedestal which stood opposite, bearing the statue of William Pitt* & which, but a little while ago, had shone with a brightness resembling the lustre [of] burnished gold.

Just as the last ray disappeared, Lord Charles Wellesley exclaimed, 'Father, I wish you would relate to us some of your adventures either in India or Spain.'*

'Very well, I will, Charles. Now listen attentively,' replied His Grace. 'Would you like to hear too, Arthur?'

'I should, very much,' answere[d] the Marquis, with a gravity & calmness which formed a striking contrast to the giddy gaiety that marred the deportment of his younger brother.

His Grace then began as follows. 'In the year & the day of the Battle [of] Salamanca,* just as the sun set & the twilight was approaching, I finished my despatches & walked forth from the convent gates of the Rector of Salamanca in order to enjoy the coolness of a Spanish evening. To this purpose I proceeded through the city till I came to the outside of its walls & then strolled heedlessly along by the clear stream of the Tormes, following as it led, until I found myself far away from the city & on the borders of a great wood, which streched over many high hills to the verge of the horizon. There was a small pathway cut through this forest, which I entred, striding over the river which had now dwindled into a diminutiv[e] rill. Strictly speaking, this was not a prudent step nor one which I should advise you, my sons, if ever you should be in the like circumstances, to take, for the evening was far advanced, & the bright light of the beautiful horizon cast an uncertain glowing glare on everything, which made travelling through a dark wood which I knew nothing of exceeding dangerous. The country was likewise much infested with daring robbers & organized banditti,* who dwelt in such lonely situations, but there was a sort of charm upon me which led me on in spite of myself.

'After I had proceeded about a quarter of a mile, I heard a sound like music at a distance which in short time dyed away, but when I had got very deep into the forest, it rose again, & then it sounded nearer. I sat down under a large, spreading maple tree, whose massive limbs & foliage were now beginning to be irradiated by the moonlight which pierced into the depths of the forest & highly illumined with its beams the thick darkness.

'I had not sat here long when, suddenly, the music which had till then sounded soft & low like the preluding of a fine musician on a sweet instrument, broke out into a loud, deep strain which resembled the pealing of a full toned organ when its rich floods of sound are rolling & swelling in the sublime Te Deum & echoing amid the lofty aisles & [?pealing] to [the] [?high] dome of some grand cathedral with a deep, solemn noise like the loud, awful rumbling & terrible thunder, or the sudden burst of that most sublime of all music, martial music, when the ringing trumpet & the rolling[drum are sounding together with the fierce onset of a brave & noble army. Then you feel the grandeur of the battle amid the lightning & roar of the cannon, the glancing of swords & lances, & the thunder of the living cataract of men & horses rushing terribly to Victory,* who stands arrayed in bloody garments with a crown of glory upon her head.

'But to proceed with my story. No sooner had this loud concert sounded than the dark forest vanished like mists of the morning before the sun's brightness, & slowly there rose upon my sight a huge mirror, in which were dimly shadowed the forms of clouds & vapours all dense

& black, rolling one over the other in dark & stormy grandeur, & among them in letters of lightning I saw the "Futurity".

'By degrees these clouds cleared away, & a fair & beautiful island appeared in their stead, rising out of the midst of a calm & peaceful ocean, & linked to it by a golden chain was anot[h]er equal in beauty but smaller. In the middle of the largest of these 2 islands was a tall & majestic female seated on a throne of ruby, crowned with roses, bearing in one hand a wreath of oak-leaves & in the other a sword, while over her the tree of liberty flourished, spreading its branches far & wide & casting the perfume of its flowers to the uttermost parts of the earth. [In] the midst of the other island there was likewise a female, who sat on an emerald throne. Her crown was formed of shamrocks, in her right hand she held an harp & her robes were of a crimson hue as if they had been dyed in blood. She was as majestic as the other, but in her countenance was some thing very sad & sorrowful, as if a terrible evil hung upon her. Over her head were the boughs of a dark cypress,* instead of the pleasant tree which shaded the other island, & sometime[s] she swept the chords of the harp, causing a wild & mournful soun[d] to issue therefrom like a death wail or dirge.

'While I was wondering at her grief, I perceived a tremendous monster rise out of the sea & land on her island. As soon as it touched the shores a lamentable cry burst forth, which shook both islands to their centre, & the ocean all round boiled furiously, as if some terrible earthquake had happened. The monster was black & hideous & the sound of his roaring was like thunder. He was clothed in the skin of wild beasts & in his forehead was branded, as with a hot iron, the word "bigotry". In one hand he held a scythe, & as soon as he entred the land the work of desolation began. All pleasantness & beauty disappeared from the face of the country, & pestilential morasses came in their stead. He seemed to pursue with inveterate fury a horrible old man who, a voice whispered in my ear, was called the Romish Religion. At first he seemed weak & impotent, but as he ran he gathered strength, & the more he was persecuted the stronger he became, till at length he began, with a terrible voice, to defy his persecutor &, at the same time, strove to break the golden chain which united the two islands.

'And now I saw the form of a warrior* approaching, whose likeness I could by no means discern, but over whom a mighty sheild was extended from the sky. He came near to the monster whose name was "bigotry" & taking a dart on which the word "justice" was written in golden characters, he flung it at him with all his might. The dart had struck in the heart & he fell with a loud groan to the earth. As soon as he had fallen, the warrior, whose brow had already many wreaths on it, was crowned by a hand which proceeded from a golden cloud with a fresh one of amaranths interwove[n] with laurel.* At the same time the two spirits arose from their thrones, &, coming towards him, they cast garlands & crowns of victory at his feet, while the[y] sung* his praises in loud & glorious notes. Meantime, the desolated land was again over-spread with pleasant pastures & green woods & sunny plains, watered by clear rivers flowing with a gentle sound over green [?rocks], while the wild harp pealed in sweetly swelling tones among the branches of the tree of liberty.

'The sound ceased & lo, I was beneath the maple tree & a nightingale was serenading me with its beautiful song, which caused me to dream of sweet music.'

CB November 21s[t]
*Anno Domini 1829**

CHAPTER THE V

The Marquis of Douro and Lord Charles Wellesley's Tale to his Little King and Queens

In the year 1722, in the pleasant month of June, four inhabitants of Fairy-land took it into their heads for a treat to pay a visit to the inhabitants of the earth. In order to accomplish this end, they took the form of mortals, but first it was necessary to obtain leave of Oberon & Titania,* their king & queen. Accordingly, they demanded an audience of their majesties & were admitted. They stated their wish & petition, which was immediately granted, & they prepared to depart.

Having descended to the earth in a cloud, they alighted in a part of England which was very mountainous & quite uninhabited. They proceeded along for some time till they came to the verge of a rock that looked down into a beautiful vale below. Through it ran a clear & pleasant stream, which followed the vale in all its narrow windings among the high, dark mountain[s] which bordered it & the massive branching trees which grew in thick clumps casting a cool & agreeable shade all over the valley. Through these it meandered with a rippling sound until, when the glen broke from its confinement among them & spread into a wide, green plain all dotted with great, white poplars & stately oaks & spangle[d] with pearly daisies & golden buttercups, among which likewise occasionally peeped out the pale primrose or the purple violet, it also expanded into a broader & deeper current, rolling or rather gliding on with a still murmur that resembled the voice of some water spirit heard from the depths of its coral palaces, when it sings in lonely silence after the sea ceased to heave & toss in terrible black beauty & on the face of the earth* Night walks in awful majesty,* all cloth[ed] in stars, while Luna sheds pale light from her silver lamp to illumine the pathway of the dark & stately queen.

In the midst of this valley there was a small thatched cottage, which had once been the pleasant abode of a flourishing husbandman, who was now dead, & his children had forsaken it one by one & the sweet spot where it stood, each to pursue his own fortune, till it was now entirely deserted & had fallen into a state of ruin & decay. The fairies proceeded down the vale towards the cottage & when they arrived there began to examine it. The walls were all grey & moss-grown. Vine tendrils were still visible among the wreaths of ivy which clasped around the door-way, & one silver star of jesamine peeped out from among the dark leaves. The little garden was all grown over with nettles & rank weed, & no trace remained of its former beauty, except a single rose bush, on which still bloomed a few half wild roses, & beside it grew a small strawberry plant with two or three scarlet strawberries upon it, forming a fine contrast to the desolation which surrounded them.

In this place the fairies determined to take up their abode, which they accordingly did, & they had not been long there when the following occurrence happened. They were sitting one evening round the fire of their hut (for being now in the form of mortals, they acted like them), listening to the wind which moaned in hollow cadences as it swept along the valley, & its voice was sometimes mingled with strange sounds which they well knew were the voices of spirits rising in the air, invisible to the dull eyes of mortals.

They were sitting, as I said before, around the fire of their hut, when suddenly they heard a low knocking at the door. One of them immediately rose to open it & a man appeared clothed in a traveller's cloak. They enquired what he wanted. He replied that he had lost his way in the glen & that, seeing the light stream across his path from their cottage, he had stopped there & now requested shelter till the morning when he might be able to pursue his journey with the advantage of daylight. His request was immediately granted, & as soon as he was seated they asked what the cause of his travelling was. He replied that if they chose he would relate to them his whole history, as he could perceive that they were persons of no ordinary description & might perhaps be able to assist him in his distress. They consented & he began as follows.

'I am the son of a gentleman of great fortun[e] & estate, who resided in one of the southernmost counties of Ireland. My father & mother were both Roman Catholics & I was brought up in that faith & continued in it until I became convinced of the error of the creed I professed. My father's confessor was a man of strange & unsociable habits, & was thought, by those among whom he dwelt, to have converse with the inhabitants of another world. He had received his education in Spain, & it was suposed that in the country he had learnt the science of necromancy.*

'The manner in which I became converted to the Protestant religion was as follows. There lived in our family an old servant who, unknown to my father, was a seceder from the Roman Catholic Church & a member of the Church of England. One day, I unexpectedly entred the room & surprised him reading his Bible. I immediately remonstrated with him on the impropriety of what he was about & desired him to leave off, telling him it was against the laws of the true church and contrary to the admonitions of our preist. He replied mildly but firmly, quoting many passages of scripture in defence of what he did & arguing in such a manner as to convince me that I was in the wrong. Next day I paid him a visit at the same hour & found him similarly employed. I had a long conversation with him, the effect of which was to induce me to search the Bible for myself. I did so and there discovered that the doctrines of the Church of England were those which most closely assimilated with the word of God. Those doctrines I accordingly determined to embrace.

'As soon as my conversion became known, my father strove to dissuade [me] from it, but I remained steadfast & [?resolute]. In a short time he ceased to trouble me. But not so with the confessor. He was constantly advancing arguments to induce me to recant, but failing, he made use of the following expedient as last resource.

'I was standing one evening in the court of my father's house, when suddenly I heard a voice whisper in my ear, "Come this night to the great moor at 12 o'clock." I turned round but could see no body. I then debated with myself what it could be & whether I should go or not. I at length determined to go & when the clock struck eleven I set off. The moor alluded to lay about four miles off. It was a wide barren heath stretching 2 leagues to the northward. In a short time I reached it. The night was very dark. No moon was visible & the stars were only dimly seen through the thin, cloudy vapours that sailed over the sky veiling the dark azure with a sombre robe & casting a melancholy gloom on the [?scene] beneath. All round me was silent, except a little stream flowing unseen among the heather with a sound resembling the hoarse, incessant murmur which the seashell retains of its native caverns, where the green billows of the deep are roaring & raging with an eternal thunder.

'I had not waited long when slowly I saw rising around me the dim form of a sacred abbey, the stately pillars, the long drawn sweeping aisles, the echoing dome & the holy altar. All arose in gradual & mysterious order while a solemn & supernatural light stole through the high arched windows & beamed full upon a tomb which stood in the centre & which I knew to be my grandfather's. I was gazing at these things in wrapt & silent astonishment, when suddenly I saw a tall white robed figure standing upon the monument. It beckoned to me with its hand. I approached. It then addressed me in the following words, "Son, why have you deserted the ancient & holy religion of your ancestors to embrace a strange one which you know not of."

'I was going to reply when, at that moment, I perceived the confessor standing near. I instantly comprehended the whole sche[me] & exclaimed in a loud voice, "Your wiles are discovered. The faith I profess is true and I well-know that this [is] all necromancy."

'When the preist heard this he flew into a terrible rage &, stamping with his foot, a fire sprung out of the ground. He then threw some perfumes on it [and] said in a voice made tremulous by governable fury, "Depart hence vile heretic!" and immediately I found my self in this valley. You know the rest.'

Here the traveller stopped, & little more is known of the story, except that the fairies restored him to his family, who became devout members of the Church of England. The preist afterwards disappeared in a very unaccountable way & the fairies no longer dwell in that little hut, of which only a mossy remnant now remains. But the tradition still lives in many a peasant's fireside tale when gloomy winter has apparelled the earth in frost & radiant snow.

. . . .

This tale was related to Little King & Queen[s], Seringpatan, Old Man Cockney, Game-keeper, Jack of all Trades & Orderly Man* by the Marquis Douro & Lord C. Wellesley, as they sat by the fire at the great hall of Strathfeildsay.

C. Bronte December 2, 1829

AN INTERESTING
PASSAGE IN THE LIVES
of Some Eminent Men of the
PRESENT Time
BY LORD
Charles Wellesley ~
JUNE the 18
1830
BY CHARLOTTE ~
BRONTE

June the 17 1830

I beleive that in great houses few know more of family concerns than servants, & even in middling establishments the case is the same. As I am generally kind to grooms, valets, footmen, lackeys, &c., &c., they often make me their confidante, entrusting me with many important secrets, which by degrees has enabled me to amass such a quantity of information respecting almost every grandee in the Glass Town that if I chose I could unveil a scene of murders, thefts, hypocrisy, perjury & so forth which can scarcely be paralleled in the annals of any other city.

There are also many who have not waded so far or deep in the slough of criminality* but are nevertheless filthily bespattered with more petty sins, such as deceit, meanness, toadism, underhand dealings, evil speaking, envy, &c. Of this latter class I purpose to make a selection, reserving the remainder for some future period, when I shall no doubt avail myself of the wonderfully extensive miscellaneous information I possess to enlighten the public mind still further on this pleasant subject.

I am aware (to use a cant phrase) that my disclosures will cause a very considerable sensation among those who are implicated in the various transactions to which I shall allude, but as I care about them, their views & actions just as much as my monkey,* all their censures will pass by me with as little effect as the zephyrs in a hot summer's day fanning a sea-surrounded rock. I shall now proceed to the subject of my present volume.

Chapter the first

One warm & sunny afternoon in August 1829 I was reposing in one of the orange groves that adorn the luxuriant vale by which Babylon the great* is girdled. Oppressed by broiling heat, I plucked listlessly the golden fruit from a graceful bough which shaded me &, flinging the bright oranges into a cool artificial rivulet flowing past, I watched their course till intervening branches hid the crystal stream from my sight. Tringia lay at my feet, dissolved in peaceful slumber, dreaming no doubt that he was in his native shades of Chili gathering rich wild grapes clustered on every vine, or sporting with his hairy brethren among the old umbra[ge] through which no glimpse of sky disturbs the profound twilight reigning for aye beneath the forest's shadow.

As I fried with heat under an African summer's sun, I continued casting up my eyes to a zenith more intensely brilliantly blue than the most flawless saphire that ever sparkled in Golconda,* like a duck in thunder wishing for some cloud, even though charged with a tropical tempest, to variegate the monotonous azure. While thus I lay, I heard some-one enter the grove & at the same instant perceived a gentleman in livery advancing towards me. On a nearer approach he raised his hat and addressed me familiarly as follows: 'Well, my lord, what is your opinion of the day? For my part, I'm on the point of being reduced to ashes with heat.'

'Oh,' said I, not wishing to coincide with him, 'it's tolerably cool, I think. You see I've been obliged to retire within this little close grove to keep myself even moderately warm.'

'Well,' returned he with a chuckling laugh, 'that's odd, & I've come here with the directly opposite purpose of sheilding my head from the fervid sunbeams.'

Disgusted at his flippancy, I was on the point of ordering him to quit the place, but then, thinking that his presence might be productive of amusement, I ordered him to sit down at some distance from me. This fellow was valet de chambre* to the well known author Captain T—,* &, as I had shown him kindness when in a destitute condition, he thought himself privileged to speak freely. He was, however, not of an ill disposition but, on the contrary, possessed a slight tincture of good nature & intelligence, for which latter reason he some times proved rather useful to me.

I asked him how his master was.

'Pretty well,' he answered, & then added slily, 'If your lordship pleases, I could relate two or three little incidents respecting him which might entertain you for half an hour.'

I consented, & the substance of his narrative is as follows. I do not give his words but merely the sense attired in the garb that I conceive fittest.

CHAPTER THE SECOND

One morning last May, as I was standing behind a tree in the avenue of my master's country house, a gentleman came riding up the road on horseback at a smart pace. When he drew nigh I perceived that it was Lieutenant B—,* chief librarian of the city. I stepped from my hiding place & did him obeisance. He asked if Captain T— was at home. I replied in the affirmative & at that instant my master appeared. They shook hands & appeared glad to see each other, but I thought there was a thing in the librarian's squint eye (for he has but one) that showed harm in his head.

They both went into the house after ordering me to cover the horse. I did so & led it up & down the avenue afterwards, till Lieutenant B— returned. When I heard them coming I slipped over the hedge & laid flat down on the other side to listen to what they would say, for I could not conjecture the reason of his coming here, which he had never been accustomed to do. They talked very low & nothing reached me but these words, which my master spoke as they parted: 'At the square at twelve at night? Very well. Goodbye.' He then went back to the house & B— cantered away.

When it was 8 o'clock in the evening, I was sent for to Captain T—. I found him in his library. He ordered me to prepare in all haste for a journey to the Glass Town, where he was to go to attend a funeral that would take place there at midnight. I thought that an uncomon time for an honest man to be buried & my curiosity quickened me. In half an hour all was ready. We set off (for I went with him) & arrived at the city before eleven. He got out of his carriage at the Fetish Inn* & there he left it with all his servants except me, whom he ordered to accompany him.

We proceeded throug[h] many narrow darksome streets till, all at once emerging from thes[e], we came to a wide square surrounded by decayed houses, none of which seemed to be inhabited save one. In an upper chamber of that a light was burning. We went into it &, passing up a ruined staircase, entred a low garret where—behold!—the librarian was standing dressed in cloak & mask. He wispered to my master & gave him the same sort of habiliments wherewith the captain presently arrayed himself.

Then he said in a low voice, 'I dread to pass through the Great Square.'

'But it must be done,' replied Lieutenant B—. 'There is no other way to the cemetery.'

After this they both quickly descended the stair & I followed.

When we got out of the house, 6 men came, all masqued (but among whom I could plainly distinguish by their gait Sergeant T— & Sergeant B—, one of whom is a lawyer & the other a bookseller. *They bore with great difficulty a very long, wide & seemingly heavy coffin. Following this as mourners, we all proceeded at a slow pace toward the Great Square. In a short time we arrived at it. About 20 or 30 noblemen & generals were standing around the image laughing & conversing gaily. Among these I could easily distinguish your father, my lord, the Duke of Wellington. None of the others appeared to mind the funeral, which stole softly along in the shade of a lofty range of houses. He, however, without discontinuing a conversation he was then holding with a dark, tall, ugly man in uniform (whose name I afterwards learnt is General Bobadill*) cast a keen glance towards it, which after wandring over all the figures fully concentred on T—. He shrank & trembled, but the Duke quickly withdrew his gaze & we moved onward. I cannot tell how many streets & lanes the procession traversed till it stopped at a house in Charles Row. There Sergeant B— rung a bell & in a few minutes his father, the great political writer, came out. As he joined us I heard him say to the librarian, 'Magrass has taken the bribe.' Then all was silence.

We quickened our pace &, by the time St Andrew's clock struck one, had arrived at a huge black marble wall where was a brass gate, strongly locked & barred. This they knocked at several times without any one appearing. Captain B—* became impatient. He stamped & muttered, 'Has the scoundrel betrayed us?'

Just then the door of a little tower built on the wall opened and a man came forth. He ran down some steps & disappeared on the other side. Presently the gate was unbolted & we beheld a vast, enclosed plain full of tombs & monuments. One of the graves were open. This we proceeded towards. It was a very deep vault full of chests. The coffin being let down & covered with earth, all went away except I & my master, who stopped behind as watchers. We continued till day-break without any disturbance & then quitted the yard also. A carriage which waited at the gate conveyed us to T—'s residence. When we arrived there, he commanded me to go to bed immediately. I obeyed but was unable to sleep, though very much fatigued, with thinking of what had occurred.

Next night we proceeded again to the cemetery. For about 2 hours no noise reached us & we were thinking of going home, but then we perceived 3 men sliding down the wall. One was Doctor H— B—, the other Young Man N— & the third Ned L—.* At this Captain T—, who is a great coward, turned pale &, though he had sworn to defend the grave, slinked off, cowering behind a monument. I followed his example, not wishing to hazard my skin for what did not concern me.

As his myrmidons approached I heard N— say, 'The lad was buried here. I think he'll be middling fresh to some that you get doctor.'

They then began to uncover the vault & in a little time turned up the coffin. T— gave an involuntary squeal at the sight, which startled the resurrectionists. They turned round & spied him trembling behind a stone. Ned dragged him out by the collar, while I crawled off unobserved to a more secure hiding place.

'How did you come here?' said H—. 'Speak or I'll dash this spade through your skull.'

'Never.'

'Hold him!' bawled N—. 'But look at this coffin! If I don't declare, it's full of books instead of bones, & here's ever so many chests crammed with the same kind of traffic.'

'They're mine!' cried T—. 'And I've buried them here for safety.'

'That's a lie!' replied H—, after glancing over them. 'These books belong to the public library. You've stole them & buried them here for secresy. I'll inform against you!'

'O don't! Don't!' exclaimed the captain. 'If you will never tell any body of this, I promise to procure you a living subject every week. Besides, Captain B—, Sergeant B—, Lieutenant B—, Sergeant T— &

Magrass the gatekeeper are all concerned as well as me in the affair, & they'll have to be executed likewise.'

'Humph, I don't much care for that,' answered H——. 'But as you say you'll get me a living subject once a week, I'll not tell. The first time, however, that you fail in the performance of that promise, or in any way displease me, your life is in my hands. Now be off!'

'I shall certainly mind,' rejoined T——. 'But remember, Doctor H——, that I also have found you engaged in not the most legal work. I have a tongue which can speak too.'

'It's safest to clap you sideway then,' said H——, & he struck him dead on the spot. Ned & N— flung the books again into the grave & covered it up & they all quitted the yard, carrying T— along with them.

After this tragical scene had been acted, I emerged from my concealed situation & returned home, which my master did also in a few days. But I have since heard him say that he spent 2 days & 2 nights in Doctor H— B—'s macerating tub.*

———————

Here my garrulous informant stopped, & after I had expressed my approbation of the ability with which he had related the affair, I left him to the solitary enjoyment of the sylvan shade within which he reclined.

After walking about a mile, I reached one of the green refreshing alleys bordered with majestic elms, limes or aloes which form public promenades for the highest circles of the metropolis. Here I beheld an assemblage of noblemen & gentlemen conversing together with great earnestness: Young Rouge,* with the body of a male mandril, the head of a jack and the dress of a buffoon; Old Rouge, the image of a hopeless insolvent; Young Bud, like walking parchment stuffed with straw or law, which you will; Old Bud, a bottle of elixir; Sergeant Tree, an absolute ape; Captain Tree, conceit personified; Lord Lofty, a buck;* Old Rouge['s] youngest son, a promising youth; &c., &c. This motley throng with bent brows & self important looks were evidently discussing no trifling topic. I perceived the Marquis of Douro, my brother, in the midst & overhead the following conversation between him & Lord Lofty.

Lofty: Well, my lord Marquis, have you heard of this little affair concerning the robbery of the public library?

D: Yes, it has suprised me, I own.

L: Brock is taken & will, I hope, be put to the torture.

D: That would be most unjustifiable cruelty in his case. No blood ought to be shed, in my opinion.

L: Well, but they might rack him. That instrument* leaves a man whole as before though a little stretched. Ha, ha, ha, ha!

Here Arthur turned from him to Captain Tree, whom he accosted thus.

D: Tree, you are, I think, more merciful. What would be your mode of proceedure?

T: Kill the wretch outright without trial or question. He may accuse innocent persons as accomplices in his crime.

I now stept forward & said, 'Aye, Tree! Kill him & all like him outright without trial or question. They might accuse such an innocent person as you, for instance, & witnesse[s] are easily to be got who could swear to seeing you in company with him on a certain night going after a black coffin not filled with flesh & blood.'

T (reddening): What do you mean, sir?

M[e]: Many a thing.

I was going on, but Arthur restrained me with, 'Charles, Charles, hush love.' He then took hold of my hand & hurried me away from the walk.

It was now evening & by the time we reached the palace, a flaming South African occident cast a transcendency of light over all the vast city that resounded with a loud murmur, & gloriously irradiated its stupendous tower, which rose encompassed with magnificent oaks now standing in undefined masses of darkness agains[t] a sky of gold. Far off the broad harbour lay dotted by innumerable white-sailed vessels. The ocean heaved in terrible beauty. Its mighty voice deepened with the hush of evening. A hundred streams of the vale pouring forth their emulous song were unheard amid that awful thunder, which rolled over the fading earth through an atmosphere of balm & fragrance. My brother & I stood on the terrace for a long time wholly absorbed in admiration, till at length Finic came to remind us that the dew was falling & colds abroad in the air.

Charles Wellesley

June the 18, 1830 C Brontë

SECOND SERIES OF THE
YOUNG MEN'S
MAGAZINE. NO
THIRD
FOR OCTOBER 1830

Edited by Charlotte Brontë

SOLD
BY
SERGEANT TREE*
AND ALL
OTHER

Booksellers in the Glass Tow[n],
Paris, Ross's Glass Town, Par-
ry's G Town & the Duke of
Wellington's Glass Town

Finished August 23 1830

Charlotte Brontë—

August 23

1830

This second series of magazines is conducted on like
principles with the first. The
same eminent authors are
also engaged to contribute for it.

CONTENTS

NO. THIRD FOR OC-

TOBER 1830 . . . . .

Finished August 23 1830

1830

CHARLOTTE

BRONTË

August 23 1830

Charlotte Brontë

A DAY AT PARRY'S PALACE

BY LORD CHARLES WELLESLEY

'Oh, Arthur!' said I, one morning last May. 'How dull this Glass Town is! I am positively dying of ennui. Can you suggest anything likely to relieve my disconsolate situation?'

'Indeed, Charles, I should think you might find some pleasant employment in reading or conversing with those that are wiser than yourself. Surely you are not so emty-headed & brainless as to be driven to the extremity of not knowing what to do!' Such was the reply to my civil question, uttered with the prettiest air of gravity imaginable.

'Oh, yes! I am, brother! So you must furnish me with some amusement.'

'Well then, Charles, you have often spoken of a visit to Captain Parry's Palace as a thing to be desired. You have now time for the accomplishment of your wish.'

'Very true, Arthur, & you deserve your weight in gold for reminding me of it.'

Next morning, I was on my way at an early hour in the direction of William Edward's country.* In less than a week I crossed the borders and was immediately struck with the changed aspect of everything. Instead of tall, strong muscular men going about seeking whom they may devour, with guns on their shoulders or in their hands, I saw none but little shiftless milk-and-water-beings, in clean blue linen jackets & white aprons. All the houses were ranged in formal rows. They contained four rooms, each with a little garden in front. No proud castle or splendid palace towered insultingly over the cottages around. No high-born noble claimed allegiance of his vassals or surveyed his broad lands with hereditary pride. Every inch of ground was enclosed with stone walls. Here & there a few regularly planted rows of trees, generally poplars, appeared, but no hoary woods or nodding groves were suffered to intrude on the scene. Rivers rushed not with foam & thunder through meads & mountains, but glided canal-like along, walled on each side that no sportive child might therein find a watery grave. Nasty factories, with their tall black chimneys breathing thick columns of almost tangible smoke, discoloured not that sky of dull, hazy, colourless hue. Every woman wore a brown stuff gown with white cap & handkerchief; glossy satin, rich velvet, costly silk or soft muslin, broke not in on the fair uniformity.

Well, 'on I travelled many a mile',* till I reached Parry's Palace. It was a square building of stone, surmounted by blue slates & some round stone pumpkins. The garden around it was of moderate dimensions, laid out in round, oval or square flower beds, [with] rows of peas, gooseberry bushes, black, red & white currant trees, some few common flowering shrubs, & a grass place to dry clothes on. All the convenient offices, such as wash-house, back-kitchen, stable and coalhouse, were built in a line & backed by a row of trees. In a paddock behind the house were feeding one cow, to give milk for the family & butter for the dairy & cheese for the table; one horse, to draw the gig, carry their majesties & bring home provisions from market; together with a calf and foal as companions for both.

As the wheels of my carriage were heard on the stone pavement of the court yard, the kitchen door opened & a little oldish maun and waman* made their appearance. They immediately ran back again at sight of my splendid (for so it must have seemed to them) equipage. A slight bustle now became audible inside the house, & in a few moments Sir Edward & Lady Emily Parry came out to welcome their newly arrived guest. They too were a little frightened at first, but I soon quitted their fears by telling them who I was.

After this explanation I was ushered into a small parlour. Tea was on the table & they invited me to partake of it. But before sitting down, Parry took from the cup-board a napkin, which he directed me to pin before my clothes lest I should dirty them, saying in a scarcely intelligible jargon that he supposed they were my best as I had come on a visit & that perhaps my mama would be angry if they got stained. I thanked him but politely declined the offer. During tea a complete silence was preserved; not a word escaped the lips of my host or hostess. When it was over little Eater was brought in, habited in a most dirty & greasy pinafore, which Lady Emily presently stripped him of and substituted a clean one in its stead, muttering in a cross tone that she wondered how Amy could think of sending the child into the parlour with such a filthy slip on.

Parry now withdrew to his study & Lady Aumly* to her work room, so that I was left alone with Eater. He stood for more than half an hour on the rug before me with his finger in his mouth, staring idiot like full in my face, uttering every now & then an odd grumbling noise, which I suppose denoted the creature's surprise. I ordered him to sit down. He laughed but did not obey. This incensed me, and heaving the poker I struck him to the ground. The scream that he set up was tremendous, but it only increased my anger. I kicked him several times & dashed his head against the floor, hoping to stun him. This failed. He only roared the louder. By this time the whole household was alarmed: master, mistress and servants came running into the room. I looked about for some means of escape but could find none.

'What hauve dou beinn douing tou de child?' asked Parry, advancing towards me with an aspect of defiance.

As I wished to stop a day longer at his palace, I was forced to coin a lie. 'Nothing [at] all,' I replied. 'The sweet little boy fell down as I was playing with him & hurt his self.'*

This satisfied the good easy man & they all retired, carrying the hateful brat still squalling & bawling along with them.

In about an hour afterwards, supper was brought in. It consisted of coffee & a very few thin slices of bread & butter. This meal, like the former, was eaten in silence, & when it was concluded we went to bed.

I rose next morning at 9 o'clock and came down just in time for breakfast, after which I took a walk through the fields. In the yard I saw Eater, surrounded by three cats, two dogs, five rabbits & six pigs, all of whom he was feeding. On my return I found a new guest had arrived in the shape of Captain John Ross.

He & Parry were conversing together, but I could understand very little of what they said. It was, however, something about 'Aun having moide Trahl a nou clouk of flouered muslin waud punk rubun ot de bottom & faul saulk belt', which he liked very much. Parry said that 'the laust dress Aumly haud moide haum wauss a boutiful pale craumson, traumed waud yaullow, groin & purple, & a fadher aun hid caup of a rauch lilac cauler.'

Dinner was set on the table precisely at twelve o'clock. The dishes were roast-beef, Yorkshire pudding, mashed potatoes, apple pie & preserved cucumbers. Ross wore a white apron during dinner. I observed that he took not the smallest notice of me, though I must necessarily have been a different object from what he was in the habit of seeing. All eat as if they had not seen a meal for three weeks, while

> The solemn hush of twilight lay
> On every tongue around.*

I felt a strong inclination to set the house on fire & consume the senseless gluttons. At the dessert each drank a single glass of wine, not a drop more, & eat a plateful of strawberries with a few sweet cakes. I expected some blow-up after the surfeit which Ross, if I might judge from his continued grunting & puffing, had evidently got, & was not disappointed. An hour subsequent to dinner, he was taken extremely sick. No doctor being at hand, death was momentarily expected & would certainly have ensued, had not the Genius Emily arrived at a most opportune period; & when the disorder had reached its crisis, she cured with an incantation & vanished.*

I only remained at Parry's Palace till the morrow, for I found my visit intolerably dull—as much so as, I fear, the reader will find this account of it. But the journey had given me some notion of things as they are, & for that reason I did not regret it. For many days after I had returned to the Glass Town my life was a very brisk one, as persons were constantly coming to hear my account of the place where I had been. I happened at that time to be in an exceedingly taciturn disposition of mind, which circumstance prevented my satisfying their curiosity by word of mouth. I have therefore had recourse to the only way of obviating the inconvenience, namely by sending this breif narrative for insertion in the Young Men's Magazine.

August 22, 1830   Farewell, Genius CW

———————————

MORNING BY MARQUIS DOURO*

LO! the light of the morning is flowing
   Through radiant portals of gold
Which Aurora in crimson robes glowing
   For the horses of fire doth unfold*

   See Apollo's burnished car
   Glorifies the east afar
   As it draws the horizon nigher
   As it climbs the heavens higher
   Richer grows the amber light
   Fairer, more intensely bright
   Till floods of liquid splendour roll
   O'er all the earth from pole to pole

Hark! the birds in the green forest bowers
   Have beheld the sun's chariot arise

And the humblest the stateliest flower[s]
    Are arrayed in more beautiful dyes

Now, while the woodland choir[s] are singing
Opening buds fresh odours flinging
And while nature's tuneful voice
Calls on all things to rejoice
I cannot join the common gladness
'Tis to me a time of sadness
All these sounds of mirth impart
Nought but sorrow to my heart

But I love evening's still quiet hour
    The whispering twilight breeze
The damp dew's invisible shower
    Conglobing in drops on the trees

Then is heard no sound or tone
But the night-bird singing lone
Peacefully adown the vale
It passes on the balmy gale
Ceases oft the pensive strain
Solemn sinking & again
Philomela* sends her song
To wander the night winds along

While silver-robed Luna* is beaming—
    Afar in the heavens on high
And her bright train of planets are gleaming
    Like gems in the dome of the sky

From the firmament above
Down they gaze with looks of love
On the minstrel all unheeding
Still their ears entranced feeding
With the notes of sweetest sound
Gushing forth on all around
Music not unfit for heaven
But to earth in mercy given
Thou dost charm the mourner's heart
Thou dost pensive joy impart

Peerless Queen of harmony
How I love thy melody

Marquis of Douro

August 22 1830

CONVERSATIONS

Marquis of Douro, Young Soult, Lord Wellesley,
Sergeant Bud, De Lisle.* Parlour in Bravey's Inn.*

Lord Wellesley

Well, De Lisle, this is the first time you have been present at our conversations & right glad I am to see a gentleman of such genius among us.

De Lisle

My lord, one of the chief pleasures which such an honnour gives me is that of being made acquainted with such distinguished personages as yourself, my Lord, & your noble brother.

Marquis of Douro

I do not know, sir, that I have had the happiness of seeing you before, but often have I seen your mind displayed in the peerless productions of your pencil, where the sublime and beautiful are set forth with a supreme mastery of execution & elevation of feeling that none but a genius of the highest order could ever hope to attain.

Lord Wellesley

Arthur, have you seen his view from the summit of the Tower of all Nations?*

Marquis of Douro

I have, Charles, & my admiration of it is unbounded. Who can conceive the thoughts & sensations of such a man, while from that aerial altitude he traced the grand lineaments of nature? None. How was he then raised above all sublunary concerns? How must his already gigantic spirit have dilated, as he saw the farthest isles & coasts drawn into the vast circle of an horizon, more extensive than that beheld from Chimborazo or Teneriffe!* De Lisle, you are already among those consecrated names that form the boast & glory of Britannia, Empress of the Waves.

De Lisle

My Lord Marquis, I cannot deserve your eulogium. Painting is but the younger sister of Poetry, that divine art which is yours.

Marquis of Douro

Mine, De Lisle? She belongs to none. She is confined to no realm, shore or empire: alike she reigns in the heart of peasant or king; painter & statuary, as well as poet, live, breathe, think, act under the celestial influence of her inspiration.

Lord Wellesley

Ochone!* Arthur, one would think M[arian] H[ume]* was Poetry in disguise.

Sergeant Bud

Well, well, the lawyer is happily free. Pray, young gentlemen, have not you lately taken a jaunt of some hundred miles into the country?

Lord Wellesley

Yes, parchment, we have. What then?

Sergeant Bud

Why, I should like to hear an account of it.

Lord Wellesley

Which I am in no humour for giving!

Young Soult

But I am & I will. We saw Nature in her fairest dress. Art has not yet built a palace in the dark hills of Jibbel Kumri, the wide desert of Sahara, the palmy plains of Fezzan, or the mountain vales which no eye but the lone traveller's hath seen.* Oh, oft as I wandered, in a delightful kind of insanity, far from the caravan, I have tout à la coup* in the midst of mountains that clave the whirlwind-swept heaven, in stern and naked grandeur, beheld glens reposing in supernatural loveliness, in the arms of circling rocks that seemed unwilling for any to seek their beauty, which was [?wildered] and enhanced by the accompaniment of unearthly objects. Strange trees grimly shook their long dark tresses over the grassy ground where stars, instead of flowers, gleamed. Clouds ever hung over them. The sun was screened by jealous hills frowning in majesty above—

> O spirits of the sky were there
> Strange enchantment filled the air
> I have seen from each dark cloud
> Which in gloom those vales did shroud

White robed beings glance & fly
& rend the curtain from the sky
I have seen their wings of light
Streaming o'er the heavens' height
I have seen them bend & kiss
Those eternal vales of bliss
& I've seen them fast enshroud
Those Edens of unfading bloom
All in mist & all in gloom
O the darkness of that night
O the grandeur of that sight
None can speak it, none can tell
Heark I hear the thunder swell
Crashing through the firmament
'Tis by wrothful spirits sent
Warning me to say no more
Now hath ceased the dreadful roar
Now a calm is all around
Not a breath and not a sound
That frozen stillness durst break
This is Nature's silent sleep
Sudden light above me springs
Sudden music round me rings
Now again the spirits dance
& again the sunbeams glance
This is light & this is mirth
All of heaven not of earth
Up hath risen purple morn
Love & Joy & life are born
I veil my eyes with a holy fear*
For the coming visions no mortal
May bear (Sinks down in a fainting fit but the Marquis
of Douro, who is sitting by, catches him in his arms & reinstates him
in a chair.)

Lord Wellesley

Ring,—ring the bell! Be quick! Bring hartshorn, cold water, vinegar, salvolatic, [?salzaikaling] and sal everything else!* The poet has
fallen into an inspiration dream! Haste, haste, if you mean to save his
life!*

Sergeant Bud

What's the matter with him? Nobody touched him that I saw of, but I suppose he is mad. Alack-a-day to be a poet!

De Lisle

His excited feelings have overcome him.

Young Soult (opening his eyes)

Where am I? Who is this so kindly bending over me? Is it you, Douro, my friend, patron, benefactor, to whom I owe more than to all the world beside?

Marquis of Douro

Be composed, my dear Soult. It is me. You should not allow your genius to gain so much ascendancy over your reason, for it exposes you more to ridicule than admiration.

Young Soult

I will try to follow your advice, my dear Douro, since I know the motives that induce you to give it.

Sergeant Bud

What ailed you? May I ask?

Young Soult

I cannot tell. My sensations at the moment of swooning were inexpressible; they were indeed 'all of heaven and not of earth'.*

Sergeant Bud

Humph! (Turning to Lord Wellesley) You look very fresh and rosy somehow. Your journey seems to have done you good.

Lord Wellesley

So it has. I never feel well in this dismal, unwholesome Glass Town.

De Lisle

For several months before you went, it much concerned me to see your white countenance and cheeks without a streak of vermeil. Now the fairest leaf of the wild rose could not surpass their bloom. Your eyes also are more radiant and your hair more glossy than ever.

Lord Wellesley

Nonsense! I hope I'm rather tawny.

De Lisle

No, of a purer white than before.

Lord Wellesley

That's a flat lie! I'm not fair. Do you think I use cosmetics, pray?

De Lisle

Yes, one: that of an incomparably sweet temper.

Lord Wellesley

You're out again, sir. Was there ever a more malignant being than I am, Arthur? Now, speak truth, honestly.

Marquis of Douro (laughing)

What! always appealing to me? As I do not know tout le monde,* it is a useless question, Charles. But I believe if what it implies was a veritable maxim, I should not love you as well as I do.

Lord Wellesley

De Lisle, you've disturbed my happiness & made me angry with Arthur, so get along, don't sit so near me!

De Lisle (aside to the Marquis of D)

Have I displeased him, do you think?

Marquis of D (aside to De Lisle)

No, no, sir, he loves flattery. You can't lay it on too thick. Butter away! The more there is, the better he will be pleased. Watch his eye: when it glares his wrath has risen, then beware; but while it sparkles, fear not, he is delighted. Never mind the knit brow, pouting lip and raging tongue; they are but so many marks of pleasure.

De Lisle

Is he as charming in private as in public?

Marquis Douro

Infinitely more so. When he and I are alone, his sweetness of manner would force the merest misanthrope to love mankind. Among strangers, he wishes to be thought less amiable than he really is.

De Lisle

That is strange. What a wayward disposition!

Lord Charles Wellesley

Young Soult & Sergeant Bud, behold those two whispering together. Ill-bred rustics! Turn about, sirs, and face the company, I say!

De Lisle

We were talking of you.

Lord Wellesley

Of me! I demand an explanation. (Enter a servant.) What do you want?

Servant

A messenger has arrived from Waterloo Palace, whom His Grace the Duke of Wellington has sent to command the Marquis of Douro's and Lord Wellesley's immediate attendance.

Lord Wellesley

Be off ape! Come, brother, we must go. What can my father want, I wonder?

Young Soult

We'll go too.

De Lisle

Might I be allowed the honour of an introduction to His Grace's august presence?

Marquis of Douro

Certainly, if you desire it, & I will present you.

De Lisle

By so doing, your lordship will confer on me a great obligation.

Sergeant Bud

It is time for me to return home.

Lord Wellesley

Come with us then. Come, come, come.
(Exeunt omnes.* Curtain falls.)

August the 23 1830
Finished August 23 1830
C Brontë Charlotte

ADVERTISEMENTS

BOOKS

PUBLISHED BY SERGEANT TREE

The Elements of LYING*
By LORD CHARLES WEL-
LESLEY in one vol., duodecimo

PRICE 2^s 6^d
With some account of those
who practise it.

———————

SOGAST, a Romance. By
CAPTAIN TREE
in 2 volumes. Oc^t. Price 20^d

———————

Orion & Arcturus,* a POEM—
LORD WELLESLEY
Recommendation: 'this is the
most beautiful poem that ever
flowed from the pen of man. The
sentiments are wholly original;
nothing is borrowed.'
                    Glass T Review

———————

An Essay on Conversation, by
THE MARQUIS DOURO
1 vol. Price 5^s

———————

Solitude, by the same. Price 10^d

———————

The Proud MAN, by Captain
TREE. Price 30ˢ. 3 vol.

ADVERTISEMENTS: SALes

TO BE SOLD: a rat-trap, by
MONSIEUR it can catch nothing
FOR it's BROKEN.

 THE ART OF BLOWing
One's Nose, is taught by
Monsieur Pretty-foot at his
house, No. 105 Blue Rose Street,
    Glass TOWN

LORD CHARLES WELLESley
hereby challenges that impudent
bragadocio,* who boasted of being
able to manage forty such as
the above whom he denominated
'a slender weed that ought
to be rooted up'.
 The Advertiser
was then incognito, at a small
tavern, named The Flame of Fire,
& he requests his insulter to
meet him in the great croft

behind Corporal Rare-lad's barn,
thirty miles east of the Glass
Town, with seconds, &c., to try
a match at fisty-cuffs.* LCW

A Feather will take an aerial
excursion, from the ale house
Sulky Boys, Dec. 9, 1830. The price
of admission will be payment for
a tankard of ale.

ALBION AND MARINA
A
TALE BY
LORD
WELLESLEY
THE
PRINCIPAL PART POS-
SESSING FACT
FOR ITS FOUNDATION
PUBLISHED
AND SOLD BY SERGEANT
TREE

And All other booksellers in—

the cheif Glass Town, Paris, &c.*

PREFACE

I have written this tale out of malignity for the injuries that have lately been offered to me. Many parts, especially the former, were composed under a mysterious influence that I cannot account for. My reader will easily recognize the characters through the thin veil which I have thrown over them. I have considerably flattered Lady Zelzia Elrington.* She is not nearly so handsome as I have represented her, & she strove far more vigorously to oust someone from another person's good graces than I say, but her endeavours failed. Albion has hitherto stood firm. What he will do I cannot pretend to even guess, but I think that Marina's incomparable superiority will prevail over her Frenchified rival who, as all the world knows, is a miller, jockey, talker, blue stocking, charioteer & beldam,* united in one blazing [?locus] of perfection. The conclusion is wholly destitute of any foundation in truth, & I did it out of revenge. Albion & Marina are both alive & well for ought I know.* One thing, however, will certainly break my heart, & that is the omission of any scandal against Tree,* but I hope my readers will pardon me for it, as I promise to make amends with usury next time I write a book.

October 12 1830   C. Wellesley
I wrote this in four hours, C B

ALBION AND MARINA
A TALE BY LORD Wellesley

There is a certain sweet little pastoral village in the south of England with which I am better acquainted than most men. The scenery around it possesses no distinguishing characteristic of romantic grandeur or wildness that might figure a way to advantage in a novel, to which high title this brief narrative sets up no pretensions.* Neither rugged, lofty rocks nor mountains dimly huge mark with frowns the undisturbed face of nature, but little peaceful valleys, low hills crowned with wood, murmuring cascades & streamlets, richly cultivated fields, farm houses, cottages & a wide river formed all the scenic features.

Every hamlet has one or more great men. This had one, but he was 'nae sheepshank'.* Every ear in the world had heard his fame,

& every tongue could bear testimony to it. I shall name him the 'Duke of Strathelleraye',* & by that name the village was likewise denominated, for more than thirty miles round every inch of ground belonged to him & every man was his retainer. The magnificent villa, or rather palace, of this noble stood on an eminence surrounded by a vast park & the embowering shade of an ancient wood, proudly seeming to claim allegiance of all the dependent country side. The mind, achievements & character of its great possessor must not, cannot, be depicted by a pen so feeble as mine, for though I could call filial love & devoted admiration to my aid, yet both would be utterly ineffective.

Though the Duke seldom himself came among his attached vassals, being detained elsewhere by important avocations, yet his lady, the Duchess, resided in the castle constantly. Of her I can only say that she was like an earthly angel. Her mind was composed of charity, beneficence, gentleness & sweetness. All, both old & young, loved her, & the blessings of those that were ready to perish came upon her ever more.*

His Grace had also two sons, who often visited Strathellraye. Of the youngest, Lord Corneilius,* every thing is said when I inform the reader that he was seventeen years of age, grave, sententious, stoical, rather haughty & sarcastic, of a fine countenance, though somewhat swarthy, long thick hair, black as the hoody's wing,* & liked nothing so well as to sit alone in moody silence, musing over the vanity of human affairs, or improving & expanding his mind by the abstruse study of the higher branches of mathematics & that sublime science, astronomy.

The eldest, Albion, Marquis of Tagus,* is the hero of my present tale. He had entred his nineteenth year. His stature was lofty; his form equal in the magnificence of its proportion[s] to that of Apollo Belvedere.* The bright wrea[th] & curls of his rich brown hair waved over a forehea[d] resembling the purest marble in the placidit[y] of its unveined whiteness. His nose & mouth were cast in the most perfect mould. But saw I never anything to equal his eye! O, I could hav[e] stood riveted with the chains of admiration, gazing for hours upon it! What clearness, depth & lucid transparency in those large orbs of radiant brown! And the fascination of his smile was irresistible, though seldom did that sunshine of the mind break the thou[ght]ful & almost melancholy expression of his nobl[e] features. He was a soldier, captain in the Royal Regiment of Horse-guards, & all his attitudes & actions were full of martial grace. His mental faculties were in exact keeping with such an exterior, being of the highest order, & though not, like his younger brother, wholly given up to study, yet he was well

versed in the ancient languages, & deeply read in the Greek & Roman
Classics, in addition to the best works in the British, German & Italian
tongues.

Such was my hero. The only blot I was ever able to discover in his
character is that of a slight fierceness or impetuosity of temper which
sometimes carried him beyond bounds, though at the slightest look
or word of command from his father he instantly bridled his passion
& became perfectly calm. No wonder the Duke should be, as he was,
proud of such a son.

About two miles from the castle there stood a pretty house, entirely
hid from view by a thick forest, in a glade of which it was situated.
Behind it was a smooth lawn fringed with odoriferous shrubs, & before,
a tasteful flower-garden. This was the abode of Sir Alured Angus,* a
Scotchman who was physician to His Grace, & though of gentlemanly
manners & demeanour, yet harsh, stern, & somewhat querelous* in
countenance and disposition. He was a widower & had but one child,
a daughter, whom I shall call Marina, which nearly resembles her true
name.

No wild rose blooming in solitude or blue bell peering from an old
wall ever equalled in loveliness this flower of the forest. The hue of her
cheek would excell the most delicate tint of the former, even when its
bud is just opening to the breath of summer, & the clear azure of her
eyes would cause the latter to appear dull as a dusky hyacinth. Also, the
silken tresses of her hazel hair, straying in light ringlets down a neck
& forehead of snow, seemed more elegant than the young tendrils of a
vine. Her dress was almost Quaker-like in its simplicity.* Pure white or
vernal green were the colours she constantly wore, without any jewels,
save one row of pearls round her neck.* She never stirred beyond the
precints of the wooded & pleasant green lane which skirted a long
cornfield near the house. There, in warm summer evenings, she would
ramble & linger, listening to the woodlark's song, & occasionally joining
her own more harmonious voice to its delightful warblings. When the
gloomy days & nights of autumn & winter did not permit these walks,
she ammused herself with drawing (for which she had an exact taste),
playing on the harp, reading the best English, French & Italian works
(both which languages she understood) in her father's extensive library,
& sometimes a little light needlework. And thus in a state of perfect
seclusion (for seldom had she even Sir Alured's company as he generally resided at London) she was quite happy, & reflected with innocent
wonder on those who could find pleasure in the noisy delights of what
is called fashionable society.

One day, as Lady Strathelleraye was walking in the wood, she met Marina and, on learning who she was, being charmed with her exquisite beauty & sweet manners, invited her to come on the morrow to the castle. She did so & there met the Marquis of Tagus. He was even more surprised & pleased with her than the Duchess &, when she was gone, asked his mother a thousand questions about her, all of which she answered to his satisfaction.

For some time after he appeared listless & abstracted. The reader will readily perceive that he had, to use a cant phrase, fallen in love. Lord Corneilius, his brother, warned him of the folly of doing so, but instead of listening to his sage admonitions, he first strove to laugh & then, frowning at him, commanded silence.

In a few days he paid a visit to Oak-wood House* (Sir Alured's mansion) & after that became more gloomy than before. His father observed this & one day as they were sitting alone remarked it to Albion, adding that he was fully acquainted with the reason. He reddened but made no answer.

'I am not, my son,' continued the Duke, 'opposed to your wishes, though certainly there is a considerable difference of rank between yourself & Marina Angus. But that difference is compensated by the many admirable qualities she possesses.'

On hearing these words, Arthur—Albion I mean—started up &, throwing himself at his father's feet, poured forth his thanks in terms of glowing gratitude, while his fine features, flushed with excitation, spoke even more eloquently than his eloquent words.

'Rise, Albion!' said the Duke. 'You are worthy of her & she of you, but both are yet too young.* Some years must elapse before your union takes place. Therefore exert your patience, my son.'

Albion's joy was slightly damped by this news, but his thankfulness & filial obedience, as well as love, forced him to acquiesce, & immediately after he quitted the room with a relieved heart & took his way towards Oak-wood House. There he related the circumstance to Marina who, though she blushed incredulously, yet in truth felt as much gladness & as great a relief from doubt, almost amounting to despair, as himself.

A few months after, the Duke of Strathelleraye determined to visit that wonder of the world, the great city of Africa: the Glass Town, of whose splendour, magnificence, extent, power, strength & riches occasional tidings came from afar, wafted by the breezes of Ocean to merry England. But to most of the inhabitants of that little isle it bore the character of a dream or gorgeous fiction. They were unable to comprehend how mere human beings could construct fabrics of such a

marvellous size & grandeur as many of the public buildings were represented to be. And as to the Tower of All Nations, few believed in its
existence. It seemed as the cities of old Nineveh or Babylon with the
temples of their gods Ninus or Jupiter Belus, their halls of Astarte &
Semele.* These most people believe to be magnified by the dim haze
of intervening ages & the exaggerating page of history, through which
mediums we behold them.

The Duke, as he had received many invitations from the Glass
Townarians, who were impatient to behold one whose renown had
spread so far & likewise possessed vast dominions near the African
coast, informed his lady, the Marquis of Tagus & Lord Corneilius that,
in a month's time, he should take his departure with them & that he
should expect them all to be prepared at that period, adding that when
they returned Marina Angus should be created Marchioness of Tagus.

Though it was a bitter trial to Albion to part with one to whom he
was now entirely devoted, yet, comforted by the last part of his father's
speech, he obeyed without murmuring. On the last evening of his stay
in Strathelleraye, he took a sad farewell of Marina, who wept as if hopeless, but suddenly restraining her greif she looked up, with her beautiful eyes irradiated by a smile that like a ray of light illumined the crystal
tears, & whispered, 'I shall be happy when you return.'

Then they parted, & Albion during his voyage over the wide ocean
often thought for comfort on her last words. It is a common superstition that the words uttered by a freind on seperating are prophetical, &
these certainly portended nothing but peace.

In due course of time they arrived at the Glass Town & were welcomed with enthusiastic cordiality. After the Duke had visited his kingdom, he returned to the cheif metropolis & established his residence
there at Salamanca Palace.*

The Marquis of Targus, from the noble beauty of his person,
attracted considerable attention wherever he went, & in a short period
he had won & attached many faithful freinds of the highest rank &
abilities. From his love of elegant literature & the fine arts in general,
painters & poets were soon among his warmest admirers. He himself
possessed a most sublime genius, but as yet its full extent was unknown
to him.

One day, as he was meditating alone on the world of waters that
rolled between him & the fair Marina, he determined to put his
feelings on paper in a tangible shape that he might hereafter show
them to her when anticipation had given place to fruition. He took his
pen & in about a quarter of an hour had completed a brief poem of

exquisite beauty. The attempt pleased him & soothed the anguish that lingered in his heart. It likewise gave him an insight into the astonishing faculties of his own mind, and a longing for immortality, an ambition of glory, seized him.

He was a devoted worshipper of the divine works that the Grecian tragedians have left for all succeeding ages to marvel at—particularly those of Sophocles the majestic—* & his mind was deeply imbued with the spirit of their eagle-like flights into higher regions than that of earth, or even Parnassus.* Being now sensible in a degree of his lofty powers, he determined, like Milton, 'to write somewhat that the gracious Muses should not willingly die',* & accordingly commenced a tragedy entitled 'Necropolis, the City of the Dead'. Here was set forth in a strain of the grandest mood of the mysteries of ancient Egyptian worship.* And he has acknowledged to me that he felt his being absorbed while he wrote it, 'even by the words [he] himself had made', so gloriously sublime is this suprising production. It is, indeed, in the words of an eminent writer (Captain Tree) 'a noble instance of the almost perfectibility of human intellect'. But there hovers over it a feeling of tender melancholy, for the image of Marina haunted his thoughts, & Amalthea,* his heroine, is but an impersonation of her. This tragedy wreathed the laurels of fame round his brow, & his after productions, each of which seemed to excel the other, added new wreaths to those which already beautified his temples.

I cannot follow him in the splendor of his literary career, nor even mention so much as the titles of his various works. Suffice it to say that he became one of the greatest poets of the age, & one of the chief motives that influenced him in his exertions for renown was to render himself worthy to possess such a treasure as Marina.* She, in whatever he was employed, was never out of his thought, & none had he yet beheld among all the ladies of the Glass Town—though rich, titled, & handsome strove by innumerable arts to gain his favour—whom he could even compare with her.

One evening he was invited to the house of Earl Creachan, where was a large party assembled. Among the guests was one lady apparently about twenty five or six years of age. In figure she was very tall, & both it & her face were of a perfectly Roman caste. Her features were regular & finely formed; her full & brilliant eye[s] jetty black, as were the luxuriant tresses of her richly curled hair. Her dark, glowing complexion was set off by a robe of crimson velvet trimmed with ermine, & a nodding plume of black ostrich feathers added to the imposing dignity of her appearance. Albion, notwithstanding her unusual comeliness, hardly noticed her, till Earl Creachan* rose & introduced her to him as the Lady Zelzia Elrington. She was the most learned & noted woman in the Glass Town, & he was pleased with this opportunity of seeing her.

For some time she entertained him with a discourse of the most lively eloquence, & indeed Madame de Stael* herself could not have gone beyond Lady Zelzia in the conversational talent, & on this occasion she exerted herself to the utmost, as she was in the presence of so distinguished a man, & one whom she seemed ambitious to please.

At length one of the guests asked her to favour the company with a song & tune on the grand piano. At first she refused, but on Albion's seconding the request rose &, taking from the drawing-room table a small volume of miscellaneous poems, opened it at one by the Marquis of Tagus. She then set it to a fine air & sung as follows, while she skilfully accompanied her voice upon the instrument:

> I think of thee when the moonbeams play
>   On the placid water's face
> For thus thy blue eyes' lustrous ray
>   Shone with resembling grace
>
> I think of thee when the snowy swan
>   Glides calmly down the stream
> Its plumes the breezes scarcely fan
>   Awed by their radiant gleam
>
> For thus I've seen the loud winds hush
>   To pass thy beauty by
> With soft caress & playful rush
>   Mid thy bright tresses fly
>
> And I have seen the loud wild birds sail
>   In rings thy head above
> While thou hast stood like lily pale
>   Unknowing of their love
>
> O for the day when once again
>   Mine eyes will gaze on thee!
> But an ocean vast a sounding main
>   An ever howling sea
> Roll us between with their billows green
>   High-tost tempestuously.

This song had been composed by Albion soon after his arrival at the Glass Town. The person addressed was Marina. The rich full tones of Lady Zelzia's voice did ample justice to the subject, & he expressed his sense of the honour she had done him in appropriate terms. When she had finished the company departed, for it was now rather late.

As Albion pursued his way homewards alone he began insensibly to meditate on her majestic charms and compare them with the gentler ones of Marina Angus. At first he could hardly tell which to give the preference to—for though he still almost idolized Marina, yet an absence of four years had considerably deadened his remembrance of her person.

While he was thus employed he heard a soft but mournful voice whisper, 'Albion!' He turned hastily round & saw the form of the identical Marina at a little distance, distinctly visible by moonlight.

'Marina! My dearest Marina!' he exclaimed, springing towards her, while joy unutterable filled his heart. 'How did you come here? Have the angels of Heaven brought you?'

So saying, he stretched out his hand, but she eluded his grasp & slowly gliding away said, 'Do not forget me. I shall be happy when you return.'

Then the apparition vanished. It seemed to have appeared merely to assert her superiority over her rival, & indeed, the moment Albion beheld her beauty, he felt that it was peerless.

But now wonder & perplexity took possession of his mind. He could not account for this vision, except by the common solution of supernatural agency, & that ancient creed his enlightened understanding had hitherto rejected until it was forced upon him by this extraordinary incident.* One thing there was, however, the interpretation of which he thought he could not mistake, & that was the repetition of her last words, 'I shall be happy when you return.' It showed that she was still alive, & that which he had seen had been her wraith. However, he made a memorandum of the day & hour, namely the 18 of June 1815, 12 o'clock at night.*

From this time the natural melancholy turn of his disposition increased, for the dread of her death before he should return was constantly [before him] and the ardency of his adoration & desire to see her again redoubled. At length, not being able any longer to bear his misery, he revealed it to his father, & the Duke, touched with his greif & the fidelity of his attachment, gave him full permission to visit England & bring back Marina with him to Africa.

I need not trouble the reader with a minute detail of the circumstances of his voyage, but shall pass on to what happened after he arrived in England.

It was a fair evening in September 1817* when he reached Strathelleraye. Without waiting to enter the halls of his fathers, he proceeded imediately to Oak-wood House. As he approached it he almost sickened when, for an instant, the thought that she might be no more passed across his mind. But summoning Hope to his aid & resting on her golden anchor, he passed up the lawn & gained the glass doors of the drawing-room.

As he drew near a sweet symphony of harp-music swelled on his ear. His heart bounded within him at the sound. He knew that no fingers but hers could create those melodious tones with which now blended the harmony of a sweet & sad but well known voice. He lifted the vine branch that shaded the door, & beheld Marina, more beautiful he thought than ever, seated at her harp & sweeping with her slender fingers the quivering chords.

Without being observed by her, as she had her face turned from him, he entred &, sitting down, leaned his head on his hand & closing his eyes, listened with feelings of overwhelming transport to the following words:

> Long my anxious ear hath listened
> For the step that ne'er returned
> And my tearful eye hath glistened
> And my heart hath duly burned
> But now I rest

> Nature's self seemed clothed in mourning
> Even the starlike woodland flower
> With its leaflets fair adorning
> Pathway of the forest bower
> Drooped its head

> From the cavern of the mountain
> From the groves that crowned the hill
> From the stream & from the fountain
> Sounds prophetic murmured still
> Betokening grief

Boding winds came fitful sighing
Through the tall & leafy trees
Birds of omen wildly crying
Sent their yells upon the breeze
               Wailing round me

At each sound I paled & trembled
At each step I raised my head
Harkening if it his resembled
Or if news that he was dead
               Were come from far

All my days were days of weeping
Thoughts of grim despair were stirred
Time on leaden feet seemed creeping
Long heart-sickness hope deferred
               Cankered my heart

Here the music & singing suddenly ceased. Albion raised his head. All was darkness, except the silver moonbeams that showed a desolate and ruined appartment, instead of the elegant parlour that a few minutes before had gladdened his sight. No trace of Marina was visible, no harp or other instrument of harmony, & the cold lunar light streamed through a void space instead of the glass door.

He sprang up & called aloud, 'Marina! Marina!' But only an echo as of empty rooms answered. Almost distracted he rushed into the open air.

A little child was standing alone at the garden gate. It advanced towards him, & said, 'I will lead you to Marina Angus. She has long removed from that house to another.'

Albion followed it till they came to a long row of tall dark trees, which led to a churchyard which they entered in, & the child vanished, leaving Albion beside a white marble tombstone on which was chiselled:

'Marina Angus. She died 18 of June 1815 at 12 o'clock pm.'

When Albion had read this he felt a pang of horrible anguish wither his heart & convulse his whole frame. With a loud groan he fell across the tomb & lay there senseless for a long time, till at length he was roused from a deathlike trance to behold the spirit of Marina, which stood beside him &, murmuring, 'Albion, I am happy, for I am at peace,' disappeared.

For a few days he lingered round her tomb, & then quitted Strathelleraye, where he was never again heard of.

The reason of Marina's death I shall breifly relate. Four years after Albion's departure tidings came to the village that he was dead. The news broke Marina's faithful heart, & the day after she was no more.

CB October 12, 1830

THE SPELL,

AN

EXTRAVAGANZA.

BY

LORD CHARLES ALBERT FLORIAN

WELLESLEY

I give you the raw material, Words, to your own ingen-
uity I leave the eliciting of the manufactured article, Sense.
Preface by lord Wellesley to a uniform edition
Of Captain Tree's Novels and Romances

PRINTED AND

PUBLISHED BY ~

JOHN TREE

BOOKSELLER AND STATIONER ~

BIBLIO - STREET

VERDOPOLIS*

Also may be had in numbers price one penny each, at Thomas Squeeze'um's book repository, in the open air, opposite the Nigger's head Stink-alley—Coomassie Square*

Charlotte Brontë June 21ˢᵗ
1834—

_____

Preface

The Duke of Zamorna should not have excluded me from Wellesley House, for the following pages have been the result of that exclusion.* Does he think I can patiently bear to be wholly seperated from my sister-in-law,* a lady whom I love & honour more than any other in Verdopolis? Does he think I can calmly endure that she, by his orders, should turn from me if I chance to meet her in public places, & when I beg a seat in her carriage that she should, smiling & shaking her head, deny me with sweet reluctance & (the unkindest cut of all) offer me the indignity of ordering a footman to remove me when I commence, by tears & cries, to give vent to my indignation in the open street? I say, does he think I am to lie down like a flogged spaniel under all this?

If such are his ideas, let him be undeceived. Here I fling him my revenge. He will not like the morsel. In this book I have tampered with his heart-strings. Perhaps a casual spectator may think that he is highly flattered & so forth—the tale, part of it at least, being told by his own wife—but to him the whole affair will be unendurable. There are passages of truth here which will make him gnash his teeth with grating agony. I am not at liberty to point out what those passages are, but he will discover them, & he will know there-by that there is one person at least in Verdopolis thoroughly acquainted with all the depths, false or true, of his double-dealing, hypocritical, close, dark, secret, half-insane character.

Serfs of Angria!* Freemen of Verdopolis! I tell you that your Tyrant & your Idol is mad! Yes, there are black veins of utter perversion of intellect born with him & running through his whole soul. He acts at times under the control of impulses that he cannot resist, displays all the strange variableness & versatility which characterize possessed lunatics, runs head-strong forwards in dark by-paths sharply angular from the straight road of common use & custom, & is, in short, an ungovernable, fiery fool.

All this is declared in my present work rather by implication than assertion. The reader will find here no lengthened passage which elaborately sets forth his outrageous peculiarities. He must gather it from the hints interwoven with the whole surface & progress of the story. When he has finished, let him shut the book &, dismissing from his mind every fictitious circumstance, let him choose such only as have self-evident marks of reality about them. Then, after due consideration, let him deliver his opinion. Is the Duke of Zamorna sane or insane?

This question I leave to his decision & in the meantime, with acknowl-
edgements for past & prayers for future favours, I remain the public's
obedient servant

C. A. F. Wellesley

THE SPELL

CHAPTER THE Iˢᵗ

The young Marquis of Almeida* is dead. This every body knows. He
has left the inheritance of two thrones vacant. Wellingtonsland and
Angria now wait for a[n] heir.

Inexorable Death! All the guards & precautions that the royal
Zamorna could put about his first-born,* his darling, the first hope of
his kingdom & the second of his father's, were unable to withstand that
scythe whose keen edge alike destroys the withered, the full-blown and
the budding flower.

In vain were the obsequious attentions of a hundred servants, the
utmost exertions of scientific skill, the maternal care of Mina Laury,
whose tenderness once raised the father* but could not raise the son to
life, the shrine-like solitude of the lone manor house,* the balmy airs
of Health breathed over its antique woods & scented dells and rushing,
rapid rivulet. And lastly, wholly vain was the energetic wish which, till
it was quenched in despair, continually filled Zamorna's soul that he,
whom he loved with an affection past the power of words to express
because he was the only son of his mother, might live & flourish to
remind him of the departed. He died, cut off early, called away before
he knew what the world was, over whose expanse his morning had risen
so fairly.

The Duke sent Lord Julius from his presence, that parental anxiety,
strained and tortured by the evident delicacy of the plant it watched,
might not become rather a check to, than an encourager of, its welfare.
I know when the grave closed on Marian, a nervous dread took possession of his mind lest the seeds of the mother's malady might have
been transmitted with existence to the child. He hated to look at its
brightly tinted cheek and sparkling eyes, its beautifully turned limbs, &
the white clear complexion beneath which veins & even arteries might
be seen meandering in wavy lines of the faintest & finest violet. I have

often heard him groan & curse on the beauty which to him brought thoughts only of unmingled bitterness, as with a heart-wrung sigh he has laid down the exquisite miniature of his own grand image, after gazing on it for a few brief moments of evanescent &, as he too well felt, unfounded exultation. 'What would I give,' he has muttered on such occasions, 'if my son had a little, a very little less of his mother's delicate loveliness! Oh, I abhor now, with my whole soul, every touch of beauty which appears too etherial for humanity; every shade in the colour of a cheek, every ray in the light of an eye, that has too much of the heavenly, too little of the earthly. Even every inflection of a voice whose sweetness goes to the heart with a sudden thrill is now to me not a cause of delight but agony.'

When the first letter came from Grassmere, intimating that the ineradicable upas-tree* of consumption had begun to put forth its shoots, he exclaimed (for I was in the room, of course unknown to him, while he perused it), 'I knew it would be so! I'm almost glad the horrors of suspense are past! I need not tamper with hope, now there is a clear unblocked path of certainty. He lingers for a few months, perhaps weeks. Aye, Florence was only eight weeks in dying. And then he finds a resting-place in that accursed vault. Yet I wish it was all over—sickness, death, burial & all! Then I might be satisfied if not happy, but till then—.' He threw himself into a chair which stood near his desk, tore out a sheet of paper, &, with the rapidity of lightning, dashed down the following lines:

My priceless Mina,
Your work is nearly completed. It has been a hard task to preserve what Destiny had marked for decay. I know how you have discharged it, & with my own lips I will hereafter declare my approbation. Watch a few days & nights longer. Just see that the last pulse has vibrated & the last breath exhaled, & then, my girl, rest from your labours. Let me hear nothing from you, not one word, not one syllable, till you think the scene is about finally to close, when he seems to have no more than perhaps a week's strength in him, that is to say, my girl, when respiration begins to rattle in his throat & the infernal brightness dies off his cheek, & his flesh (the little that remains) grows perfectly transparent, shewing no blood, but bones.* These things having come to pass, you may write & tell me. I'll annihilate the interval, if possible.

Farewell, my sweet wild-rose! Your beauty will, I fear, be faded by death-bed vigils before I next see you. Never mind, I care not

for that, & if my heart & my love be yours, I know that Mina Laury
thinks little of the light, favourable or unfavourable, in which the
rest of the world may behold her. Faithful till death (thine or mine I
mean, girl, not intermediate ones, they seem to be coming thick), I
am & ever shall be,

Your own Zamorna

Such was the reply he sent to poor Mina's timid & apprehensive epistle. A strange one! So at least I thought. He sealed & directed it, then
ordered his carriage & left Verdopolis for Angria.

Nothing could exceed the restless activity & irritable vigilance which
marked his conduct during the next five or six weeks. He is always energetic, always passionately eager in any course he pursues. Ever since I
knew him it has been his custom to give up heart & soul to the further-
ance of a favourite plan, but now he seemed to give up life also.

Even Warner could scarcely keep pace with him. He plunged
impetuously into the thick of business, sought after the most throng-
ing employment with intense solicitude, but yet hardly appeared to feel
pleasure in it when it was found. All day long he might be seen walking through the unpaved streets of Adrianopolis,* watching & actively
superintending the labours of the toiling workmen, now directing the
construction of an arch, now the craning up of some vast block of stone
or marble, standing amidst the din & tumult of uncreated squares &
terraces, whilst the deep foundations of future mansions were dug in
the stubborn soil.

Every-where the tall figure of the slender youth, in his close black
dress & unornamented cap thickly cinctured with curls, might be
seen passing along with commanding tread & bearing, controlling
all around him like the sovereign spirit of the storm. Sometimes
that shape appeared lofty against the sky, standing on a thread-like
scaffolding, a blue abyss of air on each side, before & behind the skeleton erection of an unfinished palace, honey-combed with arches, &
vast beams flung across as the divisions of state chambers, between
voids that might turn the head of a cabin-boy giddy. And here the monarch walked as fearlessly as an eagle hangs, poised above his eiry. The
eyes of his stern & swarthy subjects were often turned admiringly on
him, as he sprung like a young elk from one narrow projection to
another, & strode over the shaking beams as erectly & haughtily as if
he were crossing a hall of Wellesley-House. At other times the eye
might single him out, overtopping a throng of subordinates, gathered

round the pit of some half-sunk foundation, watching intently while a train was laid to blast the rocks beneath, &, when the whole infernal disposition was completed, giving the order to fall back in his own full & thrilling tones, lingering the last on the path of retreat, and, as the heaven-rending thunder burst up from its stony tomb in a crack that shook hill & plain, far & near, commencing the triumphant huzza, whose swell arose as the peal of the rock-quake died into groaning echos.

But when all this was past, towards evening, when the workmen had retired from the busy scene, when the architects & master-masons & carpenters had gathered together their rules, squares, compasses, &c., & departed, then might a spectator, if any at that time tarried on the scene, discern that stately form sitting solitary on the rough hewn steps of an embryo hall. All around him silent, lonely, desolate. Still as Tadmor in the wilderness,* voiceless as Tyre on the forsaken sea.* Mallet, hammer, axe & chisel all unheard. The blast-thunder of the day forgotten, the shouts of the labourers asleep, their echoing footsteps past away, & the lull of twilight stealing on a faint wind, & the low moan of the old inhabited town down from heaven, up from earth, through the becalmed region.

At such an hour Zamorna's figure would be visible, sole inhabitant of his rising city, his arms probably folded on his breast; his eyes fixed with a mingled expression of thought & vigilance (not much of sorrow) on the yellow prairie stretching east ward before him, & finding no boundary save the golden skyline; the brow of youth & beauty, clothed with a cloud of sternness that lay on it as the shadow of an ominous sky lies on the white marble wall of a palace; the fresh red lips closely met, as placidly motionless as if eternal silence had fixed them with her seal, & no token of deep emotion apparent, of any feeling, indeed, save absorbing meditation, except the varying hue of the cheek, which now & then, at long intervals, died suddenly away from its ordinary warm, bright flush to a stricken & colourless pallor. Then it might be known there was a worm gnawing at the heart, that some pang, of deadlier agony than usual, had called the blood back to its source. But ere long the pure eloquent glow would steal again over the whitened complexion, & as the Duke slightly changed his position & turned his eyes more fixedly to the dim east, or perhaps let them fall on the reedy banks of the Calabar, it was evident his spirit had, for a time at least, conquered its inward tormentor, & that plans of war-like or political ambition were once more forced into predominance over the paternal anguish whose recurrence racked him so bitterly.

He was sitting thus one evening, when a step echoed through the silent square, & Eugene Rosier advanced from the long shadows of the surrounding buildings.

'Hah!' said his master, rising up & going forward to meet him. 'Hah, Eugene! Are they come?'

'Yes, my lord; last night at ten o'clock. There were three carriages only: Miss Laury & Mr Sydney, the mourning coach with the corpse and the under-taker's barouche.'

'Eugene, enough! But where are Ernest & Emily,* and—and—you understand me, sir, the others.' This was spoken with emphasis.

Eugene bowed. 'I believe they follow to-morrow, my lord,' he replied 'His Grace went to meet them as far as Free-Town.'*

'His Grace! What! The Duke has been here then?'

'Yes, my lord, for the last four weeks, but not at Wellesley-House.'

'I wonder I have not seen him.'

'He feared a collision; the Angrian road is so public.'

Zamorna now bent his face low & sternly laid his hand on Rosier's shoulder.

'You say,' he muttered in a suppressed tone, 'that he has been about Verdopolis four weeks. Has Finic watched?'

'Aye, my lord, like a lynx, & so have I, but there was little occasion. He is circumspect in his ways.'

'Good,' said the Duke drawing himself up. 'I am satisfied, for I imagine I can depend on you, at least if I thought a moment otherwise—.' He paused and directed an awfully piercing glance on the page, who stood it manfully.

'I speak truth to you, my lord,' he said, 'for I know a lie, on that subject especially, would inevitably bring me sooner or later to the fiery draught & leaden pill. Besides, circumstances bear testimony in my favour. He dare not take the slightest advantage if he would, for he knows how grandly Your Grace could retaliate.' Rosier concluded with a slight laugh & a sly look of his ineffably mischievous eye.

'Silence!' said Zamorna, in tones nearly as deep as smothered thunder. 'How dare you jest with me, sir! I have no wish to retaliate. Retaliate! No, if he gave me cause to retaliate the matter would be all up. His life or mine would then be the only admissible cards in the great game we have so long played together. How & when will it end? I wish the stakes were swept away, by whose hand I care not.'

'By the hand that first flung them down,' muttered another voice as deep in its inflections as Zamorna's own; but instead of the full harmony which lingers in every word that falls from his lips, a discordant harsh-ness now grated on the ear.

The Duke did not appear startled by this sudden interruption. He answered calmly, without turning round, 'Aye, that would be the fittest for the work. But, my old friend, come forwards. I know your tongue, let us see your face. You need not fear intruders, unless a bat or a night heron be reckoned as such.'

'Few of those, I take it, remain <u>now</u> among the reeds of the Calabar,' replied the same voice, & a dark figure stole from behind a vast pile of mortar & stood confronting Zamorna.

'Very few,' was the reply. 'Spade, mattock & builder's-axe have rung so loud a warning to the old settlers on that plain & on those rushy shores, that scarce a wing is left now to wave between us & the horizon.'

'Spade & mattock are ringing a warning elsewhere,' replied the stranger. 'There's a grave dug in Verdopolis to-night.'

'There's a vault opened,' said the Duke. 'How does the bedral's* lantern shine in that dim subterranean aisle, & in what fashion does the key agree with its rusty wards?'

'The bedral's lantern shines bravely,' returned he. 'And it is glancing on the golden plates of three princely coffins. Should there not be room made for a fourth? The key turns as if the under-ground damps had oiled instead of hardening it, & the grave will unfold to morrow night as noiselessly as if the sick, instead of the dead, lay within its bars. But Zamorna, where must the child lie?'

'On its mother's bosom,' replied Zamorna, in sternly suppressed accents.

'Aye, & you must lay it there. She'd turn in her coffin if any other hand performed that office, Duke. Will there be many mourners at the funeral?'

'Few, I think. Tears fall scantily over a corpse of six months old.'

'So much the better. Let me reckon the tale of those likely to be present.'

'Have done with the subject!' exclaimed Zamorna in a tone of sudden passion, which till now he had restrained, either through respect or some other cause.

'I will when it pleases me,' replied his friend. 'My young lord, you'll of course see your wife on the occasion of visiting her residence. Only a thin plank of cedar & a covering of velvet will interpose between her & you. Lift them up, & the Lady Florence, the pride of the west, lies there in all her charms. Nay, not all, she's somewhat faded & wasted, it must be allowed, but if the eye be quenched, the cheek turned to clay,

& the features for ever obliterated, what does that matter to her kingly husband? He is far too faithful to love her the less for any slight failure in that beauty which he once thought matchless.'

A muttered but horrible curse broke from the Duke's lips in reply to this sarcasm. It was met by the low, inward laugh of the stranger, & he went on, 'Truly, monarch, I shall marvel if you neglect to speak with her face to face. She did not shrink from you when she placed your first-born in your arms, & why should you from her when you return that kind office? Ah, she'll look sadly at her Arthur & moan to herself when he is gone, as she did that night on leaving the Gladiator's Hall. You heard her then, but would not take pity, so she sat down in silence to fulfil her destiny, dree her weird.'*

There was a pause. Zamorna stood leaning against an upright block of stone. The light of a broad yellow moon, which was now hanging high in the placid heavens, fell full on him, & defined features as white as those of a sheeted ghost. His face was utterly bloodless, & the dark curls clustering on his forehead & temples contrasted ghastlily with the spectral paleness of what they shadowed. His eyes looked rather upwards, they were not dim with tears, but glittering with fiery defiance. The rest of his countenance was calm; it seemed as if he could overmaster the deadly & burning rage which filled him except where transparency showed the smothered flame flashing fiercely through.

'Have you done?' he at last asked, after some minutes of mutual silence.

'Yes,' said the stranger. 'I've given you a large enough dose for the present. You may digest it at your leisure. Remember that long "moan" of stricken anguish, which nearly made you repent & turn back on your path?'

'I do remember it,' said the Duke, and at the same moment he smiled. 'I remember it well, but you are mistaken, sir, if you think it made me repent, & you are mistaken still more in saying that I would not take pity on Marian's distress. That distress gratified my pride, sir, & therefore, be sure, it changed both my love & compassion, &, unless your sagacity is much at fault, you know that I told her so, & that I spent five hours of that night in reasoning with & consoling her. The dawn of the next day found her calm & resigned, almost happy, for she knew that my affection was totally unchanged, that I loved her as well as ever, & that it was that very love which caused me to take the step I had then determined on. For if I had permitted her to remain an impediment to my inclinations, I should soon have hated her—lovely, devoted & innocent as she was—& my blood ran cold at the bare imagination of that.'

'Well,' interrupted the stranger, 'these things you alledged, I suppose, in justification of your conduct.'

'Not in justification, sir. I never justified myself to any woman breathing! But I employed that reason as a means of soothing & comforting her & I am proud to say not without effect, for when the morning light glimmered through the window, in whose recess she sat for the last time by my side, it fell upon a face as placid & resigned as, a few hours before, it had been inexpressibly sad & mournful. I had wiped away all her tears. Though there was melancholy in the smile, which my final embrace called to her sweet features. There was no misery. Sir, you think I am a prey to remorse. Be undeceived. I know not what remorse is!'

'A lie! A lie!' said the unknown. 'Your heart is now torn with it! That subdued voice & ashy countenance give signs of a worm that will not die. Don't think to deceive me, Zamorna! I know you too well.'

'Yet not well enough,' replied the Duke, 'or you would know that the change in my voice & countenance is owing to hatred of yourself rather than regret for either my wife or son. I loved them both with a deeper love than words can express. Their untimely removal has, I confess, inflicted a wound that the lapse of centuries can never entirely heal, but, sir, abhorrence is stronger than grief in its sternest form, & though there may be moments, even hours, in my life when I shall forget to lament the dead, there will never be an instant when I shall cease to regard you with the bitterest detestation.'

A low malignant laugh was the stranger's only answer. He folded more closely round him the cloak in which he was enveloped, nodded to Zamorna &, gliding across the square, was quickly lost to sight.

'Hah!' said the Duke, when he was gone. 'I wish the wretch had stayed one minute longer. Though I loathe his presence so intensely, I would yet have detained him to ask what issue events are drawing to. The mystery contained in those lines I have so often heard in my infancy, & <u>once</u> since manhood's sun shone fervidly on my path, seems unfolding.

'When the wave of death's river
    Hides the rose in its bloom
When the gift & the Giver
    Lie low in the tomb

When the fresh fruit is shaken
The bright blossom blown
When the flower falls forsaken
And wither'd and lone
Then upwards to heaven
The dim cloud shall swell
The veil shall be riven
And broken the spell.

'There is more, but I forget it. Well, time is the great revealer of secrets, & no hand can delay its progress, yet it seems the sacrifice has been exacted from me & me alone. My flower & fruit are gone, while his—Good God! I am not going to wish their death, am I? No, no, that would be a black addition to the mutual pile of affliction, more tears to be wrung from a heart that has few to spare—& his, I think, would weep blood. I likewise should desire no third overshadowing of death even on that side. The cloud which has now fallen will be long ere it dissipate. Oh! Florence! Florence! My sky can never again shine as brightly as it has done. There is a continual dimness round the horizon which will not pass away.'

In bitter melancholy he paced the square &, except the sound of his measured foot-steps, all was unbroken silence for the next quarter of an hour. At the end of that time he paused.

'Eugene,' said he, 'come, I shall leave Adrianopolis immediately. My presence at Douro Villa* will, I dare say, be much missed, especially if the mourners are late in arriving. You said that He was expected to-morrow, did you not?'

Eugene answered in the affirmative & page & master departed together.

CHAPTER THE IInd

On the subsequent evening, or rather night, a message arrived from my father summoning me instantly to Waterloo-Palace. I was in bed when the servant arrived, for it was near eleven o'clock, but I rose instantly &, as soon as I was dressed, hastened to obey the mandate.

On entering the north drawing-room, where a footman informed me the Duke awaited my arrival, I found him seated with a lady, whom I presently recognized as my aunt, the Countess Seymour.* Both she and my father were dressed in deep mourning, & an air of thoughtful solemnity brooded on the brow of each. I came up to the hearth &, warming my hands at the red-bright fire for it was a somewhat chilly night, I asked, 'Is the funeral to take place this evening?'

'The funeral!' exclaimed Lady Seymour. 'Child, how did you know of the death or even sickness? Augustus has been as secret & uncommunicative as ever during the progress of the whole affair.'

'Aye, but it would be difficult for him to be so secret that I should not find him out. There are not above two or three incidents of his life which are unknown to me, & one of these must have happened before I was born.'

'Well,' said my father, 'be that as it may, your penetration has hit the mark this time. Charles, your nephew, Lord Almeida, has been dead upwards of a week. He will be buried in an hour's time. If you will solemnly promise to restrain that prying curiosity of yours which has already given your brother so much inconvenience, I may permit you to attend the funeral. But if your elfish disposition will not allow the fulfilment of such a condition, stay at home. I have no wish to subject you to any painful restraint.'

I readily promised, and then proceeded to ask my father why this discretion was so requisite.

'There will be persons there,' he said, 'whom you never saw before. It is my pleasure that you should not yet become acquainted with them, for reasons which, with all your precocity, sir, you would find a difficulty yet in comprehending. So make not the slightest attempt to discover their identity either by word, look, or sign. My severe displeasure will be the reward of disobedience.'

Again I promised, but I could not help wondering who these prohibited personages might be.

'Isabella,' continued my father, addressing Lady Seymour, 'you will take charge of him. Keep his hand fast clasped in your own, & do not let him leave your side one instant till the ceremony is over & the mourners gone.'

'I shall be careful, brother,' replied my aunt. 'For were Augustus, in his present dark & bitter mood, to notice even a prying look in his face, the consequences might be fatal.'

'He must not come near Augustus!' replied my father sternly. 'I will hazard neither his life nor that of the others. And they are so sudden & dangerous on that point, while he is so incurably inquisitive, that assuredly in case of collision the sequel would be a tragic one.' My father now struck his gold-repeater. 'It is half-past eleven, & I hear them bringing the carriage round to the private door. Come, Isabella, there is no time for delay.'

He took up his craped hat* & black gloves, which lay on a side-board and, drawing my aunt's arm through his, led her from the room & down the grand stair-case. The carriage was drawn up close under the portico, for the night was very wild & wet. Both entered. I was lifted in after by a servant. My father took me on his knee & we drove off.

Notwithstanding the noise of the wheels, the bustle of the streets around, the howling of the wind, & the incessant clattering of the rain, I fell fast asleep in my comfortable position & awoke only when the motion of the carriage ceased. We had stopped under St Michael's.* As we alighted, the great doors flew open to admit us & closed directly behind. All within was silent, lonely, &, but for the gleam of two solitary lamps, would have been shrouded in utter darkness. One of these glinted dimly from behind the curtain of the organ gallery, & the other was carried by the verger who let us in. This man wore his official stole & his face was masked.

'Are they come?' asked the Duke of Wellington.

'Yes, my lord, they are all assembled in the burial aisle.'

'Lead the way, then,' continued His Grace.

The verger obeyed &, taking his lamp, glided on before us, as we passed under the grand dome, whose vast altitude was now unseen in the thick darkness that filled the cathedral. A low note stole from the organ. As it died away others followed, & soon a requiem of Mozart's swelled with subduing solemnity through the whole void of pitch-dark air. I paused to listen. Lady Seymour seized my hand & hurried me forwards without speaking. We stopped at the door leading to the royal burial aisle of the Wellesleys. Our conductor tapped. It was opened from within & we entered. Many lamps were burning in the house of death, but all with a dim & discoloured flame, as if they loathed the air that fanned them. The vaulted walls were clearly seen. They looked dark & damp, but not slimy. Many niches were formed in them for the reception of coffins & three of these were occupied. A sepulchral urn stood before each. The centre of the aisle was occupied by a bier supporting a small coffin covered with a pall of white velvet. Round this were ranged the mourners. I obtained a full view of all as I entered, & the following is the most correct description I can give.

Dr Stanhope, the primate of Angria, stood at the head, gowned & cassocked. At his right hand, Mr Sumner in plain mourning, at his left Dr Alford,* ditto. A little in the back-ground & leaning against the wall with his arms folded, & his eyes fixed intently on the ground, appeared

Zamorna, as pale & motionless as if he too had been an image of lifeless mortality. No tear trembled in the long dark lashes that reposed
on his cheek, & his brow, as usual, wore an aspect rather of sternness
than sorrow. Close beside him stood Mina Laury. Her face & her whole
person turned, I believe unconsciously, rather away from the general
group & towards him. She wept much, but her tears flowed freest after
she had looked at the pale face of the lofty figure standing near her.

Opposite was Ernest Fitz-Arthur.* His countenance was covered
with his hands; drops trickled through his fingers; but, actuated by the
same spirit as his father, he was too proud to give way to any more audible expression of his grief. He has remarkably warm & ardent feelings
for one so young, & I saw it was a hard struggle to suppress the sorrow
with which his heart was heaving. So far all the mourners were known
to me, but at the foot of the bier were placed two with whom I was
unacquainted. A lady & a gentleman, the former shrouded in a double
veil of black crape, the latter in a cloak of sables. They whispered now
& then to each other very low, & once the lady stepped up to Zamorna.
She spoke in a soothing tone. He smiled faintly & told her to speak to
that child, pointing to Ernest, 'if she wished to comfort the afflicted'.

'No,' was her reply. 'Edward ought to weep, his playmate's death has
been a heavy loss to him. But for you, his removal may on the whole be
rather a mercy than otherwise.'

'Well, Emily,' returned he, 'you see no tear on my cheek. Poor Mina,'
& he turned to her with a look of compassion, 'is sorry for her nursling,
but I am as calm as——.' He directed a significant glance to the figure in
sables before alluded to & paused.

'Calm, Augustus!' said the lady. 'Aye, outside, but you look so deadly
white.'

'Emily,' said the Duke, 'lift up his mantle & see whether he too does
not look white?'

She shook her head & moved away.

My father now came forwards. He advanced to the two strangers.
The gentleman held out his hand, which His Grace of Wellington
grasped most warmly. The lady put aside her veil, but as she, at that
moment, turned her back to me, her features remained as much a mystery as ever. The Duke saluted her on the forehead in silence. He &
the masculine incognito then moved away to a little distance. For some
time they continued to walk in the farther part of the aisle, conversing
earnestly in subdued whispers. I could now see that the step & bearing
of the stranger were remarkably noble. His stature was lofty & his voice,
repressed as it was, sounded deep & commanding.

Ere-long the vault door reopened &, marshalled by the masked verger, Prince John of Sneachisland entered; Lord Rossendale* accompanied him. Both were, of course, attired in black. Rossendale took his station by Ernest. He regarded him with an expression of frank-hearted sympathy, but said nothing. Fitz-Arthur dashed away his tears the moment his friend entered and, biting his lip, seemed resolved to shew no more weakness. Fidena passed by Zamorna without observing him, for, as I have already said, Arthur stood a little aloof. He walked to my father & his companion &, bowing to the former, was about to take the latter's hand, saying, 'My dear Zamorna, how are you?'

A passionate & haughty repulse made him fall back a step or two. He looked round with surprise. Arthur strode hastily up to him. His face, which a moment before had been cold & colourless as marble, glowed like scarlet.

'John,' said he, convulsively grasping his arm, 'do you not know me?'

'Certainly, Arthur, I do, but for the moment not perceiving you, & observing a tall gentleman with your father I was led into a mistake. It is now, however, rectified, & as no offence was intended, so I trust none has been taken.'

The stranger, without reply & keeping his face still muffled in the shrouding cloak, resumed his station by the veiled lady.

Zamorna pressed Fidena's hand in both his, & an interval of deep silence ensued. It was broken by the grating sound of the vault key as the vergers turned it in the rusty wards.

'Are all here?' asked the Duke of Wellington, observing this action.

'All,' was the concise reply of Zamorna.

'Stanhope, commence the service,' continued His Grace.

The book was laid open, & the solemnly impressive voice of the primate soon echoed through the aisle as it consigned to dust & corruption those cold remains which the canopy of the pall & the gilded planks of the coffin alone concealed from our sight. The awful words were said: he had committed earth to earth, ashes to ashes.* The corpse was placed in its appropriate niche, & far off we heard the long stealing chords of the organ, & the softened voices of the choristers as they joined in that grand & thrilling chant, 'I know that my Redeemer liveth'.* These sounds passed mournfully away, but as they died another burst in thunder above us. It was the great bell of St Michael's, whose deep-struck toll, now clanging from its domed elevation, announced to all Verdopolis that the young heir of Angria & Wellingtonsland was laid at rest in the last home of his royal kindred. Few tears fell on the coffin of the infant prince. None from the eye of his father, none from that of his grandfather, of his uncle of Fidena, of the strangers. Mina wept, as Zamorna said, for her nursling & Fitz-Arthur for his play mate, but beside these the inheritor of two thrones could command no single tribute of regret from all his thousand future subjects.

All were about to quit the vault when the verger stepped forwards. He placed one hand on the empty bier, & rolling his eyes, which glittered like steel within the mask, over the group of mourners, he said in the deep harsh tones I had heard last night two hundred miles off:

'The wave of Death's river
   Hides the rose in its bloom
The Gift & the Giver
   Sleep low in the tomb
The fresh fruit is shaken
   The bright blossom strown
The flower lies forsaken
   And withered & lone
Then upward to heaven
   The dim cloud shall swell
The veil shall be riven
   And broken the spell
But slowly the cloud must rise
   Faint is the gale
That sighs through the muffled skies
   Breathes on the veil
High was the wanderer's power
   Wondrous his spell
It wrought in their natal hour
   Strongly & well
A might is yet on them
   No mortal can quell
A charm rests upon them
   Which none can dispel
The watch through the dark time of star & of shade,
The shadow shall vanish the starlight shall fade.'

Not one of those present looked astonished at this strange incident. Stanhope & Sumner whispered together, & Fidena muttered, 'Hah, I have heard something of this.' The rest were evidently fully acquainted with the whole mystery of the business.

All now left the vault &, lit on their path by the verger, proceed[ed] through the dark & silent cathedral to their carriages. Mina, the veiled lady & Ernest Fitz-Arthur were handed by Zamorna into his. He entered after them & they drove off. Fidena & Rossendale then departed, & the Duke of Wellington, Lady Seymour & myself remained alone with the stranger. He spoke a few words aside to the Duke in that low & very sweet tone he had used all along. He then offered his arm to my aunt. She accepted it willingly enough, & he handed her into the carriage. My father entered next, & left me standing close to the stranger.

I felt an odd kind of thrill run through me as he suddenly bent down his stately figure &, taking me in his arms, lifted me onto the carriage seat. He followed, placed himself beside me, & as the horses whipt off I felt his hand, evidently a small & slender-fingered one, laid on mine with a gentle pressure. The touch electrified me. I screamed out.

'Heavens!' said my aunt in a tone of terror.

'Good God!' exclaimed my father in one of anger. 'What are you doing, sir? You must be aware of the elf's disposition! Don't lay a finger on him! He would find you out by one of your hands.'

The stranger laughed slightly &, drawing himself a little from me, he leaned his head against the side of the carriage.

'Find him out by one of his hands,' repeated I to myself. 'Aye, there was something peculiar in that hand, something very insinuating in the feel of its warm, slight fingers, & I think familiar. I have felt them before. If I could only touch his face now—his head—it would help me to guess. I'll try. He seems not ill-disposed towards me.'

I began noiselessly to creep to his side. Already my hand had penetrated the folds of the muffling cloak; my finger touched his forehead. He started as if adder-stung, & the next moment I was stretched senseless in the bottom of the carriage.

On awaking from this dream the mild face of Lady Seymour was the first object that met my eyes. She was bending over me & my head rested on her knee. A magnificent apartment was above & around me, & the pure lustre of shaded lights slept on the walls & ceiling.

'Aunt,' said I, 'where am I?'

'In my house, Charles. In Seymour Place. Don't look so startled, child, there are none but friends round you.'

I gazed about wildly enough, I suppose, in search of the mysterious & pugnacious stranger, with whose stunning blow my temples yet tingled. Neither he nor my father, however, were visible. Some dim forms floated before my sight & a silvery murmur of tongues was in my ear, but I saw nothing distinctly.

'Keep off, children,' said my aunt. 'You oppress him with your inquisitiveness. Cecillia, hand me the salts again.'

A fresh application of this restorative brought back my senses. I rose & looked first on one side, then on the other. I had been placed on a sofa near the fire. Earl Seymour sat opposite in an arm chair, his foot (I suppose he had the gout) laid on a cushioned stool, & little Helen rubbing it gently with her hands. My other cousins, five in number, all young ladies varying in their ages from twenty to twelve, were crowded round the sofa. They were putting twenty questions to their mother in the same breath.

'Mamma, what can be the matter? Has he displeased Augustus? Who was that with our uncle? Why did he keep his face covered, mamma? Why was he so silent? Don't you think he's a strange man?' &c., &c.

'Hugh, hugh, ugh!' coughed the Earl, their father. 'Be silent, girls, & don't stun one with your larums!* I say, Isabella, order the whole crew off to bed. I permitted them to stay up so late that they might hear about the funeral, but I suppose you've nothing particular to tell. I must say it's unaccountable in that Duke of Zamorna to do every thing so privately. How many mourners were there, pray?'

She was going to answer when the door opened & Lord Fitzroy entered.

'Well, mother,' said he, coming swaggering up to the fire, 'I understand there's been bloodshed at this wonderfully select burial. You've come back with a wounded man, eh? There were so few of you that you should have been unanimous. What does Zamorna mean by excluding his relatives in this fashion? Cousins should follow cousins to the grave. Now, for my part, I never so much as saw this Lord Almeida except once, about four months since, when he was but nine weeks old, & therefore can't be expected to break my heart for the matter of his death. But then, you see, etiquette compels one to keep house on the night when one's second cousin takes a ride in the cold meat* cart, & so one might as well be trotting by the side of the vehicle to see that all's right—were it only for decency's sake.'

'For shame, brother!' said all his sisters in a breath.

'For shame! Why now, you Cecillia & Eliza & Georgiana, confess haven't you been grumbling in your own hearts that you couldn't go to Lord Richton's grand concert this evening, when the lights are glaring just opposite & if a window's flung open the music sounds quite distinctly? I'm sure you did. As for Catharine & Agnes & Helen, it's another matter they'd have to stay at home at all events.'

'My dear Fitzroy,' said Lady Seymour, 'you take the affair very much to heart. I assure you there's no such pleasure in attending a funeral at any time, but especially on so dreary a night as the present.'

'Perhaps not, mother, but it would be better than cowering in one's own ingle nook,* listening to the wind blowing a horn-pipe in the chimney & you not permitted to dance to it.'

'Fitzroy,' said Lady Cecillia, by way of changing the conversation, 'we've had one of the mourners here. He came with mamma & my uncle, but only stayed five minutes & never spoke a single word.'

'Indeed! What was he like?'

'Like the assassin in Uwins's picture* in the crimson drawing-room, for he had his face covered with a cloak.'

'Humph! Mother, you, of course, know who he was?'

'Indeed I do not! I have never seen him except muffled, as he appeared this evening. But now, children, once for all let me tell you not to trouble me with questions regarding that stranger. I shall answer none you may put to me. Come, loves, it is past one. Bid your father & me good-night. You should all have been in your chambers long since.'

The girls shook hands with & kissed their parents in succession. Fitzroy more carelessly nodded his head with rather an awkward air, for I believe the ceremony of bidding good-night in any shape was unusual to him, & left the room whistling.

In an hour's time the whole mansion from hall to attic was buried in the silence of profound sleep.

CHAPTER THE III^d

Letter from the Duchess of Zamorna
to Lady Helen Percy

Dear Grandmamma,

I have always been accustomed to make you my confidante, to tell you every-thing, to ask your advice on all subjects. I think my disposition is not very frank at least its frankness is not extended. The circle of my bosom friends I like to be small, select, strictly exclusive. My father, the Duke of Wellington, & yourself form the sphere of my concentrated strong affections. It is not in the nature of Northangerland's daughter to be very diffusive in her attachments. There are many others whom I like, many whom I admire, thousands with whom I am on good &

cheerful terms, two after whom I have hankerings of natural regard (id est my brothers, Edward & William),* but the example of my great father has prevented me from wasting among miscellaneous common-place 'connections' the esteem & tenderness which I owe only to a few. So much for affection. As for love, every drop I possess of that passion is poured out on one grand object: Zamorna has it all, & I could not, if I would, deduct an atom from his right. I wish, O, how I wish, that he could be sensible of this, that he knew how much, how deeply & how fervently I love him. Then, perhaps, he would not be so sad as he some-times is, so cold, so strange, so silent.

Grandmamma, I have now been married to the Duke half a year. It was a strange thing for me to become the wife of Zamorna! I had dreamt about him years before, seen him through the haze of his glorious poetry, conversed with him in thought, wandered with him in idea through all the scenes his works describe. For hours I have sat under the elm trees of Percy-Hall, buried [in] reveries whose continu-ally recurring theme was that youthful prince & poet. He was a wild dream a superhuman vision, a rain-bow apparition which I chased & chased over hill, & plain, & valley, ever unwearied, never successful, wholly absorbed in the vain yet delicious pursuit. When I at length saw him, when I heard him speak, when I even felt the thrilling touch of his hand, no tongue can express the emotions that almost paralyzed me with their power.

In no single thing was he like the being I had imagined to myself, & yet, as on entering the room, I saw a figure rise up as tall as Milton's Satan, as bright as his Ithuriel,* it needed not speech to furnish me with the name of that figure. My previous ideas had been all indeed sparkling, but vague & indefinite to the last degree. I had imagined him only in romantic situations. I had thought of him only as the inspired boy-minstrel, the life-giving form in a grand landscape, where stream & tree & sky & mountain, all flinging their shadows & rolling their waves, bewildered the eye with profusion of magnificence, till it carried away no distinct image of what it had rested upon.

I cannot describe how the reality affected me! It was so new, so fas-cinating, to behold my hero, my royal lyrist, mingling in the every-day scenes of genuine life. It did not lower him; it flung him out in a new light, a fresh & striking position. Every thing he did, every thing he said, however trivial, possessed enchaining interest in my eyes. I actually remember watching him with intense solicitude one day, as he was ransacking the Countess of Northangerland's desk for some papers. He flung the manuscripts out in heaps, opened the letters unscrupulously, glanced them rapidly over, laughed at some & sneered at others, tossed the seals & wax & wafers about. Then, being unable to discover the object of his search, he treated her portfolio in the same manner—opened it on the carpet, kneeling on one knee, squandered the contents about most recklessly, looking all the while so eager, his eyes lighted & his face a little flushed. There were several persons in the room, the Countess herself among the number. She regarded him very complacently & never offered to stop his proceedings. Even when he asked for the key of her cabinet, she gave it him & let him commit the same ravages there.

The first time I saw him eat, too, was an era in my life. It was one tea-time at Ellrington-Hall. I presided at table and he sat next me on a music-stool, which sort of [?sofa] he always prefers at that meal. I was so absorbed in listening to & watching him that I quite forgot to enquire whether he took tea or coffee, &c, but handed him the cup nearest my hand. It stood before him a minute without being touched.

He then said with a smile, 'Do you know, Miss Percy, you have given me a vessel of liquid which I can't taste. Milk, sugar & green tea—an intolerable compound.' So sayin[g], he emptied it into the slop-basin & requested a cup of unmixed mocha coffee.

As I hurriedly complied, he whispered to me in his own low, sweet tone. 'Be perfect in your business, Mary, before the time comes when I may be your only guest, seated opposite in a snug drawing-room with Roland & Roswal couched amicably on the rug.'*

These words made my heart throb almost audibly. I little thought then how near they were to fulfilment. The block of his existing marriage shut out any ideas of the kind—indeed that very evening the Marchioness was present. She sat at my left hand & her eyes were never off her lord. To no one else would I mention the name of that lady. I shudder whenever I think of her, not with hatred—I believe, Grandmamma, it is not in my nature to hate such a one as she was—nay, I should have loved her had she been the wife of any one else, but with horror at her ghastly fate. Were that fate to be <u>mine</u>, were Zamorna to leave me & marry another, I should die, not of consumption, but of a sudden paroxysm of life-quenching agony that would cut me down like a scythe. Good God, at times I have had glimpses of the anguish she endured so patiently. I have had sudden pangs of jealousy & moments of unutterable darkness, & while they lasted my spirit boiled in lava. I had feelings of suffocation & terrific goading sensations that almost drove me mad. And then when the creature whom I suspected to be my rival was present, I turned sheet-white with abhorrence. And when I could find Zamorna alone,

I begged him to kill me at once, & kneeled before him, and bathed his hand in tears that he himself said were scalding. He always heard me; he always pitied me; but he said I was foolish & mistaken, & tried to cheer me with his wild musical laugh—& never in vain, for that laugh, when not fierce or scornful, is a cordial itself to my ears.

But, Grandmamma, my pen has run away from me. I have written on anything rather than the subject I intended to, which is certain inconsistencies in the Duke's conduct that at times puzzle me most painfully. Since our marriage it has been my constant study, the business of my life, to watch the unfolding of his strange character, to read his heart (if I could), to become acquainted with all his antipathies that I might avoid them, & all his inclinations that I might continually follow them. Sometimes my efforts have been successful, sometimes unsuccessful, but upon the whole my attention or tact (as the Duke of Wellington calls it) has rather raised than lowered me in his good opinion. You know I am practised in this kind of silent vigilance. I used to exercise it towards my dear father. Ever since I can remember I have watched the proper moments when to speak & when to be silent. I have studied his likes & dislikes, & rigidly striven to gratify the former & avoid the latter. It was natural for me then, when I became the wife of one whom I loved so inexpressibly as Zamorna, to exert every effort in order to please him. Yet in spite of all sometimes he is unaccountably cool—not unkind, I cannot say that—but it is the kindness of a friend rather than a husband. And then he changes so suddenly. And there are other little mysterious incidents connected with these changes which no-body sees but me & which I reveal to none. An example or two will best explain my meaning.

About a week ago he came into my room one morning in travelling equipment & said he was going to Angria. He bade me good-bye very tenderly, & I felt as if I had never loved him till then. I gazed in the direction his carriage had gone long after it was invisible, & the whole day was fit for little except moping with my head on my hand. Evening came. I was too fretful to enjoy company, so instead of attending any of the numerous parties to which I was engaged, I stayed at home, sitting by the fire of the small library with splendour & comfort around & insuperable wretchedness within. I think it was about ten o'clock & my low spirits were at their depth when the door opened, & the Duke of Zamorna walked in. Astonishment & delight kept me fixed to my seat a minute. He came forward, laid his hand on the back of a chair, & looked full at me but did not speak. I was presently at his side, & my arms were clasped round his neck. He attempted to loose them, but so faintly

& smiling at the same time, that I thought he was only in play. Just then a fierce growl, almost like that of a large dog, startled me. The Duke directly shook off my hold. He held me at arm's length &, still smiling, looked through my eyes into my very heart.

'Dear Arthur,' said I, 'what happy turn in the wheel of fortune has brought you back so soon?'

'I don't know whether it is happy or not, Mary,' said he. 'You appear so much surprised to see me.'

I made no answer. There was something very singular in the expression with which he regarded me. And at that moment the apparition of Finic glided in between us &, gently yet firmly removing me from the Duke's touch, began to converse with him by means of signs. I looked on in silence as they wove their fingers into words as quickly as lightning, my lord, every now & then, fixing his speaking eyes on the mute's countenance & reading what he would say there faster than even the language of signs could inform him.

'What is all this coming to?' I asked myself. The Duke soon spoke.

'Mary,' said he, 'I ought to be at Angria. Therefore you will say nothing of this unlooked for return. I shall remain but five minutes. My purpose in entering this appartment was merely to write a letter.'

Materials stood on the table. He sat down & hastily wrote, folded & sealed a small billet. I noticed that he did not use his royal signet ring, which indeed was absent from his finger, but a small seal ring on his left hand, engraved with the arms of Wellesley, not Angria. He rose when he had finished, took his travelling-cap, which, as he placed it rather forward, threw, in conjunction with the curls that the rim pressed down, a deep shadow over his brow & eyes. He then surveyed me all over with a quick stolen, keenly penetrating glance &, uttering a careless good-night, was about to leave the room. I started towards him, hardly knowing what I was about.

'Dear Arthur,' said I, 'won't you shake hands with me before you go?'

He laughed & turned his face from me to Finic. The creature stamped & gesticulated impatiently as if he wished him to depart.

'Is that dwarf to control your motions, my lord?' said I. 'I wish he were at the bottom of the Niger!'*

'And so do I too,' was the reply. 'He is a decided bore, yet a useful one. But come, give me your hand & never mind his ill-temper.'

My hand had scarcely touched his when Finic set up a perfect yell. He jumped, contorted his hideous features, writhed as if a knife had been stuck into him, & in short exhibited every symptom of ludicrous and malignant rage. He need not have been in such alarm: I hardly felt the pressure of Zamorna's fingers, it was so slight & cold. His Grace seemed highly amused; he laughed heartily both at me & the dwarf. I thought he appeared inclined to prolong the entertainment, for he shut the door, which stood open, & once or twice approached where I stood, but then Finic began to look dangerous & to roll his white eyes most savagely.

'Hah!' said Zamorna. 'It's time to be gone, that's evident.' He hastily bid me good-night, fetched Finic a tremendous blow with the butt-end of a pistol which he drew from his breast, saying, 'Take that, dog, for your causeless clamour,' & strode out of the apartment.

Now, Grandmamma, what do you think of all this? Is it not passing strange? And this is not the only scene of the kind I have been an actor in. Twice or thrice has the same game been played over before. I cannot conceive what earthly right that dwarf has to intervene between me & my lord, much less how his haughty spirit can submit to it. Then the origin of his fits of coldness & caution I shall never be able to ascertain. They are only fits, for sometimes he is far otherwise than cold, but that makes the intervals more insufferable. Then again, generally speaking Finic hardly dares lift his eyes in his presence: he is abject & crawling as an earthworm. I verily believe Oedipus* only could solve the whole enigma.

I have written myself into a very moody humour, & it is past twelve at night, so, dear Grand-mamma, fare-well,

Your affectionate granddaughter,
Mary Henrietta Wellesley

P.S. It is a common saying that the post-script of a woman's letter always contains the pith & marrow of what she intended to write, the matter nearest her heart. I believe my present communication will offer no exception to this general rule. Doubtless you have heard of the Marquis Almeida's death. I never knew it till the news-papers formally announced the fact to the public. The name of that young prince has not once dropped from Zamorna's lips in my hearing. From the first moment of our acquaintance till now he is delicately reserved in all relating to former connections, though I fear they dwell on his mind. Well, my step-son was buried a fortnight ago at midnight, in the royal vault of Wellesley. I understand the occupants of Grassmere, together with two strangers with whom nobody is acquainted, were present at the funeral.

Grandmamma, I would just now give a thousand pounds to know who Ernest Fitz-Arthur is. Undeniably Zamorna is his father, of that

I am satisfied, for I have seen the child, but who claims the honour of being his mother? I know whom you would mention, but your guess is wrong—not M.L.* I solemnly asked Edward, & he as solemnly & most promptly replied in the negative. This assurance put me on my mettle. It roused all the latent spark[s] of female curiosity which are contained in my nature, & those are neither few nor feeble. I determined to know if I could, & I think I have been at least partially successful. Having learnt from Charles that Ernest & his guardian were still residing at Douro Villa, it came into my head, one fine evening last week, that I would take a ride over and visit them. I longed to see whether Miss Laury was so handsome, & Fitz-Arthur so much like his father as people said. It was hazardous, for I incurred the risk of my lord's displeasure if he should find me out, but curiosity, curiosity—that over-steps most obstacles with women, & as the Duke was then at Adrianopolis, two hundred miles off, I hoped there was no great danger. Well, I ordered the carriage & set out.

It was just two hours before sunset as I entered the grounds, & a serenely solemn evening that brought Percy-Hall to my remembrance. I alighted before coming in sight of the villa, as I did not wish the sound of wheels to give notice of my approach. Turning aside from the main path, I took a shorter one which wound among the trees close by the terrace-ground where the gardens are planted. All seemed so silent, so calm, & shady, & peaceful in the upper region that I could not resist the temptation of ascending its grassy slope & walking for a little while in those deep, dim alleys that opened like glimpses of Paradise far within. I wandered on, lost in thought, till, at a sudden turn, the splash of a fountain fell on my ear, & I thought a low murmur of tongues mingled with the fall of waters. Softly I stole forward. Trees grew round, &, without being myself seen, I could observe the spirits haunting these solemn groves. A Narcissus of Chantrey's,* carved in marble, was bending over the basin of the spring. Close beside, flesh & blood exquisitely in contrast with lifeless stone, sat a lady & <u>two</u> children. Yes, Grandmamma, two! When I saw that, I was really startled.

The lady I instantly recognized as Mina Laury. Her tall form, black eyes & hair, & clear brunette complexion were sufficient landmarks to go by. Handsome she certainly is, & that I do not wonder at (many of our peasantry are so), but her perfect elegance is more astonishing. She might be an earl's instead of a cottager's daughter. I trembled when I saw her, but I trembled still more when I saw the cherub-like children, a boy & girl, one four, the other perhaps two years old, so exquisitely beautiful, so full of life, their glancing curls & brilliant smiling eyes throwing into such death-like stillness the carved figure with its cold gleaming limbs & sightless orbs behind them. And then the likeness, aye, that was the bitter, the stinging ingredient that poisoned the whole lovely spectacle. I wish their eyes had been blue; I wish their hair had been flaxen; then I could have loved them, but, as it was, when I saw my own husband's features in fine miniature, when I beheld myself gazed at by his very eyes, the same remarkable, dark, transparent, sepia brown with unvarigated irids of a clear even tint, & large full pupils, their beauty sickened me. The little girl was the very counterpart of her brother, only her skin was even more delicately fair, &, mingled with the likeness of Zamorna, there was a slight alien touch that turned her features into a more feminine mould. They were lying on the edge of the fountain, floating leaves & flowers on its surface, & watching them as the whirl of the falling stream caught & sucked them into its vortex. Mina kept guard that no danger might ensue. Oh, it was a fair scene, as the mingling light & shadows of the grove fell on the whole reposing group. If I could have enjoyed it, but I could not.

Scarcely conscious what I did, I came forward, & sat down opposite Mina. 'You seem fond of children, Miss Laury,' I said.

At the sound of my voice she raised her head calmly, her countenance betrayed no surprise. Steadily surveying me she answered, 'Of my master's, I am, madam.'

'Aye, & of your master's self, too, I have no doubt,' said I, with, I believe, my father's sneer, for my heart was choking in my throat.

'Ladies equal to himself in birth & connections may say they are fond of the Duke of Zamorna,' she replied, 'but that is not the word I should use.'

'And pray what word would you use?'

'He is my master, madam, therefore I honour him.'

I laughed scornfully, for my blood was up. 'You are a hypocrite, Miss Laury,' said I. 'You do more than honour him.'

'Yes, I worship & obey him.'

'And is that all?'

'I love him.'

'Anything more?'

'I would die for him.'

'You would not!' said I. 'I could not do more & I am confident there is not a woman on earth would do as much for him as I myself.'

'Delicate, soft-bred, brittle creature,' returned she, with kindling eyes, 'that is an empty boast! The spirit might carry you far, but the body would break down at last. My Lady Duchess (for I know you by the Percy forehead & golden hair), it is not for an indulged daughter of aristocracy, for one who from her birth has hardly every breathed out of the perfumed atmosphere of palace halls, or trod elsewhere than on velvet soft carpets, to talk of serving Zamorna. She may please & entertain him & blossom brightly in his smiles, but when adversity saddens him, when there are hard duties to perform, when his brow grows dark & his voice becomes stern & sounds only in command, I warn you, he will call for another hand-maid, one whose foot is as familiar to wild heath & common as to gilded saloon, who knows the feel of a hard bed & the taste of a dry crust, who has been rudely nurtured & not shielded like a hot-house flower from every blast of chilling wind. And besides, my lady, Zamorna's work wants a heart, a mind different from yours. Beautiful patrician, with what morbid delicacy would you shrink from scenes that I have looked on unmoved? How the exotic's leaves would fold & bow down as the shadows of sorrow & death fell like night on their loveliness. The noble & high-born cannot endure grief. They fly with cowardly terror from the coming of mortality, & when it grasps them or theirs, what wild, impious wailings fill dome & turret, bower & hall. It is not so in cottages. Poverty & the necessity of labour strengthen men's souls wonderfully.' She paused.

For a minute I was too much astonished to reply. This was not the kind of language I expected from her, & at first it threw me off my guard. Northangerland's daughter, however, was not long to be baffled.

'Miss Laury,' said I, 'what right have you to rank me with the frail painted trinkets you have described. I acknowledge myself to be of noble blood, & I glory in my descent, for never, either in past or present times, has a son or daughter of the house of Percy shrunk from danger, or trembled before affliction. I know who you have in your mind, girl. I will be candid. At this moment your thoughts rest on your late mistress.'

'They do,' said she. Then, solemnly bending her large dark eyes on my face, continued, 'She was as sweet & mild & fair as you, my lady. She was as earnest as you seem to be in her devotion to the Duke. She too used to talk about her strength of mind & powers of endurance. But how silently, how rapidly, she faded when her hour came! There was no impulse in her heart which prompted her to live for him after he ceased to live for her, nor is there in yours. But listen, I hear a step. Now comes a being of the same order as yourself. Talk to her. I am too humble for such conference.'

As a sound of foot-steps approached, the flashing, lighted expression which filled Mina's countenance died away, her eyes fell, & a shadow of quiet melancholy, which is I believe habitual to her, settled on her brow.

Meantime a lady appeared advancing down the alley. She was richly dressed & her mien was stately; two others, seemingly attendants, followed behind. As she drew near I retired a little backwards, as I wished to make my observations unperceived. She was young, perhaps about nineteen, but of a rather tall figure. Her motions & port displayed an almost queenly assumption of dignity, yet her features had a soft & graceful rather than a majestic character. She resembled the most beautiful portraits I have seen of Mary Stuart* in her best days: the same fascinating turn of countenance, the same animated eyes, white neck & winning mouth. Her hair was dark glossy brown; it fell in thick ringlets over her neck & temples but did not rest on her shoulders. Her polished taper fingers were sparkling with rings, & round her neck there was a rosary of foam-white pearls, having a gold cross at the end like the one Jordan gave me when I was a little girl. This was a delightful spectacle for me, Grandmamma, was it not? However, I looked & was silent.

'Well, Mina,' said she, 'watching your charges, I perceive, as usual. You are a good girl, a valuable girl. My little Emily already appears to like you as well as Ernest, & neither of them, I fear, will be able to part with you when it is necessary. What say you, Edward?'*

'I like Mina,' replied the boy, '& I always call her Mamma when you are away. But Papa says boys should never think it impossible to do without a woman or to part with her, so when I go back to Castle Oronsay* I'll always remember Mina, but be sure, mother, I'll not cry about her.'

'But I will,' said his sister with a soft infantine lisp. 'And Mina must go back with us Mamma. Tell Papa to make her.'

'My darling,' said the lady, caressing her little dark-eyed Emily, 'I wish I could gratify you. Miss Laury, do you think it utterly impossible to accompany us?'

'I am at my master's disposal, madam,' replied Miss Laury. 'His determination must be mine.'

'Surely he will not send you back to the manor house now,' continued her interrogator, 'without either Ernest or Julius, you would die of loneliness.'

'Scarcely that,' returned Mina with a smile, 'for there would be Mrs Lancaster, [and] Mr Sumner, who remains at Keswick,* though he will no longer be an inmate at Grassmere, besides the people at the Lodge, Lady Millicent Hume, & Euphemia Lindsay* with the old dame.'

'You are quite willing to be mistress of the haunted chateau again then?'

'Yes, if the Duke commanded it. But he has hinted that Mornington-Court* will be my next destination. Grassmere Manor-House is to be shut up & consigned to the care of the steward & his wife.'

'Well,' said the lady, 'I, of course, dare not interfere with Zamorna's movements, yet I wish he would allow my children the advantage of your superintendence a little longer. My maidens here, Blanche & Harriet, are good girls, but something of the giddiest when compared with you. Well, well, it is my fault, I spoil them.'

Just then her eye fell on me for I had again drawn near.

'Hah!' said she. 'Who is that? A fair creature, by Our Lady. Don't you think, Harriet,' turning to her attendant, 'she would make a sweeter Madonna than even that celestial image in my oratory?'

'Aye, madam,' was the reply, 'but what would my lord say to such Madonnas? Would he not worship them himself, think you? And, however much you might wish for his conversion, would you employ such means to obtain it?'

She shook her head and was grave a minute, but soon returned to her former gay mood.

'Tell me your name, pretty-one,' said she, looking on me with an aspect of condescension.

I made no answer, but I felt myself tremble & turn pale with passion. So long as she abstained from addressing herself directly to me I could bear it, but when, with an air of proud affability such as a queen might use to a rosy-cheeked peasant girl, she dared to ask my name & bestow on me a half contemptuous half endearing epithet, I felt all the Percy rise in my soul. I believe she thought me a mere child, I had on only a plain satin frock & beaver hat, & you, Grandmamma, always say I look very young in that dress, not more than fifteen or sixteen perhaps. Seeing me change colour she continued, 'You are not ill I hope, my dear? Why, gracious! Harriet, see how like marble her face looks, as pale & shining as that Narcissus bending over the fountain. Blanche, be quick, sprinkle a little water on her, or she will faint.'

'Madam, madam,' whispered Miss Laury, in a hurried yet deferential tone, 'be on your guard, that is the Duchess of Zamorna.'

'The Duchess of Zamorna!' echoed the lady in a voice of strong surprise. 'Impossible! So young a creature! Why, Augustus—but I need not say anything; I was married at fifteen.'

I advanced & said, I suppose in a more energetic manner than she expected, for she stepped back & crossed herself two or three times, 'Madam, whoever you are, don't dare to say you are married, I deny it, & were Zamorna himself to swear you were his wife I would not believe him. You, Zamorna's wife? What then, that boy is his heir, for I suppose you will not disown him as your son.'

'Never!' said she, drawing Ernest toward her. 'He is indeed my son, my first-born & most cherished son. Whether he is Zamorna's heir or not, time will shew.'

'You need not equivocate,' said I, 'for I will not bear it. Do you think Alexander Percy's daughter will tamely suffer her rights to be appropriated by pretenders? No, be undeceived if such are your opinions! Woman, I hate you!'

This was said in the full sincerity of my soul. It made her tell the pearls on her rosary, but to my astonishment roused no feeling of anger, at least, no <u>apparent</u> feeling.

'I am sensible,' she returned, 'that your case appears very hard, & at present I can offer no explanation. My lips are indissolubly sealed.'

'Don't cant,' said I. 'Don't extenuate. It will admit of no explanation. Are those children Zamorna's or are they not?'

She frowned, blushed, ran her fingers from one end to the other of her beads, and was silent.

'Hah!' said I. 'You cannot say no, the mark is on them, indisputable, ineffaceable. Look at those eyes!' And between passion & grief, I burst into tears.

The lady past her hand across her brow with a gesture of weariness; she heaved a deep sigh & sat down. Ernest now addressed me.

'Leave off crying,' said he. 'I pity you very much. But why do you speak so angrily to Mamma? You make her sad. Papa would frown if he heard you. He never lets any-body say a quick word to her. She is a great lady, & would love you if you were not so cross.'

'Yes,' said little Emily, 'as much as she loves me, & you might visit her perhaps at Castle Oronsay. Papa, if you asked him, would bring you in his carriage when he comes.'

'To be sure he would,' resumed Ernest. 'Emily is quite right. But take notice, my lady, if you were a man & had spoken so to Mamma, I should hate you & you might never come to Castle Oronsay then, for the Duke, my father,' he spoke these words proudly, 'would stab you to the heart before you should enter his gates.'

These words only made me cry more. Tears now began to steal down the cheek of the lady, tears of happiness I imagine, for she had her noble boy to plead for her. At this crisis, a dark shade fell suddenly on the waters of the fountain. As I stood with my face to it & my back to the entrance of the grove it seemed to mingle with my reflected figure & far to overtop it. I knew there was some-thing behind me, but what?

My blood froze & my flesh quivered as accents, whose music was too familiar, murmured the reply in my ear. 'Mary, you are out late to-night; the sun has set a quarter of an hour. In God's name, go home.'

A dash amongst the trees followed these warning words. The reflection suddenly vanished. I turned—nothing was visible, only the boughs waved wildly in one part & a shower of roses was descending on the green walk.

'Papa, Papa,' exclaimed Ernest, & plunging amongst the agitated foliage he likewise disappeared, calling down a fresh shower of fluttering leaves from the shaken branches. I dared not follow. Nothing remained for me but instant obedience, so, bowing low, more in pride than courtesy to my still weeping rival, I returned to the carriage, which I found waiting, entered it & drove off. Here I must pause for the present. My post script has run on nearly to twice the length of my letter.

Farewell, dear grandmamma, no vicissitudes, no trials can ever make me forget you. Answer me quickly, & believe, &c., &c.
M.H. Wellesley

CHAPTER THE IVth

Dear Grandmamma,
I will now take up the thread of my narrative where I dropped it & proceed in regular order. On reaching Wellesley House after my stolen visit to Douro-Villa, I retired instantly to my apartment. The chaotic confusion of fears, hopes & conjectures which filled my mind rendered me wholly unfit for society of any kind.

Who was that lady? Was she really the wife of Zamorna, as she had as good as affirmed? Why had the Duke departed so hastily after speaking to me? Was he angry with me? How did it come to pass that, instead of being at Angria, he was in the valley of Verdopolis? And was there any likelihood of his returning to the city that night? Could I in that case summon courage to ask for an explanation? Would he give it me? Such were the questions I asked & re-asked myself, always in vain. None stood near to give me an answer. I sighed & wept & almost wished that Zamorna had ever remained a dream to me, & that the reality had never dawned in such bright but troubling glory.

There was one thing which seemed beyond a doubt, & that was the relationship of the Duke to those two children. And every look, tone

& gesture of the boy, young as he was, asserted the fact & confirmed it with indisputable testimony. While I was pondering on these things, a low sigh, as from some one close at hand, broke the train of my sad reflections. I glanced hurridly round, almost expecting to see the Duke, though his appearance is not commonly heralded by a sigh. The chamber was filled with moonlight, streaming through the large Venetian windows* over which the curtains were not yet dropped. Nothing appeared darkening that faint lustre, & I should have lapsed again into meditation had not a hand touched mine as it rested on the little flower-stand near which I sat.

Good God! My heart sprang to my throat, for at that instant the ghastly, deformed figure of Finic glided into the light, &, with a shuddering moan, sank in a heap before me. Forgetting that he could neither hear nor answer, I asked, as gently as I could, what he wanted. I cannot say that I was afraid of the creature, for he always treats me with profound respect, bowing lower than an eastern slave whenever he enters my presence, & I in return have shielded him from some annoyances arising from the antipathy of the servants to his unsightly exterior. Yet, in spite of the good-understanding which this reciprocation of kind offices has established between us, & which has only been broken by the odd system of interference mentioned in my last letter, I must confess I felt strongly inclined to ring the bell, & summon a few witnesses to behold our conference. As I was rising for this purpose, he lifted his huge head &, flinging back his matted locks so that the moonbeams had full leave to pour their revealing radiance on each wild & exaggerated feature of his unearthly visage, he fixed his eyes on mine with an expression of pathos and entreaty which I could not resist. It was the more moving because in his general moods he is sullen, ferocious, misanthropic & malignant—so, at least, the servants say, though with me he is usually gentle enough. I sat down &, patting his shaggy head in order to soothe the morbid gloom of his temperament, I again asked what he wanted, but this time it was by signs, not speech. I can converse with him pretty readily in that way, but then it's by the ordinary & well-known method, not those occult movements with which he & Zamorna hold communion in a manner intelligible only to themselves, & whose lightning rapidity so dazzles the eyes of spectators that it would be vain to attempt learning it through the medium of observation.

The following conversation ensued in terms as concise as a telegraphic despatch.

Finic (in answer to my first question): 'You have done wrong.'

Myself: 'In what?'

F[inic]: 'In your day's visit.'

M[yself]: 'What follows?'

F[inic]: 'Danger.'

M[yself]: 'Of the Duke's anger?'

F[inic]: 'Of the Duke's death.'

M[yself]: (after a pause, for this reply stunned me at first) 'What do you mean?'

F[inic]: 'What I say! The act has been so near committed that a portion, at least, if not the whole, of the penalty will be exacted.'

M[yself]: 'I do not understand you.'

F[inic]: 'Perhaps not, but it is so. You should not have been jealous. You should not have given way to curiosity. So long as Zamorna's love was yours, what mattered it if it was not wholly yours?'

'Then,' I exclaimed aloud, 'it is true, she is his wife!'

He did not hear this, & recollecting myself I put the same question in a manner he could comprehend.

'Most true,' was the reply. 'The lady of Oronsay is the Duke's wife.'

I could proceed no further. My brain whirled, my heart died within me. How long I remained in a state of torpor—torpor to every thing but a sensation of the most exquisite agony—I know not. But when I did at length arouse to something like remembrance, I looked round for Finic & saw that he was gone. A thousand questions immediately rushed on me which I wished to have asked him, & I knew it would be vain to call him back, as he never resumes a subject after he has once dismissed it.

That night sleep & I were strangers. The whole of the next day I continued in a state which you, my dear Grandmamma, may imagine, but which I cannot describe. Haunted by the shadow of that danger to my lord so vaguely hinted at, & by the still darker shadow of his apprehended displeasure, cursing my foolish jealousy while the flame of that very jealousy was kindling every moment still fiercer in my bosom watching, praying for his return yet dreading it as the herald of fresh afflictions, night came & went. The next day, & the next, and the next glided away—or rather crept as if loaded with lead. I heard no word, no syllable of him, yet dispatches arrived regularly from Adrianopolis to his secretaries here, & they were all sealed with his seal & signed with his autograph. He could not, therefore, be now at Douro-Villa. There was some consolation in that reflection.

At last, on the evening of the fifth day, he came. I was in the drawing-room surrounded with a throng of company when he entered, accompanied by my brother. Edward* looked vigorous & bright, & was evidently in the highest spirits, but alas, I saw that Zamorna was wasted, weary and wan. The curse, then, had fallen on him, & I was the cause.

So many pressed round him on his entrance that it was long before I, conscience stricken as I was, could come near enough to address him. While I stood apart I saw Maria, my sister-in-law, go fearlessly forward to welcome <u>her</u> husband, & Edward smiled on her so kindly & grasped her hand so warmly that I nearly burst into tears at the thought of the contrast my reception was likely to afford.

'Zamorna,' I heard Mr Montmorency say, 'what on earth ails you? You have been working too hard, man! Upon my word this won't do! If you stand labour no better than this, we may as well turn you over to the under-taker at once.'

'Why, Mont,' replied my husband gaily. 'I say, what on earth ails <u>you</u>? Surely you see through a jaundiced medium. It is you who need the kindness of the under-taker. As for me, the bell of St Michael's now tolling is rottenness itself when compared with the soundness of my mental and corporeal condition.'

'A mere brag!' said Montmorency, taking a long pinch of snuff. 'Mr Edward, what do you say?'

'I say he lies!' replied my brother in his decided way. 'And for the last day or two, I promise you, this same Duke of Zamorna has been forced to hear a piece of my mind respecting his want of appetite, paring of flesh, as the rare apes* say, desperately moody humours & the like absurd trash. If he does not alter, I'll wrest the sceptre out of his hand & clap a distaff* in its place.'

'O Hector!'* said the Duke in the same gay tone, unbonneting mean-time & displaying his eyes & curls as beautiful as ever, & the former flashing with even unwonted brilliancy. 'O Hector, who shall put a bridle in the mouth & a bit on thy tongue? Brother, do you see you have chased the roses from more than one fair cheek. By my honour, ladies, I am proud of your sympathy, but sweet as it is, you may spare it. Zamorna will not die yet, though all the owls on earth should croak his doom & scream his epitaph.* I'll live, by heaven, to spite <u>them</u>, to spite <u>him</u>!' This was said in a voice of fierce emphasis, & with a glance of defiance directed, not at any particular person, but at something seen rather with the mind's eye than with the bodily organs.

What could he mean? The momentary excitement passed away, & he stood as calm & cheerful as before.

Now I drew nigh. I would have spoken. I would have said something about my sorrow for his altered appearance, but the words died on my lips. I could only put my hand into his.

'Well, Mary,' said he, 'do you think me a walking skeleton, a sort of living symbol of death, as it were, a creature lingering on the surface of the earth when it ought to be asleep in her centre?'

These words shewed me that there was a morbid feeling about him, a feverish sensibility which exaggerated every idea that it caught. I only answered, 'Dear Arthur, I am glad to see you!'

'What!' he said. 'Glad to see me dying?' And turned away with an ironical laugh.

Heavily did the remainder of that party pass. Though the Duke himself was even wildly gay, yet he could not communicate a corresponding spirit to his guests. They saw it was all assumed, hollow-hearted, & all that sort of cheerfulness is more depressing to a spectator than the most determined melancholy. At length they began to depart. Group after group left the rooms; carriage after carriage rolled from the door; the full flood of 'rings & plumes & pearls'* which had inundated every appartment ebbed away till only a few scanty streamlets remained. These sunk dry also, and, as the timepiece chimed four, I made my last bow to my last retiring guest, the door closed & we were alone. We, that is, I and my lord. With a beating heart I turned towards him. Now was my time of trial, now I was to learn whether or not his anger lay heavy on me; whether, too, he could bear up against sickness as well in solitude as he had done in society. Alas, the last question was soon decided.

I saw him flung into a chair, his head hanging back in an attitude of deathly langour, his eyes closed, & his hands pressed to his forehead. The breezes of dawn were now shaking the saloon windows, & its cold light streamed through those that looked to the east, mingling in sickly unison with the pale, faded gleam of unextinguished sconce & chandelier. By this lustre I beheld my husband. It added an alien melancholy to what was already too deeply distressing in itself. I went & stood beside him. He neither looked at nor spoke to me. My heart nearly wept blood to see his eyes so quenched, his brow so darkenend, his cheek & lips so marble pale, all his glory in fact bowed in the dust of mortality. Unconsciously I bent over him; my breath stirred his hair; he opened his eyes.

'Ah, Mary,' said he, while a faint smile lit his exhausted features, 'You see I'm but in a poor way. It's vain to deny it any longer. I've struggled against the blight while I could, but now the flesh yields, though the spirit would still defy him. Sit down, love, you will not understand my wild language. I fear I shall rave terribly if delirium comes over me.'

I sat down, glad of any support which could keep me from dropping on the floor. I felt exceedingly faint & my joints shook like aspen
leaves. His kindness I now felt was worse to bear than his sternest anger
could have been. Remorse was now my portion & I felt it to be unut-
terably bitter. He drew me to his side &, resting his forehead on my
shoulder said, 'Mary, you have heard of no strange report in the city,
have you?'

I answered as well as I could, speaking in the negative.

'That is odd,' he returned. 'If the discovery had been made it would
have spread like wild-fire. But perhaps it has not, & the abhorred wretch
is taking a base advantage of some false start.'

After a momentary pause, he rose up &, pacing the room with long
& rapid strides, exclaimed, 'Who has been tampering with my private
affairs? Who has been prying into that which I chose to keep a sealed
& solemn secret? Whose hand picked the lock? Whose eye gazed on
the treasure? By all that's holy, by all that's infernal (for there's less of
heaven than hell in the business), if it be a man, I'll have the sacrifice
of his life for an atonement; if it be a woman, she's marked hence forth
with the brand of Zamorna's eternal hatred!

'Great Genii! To die now, to go down in the first burst of existence to
a cold & obscure grave, to leave all my glory ungathered, all my hopes
spread like a golden harvest, to quit the field which was ripe for the
sickle when I had just gone forth with my reapers,* to leave my kingdom desolate, my name a byword as one who promised like a God, but
fulfilled like a wretched earth-sprung man, to see all this great curse
come upon me for some villain's insolent curiosity—it would breathe
insane life into the lungs of a corpse & warm the red ice stagnating in
its veins to the heat of the boiling flood now rushing through mine! I
could swear that the pitiful crime is the work of a woman, some impulse
of malignant curiosity! Thus they have always overthrown the greatest
fabrics of man's construction! Perhaps there has been jealousy in the
matter. Hah!' And he looked at me.

At that moment I was actuated only by one feeling: a fervid wish for
the earth to rend under me and suck me in to its deepest recesses. I
shrunk together beneath his gaze, which, though I did not see, I felt as
if it had been living fire. A thousand years of happiness could never blot
this moment of intense suffering from my memory. I could not speak.
My tongue & soul were both withered. A mist spread over my eyes & a
melancholy sound moaned in my ears, through which I heard the tinkle
of a bell. Shortly after, I was sensible some one entered the room. Then
followed a dead silence. Then faint wailings, as of a human being in

bitter distress. I gradually recovered so far as to discern Finic crouched at the feet of his master, shaking his shaggy head, &, while his hands raised above it answered the signs made by Zamorna, his lips uttered the boding murmurs which had roused my attention. Their conference was not long. As it concluded the Duke approached me. Overwhelmed with terror, not knowing what I did, utterly deprived of my presence of mind, I started up & ran towards the door.

'Mary,' said he, in his deepest voice, 'come back. You surely are not afraid of bodily injury from me!'

I blindly obeyed him, more through instinct than anything else.

'Well,' he said half-playfully, 'you are the criminal, I find. You took into your head to go to Douro Villa, did you, my fair Duchess? Merely to have a look at Mina Laury & young Fitz-Arthur, with whom, by the bye madam, you had nothing to do more than you have with the inhabitants of Kamschatka.* You saw there one or two whom you did not expect to see. You were warned off the premises by myself, so at least Finic tells me. And in short, by your cursed woman's spirit of inquisitiveness, you have given my greatest enemy an advantage over me which he is now improving to your heart's content. The pains of death have laid hold on me, madam. I shall pass off ere-long, I suppose, & leave you at liberty. Don't tremble & turn pale. Here, lean on my arm, as you seem about to faint. I don't hate you, Mary. You could not help your prying weakness; it was born with you, as it is with all your sex. But then, my girl,' (& he smiled coldly & tapped my neck with ineffable contempt) 'I despise you thoroughly.'

'Arthur,' said I, gathering strength from the violence of the shock I received, 'your scorn is superfluous. I am already crushed by such a load of misery as never before bowed the head of a mortal woman to the ashes of repentance. I have sinned, but my punishment is disproportioned to my crime.'

'Poor thing,' he replied, taking my hand & regarding me with a look of mingled contempt & compassion. 'Don't accuse yourself too harshly. You have not sinned, nothing of the kind—all wretched feminine imbecility which is now shewing itself in another shape. Come madam, cannot we have a tear or two? That should have been your resource at the first approach of the storm.'

'Adrian, I cannot cry,' said I. 'My tears are all dried up with burning anguish, yet—.' I was going on, but just then they rushed at once & unbidden to my eyes. My heart swelled with suffocating sorrow. I sank on my knees &, in a voice choked with sobs, exclaimed, 'O Zamorna, do take pity on me! Forgive me this once! If I had known, if I had in the faintest degree imagined that one hair of my husband's noble head could have been injured by what I did, I would rather have cut off my right hand than stirred a step on that cursed journey!'

'I have nothing to forgive you,' he replied. 'Of course, I am well enough aware that you did not mean to harm me, only I cannot help smiling at the whole female character, so finely epitomized in you: weakness, errors, repentance. Go away, child, I can talk to you no longer. This curse is overpowering me. O, fiend! Demon! It is your time to triumph now, but I will be victor here after! Thrust me down to the tomb! I give you leave, but I'll spring up again, for the marble jaws of that devourer will not open to receive me!' He laid his hand on his heart & shuddered as if some inward pang were at that moment rending his very vitals.

How I felt no words can express. But I suppose some of my utter wretchedness appeared in my countenance, for suddenly he clasped me to him, & said, 'My dear Mary, don't look so very unhappy. There now, love, there's a kiss of perfect forgiveness. Those sad eyes will make me love them. Go to your chamber, Henrietta, & fear nothing for me. I'll wrestle it out alone. Death or victory! These torments cannot last long—I shall soon either be a corpse or convalescent. So cheer up, dearest! Forget that I said that I would despise you, & take another kiss to seal the pardon of the last.'

With these words he left me. I went up to my chamber, not to sleep you may be sure, but to brood on my sorrows, to strive in vain to unfold the dark mystery in which the whole affair was involved, & to drink up the bitter cup which remorse held to my lips.

Grandmamma, I can write no more at present, so farewell.
I am yours,
M. H. Wellesley

CHAPTER THE Vth

Extracts from the Journal of Doctor Alford, Physician in Ordinary to the Duke of Zamorna

July 1st—This morning, while I was at breakfast, a servant came in with a note, brought, he said by one of the Duchess of Zamorna's foot-men. It was in Her Grace's own slender jessamine* hand, & to the following purport.

Dear Doctor,
Come to me as soon as ever you can. I am nearly distracted. My lord, the hope of so many hearts, is, I fear in a hopeless condition. He has been ill three days, but would not permit me to call in medical aid before. What shall I do? I hardly know what I write at present. He is delirious, I think, nay I almost hope, for he will hardly suffer me to approach him. For heaven's sake, throw off all other engagements & come instantly, doctor.
Yours truly,
M. H. Wellesley

Of course I knew this summons must be followed by prompt obedience. Without a moment's delay I ordered my carriage & departed for Wellesley-House. The news was not entirely unexpected, for the last day or two paragraphs had been put forth by the public prints intimating that the Duke had returned from Adrianopolis in a very precarious state of health, & rumours had been rife in the city respecting the mysterious origin of his illness.

On my arrival I was immediately ushered into a splendid breakfast-room, where I found the Duchess. All the paraphernalia of coffee, &c, stood before her, but it was evidently untouched. She looked pale, faded, & harassed to the last degree. If it were not that her delicate Percyan features seem of that perennial nature that no sickness or sorrow can take away their loveliness, I should hardly have known her. Not the faintest flush of carmine remained on her cheek. It was totally colourless, but at the same time exquisitely fair, & her sweet hazel eyes were filled with a light of weary sadness that might have drawn tears from stones. Surely thought I, the young Duke must be ill indeed if he cannot suffer so beautiful a creature as this to approach him.

'O, doctor,' were her first words, 'I am glad to see you! Yet I fear even your skill will be in vain! It is not a common malady by which my lord's energies have been so crushed & laid prostrate. He himself declares that the hand that smote him alone can cure him, & what that hand is, heaven & the Duke can tell, but I cannot.'

'Compose yourself, my lady,' said I, for she was violently agitated. 'You are, I fear, almost as much in want of my aid as the Duke can be. Your affection has exaggerated his danger. I dare swear I shall not find him near so ill as you imagine.'

'Doctor,' she replied solemnly, 'don't say so. He is in a strange deadly way such as I never heard of before. He complains of burning fever in his veins, but externally he is cold as ice. And then, what expressions, what kindling gleams & transient ghastly clouds of feeling continually pass & repass over his countenance! O, you will shudder as I do while you watch him! And he seems, doctor, to hate me, to loathe me, & yet at times to struggle with his disgust. Aye, that is what makes me so miserable as I am. But I deserve it all! For doctor, doctor! If he dies I shall have been his—his murderess.'

She groaned & sank her head on her hands as she uttered this word. I knew not what to think. It seemed that <u>she</u> required my assistance whatever her royal husband might do. There was absolute insanity in the term she had made use of. I intreated her to be calm & offered her a little coffee to revive her.

She pushed the cup away & looking at me rather wildly said, 'Now, Doctor Alford, you see what strange things come to pass. Who would have thought that Zamorna, the god-like Zamorna, our idol, the idol of me & all my sex, would have died by the hand of one of his worshippers, his chief priestess as it were. How <u>could</u> a woman do injury to him when he is so handsome & generous, & at times so very kind. Yet it is true! I, his wife, have been his Atropos!* But, sir, don't think that I have literally dipped my hands in his blood, or Messalina-like given him poison.* No, that would be rather too bad, I should be a fiend then & not a woman. By the way, sir, do you think it possible that a mere mortal woman should harden her heart by jealousy—aye, jealousy, that's the best petrifier I know of—to that extremity of stoniness that she might, untrembling, unflinching, unrepenting, keeping always the image of her rival, a handsome woman perhaps, very like the beheaded Queen of Scots,* full before her, that she might, thus strengthened, go to Zamorna, love on her face, & love & madness in her heart, & put into his hand a cup, drugged like the one Socrates drank,* & calmly see him taste it, first smiling on her, & watch that smile pass away never to dawn more, & hear his voice as sweet as music, as sweet as that, sir,' she pulled her harp, which stood not far off, to her side & drew a single chord of the deepest & finest melody, '& as that voice failed—. But, Doctor Alford, I am supposing a case that never happened. You must not imagine that I did this, I only thought of it.

'One afternoon at Douro-Villa, or rather one evening as I was returning from thence by moonlight, the stars in the Niger you know, sir, and all as serene as I myself might have <u>looked</u>, for I have got from my father a way of looking very quiet without, when I am furious within, at that time a dream came into my head. It haunted me all the way down the valley, that my hand might, with the thought, with proper meditation on the loveliness of Mary Stuart,* & on the fidelity of her sweet

minatures, have obtained the requisite degree of steadiness to direct
either a poniard* to the heart of the omnipotent, or a bowl of poison
to his lips. But when I got home I was told that all was done, that I had
unwittingly accomplished my own intentions when I least desired it.
And then, sir, I felt what I trust you may never feel, & what I think has
almost turned my brain: there's a wide difference between purpose &
fulfilment.'

While she talked thus I made no attempt to interrupt her. She was
excited by some circumstance, apparently jealousy, to perfect phrenzy.
But could the subject on which her mind wandered be founded on
fact—. Could she in a fit of desperation—. But no, impossible! Yet
she was the daughter of Northangerland, & the Duke was known to
be wild, unstable. Perhaps under all her sweet gentle semblance there
might be as much passion pent as in the burning veins of her proud
haughty stepmother, & if so—. But I dared not pursue the supposition.
With the utmost calmness of voice & manner, I now proposed that she
should accompany me to her lord's apartment, hoping to gain some
further clue to the matter by strict observation of her deportment while
in his presence.

'I'll go, doctor,' said she, & rising quickly opened the door ere I could
reach it. With a rapid, unquiet step she crossed the hall before me.

We both ascended the staircase, covered with rich matting, threaded
a succession of galleries, thickly carpeted, & entered a large ante-
room, where a dark, foreign looking youth about fifteen years old, with
coal-black eyes & hair, & very handsome though rather spare features,
appeared in waiting.

'Eugene, Eugene,' said his lady, 'how is your master? Why are you
not with him?'

'He ordered me out, my lady, & Finic too. Not a soul has been with
him for the last half-hour.'

Without reply the Duchess past on. She softly opened the inner
door, then, pausing & speaking in a scarcely audible whisper, said,
'Enter first, sir, I dare not go further than the foot of the bed. He hates
to see me.'

I obeyed. All was still in the wide & lofty chamber, the windows darkened with long rich drapery of crimson velvet, to which the morning
sun, shining behind, gave a peculiarly vivid & brilliant appearance, the
grand state-bed surrounded with curtains of the same, all drooping in
deeply-fringed festoon folds & sweeping the floor with their glittering
gold tassels like the canopy of a royal tent. The rest of the furniture
lay in dense shadow. Only here & there a marble stand of silver lamps

glistened as pure as snow through the gorgeous gloom by which they were encompassed. Surely, thought I, this ought to defy the darts of Death if any thing can. I walked to the bedside &, taking my seat in an arm-chair which stood near, undrew the curtain.

All the clothes, the splendid counterpane, the delicate cambric sheets, were tossed & tumbled in disorder. Lying on his back but with his face turned restlessly to the ample pillow of white velvet, appeared my noble patient. He was asleep, breathing heavily, his teeth set close, his lips a little parted, his nostrils fiercely dilating & compressing as he respired, brow darkly knit, cheek flushed with the brightest hectic, his hair coming down on his temples & curling on his forehead in rich but wild profusion. I hesitated at first whether to awake him, & the Duchess, seeing me in doubt, ventured to approach. She gazed a long time at him, & then with a moan of mingled love & agony bent down &, clasping her arms round his neck, kissed his lips & cheek with passionate tenderness. He instantly awoke. So suddenly, indeed, did his eyes flash open that I doubted whether he had been really asleep.

'White witch,' said he, earnestly regarding his lady, & gently putting her from him, 'what do you wish me to do now? Oh, to submit to a doctor! I see. Well, Alford, Death fills the room. Do you think your drugs & draughts will be noxious enough to drive him out? Open the window, sir. I am dying of suffocation & internal heat! For God's sake, remove those dark, bloody curtains! Fling the sash wide, wide up & let me see the light! Let me feel the air!'

I did what he desired. A cool & gentle breeze immediately stole in. 'There,' said he, 'that is the kiss of the Niger. It rolls through the shrubbery without, & as it glides by my palace sends me this dewy salute in token of homage. I wish it would breathe fiercer & colder a thundering rush of wind, roaring down the snow-slopes of Elimbos,* would be welcome now as glory. Henrietta Wellesley, my white witch, my seraphic hypocrite! This is better than thy embrace, by the Genii! My lady's lips burned like fire!'

She turned on me a look of mute despair; he saw it.

'Rise up, Alford,' said he, '& let the Queen draw near. I have many things to say unto her & she may hear them now.'

I obeyed him; she took my seat.

'Rose of the world!' he continued. 'You have long blossomed under the palm-tree's shelter, but now an axe is laid to the root thereof & the branch of protection will soon pass away. Flower, would there not be heroism in fading with thy guardian? Drink not the dew that falls at night, wave not in the breeze that blows at dawn, open not to the light that shines at noon-day, then you'll soon be as withered as me. Aye, my scorching bride and her royal lover will consume to ashes in the same earth! Or what do you say to a suttee?* That would be better perhaps. When I am dead, erect a pile on the shores of the Calabar; let me be carried there in state. I shall be laid on the timber. Then you, Mary, will ascend, take my head on your knee, greet my cold & bloodless lips with a few of those burning kisses. No need to apply the torches: we shall of ourselves kindle into a burst of flame so vivid that, when the inhabitants of Verdopolis look out from their casements eastward, the glow of the setting, not the rising, sun* will be seen on the oriental sky-line. Hah! Queen of Angria, how would you like that?'

'I would die any death with you, Adrian,' was the fond and devoted reply.

'Would you my Percy-blossom?' said the Duke. 'No, remember, think better to begin life on a fresh tack. The incumbrance being removed, look out for another partner. Pelham,* you know, is still faithfully single; give your fair hand to him. It will be better worth his acceptance now that it has been joined to that of a monarch. Let him tie the second orange-flower garland on thy head that I circled with a diadem. Yield him up all the rights that were mine. Be gentle, obedient, dutiful to him. Be keen-sighted, Mary, see that he wanders not astray. Then, doubtless, you will be happy. Happy, did I say? Hah! But there shall be a shadow in thy sunshine, Mary. A something always darkening thy sight, an eternal blot in the eye of day, which no change of time, place or season can remove. I, from my grave, will haunt you by night, by morning & by noon-day. I will come without sound or voice, always the same, void of variation. With no thought of burning, I will stand by your side, still & motionless, with an ungrieved, unsaddened, countenance. In the hall, in the chamber, in the crowded saloon, my eye shall be ever on you. I'll follow you to your dying-bed, bow above you as the wheel of existence makes its last revolution & drink the dregs of life from lips that spoke perjury to me.'

With a look of the darkest meaning he turned on his pillow, shut his eyes, folded his arms, & was silent. The Duchess rose & left the room. I heard afterwards that she fell into a swoon on gaining her own appartment & lay two hours without sense or motion. When she was gone I again approached him. I asked him several questions, not one of which he would answer. I attempted to feel his pulse: he pushed me from him with violence. I proposed to bleed him, but no, all was in vain. The last step, however, was absolutely necessary. His fever, or whatever it was, raged so fiercely that without some measures of mercy he would have been dead before night. Aware of his refractoriness—for this was by no means the first time I had attended him at periods of critical danger—I stepped into the anti-chamber & ordered Eugene Rosier to summon one or two of his master's personal attendants. Edward Laury & the dwarf Finic soon entered.

'Well, sir,' said the former, 'I guess the Duke is fractious?'

'Very, Ned,' returned I. 'Worse than I ever saw him before. You will have a tough job of it, but if I can once get a vein open it shall not soon be stopped. The loss of a few ounces of blood will soon bring him down.'

Edward nodded & we all passed into the chamber. We had spoken low, but the ears of sick, & especially delirious, persons are often morbidly sensitive. On our entrance we found the bed & the apartment empty.

'Where is he?' said I.

'In his dressing-room,' replied Rosier coolly, & stepping to a small door covered with a curtain he attempted to open it. It was locked. The boy uttered a low whistle and muttered with a strange kind of smile, 'Mon Dieu, he'll surely not cut his own throat.'

I prepared to break open the door.

'Nay, doctor,' said Laury, 'if he means to do harm to himself, we shall not mend the matter by making a din. I know the Duke, & other folk's contrariness always fixes his mind.'

This was not to be controverted, so we stood in all the horrors of suspense about ten minutes longer. At length the door was dashed open & His Grace appeared within. He was ready dressed in his usual deep military mourning, & to a casual spectator would have appeared to be in full, vigorous health & strength. Fever, however, was burning on his cheek, & a certain dazzling & most dangerous light flickered in his eye. We all stepped back on perceiving a ready cocked pistol grasped in either hand.

'Now, Alford,' said he, 'you will bind & bleed me now, will you? Begone, sir, instantly! My malady is nothing to you; it does not come within the limits of your confined skill. I shall no longer lie waiting the issue like a helpless child, but rise & meet Death as a man should do, face to face. The die is cast. This night the stakes will be swept away either by my hand or his. No inferior player shall so much as look in. So, once more, Dr Alford, I warn you to depart quickly. The slightest attempt to oppose my will will be met by—' & he glanced at the pistols. Perceiving that coercion would only aggravate the fury of his disorder, I, for the present, thought proper to retire, first directing

Edward Laury to watch his master & not on any account permit him to leave the house. I went away satisfied that <u>poison</u> had nothing to do with his illness.

July 2nd. Read two paragraphs in the papers of today which astonished me much. The first ran thus: 'Yesterday Mr H. M. M. Montmorency Esqr gave a splendid dinner to the heads of the Angrian Party. The Duke of Zamorna & the Earl of Northangerland were both present. His Grace appeared to be in excellent health & spirits, a circumstance which fully contradicted the reports that of late have been so industriously circulated by his enemies. We are sorry, however, to say that the Duchess is much indisposed.' The second article was a long speech, purporting to have been delivered by the Duke on the previous night at a meeting of some scientific body, where he presided. The speech throughout was marked by his peculiar tone of eloquence. It was even more classic & elegant than usual, & had fewer of those fiery out-bursts of energy (of which indeed the subject did not admit) than I ever saw in an oration of his before.

These things puzzle me. I will proceed to Wellesley-House instantly & see how the case really stands.

Evening. On arriving at the young lion's magnificent den, I was shown up first, at my own request, to the Duchess. She welcomed me eagerly.

'Ah, doctor,' said she, 'you are come just in the right time. I was on the point of sending for you. Mr Abercrombie & Sir Astley Coleridge* are both up-stairs, & so are His Grace, the Duke of Wellington, & Lady Seymour. I have not been permitted to see my husband to day, but they say he is better. I hardly know how to believe them. Doctor, you will deal truly with me &, if he is really convalescent, do let me have an interview with him, though it be of only ten minutes duration.'

These words of Her Grace intimated plainly that her lord was in a dangerous, perhaps a hopeless state. They had concealed his real condition from her, perhaps in dread of its producing fatal effects. I replied evasively, but soothingly, to her request, & left the room. Edward Laury met me on the stairs.

'Did your master go out yesterday?' I immediately asked.

'Go out, sir?' was the reply. 'No, indeed. After you were gone he was worse than ever. Towards evening he grew raging mad, & till five this morning we had to hold him in bed by main force. 'Now,' continued the man calmly, but in a voice of restrained emotion, 'he may be reckoned as one that has not much more to do in this world. They are all round him waiting for the last breath as I may say.'

I passed on with an accelerated step. On pausing at the chamber door I heard a very faint sound of many whispering voices. Eugene answered to my low, scarcely audible tap. The room was darkened. A dozen persons were gathered round the bed, & two others sat at a table on which stood four lighted tapers; parchment, pens & ink lay before them. I was greeted in silence. Room was directly made for me to advance, &, on taking my station with the other medical men by the pillow, I had a full view of all who were present. The Countess Seymour sat in an armchair opposite; near her stood the Duke of Wellington, the Duke of Fidena & the Earl of Northangerland. Mr Montmorency, Mr Warner, General Thornton, Viscount Castlereagh & the Earl of Arundel formed the rest of the circle. Some grave & important matter had evidently summoned them to the young monarch's dying-bed. Deliberation, anxiety, earnest expectation sat on every brow, revealed dimly by the candle light, which at this hour seemed an unnatural substitute for the broad radiance of day.

As for Zamorna, he was stretched in the midst, still & rigid as a corpse, his countenance white, his lips livid & nothing save the motion & sparkle of his eyes indicating that he yet retained the smallest remnant of life. At my entrance, Fidena was bending over him & the subdued sound of his voice alone broke the profound hush of the appartment.

'Zamorna,' he was saying, 'though your corporeal faculties are utterly prostrated, heaven has in mercy permitted your mind to regain its balance at this last, this eleventh, hour. Once more then, I do most solemnly conjure you to settle this point while the blessing of speech remains. If you would avert the source of civil war from your kingdom, name before all these witnesses a legal successor to the crown you are now leaving.'

The pale lips of the royal youth trembled.

'You ask me,' he replied in a faint but unfaltering voice, 'that which you know not, John. I am fast departing & as soon as the shroud is round me a successor will arise without summons. Ernest follows Adrian in the number of the kings of Angria.'

'You mean Ernest Fitz-Arthur?' abruptly interposed Northangerland, on whose countenance an ominous cloud of gloom & bitterness was brooding. 'Hah! But, my lord Duke, is he your son? Is he your lawful son? Has he a legal right to the title of heir?'

A cold smile flitted across the Duke's clayey features. 'You will know in time,' he answered.

'Arthur,' pursued Fidena, 'this is a solemn hour. In the name of God, unravel this mystery! Your moments pass rapidly & none can do it save you.'

There was an interval of dead silence. Zamorna made no answer, & his face began to assume a stealing shadow.

Warner now spoke. 'I appeal to the Duke of Wellington,' he said, quickly & anxiously. 'Your Grace has yet made no attempt to extract a declaration.'

'Nor will I,' replied the Duke, determinedly. 'My son shall not have his final chance of life cut off by me.'

'Why,' began Lord Arundel, 'I think the matter is settled. Zamorna has named Fitzarthur & is not that enough? My heart burns to hear how you dare to annoy him! By heaven, he shall die in peace if I can accomplish it! To the last drop of my blood will I defend his son's rights, whether they be lawful or otherwise!'

'Silence!' said the stern Percy. 'Ernest Fitz-Arthur I say let it be, but there is a regency to appoint. Zamorna, speak once again, who shall be regent?'

'Ernest will want no regent,' answered he. 'Now I have told all, I demand rest & silence that I may gaze down on the awful gulph yawning insatiably beneath me.'

'He shall have it,' said Arundel.

'I'll stab the first man who speaks to the heart!' responded Castlereagh.

Unmoved, Northangerland went on. 'Who shall be regent?' he repeated. 'Pronounce quickly, monarch. If you die & make no sign on the subject, woe to Angria. Let a voice of lamentation be heard on every hearth, in every household. The sword of war is unsheathed & the blade will rankle in many a bosom ere Adrian be cold in his grave.'

'Bad & remorseless man!' said the Duke of Fidena, in a tone of roused indignation. 'Is this language for a deathbed, for your son-in law's, for a monarch's, for Zamorna's death-bed. I will hear no more of it, my lord! He **shall** breathe his last calmly! Arthur, my dear Arthur, turn from this world to a better. Great God! I trust a happy light shines above your path onward.'

'John,' said the Prince, 'there is no light. The river of Death alone rolls before me & its waters are pitchy dark, but I can cross them without dread, without a shudder. Is it noon?'

'Five minutes are yet to elapse,' replied the peculiarly harsh & grating voice of one of the notaries at the table.

Suddenly the Duke started up in his bed. The effect of this action was like the spring of a galvanized corpse.

'Wretch!' he exclaimed with frightful energy of voice & manner. 'Art thou there? Then I feel as if I could live still! I will defy, I will vanquish thee at last! Grapple with me, now, hand to hand, & see who shall be conqueror! Five minutes yet to elapse I thought the hour was long gone by. Courage! Hope, Zamorna! A star yet glimmers. She will not, dare not, be faithless!' The notary answered by a hollow laugh.

'I hear a sound,' continued the Duke, bending his head. 'Far off, light, rapid; no other ear can take it in. It is her tread, her own sweet fairy tread. Villain, tremble! My champion comes at last.'

'The wheels of her chariot tarry,' said the notary, rising & approaching the window. 'I look through the lattice, & no woman's robe flutters in the wind. But St Augustine's* clock shows its hand on the doomed hour. A warning of her hero's departure has, by this time, rung through all Verdopolis.'

He was silent. Every quickened ear at that moment heard a footstep. The chamber door trembled. It seemed to split asunder so impetuously was it burst open. A lady swept in. Her motion was as swift, almost as noiseless, as lightning. Instinctively we all fell back. She sank on her knees by the bed-side & hid her face on the hand which Zamorna stretched towards her.

'Ransomed,' was the only word whispered by her parting lips. The mingling bells of the city just then struck the first toll of twelve. She rose as they concluded, turned round & regarded us all with a keen, penetrating glance of her fine black eyes.

'Gentlemen,' she said, with a blush partly of excitement, & partly, as it appeared, of anger, 'I hope you will not think of remaining here. There is no need of successions being settled now. Zamorna will not die & this gloomy chamber is darkened for nothing.'

She stepped to each window in turn, hastily removed all the blinds & curtains with which they were shrouded, flung up the lattices, extinguished the candles, ordered the remaining notary to depart—one of them was already gone we knew not how—in a quick passionate voice, which he was not slow in obeying, & then again glanced impatiently at us.

'All this requires an explanation, young woman,' said the Earl of Northangerland.

'It does, my lord,' she replied, curtsying very deferentially, 'but perhaps you will allow the explanation to be postponed till my master can himself decide whether he chuses it to be given or not.'

'Mina,' said the Duke of Wellington. She started when he spoke, & the colour mounted brightly to her cheeks; immediately she was at his feet, kneeling on one knee with her head bowed on the other.

'What brought you here, my little girl?' asked the Duke in his kindliest tone.

'My lord,' she answered, 'if I am an intruder, I will return, but this morning Finic informed me that my presence might be useful to, to, to my late lady's son. And dared I sit still when <u>he</u> required that I should be active?'

'I fear you would not,' said His Grace. 'However, you are a good child, & this morning's work adds another debt to those he already owes you. He'll pay it as he did the former.'

Miss Laury shrunk as if she had been crushed to the earth. Her head dropped so low that the jetty curls rested in clusters on the carpet.

'Go & serve him, Mina,' continued the Duke. 'Spend your life in his Egyptian bondage.* His chains, I see, are locked on every limb.'

'They are,' she said, rising proudly, '& no hand but that of Death shall rend them off. His born thrall I am & will be.'

The medical gentlemen, who meantime had been examining Zamorna, now pronounced that an astonishing & most miraculous change had taken place for the better. Something like warmth had been communicated to the blood, which was again circulating freely. The pulse could now be felt; the heart had resumed its action; & the livid shadow had vanished from his face.

The deep suppressed joy of Miss Laury at this intelligence was such as I have seldom seen. She came & hung over him, & gazed into [his] eyes as if all of the universe that she cared for was contained in their dark shining spheres. It seemed as if she thought she had acquired a right to look at him undaunted, as if, for the moment, she felt he was hers by redemption. The feeling, however, scarcely appeared in her countenance before it vanished, & then again she was the doomed slave of infatuation—devoted, stricken, absorbed in one idea, finding a kind of strange pleasure in bearing the burden & carrying the yoke of him whose fascinations fettered her so strongly. The end of her being, the pride of her life seemed to consist in labouring, drudging for Zamorna. He grasped her hand & smiled upon her most sweetly, & said something in a tone of the gentlest condescension. <u>That</u>, I daresay, repaid the silly girl a hundred fold.

All now except the Duke of Wellington, the Countess Seymour, Mina, Rosier & Finic left the room. As we were descending the staircase I happened to linger a little behind on one of the landing-places. Some one called me by my name; it was Edward Laury. He stood leaning against the wall, his arms folded, his handsome face flushed, his dark eyes glancing from under his knit brows. The resemblance between daughter & father struck me forcibly.

'Doctor,' he asked, 'is not Mina Laury come?'

I answered affirmatively.

'Curse it!' said he. 'I wish the girl had half wit, & I wish too that Duke of Zamorna had half honesty! O I would hate him if I could, but then he's my king, & besides I taught him to shoot & to hunt. He was a brave, a bonnie lad, & a finer finger never touched trigger. If it hadn't been for that, if he hadn't walked by my side many a long day, many a moonlight night, over moors & along deer-tracks & wood-walks, I'd long since have riddled his bones with either cold steel or hot lead. I was a fool & waur* than a fool ever to harbour him in my bit of a hut.* I knew he was wild & heartless (heartless, that is, in some things) & yet I must needs take the viper into my very home-close* & warm it on my hearth. I've drank his venom since for my pains, & yet I still stick to him & like him, & would e'en most die for him. Idiot that I am! I'm not a woman! What for, then, can't I get his blood & run for it?'

'I have no doubt you have your reasons for acting in a better & wiser manner,' replied I, wishing to soothe him.

'Reasons! I've no reasons but his own witchery. You know doctor, how he behaved when I was wounded at the Battle of Velino.* He made me lie in his own quarters, on his own camp bed.* He examined my wound every day himself, & often when the surgeons were busy, dressed it. At night he used to wrap his cloak round him & lie down on the floor &, whatever I said, would continue to do so till I was quite well. Then he forced me to drink wine from his mess-table; I had my rations from my general's canteens. He screened me in that tough matter about Sir John Flower, now Lord Richton,* & once in a hard tussle of three to one he saved my life at hazard of his own. With all this it's impossible for me to detest him—at least not long together. Besides we are both Irishers in a way & they never bear malice. Yet, spite of all, I can't abide him at this moment, so I'll off to the west* till my blood cools.' He struck the but end of a long fowling-piece, which he held in his hand, violently against the ground, dashed down stairs, & disappeared in the hall below.

On entering the saloon, to which the other gentlemen had withdrawn, I found them all departed except Northangerland. He was sitting on a sofa near his daughter & conversing with her earnestly. Supposing myself an intruder I was about to retire; the Earl called me back.

'Doctor,' said he, 'the Duchess is anxious to see her kind, consider-ate husband. What do you say to the matter? The rest of the medical people have put their wise veto upon it.'

'I fear,' replied I, 'I shall be compelled to agree with them. Her Grace suffered too much in the last interview to hazard another so quickly.'

'Well,' said she with a sigh, 'I must submit then, I suppose, but after this day no earthly command except his own shall keep me from him.'

The Earl rose & beckoned me to a recess. 'Alford,' he commenced abruptly, 'I wish to know how long Zamorna has been ill.'

'For the four last days he has never quitted the house,' said I.

'A downright false-hood, sir!' returned Northangerland. 'How dare you say so, when yesterday I saw him at Montmorenci-Hotel in much better health than you ever restored a patient to in your life. He accompanied me after dinner to Ellrington house, & afterwards, like a fool, escorted the Countess to some absurd assembly of scientific idiots, where, according to her account, he was particularly brilliant.'

'So I read, my lord, in the papers, & I assure you the intelligence staggered me. For proof of my assertion I refer your lordship to the Duchess.'

'I need no reference,' said he, 'for she told me the same tale before your entrance, & I thought grief had somewhat affected her brain. That opinion is now transferred to you. Don't think to persuade me out of my senses, sir. I tell you, the Duke of Zamorna was in my company all yesterday afternoon & part of the evening. He looked, talked, laughed & swaggered as usual, & I never was more surprised in my life than when this morning a note from Mr Maxwell* summoned me to attend his dying bed. Then the sudden turn in his health, the behaviour of the notary, the arrival of that girl. By the bones of Scylla,* it's an infernal affair altogether!' So saying, his lordship left the room. The Duchess had already quitted it, so I summoned my carriage & returned home.

CHAPTER THE VIth

Five days elapsed. During that time Zamorna, under the tender care of Mina Laury & the skilful superintendence of Dr Alford, rapidly recovered his almost annihilated health. The Duchess, at his own request, at length received permission to see him. She was sitting at breakfast when Eugene entered & put into her hands a small twisted billet written in pencil. The hand was her husband's and the welcome words as follows:

Come to me, Mary, as soon as you will. Alford thinks an interview now not only allowable but advisable. He says you are pining to a shadow. I fear much, my sweetest, that your love has been ill-requited by me during my moments of delirium. What I said I neither know nor wish to know. Only a confused & frightful dream remains on my mind, whose details I should abhor fully to recall. I'll make up for it hereafter, so come quickly. You will find me alone in my dressing-room. I am just apparelled & have dismissed Finic.

Yours tenderly & truly, Adrian

Up started the Duchess, nearly upsetting the rose-wood stand with its burden of priceless porcelain. She flew to the door & through the hall & was just placing her foot on the stairs when a note or two of music arrested her attention. It was the tremulous vibration of a guitar, lightly & carelessly yet skilfully touched. The sounds proceeded from one of the numerous saloons whose grand portals arched the walls around her. Who could it be? She knew the style: it was familliar to her. Could the Duke—but no, impossible! Again she listened. The tune rose a wild, soft, melancholy air, monotonous, but exquisitely plaintive. It trembled, swelled, died away, breathed into life again, uttered its low lingering close, & gave place to silence.

'As I live,' said Mary, 'that is his hand! My ear is practised & cannot mistake what it has so often drank in with delight.' She stood irresolute. There was a slight shock in the circumstance of hearing sounds so unexpected echoing from a part of the house just opposite to where she imagined her lord to be—something that ruled her nerves, more so indeed than such a trivial thing would seem to warrant. Again the strings were swept & the notes of an extravaganza, just such as the Duke is accustomed to run off extempore when he happens by chance to take up his instrument, stole in quivering & liquid melody through the hall. Still the Duchess hesitated. She felt in a manner chained to the spot, but a sudden cessation of sound loosed the spell. She started, hastened to the saloon whose partially unclosed folding door had permitted egress to the music, slid it further back & entered. Zamorna was there, sure enough. He stood at a table near the upper end of the room. His guitar lay beside him & while he turned over the leaves of a large & splendidly-bound volume, he carelessly hummed the words of the tune he had just played.

Mary paused to contemplate him for appearance of ill-health: no trace of recent indisposition lingered on his kingly countenance. There was none of that langour & feebleness in his attitude or aspect which usually marks the up-riser from a sick bed. His complexion had all the fine glowing clearness which it ever wears in perfect health, & his eyes were full & bright & hawk-like, as if the quenching power of fever had never touched them.

'Death has for once been merciful,' said Henrietta, as she came forward. 'His shadow has passed away & left my noble & beautiful idol as glorious as it found him.'

The Duke, of course, looked up. It was a curious glance that he gave his lady. The vermillion lip was bit in as if to suppress the half comic smile that mantled round it; the eye-brow was raised. The light of the eye was arch, scrutinizing, rather satirical yet kind-enough: it forbade fear, yet did not invite any of that overflowing tenderness with which Mary was inclined to greet him. She stood silent, blushing & embarrassed.

'My dear Arthur,' at last she faltered out, 'why do you keep me at such a distance? Why are you so cool & strange? I <u>wish</u> I knew the reason. It should be the business of my life to labour night & day until I earned some portion of a warmer affection.'

'I'm not angry with you, Mary,' replied Zamorna, 'not I. Indeed, quite the contrary. I love you well enough, but, you little witch, what brought you to Douro Villa that evening?'

'To speak the truth, Adrian, it was curiosity. I wanted to see whether Miss Laury was so handsome, & Fitz-Arthur so like you, as people said.'

'Well, Mary,' taking her hand, '& what do you think? Is the girl a pretty one? Don't be jealous now. I solemnly swear to you that I never spoke more than three words at a time, & those of the most commonplace kind, to her in my life. She's in other hands than mine, I assure you, & if I were to come so near to her as I do now to you, such a hubbub would be raised that the Tower of Nations there would rock to its foundations. So speak freely, do you think her pretty?'

'Very pretty,' sighed poor Mary. 'And Ernest & little Emily, very, very like.'

The Duke laughed. 'Aye, so they are,' said he. 'It can't be denied. But cheer up, Mary, cheer up, the time may come when you'll not sorrow for that likeness.'

The Duchess shook her head. Tears began to steal down her fair pale cheeks. Encouraged, however, by his manner, which was gentle & friendly, though perhaps not loving, she ventured to insinuate her hand, which he held only by the tips of the fingers, further into his. An expression at that moment crossed his countenance such as she had never seen on her lord's face before. An odd, indescribable, mischievous mixture of feelings which, while it lasted, seemed almost to change the features. At the same time he pinched her hand very hard, rather unkindly, so the rings on her finger pressed against the bone & she uttered a faint exclamation of pain. Instantly the door was flung open; in bounced the ungainly figure of Finic. His small beast-like optics glared in his head like Roman candles. He mouthed, gesticulated, & capered furiously. The Duke first laughed, then hit him a sound stunning blow. He walked to the window, threw it up, sprang through the aperture & vanished among the trees of the shrubbery without.

'What brought you here, Finic?' said Mary, turning angrily to the dwarf.

He fell down before her, his hands crossed on his bosom, & his forehead touching the carpet at her feet. 'I will have no mummery!' she continued, forgetting in her displeasure that he could not understand her. 'Your conduct is very insolent, very unaccountable! No sooner have I spoken three words with my lord alone than you must enter & disturb our conversation! What do you mean? I can endure it no longer! But poor miserable wretch, I might as well talk to a statue. Let go my dress, sir,' she snatched it from him, as his long thin fingers closed slowly on the folds, &, heedless of the low wail of entreaty which he sent after her, quitted the saloon.

Eugene Rosier met her at the door. This encounter did not greatly soothe her ruffled feelings. She was in that mood (a very unusual one with her) which finds cause of irritation in every occurrence.

'What!' said she. 'Listening, I suppose, to see that I don't over-step the bounds of decorum! This is a strange state of things! I do not comprehend it & I will not bear it! Pray, sir, is it by your master's orders that I am watched so by yourself & that abortive wretch?'

'My master, madam?' replied Eugene, with a look of surprise. 'He has given me no orders, except that he wishes to know whether you could read his billet.'

'Read his billet? Yes, sir, & I have obeyed the intimation which it contained. But I might as well have remained in my own apartment, he will scarcely speak to me.'

Eugene drew up his mouth as if for a whistle. Respect for his lady, however, appeared to restrain him.

'Madam,' said he, 'the Duke desires to learn the reason of your not having visited him in his dressing-room, that's the short & long of the matter.'

'You will drive me past my patience!' returned the Duchess. 'I have visited him! He was in that saloon a minute ago & by his manner did not seem to want, or even to expect, me much.'

The page stood silent an instant. He seemed confounded, but presently a wink of the eye & a roguishly significant smile told that he had solved the riddle to his satisfaction.

'Hem! My lady,' he went on, 'his Grace, if I might venture to say so, has queer moods sometimes, but if you'll just step up stairs now, I'll wager my royal livery to a dust man's jacket he'll meet you in a different temper.'

As Rosier spoke a cough was heard within the saloon just like the Duke's.

'He is come back,' said Mary, 'I'll venture to try him again.'

She was about to open the door, when Eugene, with a temerity which he had never before ventured to display, coolly removed her hand from the lock, placed himself between her & the closed portal, & stood confronting her with a face whose boldness said plainly enough, 'you shall not re-enter this room if I can help it.'

She stepped back, perfectly astounded at his impudence. Before she could speak a yell of Finic's arose, then a laugh, the well known Ha! Ha! of Zamorna, & then an equally well-known voice exclaimed: 'Mary, fight your way through all obstacles. I am here, & I command you to come unto me.'

She sprang again to the door, again she grasped the handle.

'Madam,' said Rosier, 'I beg, I entreat, I implore, my lady, I supplicate that you will hear me one instant,' but no, she was deaf to his remonstrances. He then dismissed his face of prayer & humility, assumed a natural aspect of unblushing hardihood, drew up his slight but sinewy frame to its full height &, seizing both her hands, said, 'Now, my lady, will you go up stairs? If you say, yes, I'll fall on my knees & beg pardon for what I've already done. If you say, no, I must, I really must try my strength further. It's as much as my life is worth to lay a finger on you, but it's more than my life is worth to permit a second interview to day. The Duke may stab me for hindering you, but he'll certainly blow my brains out if I don't hinder you.'

With quivering lips, death-white cheeks & a blighting glance of passion, the Duchess broke from him & moved away. She was now the true image of her father. There was absolute malignity in the bitterness & scorn of the look she flung on her presumptuous page.

'Mon Dieu!' said he, as the haughty sweep of her robes passed by him. 'C'est fait de moi!* She'll never forgive me! This comes of being over zealous. I wish I'd let the Duke & her meet & manage it together. But then, the after-reckoning—& he's so mischievous. Why did he call out? Parbleu, that made her quite unmanageable! But she's off now, so I must try & be before hand with explaining.' So saying, he skipped across the hall & up the stair-case with his customary agility.

Mary retired to her chamber. She sat down, leant her white face on her whiter hands, & for half an hour continued utterly motionless. At length a low tap came to the door. She made no answer, but it opened & in sailed the figure of a tall gentle-woman clothed in rustling black silk. She raised her head. 'Temple,* why am I disturbed in this manner? Am I not to be safe from intrusion even in my own chamber?'

'My dear lady,' said the matron, 'you have been vexed, I see, or you would not be angry with me for coming at the Duke's command to tell you he desires your company in his dressing-room.'

'Dressing-room again!' replied the Duchess. 'How often is that word to be sounded in my ears? I say he is not in his dressing-room, &, Temple, I wonder you should bring me messages with which you were never charged. He does not wish to see me!' And now the spoiled child broke out. The young Duchess burst into tears. She sobbed & wept, & reiterated two or three times, 'I won't go! He never sent for me! He hates me!'

'My lady, my lady,' continued Mrs Temple, in a tone of alarm, 'for heaven's sake don't try him any more! He is not angry yet, but I dread to see that look of placidity begin to settle about his lips. Do take my arm, madam, for you are very much agitated, & let us go before the cloud gathers.'

'Well, well, Temple,' said Mary, for she could not long keep up that angry mood towards her servants which was so unnatural to her cheerful, indulgent temper. 'I may perhaps go soon if you'll let me alone. But then he does not want me, & that hideous dwarf Finic, & that insolent boy Eugene will break in upon us, & he will let them insult me as they like. No Temple, I won't go! I won't go!'

'Nay, my dearest lady, think it over again. If I return with that message he'll just say, "Very well, Temple, my respects to your lady, & say I am sorry I troubled her", & then he'll sit down & look like his bust in your cabinet there, & it will be many a long day before he asks to see you again.'

The Duchess returned no answer to this reasoning, but at last she rose slowly &, still weeping & with evident reluctance, resigned herself to the conduct of the worthy house-keeper, who, respectfully yet affectionately soothing and supporting her gentle mistress, led her from the room & on towards the Duke's appartments. They entered the hated dressing-room. The omnipresent Zamorna was as certainly there as he had been in the saloon, but he wore a different mood, a different aspect. Wan & wasted was the tall thin form, seated by the hearth at a table covered with books. His head with all its curls rested on a woefully attenuated hand. His brow was blanched, whitened with sickness; his cheek worn & hollow; & his full, floating eyes lit with languid light the learned page on which they rested. A portrait of the Duchess of Wellington hung over the mantle-piece—how like his mother looked her glorious son!

'Well, Temple, said he, roused by their approaching footsteps, 'you have been most successful after all, I see. Woman to woman, they know how to manage each other best! But, bless me, what is the matter? Tears, sobs, Mary? Look up, love.'

But Mary would not look up. She shrunk from him as he advanced & was going to take her from the care of Mrs Temple, turned away her face, & actually gave him a slight repulse with her hand. He was silent a minute. The awful calmness came over his before gentle countenance.

'Annabel,' said he to the housekeeper, 'explain! Your mistress seems capricious.'

'O, she will be better directly, my lord,' replied Mrs Temple. 'My lady,' in an under-tone, 'pray think what you are about. I do implore you not to trifle with your own happiness.'

'I am not trifling with my own happiness,' sobbed the Duchess. 'If he touches me, those hateful satellites of his will be on us directly, & he will leave the room, & I must remain to hear & endure what insolence they chuse to favour me with.'

'Madness,' muttered Mrs Temple. 'I never saw you in such a way before, my lady.'

'Annabel, trouble yourself no further with remonstrances,' said the Duke. 'Assist your lady back to her own room.'

He resumed his seat, again leant his head on his hand, & in a moment appeared to be thoroughly absorbed in the study which had before occupied his attention. A sense of remorse seemed now to touch the Duchess. She looked at him & for the first time perceived how pale & thin & languid sickness had left him. Immediately there was a strong revulsion of feeling. Tears flowed more rapidly than ever; her neck and bosom swelled with the choking sobs that forced their way one after the other. The waywardness of the indulged child of aristocracy took a different turn. She pushed Mrs Temple off when she offered to lead her from the chamber, went to her husband & stood beside him, trembling & weeping violently. He did not long remain unmoved by her anguish, but, soon rising, led her to a sofa, &, sitting down by her, wiped her tears with his own handkerchief.

'Annabel,' said he, 'you may go. I think we shall be right in time.'

The excellent gentlewoman smiled, but as old Bunyan says, 'the water stood in her eyes'.* As she went out she remarked with the freedom of a favourite retainer, 'Now, my lord, don't be placid. Don't be like your bust.'

'I won't, Annabel,' said he, then, with the softest smile & sweetest tone, he turned to his lady & continued, 'Well, Maria piangendo,* when is this shower to be succeeded by sunshine?'

She made no answer, but the radiant spheres under her arched brows were already flashing more cheerfully through their diamond rain.

'Ah,' said he, 'I see it will clear up. There is a light already on the horizon. Now, my love, why have you delayed so long complying with the request contained in my billet?'

'Dear, dear Arthur, have you forgot that I met you in the crimson saloon scarcely half an hour since? And you would hardly touch me, & spoke & looked so strangely, quite different to what you do now, you seemed not so pale, not so wasted.'

'Handsomer, I dare say,' interrupted he with something of a sneer.

'No, Arthur, I love you far better now. But I cannot tell how the difference is. My eyes must have been unaccountably bewildered. You appeared healthy & fresh & vigorous. I never saw you more so in my life, & these hands, O my lord, the flesh has fallen strangely from your fingers. They could not retain your rings, & yet I perfectly recollect that as you once or twice passed them across your forehead, the sunshine fell on them & they sparkled most brilliantly with jewels.'

The Duke looked disturbed. 'Stuff, child,' said he, 'you are dreaming.'

'Impossible, Arthur, here is occular demonstration. Do you remember pressing my hand very hard?'

'Pressing your hand very hard!' said he starting up. 'What business had you to come so near me? Pray, madam, was I very kind? Very cordial? Very loving? By heaven, if you say yes—.' He paused. Something seemed to agitate him greatly.

'No, my lord, you were not indeed. Your coldness made me very unhappy, & when you squeezed my hand, it seemed rather in anger than kindness, for those marks remained as a token.' She shewed him the fingers, a little bruised where the rings had rubbed against them.

'Right,' said he, 'that gives me pleasure, & yet it was most rudely & roughly done. How could I hurt such a fair & delicate hand?' And snatching it he pressed it warmly to his lips. Mary smiled through her tears.

'You do not utterly hate me then, my noble Adrian?' said she, but with a look of alarm 'Where is Finic? Will he not be interfering presently?'

'Not now, not now, Mary. But I wish to know, love, what words I made use of during that mysterious interview in the crimson saloon? Don't be surprised at my question. This whole affair must now to you appear thoroughly incomprehensible, but some time the mist may clear up. How in the first place did I receive you?'

'Very coldly, Arthur. I was prepared to throw my arms round you, but it would not do. The first look dashed & miserably confounded me. It was like cold water flung on boiling oil.'

'Right,' said the Duke, 'But go on. On what subjects did I converse?'

'You asked me among other things whether I thought Mina Laury pretty, & you told me not to be jealous, for that you had never spoken above three words at a time to her in your life.'

The Duke coughed significantly & turned away his face. It was covered with as deep a glow as the blood could now communicate to his blanched complexion.

'Did you believe me, Mary?' he asked in a low tone. She sighed & shook her head. 'Well, proceed.'

'The next thing you enquired whether I thought Fitz-Arthur like you. I said yes, & little Emily too, for indeed, my lord, they are your very miniatures.'

'Curse it!' said he, speaking between his teeth. 'I'll hear no more. Why did he—I, I mean, talk such infernal nonsense? Wrong-headed scape grace! But I'll be even with him! Time for Finic to interfere & Eugene too I say. Mary, whenever you find me in that absurd mood, revenge yourself by giving me a smart box on the ear. Do not fear either retaliation or any very lasting anger. Do it, love, I command you, & a kiss, a hundred kisses shall be your reward when I come to my right senses.'

Mary smiled at him & leaned her head on his shoulder. 'Arthur,' said she, 'I begin to think that you have a double existence. I am sure the Zamorna I saw in the saloon is not the Zamorna who now sits by me. That cared little for me; this, I will believe, nay I am sure, loves me. That was strong & in full flourish; this droops at present. But to my eyes the pale lips that now smile on me are dearer a thousand, a million times than those ruby ones that sneered at me an hour ago. These fingers feel & look very thin, but I love them far better than the white & rounded hand that lately crushed mine in its scornful clasp. Yet what am I talking about? There cannot be two Zamornas on this earth; it would not hold them! My brain is surely turned to entertain the idea for an instant! Ridiculous, impossible, chimerical! You will think me mad, Adrian!'

He laughed wildly, sweetly, but not heartily. 'Bless thee,' said he, 'I am madder myself, I think. However, no more of this just now, it is a dangerous subject. Yet the spell must be dissolving. A week ago a third part of what I have listened to patiently to day would have killed me, either with passion or horror. Leave me for the present, love, I must reconsider the events of the morning.'

He clasped her to him, kissed her tenderly, & then rose & led her to the door. She slowly, reluctantly left him. Never before had he been so deeply dear to her as now. There was something inexpressibly touching in the aspect of his stately form & noble countenance deprived of their customary brightness, but invested with a mild, wan, melancholy fascination that heretofore had been wholly foreign to him. At least of late years, for at the ages of sixteen, seventeen, eighteen & nineteen, when he was a slender, delicate-complexioned boy, thin as a lath from his rapid growth, his manners were much gentler than they are now. How has he altered since twenty! There was no grandeur in his form till that time, no martial majesty in his features. He looked elegant & effeminate & contemplative, & more like an extremely tall & beautiful girl than a bold, blustering man. Yes, hear it, ye ladies of Africa, the Duke of Zamorna was once like a girl!* That assertion seems incredible now when we look at the fiery, haughty, imperious face of the young satrap of Angria* with its quenchless, transfixing glances & rapid changes of expression in which every turn only displays pride, effrontery, & impetuosity in new & continually varied lights. He once never shewed those vices except when he was angered. And truly, Lord Douro, at the age of twelve, caught up in a whirlwind of passion, bore an appalling resemblance to the Duke of Zamorna at the age of twenty-two. In the same tantrums, how the violet veins on his white brow & whiter neck swelled & throbbed; how the clustering brown curls were tossed from their resting-places on forehead & temple, like the fore-lock of a prancing stallion. His slight, pliant form would strain & writhe while he struggled with his opponent (commonly Quashia),* as though the spirit strove in mortal agony to accomplish that by force of desire which it[s] clay casket was unequal to from fragility.

I could talk much of those times, but at present I must continue what I have now in hand. Reader, pass to the next chapter, if you are not asleep.

CHAPTER THE VIIth

The Vale of Verdopolis! That has a sweet yet kindling sound. The
Nile-swept Vale of Egypt, the rose-strewn Vale of Persia, both hold
grand & gorgeous & delicate scenes in the hollows of their mighty
bosoms, but is Cairo like the Queen of Nations? Are Candahar &
Ispahan* like the emporium of the world? No, Dear Reader. You will
think from this preamble that I am going to give a panorama description
of our valley in all its glory, all its amplitude; to tell how the wide, bright
billows of the Niger roll through banks that look down in magnificent
serenity on their own tree-dropped verdure, sloping into the illimitable
depths of skies like oceans, skirted with fertile shores, crossed with the
rippling river-waves, clouded with vanishing foam as pure & transient
as snow-wreaths.

If this is your fear dismiss it. I merely ask you to alight with me from
the six o'clock morning coach, rattling north-ward over a road like a
sea-beach, equally broad, equally even. Cry on the jarvie* to draw in
just where that pleasant shady branch-road makes itself independent of
the main-one. I am going to breakfast at Douro Villa & chuse, instead
of entering at that vast, granite gateway, which proudly opens a passage
through the huge & impregnable park-wall, & so going straight along
the carriage road, winding amid grove & lawn & avenue & open park,
even to the villa two miles up the country. I chuse, I say, instead of following this track, to take a cut across some pleasant fields I know of, to
which this tree girdled bye-path will conduct me.

Having reached the second field, I sat down at a stile over which two
lofty beeches hung their embowering branches. It was very delightful,
being early morning, the air cool & fresh, the grass green & dewy, the
flowers in the hedge-rows exhaling their sweetest perfumes. A little rill
wandered along down the sides of the pasture fields, & plenty of primroses, of wood-sorrel with their clustering leaves & faintly tinted blossoms, of vetches, wild hyacinths & geraniums budded in blushing beauty
on the borders. All was breathlessly still—that is, so far as regards the
tumultuous voice of humanity, for there were thrushes singing on the
tree tops, sky-larks warbling in the air, & rooks cawing from the rookery
of Girnington-Hall,* which was seen at a distance. The last sound was
not the least musical. To my ears it gave a sequestered country effect
to the whole landscape which I could feel & enjoy but not express. I
chose this situation to rest at because it afforded a most lovely prospect
of Douro-Villa. The hedge under which I sat was quick-set* & formed

the boundary to the park on this side. The deer could not over-leap it because it was planted much higher than their pastures and formed the sumit of a natural wall eight feet high. Leaning against a leafy bough of the beech trees, as I sat on the stile which they canopied, I could in luxurious ease contemplate all the beauty spread beneath me.

Far, far down the grounds declined in vast slopes of verdure, varied by large stately trees, brushed by the light feet of gambolling stags who, wild with the delicious freshness & fragrance of the morning, were bounding in all directions. As the huge dell descended, the foliage thickened, till it became a wood in the centre, & up from its Eden-bowers started the columns, the portico & the classic casements of the fair Grecian villa, all lifted to the early sun shine by a low knoll of shaven lawn & pleasure ground, whose light, delicate green contrasted beautifully with the darker verdure of the park & woods. Nothing could be sweeter, more elegant, more Elysiac. It had not the aspect of a fine old family seat, but it seemed like the abode of taste & refinement, & princely pride.

No landscape is complete without figures, & my pencil, or rather pen, shall now depict one or two of these animating adjuncts on the canvass. Slowly mounting the flowery hill on whose summit I was posted, I saw a fair & youthful lady. She was without bonnet. Her glowing cheek & raven curls announced Mina Laury. A little child lay in her arms, & another, Ernest Fitzarthur, ran on before her. Both these were likewise uncovered. Their ringlets danced in the morning wind, & their lovely cherub faces glowed with pleasure & exercise. Ernest was on the brow presently. He flung himself down immediately under the wall of turf when he reached it.

'Come, Mina,' he exclaimed, 'make haste, make haste! I can see all the road through the valley from here, but Papa is not coming yet. There are plenty of people & plenty of horses & some carriages covering it like little specks, but I shall know Papa by his plume when he comes, & that is not to be seen at present.'

Mina soon arrived at his post of observation. She likewise sat down & placed the little gazelle-eyed creature she carried on the grass beside her. It leaned its cheek against her smooth satin dress & looked up at her so eagerly & animatedly as if it would have spoken.

'Emily wants Mamma,' said Fitzarthur. 'And, Mina, why doesn't she come out this beautiful morning? She might, you know, with Blanche & Harriet & have a long walk in the park before Papa comes.'

'She is in her oratory, my lord,' replied Miss Laury, '& so are her gentlewomen. But we shall see her walking on the lawn after prayers are over, I dare-say.'

'Father Gonsalvi makes her pray a long while, I think,' continued Ernest. 'I should not like to be a Roman-Catholic, & Papa says I am not to be. But Emily will, & then she'll have to tell her beads every night & confess every week. I hate that confession worst of all. If Father Gonsalvi were to ask me what sins I'd committed, I would rather bite out my tongue than tell him,* wouldn't you, Mina?'

She smiled. 'Father Gonsalvi is a good man, my lord,' replied she, 'but I am not of his faith, & so it would be a hard thing to make me kneel before him in the confessional.'

'That's right, Mina. Do you know Zamorna has ordered him never to trouble you with trying to make you believe in saints & holy water?'

'What?' said Mina blushing. 'Did the Duke speak about me, did he think it worth his while——.' She stopped.

'Yes, yes,' replied Ernest very simply. 'Zamorna loves you dearly. I don't believe you think so, Mina, by your sorrowfulness, but I am sure he does. You had just been in the room for something & had gone out, & he looked at Gonsalvi very sternly & said, "Holy Father, that is a lamb that can never be gathered to the one true fold. Sir, Miss Laury is mine. Therefore, take notice, she can not be a disciple of our blessed Mother-Church. You understand me?" And Mamma's priest smiled in his quiet way & bowed low, but afterwards I saw him biting his lip, & that is a sure sign of anger with him.'

Mina answered not. Her thoughts, indeed, seemed to have wandered from the prattle of her little comforter to other & distant reminiscences, & for the moment the happy light on her countenance told that they had found rest. How touching was that interval of silence! All calm sunshine around, nothing heard but the tinkle of the hidden rivulet, the warbling of a lark unseen in ether, & the rustle of foliage wind-borne from the bottom of the dell, where a belt of forest-trees waved round the Palladian villa.

Ernest spoke again. 'Mina,' said he, 'people say Zamorna, when he was as old as me, was just like what I am now. And don't you think when I am as old as him I shall be like what he is?'

'I believe you will, my lord, in mind as well as in person.'

'Well then, Mina, never look sad any more, for I promise solemnly I'll marry you.'

Miss Laury started. 'What do you mean, child? said she, with a look of surprise & a somewhat forced laugh.

'I mean,' he returned quite seriously, 'that you would like to marry Zamorna, & so, as I shall be just like Zamorna, I shall do as well, & as he won't marry you, I will.'

'Nonsense, child, you know not what you are talking about. Pray, my Lord Ravenswood, say no more on the subject. You will make me sadder than ever if you do.'

'Not I,' was the answer. 'You <u>shall</u>, I am determined, you <u>shall</u> be Countess of Ravenswood, & we will live together at Castle Oronsay,* for twenty years hence that will be mine, you know, & I am sure, Mina, you would like the castle. It has a loch all round it & great hills, far higher than any we see here, some of them black in winter & purple in summer, & some of [them] covered with woods filled with dark close-set trees called pines. The rooms at Oronsay are not like these at Douro Villa. They have no marble on the walls or floor, & not such light, open windows. They will seem to frown at you when you first enter them, & the hall is hung with pictures of men in armour and women in whale-bone that in dark days & towards twilight look terribly grim. But you must not be afraid. They can do no harm. They are only painted. And then there are chambers in the west wing with handsomer & younger faces set in gold frames, & these are all hung with velvet, & they look out onto the castle esplanade. And, Mina, you shall sit with me by the lattices cut deep into walls as thick & solid as rocks, & in stormy days we'll watch how the clouds curl round Ben Carnach, & how the mist and rain settles on his head, and listen to the distant muttering far off among the cliffs of Arderinis. When that is heard it's a sign that there's a strong blast coming, & soon you see it bending all the trees as it roars down Glen Avon. Foam bursts on the water under us, & all the waves of Loch-Sunart seem to break in one rush at the foot of the castle-walls. Oh, I delight in such times as those, & so you will, I am sure! Now be Lady Ravenswood! Do, Mina, & you don't know how much I'll love you!'

'Beginning in good time, my boy,' said a voice close beside me, & at the same instant some one laid his hand on my shoulder, bounded over the hedge & the eight feet of turf wall, & alighted just before Mina. It was Zamorna. He had come up the fields by the same path as I had &, my attention being absorbed in listening to Fitzarthur, I had not noticed his approach. Miss Laury rose quietly up. She did not seem at all fluttered or discomposed. Ernest, with an exclamation of joy, sprang into his father's arms.

'How did you come, Papa?' said he. 'We came here to watch for you. I thought your plume would mark you from the other travellers on the valley-road & now after all you've slipped our notice.'

'Slipped your notice, sir! And no wonder when you were engaged in popping the question to that black-eyed lady! Pray, how [h]as she received the offer of your hand, heart & earldom? She does not blush—that's a bad sign.'

'I did not offer her my hand, heart & earldom, Papa, I only said I would marry her twenty years hence.'

'Tut, tut, very slack work for so early a courtship! You should have proposed tomorrow & got old Gonsalvi to knit the knot as fast as our holy Mother Church would allow. Remember, Edward, faint heart never won fair lady.'*

'Yes, I'll remember. I remember all you tell me, & generally say it afterwards when I've got an opportunity.'

'I'll be sworn you do! And so, where's Emily?'

'There, Papa, struggling to get to you like a little wild cat.'

'I meant <u>my</u> Emily, your mother; sir. But come, you small female imp. What eyes the child has! They are more startling than yours, Edward. Little antelope, don't flash them out of your head, for heaven's sake!'

He kissed his tiny image with paternal fondness, & then, still holding her in his arms, flung himself on the grass, & while she sat on his breast, Ernest rolled about him shouting & screaming with glee as his young father sometimes pushed him off, sometimes held him in a tight grasp, & nearly killed him with laughter & tickling. Meantime two large dogs came bounding from the house, up the slope. Then there was a revival of noise & play. They rushed on to their master, whining, yelping, shaking their steel collars & padlocks, licked his face, his hands unchecked, nearly worried little Emily in their gentle yet overwhelming caresses, & buried Fitz-Arthur under the large heads & dew-lap ears which they laid over his face. Zamorna encouraged them by voice & hand till at last they absolutely howled with joy. Their yells, I am sure, could be heard from the distant North-Road, & so could the Duke's 'Ha! Ha!', sometimes smothered when the hounds' tongues were brandishing about his mouth, & sometimes bursting forth in its full cordial clearness of sound.

What would the Angrians have thought could they have seen their young monarch as I saw him! Many of them, I have no doubt, were then passing in the wide highway, whence came that incessant roll of wheels almost like the rush of many waters, & continued trotting click, click of horse-hoofs which marks the proximity of a great city. At length the toll of a silver-voiced bell arose from the hollow.

'Bravo!' shouted Zamorna. 'Sirius! Condor!* Edward! Let us see who will be at the villa-vestibule first! Here, Miss Laury, take my blossom.'

He flung his daughter to Mina, & off they sprung, father, son & deer-hounds, like forms of living lightning. They dived into the wood;

the boughs seemed to shiver as they passed among them. In an instant they emerged on the other side, crossed the sunny, golden lawn swift as eagles. The marble portico received them & they vanished.

And now I left my station, dropped from an over-hanging bough of the beech tree like a squirrel, flew down the hill as lightly as any of them, passing Mina Laury in my rapid descent like a meteor & was at the hall door five minutes after them.

Zamorna was still in the entrance-hall giving some orders to a servant. As he dismissed him, I came forward. His quick eye instantly caught me.

'Charles, come hither!' said he, but I edged away from him, rather afraid of the colour which just then mounted to his face. 'Curse you!' said he striding towards me. 'What are you afraid of? I saw you eavesdropping on the stile, & if I didn't knock your brains out then, why should I now?'

'For no mortal reason on earth, Arthur,' said I. 'I hope you'll be civil to a gentleman in your own house & dole out a crumb or two of breakfast for the benefit of his appetite.'

He was stooping down looking at me very earnestly & his face was nearly in contact with mine. I kissed him—the first time I have ventured to do so for many a long year. He drew himself up directly, passed his hands across his lips as though my touch had defiled them, smiling, however, not ill-naturedly at the same time.

'Small monkey,' said he. 'Your prying eyes cannot do much harm now, so it does not matter where you go. But, sir, had I found you here a week since I would have trod you to death on the spot.'

'Very likely,' said I, & with much inward satisfaction, for my curiosity was hissing at white heat.

I followed his imperial stride as he led towards the penetralia of the mansion. Open he flung the folding-doors of one apartment in his ordinary, peremptory, all-commanding manner. The usual sweet scent of palace-saloons, mingled with the cool wildflower fragrance of a dewy summer morning, saluted my gratified nostrils as we stepped in to a large & lofty room surrounded by long windows, all open, all admitting the breath & light of rising day onto Persian carpets, alabaster vases filled with flowers, velvet hangings heavily waving in the faint, fanning air, & the other splendors of taste, wealth & aristocracy.

A lady rose to welcome us. A lovely creature, she seemed the very flower of patrician beauty, with her slight but stately figure, her fair features rounded off in curves so exquisitely delicate, her marble neck so queenly & swan-like, which a small ruff turned back shewed to fine advantage, her full, dark, liquid, blue eye[s], her wreathed, braided, curled & clustered tresses, whose bright abundance would scarce be confined by the slender gold chains wound amongst them, & above all her winning, fascinating, enchanting smile.

'Mary Stuart, Mary Stuart,'* muttered I in my delight & astonishment. A noble likeness, a dazzling eidolon! But, in the name of heaven how is that vision connected with Zamorna?'

'Well, my Catholic Emily,' said he, as they clasped hands & joined lips, 'here I am, your own, without disguise, without concealment. All is over. To night the full revelation will be made, & the coronet that has long been hovering over you shall descend on that beautiful, that high-born brow.

'I care not for that,' said she. 'I never pined after emancipation for my own sake, it was for yours. And now, if you are happy, if you feel pleasure in the unloosing of the bond, so do I. But come, you have been up all night, I daresay. This evening for severer thought, but now to breakfast. Harriet, you will attend us. Blanche may go to Miss Laury; I see her coming with Gazelle. Do you know, my lord, I have given that oriental name to little Emily? Your eyes, under her eye-brows, have such a wild, flashing eastern loveliness.'*

The Duke smiled & threw himself by Mary Stuart's side, as she sat down on a sofa near the window.

While they were sitting together I passed behind & whispered in Zamorna's ear, 'Poor Henrietta,' for my mind was horribly misgiving me.

'Poor Henrietta!' repeated he, not at all moved by the intimation.

'Aye, she would knit her little brows if she saw me now, and look so sad, so sorrowful, so imploring, & lift up that extraordinary face of hers to mine, with its small ivory nose & commanding, open forehead, & deep, gold curls. And then the hazel eyes would shine through such a storm of tears, & she would take my hand in her fairy palms & sob & moan as if her heart was breaking. But that would not do, would it Emily? It's well, I think, that Finic parted us once or twice, or else I could hardly have kept up my stoicism, though I felt more inclined to laugh than anything else. So, chase away that jealous cloud, my royal lily, & look cheerful again. Your smile, you know, I have often told you, is the talisman that binds my heart & thine in the same fillet.'

'Then you shall have it,' replied the lady, smiling most sweetly. 'And I trust its power is real & not fictitious, for to speak truth, I am half-afraid of that pretty, singular, little girl who answered me so haughtily, & assumed such proud, passionate airs with all her childish delicacy of appearance.

'But look, my lord,' she said, starting, 'there are your guests coming up the lawn. That is Edward, I am sure, so like his sister, but he has blue eyes, hers are brown; see, his very hand as he lifts it to his forehead has just the white slender aspect of hers. And the other gentleman must be Fidena, proud, grave, inexorable prince. If I were not your wife I should condescend to dread his approach.'

'By the Genii,' said Zamorna, with a low & meaning laugh, 'he does look prodigiously just, immensely rigid this morning. Ho, John! I say come hither. And you, Edward, turn your righteous footsteps from the straight path to the lateral direction of this window.'

They advanced: Edward, with rapid & impatient steps, John, more slowly. Both entered through the long low casement, & stood in [the] presence of Zamorna & the stranger lady. The Duke looked like a fiend, a handsome one, but still a true indisputable Lucifer* in the flesh. Something exceedingly sly, dark, secret & imperturbable lurked in the glance of his eye, the curl of his lip, & the whole cast of his grand countenance. Fidena regarded him calmly & steadily; Edward, with a fiery eagerness that seemed to show he was prepared for contest on the slightest opening. My brother spoke first.

'Well, gentlemen,' said he, 'I am obliged to your compliance with my wishes. Allow me to introduce to you Emily Inez Wellesley, my relation in the nearest & dearest sense of the word.'

'Your wife or sister, Arthur?' asked Fidena.

'His wife to be sure,' said Edward Percy, with a bitter sneer. 'He has provided himself with one for every day in the week, like a case of razors!'

'Edward is right,' returned Zamorna, bowing with mock civility. 'This lady is my wife.'

Fidena sat down. He leant his brow on his hand a moment, but soon looked up & said very quietly, 'Well, Adrian, and is this the intelligence you had to communicate to us? I am sorry for your fickleness of disposition, which seems, in my opinion, to border on insanity, & certainly leads you to acts marked with the stain of extreme cruelty. You have committed murder once, my young friend. I should think your feelings after that flower withered at your feet were not so enviable as to make you anxious for their revival.'

'I know what you mean, John,' replied Zamorna, with equal calmness. 'You allude to Marian. She was a sweet snow-drop, but be assured, most dignified of modern Solons,* it was no frost of mine that blighted her leaves.'

'No, no,' interrupted Mr Percy. 'She died of consumption, you know. And I suppose Mary is to walk off stage in the same way, though

she will be more likely, if my notions of her disposition are correct—&
I should like to see who dare contradict them—to draw a knife either
across her own throat or some other person's.'

'How long has that lady borne your name?' continued Fidena. 'Is
the right of precedency due to the Princess Florence, the Princess
Henrietta or the Princess Inez?'*

'Emily is the Chief Sultana,' answered Arthur. 'She has carried the
poniard at her girdle five years, young as she looks & is. But I need say
no more. Here comes a noble witness to prove my affirmation.' Just
then enter[ed] Fitz-Arthur. He walked towards his father.

'Edward, whose son are you?'

'Yours and Mamma's,' pointing to the lady.

'That's well. And how old are you?'

'Four years.'

'Good again. Now, gentlemen, what do you say to that testimony?'

'I say that you are a scoundrel,' replied Mr Percy, 'a selfish & infernal
profligate! Why did we never know of this before? Why was my sister
crowned Queen of Angria when there was one who had a prior right?
Why, since you kept it a secret for a lustrum, did you not keep it a secret
for a century? Zamorna, this matter shall not pass unchallenged! I tell
you plainly, sir, I won't be cut out from the prospect of being uncle to
a future king without a struggle. You shall have a fiery furnace to go
through before this lady can establish her claim of precedency. Look to
it! I warn you & I defy you!'

'I must say,' remarked Fidena, 'a more unprincipled & dishonour-
able transaction was never brought to light within my remembrance!
Adrian Wellesley, I am deeply grieved for you. You have chosen to walk
in paths of darkest treachery & crime. You have acted even meanly. Your
own snares are now closing you in on every side. I see nothing but shadows & dangers & universal upbraiding in the course stretching before
you. The evils of a disputed succession, the horrors of internal conflict
will form your legacy to Angria. You have brewed a bitter cup. Now, go,
& drink it to the very dregs.'*

'Well done!' exclaimed Zamorna, laughing. 'Bravo! Noble! O, for
a legion of cossacks to applaud the judgement of Rhadamanthus!*
Joachim* says the hurrah of the northern hordes was the grandest sound
to which his ears ever tingled, but I think it could scarce do justice to
that wise, good, well considered sentence of deserved condemnation.
Shall I call thee Solon or Draco,* John? Thou art bloody minded, I
think. And thou, too, our young Jupiter,* denounce vengeance, hurl thy
thunderbolts, bind Prometheus to the rock, transfix him with barbed

lightnings, & get the insatiable vulture to gnaw the irradicable liver!
Ha! Ha! Ha! Pity, Emily, they don't know how their fulminations are
wasted. Rhadamanthus, thou art on the throne in Tartarus,* but the
wailing wicked are all gone. No criminal stands awaiting thy decree.
The Furies* have flown, each on her awful errand. The hiss of their
snakes, the yell of the tortured sounds from a vast & dreary distance, no
voice save that mutters through the silence of Hades. Judge, thou art
alone. Rest, then, from thy denouncing office if it be but for a moment.
And Jupiter cease to shake Olympus with thy thunders. No one hears.
No one regards them. Gods & demigods, if such a mere mortal as I
might presume to dictate, let us appease our raging appetites before we
go further in the matter now before us. Deities as well as men are often
more savage when hungry than when full. Hebe, perform thine office!*
The mouths of the celestials water for their etherial food—. Bless me,
child! Dost not understand? Well then, to descend from our heroics:
Harriet, my girl, hand the coffee.'

He was instantly obeyed by a young & richly-dressed lady who
waited in the saloon. She gracefully presented the required beverage in china cups, ornamented with gold filigree. During breakfast,
an almost unbroken silence was maintained. Zamorna leaned back in
the sofa, regarding his two guests with a smile of the most strange &
inscrutable significancy. It was such as one might suppose a man might
assume when on the eve of accomplishing a grand piece of gullery on
an extended scale.

I think that was Mr Percy's opinion, for he suddenly rose, put down
his coffee-cup &, approaching the Duke, said with a peculiar glance,
'My good brother-in-law, take care, if you are playing off some capital, practical joke on me! I take the liberty of informing you that your
father's son is a consummate idiot. As I have a natural antipathy to
jests, & he who attempts to force them down my throat generally pays
a heavy penalty for his folly, be on your guard! This business wears a
black face at present. If the Ethiop is not quickly washed white, I'll dye
him red with the nectareous blood of your godship.'

'Eat your breakfast, Edward,' replied Zamorna. 'Here, Harriet, more
nectar, more ambrosia. Jupiter Tonans begins to mutter the moment
his supplies fail. Rhadamanthus, now, is more exemplary. I trust his
judicial bile is, by this time, diluted by streams of ameliorating
chocolate.'

The meal was soon over. When it was concluded my brother rose.
'Come,' said he, 'I move that the court do adjourn into the open air.
Percy, Fidena, follow me into the park, & we will see whether Edward's

skill can succeed in bleaching the hide of this most swart & sun-burnt Negro.'

He strode over the low window sill. His guests followed him. I thought, as the trio moved away, three finer specimens of mortality had never before stood under the sun's eye on any given square yard of our planet's surface. I watched them till they vanished amongst the thickening girdle of tall trees by which the pleasure grounds were circled. Then I turned from the window.

In about an hour's time the Duke returned alone.

'Well, Emily,' said he, 'they are gone. I have convinced them. We shall meet again this evening at Waterloo Palace. You will find them ready enough to acknowledge your royal rights then. I had most difficulty with Edward. His dread of a joke is perfectly laughable, but his impetuosity is dangerous, & his incredulity unmanageable. I don't know whether I should have succeeded had not <u>he</u> arrived most opportunely. We saw him riding through the park at a distance, & as we stood on the hill I beckoned to him. Up he came, his hand on his breast, agitatedly touching the chain & miniature, & his face alternately flushed & colourless. There was no with-standing that. Fidena grasped my hand, & Edward said, with a smile, "It was well I had not jested, for, though the reality was bad enough, a joke would have been more than the value of my life".'

'And were they <u>fully</u> satisfied then?' said the lady. 'But indeed I need not ask you. They <u>must</u> have been, and now where is <u>he</u>?'

'Gone back to the city, love, with John & Percy, so we will waive the subject till evening.'

'Charles,' turning to me, 'at nine o'clock post meridian your presence will be tolerated at Waterloo-Palace. Now leave the room. I am tired of seeing your vile inquisitive looks. Trudge this instant, I say!'

Having no alternative, I was forced to obey, which I did with a very bad grace. However, I solaced myself by repeating, 'nine o'clock, nine o'clock', & so strove to quiet my curiosity by anticipation, as a man endeavours to appease the calls of hunger by chewing tobacco. My efforts were as futile in the one case as they are generally in the other.

CHAPTER THE VIIIth

I believe General Thornton will never forget that day. The trials of Job were nothing to what he suffered during its slow, hideous, leaden progress.* A thousand times did I beg him to pull out his watch & tell me the hour. Ten thousand times did I run to the door, open, look out, & then shut it. Towards night my impatience became incontrollable. I rolled on the carpet, gnawed the fringe of the rug, screamed, kicked, &, when he attempted to chasten me with the little stick he keeps beside him for that express purpose, I seized it in my teeth & fairly bit it in two.

At last, nine o'clock found me at the vestibule of Waterloo Palace. I crossed the entrance-hall and ascended the stairs, following the train of footmen who were stationed at due distances on the landing-places, &c. I entered the north-drawing-room. It was lighted up & filled with company. A single glance sufficed to inform me that the company was all composed of the members of our own, the Fidena, & the Percy family.

My Aunt Seymour seemed to be the prima donna of the evening. She occupied the principal seat, & her gentle countenance & mild unfur-rowed brow, with its fair hair parted simply on each side, wore a look of calm & subdued gladness which it did my heart good to gaze on. Every now & then she glanced at her children, who sat in a group not far off. And when her eye turned on them, it filled instantly with a mingled light of maternal love, pride & carefulness. In the midst of my cousins Seymour, I saw William Percy. He was lying on an ottoman at the feet of the three eldest girls, Eliza & Georgiana & Cecillia. And the younger ones were clustered on the carpet round him: little Helen with her head resting on his knee, & her face raised smiling to his as he passed his hand caressingly through her thick brown curls. How his handsome countenance sparkled with animation! How his fine blue eyes filled with happiness & spirit & intellect as he conversed with those fair & noble daughters of that order from which rank, black, unnatural injus-tice alone excluded him & his more celebrated & powerful brother! I thought he devoted himself with more exclusive assiduity to Lady Cecillia Seymour than to the others, & she, I am sure, was wholly taken up with the elegant young merchant at her feet.

Cecillia is a pretty, delicate girl of mild manners & cultivated mind, very fair complexioned, like her mother, not above middle- size & slighter in stature than Eliza & Georgiana, who are tall, haughty blondes, proud of their beauty, proud of their first rate accomplish-ments, proud of their lofty lineage, proud of their semi-royal blood, proud of every thing.

I was near enough to the group to hear a little of their conversation. My elder cousins indulged themselves as usual in several lively dashing sallies, which William parried & returned with great promptitude & politeness. But it was only in answer to the low, yet sweet & cheerful voice of Cecillia that he kindled to the full exertion of his powers, & then eye, cheek, brow & voice were alike ardent, alike eloquent. I never heard him speak so much before, & I never heard anyone speak more animatedly & well. His talents & acquirements are little known because he is seldom seen except in the company of Edward. And young Rogue's imposing & fiery beauty, overbearing demeanour, omnipotent abilities, athletic strength of arm & invincible soundness of lungs are more than sufficient to dash a stronger & fiercer man than William.* When that Lord of the Ascendant is absent, he shines as the moon does at the going down of the sun:* in his presence, he is scarcely visible.

But to proceed with a more general account of the company. Near the fire-place appeared two fine representatives of croaking & narrative old age. The Marquis Wellesley & Earl Seymour sat on the same sofa, their gouty feet on foot-stools, their crutches laid beside them. I need say no more. It was an impressive scene. Opposite stood a noble contrast, Edward Percy, in all his glory, surrounded by a brilliant ring of ladies, viz., Julia Sydney, the Marchioness Louisa, his own bright, dazzling Maria, the stern Countess Zenobia—for a shadow of appalling sternness did indeed dwell on her rich Italian features, as she looked at her husband's disowned & detested son—the sweet Queen of Angria, who gazed at her brother as if she could not help loving him, yet feared to show her affection, the gentle Duchess of Fidena, with Rossendale at her knee looking as bold & princely as usual, & last not least, Lady Helen Percy, as grand in her declining as she could have been lovely in her ripening years.

Edward was talking with his accustomed energy & eloquence. He never paused in his flow of speech, never seemed at a loss for a word, but went on warming & kindling as he proceeded, his voice not boisterously high, but by no means inaudibly low. His hand every now & then raised & pushed amongst the clusters of his gold-streaked auburn ringlets, which he thrust from his forehead as if he could not bear that the intrusion of a single lock should darken its ample alabaster expanse.

At a distance from these & seated in separate recesses, I saw two groups whose appearance somewhat astonished me. One consisted of the lady of Douro-Villa, her children & their governess, Mina Laury; the other of a figure which looked startlingly like the late Marchioness of Douro. She was attired in black velvet, her snow-white arms & neck were uncovered & seemed most brilliantly fair when opposed to the sable folds of her dress. A little girl stood at the back of her chair, & beside her sat a tall gentleman in a half military blue surtout, black stock & white pantaloons. It was Lady Frances Millicent Hume,* her protégée, Euphemia Lindsay, & His Grace, the Duke of Fidena. Surely, thought I, this must be an important family affair which has caused that sightless bird to be summoned from her sequestered bower in Alderwood. I could see her lips move as she sat, but her voice was too low to reach my ear. Fidena bent over her so kindly & tenderly & bowed his stately head to listen when she spoke, & answered her with such condescending gentleness that more than one grateful tear stole from under her closed lids & down her pallid cheek, & from thence dropped like a diamond on her dress. Yet she appeared serene & happy.

Such were the company assembled within the gilded & pictured walls of the north drawing-room at Waterloo-Palace. Three were wanting to complete the tale, & for these I looked in vain. The Duke of Wellington, the Earl of Northangerland, & the King of Angria were absent. At length the former entered. All rose to salute him.

'Well,' said he, regarding them with his cordial glance & smile, 'how are you all? I hope well. It was my intention to have been with you before now, but I was detained by his lordship of Northangerland. Mr Percy, your father would not breathe under the same ceiling with you, so I have been forced to explain to him the matter which has brought you together in my library. He is digesting it now at his leisure, & in a few minutes you shall be favoured with the like information. Now sit down & wait quietly, if you can.'

He then went round, addressing a few words more particularly to each. 'Well, Emily, are you pretty well this evening? So, Millicent, having a little conversation with Fidena, I see. Aye, Julia, don't burst with curiosity, you look as if you could hardly live out the next five minutes. Louisa, you actually seem awake to night.'

'I am longing for a sight of Zamorna,' said she.

'He will come soon,' replied my father.

'Where is he? Where is he? asked several of the ladies Seymour at once.

'Silence, you girls!' observed Fitzroy. 'I say, Uncle, what's become of my cousin?'

Many now gathered round where the Duke stood, all, in fact, except Emily, Millicent, Edward Percy, the Duke of Fidena & the Countess Seymour. Amidst the confusion of question, reply, conjecture, anticipation, apprehension, &c., &c., I, who was standing near the door listening impatiently for approaching footsteps, heard a tread. At first it sounded only as of one person, but as it drew nigher the steps of two were distinctly audible. The folding doors moved a little, then there was a pause, a low & earnest whispering of voices. Again the handle turned, the portals noiselessly expanded, & two gentlemen of very lofty stature, bowing their heads slightly under the arch, crossed the threshold of the saloon. They walked towards the upper end, unobserved by any save me, & the few, above mentioned, who had not joined the general group, & placed themselves side by side near the mantle-piece. Both looked round a moment, then took off their military caps, &, turning to each other, burst into a loud & ringing laugh.

All turned as simultaneously as if the same soul had actuated each individual body. A dead stony silence succeeded the smothered rustle which this movement occasioned, but soon I heard a quick, hurried, throbbing pulsation of hearts, & saw the blood rushing to some cheeks, & fading away from others till it left them white as death.

Amongst the latter was the Queen of Angria. She leaned against the wall. Her eyes grew so fixed & glazed that they lost all expression, & seemed as soulless as those of a corpse. Her lips parted; & damp perspiration began to glisten on her forehead. Well might she be shocked, stunned, astounded! Well might all present be petrified & struck speechless!

Standing erect on the hearth, with the full flow of a blazing chandelier streaming radiantly on him & revealing every feature as distinctly as if a ray of sunlight had marked him like an index,* appeared the Duke of Zamorna, the monarch of Angria. And near at hand, so that it seemed almost to touch him, equally illuminated by that amber lustre, just as distinctly seen, just as clearly defined, appeared his wraith! For by no other name can I term that awful vision which stood beside him face to face—so like in every lineament, limb & motion, that none could tell which was the substance, which the shadow. Flesh & spirit glanced at each other, solemnly sundered: eye flashed to eye, lip curled to lip, brow darkened to brow, each refulgent-head lifted to such a haughty & equal altitude, it seemed as if, of all the brown, crimson lit curls that crowded in such bright & glossy beauty on their temples, not one could boast a hair more or less than the other. There was a universal shock given to every spectator as one of them, advancing a step forward & bowing with cool military grace, said with a lighted & laughing eye, 'Sons & daughters of the race of Wellesley, of Percy, of Fidena, you have all known Arthur Augustus Adrian Wellesley, Duke of Zamorna and Marquis of Douro & King of Angria, long. Admit to your acquaintance his twin-brother Ernest Julius Mornington

Wellesley, Duke of Valdacella, Marquis of Alhama* and heir-apparent of Wellington's Land.'

I cannot describe the scene that followed. I cannot even recollect it distinctly. My senses seemed bewildered. There was a rush towards the hearth, a burst of exclamations, a sudden out-stretching of hands, a sound of greeting & welcome, above which arose the wild, mingled laugh of the simulacri, like a trumpet swell over the roar of a cataract. It subsided soon & then I could look round me.

Mary was standing before them, gazing alternately at each with a look of agitated & puzzled yet pleasurable emotion. She was not left long in doubt. One of them caught her suddenly in his arms, &, as she sank sobbing on his breast, I heard her murmur, 'Then Zamorna is all my own! He has ever loved me! Finic did only his duty! Can I, Oh, Adrian, dare I hope for forgiveness?'

He silently pressed his lips to her forehead, & she, recollecting that many eyes were on them, blushingly turned away her face &, struggling from him, retired to a recess where she sat down as happy as renewed confidence in her lord's love & fealty could make her. Valdacella, as I must call my new-found brother, followed his sister-in-law with his eyes; a keen ironical smile began to dimple the corners of his mouth. He walked up to Miss Laury &, taking from her the little gazelle like creature she held in her lap, stept with it to the Duchess.

'Ahem!' said he, elevating his arched brows. 'You once said this little girl was very, very like her unworthy father, & said it too with a deep-drawn & most grievous sigh. I recollect I, like a prophet, foretold a time should come when you would not sorrow for that likeness. Is it come now, Henrietta? Say yes, or I'll never forgive you.'

'Indeed, but it is!' returned the Duchess, snatching the bright bud of beauty from him & kissing it warmly. 'I love little Emily now all the better for her large Zamornian orbs.'

'Valdacellian, rather you should say,' returned he. 'But here is another coming to claim your regard.'

At that moment Ernest ran up. 'Papa, Papa!' said he. 'May I call you Papa now before other people? And may I call Zamorna uncle? And may this lady go with us to Castle Oronsay? For she seems good and has left off[f] crying & I dare say she's sorry for having been angry with Mamma.'

His father smiled &, turning away, went back to the main cluster of guests. I followed him.

'Brother,' said I, 'you have not yet spoken to me. Was it not yourself who knocked me down in the carriage when we were returning from Almeida's funeral?'

He replied by taking my hand in his & squeezing it with that gentle, insinuating pressure which had, at the time, so awakened my curiosity.

'Dear, dear Ernest,' said I, 'I think I shall love you far better than Arthur.'

He curled his lip & pushed me scornfully off.

And now the demand for explanation, immediate & satisfactory explanation of all the strange, &, as yet, undeveloped mystery began to grow loud & peremptory. Cousins, aunts, uncles, &c., thronged about the Gemini,* overwhelming them with a hundred questions: 'Why had the secret been kept so long? Why had it been kept at all? Who was the Duchess of Valdacella? Where had she and her husband been living? &c., &c., &c.'

'For heaven's sake have mercy on us!' exclaimed Zamorna. 'If you will be silent, I'll tell you all I am able. Perfect satisfaction I cannot promise, but such as I have, give I unto you. Form a ring. Georgiana & Eliza, stand back, & you, Julius, leave off playing the fool with those little ones there. Helen, come to my side. Cecillia, go to William Percy. Nay, you need not blush. I mean nothing particular. Millicent, love, no one seems to be caring for you; take this seat near my aunt. Julius—curse you, get out of the way! And you too, Edward Percy! No hectoring, sir; go & bully Valdacella if you are in the humour. Effie, my fairy, look less bewildered, & put back thy yellow locks, child. Julia Sydney, Aunt Louisa, Agnes, Catherine, Fitzroy, Maria, Lily, my Empress Zenobia—one & all of you—retreat.'

When something like order & silence was restored, he commenced giving the following brief outline of explanation, leaning against the mantle-piece while he spoke, with Valdacella sitting near him & watching sharply for an opportunity to correct or add or deduct as the case might need it.

'On this day, precisely twenty two years ago,* my brother & I first opened our eyes on the troubles & pleasures of this world. What o'clock was it, Father?'

The Duke of Wellington smiled at this appeal from his tall young giant of a son, while another of equal stature at the same moment turned enquiringly to him.

'It was,' he replied, 'just five minutes past nine o'clock p.m. of the eighteenth of July 1812, that a pair of young gentlemen, who were destined severally and unitedly to give the world assurance of a scoundrel, were presented to me under the title of princes of Wellingtonsland.'

'Humph!' said Zamorna, & went on. 'Well, it so happened that Julius here, with the effrontery that marks his character, chose to take precedence of me. By a very fraction of time certainly, but sufficient to entitle him to the birth-right. Like an Esau, as he is, though I am no Jacob, yet, had my mother been a Rebecca & my father an Isaac, I would have been a willing supplanter.'*

'Curse you, no body doubts that!' interrupted Valdacella. 'Get on faster or I'll take the reins out of your hands! In fact, I will without delay. Ladies & gentlemen,' he continued, rising, 'being born, we were as like as peas: having snub noses of precisely the same dimensions, saucer eyes of equal circumference, squalling mouths each of the same cherry shape & colour.'

'I'll make yours of a redder colour & a totally nondescript shape presently,' said Zamorna, endeavouring to push Valdacella back into his seat. Julius, however, struggled against him, & a regular wrestling-match ensued.

'Tiger-cubs!' said my father, half-amused & half angry. 'You are neither of you fit to speak three consecutive words in the presence of a Christian assembly. Isabella, part them while I finish the explanation they've scarcely commenced. As one of them (I don't know which) said, they were each mere repetitions of the other from the moment of their birth, so that the women who took care of them could not tell the difference, any more than the women who now take care of them will be able to do. The instant after they were brought into the world, a tremendous storm broke over the town and Palace of Mornington, & indeed over all Wellingtonsland from one end to the other. I remember a flash of lightning glanced suddenly over their faces when I first looked at them, &, instead of screaming, they opened their large eyes, knit their diminutive brows, & seemed angrily and impudently to defy it. Throughout the night, wind, thunder & rain emulatively howled roared, rattled & splashed amongst the great castellated heap of buildings that compose Mornington-Court. For one that believed in omens, this would have been a fine subject of speculation & conjecture but as I seldom bother my head about such matters (hah, Countess, what a frown!) I went to bed (steady, my lady), & tried to go to sleep (no crime, I trust, Zenobia) as soon as ever the bustle those fellows had occasioned in every part of the house was a little subsided.

'It was dead of night, the very witching hour, all silent, all slumbering, except the elements & probably the new-sprung scions, when a tremendous clattering knock on the great door, accompanied by a furious jangling of the bell, shook the old castle till its very foundations rocked. Presently, after I heard the challenging of sentinels, & the hurrying tread of porters, the bars were withdrawn & the unhappy & belated soul without admitted. Then came a brief period of altercation. It seemed, by the obstreperous swearing & anathemizing, that the aroused menials had not found the traveller to equal the expectations raised by his pompous summons. I heard an old Scotch yeoman, seneschal of the court, Jamie Lindsay by name, the father of Harry,* my son's chancellor ("Hem! Ahem!") exclaim in his broad northern twang, "kick the auld gaberlunzie* out, for his impidence. Wha wad think o' the likes o' him a tinkler-loon, without plack or boddle,* knocking up them whilk are sae mickle his betters as us, Seneschals of the Court & Yeomen of the Dynasty Guard, forbye disturbing my leddy and the princes wi' his unchristian clishma-claver.* Kick him out, I say, and let him dee at the back o' the dyke".

'To this pitiless sentence the voice of Dennis, or as he was commonly called Dinnish Laury, ancestor of Edward Laury, sounded in audible reply: "Och, botheration, ye're not going to turn out the gintleman this a'way are ye? Not but he desarves it well for his din, & bad luck to him! But it's not them wet hard flags that any of us would chuse for a bed this same night. So, be my sowl, Jim, as it would sound ill to have it told that a gintleman had died afore the Duke's threshold, for want of shelter, on the very birth-night of our young lords, sure it's myself'll give him a lodging and a supper any-how. Come along azy, you thief of the wurlt".'

'Arthur,' interrupted the Marquis Wellesley, who had been fidgetting all the while my father uttered this piece of brogue with true Hibernian* accent & emphasis, assumed, I believe, on purpose to discompose his brother & the Countess of Northangerland who, I thought, would have died of the scorn & indignation which she dared not give vent to. 'Arthur, what can you mean by repeating to us the conversation of a couple of low-bred serving-men? Pray get forwards with the main story.'

'Oh,' said Zenobia, 'I beg my lord you will permit your royal relative to indulge in a pleasure he can so seldom enjoy. Let the great Wellington come down from his heroic elevation of king & conqueror, & Sampson-like* deign to make sport before us Philistines by showing us how they talk in Ireland.'

A quiet laugh was the Duke's only answer to this bitter sarcasm. Valdacella took Zenobia's hand &, looking into her face with that bold & mischievous smile which had so distressed Mary, observed, 'Be azy, my jewel, take things calmly & comfortably, & in return let us hear, not how they talk, but how they swear, in your country. I think an oath or two would do you good.'

She turned from him in high disdain & tryed to extricate her hand, but he held it fast.

'No frowning!' he said. 'No airs of imperiousness! If you like Augustus, you must like me; there is no choice for it. And (in a lower tone) this is not the first time I have spoken to you, & held your hand also. Often, often have words of yours, which were intended for the ear of Zamorna, been poured into that of Valdacella. And many others are in the same predicament. There is not one here, man or woman, who has not stood, sat, or walked by my side by sun-light, moon-light or candle-light, unknown to themselves, unknown indeed to the whole world but me & my twin-brother, & not always even to him. Fair Countess, frown, but you cannot hate me.'

'By my life, she shall hate you!' said Zamorna, who, while he spoke, had stolen softly behind him. And at the same instant he delivered him a smart box in the ear. Julius turned. They stood fronting each other. It was an edifying sight. Each face flushed; each brow bent; each lip bit; each eye filled with fierceness. So altogether alike, so undistinguishably similar. Tiger cubs, whelps of one litter, indeed, they looked. Fiercely malignant were their mutual glances for some seconds, but all at once something, probably the resemblance, appeared to strike them in a ludicrous point of view. They burst into a simultaneous laugh &, each bestowing on the other a short but energetic curse, strode to opposite parts of the room.

'Well,' said the Duke of Wellington, 'now that that wise pantomime is over, I will proceed. Scarcely half an hour after the castle gates had been again closed, & when all was subsiding into quietness, a fresh bustle arose in some of the distant chambers. I listened awhile &, finding that it increased instead of diminishing, I got up & dressed myself with all possible expedition. Stepping out into the corridor I was startled by a loud shriek, & skipping down the long lamp-lit passage appeared a creature of low stature & in aspect not much unlike my sons' valets Finic and Pinic, only thinner & more agile. It flung out its arms & came on laughing, shouting & yelling most infernally. I was not long in recognizing little Harry Lindsay, then about ten years old, a vile, mischievous, clever imp, who deserved horse-whipping every day of his life & every hour of that day. I asked him what was the matter—rather sternly I believe, for he shot sideways & stood at a respectful distance.

'"Come to our Minnie," said he still laughing, "my lord Duke, she's clean red-wud,* & sae are the bairns, & sae are all the women-folk. The young rottens* have fastened ilk ane on the ither's trapple* like wull-cats, & there's ane gotten amang 'em wham they canna be redd o', ane that Dinnish Laury axed ben the house. O come, come, dinna lose the sports, I maun away whild the door stands ajow." And off he darted as fast as lightning.

'I followed pretty quickly. The imp entered a chamber at the end of the corridor, whence the noise seemed to proceed. On crossing the threshold of the same room a pretty scene met my eyes. It was well lighted & I suppose, by the appearance of a cradle &c., had been fitted up for the nursery of those two tall gentlemen standing so sullenly apart from each other in separate recesses. In the very centre of the floor, just under the hanging lamp, I saw a pair of span-long candidates for limbo, the royal twins of that day's creation, rolling about in the convulsions of mortal hostility, one on the top of the other, struggling, screaming in short, sharp, shrill squeaks like small beasts of prey, striving with all their might & with an unnatural energy that made them appear possessed, each to strangle his brother. Close beside them stood a tall gaunt man in black, a quaker's broad-brimmed beaver in one hand, which he shyed* every now & then as if instigating them to fiercer combat. His countenance was very grave & serious, & his manner as he bent over them, with his hands spread on his knees, most solemnly yet ludicrously anxious. Harry Lindsay capered about in all directions, clapping his hands, grinning with delight, & exclaiming at intervals, "Huzza! Go it, rottens, that beats cock-fechtin", &c. To complete the picture, Mrs Lindsay sat weeping, wringing her hands, & audibly lamenting without attempting to separate the champions. And in the back-ground were three or four young girls in the same lachrymose condition.

'As soon as surprise would let me, I attempted to come to the rescue, but in vain. I found I could not get beyond a circular line of chalk, about three yards round, which was drawn upon the floor, & yet there was no visible impediment to stop me. So it was, however. Doubt it who dare!

'Well, the Dowager Countess of Mornington, Lady Isabella Wellesley, now Lady Seymour, Lady Isidore Hume,* our friend the Doctor Sir Alexander, then rather different to what he is now, Mr Maxwell,* young Edward Laury, Old Dennis, Jamie Lindsay, & some others were called in, but all to no purpose. I only remember that Lindsay, who was a stern old man, knocked down his son Harry & kicked him senseless out of the room, muttering at the same time something about the wickedness of giving way to carnal delight at a time when God's judgements were visibly upon us. At last the conflict ceased, seemingly from the exhaustion of the principal actors.

'The fellow in black then took them up, placed them in their cradle, walked several times round them, and afterwards in a loud, harsh, singing tone pronounced a sort of spell in rhyme, the purport of which was that, though two scions seemed to have sprung from the parent tree yet, for a length of time they should in reality be but as one; for that it should henceforth be death to them to be looked upon by mortal eyes at the same time, to have even their existence known by more than twelve persons, or to live & associate with each other. He gave to one of them (Arthur, the younger by a minute or two) the privileges of name, fame & existence, adding thereto the penalties consequent on discovery. Ernest he exempted from these, but condemned him to retirement & obscurity. He concluded by declaring that the spell should never be unloosed till the ripe fruit & the opening bud had fallen, till the gift & the giver were both departed. So saying he pulled a black card-case from his pocket, opened it, took out a card, threw it on the table, & with a low bow left the room. The card was like any ordinary note of adress & bore these words: Henri Nicolai,* Flesher & Spirit-Merchant, Styxwharf, Close by the Gates of Hades—18 of July—Cycle of Eternity.

'From that day to this the spell has wrought strongly & efficiently. Nicolai returned at times & renewed it. No human power could avail to counteract his machinations, & the consequence has been what you all see. Alhama was wholly unknown, but by no means wholly unknowing. He has been nearly as much in the society of those here present & in that of the other inhabitants of Verdopolis as his brother Douro. Their past lives are inextricably interwoven; the achievements of one cannot now be distinguished from the achievements of the other; their writings, their military actions, their political manouvers are all blended, all twisted into the same cord, a cord which none but themselves can unravel & which they will not. Even the sins, incidents & adventures of their private life are so confused & mingled that it would require a sharp eye to discover what lies to the charge of Zamorna & what to that of Valdacella. They often quarrel with, because they often cross, each other, yet the sympathy & similarity between their minds & persons is so great that, upon the whole, they agree much better than for the convenience of society it could be wished they did.

'I have now only to introduce my daughter in law, the Duchess of Valdacella, Marchioness of Alhama, & future Queen of Wellingtonsland. Come hither, Emily. She is the only child of the wealthy, aged, & patrician Duke of Morena, whose vast possessions all lie in the north of Sneachie's Land, along the shores of the Genii Sea. Ernest first saw her when he was travelling there, a boy, unattended & unknown. She was romantic; so was he. Alhama, greatly to the gratification of his own vanity, when considered only as a nameless & fortuneless adventurer, he wooed & won the heiress of all the Hills. After he had secured her oath of everlasting fidelity, the young scape-grace condescended to reveal to her the splendid mystery of his birth & doom. Of course that proved a conclusive argument both with herself & father. They were married out of hand, the bride-groom being precisely eighteen on the day of his nuptials, the bride, fifteen. Emily on the mother's side comes of the old Roman-Catholic family of the Ravenswoods & is herself a devout daughter of Holy Kirk. Since her marriage she has resided at Castle Oronsay, situated in the centre of Loch-Sunart, ten miles from the town of Kinrira* & not far from Ben-Carnach, which, with the lands round it, she laid at the feet of her royal husband as a dowry on their wedding-day. There she has had the pleasure of his company about six months out of the twelve, not more, I am certain, the rest of his time having been devoted to playing the fool & the knave with his scoundrel-colleague in Verdopolis, &c. They have two children, Ernest Edward Ravenswood Wellesley, Earl Ravenswood & Viscount Mornington, and Lady Emily Augusta Wellesley, who will be bred up a little wor-shipper of the Virgin, I presume. Now I have done. Cross-question them as you like.'

As the Duke concluded, Valdacella started up.

'Men, women and children,' said he, 'I insist upon it that you do not treat me as a stranger. I know you all, body, mind & estate. Julia, don't look incredulous—I have laughed & talked with thee for hours, almost for days together. Edward Percy, thou knowest that I know thee; so dost thou, sister Henrietta. Georgiana & Eliza, no need of your assumed reserves, I have your proud hearts in my hand. Zenobia, you have as often studied the ancients & devoured the moderns with Julius as with Augustus. My Lady of Fidena, I was the acquaintance of Lily Hart* & not Zamorna. Millicent, Oramare is certainly Zamorna's and so is Alderwood,* & he married his Florence the year after I married my Inez. But for all that, Ernest's hand has often led & guided yo[ur] happiness, of spending a day with you at Alnwick-Castle scarcely a month since. Aunt Louisa, Julius has teased you as often as Arthur. Maria, Douro & Alhama are as one. Since your marriage you have promised to be my sister, & before that Zamorna was not more frequently your Ilderim* than I was. Tell Edith she lectured me with her gentle voice & solemn eyes last night. Tell Arundel, he gave an oath of friendship to me written in his own blood. By heaven, you sha[ll] receive me as an old-long-tryed associate or I'll make some of you repent it!' He ceased.

They all declared their readiness to acquiesce at once in his wishes, & amidst the renewed bustle of congratulations, surprise & pleasure, I beg leave to drop the curtain. . . . .

P.S. A novel can scarcely be called a novel unless it ends in a marriage, therefore I herewith tack to, add & communicate the following post-scriptum, which may perhaps be pronounced the only real piece of information contained in the book.

Yesterday married in St Augustin's Cathedral by the Right Reverend Doctor Stanhope, Primate of all Angria, Captain William Percy of the Royal Life Guards of Angria & aide-de-camp to His Grace the Duke of Zamorna, to Lady Cecillia, daughter of Earl Seymour and niece to the Duke of Wellington. We understand the monarch of Wellingtonsland, to testify his approbation of the bride-groom's conduct in quitting a commercial for a military life, presented him after the ceremony with a check for 100,000 £ sterling. The bride's dowry amounted to 80,000 £, in addition to which she will shortly come into possession of an estate of nearly 3,000 £ a year left her by her uncle the late Colonel Vavasour Seymour, whose favourite neice she was. We have not heard what share of profits the celebrated young eastern merchant Mr Percy has allowed as his brother's share. It is said on the Exchange that Young Rogue declared openly, the clerk's salary should be punctually paid but not a stiver more.*

Vale, reader, Cecillia Seymour & William Percy make a fair & loving couple. Here's health, wealth, happiness & long life to them.

                                        Reader, I am thine
                                        C. A. F. Wellesley

                                                        Charlotte Brontë

July 21st 1834

N.B. I think I have redeemed my pledge. I think I have proved the Duke of Zamorna to be partially insane—by a circuitous & ambiguous road certainly—but still by one in which no traveller can be lost. Reader, if there is no Valdacella, there ought to be one. If the young King of Angria has no alter ego he ought to have such a convenient representative, for no single man, having one corporeal & one spiritual nature, if these were rightly compounded without any mixture of pestilential ingredients, should, in right reason & in the ordinance of common sense & decency, speak & act in that capricious, double-dealing, unfathomable, incomprehensible, torturing, sphinx-like manner which he constantly assumes for reasons known only to himself. I say my brother has too many reins in his hands—believe me or understand me who will. He has gathered the symbols of dominion in a mighty grasp; he strains all the energy, all the power, all the talent of his soul to retain them. He struggles, he ponders, night & day, morning & evening, to hold the empire he has established in so many lands, so many hearts, so many interests. He strives to keep them under one rule & government & to prevent them, if possible, from coming into collision. His brain throbs, his blood boils, when they wince and grow restive under his control—which they often do—for should they once break loose, should the talisman of his influence once fail—! Mighty Genii, draw a veil over the scene! There is a sound, a stun, a crash, a smothered but deep, dull, desperate peal of thunder heard amidst the volumed fold of clouds which hide & pervade futurity. But farther I dare not look, more I dare not hear.

Reader, what say you to the image of a crowned maniac, dying dethroned, forsaken, desolate, in the shrieking gloom of a mad-house. No light around him but the discouloured beam which falls through grated windows on scattered straw; his kingdom gone, his crown a mockery, those who worshipped him dead or estranged: 'All earth a dreary void to him, All heaven a cloud of gloom.'*

O, Zamorna! Think not of the field of battle, think not of the trampling of horses & garments rolled in blood, nor of the death-bed amids[t] piles of slain, with 'Victory' for the last sound lingering in thine ear, and a song of triumph for thy burial hymn. Trumpets may pour the dirge for the captains of thine armies, 'Arise' may be their battle-shout, & thy sun their exalting standard,* while thou art mouldering in earth, utterly forgotten or remembered only to be despised—Zamorna, a young man of promise. He attempted, however, more than he could perform; his affairs grew embarrassed & perplexed; he became insane & died in a private mad-house at the early age of twenty-two.

C. Brontë
July 21st 1834

'We wove a web in childhood'

We wove a web in childhood,
A web of sunny air;
We dug a spring in infancy
Of water pure and fair.

We sowed in youth a mustard seed,*
We cut an almond rod;*
We are now grown up to riper age—
Are they withered in the sod?

Are they blighted failed and faded?
Are they mouldered back to clay?
For life is darkly shaded
And its joys fleet fast away.

Faded! The web is still of air
But how its folds are spread,
And from its tints of crimson clear
How deep a glow is shed.
The light of an Italian sky
Where clouds of sunset lingering lie
Is not more ruby-red.

But the spring was under a mossy stone,
Its jet may gush no more.
Heark! Sceptic bid thy doubts be gone,
Is that a feeble roar
Rushing around thee? Lo! The tides
Of waves where armed fleets may ride
Sinking and swelling, frowns & smiles,
An ocean with a thousand isles
And scarce a glimpse of shore.

The mustard-seed on distant land
Bends down a mighty tree,*
The dry unbudding almond-wand
Has touched eternity.
There came a second miracle

Such as on Aaron's sceptre fell,*
And sapless grew like life from death:
Bud, bloom & fruit in mingling wreath
All twined the shrivelled off-shoot round,
As flowers lie on the lone grave-mound.*

Dream that stole o'er us in the time
When life was in its vernal clime,
Dream that still faster o'er us steals
As the mild star of spring declining,
The advent of that day reveals
That glows in Sirius'* fiery shining—
Oh! as thou swellest and as the scenes
Cover this cold world's darkest features,
Stronger each change my spirit weans
To bow before thy god-like creatures.

When I sat 'neath a strange roof-tree*
With nought I knew or loved around me,
Oh how my heart shrank back to thee—
Then I felt how fast thy ties had bound me.

That hour, that bleak hour when the day
Closed in the cold autumnal gloaming,
When the clouds hung so bleak & drear & grey
And a bitter wind through their folds was roaming,

There shone no fire on the cheerless hearth,
In the chamber there gleam'd no taper's twinkle.
Within neither sight nor sound of mirth,
Without but the blast & the sleet's chill sprinkle.

Then sadly I longed for my own dear home,
For a sight of the old familiar faces.
I drew near the casement & sat in its gloom
And looked forth on the tempest's desolate traces.

Ever anon that wolfish breeze
The dead leaves & sere from their boughs was shaking,

And I gazed on the hills through the leafless trees
And felt as if my heart was breaking.

Where was I ere an hour had past:
Still list'ning to that dreary blast,
Still in that mirthless lifeless room
Cramped, chilled & deadened by its gloom?

No! Thanks to that bright, darling dream,
Its power had shot one kindling gleam,
Its voice had sent one wakening cry
And bade me lay my sorrows by,
And called me earnestly to come
And borne me to my moorland home.
I heard no more the senseless sound
Of task & chat that hummed around;
I saw no more that grisly night
Closing the day's sepulchral light.

The vision's spell had deepened o'er me:
Its lands, its scenes were spread before me.
In one short hour a hundred homes
Had roofed me with their lordly domes,
And I had sat by fires whose light
Flashed wide o'er halls of regal height,
And I had seen those come & go
Whose forms gave radiance to the glow.
And I had heard the matted floor
Of ante-room & corridor
Shake to some half-remembered tread,
Whose haughty firmness woke even dread,
As through the curtained portal strode
Some spurred & fur-wrapped demi-god,*
Whose ride through that tempestuous night
Had added somewhat of a frown
To brows that shadowed eyes of light,
Fit to flash fire from Scythian crown,*
Till sweet salute from lady gay
Chased that unconscious scowl away.
And then, the savage fur-cap doffed,

The Georgian mantle* laid aside,
The satrap* stretched on cushion soft,
His lov'd & chosen by his side,
That hand, that in its horseman's glove
Looked fit for nought but bridle rein,
Caresses now its lady-love
With fingers white that shew no stain
They got in hot & jarring strife,
When hate or honour warred with life—
Nought redder than the roseate ring
That glitters fit for eastern king.

In one proud household, where the sound
Of life & stir rang highest round,
Hall within hall burned starry bright
And light gave birth to richer light.
Grandly its social tone seemed strung,
Wildly its keen excitement rung,
And hundreds mid its splendors free
Moved with unfettered liberty,
Not gathered to a lordly feast,
But each a self-invited guest—
It was the kingly custom there
That each at will the house should share.

I saw the master not alone,
He crossed me in a vast saloon,
Just seen, then sudden vanishing
As laughingly he joined the ring
That closed around a dazzling fire
& listened to a trembling lyre.
He was in light & licensed mood,
Fierce gaiety had warmed his blood,
Kindled his dark & brilliant eye,
And toned his lips' full melody

I saw him take a little child
That stretched its arms & called his name.
It was his own, & half he smiled
As the small eager creature came

Nestling upon his stately breast,
And its fair curls & forehead laying
To what but formed a fevered nest—
Its father's cheek where curls were straying
Thicker & darker on a bloom
Whose hectic brightness boded doom.*

He kissed it, and a deeper blush
Rose to the already crimson flush,
And a wild sadness flung its grace
Over his grand & Roman face.
The little, heedless, lovely thing
Lulled on the bosom of a king
Its fingers mid his thick locks twining,
Pleased with their rich & wreathed shining,
Dreamed not what thoughts his soul were haunting,
Nor why his heart so high was panting.

I went out in a summer night,
My path lay o'er a lonesome waste;
Slumb'ring & still in clear moon-light,
A noble road was o'er it traced.

Far as the eye of man could see
No shade upon its surface stirred,
All slept in mute tranquillity,
Unbroke by step or wind or word.

That waste had been a battle-plain;
Head-stones were reared in the waving fern.
There they had buried the gallant slain
That dust to its own dust might return.*

And one black marble monument
Rose where the heather was rank & deep;
Its base was hid with the bracken & bent,*
Its sides were bare to the night-wind's sweep.

A Victory carved in polished stone,
Her trumpet to her cold lips held,

And strange it seemed as she stood alone
That not a single note was blown,
That not a whisper swelled.

It was Camalia's ancient field*—
I knew the desert well,
For traced around a sculptured shield
These words the summer moon revealed:
  'Here brave Macarthy fell!
The men of Keswick leading on.
Their first, their best, their noblest one,
  He did his duty well.'*

I now heard the far clatter of hoofs on the hard & milk-white road, the great high-way that turns in a bend from Free-Town* and stretches on to the West. Two horse-men rode slowly up in the moonlight & leaving the path struck deep into the moor, galloping through heather to their chargers' breasts.

'Hah!' said one of them as he flung himself from his steed & walked forward to the monument. 'Hah! Edward, here's my kinsman's tomb.* Now for the bugle sound! He must have his requiem or he will trouble me. The bell tolled for him in Alderwood on the eve of the conflict. I heard it myself &, though then but a very little child, I remember well how my mother trembled as she sat in the drawing-room of the manor house & listened while that unaccountable & supernatural sound was booming so horribly through the woods. Edward begin.'

Never shall I, Charlotte Brontë, forget what a voice of wild & wailing music now came thrillingly to my mind's—almost to my body's—ear; nor how distinctly I, sitting in the schoolroom at Roe Head, saw the Duke of Zamorna leaning against that obelisk, with the mute marble Victory above him, the fern waving at his feet, his black horse turned loose grazing among the heather, the moonlight so mild & so exquisitely tranquil, sleeping upon that vast & vacant road, & the African sky quivering & shaking with stars expanded above all. I was quite gone. I had really utterly forgot where I was and all the gloom & cheerlessness of my situation. I felt myself breathing quick and short as I beheld the Duke lifting up his sable crest, which undulated as the plume of a hearse waves to the wind, & knew that that music which seems as mournfully triumphant as the scriptural verse

'Oh Grave where is thy sting;
   Oh Death where is thy victory'*

was exciting him & quickening his ever rapid pulse.

'Miss Brontë, what are you thinking about?' said a voice that dissipated all the charm, & Miss Lister* thrust her little, rough black head into my face! 'Sic transit' &c.

C Brontë Dec^{br} 19th
Haworth 1835

THE ROE HEAD JOURNAL

1. 'Well, here I am at Roe Head'

Well, here I am at Roe-Head. It is seven o'clock at night. The young ladies are all at their lessons, the school-room is quiet, the fire is low. A stormy day is at this moment passing off in a murmuring and bleak night. I now assume my own thoughts. My mind relaxes from the stretch on which it has been for the last twelve hours & falls back onto the rest which no-body in this house knows of but myself. I now, after a day of weary wandering, return to the ark which for me floats alone on the face of this world's desolate & boundless deluge.* It is strange. I cannot get used to the ongoings that surround me. I fulfil my duties strictly & well. I must, so to speak. If the illustration be not profane—as God was not in the wind nor the fire nor the earth-quake so neither is my heart in the task, the theme or the exercise. It is the still small voice* alone that comes to me at eventide, that which like a breeze with a voice in it [comes] over the deeply blue hills & out of the now leafless forests & from the cities on distant river banks of a far & bright continent.* It is that which takes my spirit & engrosses all my living feelings, all my energies which are not merely mechanical &, like Haworth & home, wakes sensations which lie dormant elsewhere.

Last night I did indeed lean upon the thunder-wakening wings of such a stormy blast as I have seldom heard blow, & it whirled me away like heath in the wilderness* for five seconds of ecstasy. And as I sat by myself in the dining-room while all the rest were at tea, the trance seemed to descend on a sudden, & verily this foot trod the war-shaken shores of the Calabar & these eyes saw the defiled & violated Adrianopolis,* shedding its lights on the river from lattices whence the invader looked out & was not darkened.* I went through a trodden garden whose groves were crushed down. I ascended a great terrace, the marble surface of which shone wet with rain where it was not darkened by the crowds of dead leaves, which were now showered on & now swept off by the vast & broken boughs which swung in the wind above them. Up I went to the wall of the palace, to the line of latticed arches which shimmered in light. Passing along quick as thought, I glanced at what the internal glare revealed through the crystal.

There was a room lined with mirrors, & with lamps on tripods, & very [?decorated] & splendid couches, & carpets, & large half lucid vases white as snow, thickly embossed with whiter mouldings, & one large picture in a frame of massive beauty representing a young man* whose gorgeous & shining locks seemed as if they would wave on the breath & whose eyes were half hid by the hand, carved in ivory, that shaded them & supported the awful looking coron[al]* head. A solitary picture, too great to admit of a companion—a likeness to be remembered, full of beauty not displayed, for it seemed as if the form had been copied so often in all imposing attitudes that at length the painter, satiated with its luxuriant perfection, had resolved to conceal half & make the imperial giant bend & hide, under his cloud like tresses, the radiance he was grown tired of gazing on.

Often had I seen this room before and felt, as I looked at it, the simple and exceeding magnificence of its single picture, its five colossal cups of sculptured marble, its soft carpets of most deep and brilliant hues, & its mirrors broad, lofty & liquidly clear. I had seen it in the stillness of evening when the lamps so quietly & steadily burnt in the tranquil air & when their rays fell upon but one living figure: a young lady,* who generally at that time appeared sitting on a low sofa, a book in her hand, her head bent over it as she read, her light brown hair dropping in loose & unwaving curls, her dress falling to the floor as she sat in sweeping folds of silk. All stirless about her, except her heart softly heaving under her dark satin bodice, & all silent, except her regular and very gentle respiration. The haughty sadness of grandeur beamed out of her intent, fixed, hazel eye, &, though so young, I always felt as if I dared not have spoken to her, for my life. How lovely were the lines of her straight, delicate features. How exquisite was her small & rosy mouth. But how very proud her white brow, spacious & wreathed with ringlets, & her neck, which though so slender had the superb curve of a queen's about the snowy throat! I knew why she chose to be alone at that hour & why she kept that shadow in the golden frame to gaze on her, & why she turned sometimes to her mirrors & looked to see if her loveliness & her adornments were quite perfect.

However, this night she was not visible—no—but neither was her bower void. The red ray of the fire flashed upon a table covered with wine flasks, some drained and some brimming with the crimson juice. The cushions of a voluptuous ottoman, which had often supported her slight fine form, were crushed by a dark bulk flung upon them in drunken prostration. Aye, where she had lain imperially robed and decked with pearls, every waft of her garments as she moved diffusing perfume, her beauty slumbering & still glowing as dreams of him for whom she kept herself in such hallowed & shrine-like separation wandered over her

soul, on her own silken couch a swarth & sinewy moor intoxicated to
ferocious insensibility had stretched his athletic limbs, weary with was-
sail and stupified with drunken sleep. I knew it to be Quashia himself,
and well could I guess why he had chosen the Queen of Angria's sanc-
tuary for the scene of his solitary revelling.* While he was full before
my eyes, lying in his black dress on the disordered couch, his sable
hair dishevelled on his forehead, his tusk-like teeth glancing vindic-
tively through his parted lips, his brown complexion flushed with wine
& his broad chest heaving wildly as the breath issued in snorts from
his distended nostrils, while I watched the fluttering of his white shirt
ruffles starting through the more than half-unbuttoned waistcoat &
beheld the expression of his Arabian countenance savagely exulting*
even in sleep—Quamina, triumphant lord in the halls of Zamorna! in
the bower of Zamorna's lady!—while this apparition was before me, the
dining-room door opened and Miss W[ooler]* came in with a plate of
butter in her hand. 'A very stormy night, my dear!' said she.

'It is, ma'am,' said I.

Feby the 4th 1836

2. 'Now as I have a little bit of time'

*Friday afternoon**
Now as I have a little bit of time, there being no French lessons this
afternoon, I should like to write something. I can't enter into any continued narrative—my mind is not settled enough for that—but if I
could call up some slight & pleasant sketch, I would amuse myself by
jotting it down.

Let me consider the other day. I appeared to realize a delicious,
hot day in the most burning height of summer. A gorgeous afternoon
of idleness & enervation descending upon the hills of our Africa. An
evening enfolding a sky of profoundly deep blue & fiery gold about the
earth.

Dear me! I keep heaping epithets together and I cannot describe
what I mean. I mean a day whose rise, progress & decline seem
made of sunshine. As you are travelling you see the wide road before
you, the fields on each side & the hills far, far off, all smiling, glowing in the same amber light, and you feel such an intense heat, quite
incapable of chilling damp or even refreshing breeze. A day when fruits
visibly ripen, when orchards appear suddenly to change from green to
gold.

Such a day I saw flaming over the distant Sydenham Hills in Hawkscliffe Forest.* I saw its sublime sunset pouring beams of crimson through the magnificent glades. It seemed to me that the war was over,* that the trumpet had ceased but a short time since, and that its last tones had been pitched on a triumphant key. It seemed as if exciting events—tidings of battles, of victories, of treaties, of meetings of mighty powers—had diffused an enthusiasm over the land that made its pulses beat with feverish quickness. After months of bloody toil, a time of festal rest was now bestowed on Angria. The noblemen, the generals and the gentlemen were at their country seats, & the Duke, young but war-worn, was at Hawkscliffe.

A still influence stole out of the stupendous forest, whose calm was now more awful than the sea-like rushing that swept through its glades in time of storm. Groups of deer appeared & disappeared silently amongst the prodigious stems, & now & then a single roe glided down the savannah park, drank of the Arno & fleeted back again.

Two gentlemen in earnest conversation were walking in St Mary's Grove, & their deep commingling tones, very much subdued, softly broke the silence of the evening. Secret topics seemed to be implied in what they said, for the import of their words was concealed from every chance listener by the accents of a foreign tongue. All the soft vowels of Italian articulation* flowed from their lips, as fluently as if they had been natives of the European Eden. 'Henrico' was the appellative by which the taller & the younger of the two addressed his companion, & the other replied by the less familiar title of 'Monsignore'.* That young signore, or lord, often looked up at the Norman towers of Hawkscliffe, which rose even above the lofty elms of St Mary's Grove. The sun was shining on their battlements, kissing them with its last beam that rivalled in hue the fire-dyed banner* hanging motionless above them.

'Henrico,' said he, speaking still in musical Tuscan, 'this is the 29th of June.* Neither you nor I ever saw a fairer day. What does it remind you of? All such sunsets have associations.'

Henrico knitted his stern brow in thought & at the same time fixed his very penetrating black eye on the features of his noble comrade, which, invested by habit and nature with the aspect of command & pride, were at this sweet hour relaxing to the impassioned & fervid expression of romance. 'What does it remind you of, my lord?' said he briefly.

'Ah! Many things, Henrico! Ever since I can remember, the rays of the setting sun have acted on my heart, as they did on Memnon's wondrous statue.* The strings always vibrate; sometimes the tones swell in harmony, sometimes in discord. They play a wild air just now—but sweet & ominously plaintive. Henrico, can you imagine what I feel when I look into the dim & gloomy vistas of this my forest & at yonder turrets which the might of my own hands has raised—not the halls of my ancestors, like hoary Mornington? Calm diffuses over this wide wood a power to stir & thrill the mind such as words can never express. Look at the red west! The sun is gone, & it is fading to gas & into those mighty groves, supernaturally still & full of gathering darkness. Listen how the Arno moans!'

3. 'All this day I have been in a dream'

Friday Augst 11th*—All this day I have been in a dream, half miserable & half ecstatic: miserable because I could not follow it out uninterruptedly; ecstatic because it shewed almost in the vivid light of reality the ongoings of the infernal world.* I had been toiling for nearly an hour with Miss Lister, Miss Marriott & Ellen Cook,* striving to teach them the distinction between an article and a substantive. The parsing lesson* was completed, a dead silence had succeeded it in the school-room, & I sat sinking from irritation & weariness into a kind of lethargy.

The thought came over me: am I to spend all the best part of my life in this wretched bondage, forcibly suppressing my rage at the idleness, the apathy and the hyperbolical & most asinine stupidity of those fat-headed oafs, and on compulsion assuming an air of kindness, patience & assiduity? Must I from day to day sit chained to this chair, prisoned with in these four bare walls, while these glorious summer suns are burning in heaven & the year is revolving in its richest glow & declaring at the close of every summer day [that] the time I am losing will never come again?

Stung to the heart with this reflection, I started up & mechanically walked to the window. A sweet August morning was smiling without. The dew was not yet dried off the field. The early shadows were stretching cool & dim from the hay-stack & the roots of the grand old oaks & thorns scattered along the sunk fence. All was still, except the murmur of the scrubs about me over their tasks. I flung up the sash. An uncertain sound of inexpressible sweetness came on a dying gale from the south. I looked in that direction. Huddersfield & the hills beyond it were all veiled in blue mist; the woods of Hopton & Heaton Lodge were clouding the water's-edge; & the Calder,* silent but bright, was shooting among them like a silver arrow. I listened. The sound sailed full & liquid down the descent. It was the bells of Huddersfield parish church. I shut the window & went back to my seat.

Then came on me, rushing impetuously, all the mighty phantasm that we had conjured from nothing to a system strong as some religious creed. I felt as if I could have written gloriously—I longed to write. The spirit of all Verdopolis, of all the mountainous North, of all the woodland West, of all the river-watered East* came crowding into my mind. If I had had time to indulge it, I felt that the vague sensations of that moment would have settled down into some narrative better at least than any thing I ever produced before. But just then a dolt came up with a lesson. I thought I should have vomited.

In the afternoon, Miss E— L—* was trigonometrically œcumenical* about her French lessons. She nearly killed me between the violence of the irritation her horrid wilfulness excited and the labour it took to subdue it to a moderate appearance of calmness. My fingers trembled as if I had had twenty four hours tooth-ache, & my spirits felt worn down to a degree of desperate despondency. Miss Wooler tried to make me talk at tea time and was exceedingly kind to me, but I could not have roused if she had offered me worlds. After tea we took a long weary walk. I came back abymé* to the last degree, for Miss L— & Miss M—t had been boring me with their vulgar familiar trash all the time we were out. If those girls knew how I loathe their company, they would not seek mine so much as they do.

The sun had set nearly a quarter of an hour before we returned and it was getting dusk. The ladies went into the school-room to do their exercises & I crept up to the bed-room to be <u>alone</u> for the first time that day. Delicious was the sensation I experienced as I laid down on the spare-bed & resigned myself to the luxury of twilight & solitude. The stream of thought, checked all day, came flowing free & calm along its channel. My ideas were too shattered to form any defined picture, as they would have done in such circumstances at home, but detached thoughts soothingly flitted round me, & unconnected scenes occurred and then vanished, producing an effect certainly strange but, to me, very pleasing.

The toil of the day, succeeded by this moment of divine leisure, had acted on me like opium & was coiling about me a disturbed but fascinating spell, such as I never felt before. What I imagined grew morbidly vivid. I remember I quite seemed to see, with my bodily eyes, a lady standing in the hall of a gentleman's house, as if waiting for some one.

It was dusk, & there was the dim outline of antlers with a hat & a rough great-coat upon them. She had a flat candle-stick in her hand & seemed coming from the kitchen or some such place. She was very handsome. It is not often we can form from pure idea faces so individually fine. She had black curls, hanging rather low on her neck, & very blooming skin, & dark, anxious looking eyes. I imagined it the sultry close of a summer's day, and she was dressed in muslin—not at all romanticly—a flimsy, printed fabric with large sleeves & a full skirt.

As she waited, I most distinctly heard the front door open & saw the soft moonlight disclosed upon a lawn outside, & beyond the lawn at a distance I saw a town with lights twinkling through the gloaming. Two or three gentlemen entered, one of whom I knew by intuition to be called Dr Charles Brandon and another William Locksley Esqr.* The doctor was a tall, handsomely built man, habited in cool, ample looking white trowsers and a large straw hat, which, being set on one side, shewed a great deal of dark hair & a sun-burnt but smooth and oval cheek. Locksley & the other went into an inner room, but Brandon stayed a minute in the hall. There was a bason of water on a slab, & he went & washed his hands, while the lady held the light.

'How has Ryder borne the operation?' she asked.

'Very cleverly. He'll be well in three weeks,' was the reply. 'But Lucy won't do for a nurse at the hospital. You must take her for your head servant, to make my cambric fronts & handkerchiefs, & to wash & iron your lace aprons. Little silly thing, she fainted at the very sight of the instruments.'

Whilst Brandon spoke, a dim concatenation of ideas describing a passage in some individual's life, a varied scene in which persons & events, features & incidents, revolved in misty panorama,* entered my mind. The mention of the hospital, of Ryder, of Lucy, each called up a certain set of reminiscences, or rather fancies. It would be endless to tell all that was at that moment suggested.

Lucy first appeared before me as sitting at the door of a lone cottage on a kind of moorish waste, sorrowful & sickly—a young woman with those mild, regular features that always interest us, however poorly set off by the meanness of surrounding adjuncts. It was a calm afternoon. Her eyes were turned towards a road crossing the heath. A speck appeared on it far, far away. Lucy smiled to herself as it dawned into view, & while she did so there was some thing about her melancholy brow, her straight nose & faded bloom that reminded me of one who might, for anything I at that instant knew, be dead & buried under the newly plotted sod.* It was this likeness & the feeling of its existence that had called Dr Brandon so far from his bodily circle & that made him now, when he stood near his patient, regard her meek face, turned submissively & gratefully to him, with tenderer kindness than he bestowed on employers of aristocratic rank & wealth.

No more. I have not time to work out the vision. A thousand things were connected with it, a whole country, statesmen & kings, a revolution, thrones & princedoms subverted & reinstated.*

Meantime, the tall man washing his bloody hands in a bason & the dark beauty standing by with a light remained pictured on my mind's eye with irksome & alarming distinctness. I grew frightened at the vivid glow of the candle, at the reality of the lady's erect & symmetrical figure, of her spirited & handsome face,* of her anxious eye watching Brandon's & seeking out its meaning, diving for its real expression through the semblance of severity that habit & suffering had given to his stern aspect.

I felt confounded & annoyed. I scarcely knew by what. At last I became aware of a feeling like a heavy weight laid across me. I knew I was wide awake & that it was dark, & that, moreover, the ladies were now come into the room to get their curl-papers. They perceived me lying on the bed & I heard them talking about me. I wanted to speak, to rise—it was impossible. I felt that this was a frightful predicament—that it would not do. The weight pressed me as if some huge animal had flung itself across me.* A horrid apprehension quickened every pulse I had. 'I must get up', I thought, & I did so with a start. I have had enough of morbidly vivid realizations. Every advantage has its corresponding disadvantage. Tea's read[y]. Miss Wooler is impatient.

October 14th 1836

4. 'I'm just going to write because I cannot help it'

I'm just going to write because I cannot help it. Wiggins might indeed talk of scriblomania* if he were to see me just now, encompassed by the bulls (query calves of Bashan*), all wondering why I write with my eyes shut—staring, gaping. Hang their astonishment! A. C—k on one side of me, E. L—r on the other and Miss W—r* in the back-ground. Stupidity the atmosphere, school-books the employment, asses the society.* What in all this is there to remind me of the divine, silent, unseen land of thought, dim now & indefinite as the dream of a dream, the shadow of a shade?

There is a voice,* there is an impulse that wakens up that dormant power, which in its torpidity I sometimes think dead. That wind, pouring in impetuous current through the air, sounding wildly, unremittingly from hour to hour, deepening its tone as the night advances, coming not in gusts, but with a rapid gathering stormy swell.* That wind I know is heard at this moment far away on the moors at Haworth. Branwell & Emily hear it, and as it sweeps over our house, down the church-yard & round the old church, they think perhaps of me & Anne.*

Glorious! That blast was mighty. It reminded me of Northangerland.* There was something so merciless in the heavier rush that made the very house groan as if it could scarce bear this acceleration of impetus. O, it has wakened a feeling that I cannot satisfy! A thousand wishes rose at its call which must die with me, for they will never be fulfilled. Now I should be agonized if I had not the dream to repose on. Its existences, its forms, its scenes do fill a little of the craving vacancy. Hohenlinden! Childe Harold! Flodden Field! The burial of Moore!* Why cannot the blood rouse the heart, the heart wake the head, the head prompt the hand* to do things like these? Stuff! Pho!

I wonder if Branwell has really killed the Duchess.* Is she dead? Is she buried? Is she alone in the cold earth on this dreary night, with the ponderous, gold coffin plate on her breast, under the black pavement of a church, in a vault closed up with lime mortar? Nobody near where she lies—she who was watched through months of suffering as she lay on her bed of state now quite forsaken because her eyes are closed, her lips sealed and her limbs cold & rigid. The stars, as they are fitfully revealed through severed clouds, looking in through the church windows on her monument.

A set of wretched thoughts are rising in my mind. I hope she's alive still, partly because I can't abide to think how hopelessly & cheerlessly she must have died, and partly because her removal, if it has taken place, must have been to North—d like the quenching of the last spark that averted utter darkness.*

What are Zenobia's* thoughts among the stately solitudes of Ennerdale? She's by herself now in a large, lofty room that thirty years ago used nightly to look as bright & gay as it now looks lone & dreary. Her mother was one of the beauties of the West. She's sleeping in the dust of a past generation. And there is her portrait—a fine woman at her toilette. Vanity dictated that attitude. Paulina* was noted for her profuse raven tresses, and the artist has shewn her combing them all out, the heavy locks uncurled & loose, falling over her white arms as she lifts them to arrange the dishevelled masses. There for nine & twenty years has that lovely Spaniard sat, looking down on the saloon that used to be her drawing-room. Can she see her descendant, a nobler edition of her self—the woman of a haughty & violent spirit—seated at that table medi[t]ating how to save her pride & crush her feelings? Zenobia is not easily warped by imagination. Yet she feels unconsciously the power of ——*

5. 'My compliments to the weather'

My compliments to the weather. I wonder what it would be at? Snow and sunshine? But, however, let me forget it. I've sat down for the purpose of calling up spirits from the vasty deep* and holding half an hour's converse with them. Hush! there's a knock at the gates of thought and Memory ushers in the visitors. The visitors! There's only one: a tall gentleman with a presence, in a blue surtout & jane trowsers.*

'How do you do, sir? I'm glad to see you, take a seat. Very uncommon weather this, sir! How do you stand the changes?'

The gentleman, instead of answering, slowly divests his neck & chin of the folds of a large black silk handkerchief, deposits the light cane he carried in a corner, assumes a seat with deliberate state &, bending his light-brown, beetling eye-brows over his lighter blue, menacing eyes, looks fixedly at me.

'Scarcely civil, sir. What's your name?'

'John of the Highlands,'* answers the gentleman in a voice whose depth of base makes the furniture vibrate. 'John of the Highlands. You called me and I am come. Now what's your business?'

'Your servant Mr Saunderson,'* says I. 'Beg your pardon for not recognizing you at once, but really you've grown so exceedingly mild-looking and unsaturnine since I saw you last, and you do look so sweet-tempered. How's Mrs Saunderson, and how are the old people & the dear little hope of all the Saundersons?'

'Pretty well, thank ye. I'll take a little snuff, if ye have any—my box is empty.' So saying, Mr Saunderson held out his empty gold mull, which I speedily filled with black rappee.* The conversation then proceeded.

'What news is stirring in your parts?' I asked.

'Nothing special,' was the answer. 'Only March has left the Angrians madder than ever.'*

'What, they're fighting still are they?'

'Fighting! Aye and every man amongst them has sworn by his hilts* that he'll continue fighting whilst he has two rags left stitched together upon his back.'

'In that case I should think peace would soon be restored,' said I.

Mr Saunderson winked. 'A very sensible remark,' said he. 'Mr Wellesley Senr* made me the fellow to it last time I saw him.'

'The sinews of war not particularly strong in the East?' I continued.

M^r S—n winked again and asked for a pot of porter. I* sent for the beverage to the Robin-Hood across the way, & when it was brought Mr Saunderson, after blowing off the froth, took a deep draught to the health of 'the brave and shirtless!' I added in a low voice 'to the vermined & victorious!' He heard me & remarked with a grave nod of approbation, 'very jocose'.

After soaking a little while, each in silence, Mr Saunderson spoke again—*

Mr Saunderson did <u>not</u> speak again. He departed like the fantastic creation of a dream. I was called to hear a lesson, & when I returned to my desk again I found the mood which had suggested that allegorical whim was irrevocably gone. A fortnight has elapsed since I wrote the above. This is my first half hour's leisure since then and now, once more on a dull Saturday afternoon, I sit down to try to summon round me the dim shadows, not of coming events, but of incidents long departed, of feelings, of pleasures, whose exquisite relish I sometimes fear it will never be my lot again to taste.

How few would believe that from sources purely imaginary such happiness could be derived. Pen cannot pourtray the deep interest of the scenes, of the continued trains of events, I have witnessed in that little room with the low, narrow bed & bare, white-washed walls, twenty miles away.* What a treasure is thought! What a privilege is reverie. I am thankful that I have the power of solacing myself with the dream of creations whose reality I shall never behold. May I never lose that power! May I never feel it growing weaker! If I should, how little pleasure will life afford me—its lapses of shade are so wide, so gloomy, its gleams of sunshine so limited & dim!

Remembrance yields up many a fragment of past twilight hours spent in that little, unfurnished room. There have I sat on the low bed-stead, my eyes fixed on the window, through which appeared no other landscape than a monotonous stretch of moorland, a grey church tower rising from the centre of a church-yard so filled with graves that the rank weed & coarse grass scarce had room to shoot up between the monu-ments. Over these hangs in the eye of memory a sky of such grey clouds as often veil the chill close of an October day, & low on the horizon, glances at intervals through the rack* the orb of a lurid & haloed moon.

Such was the picture that threw its reflection upon my eye, but com-municated no impression to my heart. The mind knew but did not feel its existence. It was away. It had launched on a distant voyage. Haply it was nearing the shores of some far & unknown island, under whose cliffs no bark had ever before cast anchor. In other words, a long tale was perhaps then evolving itself in my mind, the history of an ancient & aristocratic family—the legendary records of its origin, not pre-served in writing but delivered from the lips of old retainers, floating in tradition up & down the woods & vales of the earldom or dukedom or barony. The feeling of old oak avenues planted by the ancestors of three hundred years ago, of halls neglected by the present descendants, of galleries peopled with silent pictures, no longer loved & valued, for none now live who remember the substance of those shadows.

Then with a parting glance at the family-church, with a thought reverting to the wide, deep vault beneath its pavement, my dream shifted to some distant city, some huge, imperial metropolis, where the descendants of the last nobleman, the young lords & ladies, shine in gay circles of patricians. Dazzled with the brilliancy of courts, haply with the ambition of senates, sons & daughters have almost forgotten the groves where they were born & grew. As I saw them—stately & hand-some, gliding through those saloons where many other well-known forms crossed my sight, where there were faces looking up, eyes smil-ing & lips moving in audible speech, that I knew better almost than my brother & sisters, yet whose voices had never woke an echo on this world, whose eyes had never gazed upon that day-light—what glori-ous associations crowded upon me, what excitement heated my face & made me clasp my hands in ecstasy!

I too forgot the ancient country seat. I forgot the great woods with their lonely glades peopled only by deer. I thought no more of the Gothic-chapel under whose floor mouldered the bones of a hundred barons. What then to me were the ballads of the grand-mothers, the tales of the grey-headed old men of that remote village on the Annesley Estate?*

I looked at Lady Amelia, the eldest daughter, standing by a wide, lofty window, descending by marble steps on to a sunshiny lawn amidst a flush of rose-trees in bloom, a lady of handsome features & full growth. Just now she is exquisitely beautiful, though that extreme brightness

which excitement & happiness are bestowing will soon pass away. I see
the sweep of her light, summer dress, the fall & waving of her curled
hair on her neck, the unaccustomed glow of her complexion & shine
of her smiling eyes. I see them now—she is looking round at that ring
of patricians. She is hearing her brother tell over the names & titles of
many that are become the darlings of fame, the monarchs of mind. She
has been introduced to some. As they pass, they speak to her.

I hear them speak as well as she does. I see distinctly their figures,
and though alone I experience all the feelings of one admitted for the
first time into a grand circle of classic beings, recognizing by tone, gesture and aspect hundreds whom I never saw before, but whom I have
heard of and read of many a time. And is not this enjoyment? I am
not accustomed to such magnificence as surrounds me, to the gleam
of such large mirrors, to the beauty of marble figures, to soft, foreign
carpets, to long, wide rooms, to lofty gilded ceilings. I know nothing of
people of rank & distinction, yet there they are before me in throngs,
in crowds. They come; they go; they speak; they beckon; & that not like
airy phantoms but as noblemen & ladies of flesh & blood.

There is an aim in all. I know the house. I know the square it stands
in. I passed through it this day. I ascended the steps leading to the
vestibule. I saw the porter at the door. I went along hall & gallery till
I reached this saloon. Is it not enjoyment to gaze around upon those
changeful countenances, to mark the varied features of those high-born
& celebrated guests, some gay & youthful, some proud, [?cold] & middle-aged, a few bent & venerable, here & there a head throwing the rest
into shade, a bright, perfect face, with eyes & bloom & divine expression, whose realization thrills the heart to its core?

There is one just now crossing—a lady. I will not write her name,
though I know it. No history is connected with her identity. She is not
one of the transcendantly fair & inaccessibly sacred beings whose fates
are interwoven with the highest of the high, beings I am not alluding to
in this general picture. Far from home I cannot write of them, except in
total solitude. I scarce dare think of them.*

This nameless & casual visitant has crossed the drawing-room & is
standing close by Lady Amelia. She is looking up & speaking to her. I
wish I could trace the picture, so vivid, so obvious at this moment. She
is a native of the East. I never saw a richer specimen of an Angrian lady,
with all the characteristics of her country, woman in such perfection.

She is rather tall, well & roundly formed, with plump neck & shoulders as white as drift snow, profuse tresses in coulour almost red, but
fine as silk & lying in soft curls upon her cheeks & round her forehead.

The sweetness of the features thus shaded is inexpressible: the beautiful little mouth, the oval chin & fine animated eyes, the frank, cheerful look, the clear skin with its pure healthy bloom. The dress of light blue satin, beautifully contrasting with her hair & complexion; the pearls circling her round, white wrist; the movements of her figure, not marked by the inceding grace of the West, but unstudied, prompt & natural; her laugh always ready; the sound of her voice—her rapid, rather abrupt, but sweet & clear utterance, possessing a charm of its own, very different from the rich, low, subdued melody that flows from the lips of Senegambia's daughters; the quick glances of her eye, indicating a warm & excitable temperament; the mingled expression of good nature & pride, spirit & kind-heartedness predominating in every feature. All these are as clearly before me as Anne's quiet image, sitting at her lessons on the opposite side of the table.*

Jane Moore, that is her name, has long been celebrated as a beauty all over the province of Arundel, amongst whose green swells of pasture her father's handsome new mansion* lies, with all its pleasant grounds & young plantations on this warm spring-day opening their delicate foliage as rapidly as the forests of Kentucky.* George Moore Esqr is a rising man, one of those whose fortunes were made on the night Angria was declared a kingdom. He is a mercantile man moreover & has a huge warehouse down at Doverham,* & a vessel or two lying in the docks, built by himself & christened the Lady Jane after his fair daughter. She is no petted only child. Moore, like a true Angrian, has given to the State some half dozen of stout youths and an equal number of well-grown girls, most of whom, now grave professional men & dignified young matrons, are married into the first families of the province, & each established in a hall of their own amongst the prairies.*

But Jane is the youngest, the prettiest, the rose of the whole bouquet. She has been the most highly educated, & by nature she was one of those whose minds, manners & appearance must tend to elevate them wherever they go. Jane has ambition enough about her to scorn any offer that does not comprise a coronet—and it must be an Angrian coronet too.* And there must be wealth & estates, & a noble mansion & servants & carriages & all the other means & appliances a dashing beauty can be supposed to require to set her off.

I am afraid Jane Moore, notwithstanding her natural quickness & high education, has none of the deep refined romance of the West. I am afraid she scarcely knows what it means. She is as matter of fact as any manufacturer of Edwardston* & likes as well to receive her penny's-worth for her penny. With undisguised frankness, she acknowledges

that this world would be nothing without a flash & glitter now & then. If
Jane does any thing well, she eminently likes to be told so. She delights
in society—not for worlds would she live alone. She has no idea
even of playing a tune or singing a melancholy stanza to herself by
twilight. Once or twice she has by some chance found herself alone
in the evening, about dusk, in the large parlour at Kirkham-Wood, &
she has gone to the window & looked out at the garden clustered over
with dewy buds, & at the lawn carpeted with mossy verdure, & at the
carriage walk winding down to the gate, & beyond that at the wide &
sweeping swell of grazing country, all green, all opening with a smile to
the moon light beaming from the sky upon it. And as Jane looked, some
unaccustomed feeling did seem to swell in her heart, but if you had
asked her why her eyes glistened so, she would not have answered, 'the
moonlight is so lovely', but 'Angria is such a glorious land!'

Then as Miss Moore turned from the window & looked round on
the deserted room, with the restless firelight flickering over its walls &
making the pictures seem to stir in their frames, as she rose & threw
herself into her father's arm-chair & sat in silence listening for his
tread, perhaps she might fall into abstracted reverie & begin to recall
former days, to remember her eldest sister who died when she was a
child, to think of the funeral-day, of the rigid & lengthened corpse laid
in its coffin on the hall-table, of the servants pressing round to gaze on
Miss Harriet for the last time, of the kiss that she herself was bidden to
give the corpse, of the feeling which then first gushed into her childish
& volatile heart that Harriet had left them for ever.*

She recollects the contrast that struck upon her mind of her dead &
of her living sister, the tall girl of eighteen who had left school, who was
privileged always to be in the drawing-room when Mr & Mrs Kirkwall
& Sir Frederic & Lady Fala* came to pay their annual visit, who had
her own dressing-room with her toilette table & her dressing case, who
used so kindly to come into the nursery sometimes after dinner & bring
them all down into the parlour, where she would sing for them & play
marches & waltzes on the piano. Very lovely and a little awful did she
then seem to the eye of Jane. Her superior stature, her handsome dress,
her gold watch & chain, her powers of drawing & playing & reading
French & Italian books, all tended to invest her with the character of a
being of a superior order.

With these reminiscences comes one of a rumour Jane used to
hear whispered by the house-maid to the nurse, that her sister was to
be married to Mr Charles Kirkwall—& therewith steps in Charles's
image: a tall, young man, who in those days was no unfrequent visitor

at the Hall. He always attended Miss Moore in her walks & rides: often from the nursery window has Jane seen them both mounted on horseback & dashing down the avenue. She remembers her sister's figure as she bent over the neck of her beautiful mare, Jessy, her long curls & veil & her purple habit streaming in the wind. And she remembers Charles too, his keen features & penetrating eye, always watching Miss Moore.

Then from those forms of life, from Harriet's mild & pleasing face as it was in health, never very blooming but lighted with soft, grey eyes of sweetest lustre, Jane's memory turns to the white, shrunk, sightless corpse. She starts & a tear falls on her silk frock. Ask her what she's crying for. 'Because I'm so low-spirited with being alone,' she will answer. Such is not Jane Moore's element; the inspiration of twilight—solitude—melancholy musing—is alien from her nature.

Step into this great assembly room full of Angrian grandees. A public ball is given in celebration of the third anniversary of Independence. What light! What flashing of jewels & w[e]aring of scarlet* scarfs & plumes! What a tumultuous swell of melody! It is from a single instrument & the air is one of triumph. It proceeds from that recess. You cannot see the grand-piano for the ring of illustrissima* crowding round it. Listen! A voice electrically sweet & thrilling in its tones. Angria's glorious Song of Victory, 'Sound the Loud Timbrel!'*

Come nearer, lift up your eyes & look at the songstress. You know her, plumed, robed in vermilion, with glowing cheek & large blue eye eloquently telling what feelings the gales of Angria breathe into her daughters—Jane Moore. That feeling will not last. It will die away into oblivion as the echoes of those chords die away into silence. That expression too will leave your eye, that flush, your cheek, & you will look round & greet with a careless laugh the first word of flattery uttered by that dandy at your elbow. Yet your spirit can take a high tone. It can respond to an heroic call. You are not all selfish vanity, all empty shew. You are a handsome, generous, clever, flashy, proud, overbearing woman.

6. 'About a week since I got a letter from Branwell'

About a week since I got a letter from Branwell containing a most exquisitely characteristic epistle from Northangerland to his daughter. It is astonishing what a soothing and delightful tone that letter seemed to speak. I lived on its contents for days. In every pause of employment it came chiming in like some sweet bar of music, bringing with it agreeable thoughts such as I had for many weeks been a stranger to—some representing scenes such as might arise in consequence of that unexpected letter, some unconnected with it, referring to other events, another set of feelings. These were not striking & stirring scenes of incident—no, they were tranquil & retired in their character, such as might every day be witnessed in the inmost circles of highest society.

A curtain seemed to rise and discover to me the Duchess, as she might appear when newly risen and lightly dressed for the morning, discovering her father's letter in the contents of the mail which lies on her breakfast-table. There seems nothing in such an idea as that, but the localities of the picture were so graphic, the room so distinct, the clear fire of morning, the window looking upon no object but a cold October sky, except when you draw very near and look down on a terrace far beneath, &, at a still dizzier distance, on a green court with a fountain and rows of stately limes—beyond, a wide road, a wider river and a vast metropolis—you feel it to be the Zamorna Palace, for buildings on buildings piled round embosom this little, verdant circle, with its marble basin to receive the jet, and its grove of mellowing foliage. Above fifty windows look upon the court, admitting light into you know not what splendid and spacious chambers.

The Duchess has read that letter, and she is following the steps of the writer—she knows not where, but with a vague idea that it is through no pleasant scenes. In strange situations her imagination places him—in the inn of a sea-port town, sitting alone on a wet and gusty autumn night, the wind bringing up the ceaseless roar of the sea—of the Atlantic to whose grim waves he will tomorrow commit himself in that steamer*—hissing amongst a crowd of masts in the harbour. She looks from the window and there is the high roof and lordly front of Northangerland-House, towering like some great theatre above the streets of Adrianopolis. The owner of that pile is a homeless man.

MINA LAURY

I

The last scene in my last book concluded within the walls of Alnwick House,* and the first scene in my present volume opens in the same place. I have a great partiality for morning pictures—there is such a freshness about everybody & everything before the toil of the day has worn them. When you descend from your bedroom, the parlour door looks so clean, the fire so bright, the hearth so polished, the furnished breakfast table so tempting. All these attractions are diffused over the oak-panelled room with the glass door to which my readers have before had frequent admission. The cheerfulness within is enhanced by the dreary, wildered look of all without.* The air is dimmed with snow careering through it in wild whirls, the sky is one mass of congealed tempest—heavy, wan & icy, the trees rustle their frozen branches against each other in a blast bitter enough to flay alive the flesh that should be exposed to its sweep. But hush! the people of the house are up. I hear a step on the stairs. Let us watch the order in which they will collect in the breakfast room.

First, by himself, comes an individual in a furred morning-gown of crimson damask,* with his shirt-collar open & neck-cloth thrown by, his face fresh & rather rosy than otherwise, partly perhaps with health but chiefly with the cold water in which he has been performing his morning's ablutions, his hair fresh from the toilette—plenty of it & carefully brushed & curled—his hands clean & white & visibly as cold as icicles. He walks to the fire rubbing them. He glances towards the window meantime & whistles as much as to say, 'It's a rum morning.' He then steps to a side-table, takes up a newspaper of which there are dozens lying folded & fresh from the postman's bag, he throws himself into an arm-chair & begins to read. Meantime, another step & a rustle of silks. In comes the Countess Zenobia with a white gauze turban over her raven curls & a dress of grey. 'Good morning Arthur,' she says in her cheerful tone, such as she uses when all's right with her.

'Good morning, Zenobia,' answers the Duke, getting up, and they shake hands & stand together on the rug. 'What a morning it is!' he continues. 'How the snow drifts! If it were a little less boisterous I would make you come out & have a snow-balling match with me just to whet your appetite for breakfast.'

'Aye,' said the Countess. 'We look like two people adapted for such child's-play, don't we?' and she glanced with a smile first at the 'great blethering King of Angria' (see Harlaw*) and then at her own comely & portly figure.

'You don't mean to insinuate that we are too stout for such exercise?' said His Majesty.

Zenobia laughed. 'I am, at any rate,' said she, &, 'Your Grace is in most superb condition—what a chest!'

'This will never do,' returned the Duke shaking his head. 'Wherever I go they compliment me on my enlarged dimensions. I must take some measures for reducing them within reasonable bounds. Exercise & Abstinence, that is my motto.'

'No, Adrian—let it be "Ease and Plenty",' said a much softer voice, replying to His Grace. A third person had joined the pair & was standing a little behind, for she could not get her share of the fire, being completely shut out by the Countess with her robes & the Duke with his morning gown. This person seemed but a little & slight figure when compared with these two august individuals, & as the Duke drew her in between them, that she might at least have a sight of the glowing hearth, she was almost lost in the contrast.

'Ease & Plenty!' exclaimed His Grace. 'So you would have a man mountain* for your husband at once.'

'Yes, I should like to see you really very stout. I call you nothing now—quite slim—scarcely filled up.'

'That's right!' said Zamorna. 'Mary always takes my side.'

Lady Helen Percy now entered, & shortly after, the Earl, with slow step & in silence took his place at the breakfast-table. The meal proceeded in silence. Zamorna was reading. Newspaper after newspaper he opened, glanced over & threw on the floor. One of them happened to fall over Lord Northangerland's foot. It was very gently removed as if there was contamination in the contact.

'An Angrian print I believe,' murmured the Earl. 'Why do they bring such things to the house?'

'They are my papers,' answered his son-in-law, swallowing at the same moment more at one mouthful than would have sufficed his father for the whole repast.

'Yours! What do you read them for? To give you an appetite? If so, they seem to have answered their end. Arthur, I wish you would masticate your food better—'

'I have not time. I'm very hungry. I eat but one meal all yesterday.'

'Humph! and now you're making up for it I suppose. But pray put that newspaper away.'

'No, I wish to learn what my loving subjects are saying about me.'

'And what are they saying, pray?'

'Why, here is a respectable gentleman who announces that he fears his beloved monarch is again under the influence of that baleful star whose ascendancy has already produced such fatal results to Angria—wishing to be witty he calls it the North Star.* Another insinuates that their gallant sovereign, though a Hector in war, is but a Paris in peace. He talks something about Sampson & Delilah, Hercules & the distaff,* & hints darkly at the evils of petticoat government—a hit at you, Mary. A third mutters threateningly of hoary old ruffians who, worn with age & excess, sit like Bunyan's Giant Pope* at the entrances of their dens & strive by menace or promise to allure passengers within the reach of their bloody talons.'

'Is that me?' asked the Earl quietly.

'I've very little doubt of it,' was the reply. 'And there is a fourth print, the *War Despatch*, noted for the ardour of its sentiments, which growls a threat concerning the power of Angria to elect a new sovereign whenever she is offended with her old one. Zenobia, another cup of coffee if you please.'

'I suppose you're frightened,' said the Earl.

'I shake in my shoes,' replied the Duke. 'However there are two old sayings that somewhat cheer me—"More noise than work", "Much cry & little wool".* Very applicable when properly considered, for I always called the Angrians hogs & who am I except the Devil that shears them?'

Breakfast had been over for about a quarter of an hour. The room was perfectly still. The Countess & Duchess were reading those papers Zamorna had dropped, Lady Helen was writing to her son's agent, the Earl was pacing the room in a despondent mood; as for the Duke, no one well knew where he was, or what he was doing. He had taken himself off, however. Ere long his step was heard descending the staircase, then his voice in the hall giving orders, & then he re-entered the breakfast-room, but no longer in morning costume. He had exchanged his crimson damask robe for a black coat & checked pantaloons. He was wrapped up in a huge blue cloak with a furred collar—a light fur cap rested on his brow—his gloves were held in his hands—in short he was in full travelling costume.

'Where are you going?' asked the Earl, pausing in his walk.

'To Verdopolis, & from thence to Angria,' was the reply.

'To Verdopolis, & in such weather!' exclaimed the Countess, glancing towards the wild whitened tempest that whirled without. Lady Helen looked up from her writing.

'Absurd, my Lord Duke! You do not mean what you say.'

'I do. I must go. The carriage will be at the door directly. I'm come to bid you all good-bye.'

'And what is all this haste about?' returned Lady Helen rising.

'There is no haste in the business, madam. I've been here a week. I intended to go today.'

'You never said anything about your intention.'

'No, I did not think of mentioning it—but they are bringing the carriage round. Good morning, madam.'

He took Lady Helen's hand & saluted her as he always does at meeting & parting. Then he passed to the Countess.

'Good-bye Zenobia. Come to Ellrington House as soon as you can persuade our friend to accompany you.'

He kissed her, too. The next in succession was the Earl.

'Farewell, sir, & be d——d to you. Will you shake hands?'

'No. You always hurt me so. Good morning. I hope you won't find your masters quite so angry as you expect them to be, but you do right not to delay attending to their mandates. I'm sorry I have been the occasion of your offending them.'

'Are we to part in this way?' asked the Duke. 'And won't you shake hands?'

'No!'

Zamorna coloured highly, but turned away & put on his gloves. The barouche stood at the door. The groom & the valet were waiting, & the Duke, still with a clouded countenance, was proceeding to join them when his wife came forwards.

'You have forgotten me, Adrian,' she said in a very quiet tone, but her eye meantime flashing expressively. He started, for in truth he had forgotten her. He was thinking about her father.

'Good bye then, Mary,' he said, giving her a hurried kiss & embrace. She detained his hand.

'Pray how long am I to stay here?' she asked. 'Why do you leave me at all? Why am I not to go with you?'

'It is such weather!' he answered. 'When the storm passes over I will send for you.'

'When will that be?' pursued the Duchess, following his steps as he strode into the hall.

'Soon—soon my love—perhaps in a day or two. There now, don't be unreasonable. Of course you cannot go to day.'

'I can & I will,' answered the Duchess quickly. 'I have had enough of Alnwick. You shall not leave me behind you.'

'Go into the room, Mary. The door is open & the wind blows on you far too keenly. Don't you see how it drifts the snow in?'

'I will not go into the room. I'll step into the carriage as I am if you refuse to wait till I can prepare. Perhaps you will be humane enough to let me have a share of your cloak.'

She shivered as she spoke. Her hair & her dress floated in the cold blast that blew in through the open entrance, strewing the hall with snow & dead leaves. His Grace, though he was rather stern, was not quite negligent of her, for he stood so as to screen her in some measure from the draught.

'I shall not let you go, Mary,' he said. 'So there is no use in being perverse.'

The Duchess regarded him with that troubled, anxious glance peculiar to herself.

'I wonder why you wish to leave me behind you?' she said.

'Who told you I wished to do so?' was his answer. 'Look at the weather & tell me if it is fit for a delicate little woman like you to be exposed to?'

'Then,' murmured the Duchess, wistfully glancing at the January storm, 'you might wait till it is milder. I don't think it will do Your Grace any good to be out to day.'

'But I must go, Mary. The Christmas Recess is over & business presses.'

'Then do take me. I am sure I can bear it.'

'Out of the question. You may well clasp those small, silly hands—so thin I can almost see through them—and you may well shake your curls over your face, to hide its paleness from me, I suppose. What is the matter—crying? Good! what the d—l am I to do with her? Go to your father, Mary. He has spoilt you.'

'Adrian, I cannot live at Alnwick without you,' said the Duchess earnestly. 'It recalls too forcibly the very bitterest days of my life. I'll not be separated from you again except by violence.' She took hold of his arm with one hand, while with the other she was hastily wiping away the tears from her eyes.

'Well, it will not do to keep her any longer in this hall,' said the Duke & he pushed open a side-door which led into a room that during his stay he had appropriated for his study. There was a fire in it & a sofa drawn to the hearth. There he took the Duchess, &, having shut the door, recommended the task of persuasion, which was no very easy one, for his own false play, his alienations & his unnumbered treacheries had filled her mind with hideous phantasms of jealousy, had weakened her nerves & made them prey to a hundred vague apprehensions—fears that never wholly left her, except when she was actually in his arms or at least in his immediate presence.

'I tell you, Mary,' he said, regarding her with a smile half-expressive of fondness, half of vexation, 'I tell you I will send for you in two or three days.'

'And you will be at Wellesley House when I get there? You said you were going from Verdopolis to Angria?'

'I am, & probably I shall be a week in Angria, not more.'

'A week! and Your Grace considers that but a short time? To me it will be most wearisome. However, I must submit. I know it is useless to oppose Your Grace—but I could go with you, and you should never find me in the way. I am not often intrusive on Your Grace.'

'The horses will be frozen if they stand much longer,' returned the Duke, not heeding her last remark. 'Come, wipe your eyes and be a little philosopher for once. There, let me have one smile before I go. A week will be over directly. This is not like setting out for a campaign.'

'Don't forget to send for me in two days,' pleaded the Duchess as Zamorna released her from his arms.

'No, no. I'll send for you to-morrow if the weather is settled enough—and,' half mimicking her voice, 'don't be jealous of me, Mary—unless you're afraid that the superior charms of Enara & Warner & Kirkwall & Richton & Thornton will seduce me from my allegiance to a certain fair-complexioned brown-eyed young woman in whom you are considerably interested. Good-bye.'

He was gone. She hurried to the window—he passed it—in three minutes the barouche swept with muffled sound round the lawn—shot down the carriage road & was quickly lost in the thickening whirl of the snow-storm.

Late at night, the Duke of Zamorna reached Wellesley House. His journey had been much delayed by the repeated change of horses which the state of the roads rendered necessary. So heavy & constant had been the fall of snow all day that in many places they were almost blocked up, & he and his valet had more than once been obliged to alight from the carriage & wade through the deep drifts far above the knee. Under such circumstances any other person would have stopped for the night at some of the numerous excellent hotels which skirt the way, but His Grace is well known to be excessively pig-headed, and the more obstacles are thrown in the way of any scheme he wishes to execute, the more resolute he is in pushing on to the attainment of his end. In the prosecution of this journey he had displayed a particular wilfulness. In vain when he had alighted at some inn to allow time for a change of horses, Rosier had hinted the propriety of a longer stay, in vain he had recommended some more substantial refreshment than the single glass of Madeira & the half-biscuit wherewith his noble master tantalized rather than satisfied the cravings of a rebellious appetite. At last, leaving him to the enjoyment of obstinancy & starvation in a large saloon of the inn, which his Grace was traversing with strides that derived their alacrity partly from nipping cold & partly from impatience, Eugene himself had sought the traveller's room, & while he devoured a chicken with champagne he had solaced himself with the muttered objurgation, 'Let him starve & be d—d!'

Flinging himself from the barouche, the Duke—in no mild mood—passed through his lighted halls, whose echoes were still prolonging the last stroke of midnight, pealed from the house-bell just as the carriage drew up under the portico. Zamorna seemed not to heed the call to immediate repose which that sound conveyed, for turning as he stood on the first landing-place of the wide, white marble stairs—with a bronze lamp pendant above him & a statue standing in calm contrast to his own figure—he called out, 'Rosier! I wish Mr Warner to attend me instantly. See that a messenger is despatched to Warner Hotel.'

'To night, does Your Grace mean?' said the valet.

'Yes sir.'

Monsieur Rosier reposed his tongue in his cheek but hastened to obey.

'Hutchinson, send your deputy directly—you heard His Grace's orders—& Hutchinson tell the cook to send a tumbler of hot negus into my room. I want something to thaw me. And tell her to toss me up a nice hot *petit souper—a fricandeau de veau* or an omelette. And carry my compliments to Mr Greenwood & say I shall be happy to have the honour of his company in my salon half an hour hence. And, above all things, Hutchinson'—here the young gentleman lowered his tone to a more confidential key—'give Mademoiselle Harriette a hint that I am returned—very ill, you may say, for I've got a cursed sore throat with being exposed to this night air. Ah! there she is! I'll tell her myself.'

As the omnipotent Eugene spoke, a young lady carrying a china ewer appeared crossing the gallery which ran round this inner hall. The French *garçon* skipped up the stairs like a flea.

'*Ma belle!*' he exclaimed, '*permettez moi porte cette cruse-là!*'*

'No, monsieur, no,' replied the young lady laughing & throwing back her head which was covered with very handsome dark hair finely curled. 'I will carry it—it is for the Duke.'

'I must assist you,' returned the gallant Rosier, & then, 'I shall earn a kiss for my services.'

But the damsel resisted him & stepping back shewed to better advantage a pretty foot and ancle, well displayed by a short, full petticoat of pink muslin & a still shorter apron of black silk. She had also a modest handkerchief of thin lace on her neck. She wore no cap, had good eyes, comely features and a plump round figure. A very interesting love scene was commencing in the seclusion of the gallery, when a bell rung very loudly.

'God! it's the Duke!' exclaimed Rosier. He instantly released his mistress & she shot away like an arrow towards the inner chambers. Eugene followed her very cautiously—somewhat jealously, perhaps. Threading her path through a labyrinth of intermediate rooms, she came at last to the royal chamber & thence a door opened direct to the royal dressing-room. His Grace was seated in an arm-chair by his mirror—an enormous one taking him in from head to foot. He looked cursedly tired & somewhat wan, but the lights & shadows of the fire were playing about him with an animating effect.

'Well, Harriet,' he said as the housemaid entered his presence. 'I wanted that water before. Put it down & pour me out a glass. What made you so long in bringing it?'

Harriet blushed as she held the refreshing draught to her royal master's parched lips. (He was too lazy to take it himself.) She was going to stammer out some excuse, but meantime the Duke's eye had reverted to the door & caught the dark vivacious aspect of Rosier.

'Ah!' he said. 'I see how it is! Well, Harriet, mind what you're about. No giddiness! You may go now, & tell your swain to come forwards on pain of having his brains converted into paste.'

Eugene strutted in humming aloud—in no sort abashed or put to the blush. When Harriet was gone, the Duke proceeded to lecture him, the valet meantime coolly aiding him in the change of his travelling-dress, arrangement of his hair, &c.

'Dog,' began the saintly master, 'take care how you conduct yourself towards that girl; I'll have no improprieties in my house, none.'

'If I do but follow your Grace's example, I cannot be guilty of improprieties,' snivelled the valet, who being but too well-acquainted with many of his master's weaknesses is sometimes permitted a freedom of speech few others would attempt.

'I'll make you marry her at all risks if you once engage her affections,' pursued Zamorna.

'Well,' replied Rosier, 'if I do marry her and if I don't like her, I can recompense myself for the sacrifice.'

'Keep within your allotted limits, my lad,' remarked the Duke quietly.

'What does your Grace mean? Matrimonial limits or limits of the tongue?'

'Learn to discern for yourself!' returned his master, enforcing the reply by a manual application that sent Monsieur to the other side of the room. He speedily gathered himself up & returned to his employment of combing out the Duke's long and soft curls of dark brown hair.

'I have a particular interest in your Harriet,' remarked Zamorna benevolently. 'I can't say that the other handmaids of the house often cross my sight, but now and then I meet that nymph in a gallery or a passage, and she always strikes me as being very modest & correct in her conduct.'

'She was first bar-maid at Stancliffe's Hotel in Zamorna* not long since,' insinuated Rosier.

'I know she was, sir. I have reason to remember her in that station. She once gave me a draught of cold water, when there was not another human-being in the world who would have lifted a finger to do me even that kindness.'

'I've heard Mademoiselle tell that story,' replied Eugene. 'It was when Your Grace was taken prisoner of war before MacTerroglen, & she told how Your Grace rewarded her afterwards when you stopped six months ago at Stancliffe's & gave her a certificate of admission to the royal household—and into the bargain, if Mademoiselle speaks the truth, Your Grace gave her a kiss from your own royal lips.'

'I did & be d—d to you, sir. The draught of water she once gave me & the gush of kind-hearted tears that followed it were cheaply rewarded by a kiss.'

'I should have thought so,' replied Rosier, 'but perhaps she did not. Ladies of title sometimes pull each others' ears for Your Grace's kisses, so I don't know how a simple bar-maid would receive them.'

'Eugene, your nation have a penchant for suicide. Go & be heroic,' returned Zamorna.

'If Your Grace has done with me, I will obey your wishes & immediately seek my quietus in a plate of ragout of paradise & such delicate claret as the vintages of la belle France yield when they are in a good humour.'

As the illustrious valet withdrew from the presence of his still more illustrious master, a different kind of personage entered by another door—a little man enveloped in a fur cloak. He put if off and, glancing round the room, his eye settled upon Zamorna. Released from the cumbrous costume of his journey, Zamorna was again enveloped in his crimson damask robe, half-reclined on the mattress of a low & hard couch, his head of curls preparing to drop on to the pillow & one hand just drawing up the coverlet of furs & velvet. Warner beheld him in the act of seeking his night's repose.

'I thought Your Grace wanted me on business!' exclaimed the minister. 'And I find you in bed!'

Zamorna stretched his limbs, folded his arms across his chest, buried his brow, cheek & dark locks in the pillow, & in a faint voice requested Warner to 'arrange that coverlet for her was too tired to do it'. The Premier's lip struggled to repress a smile. This was easily done, for the said lip was unaccustomed to that relaxation.

'Has Your Majesty dismissed Monsieur Rosier, & have you sent for me to fulfil the duties of that office he held about Your Majesty's person?'

'There, I'm comfortable,' said the Duke, as the drapery fell over him arranged to his satisfaction. 'Pray, Warner, be seated.'

Warner drew close to His Grace's bedside an arm-chair & threw himself into it. 'What', said he, 'have you been doing? You look extremely pale—have you been raking?'*

'God forgive you for the supposition. No, I have been fagging myself to death for the good of Angria.'

'For the good of Angria, my lord? Aye, truly there you come to the point—& it is I suppose for the good of Angria that you go to Alnwick & spend a week in the sick room of Lord Northangerland?'

'How dutiful of me Howard! I hope my subjects admire me for it.'

'My lord Duke, do not jest. The feeling which has been raised by that ill-advised step is no fit subject for levity. What a strange mind is yours which teaches you to rush headlong into those very errors which your enemies are always attributing to you! It is in vain that you now & then display a splendid flash of talent when the interstices, as it were, of your political life are filled up with such horrid bungling as this.'

'Be easy, Howard. What harm have I done?'

'My lord, I will tell you. Has it not ever been the bitterest reproach in the mouth of your foes that you are a weak man liable to be influenced & controlled. Have not Ardah & Montmorency a thousand times affirmed that Northangerland guided, ruled, infatuated you? They have tried to bring that charge home to you—to prove it—but they could not, & you, with all Christian charity, have taken the trouble off their hands. You have proved it beyond dispute or contradiction.'

'As how my dear Howard?'

'My lord, you see it, you feel it yourself. In what state was Angria last year at this time? You remember it laid in ashes—plague & famine & slaughter, struggling with each other which should sway the sceptre that disastrous war had wrested from your own hand—and I ask, my lord, who had brought Angria to this state?'

'Northangerland!' replied Zamorna promptly.

'Your Grace has spoken truly—& knowing this, was it weakness or was it wickedness which led you to the debauched traitor's couch and taught you to bend over him with the tenderness of a son to a kind father?' Warner paused for an answer but none came. He continued, 'That the man is dying I have very little doubt—dying in that premature decay brought on by excesses such as would have disgraced any nature, aye, even that of an unreasoning beast. But ought you not to have let him meet death alone, in that passion of anguish & desolation which is the just meed for crime, for depravity like his? What call was there for you to go and count his pulses? Can you prolong their beat? Why should you mingle your still pure breath with his last contaminated gasps? Can you purify that breath which debauchery has so sullied? Why should you commit your young hand to the touch of his clammy nerveless fingers? Can the contact infuse vitality into his veins or vigour into his sinews? Had you not the strength of mind to stand aloof & let him who has lived the slave of vice die the victim of the disease?'

The Duke of Zamorna raised himself on his elbow.

'Very bad language this Howard,' said he. 'And it won't do. I know very well what the reformers and the constitutionalists & my own opinionated & self-complacent Angrians have been saying because I chose to spend my Christmas recess at Alnwick. I knew beforehand what they would say—& above all I knew in particular what you would say. Now it was not in defiance of either public or private opinion that I went. Neither was it from the working of any uncontrollable impulse. No, the whole matter was the result of mature reflection. My Angrians have certain rights over me. So have my ministers. I also have certain rights independent of them, independent of any living thing under the firmament of Heaven. I claim the possession of my reason. I am neither insane nor idiotic, whatever the all-accomplished Harlaw may say to the contrary, & in two or three things I will, whilst I retain that valuable possession, judge for myself. One of these is the degree of intimacy which I choose to maintain with Lord Northangerland. In a public sense, I have long done with him. The alienation cost me much, for in two or three particular points his views & mine harmonized, & neither could hope to find a substitute for the other in the whole earth beside. However, though it was like tearing up something whose roots had taken deep hold in my very heart of hearts, the separation was made—& since it was finally completed, by what glance or look or word have I sighed for a reunion? I have not done so & I cannot do so. My path I have struck out & it sweeps far away out of sight of his. The rivers of blood Angria shed last year, & the hills of cold carnage which she piled up before the shrine of Freedom, effectually, eternally divide Northangerland's spirit from mine. But in the body we may meet—we shall meet—till death interposes. I say, Warner, no sneers of my foes nor threats from my friends, no murmurs from my subjects, shall over-rule me in this matter.

'Howard, you are a different man from Northangerland, but let me whisper to you this secret. You also love to control, & if you could you would extend the energies of that keen haughty mind, till they surrounded me & spell-bound my will & actions within a magic circle of your own creating. It will not do, it will not do. Hate Northangerland if you please—abhor him, loathe him. You have a right to do so. He has more than once treated you brutally, spoken of you grossly. If you feel so inclined & if an opportunity should offer, you have a right to pistol him. But, sir, do not dare to impose your private feelings on me, to call upon me to avenge them. Do it yourself! In you the action would be justifiable, in me dastardly. Neither will I bend to Ardah or to the defiled cuckhold Montmorency. I will not at their bidding give up the best feelings of a very bad nature—I will not crush the only impulses that enable me to be endured by my fellow-men—I will not leave the man who was once my <u>comrade</u>—my <u>friend</u>—to die in unrelieved agony because Angria mutinies & Verdopolis sneers. My heart, my hand, my energies belong to the public—my feelings are my own. Talk no more on the subject.'

Warner did not. He sat & gazed in silence on his master, who with closed eyes & averted head seemed composing himself to slumber. At last he said aloud: 'A false step, a false step! I would die on the word!'

Zamorna woke from his momentary doze.

'You have papers for me to sign & look over, I daresay, Howard. Give me them. I wish to dispatch arrears to-night, as it is my intention to set

off for Angria. I wish to ascertain in person the state of feeling there &
to turn it into its legitimate channel.'

Warner produced a green bag well filled. The Duke raised himself
on his couch & collecting his wearied faculties proceeded to the task. A
silence of nearly an hour ensued, broken only by occasional monosyl-
lables from the King & minister as papers were presented & returned.
At length Warner locked the padlock with which the bag was secured,
& saying, 'I recommend Your Majesty to sleep', rose to reassume his
cloak.

'Warner,' said the Duke with an appearance of nonchalance, 'where
is Lord Hartford? I have seen nothing of him for some time.'

'Lord Hartford, my lord! Lord Hartford is a fool & affects delicacy
of the lungs. His health, forsooth, is in too precarious a state to allow
of any attention to public affairs & he has withdrawn to Hartford Hall
there to nurse his maudlin folly in retirement.'

'What, the maudlin folly of being ill? You are very unsparing
Howard.'

'Ill, sir! The man is as strong & sound as you are. All trash! It is the
effects of his ruling passion, sir, which will pursue him to hoar age, I
suppose. Lord Hartford is love-sick, my lord Duke—the superannuated profligate!'

'Did he tell you so?'

'No, indeed he dared not—but Lord Richton insinuated as much in
his gossipy way. I will cut Lord Hartford, sir—I despise him! He ought
to be sent to Coventry.'*

'How very bitter you are, Warner! Be more moderate. Meantime,
good-night.'

'I wish Your Grace a very good night. Take care that you sleep
soundly & derive refreshment from your slumbers.'

'I will do my best,' replied the Duke laughing. Warner having
clasped on his cloak with-drew. Could he have watched unseen by the
couch of his master for two hours longer, he would have repined at the
hidden feeling that prevented the lids from closing over those dark &
restless eyes. Long Zamorna lay awake. Neither youth nor health nor
weariness could woo sleep to his pillow. He saw his lamp expire. He saw
the brilliant flame of the hearth settle into ruddy embers, then fade,
decay, & at last perish. He felt silence & total darkness close round him.
But still the unslumbering eye wandered over images which the fiery
imagination pourtrayed upon vacancy. Thought yielded at last & sleep
triumphed. Zamorna lay in dead repose amidst the hollow darkness of
his chamber.

*

Lord Hartford sat by himself after his solitary dinner with a decanter of champagne & a half filled glass before him. There was also a newspaper spread out on which his elbow leaned and his eye rested. The noble lord sat in a large dining-room, the windows of which looked upon a secluded part of his own grounds—a part pleasant enough in summer leafiness & verdure, but dreary now in the cold white clothing of winter. Many a time had this dining-room rung with the merriment of select dinner-parties, chosen by the noble bachelor from his particular friends, & often had the rum physiognomies of Richton, Arundel, Castlereagh & Thornton been reflected in the mirror-like surface of that long dark polished mahogany table at whose head Edward Hartford now sat alone. Gallant & gay, & bearing on his broad forehead the very brightest & greenest laurels Angria had gathered on the banks of the Cirhala,* he had retired with all his blushing honours thick upon him from the council, the court, the salon. He had left Verdopolis in the height of the most dazzling season it had ever known & gone to haunt like a ghost his lonely halls in Angria. Most people thought the noble General's brains had suffered some slight injury amid the hardships of the late campaign. Richton [was] among the number who found it impossible to account for his friend's conduct upon any other supposition.

As the dusk closed & the room grew more dismal, Hartford threw the newspaper from him, poured out a bumper of amber-coloured wine & quaffed it off to the memory of the vintage that produced it. According to books, men in general soliloquize when they are by themselves & so did Hartford—

'What the d—l,' he began, 'has brought our lord the King down to Angria? That drunken editor of the *War Despatch* gives a pretty account of his progress—hissed, it seems, in the streets of Zamorna, & then, like himself, instead of getting through the town as quietly as he could, bidding the postillions halt before Stancliffe's & treating them to one of his fire & gunpowder explosions! What a speech, beginning "My lads what a d—d set you are! Unstable as water! you shall never excel!" It's odd, but that western dandy knows the genius of our land.* "Take the bull by the horns"*—that's his motto. Hitherto his tactics have succeeded but I think it says somewhere, either in Revelations or the Apocrypha, the end is not yet.* I wish he'd keep out of Angria.'

Here a pause ensued, & Hartford filled it up with another goblet of the golden wine.

'Now,' he proceeded. 'I know I ought not drink this Guanache.* It is a kindling sort of draught & I were better take to toast & water—but

Lord bless me! I've got a feeling about my heart I can neither stifle nor tear away, & I would fain drown it. They talk of optical delusions—I wonder what twisting of the nerves it is that fixes before my eyes that image which neither darkness can hide nor light dissipate? Some demon is certainly making a bonfire of my inwards. The burning thrill struck through all my veins to my heart with that last touch of the little warm soft hand—by heaven, nearly a year ago—& it has never left me since. It wastes me. I'm not half the man I was, but I'm handsome still!'

He looked up at a lofty mirror between the two opposite windows. It reflected his dark, commanding face with the prominent profile, the hard forehead, the deep expressive eye, the mass of raven hair & whisker & mustache, the stately aspect & figure, the breadth of chest & length of limb. In short, it gave back to his sight as fine a realization of soldier & patrician majesty as Angria ever produced from her ardent soil. Hartford sprang up.

'What should I give up hope for?' he said rapidly pacing the room. 'By G—d, I think I could make her love me! I never yet have told her how I adore her. I've never offered her my title & hand & my half-phrenzied heart—but I will do it! Who says it is impossible she should prefer being my wife to being His mistress? The world will laugh at me—I don't care for the world—it's inconsistent with the honour of my house. I've burnt the honour of my house & drank its ashes in Guanache. It's dastardly to meddle with another man's matters—another man who has been my friend, with whom I have fought & feasted, suffered & enjoyed. By G—d it is, I know it is, & if any man but myself had dared to entertain the same thought I'd have called him out. But Zamorna leaves her & cares no more about her—except when she can be of use to him—than I do for that silly Christmas rose on the lawn shrivelled up by the frost. Besides, every man for himself. I'll try & if I do not succeed I'll try again & again—she's worth a struggle. Perhaps, meantime, Warner or Enara will send me an invitation to dine on bullets for two—or perhaps I may forget the rules of the drill, & present & fire not from but at myself—in either case I get comfortably provided for & that torment will be over which now frightens away my sleep by night & my sense by day.'

This was rather wild talk but his lordship's peculiar glance told that wine had not been without its effect. We will leave him striding about the room & maddening under the influence of his fiery passions. A sweet specimen of an aristocrat!

*

Late one fine, still evening in January the moon rose over a blue
summit of the Sydenham Hills & looked down on a quiet road winding from the hamlet of Rivaulx.* The earth was bound in frost—hard,
mute & glittering. The forest of Hawkscliffe was as still as a tomb, &
its black leafless wilds stretched away in the distance & cut off with a
hard serrated line the sky from the country. That sky was all silver blue,
pierced here & there with a star like a diamond. Only the moon softened it, large, full, golden. The by-road I have spoken of received her
ascending beam on a path of perfect solitude. Spectral pines & vast old
beech trees guarded the way like sentinels from Hawkscliffe. Farther on
the rude track wound deep into the shades of the forest, but here it was
open & the worn causeway bleached with frost ran under an old wall
grown over with moss & wild ivy. Over this scene the sun of winter had
gone down in cloudless calm, red as fire & kindling with its last beams
the windows of a mansion on the verge of Hawkscliffe. To that mansion the road in question was the shortest cut from Rivaulx—& here a
moment let us wait, wrapped it is to be hoped in furs, for a keener frost
never congealed the Olympian.

Almost before you are aware, a figure strays up the causeway at a
leisurely pace, musing amid the tranquillity of evening. Doubtless that
figure must be an inmate of the before-mentioned mansion, for it is
an elegant & pleasing object. Approaching gradually nearer, you can
observe more accurately. You see now a lady of distinguished carriage,
straight & slender, something inceding & princess-like in her walk but
unconsciously so. Her ancles are so perfect & her feet—if she tryed
she could scarce tread otherwise than she does, lightly, firmly, erectly.
The ermine muff, the silk pelisse, the graceful & ample hat of dark
beaver, suit & set off her slight, youthful form. She is deeply veiled—you
must guess at her features. But she passes on, and a turn of the road
conceals her.

Breaking up the silence, dashing in on the solitude comes a horseman.
Fire flashes from under his steed's hoofs out of the flinty road. He rides
desperately. Now & then he rises in his stirrups & eagerly looks along
the track as if to catch sight of some object that has eluded him. He sees
it & the spurs are struck mercilessly into his horse's flanks. Horse &
rider vanish in a whirlwind.

The lady passing through the iron gates had just entered upon the
demesne of Hawkscliffe. She paused to gaze at the moon, which now
fully risen looked upon her through the boughs of a superb elm. A
green lawn lay between her & the house & there its light slumbered

in gold. Thundering behind her came the sound of hoofs &, bending low to his saddle to avoid the contact of oversweeping branches, that wild horseman we saw five minutes since rushed upon the scene. Harshly curbing the charger, he brought it almost upon its haunches close to the spot where she stood.

'Miss Laury! Good evening!' he said.

The lady threw back her veil, surveyed him with one glance, & replied, 'Lord Hartford! I am glad to see you my lord. You have ridden fast—your horse foams—any bad news?'

'No!'

'Then you are on your way to Adrianopolis, I suppose. You will pass the night here?'

'If you ask me I will.'

'If I ask you! Yes, this is the proper half-way house between the capitals. The night is cold, let us go in.'

They were now at the door. Hartford flung himself from his saddle, a servant came to lead the over-ridden steed to the stables, & he followed Miss Laury in.

It was her own drawing-room to which she led him—just such as scene as is most welcome after the contrast of a winter evening's chill—not a large room, simply furnished, with curtains & couches of green silk, a single large mirror, a Grecian lamp dependent from the centre, softly burning now & mingling with the warmer illumination of the fire, whose brilliant glow bore testimony to the keenness of the frost.

Hartford glanced round him. He had been in Miss Laury's drawing-room before, but never as her sole guest. He had, before the troubles broke out, more than once formed one of a high & important trio, whose custom it was to make the Lodge of Rivaulx* their occasional rendezvous. Warner, Enara & himself had often stood on that hearth in a ring round Miss Laury's sofa, & he recalled now her face looking up to them, with its serious, soft intelligence that blent no woman's frivolity with the heartfelt interest of those subjects on which they conversed. He remembered those first kindlings of the flame that now devoured his life, as he watched her beauty & saw the earnest enthusiasm with which she threw her soul into topics of the highest import. She had often done for these great men what they could get no man to do for them. She had kept their secrets & executed their wishes as far as in her lay, for it had never been her part to counsel. With humble feminine devotedness, she always looked up for her task to be set, & then not Warner himself could have bent his energies more resolutely to the fulfilment of that task than did Mina Laury.

Had Mina's lot in life been different, she never would have interfered in such matters. She did not interfere now; she only served—nothing like intrigue had ever stained her course in politics. She told her directors what she had done & she asked for more to do, grateful always that they would trust her so far as to employ her, grateful too for the enthusiasm of their loyalty; in short, devoted to them heart & mind, because she believed them to be devoted as unreservedly to the common master of all. The consequences of this species of deeply confidential intercourse between the statesmen and their beautiful lieutenant had been intense & chivalric admiration on the part of Mr Warner, strong fond attachment on that of General Enara, & on Lord Hartford's the burning brand of passion. His Lordship had always been a man of strong & ill-regulated feelings & in his youth (if report may be credited) of somewhat dissolute habits, but he had his own ideas of honour strongly implanted in his breast, & though he would not have scrupled if the wife of one of his equals or the daughter of one of his tenants had been in the question yet, as it was, he stood beset & nonplussed.

Miss Laury belonged to the Duke of Zamorna. She was indisputably his property, as much as the Lodge of Rivaulx or the stately woods of Hawkscliffe, & in that light she considered herself. All his dealings with her had been on matters connected with the Duke, & she had ever shown an habitual, rooted, solemn devotedness to his interest, which seemed to leave her hardly a thought for anything else in the world beside. She had but one idea—Zamorna, Zamorna! It had grown up with her, become a part of her nature. Absence, coldness, total neglect for long periods together went for nothing. She could no more feel alienation from him than she could from herself. She did not even repine when he forgot her, any more than the religious devotee does when his deity seems to turn away his face for a time & leave him to the ordeal of temporal afflictions. It seemed as if she could have lived on the remembrance of what he had once been to her without asking for anything more.

All this Hartford knew & he knew too that she valued himself in proportion as she believed him to be loyal to his sovereign. Her friendship for him turned on this hinge: 'We have been fellow-labourers & fellow-sufferers together in the same good cause.' These were her own words, which she had uttered one night as she took leave of her three noble colleagues just before the storm burst over Angria. Hartford had noted the expression of her countenance as she spoke, & thought what a young & beautiful being thus appealed for sympathy with minds scarcely like her own in mould.

However let us dwell no longer on these topics. Suffice it to say that Lord Hartford, against reason & without hope, had finally delivered himself wholly up to the guidance of his vehement passions, & it was with the resolution to make one desperate effort in the attainment of their end that he now stood before the lady of Rivaulx.

Above two hours had elapsed since Lord Hartford had entered the house. Tea was over, & in the perfect quiet of evening he & Miss Laury were left together. He sat on one side of the hearth, she on the other, her work-table only between them, & on that her little hand rested within his reach. It was embedded on a veil of lace, the embroidering of which she had just relinquished for a moment's thought. Lord Hartford's eye was fascinated by the white soft fingers. His whole heart at the moment was in a tumult of bliss—to be so near—to be received so benignly, so kindly! He forgot himself. His own hand closed half involuntarily upon hers.

Miss Laury looked at him. If the action had left any room for doubt of its significancy, the glance which met hers filled up all deficiencies—a wild fiery glance as if his feelings were wrought up almost to delirium. Shocked for a moment, almost overwhelmed, she yet speedily mastered her emotions, took her hand away, resumed her work, & with head bent down seemed endeavouring to conceal embarrassment under the appearance of occupation. The dead silence that followed would not do, so she broke it, in a very calm, self-possessed tone.

'That ring, Lord Hartford, which you were admiring just now, belonged once to the Duchess of Wellington.'

'And was it given you by her son?' asked the General bitterly.

'No my lord. The Duchess herself gave it me a few days before she died. It has her maiden name, Catherine Pakenham,* engraved within the stone.'

'But,' pursued Hartford, 'I was not admiring the ring when I touched your hand. No, the thought struck me, if ever I marry I should like my wife's hand to be just as white & snowy & taper as that.'

'I am the daughter of a common soldier,* my lord, & it is said that ladies of high descent have fairer hands than peasant women.'

Hartford made no reply. He rose restlessly from his seat & stood leaning against the mantle-piece.

'Miss Laury, shall I tell you which was the happiest hour of my life?'

'I will guess my lord. Perhaps when the bill passed which made Angria an independent kingdom?'

'No,' replied Hartford with an expressive smile.

'Perhaps, then, when Lord Northangerland resigned the seals*—for I know you & the Earl were never on good terms.'

'No. I hated his lordship, but there are moments of deeper felicity even than those which see the triumph of* a fallen enemy.'

'I will hope then it was at the Restoration.'*

'Wrong again. Why, madam, young as you are, your mind is so used to the harness of politics that you can imagine no happiness or misery unconnected with them. You remind me of Warner.'

'I believe I am like him,' returned Miss Laury. 'He often tells me so himself. But I live so with men & statesmen, I almost lose the ideas of a woman.'

'Do you?' muttered Hartford with the dark, sinister smile peculiar to him. 'I wish you would tell the Duke so next time you see him.'

Miss Laury passed over this equivocal remark & proceeded with the conversation.

'I cannot guess your riddle, my lord, so I think you must explain it.'

'Then, Miss Laury, prepare to be astonished. You are so patriotic, so loyal, that you will scarcely credit me when I say that the happiest hour I have ever known fell on the darkest day in the deadliest crisis of Angria's calamities.'

'How, Lord Hartford?'

'Moreover, Miss Laury, it was at no bright period of your own life. It was to you an hour of the most acute agony, to me one of ecstasy.'

Miss Laury turned aside her head with a disturbed air & trembled. She seemed to know to what he alluded.

'You remember the first of July,—36?' continued Hartford.

She bowed.

'You remember that the evening of that day closed in a tremendous storm?'

'Yes, my lord.'

'You recollect how you sat in this very room by this fireside, fearful of retiring for the night lest you should awake in another world in the morning? The country was not then as quiet as it is now. You have not forgotten the deep explosion which roared up at midnight, & told you that your life & liberty hung on a thread, that the enemy had come suddenly upon Rivaulx & that we who lay there to defend the forlorn hope were surprised & routed by a night attack? Then, madam, perhaps you recollect the warning which I brought you at one o'clock in the morning, to fly instantly, unless you chose the alternative of infamous captivity in the hands of Jordan.* I found you here, sitting by a black hearth without fire, & Ernest Fitz-Arthur lay on your knee asleep. You told me you had heard the firing, & that you were waiting for some communication from me, determined not to stir without orders lest a precipitate step on your part should embarrass me. I had a carriage already in waiting for you. I put you in & with the remains of my defeated followers escorted you as far as Zamorna. What followed after this, Miss Laury?'

Miss Laury covered her eyes with her hand. She seemed as if she could not answer.

'Well,' continued Hartford. 'In the midst of darkness & tempest & while the whole city of Zamorna seemed changed into a hell— peopled with fiends & inspired with madness—my lads were hewed down about you and your carriage was stopped. I very well remember what you did—how franticly you struggled to save Fitz-Arthur, & how you looked at me when he was snatched from you. As to your own preservation—that I need not repeat—only my arm did it. You acknowledge that, Miss Laury?'

'Hartford I do. But why do you dwell on that horrible scene?'

'Because I am now approaching the happiest hour of my life. I took you to the house of one of my tenants whom I could depend upon, and just as morning dawned you & I sat together & alone in the little chamber of a farmhouse, and you were in my arms, your head upon my shoulder & weeping out all your anguish on a breast that longed to bleed for you.'

Miss Laury agitatedly rose. She approached Hartford.

'My lord, you have been very kind to me, and I feel very grateful for that kindness. Perhaps sometime I may be able to repay it. We know not how the chances of fortune may turn. The weak have aided the strong, & I will watch vigilantly for the slightest opportunity to serve you. But do not talk in this way. I scarcely know whither your words tend.'

Lord Hartford paused a moment before he replied. Gazing at her with bended brows & folded arms, he said: 'Miss Laury, what do you think of me?'

'That you are one of the noblest hearts in the world,' she replied unhesitatingly.

She was standing just before Hartford, looking up at him, her hair in the attitude falling back from her brow, shading with exquisite curls her temples & her slender neck, her small sweet features with that high seriousness deepening their beauty, lit up by eyes so large, so dark, so swimming, so full of pleading benignity, of an expression of alarmed regard, as if she at once feared for and pitied the sinful abstraction of a great mind. Hartford could not stand it. He could have borne female anger or terror, but the look of enthusiastic gratitude softened by compassion nearly unmanned him. He turned his head for a moment aside, but then passion prevailed. Her beauty, when he looked again, struck through him, maddening sensation whetted to acuter power by a feeling like despair.

'You shall love me!' he exclaimed desperately. 'Do I not adore you? Would I not die for you? And must I in return receive only the cold regard of friendship? I am no Platonist,* Miss Laury. I am not your friend. I am—hear me, madam—your declared lover! Nay, you shall not leave me, by heaven! I am stronger than you are!'

She had stepped a pace or two back, appalled by his vehemence. He thought she meant to withdraw & determined not to be so balked. He clasped her at once in both his arms & kissed her furiously rather than fondly. Miss Laury did not struggle.

'Hartford,' said she, steadying her voice though it faltered in spite of her effort. 'This must be our parting scene. I will never see you again if you do not restrain yourself.'

Hartford saw that she turned pale & he felt her tremble violently. His arms relaxed their hold. He allowed her to leave him. She sat down on a chair opposite, & hurriedly wiped her brow which was damp & marble pale.

'Now Miss Laury,' said his lordship. 'No man in the world loves you as I do. Will you accept my title & my coronet? I fling them at your feet.'

'My lord, do you know whose I am?' she replied in a hollow & very suppressed tone. 'Do you know with what a sound those proposals fall on my ear, how impious & blasphemous they seem to be? Do you at all conceive how utterly impossible it is that I should ever love you? The scene I have just witnessed has given a strange wrench to all my accustomed habits of thought. I thought you a true-hearted, faithful man—I find that you are a traitor.'

'And do you despise me?' asked Hartford.

'No, my lord, I do not.'

She paused & looked down. The colour rose rapidly into her pale face. She sobbed—not in tears but in the overmastering approach of an impulse born of a warm & western heart.* Again she looked up. Her eyes had changed their aspect, beaming with a wild bright inspiration—truly, divinely Irish.

'Hartford!' she said. 'Had I met you long since, before I left Ellibank & forgot the St Cyprian & dishonoured my father,* I would have loved you. O, my lord, you know not how truly! I would have married you & made it the glory of my life to cheer & brighten your hearth. But I cannot do so now, never. I saw my present master when he had scarcely attained manhood. Do you think, Hartford, I will tell you what feelings I had for him? No tongue could express them. They were so fervid, so glowing in their colour that they efface everything else. I lost the power of properly appreciating the value of the world's opinion, of discerning the difference between right & wrong. I have never in my life contradicted Zamorna, never delayed obedience to his commands. I could not. He was something more to me than a human being. He superseded all things—all affections, all interests, all fears or hopes or principles. Unconnected with him my mind would be a blank—cold, dead, susceptible only of a sense of despair. How I should sicken if I were torn from him & thrown to you! Do not ask it. I would die first. No woman that ever loved my master could consent to leave him. There is nothing like him elsewhere. Hartford, if I were to be your wife, if Zamorna only looked at me, I should creep back like a slave to my former service. I should disgrace you as I have long since disgraced all my kindred. Think of that, my lord, & never say you love me again.'

'You do not frighten me,' replied Lord Hartford hardily. 'I would stand that chance, aye, & every other, if I only might see, at the head of my table in that old dining-room at Hartford Hall, yourself as my wife & lady. I am called proud as it is, but then I would shew Angria to what pitch of pride a man might attain, if I could, coming home at night, find Mina Laury waiting to receive me, if I could sit down & look at you with the consciousness that your exquisite beauty was all my own, that that cheek, those lips, that lovely hand might be claimed arbitrarily & you dare not refuse me. I should then feel happy.'

'Hartford, you would be more likely when you came home to find your house vacant & your hearth deserted. I know the extent of my own infatuation. I should go back to Zamorna & entreat him on my knees to let me be his slave again.'

'Madam,' said Hartford frowning, 'you dared not if you were my wife. I would guard you.'

'Then I should die under your guardianship. But the experiment will never be tried.'

Hartford came near, sat down by her side & leant over her. She did not shrink away.

'Oh!' he said. 'I am happy. There was a time when I dared not have come so near you. One summer evening, two years ago, I was walking in the twilight amongst those trees on the lawn, & at a turn I saw you sitting at the root of one of them by yourself. You were looking up at a star which was twinkling above the Sydenhams. You were in white. Your hands were folded on your knee & your hair was resting in still, shining curls on your neck. I stood and watched. The thought struck me—if that image sat now in my own woods, if she were something in which I had an interest, if I could go & press my lips to her brow & expect a smile in answer to the caress, if I could take her in my arms & turn her thoughts from that sky with its single star and from the distant country to which it points (for it hung in the west & I knew you were thinking about Senegambia), if I could attract those thoughts & centre them all in myself, how like heaven would the world become to me. I heard a window open & Zamorna's voice called through the silence "Mina!" The next moment I had the pleasure of seeing you standing on the lawn, close under this very casement, where the Duke sat leaning out, & you were allowing his hand to stray through your hair, & his lips—'

'Lord Hartford!' exclaimed Miss Laury, colouring to the eyes. 'This is more than I can bear. I have not been angry yet. I thought it folly to rage at you because you said you loved me, but what you have just said is like touching a nerve. It overpowers all reason. It is like a stinging taunt which I am under no obligation to endure from you. Every one knows what I am—but where is the woman in Africa who would have acted more wisely than I did if under the same circumstances she had been subject to the same temptations?'

'That is,' returned Hartford, whose eye was now glittering with a desperate reckless expression, 'where is the woman in Africa who would have said no to young Douro, when amongst the romantic hills of Ellibank he has pressed his suit on some fine moonlit summer night, & the girl & boy have found themselves alone in a green dell, here & there a tree to be their shade, far above the stars for their sentinels, & around the night for their wide curtain.'

The wild bounding throb of Miss Laury's heart was visible through her satin bodice. It was even audible as for a moment Hartford ceased his scoffing to note its effect. He was still close by her & she did not move from him. She did not speak. The pallid lamplight shewed her lips white, her cheek bloodless.

He continued unrelentingly & bitterly: 'In after times, doubtless, the woods of Hawkscliffe have witnessed many a tender scene, when the King of Angria has retired from the turmoil of business & the teazing of matrimony to love & leisure with his gentle mistress.'

'Now, Hartford, we must part,' interrupted Miss Laury. 'I see what your opinion of me is & it is very unjust, but not one which I willingly hear expressed. You have cut me to the heart. Good bye. I shall try to avoid seeing you for the future.'

She rose. Hartford did not attempt to detain her. She went out. As she closed the door he heard the bursting, convulsive gush of feelings which his taunts had wrought up to agony.

Her absence left a blank. Suddenly the wish to recall, to soothe, to propitiate her, rose in his mind. He strode to the door & opened it. There was a little hall or rather a wide passage without, in which one large lamp was quietly burning. Nothing appeared there, nor on the staircase of low broad steps in which it terminated. She seemed to have vanished.

Lord Hartford's hat & horseman's cloak lay on the side slab. There remained no further attraction for him at the Lodge of Rivaulx. The delirious dream of rapture which had intoxicated his sense broke up & disappeared, his passionate stern nature maddened under disappointment. He strode out into the black & frozen night, burning in flames no ice could quench. He ordered & mounted his steed &, dashing his spurs with harsh cruelty up to the rowels* into the flanks of the noble war-horse which had borne him victoriously through the carnage of Westwood & Leyden, he dashed in furious gallop down the road to Rivaulx.

The frost continued unbroken & the snow lay cold & cheerless all over Angria. It was a dreary morning. Large flakes were fluttering slowly down from the sky, thickening every moment. The trees around a stately hall, lying up among its grounds at some distance from the road-side, shuddered in the cutting wind that at intervals howled through them. We are now on a broad and public road. A great town lies on our left hand, with a deep river sweeping under the arches of a bridge. This is Zamorna & that house is Hartford Hall.

The wind increased, the sky darkened, & the bleached whirl of a snow-storm began to fill the air. Dashing at a rapid rate through the tempest, an open travelling carriage swept up the road. Four splendid greys & two mounted postillions gave the equipage an air of aristocratic style. It contained two gentlemen, one a man of between thirty or forty, having about him a good deal of the air of a nobleman, shawled to the eyes & buttoned up in at least three surtouts, with a water-proof white beaver hat, an immense mackintosh cape & beaver gloves.* His countenance bore a half rueful, half jesting expression. He seemed endeavouring to bear all things as smoothly as he could, but still the cold east wind & driving snow evidently put his philosophy very much to the test. The other traveller was a young high-featured gentleman with a pale face & accurately arched dark eyebrows. His person was carefully done up in a vast roquelaire of furs. A fur travelling cap decorated his head, which, however, Nature had much more effectively protected by a profusion of dark chestnut ringlets, now streaming long & thick in the wind. He presented to the said wind a case of bared teeth firmly set together & exposed in a desperate grin. They seemed daring the snow flakes to a comparison of whiteness.

'Oh,' groaned the elder traveller, 'I wish your Grace would be ruled by reason. What could possess you to insist on prosecuting the journey in such weather as this?'

'Stuff, Richton, an old campaigner like you ought to make objections to no weather. It's d—d cold though. I think all Greenland's coming down upon us. But you're not going to faint, are you, Richton? What are you staring at so? Do you see the d—l?'

'I think I do,' replied Lord Richton. 'And really, if your Grace will look two yards before you, you will be of the same opinion.'

The carriage was now turning that angle of the park-wall where a lodge on each side, overhung by some magnificent trees, formed the supporters to the stately iron gates opening upon the broad carriage-road which wound up through the park. The gates were open & just outside on the causeway of the high-road stood a tall, well-dressed man in a blue coat with military pantaloons of grey having a broad stripe of scarlet down the sides. His distinguished air, his handsome dark face, & his composed attitude—for he stood perfectly still with one hand on his side—gave singular effect to the circumstance of his being without hat. Had it been a summer day one would not so much have wondered at it, though even in the warmest weather it is not usual to see gentlemen parading the public roads uncovered. Now as the keen wind rushed down upon him through the boughs of the lofty trees arching the park-portal, and as the snow-flakes settled thick upon the short raven curls of his hair, he looked strange indeed.

Abruptly stepping forward, he seized the first leader of the chariot by the head & backed it fiercely. The postillions were about to whip on, consigning the hatless & energetic gentleman to that fate which is sought by the worshippers of Juggernaut,* when Lord Richton called out to them, 'For God's sake to stop the horses!'

'I think they are stopped with a vengeance,' said his young companion. Then leaning forward with a most verjuce expression on his pale

face, he said, 'Give that gentleman half a minute to get out of the way &
then drive on forward like d—ls.'

'My lord Duke,' interposed Richton, 'do you see who it is? Permit
me to solicit a few minutes' forbearance. Lord Hartford must be ill. I
will alight & speak to him.'

Before Richton could fulfil his purpose, the individual had let go
his hold & stood by the side of the chariot. Stretching out his clenched
hand with a menacing gesture, he addressed Zamorna thus:

'I've no hat to take off in Your Majesty's presence, so you must excuse
my rustic breeding. I saw the royal carriage at a distance & so I came out
to meet it something in a hurry. I'm just in time, God be thanked! Will
Your Grace get out & speak to me? By the Lord, I'll not leave this spot
alive without an audience.'

'Your lordship is cursedly drunk,' replied the Duke, keeping his
teeth as close shut as a vice. 'Ask for an audience when you're sober.
Drive on, postillions!'

'At the peril of your lives!' cried Hartford, & he drew out a brace of
pistols, cocked them, & presented one at each postillion.

'Rosier! my pistols!' shouted Zamorna to his valet, who sat behind, &
he threw himself at once from the chariot & stood facing Lord Hartford
on the high road.

'It is Your Grace that is intoxicated,' retorted the nobleman. 'And I'll
tell you with what—with wine of Cyprus or Cythera.* Your Majesty is
far too amorous, you had better keep a harem!'

'Come, sir,' said Zamorna in lofty scorn, 'this won't do. I see you are
mad. Postillions, seize him, & you, Rosier, go up to the Hall & fetch five
or six of his own domestics. Tell them to bring a strait waistcoat if they
have such a thing.'

'Your Grace would like to throw me into a dungeon,' said Hartford,
'but this is a free country, & we will have no western despotism. Be so
good as to hear me, my lord Duke, or I will shoot myself.'

'Small loss,' said Zamorna, lifting his lip with a sour sneer.

'Do not aggravate his insanity,' whispered Richton. 'Allow me to
manage him, my lord Duke. You had better return to the carriage, & I
will accompany Hartford home.' Then turning to Hartford, 'Take my
arm, Edward, & let us return to the house together. You do not seem
well this morning.'

'None of your snivel,' replied the gallant nobleman. 'I'll have satisfaction. I'm resolved on it. His Grace has injured me deeply.'

'A good move,' replied Zamorna. 'Then take your pistols, sir, & come
along. Rosier, take the carriage back to the town. Call at Dr Cooper's &

ask him to ride over to Hartford Hall. D—n you, sir, what are you staring at? Do as I bid you.'

'He is staring at the propriety of the monarch of a kingdom fighting
a duel with a madman,' replied Richton. 'If Your Grace will allow me
to go, I will return with a detachment of police & put both the sovereign
& the subject under safe ward.'*

'Have done with that trash!' said Zamorna angrily. 'Come on, you
will be wanted for a second.'

'Well,' said Richton, 'I don't wish to disoblige either Your Grace or
my friend Hartford, but it's an absurd & frantic piece of business. I
beseech you to consider a moment. Hartford, reflect—what are you
about to do?'

'To get vengeance for a thousand wrongs & sufferings,' was the reply.
'His Grace has dashed my happiness for life.'

Richton shook his head. 'I must stop this work,' he muttered to
himself. 'What demon is influencing Edward Hartford—& Zamorna
too, for I never saw such a fiendish glitter as that in his eyes just
now—strange madness!'

The noble Earl buttoned his surtout still closer & then followed the
two other gentlemen, who were already on their way to the house. The
carriage meantime drove off according to orders in the direction of
Zamorna.

Lord Hartford was not mad, though his conduct might seem to betoken
such a state of mind. He was only desperate. The disappointment of
the previous night had wrought him up to a pitch of rage & recklessness whose results, as we have just seen them, were of such a nature
as to convince Lord Richton that the doubts he had long harboured
of his friend's sanity were correct. So long as his passion for Miss
Laury remained unavowed & consequently unrejected, he had cherished a dreamy kind of hope that there existed some chance of success.
When wandering through his woods alone, he had fed on reveries of
some future day when she might fill his halls with the bliss of her presence and the light of her beauty. All day her image haunted him. It
seemed to speak to & look upon him with that mild friendly aspect he
had ever seen her wear, & then, as imagination prevailed, it brought
vividly back that hour when in a moment almost of despair her feminine weakness had thrown itself utterly on him for support & he had
been permitted to hold her in his arms & take her to his heart. He
remembered how she looked when, torn from danger & tumult, rescued
from hideous captivity, he carried her up the humble stair-case of a

farm-house, all pale & shuddering, with her long black curls spread dishevelled on his shoulder & her soft cheek resting there as confidingly as if he had indeed been her husband. From her trusting gentleness in those moments he drew blissful omens, now alas utterly belied. No web of self-delusion could now be woven. The truth was too stern. & besides, he had taunted her, hurt her feelings, & alienated forever her grateful friendship.

Having thus entered more particularly into the state of his feelings, let me proceed with my narrative.

The appartment into which Lord Hartford shewed his illustrious guest was that very dining-room where I first represented him sitting alone & maddening under the double influence of passion & wine. His manner now was more composed, and he demeaned himself even with lofty courtesy towards his sovereign. There was a particular chair in that room which Zamorna had always been accustomed to occupy when in happier days he had not unfrequently formed one of the splendid dinner-parties given at Hartford Hall. The General asked him to assume that seat now but he declined, acknowledging the courtesy only by a slight inclination of the head, & planted himself just before the hearth, his elbow leaning on the mantle-piece & his eyes looking down. In that position the eye-lids & the long fringes partly concealed the sweet expression of vindictiveness lurking beneath. But still, aided by the sour curl & pout of the lip, the passionate dishevelment of the hair & flushing of the brow, there was enough seen to stamp his countenance with a character of unpleasantness more easily conceived than described.

Lord Hartford, influenced by his usual habits, would not sit whilst his monarch stood, so he retired with Richton to the deeply embayed recess of a window. That worthy & prudent personage, bent upon settling this matter without coming to the absurd extreme now contemplated, began to reason with his friend on the subject.

'Hartford,' he said, speaking soft & low so that Zamorna could not overhear him, 'let me entreat you to consider well what you are about to do. I know that the scene which we have just witnessed is not the primary cause of the dispute between you & His Grace there, which is now about to terminate so fatally. I know that circumstances previously existed which gave birth to bitter feelings on both sides. I wish, Hartford, you would reconsider the steps you have taken. All is in vain: the lady in question can never be yours.'

'I know that, sir, & that is what makes me frantic. I have no motive left for living & if Zamorna wants my blood, let him have it.'

'You may kill him,' suggested Richton, 'and what will be the consequences then?'

'Trust me,' returned Hartford. 'I'll not hurt him much, though he
deserves it—the double-dyed infernal western profligate! But the fact
is he hates me far more than I hate him. Look at his face now reflected
in that mirror. God! he longs to see the last drop of blood I have in my
heart.'

'Hush! he will hear you,' said Richton. 'He certainly does not look
very amiable, but recollect you are the offender.'

'I know that,' replied Hartford gloomily. 'But it is not out of spite to
him that I wish to get his mistress. & how often in the half-year does he
see her or think about her? Grasping dog! Another king when he was
tired of his mistress would give her up—but he!—I think I'll shoot
him straight through the head. I would if his death would only win me
Miss Laury.'

That name, though spoken very low, caught Zamorna's ear, & he at
once comprehended the nature of the conversation. It is not often that
he had occasion to be jealous & as it is so rare so also it is a remarkably
curious & pretty sight to see him under the influence of that passion.
It worked in every fibre of his frame & boiled in every vein—blush
after blush deepened the hue of his cheek: as one ended another darker
crimson followed (this variation of colour resulting from strong emotion has been his wonted peculiarity from childhood). His whiskers
twined & writhed, & even the very curls seemed to stir on his brow.
Turning to Hartford, he spoke—

'What drivelling folly have you let into your head, sir, to dare to
look at any thing which belonged to me? Frantic idiot! To dream that I
should allow a coarse Angrian squire to possess anything that had ever
been mine—as if I knew how to relinquish! G—d d—n your gross-
ness! Richton, you have my pistols? Bring them here directly. I will
neither wait for doctors nor anybody else to settle this business.'

'My lord Duke!' began Richton.

'No interference, sir!' exclaimed His Grace. 'Bring the pistols!'

The Earl was not going to stand this arbitrary work. 'I wash my
hands of this bloody affair,' he said sternly, placing the pistols on the
table, & in silence he left the room.

The demon of Zamorna's nature was now completely roused.
Growling out his words in a deep & hoarse tone almost like the smothered roar of a lion, he savagely told Hartford to measure out his ground
in this room, for he would not delay the business a moment. Hartford
did so, without remonstrance or reply.

'Take your station!' thundered the barbarian.

'I have done so,' replied his lordship, 'and my pistol is ready.'

'Then fire!'

The deadly explosion succeeded, the flash & the cloud of smoke.

While the room still shook to the sound, almost before the flash had expired & the smoke burst after it, the door slowly opened & Lord Richton reappeared, wearing upon his face a far more fixed & stern solemnity than I ever saw there before.

'Who is hurt?' he asked.

There was but one erect figure visible through the vapour, & the thought thrilled through him, 'The other may be a corpse.'

Lord Hartford lay across the doorway, still & pale.

'My poor friend!' said Lord Richton &, kneeling on one knee, he propped against the other the wounded nobleman, from whose lips a moan of agony escaped as the Earl moved him.

'Thank God he is not quite dead!' was Richton's involuntary exclamation, for though a man accustomed to scenes of carnage on gory battle-plains, & though of enduring nerves & cool resolution, he felt a pang at this spectacle of fierce manslaughter amid scenes of domestic peace. The renowned & gallant soldier, who had escaped hostile weapons & returned unharmed from fields of terrific strife, lay as it seemed dying, under his own roof. Blood began to drop on to Richton's hand & a large crimson stain appeared on the ruffles of his shirt. The same ominous dye darkened Lord Hartford's lips & oozed through them when he made vain efforts to speak. He had been wounded in the region of the lungs.

A thundering knock & a loud ring at the door-bell now broke up the appalling silence which had fallen. It was Dr Cooper.* He speedily entered, followed by a surgeon with instruments &c. Richton silently resigned his friend to their hands & turned for the first time to the other actor in this horrid scene.

The Duke of Zamorna was standing by a window, coolly buttoning his surtout over the pistols which he had replaced in his breast.

'Is Your Majesty hurt?' asked Richton.

'No sir. May I trouble you to hand me my gloves?'

They lay on a side-board near the Earl. He politely complied with the request, handing over at the same time a large shawl or scarf of crimson silk which the Duke had taken from his neck. In this he proceeded to envelope his throat & a considerable portion of his face, leaving little more visible than the forehead, eyes & high Roman nose. Then drawing on his gloves he turned to Dr Cooper.

'Of what nature is the wound, sir? Is there any likelihood of Lord Hartford's recovery?'

'A possibility exists that he may recover, my lord Duke, but the wound is a severe one. The lungs have only just escaped.'

The Duke drew near the couch on which his general had been raised, looked at the wound then under the operation of the surgeon's probing knife & transferred his glance from the bloody breast to the pallid face of the sufferer. Hartford, who had borne the extraction of the bullet without a groan & whose clenched teeth & rigid brow seemed defying pain to do its worst, smiled faintly when he saw his monarch's eye bent upon him with searching keenness. In spite of the surgeon's prohibition, he attempted to speak.

'Zamorna,' he said, 'I have got your hate, but you shall not blight me with your contempt. This is but a little matter. Why did you not inflict more upon me, that I might bear it without flinching? You called me a coarse Angrian squire ten minutes since. Angrians are men as well as westerns.'

'Brutes, rather,' replied Zamorna. 'Faithful, gallant, noble brutes.'

He left the room, for his carriage had now returned and waited at the door. Before Lord Richton followed him, he stopped a moment to take leave of his friend.

'Well,' murmured Hartford as he feebly returned the pressure of the Earl's hand, 'Zamorna has finished me, but I bear him no ill-will. My love for his mistress was involuntary. I am not sorry for it now. I adore her to the last. Flower, if I die give Miss Laury this token of my truth.' He drew off the gold ring from his little finger & gave it into Richton's hand. 'Good G——d!' he muttered turning away. 'I would have endured Hell's torments to win her love. My feelings are not changed; they are just the same—passion for her, bitter self-reproach for my treachery to her master. But he has paid himself in blood, the purest coin to a Western. Farewell Richton.'

They parted without another word on either side. Richton joined the Duke, sprung to his place in the carriage & off it swept like the wind.

II

Miss Laury was sitting after breakfast in a small library. Her desk* lay before her & two large ruled quartos filled with items & figures which she seemed to be comparing. Behind her chair stood a tall, well-made, soldierly young man with light hair. His dress was plain &

gentlemanly—the epaulette on one shoulder alone indicated an official capacity. He watched with a fixed look of attention the movements of the small finger which ascended in rapid calculation the long columns of accounts. It was strange to see the absorption of mind expressed in Miss Laury's face, the gravity of her smooth white brow shaded with drooping curls, the scarcely perceptible & unsmiling movement of her lips—though those lips in their rosy sweetness seemed formed only for smiles. Edward Percy at his ledger could not have appeared more completely wrapt in the mysteries of practice* and fractions. An hour or more lapsed in this employment, the room meantime continuing in profound silence, broken only by an occasional observation addressed by Miss Laury to the gentleman behind her, concerning the legitimacy of some item or the absence of some stray farthing wanted to complete the accuracy of the sum total. In this balancing of the books she displayed a most business-like sharpness & strictness. The slightest fault was detected and remarked on, in few words but with a quick searching glance. However, the accountant had evidently been accustomed to her surveillance, for on the whole his books were a specimen of arithmetical correctness.

'Very well,' said Miss Laury as she closed the volumes. 'Your accounts do you credit, Mr O'Neill. You may tell His Grace that all is quite right. Your memoranda tally with my own exactly.'

Mr O'Neill bowed. 'Thank you, madam. This will bear me out against Lord Hartford. His lordship lectured me severely last time he came to inspect Fort Adrian.'

'What about?' asked Miss Laury, turning aside her face to hide the deepening of colour which overspread it at the mention of Lord Hartford's name.

'I can hardly tell you, madam, but his lordship was in a savage temper. Nothing could please him—he found fault with everything & everybody. I thought he scarcely appeared himself & that has been the opinion of many lately.'

Miss Laury gently shook her head. 'You shall not say so, Ryan,' she replied in a soft tone of reproof. 'Lord Hartford has a great many things to think about, and he is naturally rather stern. You ought to bear with his tempers.'

'Necessity has no law,* madam,' replied Mr O'Neill with a smile, '& I must bear with them. But his lordship is not a popular man in the army. He orders the lash so unsparingly. We like the Earl of Arundel ten times better.'

'Ah!' said Miss Laury smiling. 'You & I are Westerns, Mr O'Neill—Irish & we favour our countrymen—but Hartford is a gallant commander. His men can always trust him. Do not let us be partial.'

Mr O'Neill bowed in deference to her opinion, but smiled at the same time as if he doubted its justice. Taking up his books, he seemed about to leave the room. Before he did so, however, he turned & said: 'The Duke wished me to inform you, madam, that he would probably be here about four or five o'clock in the afternoon.'

'To day?' asked Miss Laury in an accent of surprise.

'Yes, madam.'

She paused a moment, then said quickly, 'Very well, sir.'

Mr O'Neill now took his leave, with another low & respectful obeisance. Miss Laury returned it with a slight abstracted bow. Her thoughts were all caught up & hurried away by that last communication. For a long time after the door had closed she sat with her head on her hand, lost in a tumultuous flush of ideas, anticipations awakened by that simple sentence, 'The Duke will be here to-day.'

The striking of a time-piece roused her. She remembered that twenty tasks waited her direction. Always active, always employed, it was not her custom to waste many hours in dreaming. She rose, closed her desk & left the quiet library for busier scenes.

Four o'clock came & Miss Laury's foot was heard on the stair-case, descending from her chamber. She crossed the large, light passage—such an apparition of feminine elegance & beauty! She had dressed herself splendidly. The robe of black satin became at once her slender form, which it envelloped in full & shining folds, & her bright blooming complexion, which it set off by the contrast of colour. Glittering through her curls there was a band of fine diamonds, & drops of the same pure gem trembled from her small, delicate ears. These ornaments, so regal in their nature, had been the gift of royalty, & were worn now chiefly for the associations of soft & happy moments which their gleam might be supposed to convey.

She entered her drawing-room & stood by the window. From thence appeared one glimpse of the high-road visible through the thickening shades of Rivaulx. Even that was now almost concealed by the frozen mist in which the approach of twilight was wrapt. All was very quiet, both in the house & in the wood. A carriage drew near. She heard the sound. She saw it shoot through the fog. But it was not Zamorna. No, the driving was neither the driving of Jehu the son of Nimshi,* nor that of Jehu's postillions. She had not gazed a minute before her experienced eye discerned that there was something wrong with the horses. The harness had got entangled, or they were frightened. The coachman had lost command over them; they were plunging violently.

She rung the bell. A servant entered. She ordered immediate assistance to be despatched to that carriage on the road. Two grooms presently* hurried down the drive to execute her commands, but before they could reach the spot, one of the horses in its gambols had slipped on the icy road & fallen. The others grew more unmanageable, & presently the carriage lay overturned on the road side. One of Miss Laury's messengers came back. She threw up the window that she might communicate with him more readily.

'Any accident?' she asked. 'Anybody hurt?'

'I hope not much, madam.'

'Who is in the carriage?'

'Only one lady, and she seems to have fainted. She looked very white when I opened the door. What is to be done, madam?'

Miss Laury, with fresh Irish frankness, answered directly, 'Bring them all into the house. Let the horses be taken into the stables & the servants—how many are there?'

'Three, madam. Two postillions & a footman—it seems quite a gentleman's turn-out, very plain but quite slap up. Beautiful horses.'

'Do you know the liveries?'

'Can't say, madam. Postillions grey & white, footmen in plain clothes. Horses frightened at a drove of Sydenham oxen they say—very spirited nags.'

'Well, you have my orders. Bring the lady in directly & make the others comfortable.'

'Yes madam.'

The groom touched his hat & departed. Miss [Laury] shut her window. It was very cold. Not many minutes elapsed before the lady, in the arms of her own servants, was slowly brought up the lawn & ushered into the drawing-room.

'Lay her on the sofa,' said Miss Laury.

She was obeyed. The lady's travelling cloak was carefully removed, & a thin figure became apparent, in a dark silk dress. The cushions of down scarcely sunk under the pressure, it was so light.

Her swoon was now passing off. The genial warmth of the fire, which shone full on her, revived her. Opening her eyes, she looked up at Miss Laury's face, who was bending close over her & wetting her lips with some cordial. Recognizing a stranger, she shyly turned her glance aside & asked for her servants.

'They are in the house, madam, & perfectly safe. But you cannot pursue your journey at present. The carriage is much broken.'

The lady lay silent. She looked keenly round the room & seeing the perfect elegance of its arrangement, the cheerful & tranquil glow of its hearthlight, she appeared to grow more composed. Turning a little on the cushions which supported her & by no means looking at Miss Laury but straight the other way, she said, 'To whom am I indebted for this kindness? Where am I?'

'In a hospitable country, madam. The Angrians never turn their backs on strangers.'

'I know I am in Angria,' she said quickly. 'But where? What is the name of the house, who are you?'

Miss Laury coloured slightly. It seemed as if there was some undefined reluctance to give her real name. That, she knew, was widely celebrated—too widely. Most likely the lady would turn from her in contempt if she heard it & Miss Laury felt she could not bear that.

'I am only the housekeeper,' she said. 'This is a shooting Lodge belonging to a great Angrian proprietor.'

'Who?' asked the lady, who was not to be put off by indirect answers.

Again Miss Laury hesitated. For her life she could not have said, 'His Grace the Duke of Zamorna.' She replied hastily, 'A gentleman of Western extraction, a distant branch of the great Pakenhams*—so at least the family records say, but they have been long naturalized in the east.'

'I never heard of them,' replied the lady. 'Pakenham: that is not an Angrian name.'

'Perhaps, madam, you are not particularly acquainted with this part of the country?'

'I know Hawkscliffe,' said the lady, '& your house is on the very borders, within the royal liberties,* is it not?'

'Yes madam. It stood there before the great Duke bought up the forest manor, & His Majesty allowed my master to retain this Lodge & the privilege of sporting in the chase.'

'Well, and you are Mr Pakenham's housekeeper?'

'Yes madam.'

The lady surveyed Miss Laury with another furtive side-glance of her large, majestic eyes. Those eyes lingered upon the diamond earrings, the bandeau of brilliants that flashed from between the clusters of raven curls, then passed over the sweet face, the exquisite figure of the young housekeeper, & finally were reverted to the wall with an expression that spoke volumes. Miss Laury could have torn the dazzling pendants from her ears. She was bitterly stung. 'Every body knows me,' she said to herself. ' "Mistress", I suppose, is branded on my brow.'

In her turn she gazed on her guest. The lady was but a young creature, though so high & commanding in her demeanour. She had very small & feminine features, handsome eyes, a neck of delicate curve & hue, fair, long, graceful little snowy aristocratic hands & sandalled feet to match. It would have been difficult to tell her rank by her dress. None of those dazzling witnesses appeared which had betrayed Miss Laury. Any gentleman's wife might have worn the gown of dark blue silk, the tinted gloves of Parisian kid & the fairy sandals of black satin in which she was attired.

'May I have a room to myself?' she asked, again turning her eyes with something like a smile toward Miss Laury.

'Certainly, madam. I wish to make you comfortable. Can you walk up stairs?'

'Oh yes!'

She rose from the couch, &, leaning upon Miss Laury's offered arm in a way that shewed she had been used to that sort of support, they both glided from the room. Having seen her fair but somewhat haughty guest carefully laid on a stately crimson bed in a quiet & spacious chamber, having seen her head sink with all its curls onto the pillow of down, her large shy eyes close under their smooth eyelids, & her little slender hands fold on her breast in an attitude of perfect repose, Miss Laury prepared to leave her. She stirred.

'Come back a moment,' she said. She was obeyed: there was something in the tone of her voice which exacted obedience. 'I don't know who you are,' she said, 'but I am very much obliged to you for your kindness. If my manners are displeasing, forgive me. I mean no incivility. I suppose you will wish to know my name. It is Mrs Irving—my husband is a minister in the Northern Kirk.* I come from Sneachiesland. Now you may go.'

Miss Laury did go. Mrs Irving had testified incredulity respecting her story, & now she reciprocated that incredulity. Both ladies were lost in their own mystification.

Five o'clock now struck. It was nearly dark. A servant with a taper was lighting up the chandeliers in the large dining-room, where a table spread for dinner received the kindling lamp-light upon a starry service of silver. It was likewise magnificently flashed back from a splendid sideboard, all arranged in readiness to receive the great, the expected guest.

Tolerably punctual in keeping an appointment when he means to keep it at all, Zamorna entered the house as the fairy-like voice of a musical-clock in the passage struck out its symphony to the pendulum. The opening of the front-door, a bitter rush of the night wind, & then the sudden close & the step advancing forwards were the signals of his arrival. Miss Laury was in the dining-room looking round & giving the last touch to all things. She just met her master as he entered. His cold lip pressed to her forehead & his colder hand clasping hers brought the sensation which it was her custom of weeks & months to wait for, and to consider, when attained, as the ample recompense for all delay, all toil, all suffering.

'I am frozen, Mina,' said he. 'I came on horseback for the last four miles and the night is like Canada.'

Chafing his icy hand to animation between her own warm supple palms, she answered by the speechless but expressive look of joy, satisfaction, idolatry, which filled & overflowed her eyes.

'What can I do for you, my lord?' were her first words, as he stood by the fire rubbing his hands cheerily over the blaze. He laughed.

'Put your arms round my neck, Mina, & kiss my cheek as warm & blooming as your own.'

If Mina Laury had been Mina Wellesley she would have done so, & it gave her a pang to resist the impulse that urged her to take him at his word. But she put it by and only diffidently drew near the arm-chair into which he had now thrown himself & began to smooth & separate the curls which were matted on his temples. She noticed, as the first smile of salutation subsided, a gloom succeeded on her master's brow, which, however he spoke or laughed afterwards, remained a settled characteristic of his countenance.

'What visitors are in the house?' he asked. 'I saw the groom rubbing down four black horses before the stables as I came in. They are not of the Hawkscliffe stud, I think?'

'No my lord. A carriage was overturned at the Lawn Gates about an hour since, & as the lady who was in it was taken out insensible, I ordered her to be brought up here and her servants accommodated for the night.'

'And do you know who the lady is?' continued His Grace. 'The horses are good—first rate.'

'She says her name is Mrs Irving & that she is the wife of a Presbyterian minister in the North, but—'

'You hardly believe her?' interrupted the Duke.

'No,' returned Miss Laury. I must say I took her for a lady of rank. She has something highly aristocratic about her manners & aspect, & she appeared to know a good deal about Angria.'

'What is she like?' asked Zamorna. 'Young or old, handsome or ugly?'

'She is young, slender, not so tall as I am, and I should say rather elegant than handsome—very pale, cold in her demeanour. She has a small mouth & chin, & a very fair neck.'

'Humph! a trifle like Lady Stuartville,' replied His Majesty. 'I should not wonder if it is the Countess. But I'll know. Perhaps you did not say to whom the house belonged, Mina?'

'I said,' replied Mina, smiling, 'the owner of the house was a great Angrian proprietor, a lineal descendant of the Western Pakenhams, & that I was his housekeeper.'

'Very good! She would not believe you. You look like an Angrian country gentleman's dolly. Give me your hand, my girl. Are you not as old as I am?'

'Yes, my lord Duke. I was born on the same day, an hour after Your Grace.'

'So I have heard, but it must be a mistake. You don't look twenty & I am twenty-five. My beautiful Western—what eyes! Look at me, Mina, straight & don't blush.'

Mina tryed to look but she could not do it without blushing. She coloured to the temples.

'Pshaw!' said His Grace pushing her away. 'Pretending to be modest! My acquaintance of ten years cannot meet my eye unshrinkingly. Have you lost that ring I once gave you, Mina?'

'What ring, my lord? You have given me many.'

'That which I said had the essence of your whole heart & mind engraven in the stone as a motto.'

'FIDELITY?' asked Miss Laury, & she held out her hand with a graven emerald on the forefinger.

'Right' was the reply. 'Is it your motto still?' And with one of his hungry, jealous glances he seemed trying to read her conscience. Miss Laury at once saw that late transactions were not a secret confined between herself & Lord Hartford. She saw His Grace was unhinged & strongly inclined to be savage. She stood & watched him with a sad, fearful gaze.

'Well,' she said turning away after a long pause, 'if Your Grace is angry with me I've very little to care about in this world.'

The entrance of servants with the dinner prevented Zamorna's answer. As he took his place at the head of the table, he said to the man who stood behind him: 'Give Mr Pakenham's compliments to Mrs Irving, and say that he will be happy to see her at his table, if she will honour him so far as to be present there.'

The footman vanished. He returned in five minutes.

'Mrs Irving is too much tired to avail herself of Mr Pakenham's kind invitation at present, but she will be happy to join him at tea.'

'Very well,' said Zamorna, then looking round, 'Where is Miss Laury?'

Mina was in the act of gliding from the room but she stopped mechanically at his call.

'Am I to dine alone?' he asked.

'Does Your Grace wish me to attend you?'

He answered by rising & leading her to her seat. He then resumed his own, & dinner commenced. It was not till after the cloth was withdrawn & the servants had retired that the Duke, whilst he sipped his single glass of champagne, recommenced the conversation he had before so unpleasantly entered upon.

'Come here—my girl,' he said drawing a chair close to his side. Mina never delayed, never hesitated, through bashfulness or any other feeling, to comply with his orders.

'Now,' he continued, leaning his head towards her & placing his hand on her shoulder, 'are you happy, Mina? Do you want anything?'

'Nothing my lord.'

She spoke truly. All that was capable of yielding her happiness on this side of eternity was at that moment within her reach. The room was full of calm. The lamps burnt as if they were listening. The fire sent up no flickering flame, but diffused a broad, still, glowing light over all the spacious saloon. Zamorna touched her—his form & features filled her eye, his voice her ear, his presence her whole heart. She was soothed to perfect happiness.

'My Fidelity' pursued that musical voice. 'If thou hast any favour to ask, now is the time. I'm all concession, as sweet as honey, as yielding as a lady's glove. Come, Esther, what is thy petition & thy request? Even to the half of my kingdom it shall be granted.'*

'Nothing,' again murmured Miss Laury. 'Oh, my lord, nothing. What can I want?'

'Nothing!' he repeated. 'What, no reward for ten years' faith & love & devotion, no reward for the companionship in six months' exile, no recompense to the little hand that has so often smoothed my pillow in sickness—to the sweet lips that have many a time in cool & dewy health been pressed to a brow of fever, none to the dark Milesian* eyes that once grew dim with watching through endless nights by my couch of delirium? Need I speak of the sweetness & fortitude that cheered sufferings known only to thee & me, Mina, of the devotion that gave me bread when thou wast dying with hunger & that scarcely more than a year since? For all this & much more must there be no reward?'

'I have had it,' said Miss Laury. 'I have it now.'

'But,' continued the Duke, 'what if I have devised something worthy of your acceptance? Look up now & listen to me.'

She did look up, but she speedily looked down again—her master's eye was insupportable. It burnt absolutely with infernal fire. 'What is he going to say?' murmured Miss Laury to herself & she trembled.

'I say, love,' pursued the individual drawing her a little closer to him, 'I will give you as a reward a husband—don't start now—& that husband shall be a nobleman, & that nobleman is called Lord Hartford! Now, madam, stand up & let me look at you.'

He opened his arms & Miss Laury sprang erect like a loosened bow.

'Your Grace is anticipated!' she said. 'That offer has been made me before. Lord Hartford did it himself three days ago.'

'And what did you say, madam? Speak the truth, now. Subterfuge won't avail you.'

'What did I say? Zamorna, I don't know—it little signifies. You have rewarded me, my lord Duke, but I cannot bear this—I feel sick.'

With a deep, short sob she turned white, & fell close by the Duke, her head against his foot. This was the first time in her life that Mina Laury had fainted, but strong health availed nothing against the deadly struggle which convulsed every feeling of her nature when she heard her master's announcement. She believed him to be perfectly sincere. She thought he was tired of her and she could not stand it.

I suppose Zamorna's first feeling when she fell was horror, & his next I am tolerably certain was intense gratification. People say I am not in earnest when I abuse him, or else I would here insert half a page of deserved vituperation, deserved & heart-felt. As it is, I will merely relate his conduct without note or comment. He took a wax taper from the table & held it over Miss Laury. Here could be no dissimulation. She was white as marble & still as stone. In truth, then, she did intensely love him, with a devotion that left no room in her thoughts for one shadow of an alien image.

Do not think, reader, that Zamorna meant to be so generous as to bestow Miss Laury on Lord Hartford. No, trust him—he was but testing in his usual way the attachment which a thousand proofs, daily given, ought long ago to have convinced him was undying. While he yet gazed she began to recover. Her eye-lids stirred & then slowly dawned from beneath the large black orbs that scarcely met his before they filled to over-flowing with sorrow. Not a gleam of anger, not a whisper of reproach. Her lips & eyes spoke together no other language than the simple words, 'I cannot leave you.'

She rose feebly & with effort. The Duke stretched out his hand to assist her. He held to her lips the scarcely-tasted wine-glass.

'Mina,' he said, 'are you collected enough to hear me?'

'Yes my lord.'

'Then listen. I would much sooner give half—aye, the whole—of my estates to Lord Hartford than yourself. What I said just now was only to try you.'

Miss Laury raised her eyes & sighed like one awaking from some hideous dream, but she could not speak.

'Would I,' continued the Duke, 'would I resign the possession of my first love to any hands but my own? I would far rather see her in her coffin. And I would lay you there as still, as white & much more lifeless than you were stretched just now at my feet, before I would for threat, for entreaty, for purchase, give to another a glance of your eye or a smile from your lip. I know you adore me now, Mina, for you could not feign that agitation, & therefore I will tell you what proof I gave yesterday of my regard for you. Hartford mentioned your name in my presence, & I revenged the profanation by a shot which sent him to his bed little better than a corpse.'

Miss Laury shuddered. But so dark & profound are the mysteries of human nature, ever allying vice with virtue, that I fear this bloody proof of her master's love brought to her heart more rapture than horror. She said not a word, for now Zamorna's arms were again folded round her & again he was soothing her to tranquillity by endearments & caresses that far away removed all thought of the world, all past pangs of shame, all cold doubts, all weariness, all heart-sickness resulting from hope long deferred. [He] had told her that she was his first love & now she felt tempted to believed that she was likewise his only love. Strong-minded beyond her sex, active, energetic & accomplished in all other points of view—here she was weak as a child. She lost her identity. Her very life was swallowed up in that of another.

There came a knock to the door. Zamorna rose & opened it. His valet stood without.

'Might I speak with Your Grace in the ante-room?' asked Monsieur Rosier, in somewhat of a hurried tone. The Duke followed him out.

'What do you want with me sir? Anything the matter?'

'Ahem!' began Eugene, whose countenance expressed much more embarrassment than is the usual characteristic of his dark sharp physiognomy. 'Ahem! My lord Duke, rather a curious spot of work—a complete conjuror's trick, if Your Grace will allow me to say so.'

'What do you mean sir?'

'Sacré! I hardly know. I must confess I felt a trifle stupefied when I saw it.'

'Saw what? Speak plainly, Rosier.'

'How Your Grace is to act I can't imagine,' replied the valet, 'though indeed I have seen Your Majesty double wonderfully well when the case appeared to me extremely embarrassing. But this I really thought extra—I could not have dreamt—'

'Speak to the point, Rosier or—' Zamorna lifted his hand.

'Mort de ma vie!' exclaimed Eugene. 'I will tell Your Grace all I know. I was walking carelessly through the passage about ten minutes since when I heard a step on the stairs, a light step as if of a very small foot. I turned & there was a lady coming down. My lord, she was a lady!'

'Well sir, did you know her?'

'I think, if my eyes were not bewitched, I did. I stood in the shade, screened by a pillar, & she passed very near without observing me. I saw her distinctly & may I be d—d this very moment if it was not—'

'Who sir?'

'The Duchess!'

There was a pause, which was closed by [a] clear & remarkably prolonged whistle from the Duke. He put both his hands into his pockets & took a leisurely turn through the room.

'You're sure, Eugene?' he said. 'I know you dare not tell me a lie in such matters, because you have a laudable & natural regard to your proper carcase. Aye, it's true enough, I'll be sworn—Mrs Irving, wife of a minister in the North—a satirical hit at my royal self, by G—d! Pale, fair neck, little mouth & chin—very good. I wish that same little mouth & chin were about a hundred miles off. What can have brought her? Anxiety about her invaluable husband—could not bear any longer without him—obliged to set off to see what he was doing. It's as well that turnspit Rosier told me however. If she had entered the room unexpectedly about five minutes since—God! I should have had no resource but to tie her hand and foot. It would have killed her. What the D—l shall I do? Must not be angry; she can't do with that sort of thing just now. Talk softly, reprove her gently, swear black & white to my having no connection with Mr Pakenham's housekeeper.'

Ceasing his soliloquy the Duke turned again to his valet.

'What room did her Grace go into?'

'The drawing-room my lord. She's there now.'

'Well, say nothing about it, Rosier, on pain of sudden death. Do you hear sir?'

Rosier laid his hand on his heart, & Zamorna left the room to commence operations.

Softly unclosing the drawing-room door, he perceived a lady by the hearth. Her back was towards him, but there could be no mistake. The whole turn of form, the style of dress, the curled auburn head, all were attributes but of one person—of his own unique, haughty, jealous little Duchess. He closed the door as noiselessly as he had opened it and stole forwards. Her attention was absorbed in something, a book she had picked up. As he stood unobserved behind her he could see that her eye rested on the fly leaf, where was written in his own hand—

> Holy St Cyprian! thy waters stray
>   With still and solemn tone,
> And fast my bright hours pass away
> And somewhat throws a shadow grey,
> Even as twilight closes day
>   Upon thy waters lone.
>
> Farewell! if I might come again,
>   Young as I was & as free,
> And feel once more in every vein
> The fire of that first passion reign
> Which sorrow could not quench, nor pain,
>   I'd soon return to thee;
> But while thy billows seek the main
>   That never more may be!

This was dated 'Mornington—1829'.* The Duchess felt a hand press her shoulder & she looked up. The force of attraction had its usual results & she clung to what she saw.

'Adrian! Adrian!' was all her lips would utter.

'Mary, Mary,' replied the Duke allowing her to hang about him. 'Pretty doings! What brought you here? Are you running away, eloping, in my absence?'

'Adrian, why did you leave me? You said you would come back in a week & it's eight days since. I could not bear any longer. I have never slept nor rested since you left me. Do come home!'

'So you actually have set off in search of a husband,' said Zamorna laughing heartily, '& been overturned & obliged to take shelter in Pakenham's shooting-box!'

'Why are you here, Adrian?' inquired the Duchess, who was far too much in earnest to join in his laugh. 'Who is Pakenham & who is that person who calls herself his housekeeper? & why do you let anybody live so near Hawkscliffe without ever telling me?'

'I forgot to tell you,' said his Grace. 'I've other things to think about when those bright hazel eyes are looking up to me. As for Pakenham, to tell you the truth, he's a sort of left hand cousin* of your own, being natural son to the old Admiral, my uncle in the south, & his housekeeper is his sister. Voilà tout. Kiss me now.'

The Duchess did kiss him, but it was with a heavy sigh. The cloud of jealous anxiety hung on her brow undissipated.

'Adrian, my heart aches still. Why have you been staying so long in Angria? O, you don't care for me! You have never thought how miserably I have been longing for your return. Adrian—' She stopped & cryed.

'Mary, recollect yourself,' said His Grace. 'I cannot be always at your feet. You were not so weak when we were first married. You let me leave you often then without any jealous remonstrance.'

'I did not know you so well at that time,' said Mary, '& if my mind is weakened, all its strength has gone away in tears & terrors for you. I am neither so handsome nor so cheerful as I once was, but you ought to forgive my decay because you have caused it.'

'Low spirits!' returned Zamorna. 'Looking on the dark side of matters! God bless me, the wicked is caught in his own net. I wish I could add, "yet shall I withal escape".* Mary, never again reproach yourself with loss of beauty till I give the hint first. Believe me now, in that & every other respect you are just what I wish you to be. You cannot fade any more than marble can—at least not to my eyes—& as for your devotions & tenderness, though I chide its excess sometimes because it wastes & bleaches you almost to a shadow, yet it forms the very firmest chain that binds me to you. Now cheer up! Tonight you shall go to

Hawkscliffe; it is only five miles off. I cannot accompany you because I have some important business to transact with Pakenham which must not be deferred. To-morrow I will be at the castle before dawn. The carriage shall be ready. I will put you in, myself beside you. Off we go straight to Verdopolis & there for the next three months I will tire you of my company morning, noon & night. Now, what can I promise more? If you choose to be jealous of Henri Fernando, Baron of Etrei, or John, Duke of Fidena, or the fair Earl of Richton—who, as God is my witness, has been the only companion of my present peregrination—why, I can't help it. I must then take to soda-water & despair, or have myself petrified & carved into an Apollo* for your dressing-room. Lord, I get not credit with my virtue!'

By dint of lies & laughter, the individual at last succeeded in getting all things settled to his mind. The Duchess went to Hawkscliffe that night, & keeping his promise for once he accompanied her to Verdopolis next morning.

Lord Hartford lies still between life & death. His passion is neither weakened by pain, piqued by rejection, nor cooled by absence.* On the iron nerves of the man are graven an impression which nothing can efface. Warner curses him, Richton deplores.

For a long space of time,* good-bye, reader. I have done my best to please you, & though I know that through feebleness, dullness & iteration, my work terminates rather in failure [than] triumph, yet you are bound to forgive, for I have done my best.

C Brontë Jany 17th

Haworth 1838

CAROLINE VERNON

I

When I concluded my last book I made a solemn resolve that I would write no more till I had somewhat to write about, & at the time I had a sort of notion that perhaps many years might elapse before aught should transpire novel & smart enough to induce me to resume my relinquished pen. But lo you! Scarce three moons have waxed & waned* ere

'the creature's at his dirty work again.'*

And yet it is no novelty—no fresh & startling position of affairs—that has dipped my quill in ink & spread the blank sheet before me. I have but been looking forth as usual over the face of society. I have but been eating my commons in Chapel Street—dressing & dining out daily—reading newspapers—attending the Theatres nightly—taking my place about once a week in the fire-flaught* Angrian Mail—rushing as far as Zamorna*—sometimes continuing my career till I saw the smoke of Adrianopolis. Snatching a look at the staring shops & raw new palaces of that Great Baby Capital, then like a water-god taking to the Calabar—not however robing myself in flags & crowning myself with sedge,* but with a ticket in my fist—getting on board a steamer & away, all fizz & foam, down past Mouthton & coasting it along by Doverham* back to Verdopolis again. When subdued by a fit of pathos & sentimentalities, I've packed a hamper with sandwiches & gone to Alnwick* or somewhere there awa'. But I'll try that no more, for last time I did it—chancing to sit down under a willow* in the grounds to eat a cold fowl & drink a bottle of ginger-beer—I made use of the pedestal of a statue for my table, whereat a keeper thought fit to express himself eminently scandalized & in an insolent manner to give notice that such liberties were not permitted at the castle, that strangers were excluded from this part the grounds, that the statue was considered a valuable piece of sculpture—being the likeness of some male or female of the house of Wharton who had died twenty years ago*—with a lot of rhodomontade* all tending to shew that I had committed sacrilege or something like it by merely placing a mustard-glass & pepper box, with a dinner-bun & knife & fork, at the base of a stupid stone idol representing somebody in their chemise gazing fatuitously at their own naked toes.

Howsumdiver,* even in this course of life I've seen & heard a summat that, like the notes of a tourist, may sell when committed to paper.* Lord, a book-wright need never be at a loss! One can't expect earthquakes & insurrections every-day.

There's not always
>   An Angrian campaign going on in the rain,
>   Nor a Gentleman Squire lighting his fire
>   Up on the moors with his blackguards & boors,*
>   Nor a Duke & a lord drawing the sword,
>   Hectoring & lying the whole world defying,
>   Then sitting down crying.

There's not always
>   A Shopkeeper militant coming out iligant,*
>   With King Boy & King Jack both genteely in black
>   Forming Holy Alliance & breathing defiance,
>   Nor a Prince finding brandy every day coming handy,
>   While he's conquering of lands with his bold nigger bands
>   Like a man of his hands.*

There's not always
>   A Death & a Marriage—a Hearse & a Carriage,
>   A Bigamy cause—A King versus laws,
>   Nor a short Transportation for the good of the nation,
>   Nor a speedy returning mid national mourning,
>   While him & his father refuse to foregather
>   'Cause the Earl hadn't rather.*

Reader, these things don't happen every day. It's well they don't, for a constant recurrence of such stimulus would soon wear out the public stomach & bring on indigestion. But surely one can find something to talk about, though miracles are no longer wrought in the world. Battlefields, it is true, are now growing corn—according to a paragraph in a Westland newspaper which I had a while since in my hand: 'Barley & oats are looking well in the neighbourhood of Leyden & all the hay is carried from the fields about Evesham. Nay, they tell us the navigation of the Cirhala is about to be improved by a canal, which will greatly facilitate the conveyance of goods up the country, & that subscriptions are on foot for erecting a new & commodious Piece-Hall in the borough of Westwood.'* What then, is all interest to stagnate because blood has ceased to flow? Has life no variety now? Is all crime the child of war? Does Love fold his wings when Victory lowers her pennons?* Surely not! It is true a tone of respectability has settled over society—a business-like calm. Many that were wild in their youth have grown rational & sober. I really trust morals—even court morals—have improved. We hear of no out-breaks now—some small irregularities, indeed, of a certain very elevated nobleman* are occasionally rumoured in the public ear, but habit with him has become second nature, & the exquisite susceptibility of his feelings is too well known to need comment—& elsewhere there is certainly a change, a reformation. And let us now, who have so long gazed on glaring guilt, solace ourselves with a chastened view of mellowed morality.

CHAPTER Ist

On the morning of the 1st of July a remarkable event happened at Ellrington-House. The Earl & Countess were both eating their breakfast—at least the Countess was, the Earl was only looking at his—when all at once the Earl, without previous warning or apparent cause, laughed!

Now the scene of this singular occurrence was the Countess's own dressing-room. Her ladyship had that morning coaxed his lordship to rise early with the intention that, as it was a very fine summer day, they should take a drive out to Alnwick for the benefit of his lordship's health & spirits. For about a fortnight or three weeks past his lordship had ceased certain eccentric deviations from his lawful path: the saloons—I should rather say the boudoirs—of certain noble mansions had vainly waited to reverberate the gentle echo of his voice & step. Mesdames Greville, Lalande & St James* had been mourning like nightingales on their perches, or like forsaken turtle-doves cooing soft reproaches to their faithless mate. He came not, & bootless was the despatch of unnumbered tender billets, charged at once with sighs & perfumes & bedewed with tears & rose-water. More than one such delicate messenger had been seen shrivelling 'like a parched scroll'* in the grate of his lordship's appartment, & answer there was none. Sick of music, surfeited with sentiment, the great ex-president* had come home to his unmusical, plain-spoken Countess. The roll of languishing eyes gave him the exies,* so he sought relief in the quick, piercing glances that bespoke more hastiness than artifice of temper. Her ladyship was very cross-gained & intractable at first—she would not come to at all for about a week—but after the Earl had exhibited a proper modicum of hopeless melancholy & lain on the sofa for two or three days in half real half-feigned illness, she began first to look at him then to pity him, then to speak to him, & last of all to make much of him & caress him. This re-awakened interest was at its height about the time when my chapter opens. On the very morning in question she had been quite disquieted to see how little appetite her noble help-mate evinced for his breakfast, & when, after an unbroken silence of about half an hour, he all at once, while looking down at his untasted cup, dissipated that silence by a laugh—an unexpected, brief, speechless but still indisputable laugh—Zenobia was half alarmed.

'What is it Alexander?' said she. 'What do you see?'

'You & that's enough in all conscience,' answered the Earl, turning upon her an eye that had more of sarcasm than mirth in it & more of languor than either.

'Me! Are you laughing at me then?'

'Who I? No.' And he relapsed again into silence—a silence so pensive & dejected that the worthy Countess began to doubt her ears & to think she had only fancied the laugh which still rung in them. Breakfast being concluded she rose from table &, advancing to the window, drew up the blind which had hitherto screened the sunshine. She opened the sash top & a free admission of morning light & air cheered the apartment. It was a fine day—too bright & summer-like for a city. Every heart & every eye under the influence of such a day longs for the country.

'Let the carriage be got ready quickly,' said the Countess, turning to a servant who was clearing the breakfast-table. And as the servant closed the door she sat down at her glass to complete the arrangement of her dress, for as yet she was only en déshabillé.* She had platted & folded her hair & thought with some pride that its sable profusion became her handsome features as well now as it had done ten years ago. She had adjusted her satin apparel to a shape that, though it might not befit a sylph, did well enough for a fine tall woman who had the weight of as much pride & cholor to support as would overwhelm any two ordinary mortals. She had put on her watch & was embellishing her white, round hands with sundry rings when the profound hush which had till now attended her operations was interrupted by a repetition of that low involuntary laugh.

'My lord!' exclaimed the Countess turning quickly round. She would have started if her nerves would have permitted such a proof of sensitiveness.

'My lady!' was the dry answer.

'Why do you laugh?' said she.

'Don't know.'

'Well, but what are you laughing at?'

'Can't tell.'

'Are you ill? Is it hysterical?'*

'I'm never in rude health that I know of, Zenobia, but as to hysterics—ask Miss Delph.'*

With a gesture of scorn the Countess turned again to her glass. Wrath is seldom prudent and as her ladyship's was vented upon her hair—on which she had so recently lavished such care & taste—combs & fillets flew, & the becoming braids which had wreathed her temples & brow quickly floated in a confused cloud of darkness over her shoulders.

Again the Earl laughed, but now it was evidently at her. He approached her toilette &, leaning on the back of the arm-chair she filled (emphatically I say filled, for indeed there was no room for anybody else), he began to talk. 'Softly, Zenobia. I thought you had done your hair. It was well enough, rather a little sombre or so—not quite enough in the floating, airy tendril style—but then, that requires a lightish figure & yours—ahem!'

Here the glass was shifted with a hasty movement, the brush thrown down & the comb snatched up with emphatic promptitude.

The Earl continued with gentleness. 'The Furies, I believe, had hair of live snakes,'* said he. 'What a singular taste! How was it, eh, Zenobia? Eh?'

'How was it my lord! What do you mean? I have not the honour of understanding your lordship.'

'Don't know exactly what I meant. It was some dim notion of analogy haunting my mind that made me put the question. I've so many embryo ideas now a-days, Zenobia, that are crushed, blighted by the stormy climate I live in. Gentler nurture, a little soft sunshine & quiet showers might encourage the infant buds to expand, & in the tender shining after rain I might now & then say a good thing—make a hit—but as it is I daren't speak lest I should be snapped up & snarled at out of all reason. It makes me quite low.'

The Countess, as she brushed her tresses, whisked a thick dark mass over her face to conceal the smile she could not repress. 'You're hardly used,' said she.

'But Zenobia,' pursued the Earl, 'I've something to tell, something to shew you.'

'Indeed my lord?'

'Aye, we all love them that love us,* Zenobia.'

'Do we?' was the succinct answer.

'And,' pursued his lordship with pathos, 'When we've neglected an attached friend—you know, turned a cold shoulder to him, kicked him perhaps by mistake—how touching it is to find that after long years of separation & misunderstanding he still remembers us & is still willing to borrow that half-crown he has asked for seventy & seven times* & has seventy & seven times been refused. Zenobia, they brought me [this] letter last night.'

'Who my lord?'

'The people—James I think—I don't often get a letter you know—Mr Steaton* manages these things.'

'And I suppose your letter is from Zamorna.'

'Oh no, Mr Steaton generally relieves me of the trouble of correspondence in that quarter—besides I think his documents are more frequently addressed to you than me. I object, you know, to his style—it is unpleasant—smells so very strong of oat-cake & grouse.'

'Alexander!' expostulated Zenobia.

'And then,' continued the Earl, 'you forget that he is in the country at present, & therefore too fully occupied in devising a new compost for Thornton's beans, farming Warner's turnips & curing the rot in Sir Markham Howard's sheep to think of writing letters. Besides, his own hay about Hawkscliffe is not all carried, &, depend on it, he's making the most of this fine morning out in his shirt sleeves, with a straw hat on his head, swearing at the hay-tenters,* now & then giving a hand to help to load the waggons, & at noon & drinking-time sitting down on a cock* to eat his bread & cheese & drink his pot of ale like a king & a clod-hopper. Can't you fancy him, Zen, all in a muck of sweat, for it's hard work & hot weather, arrayed in his shirt & white tights & nothing else & then you know "at the close of the day when the hamlet is still"* going with his dear brother in arms Lord Arundel to take a prudent dip & swim in the beck—& coming out with a bad inflamation occasioned by a sudden check of the perspiration, & going home to be blistered & bled ad libitum* & then with interesting wilfulness insisting on t'other tankard and a fresh go of bathing when he's in a raging fever, & being very properly yielded to—allowed to have his way & so waxing delirious, cutting his throat & walking off stage with a flourish of trumpets worthy of the most mighty & magnanimous monarch that ever understood dog-diseases or practised the noble science of farrier?'

'Who is that letter from please, my lord?'

'Ah, the letter. You shall read it & the signature will tell you who it is from.' His lordship took out his pocket-book & handed therefrom a singularly folded epistle, directed in a large black autograph, whose terrible down-strokes, cross-dashes & circular flourishes seemed to defy all hands—mercantile, genteel & juvenile—that ever existed.* The Countess read as follows:

Boulogne June 29th 1839

Daddy Long-legs,*

      Sober I am & sober I have been, and by the bleached bones of my fathers sober I mean to be to the end of the chapter. Aye, by the bones of my fathers & by their souls, their burning souls—which in the likeness of game-cocks cropped & spurred are even now sitting on my right hand and on my left* & crowing aloud for vengeance!

The night was dark when I saw them. It lightened & there was thunder. Who bowed from the cloud as it rolled? Who spake a word in mine ear? Did'st not thou, O dark but comely one, Sai Too-Too* & thou, the brother of my mother's grand-mother, Sambo Mungo Anamaboo.*

I'll tell ye what—ye're a cozening old rascal! Ye never made me a promise in your life but you broke it. Deny that, deny it I say, will ye? Give me the lie—beard me—spit i' my face—tweak my nose. Come on! I'm your man! Up with your daddles!* Who's afraid? What's the fun?

The marrow of the affair—the root of the matter—is this: a more scoundrelly set of men than some that I could mention were never beheld, nor a more horrifying series of transactions than some that I have in my eye. Why, the earth reels, the heavens stagger,* the seas totter to their downfall, & old Ocean himself trembles* in his highest hills & shudders horror-struck through all his woods.

To come to the point at once—may I forget myself & be counted as a child of perdition* if the present generation be not very little better than the last. Why, I remember when there was a Bible in every house & as much brandy sold for a cab of dove's dung* as you could buy now for half a sovereign. The fact is, & I am certain of it, religion's not popular—real genuine religion I mean. I've seen more Christianity in the desert than it would be worth any man's while to take account of.

Daddy, where are you? There seems to be a kind of a darkness, a sort of a mist in the hoyle*—a round-about whirligig circumferential cloudiness. Prop the leg of this here table, will ye daddy, it's sinking with me through the floor? Snuff out the candlestick—there, we've a better light now—we write steadier. Hark ye then, the play's nearly played out.*

Bloody old robber! You walk in silks & velvets & live in a diamond house with golden windows, while I have foxes & holes, & the birds of the air have neither.* You toil & spin while I am Solomon in all his glory arrayed like one of these.* But I warn you, Scaramouch,* you'd better provide for me, for my wife must share my poverty & then what will you say? I've made up my mind to marry. I tell you, it's a done thing, & the Queen of Heaven* herself shouldn't prevail on me to alter it.

Beautiful & benign being! Thou pinest in captivity! Loved lady of my heart, thou weepest in the prison house!* But heaven opens & thy bridegroom waits.* She shall be mine!

Won't you give your consent, old scum? You promised me another, but she, 'like a lily drooping, bowed her head & died'*—at least as good as died, for was not that a living death that consigned her to the arms of a numb-scull?

> A better lot is thine, fair maid,*
>   A happier lot is thine,
> And who would weep in dungeon shade
>   Whom fate had marked for mine?
>   Come, do not pine,
> But fly to arms that open to receive
>   Thy youthful form divine.
> Clasped to this heart of fire thoul't never grieve,
>   No, thou shalt shine
> Happy as houris fair—that braid their hair
>   Glorious in Eden's bowers*
>   Where noxious flowers
> With fragrant reptiles twine.
> But thou, my blooming gem, wilt far out-flourish them,
>   My radiant Caroline!

Now, daddy, what d'ye say to that? Shew her them lines & see if they won't plead my cause for me. She's young, you say, the more need she has of a father. And won't I be both father & husband to her in one? 'tother was not much older when you gave me the refusal of her fair snow-white hand. True, I rejected her—but what then? I'd my eye on the younger, softer bud. Caroline's a more alluring name than

Mary—more odoriferously & contumaciously musical. Then, she loves me—so did the other you'll say—desperately—divinely—I know it, old cock, I know it! I have it under her hand, sealed & signed in legal form, but this sweet blossom, this little fluttering, fickle, felicitous, fairy, this dear, delicious, delirious morsel, comes into my arms & announces her intention of marrying me straight away off-hand, whether I will or no!

I'll be moderate on the subject of settlements: a handsome house, ten thousand a year, the custody of your will & the making of it all over again according to my own directions—that's what I want & what I'll have. Answer by return of post & enclose a letter from my lovely one—also a bank-note or two. In the shadows of approaching sunrise & the profound roar of the storm when it subsides to silence—in Love's intoxication—Hope's fury & Despair's wild madness—in Beauty's blaze—in Eden's bliss—in Hell's troubled & terrific turbulence—in Death's deep & dangerous delirium—

I am & was not a squire of high degree

Q in the corner*

'You know the fine Roman hand,* I presume,' said the Earl, when his Countess had finished reading this surprising lucubration.

'Yes, Quashia of course. But who does he mean? What is he driving at?'

'He wants to marry a little girl of ten or eleven years old,' returned Northangerland.

'What Miss Vernon?' said her ladyship, uttering the name between her teeth.

'Aye'

'And is Miss Vernon no more than ten or eleven?'

'No, I think not.'

A servant just then entered to announce the carriage. The Countess went on dressing herself very fast & looking very red & choleric. While she finished her toilette, Northangerland stood by the window thinking. His thoughts were wound up by a word that seemed to burst involuntarily from his lips. It was 'D—n—t—n!' He then asked his wife where she was going.

She said, 'to Alnwick.'

'No,' he replied. 'I'll go to Angria. Bid them turn the horses' heads east.' Mr Jas Shaver brought his hat & gloves & he went down into the hall & so vanished.

CHAPTER II.

Zamorna was literally standing in a hay-field—just below the house at Hawkscliffe—talking to a respectable man in black. It was a hot afternoon & he wore a broad-brimmed hat of straw & though not exactly in his shirt-sleeves, yet a plaid jacket & trowsers testified but a remote approximation to full dress.

It was a large field and at the further end about a score of hay-makers, male & female, were busily engaged at their work. Zamorna, leaning against the trunk of a fine tree with a dog laid on the hay at his feet, was watching them—especially his eyes followed one or two smart, active girls who were amongst the number of the tenters. At the same time he talked to his companion & thus their conversation ran.

'I reckon now,' said the respectable man in black, 'if your Grace gets this hay well in it'll be a varry* fair crop.'

'Yes it's good land,' returned the monarch.

'Varry good grazing land. I sud thing grain would hardly answer so weel. Have ye tried it wi' ony mak o' corn seed?'

'There's a croft* on the other side of the beck* where the soil is just like this. I sowed it with red wheat last spring & it's bearing beautifully now.'

'Humph! Wha ye see ye cannot err mich, for where trees grow as they do here, there's hardly ony mak o' grain but what'll prosper. I find t'truth o' that at Girnington. Now up i't North, about Mr Warner's place, it's clear different.'

'Yes, Warner has a great deal of bother with tillage & manure. That bog-soil is so cold & moist it rots the seed instead of cherishing it. Well my lass are you tired?' going forward & speaking to a tight* girl with cheeks like a rose, who with her rake had approached nearer to the royal station.

'Nay, sir,' was the answer, while the young rustic's vanity, gratified by the notice of a fine gentleman with whiskers & moustaches, sent a deeper colour than ever to her brown healthy complexion.

'But it's hot, don't you think so?' continued His Grace.

'Nay not so varry.'

'Have ye been working all day among the hay?'

'Nay nobbut sin' nooin.'

'It is Hawkscliffe Fair to-morrow, is not it my lass?'

'Yes, sir, they call't so.'

'And you'll go there no doubt?'

'I happen sall,' giggling & working with her rake very busily to conceal her embarrassment.

'Well, there's something to buy a fairing* with.'

There was a show of reluctance to accept the present which was tendered, but his Grace said 'Pshaw!' & pressed it more urgently, so the damsel suffered her fingers to close upon it & as she put it in her pocket dropped two or three short quick curtsies in acknowledgement.

'You'd give me a kiss I daresay if that gentleman were not by,' said Zamorna, pointing to his friend, who regarded the scene with an expression that shewed he thought it excellent fun. The lass looked up at both the gentlemen, coloured again very deeply & laughing began to withdraw in silence. Zamorna let her go.

'There's a deal of vanity there,' said he, as he returned to the oak-tree.

'Aye & coquetry too. Look, the witch is actually turning back & surveying me with the corner of her eye.'

'I doubt she's a jilt,'* replied Thornton.

His Grace pushed out his under lip, smiled & said something about 'Palace & Cottage' & 'very little difference'.

'But she's a bonny lass,' pursued the Laird of Girnington.

'Tight & trim & fresh & healthy,' was the reply.

'There's mony a lady would be glad to exchange shapes with her,' remarked Sir Wilson again.

'Varry like,' said His Grace, leaning lazily against the trunk & looking down with a bantering smile at Thornton as he imitated his tone.

'Does Your Grace know the lass's name?' asked the General, not noticing his master's aspect.

A pause, closed by a laugh, was the answer.

Thornton turned to him in surprise.

'What the D—l!' said he hastily when he saw the sarcasm expressed by eye & lip. 'Does your Grace mean to insinuate—'

'Nay Thornton—be cool—I'm only thinking what a soft heart you have.'

'Nonsense, nonsense,' returned Sir Wilson. 'But Your Grace is like to have your own cracks, as if I had spoken to t'lass when it was all your majesty 'at cannot let ought be under thirty—'

'Cannot I? That's a lie! Here I stand & I care as much for that foolish little jilt or any other you can mention—high or low—as Bell here at my feet does. Bell's worth them all. Hey, old girl—there's some truth in thy carcase. There, there. Down now, that's enough.'

'I know yer Grace is steadier nor you used to be—& that's raight enough—but you <u>have</u> been wild.'

'Never!' was the unblushing rejoinder.

'But I knaw better.'

'Never by G—d, never!' repeated His Grace.

'O whah!' said Thornton coolly. 'Your Majesty's a right to lie abaat yese'h. It's nought to me 'at I know on.'*

Could it possibly have been Quashia's mad letter which induced Lord Northangerland to set off then & there to Hawkscliffe at the far end of Angria—a house & a country where he had not shewn his nose for years? His lordship's movements are often very inexplicable but this, as Mr Jas Shaver expressed it (when he received sudden orders to pack up the Earl's dressing case & wardrobe), was the 'beat 'em of all'.

The Countess offered to go with her lord, but he made answer that she 'had better not'. So he put himself into the carriage solus, & solus he continued through the whole of the journey. Neither did he speak word to man or beast, except to desire them 'to get on'. And get on they did, for they stopped neither day nor night till half the breadth of Angria was traversed & the Moray-Hills began to undulate on the Horizon. He did not travel incognito & of course he was known at every inn & ale-house where the horses got a pail-ful of meal & water & the postillions a bottle of Madeira. Trivial preparations were commenced in Zamorna for a riot & a stoning, but before Mr Edward Percy could loose his mill & furnish his people with brick-bats the object of filial attention* was a mile out of town & clearing the woods of Hartford in a whirlwind of summer dust. His progress was similarly hailed at the other towns & villages that intercepted his route. At Islington a dead cat, nimble as when alive, leapt up at the carriage window & broke it. At Grantley the hissing & yelling rivalled the music of a legion of cats, & at Rivaux the oblations of mud offered to his divinity were so profuse as to spread over the chariot pannels a complete additional coating of varnish. Whether the Earl derived pleasure or vexations from these little testimonials of national regard it would be hard to say, inasmuch as the complexion of his countenance varied no more than the hue of his coat, & his brow & features looked evermore to the full as placid as the glass-face of a repeater which he held in his hand & continually gazed at.

One thinks there is something pleasant in slowly approaching solitude towards the close of a bustling journey. Driving over the burning pavements, through the smoke & filth of manufacturing towns in the

height of summer, must form one would fancy no unimpressive preparation for the entrance on a fine green country of woods where everything seems remote, fresh & lonely. Yet for all Jas Shaver Esqre could see
in Lord Northangerland & for all Lord Northangerland could remark
in Jas Shaver, neither of these illustrious persons found any remarkable
difference when a July afternoon saw their carriage entering the vast &
silent domain of Hawkscliffe—town & tumult being left far behind—&
only a rustling of trees & a trickling of becks being audible.

Where the habitation of man is fixed, there are alway signs of its
proximity—the perfect freshness of Nature disappears, her luxuriance
is cleared away—& so erelong Hawkscliffe began to break into glades.
The path grew rolled & smooth, & more frequent prospects of distant
hills burst through the widening glimpses of foliage. Out at last they
rolled upon a broad & noble road as well beaten, as white & as spacious
as the far-distant highway from Zamorna to Adrianopolis. That track,
however, seems endless, but this at the close of about a hundred yards
was crossed by the arch of an architectural gateway. The turret on each
side served for a lodge, & the heavy iron gates were speedily flung back
by the keeper. As the carriage paused for a moment ere it shot through,
the yelping of a kennel of hounds was heard somewhere near, & a large
Newfoundlander laid under the lodge-porch rose up & gave a deep-
mouthed bark of welcome.*

Beyond these gates there was no more forest, only detatched clumps
of trees & vast solitary specimens varying the expanse of a large &
wild park which ascended & half-clothed with light verdure the long
aclivity of one of the Sydenhams. The remoter hills of the same range
rolled away clad in dusky woodland till distance softened them & the
summer sky embued them with intense violet. Near the centre of the
park stood Hawkscliffe-House, a handsome pile but by no means so
large nor so grand as the extent of the grounds seemed to warrant. It
could not aspire to the title neither of palace nor castle: it was merely
a solitary hall, stately from its loneliness & pleasant from the sunny &
serene effect of the green region which expanded round it. Deer, a herd
of magnificent cattle & a troop of young unbroken horses shared the
domain between them.

As the carriage stopped at the front-door Northangerland put up his
repeater,* whose hand was pointing to six o'clock p.m., & the steps being
let down & door opened he alighted & quietly walked into the house. He
had got half through the hall before he asked a question of any servant,
but the butler advancing with a bow enquired to what appartment he
should conduct him. North[angerland] stopped as if at fault.

'Perhaps I am wrong,' said he. 'This is not Hawkscliffe.' And he looked dubiously round on the plain unadorned walls & oak-painted doors about him, so unlike the regal splendours of Victoria Square. A noble branch of stag's antlers seemed to strike him with peculiar horror. He recoiled instantly &, muttering something indistinct about 'Angrian squire's den & strange mistake', he was commencing a precipitate retreat to his carriage when James Shaver interposed.

'Your Lordship is in the right,' said he whispering low. 'This is the royal residence' (with a sneer) 'but country plainness—no style kept up—fear I shan't be able to muster proper accommodations for your lordship.'

'James,' said the Earl after a pause, 'will you ask those people where the Duke of Zamorna is?' James obeyed.

'Gone out,' was the reply, 'His Grace is generally out all day.'

And where was the Duchess?

'Gone out too, but most likely would be back presently.'

'Shew me into a room,' said the Earl. And his lordship was ushered into a library where, without looking round him, he sat down, his back to the window & his face to an enormous map unrolled & covering half the opposite wall. There was nothing else in the room except books—a few chairs—a desk & a table loaded with pamphlets & papers—no busts or pictures, or any of the other elegant extras commonly seen in a nobleman's library. A large quarto lay on the floor at Northangerland's feet. He kicked it open with a slight movement of his toe. It was full of gay feathers, coloured wools & brilliant flies for fishing. Another & apparently still slighter movement sufficed to discharge the volume to the other end of the room. It fell by a row of thick volumes standing side by side in the lowest shelf of books—the words *Agricultural Magazine* glittered in gilt letters on the back of each. When Northangerland was quite tired of sitting he got up and restlessly paced through the appartment. Pausing at a side-table where a small book was lying open, he began mechanically to finger the leaves—it was the planter's vade-mecum.* Northangerland withdrew his fingers as if they had been burnt. On the same table lay two packets neatly tied up & labelled 'Sample of red wheat from General Thornton', 'Sample of oats from Howard'. The Earl was still gazing at these packets—riveted by them apparently as if they had been the two eyes of a basilisk—when a shade crossed the window outside.

Soon after, somebody was heard entering by the front-door. A word or two passed in the hall, & then a step quietly approached the library.

It was the Duchess who came. She went to her father & he had to stoop to give the kiss for which she looked up in silent eagerness.

'I thought it was a farm-house,' said he, when he had held her a moment & surveyed her face, 'but I suppose, Mary, you don't milk cows.'

'How long have you been here?' returned his daughter, evading his sarcasm with a smile. 'They should have fetched me in before. I was only walking down the avenue.'

'Down the yard, I thought you would say,' continued the Earl. 'Surely, Mary, you term that a croft' (pointing to the park) 'and this bigging* we are in no doubt is called the grange. Have you a room to yourself, or [do] you sit in the house* & eat your porridge with the ploughmen & dairy-maids?'

The Duchess still smiled & she slipped the obnoxious packets into a drawer.

'Is there a small inn in the place?' went on her father. 'Because if there is, I'll put up there. You know I can't eat bacon & eggs, & though your kitchen may be very comfortable it will smell perhaps of the stables, which you know comes close up to the door for convenience sake, because when the big farmer comes home from the market a trifle sprung* or so—it's more convenient to dismount him rather nigh the house, as he's a good weight to carry in.'

'Don't father,' said the Duchess as, half-vexed, she held her head down, looking at her father's hand, which she retained in hers, & pulling the ring from his little finger.

'Whether is he a better horse-jockey or cow-jobber?' enquired the inexorable Northangerland. 'Does he kill his own meat or he buys it? Does he feed pigs, Mary?'

The Duchess pouted.

'I should like to see him riding home a horse-back, after driving a hard bargain down at Grantley there, about a calf which he is to bring home in a rope.* The excellent fellow, of course, will be very drunk—extremely so—for the bargain has been on & off at least ten times & it took at least sixteen tumblers of whiskey & water to consolidate it in the end. Then the calf will be amazingly contrary—as bad to get on as himself—& what with tumbling from his saddle, rolling in the mud, fighting with his bargain, &c., he will I should imagine cut much such a figure as I have seen that fool Arthur O'Connor do under similar circumstances.'

'Hush Father!' said the Duchess earnestly. 'Don't talk so—I hear him in the passage. Now pray—' She had not time to complete her

entreaty when the door was promptly opened & His Grace walked in.
Some dogs walked in too. The whole party, equally heedless of who
might or might not be in the room, advanced to a cabinet with some
drawers in it. And while the Duke sought in one of the drawers for a
coil of gut that he wanted for his line, the dogs pushed their noses in
his face as he stooped down or smelt at his pannier which he had laid
on the carpet.

'Be quiet, Juno,' said Zamorna, putting a large pointer from him
whose caresses interrupted him in his sedulous search, then calling to
somebody in the passage, 'William, tell Homes I can't find the tackle. It
must be at his Lodge—but I shall not want it to night, so he may send
it up first thing to-morrow-morning.'

'Very well my lord,' answered a gruff voice without.

Zamorna shut up the drawers. 'O stop!' said he, speaking suddenly
to himself. 'I had almost forgotten.' He walked quickly out of the
room.

'William!' standing on the front-door steps & calling down the
Park.

'Yes please Your Grace.'

'You may give my compliments to Homes & say that the river has
been poached on. I was fishing there to day & I only got three trout.
Tell him he's a d—d idle dog & keeps no right look-out at all when
I'm away, but things must be managed differently. I'll have law & order
observed here, or else I'll try for it.'

He came back crossing the passage with firm even stride. He entered
the library again rather more deliberately. He had now time to notice
that it was occupied by other persons besides himself & his dogs—his
wife caught his eye first. 'Well Mary have you been walking?'

'Yes.'

'Rather late, is not it? You should mind not to be out after sunset.'

'It was very warm.'

'Yes, fine weather,' & he pulled off his gloves & began to take his long
fishing rod to pieces.

As he was busily intent on dissengaging the hook from the line
Northangerland advanced a little step from the sort of recess where
he had been standing. Zamorna, attracted by the movement, turned.
He looked keenly, pausing from his employment. He was obviously astonished for a moment at this unexpected apparition of his
father-in-law—only for a moment. There was no salutation on either
side—Zamorna stared—Northangerland gazed coolly. Zamorna turned
his back, went on disjointing his rod, hung up that & his pannier, took

off a broad brimmed straw hat which had hitherto diademed his head,
& then at last as he sat down in an arm-chair by the table, found time to
ask when the Earl had arrived.

'I didn't look at the clock,' was the answer, and, 'Yet faith I remember I did—it was about six this evening.'

'Hum. Have ye had any dinner? We dine early, seldom later than three.'*

'James gave me a biscuit in the carriage—& 'tis as well he did so, for as I've been remarking to Mrs Wellesley I can't take porridge or fried bacon.'

'No, nor omlets & pâtés either for that matter,' muttered the Duke in an under-tone. 'Nor hardly a mouthful of any Christian edible under the sun.' Then he continued aloud, 'Pray have ye been ordered to take a journey here for your health?'

'What! To a fish-monger's & farrier's? No! Stale herring gives me the nausea. I'm come on business—but may that basket of stinking sprat be sent away?' pointing to the pannier & holding a perfumed cambric handkerchief to his nose.

'It's fresh trout,' answered his son calmly. 'But you're a valetudinarian & must be excused for having sickly antipathies. Come, I'll humour you for once.' He rung the bell & the nuisance was quickly removed.

'How did you get along through the country?' continued the Duke, taking up a newspaper & unfolding it. 'Were you much fêted & flattered? Or they forgot to ring the bells & call out the bands in your honour?'

'I don't remember,' responded Northangerland.

'Don't you? Humph! But perhaps your postillions & horses will. I have some dim notion that the kennel rubbish of Edwardston & Zamorna & Islington & some of those places has been made uncommon useful not so long since.'

The Duchess here approached His Grace's chair &, leaning over the back as if to look at the newspaper which he was still reading or feigning to read, she whispered, 'Don't try to vex him to-night Adrian. I am sure he's tired with his journey.'

The Duke merely seated her beside him &, resting his hand on her shoulder, went on talking. 'Where d'ye think you're most popular now, sir?' said he.

'With a small handful of coloured men under the command of Mr Kashna,'* returned Northangerland.

'Long may your popularity be confined to that limited & devoted band,' rejoined his dutiful son.

'What for, Arthur?' enquired the Earl in a gentle, insinuating tone.

'Because you'll never more be fit for the confidence of decent Christians.'

'Was I once?'

'Not that I can remember.'

'No, only for such debauched dogs as Douro—the dandy,' retorted Northangerland.

'Could you get up a meeting now any where in Angria or form a Society for the Diffusion of Genuine Vitality?'*

'I could if my dear young friend Arthur Wellesley would stick the bills* as he used to do.'

'Arthur Wellesley, instead of sticking the bills, now would stick the whole concern*—aye to the D—l.'

'As he does everything else he meddles with!' said Northangerland, closing the verbal sparring-match with a gentle nicher.

His son's reply was prevented by the Duchess, who sat between the combatants trembling with anxiety lest this skirmish of words should overstep the brink of mere sarcasm & plunge into invective.

'Well,' said the Duke, in answer to her silent entreaty for forbearance, 'he shall have it his own way this time in consideration that he's done up with riding a few miles in an easy carriage like a bed. But I'll balance the reckoning to-morrow.'

'Good-night Mary,' said the Earl rising abruptly. She followed her father from the room & the Duke, being left by himself, rang for candles & sat down to write a lot of letters.

CHAPTER III.

Well, reader, you have not yet heard what business it was that brought Northangerland all that long way from Ellrington House to Hawkscliffe-Hall. But you shall if you'll suppose it to be morning & step with the Earl out of this little parlour where the Duchess is at work, sitting by a window surrounded with roses.

As soon as ever Zamorna had had his breakfast he had set off & the Earl was now following him. Fortunately he met him on the steps at the front door, leaning against the pillar & enjoying the morning sunshine & the prospect of his wild park but half-reclaimed from the forest for one tranquil moment before starting on a day-long campaign in the fields.

'Where are you going, Arthur?' asked the Earl.

'To that wood beyond the river.'

'What to do there?'

'To see some young trees transplanted.'

'Will there be an earthquake if you defer that important matter until I have spoken a word with you on a trivial business of my own?'

'Perhaps not. What have you to say?'

Northangerland did not immediately answer. He paused, either from reluctance to commence or from a wish to ascertain that all was quiet & safe around & that no intruder was nigh. The Hall behind was empty; the grounds in front were still dewy & solitary. He & his son-in-law stood by themselves—there was no listener.

'Well, why don't you begin?' repeated Zamorna, who was whistling carelessly & evincing no inclination to attach special importance to the coming communication.

When our own minds are intensely occupied with a subject we are apt to imagine that those near us are able to pry into our thoughts. The side-glance with which Northangerland viewed his son was strange, dubious & distorted. At last he said in a remarkable tone, 'I wish to know how my daughter Caroline is?'

'She was very well when I saw her last,' replied the Duke of Zamorna, not moving a muscle, but looking straight before him at the waving & peaked hills which marked the unclouded horizon. There was another pause. Zamorna began his whistle again. It was more studiedly careless than before, for whereas it had just flowed occasionally into a pensive strain it now only mimicked rattling & reckless airs broken into fragments.

'My daughter must be grown,' continued Northangerland.

'Yes healthy children always grow.'

'Do you know anything about the progress of her studies? Is she well educated?'

'I took care that she should be provided with good masters, & from their report I should imagine she has made very considerable proficiency for her age.'

'Does she evince any talent? Musical talent she ought to inherit.'*

'I like her voice,' answered Zamorna. 'And she plays well enough too for a child.'

Northangerland took out a pocket book—he seemed to calculate in silence for a moment &, writing down the result with a silver pencil-case,* he returned the book to his pocket, quietly remarking, 'Caroline is fifteen years old.'

'Aye, her birth-day was the first or second of this month, was it not?' returned Zamorna. 'She told me her age the other day—I was surprised. I thought she had hardly been more than twelve or thirteen.'

'She looks childish then, does she?'

'Why no. She is well-grown & tall, but time in some cases cheats us. It seems only yesterday when she was quite a little girl.'

'Time has cheated me,' said the Earl. There was another pause. Zamorna descended the steps.

'Well good-morning,' said he. 'I'll leave you for the present.' He was moving off, but the Earl followed him.

'Where is my daughter?' asked he. 'I wish to see her.'

'O, by all means. We can ride over this afternoon—the house is not above three miles off.'

'She must have a separate establishment instantly,' pursued the Earl.

'She has,' said Zamorna. 'That is, in conjunction with her mother.'

'I shall either have Selden-House or Eden-Hall* fitted up for her,' continued his lordship without heeding this remark. He & his son-in-law were now pacing slowly through the ground side by side. Zamorna fell a little into the rear. His straw hat was drawn over his eyes & it was not easy to tell with what kind of a glance he regarded his father-in-law.

'Who is to go with her & take care of her?' he asked after a few minutes silence. 'Do you mean to retire into the north or south yourself & take up your abode at Eden-Hall or Selden-House?'

'Perhaps I may.'

'Indeed! And will Zenobia adopt her & allow the girl to live under the same roof without the penalty of a daily chastisement?'

'Don't know. If they can't agree, Caroline must marry—but I think you once told me she was not pretty.'

'Did I? Well, tastes differ, but the girl is a mere child, she may improve. In the meantime, to talk of marrying her is rather good. I admire the idea. If she were my daughter, sir, she should not marry these ten years, but the whole scheme sounds excessively raw, just like one of your fantastic expensive whims. About establishments—you know nothing of management nor of the value of money, you never did—'

'She must be established. She must have her own servants & carriage & allowance,' repeated the Earl.

'Fudge!' said the Duke impatiently.

'I have spoken to Steaton, & matters are in train,' continued his father-in-law in a deliberate tone.

'Unbusiness-like, senseless ostentation!' was the reply. 'Have you calculated the expense, sir?'

'No. I've only calculated the fitness of things.'

'Pshaw!'

Both gentlemen pursued their path in silence. Northangerland's face looked serene but extremely obstinate. Zamorna could compose his features but not his eye—it was restless & glittering.

'Well,' he said after the lapse of some minutes, 'do as you like. Caroline is your daughter, not mine, but you go to work strangely—that is, according to my notions as to how a young susceptible girl ought to be managed.'

'I thought you said she was a mere child.'

'I said, or I meant to say, I considered her as such. She may think herself almost a woman. But take your own way—give her this separate establishment, give her money & servants & equipages—& see what will be the upshot.'

Northangerland spoke not. His son-in-law continued.

'It would be only like you, like your unaccountable frantic folly, to surround her with French society, or Italian if you could get it. If the circle in which you lavished your own early youth were now in existence, I very* believe you'd allow Caroline to move as a queen in its centre.'

'Could my little daughter be the queen of such a circle,' asked Northangerland. 'You said she had no beauty & you spoke as if her talents were only ordinary.'

'There,' replied his son, 'that question confirms what I say. Sir,' he continued, stopping & looking full at Northangerland & speaking with marked emphasis, 'If your fear is that Caroline will not have beauty sufficient to attract licentiousness, & imagination warm enough to understand approaches, to meet them & kindle at them, & a mind & passions strong enough to carry her a long way in the career of dissipation if she once enters it—set yourself at rest, for she is or will be fit for all this & much more.'

'You may as well drop that assumed tone,' said Northangerland, squinting direfully at his comrade. 'You must be aware that I know Your Royal Grace & cannot for a moment be deluded into the supposition that you are a saint or even a repentant sinner.'

'I'm not affecting either saintship or repentance,' replied the Duke. 'And I'm well aware that you know me. But I happen to have taken some pains with the education of Miss Vernon. She has grown up an interesting clever girl & I should be sorry to hear of her turning out no better than she should be—to find that I have been rearing & training a mistress for some blackguard Frenchman—& this or something worse would certainly be the result of your plans. I have studied her character. It is one that ought not to be exposed to dazzling temptation. She is at once careless & imaginative—her feelings are mixed with her passions—both are warm & she never reflects. Guidance like yours is not what such a girl ought to have. She could ask you for nothing which you would not grant. Indulgence would foster all her defects. When she found that winning smiles & gentle words passed current for reason & judgement, she would speedily purchase her whole will with that cheap coin & that will would be as wild as the wildest bird—as fantastic & perverse as if the caprice & perversity of her whole sex were concentrated in her single little head & heart.'

'Caroline has lived in a very retired way hitherto, has she not?' asked Northangerland, not at all heeding the Duke's sermonizing.

'Not at all too retired for her age,' was the reply. 'A girl with lively spirits & good health needs no company until it is time for her to be married.

'But my daughter will be a little rustic!' said the Earl. 'A milkmaid—she will want manners when I want to introduce her to the world.'

'Introduce her to the world!' repeated Zamorna impatiently. 'What confounded folly! And I know in your own mind you are attaching as much importance to the idea of bringing out this half-grown school-girl—providing her with an establishment & all that sort of humbug—as if it were an important political manœuvre on the issue of which the existence of half a nation depended.

'Oh!' replied the Earl with a kind of dry, brief laugh. 'I assure you, you quite underrate my ideas on the subject. As to your political manœuvres, I care nothing at all about them—but if my Caroline should turn out a fine woman, handsome & clever, she will give me pleasure. I shall once more have a motive for assembling a circle about me to see her mistress & directress of it.'

An impatient 'Pshaw!' was Zamorna's sole answer to this.

'I expect she will have a taste for splendour,' continued the Earl, '& she must have the means to gratify it.'

'Pray what income do you intend to allow her?' asked his son.

'Ten thousand per annum to begin with.'

Zamorna whistled & put his hands in his pockets. After a pause he said, 'I shall not reason with you, for on this subject you're just a natural-born fool incapable of understanding reason. I'll just let you go on your own way without raising a hand either to aid or oppose you.

You shall take your little girl just as she is. Strip her of her frock & sash & put on a gown & jewels—take away her child's playthings & give her a carriage & an establishment—place her in the midst of one of your unexceptionable Ellrington-House or Eden Hall coteries—& see what will be the upshot. God d—n! I can hardly be calm about it! Well enough do I know what she is now—a pretty, intelligent, innocent girl, & well enough can I guess what she will be some few years hence—a beautiful, dissipated, dissolute woman—one of your syrens—your Donna Julias, your Signora Cecillias.* Faugh!

'Good-morning Sir! We dine at three. After dinner we'll take a ride over to see Miss Vernon.' His Grace jumped over a field wall &, as he walked away very fast, he was soon out of sight.

CHAPTER IV

Punctually at three o'clock dinner was served in a large antique dining-room at Hawkscliffe, whose walls, rich in carved oak & old pictures, received a warm dim glow from the bow-window screened with amber curtains. While one footman removed the silver covers from two dishes, another opened the folding door to admit a tall middle aged gentleman, with a very sweet young lady resting on his arm & another gentleman walking after. They seated themselves & when they were seated there was as much an air of state about the table as if it had been surrounded by a large party, instead of this select trio. The gentlemen, as it happened, were both very tall. They were both, too, dressed in black, for the young man had put off the plaid jacket & checked trowsers which it was his pleasure to sport in the morning & had substituted in their stead the costume of a well-dressed clergy-man. As for the young lady, a very fair neck & arms, well displayed by a silk dress made low & with short sleeves, were sufficient of themselves to throw an air of style & elegance over the party. Besides that, her hair was beautiful & profusely curled, & her mien & features were exceedingly aristocratic & exclusive.

Very little talk passed during dinner. The younger gentleman eat* uncommon well; the elderly one trifled a considerable time with a cer-tain mess in a small silver tureen which he did not eat. The young lady drank wine with her husband when he asked her & made no bones of some three or four glasses of champagne. The Duke of Zamorna looked as grave as a judge. There was an air about him, not of unhappiness, but as if the cares of a very large family rested on his shoulders. The Duchess was quiet—she kept glancing at her help-mate from under her eye-lids. When the cloth was taken away & the servants had left the room, she asked him if he was well—a superfluous question, one would think, to look at His delicate Grace's damask complexion & athletic form, & to listen to his sounding, steady voice. Had he been in a good humour he would have answered her question by some laughing banter about her over-anxiety. As it was he simply said he was well. She then enquired if he wished the children to come down. He said no, he should hardly have time to attend to them that afternoon. He was going out directly.

'Going out! What for?' There was nothing to call him out.

Yes, he had a little business to transact.

The Duchess was nettled, but she swallowed her vexation & looked calm upon it.

'Very well,' said she. 'Your Grace will be back to tea I presume?'

'Can't promise indeed, Mary.'

'Then I had better not expect you till I see you.'

'Just so. I'll return as soon as I can.'

'Very well,' said she, assuming as complacent an air as she possibly could, for her tact told her this was not a time for the display of wife-like petulance & irritation—what would amuse His Grace in one mood she knew would annoy him in another. So she sat a few minutes longer, made one or two cheerful remarks on the weather & the growth of some young trees His Grace had lately planted near the window, & then quietly left the table. She was rewarded for this attention to the Duke's humours by his rising to open the door for her. He picked up her handkerchief too, which she had dropped, & as he returned it to her he favoured her with a peculiar look & smile, which as good as said he thought she was looking very handsome that afternoon. Mrs Wellesley considered that glance sufficient compensation for a momentary chagrin, therefore she went into her drawing-room &, sitting down to the piano, soothed away the remains of irritation with sundry soft songs & solemn psalm tunes which, better than gayer music, suited her own fine, melancholy voice.

She did not know where Northangerland & Zamorna were going, nor what it was that occupied their minds, or she would not have sung at all—most probably, could she have divined the keen interest which each took in little Caroline Vernon she would have sat down & cryed. It is well for us that we cannot read the hearts of our nearest friends. It is an old saying 'where ignorance is bliss 'tis folly to be wise',* & if it makes us happy to believe that those we love unreservedly give us in return affections unshared by another, why should the veil be withdrawn & a triumphant rival be revealed to us? The Duchess of Zamorna knew that such a person as Miss Vernon existed, but she had never seen her. She imagined that Northangerland thought & cared little about her—& as to Zamorna, the two ideas of Caroline & the Duke never entered her head at the same time.

While Mrs Wellesley sung to herself—'Has sorrow thy young days shaded'*—& while the sound of her piano came through closed doors with a faint sweet effect, Mr Wellesley Junr & Mr Percy Senior sat staring opposite to each other like two bulls. They didn't seem to have a word to say, not a single word—but Mr Wellesley manifested a disposition to take a good deal of wine, much more than was customary with him, & Mr Percy seemed to be mixing & swallowing a number of little tumblers of brandy & water. At last Mr Wellesley asked Mr Percy whether he meant to stir his stumps that afternoon or not? Mr Percy said he felt very well where he was but, however, as the thing must be done some day, he thought they had better shog.* Mr Wellesley intimated that it was not his intention to make any further objection & that therefore Mr Percy should have his way, but he further insinuated that that way was the direct road to hell & that he wished with all his heart Mr Percy had already reached the end of his journey, only it was a pity a poor foolish little thing like Caroline Vernon should be forced to trot off along with him.

'You, I suppose,' said Mr Percy drily, 'would have taken her to heaven. Now I've an odd sort of a crotchetty notion that the girl will be safer in hell with me than in heaven with thee, friend Arthur.'

'You consider my plan of education defective, I suppose,' said His Grace with the air of a schoolmaster.

'Rather,' was the reply.

'You're drinking too much brandy & water,' pursued the royal mentor.

'And you have had quite enough champagne,' responded his friend.

'Then we'd better both be moving,' suggested the Duke, & he rose, rung the bell & ordered horses. Neither of them were quite steady when they mounted their saddles &, unattended by servants, started from the front door at a mad gallop as if they were chasing wild-fire.*

People are not always in the same mood of mind & thus, though Northangerland & Zamorna had been on the point of quarrelling in the morning, they were wondrous friends this afternoon—quite jovial—the little disagreement between them as to the mode of conducting Miss Caroline's future education was allowed to rest.

Indeed, Miss Caroline herself seemed quite forgotten. Her name was never mentioned as they rode on through sombre Hawkscliffe, talking fast & high & sometimes laughing loud—I don't mean to say that Northangerland laughed loud, but Zamorna did, very frequently. For a little while it was Ellrington & Douro resuscitated. Whether champagne & brandy had any hand in bringing about this change I can't pretend to decide. However neither of them were ree,* they were only gay; their wits were all about them, but they were sparkling.

We little know what fortune the next breath of wind may blow us, what strange visitor the next moment may bring to our door—so Lady Louisa Vernon may be thinking just now, as she sits by her fireside in this very secluded house, whose casements are darkened by the boughs of large trees. It is near seven o'clock, & the cloudy evening is closing in somewhat comfortless & chill—more like October than July. Her ladyship consequently has the vapours,* in fact she has had them all day. She imagines herself very ill—though what her ailments are she can't distinctly say—so she sits up-stairs in her dressing-room, with her head reclined on a pillow & some drops & a smelling-bottle close at hand. Did she but know what step was now near her door—even at her threshold—she would hasten to change her dress & comb her hair, for in that untidy deshabille, with that pouting look & those dishevelled tresses, her ladyship looks haggard.

'I must go to bed Elise—I can't bear to sit up any longer,' says she to her French maid, who is sewing in a window recess near.

'But your ladyship will have your gown tryed on first?' answered the girl. 'It is nearly finished.'

'Oh no, nonsense! What is the use of making gowns for me? Who will see me wear them? My God! Such barbarous usage as I receive [from] that man who has no heart!'

'Ah, madame!' interposed Elise. 'He has a heart—don't doubt it! Attendez un peu—Monsieur loves you jusqu'à [la] folie.'*

'Do you think so, Elise?'

'I do! He looks at you so fondly.'

'He never looks at me at all—I look at him.'

'But when your back is turned, madame, then he measures you with his eyes.'

'Aye scornfully!'

'Non, avec tendresse, avec ivresse.'*

'Then why doesn't he speak? I'm sure I've told him often enough that I am very fond of him—that I adore him, though he is so cold & proud & tyrannical & cruel.'

'C'est trop modest,'* replied Elise very sagely. Apparently this remark struck her ladyship in a ludicrous point of view,—she burst into a laugh.

'I can't quite swallow that either,' said she. 'You are almost an idiot, Elise. I daresay you think he loves you too. Ecoutez la fille! C'est un homme dur. Quant'à l'amour il ne sait guère qu'est-ce que c'est. Il regarde les femmes comme des esclaves—il s'amuse de leur beauté pour un instant et alors il les abandonne. Il faut haïr un tel homme & l'éviter. Et moi je le haïs—beaucoup—oui je le déteste. Hélas combien! Il est différent de mon Alexandre. Elise, souvenez-vous de mon Alexandre—du beau Northangerland!'

'C'était fort gentil,' responded Elise.

'Gentil!' ejaculated her ladyship. 'Elise, c'était un ange. Il me semble que je le vois—dans cette chambre même—avec ses yeux bleus, sa physiognomy qui exprimait tant de douceur—et son front de marbre environné des cheveux châtains.'

'Mais le Duc a des cheveux châtains aussi,' interposed Elise.

'Pas comme ceux de mon preux Percy,'* sighed her faithful ladyship, and she continued in her own tongue, 'Percy had so much soul, such a fine taste—il sut apprécier mes talents.* He gave me trinkets—his first present was a brooch like a heart, set with diamonds. In return he asked for a lock of his lovely Allan's hair—my name was Allan then, Elise—I sent him such a long streaming tress! He knew how to receive the gift like a gentleman—he had it plaited into a watch-guard. And the next night I acted at the Fidena theatre. When I came onto the stage—there he was in a box just opposite—with the black braid across his breast! Ah, Elise! talk of handsome men—he was irresistible in those days! Stronger & stouter than he is now—such a chest he shewed & he used to wear a green Newmarket coat* & a white beaver—well, anything became him. But you can't think, Elise, how all the gentlemen admired me when I was a girl—what crowds used to come to the theatre to see me act—& how they used to cheer me. But he never did, he only looked—ah, just as if he worshipped me. And when I used to clasp my hands & raise my eyes just so, & shake back my hair in this way, which I often did in singing solemn things, he seemed as if he could hardly hold from coming on to the stage & falling at my feet—& I enjoyed that.

'The other actresses did envy me so! There was a woman called Morton whom I always hated—so much, I could have run a spit through her, or stuck her full of needles any-day—& she & I once quarrelled about him. It was in the green-room. She was dressing for a character—she took one of her slippers & flung it at me. I got all my fingers into her hair & I twisted them round & round & pulled & dragged till she was almost in fits with pain—I never heard anybody scream so. The Manager tryed to get me off, but he couldn't—nor could anybody else. At last he said, "Call Mr Percy, he's in the saloon." Alexander came, but he had had a good deal of wine, & Price the manager couldn't rightly make him comprehend what he wanted him for. He was in a swearing passionate humour & he threatened to shoot Price for attempting to humbug him, as he said. He took out his pistols & cocked them. The green-room was crowded with actors & actresses & dressers—every-body was so terrified—they appealed to me to go & pacify him. I was so proud to shew my influence before them all—I knew that, drunk as he was, I could turn him round my little finger. So at last I left Morton, with her head almost bald & her hair torn off by handfuls, & went to the Drover.* I believe he would really have shot Price if I hadn't stopped him. But I soon changed his mood. You can't think, Elise, what power I had over him. I told him I was frightened of his pistols & began to cry. He laughed at me first & when I cryed more he put them away. Lord George, poor man, was standing by watching—I did used to like to coquette between Vernon* & Percy. Ah, what fun I had in those days! But it's all gone by now—nothing but this dismal house & that garden with its high wall like a convent & these great dark trees always groaning & rustling. Whatever have I done to be punished so?' Her ladyship began to sob.

'Monseigneur will change all this,' suggested Elise.

'No—no. That's worst of all!' returned her ladyship. 'He does not know how to change—such an impenetrable iron-man, so austere & sarcastic. I can't tell how it is I always feel glad when he comes. I always wish for the day to come round when he will visit us again, & every time I hope he'll be kinder & less stately & laconic & abrupt, & yet when he does come I'm so tormented with mortification & disappointment. It's all nonsense looking into his handsome face—his eyes won't kindle any more than if they were of glass. It's quite in vain that I go & stand by him & speak low—he won't bend to listen to me, though I'm so much less than him. Sometimes when he bids me good bye I press his hand tenderly; I'm very cold, distant—it makes no difference—he does not seem to notice the change. Sometimes I try to provoke him, for if he would only be exceedingly savage I might fall into great terror & faint, & then perhaps he would pity me afterwards. But he won't be provoked—he smiles as if he were amused at my anger & that smile of his is so—I don't know what—vexing, maddening—it makes him look so handsome—& yet it tears one's heart with passion. I could draw my nails down his face till I had scraped it bare of flesh. I could give him some arsenic in a glass of wine.

'O, I wish something would happen—that I could get a better hold of him. I wish he would fall desperately sick in this house, or shoot himself by accident so that he would be obliged to stay here & let me nurse him. It would take down his pride if he were so weak that he could do nothing for himself. And then, if I did everything for him he would be thankful—perhaps he would begin to take a pleasure in having me with him, & I could sing his kind of songs & seem to be very gentle. He'd love me—I'm sure he would! If he didn't, & if he refused to let me wait on him, I'd come at night to his room & choke him while he was asleep—smother him with the pillow—as Mr Ambler used to smother me when he had the part of Othello & I had that of Desdemona.* I wonder if I daren't do such a thing—'

Her ladyship paused for a minute as if to meditate on the moral problem she had thus proposed for her own solution. Erelong she proceeded.

'I should like to know now how he behaves towards people that he does love—if indeed he ever loved anybody. His wife now—does he always keep her at a distance? And they say he has a mistress or two—I've heard all sorts of queer stories about him. It's very odd—perhaps he likes only blondes. But no, Miss Gordon* was as dark as me, & eight years ago what a talk there was in the north about him & her—he was a mere school-boy then to be sure. I remember hearing Vernon & O'Connor bantering Mr Gordon about it, & they joked him for being cut out by a beardless lad. Gordon did not like the joke—he was an ill-tempered man that.

'Elise, you're making my gown too long. You know I always like rather short skirts. Morton used to wear long ones because, as I often told her, she'd ugly thick ancles. My ancles now were a straw-breadth less circumference than Julia Corelli's, who was the first figurante at the Verdopolitan Opera.* How vexed Corelli was that night that we measured & my ancles were found to be slimmer than hers! Then neither she nor any of the other dancers could put on my shoe. And—its a fact, Elise—a colonel in the army stole a little black satin slipper of mine & wore it a whole week in his cap as a trophy. Poor man—Percy challenged him—they had such a dreadful duel across a table. He was shot dead—they called him Markham Sydenham Markham. He was an Angrian.'

'Madame c'est finie,' said Elise, holding up the gown which she had just completed.

'O well, put it away. I can't try it on. I don't feel equal to the fatigue—my head's so bad & I've such a faintness—& such a fidgetty restlessness. What's that noise?'

A distant sound of music in a room below was heard—a piano very well touched.

'Dear, dear! There's Caroline strumming over that vile instrument again. I really <u>cannot</u> bear it & so it doesn't signify. That girl quite distracts me with the racket she keeps up.'

Here her ladyship rose very nimbly &, going to the top of the stairs which was just outside her room, called out with much power of lungs, 'Caroline! Caroline!'

No answer except a brilliant bravura run down the keys of the piano.

'Caroline!' was reiterated. 'Give up playing this instant! You know how ill I have been all day, & yet you will act in this way.'

A remarkably merry jig responded to her ladyship's objurgations, & a voice was heard far off saying, 'It will do you good, Mamma!'

'You are very insolent,' cried the fair invalid, leaning over the bannisters. 'Your impertinence is beyond bearing. You will suffer for it one day. You little forward peice, do as I bid you!'

'So I will, directly,' replied the voice. 'I have only to play "Jim Crow"* & then—' & 'Jim Crow' was played with due spirit & sprightliness.

Her ladyship cryed once again with a volume of voice that filled the whole house, 'D'ye know I'm your mother, madam? You seem to think you are grown out of my control. You have given yourself fine impudent airs of late—it's high time your behaviour was looked to I think! Do you hear me?'

While 'Jim Crow' was yet jigging his round, while Lady Vernon, bent above the bannisters, was still shaking the little passage with her voice, the wire of the door-bell vibrated. There was a loud ring & there after a pealing aristocratic knock. 'Jim Crow' & Lady Louisa were silenced simultaneously. Her ladyship affected a precipitate retreat to her dressing-room. It seemed also as if Miss Caroline were making herself scarce, for there was a slight rustle & run heard below, as of someone retiring to hidden regions.

I need not say who stood without. Of course it was Messrs Percy & Wellesley. In due time the door was opened to them by a man-servant & they walked straight on to the drawing-room. There was no one to receive them in that appartment, but it was evident somebody had lately been there. An open piano & a sheet of music with a grinning, capering nigger lithographed on the title-page, a capital good fire, an easy chair drawn close to it—all gave direct evidence to that effect. His Grace the Duke of Zamorna looked warily round—nothing alive met his eye. He drew off his gloves &, as he folded them one in the other, he walked to the hearth. Mr Percy was already bent over a little work-table near the easy chair. Pushed out of sight under a drapery of half-finished embroidery there was a book—Percy drew it out. It was a novel, & by no means a religious one either. While Northangerland was turning over the leaves Zamorna rung the bell.

'Where is Lady Vernon?' he asked of the servant who answered it.

'Her ladyship will be down stairs directly. I have told her Your Grace is here.'

'And where is Miss Caroline?'

The servant hesitated. 'She's in the passage,' he said, half-smiling & looking behind him. 'She's rather bashful, I think, because there's company with Your Grace.'

'Tell Miss Vernon I wish to see her, will you Cooper,' replied the Duke.

The footman withdrew. Presently the door re-opened very slowly. Northangerland started & walked quickly to the window, where he stood gazing intently into the garden. Meantime he heard Zamorna say, 'How do you do?' in his deep, low voice—most thrilling when it is most subdued.

Somebody answered, 'Very well, thank ye,' in an accent indicating girlish mauvaise honte* mixed with pleasure.

There was then a pause. Northangerland turned round. It was getting dusk, but daylight enough remained to shew him distinctly what sort of a person it was that had entered the room & was now standing by the fire-place looking as if she did not exactly know whether to sit down or to remain on her feet. He saw a girl of fifteen, exceedingly well grown & well-made of her age—not thin or delicate, but on the contrary very healthy & very plump. Her face was smiling. She had fine dark eyelashes & very handsome eyes. Her hair was almost black—it curled as Nature let it, though it was now long & thick enough to be trained according to the established rules of art. This young lady's dress by no means accorded with her years & stature. The short-sleeved frock, worked trousers* & streaming sash would better have suited the age of nine or ten than that of fifteen. I have intimated that she was somewhat bashful & so she was, for she would neither look Zamorna nor Northangerland in the face. The fire & the rug were the objects of her fixed contemplation, yet it was evident that it was only the bashfulness of a raw school-girl unused to society. The dimpled cheek &

arch, animated eye indicated a constitutional vivacity which a very little encouragement would soon foster into sprightly play enough—perhaps it was a thing rather to be repressed than fostered.

'Won't you sit down,' said Zamorna, placing a seat near her. She sat down. 'Is your mamma very well?' he continued.

'I don't know. She's never been down to day, & so I haven't seen her.'

'Indeed! You should have gone up-stairs & asked her how she did.'

'I did ask Elise & she said madame had the megrims.'

Zamorna smiled & Northangerland smiled too.

'What have you been doing then all day?' continued the Duke.

'Why I've been drawing & sewing. I couldn't practise because Ma said it made her head ache.'

'What is "Jim Crow" doing on the piano then?' asked Zamorna.

Miss Vernon giggled. 'I only just jigged him over once,' she replied. 'And Ma did fly! She never likes "Jim Crow".'

Her guardian shook his head. 'And have you never walked out this fine day?' he continued.

'I was riding on my pony most of the morning.'

'Oh you were! Then how did the French & Italian lessons get on in that case.'

'I forgot them,' said Miss Caroline.

'Well,' pursued the Duke, 'look at this gentleman now & tell me if you know him.'

She raised her eyes from the carpet & turned them furtively on Percy—frolic & shyness was the mixed expression of her face as she did so. 'No' was her first answer.

'Look again,' said the Duke, & he stirred the fire to elicit a brighter glow over the now darkening appartment.

'I do!' exclaimed Caroline as the flame flashed over Northangerland's pallid features & marble brow. 'It's Papa!' she said, rising. And without agitation or violent excitement she stepped across the rug towards him. He kissed her. The first minute she only held his hand, & then she put her arms round his neck & would not leave him for a little while, though he seemed oppressed & would have gently put her away.

'You remember something of me then,' said the Earl at last, loosening her arms.

'Yes, Papa, I do.' She did not immediately sit down, but walked two or three times across the room, her colour heightened & her respiration hurried.

'Would you like to see Lady Vernon to-night?' asked Zamorna of his father-in-law.

'No, not to-night. I'd prefer being excused.'

But who was to prevent it? Rustle & sweep,—a silk gown traversed the passage—in she came.

'Percy! Percy! Percy,' was her thrice repeated exclamation. 'My own Percy! Take me again! Oh, you shall hear all—you shall! But I'm safe now, you'll take care of me. I've been true to you, however.'

'God bless me, I shall be choked!' ejaculated the Earl, as the little woman vehemently kissed & embraced him. 'I never can stand this!' he continued. 'Louisa just be quiet will ye?'

'But you don't know what I've suffered!' cryed her ladyship. 'Nor what I've had to contend against. He has used me so ill, & all because I couldn't forget you.'

'What! The Duke there?' asked Percy.

'Yes, yes! Save me from him! Take me away with you! I cannot exist if I remain in his power any longer!'

'Ma, what a fool you are!' interposed Caroline very angrily.

'Does he make love to you?' said the Earl.

'He persecutes me! He acts in a shameful, unmanly, brutal manner.'

'You've lost your senses Ma,' said Miss Vernon.

'Percy, you love me, I'm sure you do,' continued her ladyship. 'O protect me! I'll tell you more when we've got away from this dreadful place.'

'She'll tell you lies!' exclaimed Caroline in burning indignation. 'She's just got up a scene, Papa, to make you think she's treated cruelly, & nobody ever says a word against her.'

'My own child is prejudiced & made to scorn me,' sobbed the little actress. 'Every source of happiness I have in the world is poisoned & all from his revenge because—'

'Have done, Mama!' said Caroline promptly. 'If you are not quiet I shall take you up-stairs.'

'You hear how she talks!' cryed her ladyship. 'My own daughter, my darling Caroline—ruined, miserably ruined!'

'Papa, Mama's not fit to be out of her room, is she?' again interrupted Miss Vernon. 'Let me take her in my arms & carry her up-stairs. I can do it easily.'

'I'll tell you all!' almost screamed her ladyship. 'I'll lay bare the whole vile scheme. Your father shall know you, Miss—what you are & what <u>he</u> is! I never mentioned the subject before, but I've noticed, & I've laid it all up, & nobody shall hinder me from proclaiming your baseness aloud.'

'Good heavens! This won't do!' said Caroline, blushing as red as fire. 'Be silent, Mother! I hardly know what you mean, but you seem to be possessed. Not another word now. Go to bed, do. Come, I'll help you to your room.'

'Don't fawn, don't coax!' cried the infuriated little woman. 'It's too late! I've made up my mind. Percy, your daughter is a bold, impudent minx! Young as she is—she's a—'

She could not finish the sentence. Caroline fairly capsized her mother, took her in her arms & carried her out of the room. She was heard in the passage calling Elise & firmly ordering her to undress her lady & put her to bed. She locked the door of her bed-room, & then she came down stairs with the key in her hand. She did not seem to be aware that she had done anything at all extraordinary, but she looked very much distressed & excited.

'Papa, don't believe Mamma,' were her first words as she returned to the drawing-room. 'She talks such mad stuff when she's in a passion, & sometimes she seems as if she hated me—I can't tell why. I'm never insolent to her—I only make fun sometimes.' Miss Vernon lost command over herself & burst into tears. His Grace of Zamorna, who had been all this time a perfectly silent spectator of the whole strange scene, rose & left the room. Miss Vernon sobbed more bitterly when he was gone.

'Come here, Caroline,' said Northangerland. He placed his daughter on a seat close to his side & patted her curled hair soothingly. She gave up crying very soon & said, smiling, she didn't care a fig about it now, only Mamma was so queer & vexatious. 'Never mind her, Caroline,' said the Earl. 'Always come to me when she's cross. I can't do with your spirit being broken by such termagant whims. You shall leave her & come & live with me.'

'I wonder what in the world Mama would do quite by her self,' said Caroline. 'She would fret away to nothing. But to speak truth, Papa, I really don't mind her scolding—I'm so used to it. It does not break my spirit at all. Only she set off on a new tack just now. I did not expect it. She never talked in that way before.'

'What did she mean, Caroline?'

'I can't tell. I've almost forgot what she did say now, Papa, but it put me into a regular passion.'

'It was something about the Duke of Zamorna,' said Northangerland quietly.

Caroline's excitement returned. 'She's lost her senses,' she said. 'Such wild, mad trash!'

'What mad trash?' asked Percy. 'I heard nothing but half sentences, which amazed me I confess, but certainly didn't inform me.'

'Nor me either,' replied Miss Vernon. 'Only I had an idea she was going to tell some tremendous lie.'

'Of what nature?'

'I can't tell, Papa—I know nothing about it. Ma vexed me.'

There was a little pause. Then Northangerland said:

'Your mother used to be fond of you Caroline when you were a little child. What is the reason of this change? Do you provoke her unnecessarily?'

'I never provoked her but when she provokes me worse. She's like as if she was angry with me for growing tall, & when I want to be dressed more like a woman & to have scarfs & veils & such things, it does vex her so. Then, when she's raving & calling me vain & conceited—& a hussey—I can't help sometimes letting her hear a bit of the real truth.'

'And what do you call the real truth?'

'Why, I tell her that she's jealous of me, because people will think she is old if she has such a woman as I am for her daughter.'

'Who tells you you are a woman Caroline?'

'Elise Touquet. She says I'm quite old enough to have a gown & a watch & a desk & a maid to wait on me. I wish I might. I'm quite tired of wearing frocks & sashes & indeed, Papa,—they're only fit for little girls. Lord Enara's children came here once, & the eldest, Senora Maria as they call her, was quite fashionable compared to me, & she's only fourteen—more than a year younger than I am. When the Duke of Zamorna gave me a pony, Mamma would hardly let me have a riding habit. She said a skirt was quite sufficient for a child, but His Grace said I should have one & a beaver too—& I got them! Eh, how Ma did go on! She said the Duke of Zamorna was sending me to ruin as fast as I could go, & whenever I put them on to ride out, she plays up beautifully. You shall see me wear them to-morrow, Pa—if I may ride somewhere with you. Do let me!'

Northangerland smiled. 'Are you very fond of Hawkscliffe?' he asked after a brief interval of silence.

'Yes, I like it well enough. Only I want to travel somewhere. I should like when winter comes to go to Adrianopolis, & if I were a rich lady I'd have parties & go to the theatre & opera every-night—as Lady Castlereagh does. Do you know Lady Castlereagh, Papa?'

'I've seen her.'

'And have you seen Lady Thornton too?'

'Yes.'

'Well—they're both very fine fashionable ladies aren't they?'

'Yes.'

'And very handsome too. Do you think them handsome?'

'Yes.'

'Which is the best looking & what are they like? I often ask the Duke of Zamorna what they're like, but he'll tell me nothing, except that Lady Castlereagh is very pale & that Lady Thornton is extremely stout. But Elise Touquet, who was Lady Castlereagh's dress-maker once, says they're beautiful. Do you think them so?'

'Lady Thornton is very well,' replied Northangerland.

'Well, but has she dark eyes & a Grecian nose?'

'I forget,' answered the Earl.

'I should like to be exceedingly beautiful,' pursued Caroline. 'And to be very tall—a great deal taller than I am—& slender. I think I'm a great deal too fat. And fair—my neck is so brown Ma says I'm quite a negro—& I should like to be dashing & to be very much admired. Who is the best-looking woman in Verdopolis, Papa?'

Northangerland was considerably non-plussed. 'There are so many, it's difficult to say,' he answered. 'Your head runs very much on these things Caroline.'

'Yes. When I walk out in the wood by myself I build castles in the air & I fancy all how beautiful & rich I should like to be & what sort of adventures I should like to happen to me—for you know, Papa, I don't want a smooth, common place life, but something strange & unusual.'

'Do you talk in this way to the Duke of Zamorna?' asked Mr Percy.

'In what way, Papa?'

'Do you tell him what kind of adventures you should like to encounter & what sort of nose & eyes you should choose to have?'

'Not exactly. I sometimes say I'm sorry I'm not handsome & that I wish a fairy would bring me a ring or a magician would appear & give me a talisman like Aladdin's lamp* that I could get everything I want.'

'And pray what does His Grace say?'

'He says time & patience will do much—that plain girls with manners & sense often make passable women & that he thinks reading Lord Byron has half-turned my head.'

'You do read Lord Byron then?'

'Yes, indeed I do—& Lord Byron & Bonaparte & the Duke of Wellington & Lord Edward Fitzgerald* are the four best men that ever lived.'

'Lord Edward Fitzgerald? Who the D—l is he?' asked the Earl in momentary astonishment.

'A young nobleman that Moore wrote a life about,' was the reply. 'A regular Grand Republican. He would have rebelled against a thousand tyrants if they'd dared to trample on him. He went to America because he wouldn't be hectored over in England & he travelled in the American Forests, & at night he used to sleep on the ground like Miss Martineau.'*

'Like Miss Martineau!' exclaimed the Earl, again astounded out of his propriety.

'Yes, Papa—a lady who must have been the cleverest woman that ever lived. She travelled like a man to find out the best way of governing a country. She thought a republic far the best & so do I. I wish I had been born an Athenian.* I would have married Alcibiades*—or else Alexander the Great.* I do like Alexander the Great!'

'But Alexander the Great was not an Athenian—neither was he a republican,' interposed the Earl in a resigned, deliberate tone.

'No, Papa, he was a Macedonian I know—& a king too—but he was a right kind of king—martial & not luxurious & indolent. He had such power over all his army they never dared mutiny against him, though he made them suffer hardships.* And he was such an heroic man! Hephæstion* was nearly as nice as he was though; I always think he was such a tall slender elegant man. Alexander was little—what a pity!'

'What other favourites have you?' asked Mr Percy.

The answer was not quite what he expected. Miss Caroline, who probably had not often an opportunity of talking so unreservedly, seemed to warm with her subject. In reply to her excellent father's question, the pent up enthusiasm of her heart came out in full tide. The reader will pardon any little inconsistencies he may observe in the young lady's declaration.

'O, Papa, I like a great many people! But soldiers most of all. I do adore soldiers! I like Lord Arundel, Papa, & Lord Castlereagh & General Thornton, & General Henri Fernando di Enara* & I like all gallant rebels. I like the Angrians because they rebelled in a way against the Verdopolitans. Mr Warner is an insurgent & so I like him. As to Lord Arundel, he's the finest man that can be. I saw a picture of him once on horseback—he was reining in his charger & turning round with his hand stretched out—speaking to his regiment—as he did before he charged at Leyden—he was so handsome.'*

'He is silly,' whispered Northangerland very faintly.

'What, Pa!'

'He is silly, my dear. A big man, but nearly idiotic—calfish—quite heavy & poor-spirited. Don't mention him.'

Caroline looked as blank as the wall. She was silent for a time. 'Bah!' said she at last. 'That's disagreeable.' And she curled her lip as if nauseating the recollection of him. Arundel was clearly done for in her opinion.

'You are a soldier, aren't you, Papa?' she said erelong.

'No, not at all.'

'But you are a rebel & a republican,' continued Miss Vernon. 'I know that, for I've read it over & over again.'

'Those facts won't deny,' said Northangerland.

She clapped her hands & her eyes sparkled with delight. 'And you're a pirate* & a democrat too,' said she. 'You scorn worn out constitutions & old rotten monarchies, & you're a terror to those ancient doddered kings up at Verdopolis—that crazy ill-tempered old fellow Alexander* dreads you I know. He swears in broad Scotch whenever your name is mentioned. Do get up an insurrection Papa & send all those doting constitutionalists to Jericho!'*

'Rather good for a young lady that has been educated under royal auspices,' remarked Northangerland. 'I suppose these ideas on politics have been carefully instilled into you by His Grace of Zamorna, eh Caroline?'

'No, I've taken them all up myself. They're just my unbiassed principles.'

'Good!' again said the Earl & he could not help laughing quietly, while he added in an undertone, 'I suppose it's hereditary then—rebellion runs in the blood.'

By this time the reader will have acquired a slight idea of the state of Miss Caroline Vernon's mental developement & will have perceived that it was as yet only in the chrysalis form—that in fact she was not altogether so sage, steady & consistent as her best friends might have wished. In plain terms, mademoiselle was evidently raw, flighty & romantic—only there was a something about her, a flashing of her eye, an earnestness, almost an impetuosity of manner, which I cannot convey in words & which yet if seen must have irresistibly impressed the spectator that she had something of an original & peculiar character under all her rubbish of sentiment & inconsequence. It conveyed the idea that though she told a great deal, rattled on—let out—concealed neither feeling nor opinion—neither predilection nor antipathy—it was still just possible that something might remain behind, which she did not choose to tell nor even to hint at. I don't mean to say that she'd any love secret, or hate-secret either, but she'd sensations somewhere that were stronger than fancy or romance. She shewed it when she stepped across the rug to give her father a kiss & could not leave him for a minute. She shewed it when she blushed at what her mother said & in desperation lest she should let out more whisked her out of the room in a whirlwind. All the rattle about Alexander & Alcibiades & Lord Arundel & Lord Edward Fitzgerald was of course humbug—the rawest hash of ideas imaginable, yet she could talk better sense if she liked & often did do so when she was persuading her mother to reason. Miss Caroline had a fund of vanity about her, but it was not yet excited. She really did not know that she was good-looking but rather, on the contrary, considered herself unfortunately plain. Sometimes indeed she ventured to think that she had a nice foot & ancle & a very little hand, but then, alas, her form was not half slight & sylph-like enough for beauty according to her notions of beauty, which of course like those of all school-girls approached the farthest extreme of the thread-paper & may-pole style.* In fact she was made like a model. She could not but be graceful in her movements, she was so perfect in her proportions. As to her splendid eyes—dark enough & large enough to set twenty poets raving about them—her sparkling, even teeth & her profuse tresses—glossy curling & waving—she never counted these as beauties. They were nothing. She had neither rosy cheeks nor a straight Grecian nose, nor an alabaster neck, & so she sorrowfully thought to herself she could never be considered as a pretty girl. Besides, no one ever praised her, ever hinted that she possessed a charm. Her mother was always throwing out strong insinuations to the contrary &, as to her royal guardian, he either smiled in silence when she appealed to him, or uttered some brief & grave admonition to think less of physical & more of moral attraction.

It was after eleven when Caroline bade her papa good-night. His Grace the Duke did not make his appearance again that evening in the drawing-room. Miss Vernon wondered often what he was doing so long up-stairs but he did not come. The fact is, he was not up-stairs but comfortably enough seated in the dining-room, quite alone with his hands in his pockets, a brace of candles on the table by him unsnuffed & consequently burning rather dismally dim. It would seem he was listening with considerable attention to the various little movements in the house, for the moment the drawing-room door opened he rose, & when Caroline's 'Good-night, Papa' had been softly spoken & her step had crossed the passage & tripped up the stair-case, Mr Wellesley emerged from his retreat. He went straight to the appartment Miss Vernon had just left.

'Well,' said he, appearing suddenly before the eyes of his father-in-law. 'Have ye told her?'

'Not exactly,' returned the Earl. 'But I will do to-morrow.'

'You mean it still then?' continued His Grace, with a look indicating thunder.

'Of course I do.'

'You're a d—d noodle,' was the mild reply & therewith the door banged to & the Majesty of Angria vanished.

CHAP V

To-morrow came. The young lover of rebels & regicides awoke as happy as could be. Her father, whom she had so long dreamed about, was at last come. One of her dearest wishes had been realized & why might not others in due course of time? While Elise Touquet dressed her hair she sat pondering over a reverie of romance—something so delicious, yet so undefined—I will not say that it was all love, yet neither will I affirm that love was entirely excluded there-from—something there was of a hero, yet a nameless a formless a mystic being, a dread shadow—that crowded upon Miss Vernon's soul, haunted her day & night when she had nothing useful to occupy her head or her hands. I almost think she gave him the name of Ferdinand Alonzo FitzAdolphus,* but I don't know. The fact was he frequently changed his designation, being some-times no more than simple Charles Seymour or Edward Clifford,* & at other times soaring to the title of Harold, Aurelius Rinaldo Duke of Montmorency di Valdacella*—a very fine man no doubt, though whether he was to have golden or raven hair or straight or aquiline pro-boscis she had not quite decided. However, he was to drive all before him in the way of fighting, to conquer the world & build himself a city like Babylon*—only it was to be in the Moorish style, & there was to be a palace called the Alhambra,* where Mr Harold Aurelius was to live, taking upon himself the title of Caliph & she, Miss C. Vernon, the professor of republican principles, was to be his chief lady & to be called the Sultana Zara Esmerelda, with at least a hundred slaves to do her bidding. As for the gardens of roses & the halls of marble & the diamonds & the pearls & the rubies, it would be vanity to attempt a description of such heavenly sights—the reader must task his imagin-ation & try if he can conceive them.

In the course of that day Miss Vernon got something better to think of than the crudities of her over-stretched fancy. That Day was an era in her life. She was no longer to be a child—she was to be acknowledged a woman. Farewell to captivity where she had been reared like a bird! Her father was come to release her & she was to go with him to be his daughter & his darling. The Earl's splendid houses which she had never entered were to be opened to her & she was to be almost mistress there. She was to have servants & wealth & whatever delighted her eye she was to ask for & receive. She was to enter life, to see society, to live all the winter in a great city—Verdopolis—to be dressed as gaily as the gayest ladies, to have jewels of her own, to vie even with those demi-goddesses the Ladies Castlereagh & Thornton. It was too much—she could hardly realize it.

It may be supposed from her enthusiastic character that she received this intelligence with transport, that as Northangerland unfolded these coming glories to her view she expressed her delight & astonishment & gratitude in terms of extacy, but the fact is she sat by the table with her head on her hand listening to it all with a very grave face. Pleased she was, of course, but she made no stir. It was rather too important a matter to clap her hands about. She took it soberly. When the Earl told her she must get all in readiness to set off early to-morrow she said, 'To-morrow, Papa!' & looked up with an excited glance.

'Yes, early in the morning.'

'Does Mamma know?'

'I shall tell her.'

'I hope she'll not take it to heart,' said Caroline. 'Let her go with us for about a week or so Papa—it will be so dreary to leave her behind.'

'She's not under my control,' replied Percy.

'Well,' continued Miss Vernon, 'if she were not so excessively perverse & bad to manage as she is I'm sure she might get leave to go, but she makes the Duke of Zamorna think she's out of her wits by her frantic ways of going on, & he says she's not fit to be let loose on society. Actually, Papa, one day when the Duke was dining with us she started up without speaking a word in the middle of dinner & flew at him with a knife. He could hardly get the knife from her & afterwards he was obliged to tell Cooper to hold her hands. And another time she brought him a glass of wine & he just tasted it & threw the rest at the back of the fire. He looked full at her, & Mamma began to cry & scream as if somebody was killing her. She's always contriving to get laudanum & prussic acid* & such trash. She says she'll murder either him or herself, & I'm afraid if she's left quite alone she'll really do some harm.'

'She'll not hurt herself,' replied the Earl. 'And as to Zamorna, I think he's able to mind his own affairs.'

'Well,' said Miss Vernon, 'I must go & tell Elise to pack up.' And she jumped up & danced away as if care laid but lightly on her.

I believe the date of these present transactions is July, but I've almost forgotten. If so, summer-days were not gone by, nor summer evenings either & it is with a summer evening that I have now to do. Miss Caroline Vernon, alias Percy, had finished her packing-up & she had finished her tea too. She was in the drawing-room alone & she was sitting in the window-seat as quiet as a picture. I don't exactly know where the other inmates of the house were, but I believe Mr Percy was with Lady Louisa, & Lady Louisa was in her own room—as sick as you please. Whether at this particular moment of time she was playing the houri* or the fiend—kissing or cuffing the Earl, her lover, I really can't tell—neither as far as I know does it much signify. However, be that as it may, Caroline was by herself, & also she was very still & pensive. What else could she be, looking out on to the quiet walks of that garden & on to that lawn where the moon is already beginning dimly to shine? A summer moon is yellow & a summer evening sky is often more softly blue than pen can describe, especially when that same moon is but newly risen & when its orb hangs low & large over a back-ground of fading-hills & looks into your face from under the boughs of forest beeches. Miss Caroline Vernon is to leave Hawkscliffe to-morrow, so she is drinking in all its beauties to-night.

So you suppose reader, but you're mistaken. If you observe her eyes, she's not gazing, she's watching; she's not contemplating the moon, she's following the motions of that person who, for the last half hour, has been leisurely pacing up & down that gravel walk at the bottom of the garden. It is her guardian, & she is considering whether she shall go & join him & have a bit of talk with him for the last time—that is for the last time at Hawkscliffe, she's by no means contemplating anything like the solemnity of an eternal separation. This guardian of hers has a blue frock-coat on, white inexpugnables* & a stiff black stock; consequently he considerably resembles that angelic existence called a military man. You'll suppose Miss Vernon considers him handsome, because other people do—all the ladies in the world you know hold the Duke of Zamorna to be matchless, irresistible—but Miss Vernon doesn't think him handsome. In fact, the question of his charms has never yet been mooted in her mind. The idea as to whether he is a god of perfection or a demon of defects has not crossed her intellect once. Neither has she once compared him with other men. He is himself—a kind of abstract isolated being, quite distinct from aught beside under the sun. He can't be handsome, because he has nothing at all in common with Messrs

Ferdinand Alonzo Fitzadolphus, Harold Aurelius Rinaldo & company. His complexion is not like a lady's, nor has he cheeks tinged with transparent roses, nor glossy golden hair nor blue eyes. The Duke's whiskers & moustaches are rather terrible than beautiful, & the Duke's high mien & upright port & carriage are more awful than fascinating—& yet Miss Caroline is only theoretically afraid of him. Practically, she is often familiar enough—to play with the lion's mane is one of her greatest pleasures. She would play with him now, but he looks grave & is reading a book.

It seems, however, that Miss Vernon has at length conquered her timidity, for lo, as the twilight deepens & the garden is all dim & obscure, she with her hat on comes stealing quietly out of the house, & through the shrubs, the closed blossoms & dewy leaves, trips like a fairy to meet him. She thought she would surprise him, so she took a circuit & came behind. She touched his hand before he was aware. Cast-iron, however, can't be startled, & so no more was he.

'Where did you come from?' said the guardian, gazing down from supreme altitude upon his ward, who passed her arm through his & hung upon him according to her custom when they walked together.

'I saw you walking by yourself & so I thought I'd come & keep you company,' she replied.

'Perhaps I don't want you,' said the Duke.

'Yes you do. You're smiling, & you've put your book away as if you meant to talk to me instead of reading.'

'Well, are you ready to set off to-morrow?' he asked.

'Yes all is packed.'

'And the head & the heart are in as complete a state of preparation as the trunk I presume?' continued His Grace.

'My heart is wae,'* said Caroline. 'At last of all I'm sorry to go—especially this evening. I was not half so sorry in the middle of the day while I was busy, but now—'

'You're tired & therefore low-spirited. Well, you'll wake fresh in the morning & see the matter in a different light. You must mind how you behave Caroline when you get out into the world. I shall ask after you sometimes.'

'Ask after me? You'll see me! I shall come to Victoria-Square* almost constantly when you're in Verdopolis.'

'You will not be in Verdopolis longer than a few days.'

'Where shall I be, then?'

'You will go either to Paris, or Fidena or Rossland.'*

Caroline was silent.

'You will enter a new sphere,' continued her guardian, '& a new circle of society, which will mostly consist of French-people. Don't copy the manners of the ladies you see at Paris or Fontainebleau.* They are most of them not quite what they should be. They have very free, obtrusive manners, & will often be talking to you about love & endeavouring to make you their confidante. You should not listen to their notions on the subject, as they are all very vicious & immodest. As to the men, those you will see will be almost universally gross & polluted—avoid them.'

Caroline spoke not.

'In a year to two your Father will begin to talk of marrying you,' continued her Guardian, '& I suppose you think it would be the finest thing in the world to be married. It is not at all impossible that your father may propose a Frenchman for your husband. If he does, decline the honour of such a connexion.'

Still Miss Vernon was mute.

'Remember always,' continued His Grace, 'that there is one nation under heaven filthier even than the French—that is the Italians. The women of Italy should be excluded from your presence & the men of Italy should be spurned with disgust even from your thoughts.'

Silence still. Caroline wondered why his Grace talked in that way. He had never been so stern & didactic before.* His allusions to matrimony &c. too confounded her. It was not that the idea was one altogether foreign to the young lady's mind—she had most probably studied the subject now & then in those glowing day-dreams before hinted at. Nay, I would not undertake to say how far her speculations concerning it had extended, for she was a daring theorist, but as yet these thoughts had all been secret & untold—her guardian was the last person to whom she would have revealed their existence—& now it was with a sense of shame that she heard his grave counsel on the subject. What he said too about the French ladies & the Italian men & women made her feel very queer. She could not for the world have answered him & yet she wished to hear more. She was soon gratified.

'It is not all improbable,' pursued His Grace after a brief pause, during which he & Caroline had slowly paced the long terrace-walk at the bottom of the garden which skirted a stately aisle of trees, 'it is not at all improbable that you may meet occasionally in society a lady of the name of Lalande & another of the name of St James,* & it is most likely that these ladies will shew you much attention—flatter you—ask you to sing or play—invite you to their houses, introduce you to their particular circles & offer to accompany you to public places. You must decline it all.'

'Why?' asked Miss Vernon.

'Because,' replied the Duke, 'Madame Lalande & Lady St James are easy about their characters, their ideas on the subject of morality are very free. They would get you into their boudoirs, as the ladies of Paris call the little rooms where they sit in a morning & read gross novels, & talk over their own secrets with their intimate friends. You would hear of many love-intrigues & of a great deal of amorous manœuvering. You would get accustomed to impudent conversation & perhaps become involved in foolish adventures which would disgrace you.'

Zamorna still had all the talk to himself, for Miss Vernon seemed too busily engaged in contemplating the white pebbles on which the moon was shining that lay here & there on the path at her feet to take much share in the conversation.

At last she said in rather a low voice, 'I never intended to make friends with any Frenchwomen & I always thought that when I was a woman I would visit chiefly with such people as Lady Thornton & Mrs Warner & that lady who lives about two miles from here—Miss Laury—they are all very well-behaved are they not?'

Before the Duke answered this question he took out a red-silk hand-kerchief & blew his nose. He then said, 'Mrs Warner is a remarkably decent woman. Lady Thornton is somewhat too gay & flashy—in other respects I know no harm in her.'

'And what is Miss Laury like?' asked Caroline.

'What is she like? She is rather tall & pale.'

'But I mean, what is her character? Ought I to visit with her?'

'You will be saved the trouble of deciding on that point as she will never come in your way—she always resides in the country.'

'I thought she was very fashionable,' continued Miss Vernon, 'for I remember when I was in Adrianopolis I often saw pictures of her in the shops & I thought her very nice-looking.'

The Duke was silent in his turn.

'I wonder why she lives alone?' pursued Caroline, 'and I wonder she has no relations. Is she rich?'

'Not very.'

'Do you know her?'

'Yes.'

'Does Papa?'

'No.'

'Do you like her?'

'Sometimes.'

'Why don't you like her always?'

'I don't always think about her.'

'Do you ever go to see her?'

'Now & then.'

'Does she ever give parties?'

'No.'

'I believe she's rather mysterious & romantic,' continued Miss Vernon. 'She's a romantic look in her eyes—I should not wonder if she has had adventures.'

'I daresay she has,' remarked her Guardian.

'I should like to have some adventures,' added the young lady. 'I don't want a dull droning life.'

'You may be gratified,' replied the Duke. 'Be in no hurry—you are young enough yet, life is only just opening.'

'But I should like something very strange & uncommon, something that I don't at all expect.'

Zamorna whistled.

'I should like to be tried to see what I had in me,' continued his ward. 'O, if I were only rather better looking—adventures never happen to plain fat people!'

'No—not often.'

'I'm so sorry I'm not as pretty as your wife, the Duchess. If she had been like me she would never have been married to you.'

'Indeed, how do you know that?'

'Because I'm sure you would not have asked her. But she's so nice & fair, & I'm all dark—like a mulatto, Mamma says.'

'Dark yet comely,' muttered the Duke involuntarily, for he looked down at his ward & she looked up at him & the moonlight disclosed a clear forehead, pencilled with soft dusk curls, dark & touching eyes, & a round youthful cheek, smooth in texture & fine in tint as that of some portrait hung in an Italian palace where you see the raven eyelash & southern eye relieving a complexion of pure colourless olive, & the rosy lips smiling brighter & warmer for the absence of bloom elsewhere.

Zamorna did not tell Miss Vernon what he thought—at least not in words, but when she would have ceased to look up at him & returned to the contemplation of the scattered pebbles he retained her face in that raised attitude by the touch of his finger under her little oval chin. His Grace of Angria is an artist: it is probable that that sweet face, touched with soft lunar light, struck him as a fine artistical study.

No doubt it is terrible to be looked fixedly at by a tall powerful man who knits his brows, & whose dark hair & whiskers & moustaches combine to shadow the eyes of a hawk & the features of a Roman statue. When such a man puts on an expression that you can't understand—stops suddenly as you are walking with him alone in a dim garden—removes your hand from his arm & places his hand on your shoulder—you are justified in feeling nervous & uneasy.

'I suppose I've been talking nonsense,' said Miss Vernon, colouring & half-frightened.

'In what way?'

'I've said something about my sister Mary that I shouldn't have said.'

'How?'

'I can't tell, but you don't like her to be spoken of perhaps. I remember now you once said that she & I ought to have nothing to do with each other & you would never take me to see her.'

'Little simpleton!' remarked Zamorna.

'No,' said Caroline, deprecating the scornful name with a look & smile; & shewed her transient alarm was evaporating. 'No, don't call me so.'

'Pretty little simpleton. Will that do?' said her guardian.

'No, I'm not pretty.'

Zamorna made no reply—whereat, to confess the truth, Miss Vernon was slightly disappointed, for of late she had begun to entertain some latent embryo idea that His Grace did think her not quite ugly. What grounds she had for supposing so it would not be easy to say: it was an instinctive feeling & one that gave her little vain female heart too much pleasure not to be encouraged & fostered as a secret prize. Will the reader be exceedingly shocked if I venture to conjecture that all the foregoing lamentations about her plainness, were uttered with some half-defined intent of drawing forth a little word or two of cheering praise? Oh, human nature! human nature! And, oh inexperience! In what an obscure, dim, unconscious dream Miss Vernon was envelloped! How little she knew of herself! However, time is advancing & the hours—those 'wild-eyed charioteers' as Shelley calls them*—are driving on. She will gather knowledge by degrees. She is one of the gleaners of grapes in that vineyard where all man & woman-kind have been plucking fruit since the world began—the vineyard of experience. At present, though, she rather seems to be a kind of Ruth in a corn-field—nor does there want a Boaz to complete the picture,* who also is well-disposed to scatter handfuls for the damsel's special benefit. In other words, she has a mentor who, not satisfied with instilling into her mind the precepts of wisdom by words, will if not prevented by others do his best to enforce his verbal admonitions by practical illustrations that will dissipate the mists on her vision at once & shew her, in light both broad & burning,* the mysteries of humanity now hidden—its passions &

sins & sufferings, all its passages of strange error & all its after-scenes of agonized atonement. A skilful preceptor is that same—one accustomed to tuition. Caroline has grown up under his care a fine & accomplished girl—unspoilt by flattery, unused to compliment, unhackneyed in trite fashionable conventionalities, fresh, naïve & romantic—really romantic—throwing her heart & soul into her dreams, longing only for an opportunity to do what she feels she could do—to die for somebody she loves—that is, not actually to become a subject for the undertaker, but to give up heart, soul, sensations to one adored hero, to lose independent existence in the perfect adoption of her lover's being. This is all very fine, isn't it reader? Almost as good as the notion of Mr Rinaldo Aurelius! Caroline has yet to discover that she is as clay in the hands of the potter*—that the process of moulding is even now advancing—& that erelong she will be turned off the wheel a perfect polished vessel of grace.

Mr Percy Senr had been a good while up-stairs. Lady Louisa had talked him nearly deaf, so at last he thought he would go down into the drawing-room by way of change & ask his daughter to give him a tune on the piano. That same drawing-room was a nice little place, with a clean bright fire, no candles, & the furniture shining in a quiet glow. But however, as there was nobody there, Mr Percy regarded the vacant sofa, the empty easy-chair & the mute instrument with an air of gentle discontent. He would never have thought of ringing & asking after the missing individual, but however as a footman happened to come in with four wax candles he did just enquire where Miss Vernon was. The footman said he really didn't know, but he thought she was most likely gone to bed, as he had heard her saying to Mademoiselle Touquet that she was tired of packing. Mr Percy stood a little while in the room. Erelong he strayed into the passage, laid his hand on a hat & wandered placidly into the garden. Mr Percy was very poetical in his youth. Consequently he must have been very much smitten with the stillness of the summer night—the fine, dark, unclouded blue of the sky, & the glitter of the pin-point stars that swarmed over it like mites—all this must have softened his spirit, not to mention anything of a full moon, which was up a good way in the element just opposite & gazed down on him as he stood on the front door-steps, just as if she mistook him for Endymion.*

Mr Percy, however, would have nothing to say to her. He pulled the brim of his hat a trifle lower down on his forehead & held the noiseless tenor of his way* amongst the shades & flowers of the garden. He was just entering the terrace walk when he heard somebody speak.

The voice came from a dim nook where the trees were woven into a bower & a seat was placed at their roots.

'Come, it is time for you to go in,' were the words. 'I must bid you good-bye.'

'But won't you go in too?' said another voice, pitched [in] rather a different key to that of the first speaker.

'No, I must go home.'

'But you'll come again in the morning before we set off.'

'No.'

'Won't you?'

'I cannot.'

There was silence. A little suppressed sound was heard like a sob.

'What is the matter Caroline? Are you crying?'

'O I am so sorry to leave you! I knew when Papa told me I was to go I should be grieved to bid you good-bye—I've been thinking about it all day. I can't help crying.'

The sound of weeping filled up another pause.

'I love you so much,' said the mourner. 'You don't know what I think about you or how much I've always wanted to please you or how I've cryed by myself whenever you've seemed angry with me. Or what I'd give to be your little Caroline & to go with you through the world. I almost wish I'd never grown a woman, for when I was a little girl you cared for me far more than you do now. You're always grave now.'

'Hush & come here to me,' was the reply, breathed in a deep tender tone. 'There, sit down as you did when you <u>were</u> a little girl. Why do you draw back?'

'I don't know. I didn't mean to draw back.'

'But you always do, Caroline, now when I come near you, & you turn away your face from me if I kiss you, which I seldom do, because you are too old to be kissed & fondled like a child.'

Another pause succeeded, during which it seemed that Miss Vernon had had to struggle with some impulse of shame, for her guardian said when he resumed the conversation, 'Nay now, there is no need to distress yourself & blush so deeply. And I shall not let you leave me at present, so sit still.'

'You are so stern,' murmured Caroline. Her stifled sobs were heard again.

'Stern am I? I could be less so, Caroline, if circumstances were somewhat different. I would leave you little to complain of on that score.'

'What would you do?' asked Miss Vernon.

'God knows!'

Caroline cried again, for unintelligible language is very alarming.

'You must go in, child,' said Zamorna. 'There will be a stir if you stay here much longer. Come a last kiss.'

'Oh, my lord!' exclaimed Miss Vernon, & she stopped short as if she had uttered that cry to detain him & could say no more. Her grief was convulsive.

'What Caroline?' said Zamorna, stooping his ear to her lips.

'Don't leave me so—my heart feels as if it would break.'

'Why?'

'Oh, I don't know.' Long was the paroxysm of Caroline's sore distress. She could not speak; she could only tremble & sob wildly. Her mother's excitable temperament was roused within her. Zamorna held her fast in his arms, & sometimes he pressed her more closely, but for a while he was as silent as she was.

'My little darling,' he said, softening his austere tone at last. 'Take comfort. You will see or hear from me again soon. I rather think neither mountains nor woods nor seas will form an impassable barrier between you & me—no, nor human vigilance either. The step of separation was delayed till too late. They should have parted us a year or two ago Caroline, if they had meant the parting to be a lasting one. Now leave me. Go in.' With one final kiss he dismissed her from his arms. She went. The shrubs soon hid her. The opening & closing of the front door announced that she had gained the house.

Mr Wellesley was left by himself on the terrace-walk. He took a cigar out of his pocket, lighted it by the aid of a Lucifer-match,* popped it into his mouth &, having reared himself up against the trunk of a large beech, looked as comfortable & settled as possible. At this juncture he was surprised by hearing a voice at his elbow gently inquiring whether his mother knew he was out?* He had barely to turn his head to get a view of the speaker, who stood close to his side—a tall man, with a pale aspect & a particular expression in his eyes which shewed a good deal of their whites & were turned laterally on to Mr Wellesley.

II

CHAP—I

We were talking of a young lady of the name of Miss Caroline Vernon, who by herself & her more partial friends, was considered to have pretty nigh finished her education—who consequently was leaving retirement & on the point of taking her station, somewhere, in some circle of some order of highly fashionable society. It was in July when affairs reached this climax. It is now November, nearly December, & consequently a period of about four months has lapsed in the interim.* We are not to suppose that matters have all this while remained in statu quo*—that Miss Caroline has been standing for upwards of a quarter of a year with her foot on the carriage-step, her hand on the lackey's arm, her eyes pathetically & sentimentally fixed on the windows & chimnies of the convent-like place she is about to leave for good—all in a cataleptic condition of romantic immutability. No, be assured the young person sighed over Hawkscliffe but once, wept two tears on parting with a groom & a pony she had been on friendly terms with, wondered thrice what her dear mama would do without any-body to scold, for four minutes had a childish feeling of pity that she should be left behind, sat a quarter of an hour after the start in a fit of speechless thought she did not account for, & all the rest of the way was as merry as a grig.*

One or two instances did indeed occur on their route through Angria which puzzled her a little. In the first place, she wondered to hear her noble father give orders, whenever they approached a town, that the carriage should be taken through all sorts of odd, narrow bye-ways so as to avoid the streets, & when she asked the reason of this, he told her with a queer sort of smile that the people of Angria were so fond of him he was afraid that a recognition of the arms on his carriage might be attended with even a troublesome demonstration of their affection. When towards evening they entered the city of Zamorna, which they were necessitated to pass through because it lay directly in their way, Miss Caroline was surprised to hear all sorts of groans & yells uttered by grimy looking persons in paper-caps who seemed to gather about the lamp-posts* & by the shop windows as they passed along. She was almost confounded when, as the carriage stopped a moment at a large hotel, an odd kind of howl broke from a crowd of persons who had quickly collected by the door, & at the same instant the window of plate-glass on her right-hand shivered with a crash & an ordinary-sized brick-bat leapt through it & settled on her lap, spoiling a pretty silk frock which she had on & breaking a locket which was a keep-sake & which she very much valued.

It will now be a natural question in the reader's mind what has Miss Vernon been about during the last four months. Has she seen the world? Has she had any adventures? Is she just the same as she was? Is there any change? Where has she been? Where is she now? How does the globe stand in relation to her & she in relation to the globe?

During the last four months, reader, Miss Vernon has been at Paris. Her father had a crotchety, undefined notion that it was necessary she should go there to acquire a perfect finish. And in fact he was right in that notion, for Paris was the only place to give her what he wished her to have—the ton,* the air, the elegance, of those who were highest on the summit of fashion. She changed fast in the atmosphere of Paris. She saw quickly into many things that were dark to her before. She learnt life & unlearnt much fiction. The illusions of retirement were laid aside with a smile, & she wondered at her own rawness when she discovered the difference between the world's reality & her childhood's romance. She had a way of thinking to herself & of comparing what she saw with what she had imagined. By dint of shrewd observation she made discoveries concerning men & things which sometimes astounded her. She got hold of books which helped her in the pursuit of knowledge. She lost her simplicity by this means & she grew knowing & in a sense reflective. However, she had talent enough to draw from her theories a safe practice, & there was something in her mind or heart or imagination which, after all, filled her with wholesome contempt for the goings on of the bright refined world around her. People who have been brought up in retirement don't soon get hackneyed to society: they often retain a notion that they are better than those about, that they are not of their sort & that it would be a letting-down to them to give the slightest glimpse of their real natures & genuine feelings to the chance associates of a ball-room.

Of course Miss Caroline did not forget that there was such a thing in the world as love. She heard a great deal of talk about that article amongst the gallant monsieurs & no less gallant madames around her. Neither did she omit to notice whether she had the power of inspiring that super fine passion. Caroline soon learnt that she was a very attractive being & that she had that power in a very high degree. She was told that her eyes were beautiful—that her voice was sweet—that her complexion was clear & fine—that her form was a model. She was told all this without mystery, without reserve. The assurance flattered her highly & made her face burn with pleasure, & when by degrees she ascertained that few even of the prettiest women in Paris were her equals, she began to feel a certain consciousness of power, a certain security of pleasing more delicious & satisfactory than words can describe. The circumstance of her high parentage gave her éclat:* Northangerland is a kind of king in Paris, & his youthful daughter received from her father's followers the homage of a princess. In the French fashion they hailed her as a rising & guiding star of their faction—the Dupins, the Barrases & the Bernadottes* called her a new planet in the Republican Heaven. They knew what an ornament to their dark revolutionary coteries a lady so young & intelligent must be. And it will be no matter of wonder to the reader when I say that Miss Vernon received their homage, imbibed their sentiments & gave heart & soul to the politics of the faction that called her father its leader.

Her career at Paris soon assumed the aspect of a triumph after she had made one or two eloquent & enthusiastic declarations of her adoration for republics & her scorn of monarchies. She began to be claimed by the jeunes gens* of Paris as their queen & goddess. She had not yet experience enough to know what sort of a circle she [had] gathered round her, though she guessed that some of those sons of young France who thronged about her sofa in the saloon & crowded her box at the theatre were little better than regular mauvais sujets.* Very different, indeed, were these from the polite, grimacing, men-monkeys* of the old regime. There was a touch of the unvarnished blackguard about most of them—infinitely more gross & unequivocal than is to be met with in any other capital of civilized Europe. Miss Vernon—who was tolerably independent in her movements because her father restrained her very little & seemed to trust with a kind of blind confidence to I know not what conservative principle in his daughter's mind—Miss Vernon, I say, often at concerts & nightly soirées, met & mingled with troops of these men. She also met with a single individual who was as bad as the worst of the jeunes gens. He was not a Frenchman, however, but a countryman of her father's & a friend of his first youth. I allude to Hector Montmorency Esqre.

She had seen Mr Montmorency first at an evening party at Sir John Denard's Hotel in a Grand Reunion of the Northangerland faction. As usual, her seat was surrounded by the youngest & handsomest men in the room, & as usual she was engaged in impassioned & declamatory conversation on the desperate politics of her party, & whenever she turned her head she noticed a man of middle age, of strong form & peculiar sinister, sardonic aspect, standing with his arms folded, gazing hard at her. She heard him ask Sir John Denard in the French language who the De—l cette jolie petite fille à cheveux noirs* could possibly be. She did not hear Sir John's reply—it was whispered—but directly afterwards she was aware of some one leaning over her chair-back. She looked up. Mr Montmorency's face was bending over her.

'My young lady,' said he, 'I have been looking at you for a good while, & I wondered what on earth it could possibly be in your face that reminded me so of old times. I see how it is now, as I've learnt your name—you're Northangerland's & Louisa's child I understand. Hum! You're like to do them credit. I admire this. It's a bit in Augusta's way.* I dare say your father'll admire it too. You're in a good line—nice young men you have about you. Could you find in your heart to leave them a minute & take my arm for a little promenade down the room?'

Mr Montmorency offered his arm with the manner & look of a gentleman of the west.* It was accepted for, strange to say, Miss Vernon rather liked him—there was an off-hand gallantry in his mien which took her fancy at once. When the honourable Hector had got her to himself he began to talk to her in a half free, half confidential strain. He bantered her on her numerous train of admirers. He said one or two warm words about her beauty. He tried to sound the depth of her moral principles, & when his experienced eye & ear soon discovered that she was no Frenchwoman & no callous & hackneyed & well-skilled flirt, that his hints did not take & his innuendos were not understood, he changed the conversation & began to inquire about her education—where she had been reared & how she had got along in the world. Miss Vernon was as communicative as possible. She chattered away with great glee about her mother & her masters, about Angria & Hawkscliffe, but she made no reference to her guardian. Mr Montmorency inquired whether she was at all acquainted with the Duke of Zamorna. She said she was a little. Mr Montmorency then said he supposed the Duke wrote to her sometimes. She said, 'No, never.' Mr Montmorency said he wondered at that, & meantime he looked into Miss Vernon's face as narrowly as if her features had been the Lord's Prayer written within the compass of a sixpence.* There was nothing particular to be seen except a smooth brunette complexion & dark eyes looking at the carpet. Mr Montmorency remarked—in a random, careless way—that the Duke was a sad hand in some things. Miss Vernon asked in what.

'About women,' replied Montmorency bluntly & coarsely.

After a momentary pause she said, 'Indeed!' And that was all she did say. But she felt such a sensation of astonishment, such an electrical, stunning surprise that she hardly knew for a minute where [she] was. It was the oddest, the most novel thing in the world for her to hear her guardian's character freely canvassed—to hear such an opinion expressed concerning him as that Mr Montmorency had so nonchalantly uttered was strange to a degree. It gave a shock to her ordinary way of thinking—it revolutionized her ideas. She walked on through

the room, but she forgot for a moment who was round her or what she
was doing.

'Did you never hear that before?' asked Mr Montmorency after a
considerable interval, which he had spent humming a tune which a lady
was singing to a harp.

'No.'

'Did you never guess it? Has not His Grace a rakish, impudent air
with him?'

'No, quite different.'

'What! He sports the Simon Pure* does he?'

'He's generally rather grave & strict.'

'Did you like him?'

'No—yes—no—not much.'

'That's queer! Several young ladies have liked him a good deal too
well. I daresay you've seen Miss Laury now, as you lived at
Hawkscliffe.'

'Yes.'

'She's his mistress.'

'Indeed!' repeated Miss Vernon after the same interregnum of
appalled surprise.

'The Duchess has not particularly easy times of it,' continued
Montmorency. 'She's your half-sister, you know.'

'Yes.'

'But she knew what she had to expect before she married him, for
when he was Marquis of Douro he was the most consumed black-guard
in Verdopolis.'

Miss Caroline in silence heard, & in spite of the dismay she felt
wished to hear more. There is a wild interest in thus suddenly seeing
the light rush in on the character of one well known to our eyes, but
as we discover utterly unknown to our minds. The young lady's feelings were not exactly painful, they were strange, new & startling—she
was getting to the bottom of an unsounded sea & lighting on rocks she
had not guessed at. Mr Montmorency said no more in that conversation—he left Miss Vernon to muse over what he had communicated.
What his exact aim was in thus speaking of the Duke of Zamorna it
would be difficult to say—he added no violent abuse of him, nor did he
attempt to debase his character as he might easily have done—he left the
subject there. Whether his words lingered in the mind of the listener
I can hardly say. I believe they did, for though she never broached the
matter to any one else or again applied to him for farther information, yet she looked into magazines & into newspapers, she read every

passage & every scrap she could find that referred to Zamorna & Douro, she weighed & balanced & thought over every thing, & in a little while, though removed five hundred miles from the individual whose character she studied, she had learnt all that other people know of him & saw him in his real light—no longer as a philosopher & apostle, but as—I need not tell my readers what they know or at least can guess. Thus did Zamorna cease to be an abstract principle in her mind—thus did she discover that he was a man vicious like other men. Perhaps I should say more than other men—with passions that sometimes controlled him, with propensities that were often stronger than his reason, with feelings that could be reached by beauty, with a corruption that could be roused by opposition. She thought of him no longer as 'the stoic of the woods, the man without a tear'* but as—don't let us bother ourselves with considering as what.

When Miss Vernon had been about a quarter of a year in Paris she seemed to grow tired of the society there. She begged her father to let her go home, as she called it, meaning to Verdopolis. Strange to say, the Earl appeared disquieted at this request. At first he would not listen to it. She refused to attend the soirées [?or] frequent the Opera. She said she had had enough of the French people. She spent the evenings with her father & played & sung to him. Northangerland grew very fond of her, & as she continued her entreaties to be allowed to go home, often soliciting him with tears in her eyes, he slowly gave way & at length yielded a hard-wrung & tardy assent. But though his reluctance was overruled it was evidently not removed. He would not hear her talk of Verdopolis—he evidently hated the thoughts of her return thither. He seemed disturbed when she secluded herself from society & declined invitations. All this to an ordinary observer would seem to partake of a tincture of insanity, for well did his lordship know the character of those circles in which his daughter moved—the corrupt morality, the cold systematic dissoluteness universal there—yet he never hinted a word of advice or warning to her. He let her go seemingly unwatched & unguarded. He shewed no anxiety about her till the moment when she wished to withdraw from the vitiated atmosphere, & then he demurred & frown[ed] as though she had asked to enter into some scene of temptation instead of to retire from it. In spite of this seeming paradox, however, the probability is that Northangerland knew what he was about. He was well acquainted with the materials he had to work upon, & as he said himself he deemed that Caroline was safer as the prima-donna of a Parisian saloon than as the recluse of a remote lodge in Angria. But Northangerland is not proof to a soft imploring voice & a mournful look. Miss Vernon loathed Paris & pined after Verdopolis, & she got her way. One evening, as she kissed her father good-night, he said she might give what orders she pleased on the subject of departure. A very few days after, a packet freighted with the Earl & his household were steaming across the Channel.

CHAP. II

Northangerland was puzzled & uncomfortable when he got his daughter to Verdopolis. He evidently did not like her to remain there. He never looked settled or easy. There was no present impediment to her residing at Ellrington-House, because the Countess happened to be then staying in Angria, but when Zenobia came home Caroline must quit. Other considerations also disturbed the calm of the Earl's soul—by him untold, by his daughter unsuspected.

Mr Percy has his own peculiar way of expressing his dissatisfaction. Rarely does a word drop from his lips which bears the tone of expostulation, of reproof or even command. He does it all by looks & movements which the initiated only can understand. Miss Vernon discerned a difference in him, but could not dive to the origin thereof. When she came to him with her bonnet on, dressed to go out & looking, as her mirror had told her, very pretty & elegant, he did not express even his usual modicum of quiet pleasure. He would insinuate that the day was wet or cold, or windy or in some way unfit for an excursion. When she came to his drawing-room after tea & said she had no where to go & was come to spend the evening with him, he gave her no welcome—hardly smiled, only sat passive. Now his daughter Mary would have keenly felt such coldness, & would have met it with silent pride & bitter regret, but Caroline had no such acute sensitiveness, no such subtle perception. Instead of taking the matter home to herself & ascribing this change to something she had done or left undone, she attributed it to her father's being ill or in low spirits, or annoyed with business. She could not at all conceive that he was angry with her, & accordingly, in her carressing way, she would put her arms round his neck & kiss him. And though the Earl received the kiss more like a peice of sculpture than anything living, Caroline instead of retiring in silence would begin some prattle to amuse him, & when that failed of its effect she would try music. And when he asked her to give up playing she would laugh & tell him he was as capricious as mamma. And when nothing at all would do, she would take a book, sit down at his feet & read to herself. She was so engaged one evening when Mr Percy said after a long, long lapse of silence, 'Are you not tired of Verdopolis Caroline?'

'No,' was the answer.

'I think you had better leave it,' continued the Earl.

'Leave it, Papa, when winter is just coming on?'

'Yes.'

'I have not been here three weeks,' said Miss Vernon.

'You will be as well in the country,' replied her father.

'Parliament is going to meet & the season is beginning,' pursued she.

'Are you turned a monarchist?' asked the Earl. 'Are you going to attend the debates & take interest in the divisions?'

'No, but town will be full.'

'I thought you had had enough of fashion & gaiety at Paris.'

'Yes, but I want to see Verdopolitan gaiety.'

'Eden-Cottage* is ready,' remarked Northangerland.

'Eden-Cottage, Papa?'

'Yes, a place near Fidena.'

'Do you wish to send me there, Papa?'

'Yes.'

'How soon?'

'Tomorrow or the day after if you like.'

Miss Vernon's face assumed an expression which it would be scarcely correct to describe by softer epithets than dour & drumly.* She said with an emphatic, slow enunciation, 'I should not like to go to Eden-Cottage.' Northangerland made no remark. 'I hate the north extremely,' she pursued, '& have no partiality to the Scotch.'*

'Selden-House is ready too,' said Mr Percy.

'Selden-House is more disagreeable to me still!' replied his daughter.

'You had better reconcile yourself either to Fidena or Rossland,' suggested Mr Percy quietly.

'I feel an invincible repugnance to both!' was her reply, uttered with a self-sustained haughtiness of tone almost ludicrous from such lips.

Northangerland is long-suffering. 'You shall choose your own retreat,' said he. 'But as it is arranged that you cannot long remain in Verdopolis it will be well to decide soon.'

'I would rather remain at Ellrington-House,' responded Mademoiselle Vernon.

'I think I intimated that would not be convenient,' answered her Father.

'I would remain another month,' said she.

'Caroline!' said a warning voice. Percy's light eye flickered.

'Papa, you are not kind.' No reply followed. 'Will I be banished to Fidena?' muttered the rebellious girl to herself.

Mr Percy's visual organs began to play at cross-purposes—he did not like to be withstood in this way.

'You may as well kill me as send me to live by myself at the end of the world where I know nobody except Denard, an old grey badger.'*

'It is optional whether you go to Fidena,' returned Percy. 'I said you might choose your station.'

'Then I'll go & live at Paquena in Angria. You have a house there Papa.'

'Out of the question.' said the Earl.

'I'll go back to Hawkscliffe then.'

'O no! You can't have the choice of that—you are not wanted there.'

'I'll live in Adrianopolis then, at Northangerland-House.'

'No.'

'You said I might have my choice, Papa, & you contradict me in everything.'

'Eden-Cottage is the place,' murmured Percy.

'Do—do let me stay in Verdopolis!' exclaimed Miss Vernon after a pause of swelling vexation. 'Papa do—be kind & forgive me if I'm cross.' Starting up, she fell to the argument of kisses & she also cryed abundantly. None but Louisa Vernon or Louisa Vernon's daughter would have thought of kissing Northangerland in his present mood.

'Just tell why you won't let me stay, Papa,' she continued. 'What have I done to offend you? I only ask for another month, or another fortnight, just to see some of my friends when they come to Verdopolis.'

'What friends, Caroline?'

'I mean some of the people I know.'

'What people do you know?'

'Well, only two or three, & I saw in the newspaper this morning that they were expected to arrive in town very soon.'

'Who, Caroline?'

'Well, some of the Angrians—Mr Warner & General Enara & Lord Castlereagh. I've seen them many a time you know Papa, & it would be only civil to stop & call on them.'

'Won't do, Caroline,' returned the Earl.

'Why won't it do, Papa? It's only natural to wish to be civil is[n't] it?'

'You don't wish to be civil, & we'd better say no more about it. I prefer your going to Fidena the day after to-morrow at the farthest.'

Caroline sat mute for a moment, then she said, 'So, I am <u>not</u> to stay in Verdopolis & I <u>am</u> to go to Eden-Cottage.'

'Thou hast said it,' was the reply.

'Very-well,' she rejoined quickly. She sat looking at the fire for another minute, then she got up, lit her candle, said good night & walked up-stairs to bed. As she was leaving the room, she accidentally hit her forehead a good knock against the side of the door—a considerable organ* rose in an instant. She said nothing, but walked on. When she got to her own room the candle fell from its socket & was extinguished. She neither picked it up nor rang for another. She undressed in the dark & went to bed ditto. As she lay alone with night round her, she began to weep. Sobs were audible a long time from her pillow—sobs not of grief but of baffled will & smothered passion. She could hardly abide to be thus thwarted, to be thus forced from Verdopolis when she would have given her ears to be allowed to stay. The reader will ask why she had her heart so fixedly on this point. I'll tell him plainly & make no mystery of it.

The fact was she wanted to see her guardian. For weeks, almost months, she had felt an invincible inclination to behold him again by the new lights Mr Montmorency had given her as to his character. There had also been much secret enjoyment in her mind from the idea of shewing herself to him, improved as she knew she was by her late sojourn in Paris. She had been longing for the time of his arrival in town to come, & that very morning she had seen it announced in the newspaper that orders had been given to prepare Wellesley-House for the immediate reception of His Grace the Duke of Zamorna & suite, & that the noble Duke was expected in Verdopolis before the end of the week. After reading this Miss Caroline had spent the whole morning in walking in the garden behind Ellrington-House reverieing* on the interesting future she imagined to be in store for her—picturing the particulars of her first interview with Mr Wellesley, fancying what he would say—whether he would look as if he thought her pretty, whether he would ask her to come & see him at Wellesley House—if she should be introduced to the Duchess, how the Duchess would treat her, what she would be like, how she would be dressed, etcetera etceterorum. All this was now put a stop to—cut off, crushed in the bud—& Miss Caroline was thereupon in a horrid bad temper, choked almost with obstinacy & rage & mortification. It seemed to her impossible that she could endure the disappointment—to be torn away from a scene where there was so much of pleasure & exiled into comparative dark, blank solitude was frightful. How could she live? After long musing in midnight silence she said half-aloud, 'I'll find some way to alter matters,' & then she turned on her pillow & went to sleep.

Two or three days elapsed. Miss Vernon, it seemed, had not succeeded in finding a way to alter matters, for on the second day she was obliged to leave Ellrington-House, & she took her departure in tearless taciturnity, bidding no one good by except her father, & with him she just shook hands & offered him no kiss. The Earl did not half like her look & manner—not that he was afraid of anything tragic, but she seemed neither fretful nor desponding. She had the air of one who had laid a plan & hoped to compass her ends yet. She scrupled not to evince continued & haughty displeasure towards his lordship, & her anger was expressed with all her mother's temerity & acrimony—with something too of her mother's whimsicality, but with none of her fickleness. She seemed quite unconscious of any absurdity in her indignation, though it produced much the same effect as if a squirrel had thought proper to treat a Newfoundland dog with lofty hauteur. Northangerland smiled when her back was turned. Still, he perceived that there was character in all this & he felt far from comfortable. However, he had written to Sir John Denard, desiring him to watch her during her stay at Eden-Cottage, & he knew Sir John dared not be a careless sentinel.

The very morning after Miss Vernon's departure Zenobia, Countess of Northangerland, arrived at Ellrington-House & in the course of the same day a cortège of six carriages conveyed the Duke & Duchess of Zamorna, their children & household to the residence in Victoria Square. Mr Percy had made the coast clear only just in time.

CHAP. III.

One day when the Duke of Zamorna was dressing to go and dine in state at Waterloo-Palace—with some much more respectable company than he was accustomed to associate with—his young man, Mr Rosier, said as he helped him on with his Sunday coat, 'Has Your Grace ever noticed that letter on the mantle-piece?'

'What letter? No. Where did it come from?'

'It's one that I found on Your Grace's library-table the day we arrived in town—that's nearly a week ago—& as it seemed to be from a lady

I brought it up here intending to mention it to Your Grace, & somehow it slipped down between the toilet & the wall & I forgot it till this morning when I found it again.'

'You're a blockhead! Give me the letter.'

It was handed to him. He turned it over & examined the superscription & seal—it was a prettily folded, satin-paper production, nicely addressed & sealed with the impression of a cameo. His Grace cracked the pretty classic head, unfolded the document & read.

My lord Duke

I am obliged to write to you because I have no other way of letting you know how uncomfortable everything is. I don't know whether you will expect to find me in Verdopolis, or whether you've ever thought about it, but I'm not there. At least I shall not be there to-morrow, for Papa has settled that I am to go to Eden-Cottage near Fidena & live there all my life, I suppose. I call this very unreasonable, because I have no fondness for the place & no wish ever to see it, & I know none of the people there except an old, plain person called Denard, whom I exceedingly dislike. I have tryed all ways to change Papa's mind, but he has refused me so often that I think it would shew a want of proper spirit to beg any longer. I intend, therefore, not to submit, but to do what I can't help doing—though I shall let Papa see that I consider him very unkind & that I should be very sorry to treat him in such a way. He was quite different at Paris & seemed as if he had too much sense to contradict people & force them to do things they have a particular objection to. Will Your Grace be so kind as to call on Papa & recommend him to think better of it & let me come back to Verdopolis? It would perhaps be as well to say that very likely I shall do something desperate if I am kept long at Eden-Cottage—I know I cannot bear it, for my whole heart is in Verdopolis. I had formed so many plans which are now all broken up. I wanted to see Your Grace. I left France because I was tired of being in a country where I was sure you would not come, & I disliked the thought of the sea being between Your Grace & myself. I did not tell Papa that this was the reason I wished to remain in Verdopolis, because I was afraid he would think me silly as he does not know the regard I have for you.

I am in a hurry to finish this letter as I wish to send it to Wellesley-House without Papa knowing, & then you will find it there when you come. Your Grace will excuse faults because I have never been much accustomed to writing letters, though I am nearly sixteen years old. I know I have written in much too childish a way. However,

I cannot help it, & if Your Grace will believe me, I talk & behave much more like a woman than I did before I went to Paris, & I can say what I wish to say much better in speaking than I can in a letter. This letter for instance is all contrary to what I had intended. I had not meant to tell Your Grace that I cared at all about you. I had intended to write in a reserved, dignified way that you might think I was changed—which I am I assure you—for I have by no means the same opinion of you that I once had, & now that I recollect myself, it was not from pure friendship that I wished to see you, but chiefly from the desire I had to prove that I had ceased to respect Your Grace so much as formerly. You must have a great deal of cover in your character which is not a good sign.

I am, my lord Duke

Your obedient servant

Caroline Vernon

P.S. I hope you will be so kind as to write to me—I shall count the hours & minutes till I get an answer. If you write directly it will reach me the day after tomorrow. Do write! My heart aches. I am so sorry & so grieved. I had thought so much about meeting you—but perhaps you don't care much about me & have forgotten how I cryed the evening before I left Hawkscliffe—not that this signifies or is of the least consequence—I hope I can be comfortable whoever forgets me, & of course you have a great many calls on your thoughts, being a sort of king—which is a great pity—I hate kings. It would conduce to your glory if you would turn Angria into a Commonwealth & make yourself Protector. Republican principles are very popular in France. You are not popular there—I heard you very much spoken against. I never defended you—I don't know why—I seemed as if I disliked to let people know that I was acquainted with you. Believe me, Yours respectfully, C.V.

Zamorna, having completed the perusal of this profound & original document, smiled—thought a minute—smiled again—popped the epistle into the little drawer of a cabinet which he locked—pulled down his brief black silk waistcoat—adjusted his stock—settled himself in his dress-coat—ran his fingers three times through his hair—took his hat & new light lavender kid gloves—turned a moment to a mirror—backed—erected his head—took a survey of his whole longitude from top to toe—walked down stairs—entered a carriage that was waiting for him—sat back with folded arms & was whirled away to Waterloo Palace. He dined very heartily with a select gentleman party, consisting of His Grace the Duke of Wellington, His Grace the Duke of Fidena, the Right Honourable the Earl of Richton, the Right Honourable Lord St Clair, General Grenville & Sir R. Weaver Pelham. During the repast he was too fully occupied in eating to have time to commit himself much by any marked indecorum of behaviour, & even when the cloth was withdraw[n] & the wine placed on the table he comported himself pretty well for some-time, seeming thoughtful & quiet. After a while he began to sip his glass of champagne & crack his walnuts with an air of easy impudence much more consistent with his usual habits. Erelong he was heard to laugh to himself at some steady constitutional conversation going on between General Grenville & Lord St Clair. He likewise leaned back in his chair, stretched his limbs far under the table & yawned. His noble father remarked to him aside that if he were sleepy he knew the way upstairs to bed & that most of the guests there present would consider his room fully an equivalent for his company. He sat still, however, & before the party were summoned to coffee in the drawing room he had proceeded to the indecent length of winking at Lord Richton across the table. When the move was made from the dining-room, instead of following the rest upstairs he walked down into the hall—took his hat—opened the door, whistling, to see if it was a fine night, having ascertained that it was—turned out into the street without carriage or servant & walked home with his hands in his breeches pockets, grasping fast hold of a bob & two joeys.*

He got home in good time—about eleven o'clock—as sober as a water-cask, let himself in by the garden-door at the back of Wellesley-House & was ascending the private stair-case in a most sneaking manner—as if he was afraid of some-body hearing him & wanted to slink to his own den unobserved—when hark! A door opened in the little hall behind him. It was Her Grace the Duchess of Zamorna's drawing-room door. Mr Wellesley had in vain entered from the garden like a thief & trodden across the hall like a large tom-cat & stepped on his toes like a magnified dancing-master as he ascended the softly carpeted stairs. Some persons' ears are not to be deceived & in a quiet hour of the night, when people are sitting alone, they can hear the dropping of a pin within doors or the stirring of a leaf without.

'Adrian!' said one below, & Mr Wellesley was obliged to stop mid-way up the stairs.

'Well Mary?' he replied, without turning round or commencing a descent.

'Where are you going?'

'Up stairs I rather think. Don't I seem to be on that tack?'

'Why did you make so little noise in coming in?'

'Do you wish me to thunder at the door like a battering-ram, or come in like a troop of horse?'

'Now that's nonsense Adrian. I suppose the fact is you're not well. Now just come down & let me look at you.'

'Heaven preserve us! There's no use in resisting. Here I am!' He descended & followed the Duchess from the hall to the room to which she retreated.

'Am I all here, do you think?' he continued, presenting himself before her. 'Quite as large as life?'

'Yes, Adrian, but—'

'But what? I presume there's a leg or an arm wanting—or my nose is gone—or my teeth have taken out a furlough—or the hair of my head has changed colour—eh? Examine well & see that your worser half is no worse than it was.'

'There's quite enough of you, such as you are,' said she. 'But what's the matter with you? Are you sure you've been to Waterloo-Palace?'

'Where do you think I have been? Just let us hear. Keeping some assignation I suppose. If I had, I would not have come home so soon, you may be pretty certain of that.'

'Then you have been only to Waterloo-Palace?'

'I rather think so. I don't remember calling any-where else.'

'And who was there? And why did you come home by yourself without the carriage? Did the rest leave when you did?'

'I've got a head-ache, Mary.' This was a lie, told to awaken sympathy & elude further cross-examination.

'Have you Adrian? Where?'

'I think I said I had a <u>head</u>-ache. Of course it would not be in my great toe.'

'And was that the reason you came away so soon?'

'Not exactly. I remembered I had a love-letter to write.'

This was pretty near the truth. The Duchess however believed the lie & disregarded the truth. The matter was so artfully managed that jest was given for earnest & earnest for jest.*

'Does your head ache very much?' continued the Duchess.

'Deucedly.'

'Rest it on this cushion.'

'Hadn't I better go to bed, Mary?'

'Yes, & perhaps if I was to send for Sir Richard Warner—you may have taken cold.'

'Oh no, not to-night. We'll see to-morrow morning.'

'Your eyes don't look heavy Adrian.'

'But they feel so, just like bullets.'

'What kind of a pain is it?'

'A shocking bad one.'

'Adrian, you are laughing. I saw you turn away your head & smile.'

His Grace smiled without turning away his head—that smile confessed that his head-ache was a sham. The Duchess caught its meaning quickly. She caught also an expression in his face which indicated that he had changed his mood since he came in & that he was not so anxious to get away from her as he had been. She had been standing before him—she now took his hand. Mary looked prettier than any of her rivals ever did. She had finer features, a fairer skin, more eloquent eyes. No hand more soft & delicate had ever closed on the Duke's than that which was detaining him now. He forgot her superiority often & preferred charms which were dim to hers. Still she retained the power of wakening him at intervals to a new conscious- ness of her price, & His Grace would every now & then discover with surprise that he had a treasure always in his arms that he loved better a great deal than the far-sought gems he dived amongst rocks so often to bring up.

'Come, all's right,' said His Grace, sitting down, & he mentally added, 'I shall have no time to write a letter to-night—it's perhaps as well let alone.' Dismissing Caroline Vernon with this thought he allowed himself to be pleased by her elder & fairer sister Mary.

The Duchess appeared to make no great bustle or exertion in effect- ing this, nor did she use the least art or agacerie,* as the French call it—which indeed she full well knew with the subject she had to manage would have instantly defeated its own end. She simply took a seat near the arm-chair into which His Grace had thrown himself, inclined her- self a little towards him, & in a low agreeable voice began to talk on mis- cellaneous subjects of a household & family nature. She had something to say about her children & some advice to ask. She had also quietly to inquire into His Grace's opinion on one or two political points, & to communicate her own notions respecting divers matters under discus- sion—notions she never thought of imparting to any living ear except that of her honourable spouse, for in everything like gossip & chit- chat the Duchess of Zamorna is ordinarily the most reserved person immaginable.

To all this the Duke hearkened almost in silence, resting his elbow on the chair & his head on his hand, looking sometimes at the fire & sometimes at his wife. He seemed to take her talk as though it were a kind of pleasant air on a flute, & when she expressed herself with a certain grave naïve simplicity—which is a peculiar characteristic of her familiar conversation which she seldom uses but can command at will—he did not smile but gave her a glance which somehow said that those little original touches were his delight. The fact was she could if she liked have spoken with much more depth & sense. She could have rounded her periods like a blue* if she had had a mind & discussed topics worthy of a member of parliament. But this suited better. Art was at the bottom of the thing after all—it answered. His Grace set some store on her as she sat telling him everything that came into her mind in a way which proved that he was the only person in whom she reposed this confidence—now & then but very seldom, raising her eyes to his—& then her warm heart mastered her prudence, & a glow of extreme ardour confessed that he was so dear to her that she could not long feign indifference or even tranquillity while thus alone with him, close at his side.

Mr Wellesley could not help loving his Mary at such a moment & telling her so too, & I daresay asseverating with deep oaths that he had never loved any other lady half so well—nor ever seen a face that pleased his eye so much or heard a voice that filled his ear with such sweetness. That night she certainly recalled a wanderer. How long it will be before the wish to stray returns again is another thing. Probably circumstances will decide this question—we shall see if we wait patiently.

CHAP IV

Louisa Vernon sixteen years ago gave the name of Eden to her romantic cottage at Fidena, not one would suppose from any resemblance the place bears to the palmy shades of an Asiatic paradise, but rather because she there spent her happiest days in the society of her lover, Mr Percy, the Drover, & because that was the scene where she moved as a queen in the midst of a certain set & enjoyed that homage & adulation whose recollection she to this day dwells on with fondness & whose absence she pines over with regret.

It was not with her mother's feelings that Caroline Vernon viewed the place when she arrived there late on a wet & windy November night—too dark to shew her the amphitheatre of Highlands towards which her cottage looked, for the mountains had that evening muffled their brows in clouds instead of crowning them 'with the wandering star'.* Caroline, as may be supposed, cherished other feelings towards the place than her mother would have done—other than she herself might very probably have entertained had the circumstances attending her arrival there been somewhat different—had the young lady, for instance, made it her resting-place in the course of a bridal tour. Had she come to spend her honeymoon amid that amphitheatre of Highlands towards which the cottage looked she might have deigned to associate some high or soft sensation with the sight of those dim mountains—only the portals, as it were, to a far wilder region beyond, especially when in an evening 'they crowned their blue brows with the wandering star'. But Miss Caroline had arrived on no bridal tour. She had brought no inexpressibly heroic-looking personage as her camarade de voyage & also her camarade de vie.* She came a lonely exile, a persecuted & banished being according to her own notions, & this was her Siberia & not her Eden.*

Prejudiced thus, she would not for a moment relax in her detestation of the villa & the neighbourhood. Her heaven for that season she had decided was to be Verdopolis—there were her hopes of pleasure—there were all the human beings on earth in whom she felt any interest—there were those she wished to live for, to dress for, to smile for. When she put on a becoming frock here, what was the good of it? Were those great staring mountains any judges of dress? When she looked pretty, who praised her? When she came down of an evening to her sitting-room, what was there to laugh with her, to be merry with her? Nothing but arm-chairs & ottomans & a cottage piano. No hope here of happy arrivals, of pleasant rencontres.*

Then she thought if she were but at that moment passing through the folding-door of a saloon at Ellrington-House, perhaps just opposite to her—by the marble fire-place—there would be somebody standing that she should like to see—perhaps nobody else in the room. She had imagined such an interview. She had fancied a certain delightful excitement & surprise connected with the event. The gentleman would not know her at first—she would be so changed from what she was five months ago. She was not dressed like a child now, nor had she the air & tournure* of a child. She would advance with much state. He would perhaps move to her slightly. She would give him a glance, just to be quite certain who it was. It would of course be him & no mistake, & he would have on a blue frock coat & white irreproachables* & would be very much bewhiskered & becurled as he used to be. Also, his nose would be in no wise diminished or impaired: it would exhibit the same aspect of a tower looking towards Lebanon* that it had always done. After a silent

inspection of two or three minutes he would begin to see daylight—&
then came the recognition. There was a curious uncertainty about this
scene in Miss Caroline's imagination. She did not know exactly what
His Grace would do or how he would look. Perhaps he would only say,
'What, Miss Vernon, is it you?' & then shake hands. That, the young
lady thought, would be sufficient if there was anybody else there; but if
not—if she found His Grace in the saloon alone—such a cool acknowledgement of acquaintanceship would never do. He must call her his
little Caroline & must bestow at least one kiss. Of course there was no
harm in such a thing—wasn't she his ward? And then there came the
outline of an idea of standing on the rug talking to him, looking up
sometimes to answer his questions about Paris & being sensible how
little she was near him. She hoped nobody would come into the room,
for she remembered very well how much more freely her guardian used
to talk to her when she took a walk with him alone than when there were
other persons by.

So far Caroline would get in her reverie & then something would
occur to rouse her—perhaps the tinkling fall of a cinder from the grate.
To speak emphatically, it was then dickey with all these dreams.* She
awoke & found herself at Fidena & knew that Verdopolis & Ellrington-
House were just three hundred miles off, & that she might wear her
heart with wishes—but could neither return to them nor attain the
hope of pleasure they held forth. At this crisis Miss Vernon would sit
down & cry, & when a cambric handkerchief had been thoroughly wet
she would cheer up again at the remembrance of the letter she had left
at Wellesley House & commence another reverie on the effects that profound lucubration was likely to produce. Though day after day elapsed
& no answer was returned, & no messenger came riding in breathless
haste, bearing a recall from banishment, she still refused to relinquish
this last consolation. She could not believe that the Duke of Zamorna
would forget her so utterly as to neglect all notice of her request.
But three weeks elapsed & it was scarcely possible to hope any longer.
Her father had not written for he was displeased with her. Her Guardian
had not written, for her sister's charms had succeeded in administer-
ing a soft opiate to his memory, which for the time lulled to sleep all
recollection of every other female face & deadened every faithless wish
to roam.

Then did Miss Caroline begin to perceive that she was despised & cast
off, even as she herself hid away a dress that she was tired of or a scarf
that had become frayed & faded. In deep meditation—in the watches
of the night*—she discerned at first by glimpses & at last clearly that

she was not of that importance to the Earl of Northangerland & the Duke of Zamorna which she had vainly supposed herself to be.

'I really think,' she said to herself doubtfully, 'that because I am not Papa's proper daughter but only his natural daughter—& Mamma was never married to him—he does not care much about me. I suppose he is proud of Mary Henrietta because she married so highly & is considered so beautiful & elegant. And the Duke of Zamorna just considers me as a child whom he once took a little trouble with in providing her with masters & getting her taught to play a tune on the piano, & to draw in French chalk & to speak with a correct Parisian accent, & to read some hard, dry, stupid, intricate Italian poetry. And now that I'm off his hands he makes no more account of me than of one of those ricketty little Flowers* whom he sometimes used to take on his knee a few minutes to please Lord Richton. Now this will never do! I can't bear to be considered in this light! But how do I wish him to regard me? What terms should I like to be on with him? Really, I hardly know. Let me see. I suppose there's no harm in thinking about it at night to oneself when one can't sleep but is forced to lie awake in bed looking into the dark & listening to the clock strike hour after hour.' And having thus satisfied herself with the reflection that silence could have no listener & solitude no watcher, she turned her cheek to her pillow &, shrouding her eyes even from the dim outline of a large window which alone relieved the midnight gloom of her chamber, she would proceed thus with her thoughts.

'I do believe I like the Duke of Zamorna very much. I can't exactly tell why. He is not a good man, it seems, from what Mr Montmorency said, & he is not a particularly kind or cheerful man. When I think of it, there were scores of gentlemen at Paris who were a hundred times more merry & witty & complimentary than ever he was. Young Vaudeville & Troupeau said more civil things to me in half an hour than ever he did in all his life. But still I like him so much—even when he is behaving in this shameful way. I think of him constantly. I thought of him all the time I was in France. I can't help it. I wonder whether—' She paused in her mental soliloquy, raised her head & look[ed] forth into her chamber. All was dark & quiet. She turned again to her pillow. The question which she had thrust away returned, urging itself on her mind: 'I wonder whether I love him? O, I do!' cryed Caroline starting up in fitful excitement. 'I do, & my heart will break. I'm very wicked,' she thought, shrinking again under the clothes. 'Not so very,' suggested a consolatory reflection. 'I only love him in this way: I should like always to be with him & always to be doing something that would please him.

I wish he had no wife, not because I want to be married to him, for that is absurd, but because if he were a bachelor he would have fewer to think about & then there would be more room for me. Mr Montmorency seemed to talk as if my sister Mary was to be pitied. Stuff! I can't imagine that! He must have loved her exceedingly when they were first married at any rate, & even now she lives with him & sees him & talks to him. I should like a taste of her unhappiness, if she would be Caroline Vernon for a month & let me be Duchess of Zamorna. If there was such a thing as magic & if His Grace could tell how much I care for him & could know how I am lying awake just now & wishing to see him, I wonder what he would think? Perhaps he would laugh at me & say I was a fool. O why didn't he answer my letter? What makes Papa so cruel? How dark it is! I wish it was morning—the clock is striking only one. I can't go to sleep. I'm so hot & so restless. I could bear now to see a spirit come to my bed-side and ask me what I wanted—wicked or not wicked I would tell all—& beg it to give me the power to make the Duke of Zamorna like me better than ever he liked any body in the world before. And I would ask it to unmarry him & change the Duchess into Miss Percy again & he should forget her & she should not be so pretty as she is. And I believe—yes, in spite of fate—he should love me & be married to me. Now then, I'm going mad, but there's the end of it.'

Such was Miss Vernon's midnight soliloquy & such was the promising frame of mind into which she had worked herself by the time she had been a month at Fidena. Neglect did not subdue her spirit; it did not weaken her passions. It stung the first into such desperate action that she began to scorn prudence & would have dared anything—reproach, disgrace, disaster—to gain what she longed for. And it worked the latter into such a ferment that she could rest neither day nor night. She could not eat; she could not sleep. She grew thin. She began to contemplate all sorts of strange, wild schemes. She would assume a disguise; she would make her way back to Verdopolis; she would go to Wellesley-House & stand at the door & watch for the Duke of Zamorna to come out. She would go to him hungry, cold & weary, & ask for something. Perhaps he would discover who she was, & then surely he would at least pity her. It would not be like him to turn coldly away from his little Caroline, whom he had kissed so kindly when they had last parted on that melancholy night at Hawkscliffe. Having once got a notion like this into her head, Miss Vernon was sufficiently romantic, wilful & infatuated to have attempted to put it into execution—in fact, she had resolved to do so. She had gone so far as to bribe her maid by a present of her watch—a splendid trinket set with diamonds—to procure her a suit of boy's clothes from a tailor's at Fidena. That watch might have been worth two hundred guineas; the value of the clothes was at the utmost six pounds. This was just a slight hereditary touch of lavish folly. With the attire thus dearly purchased she had determined to array herself on a certain day, slip out of the house unobserved, walk to Fidena four miles, take the coach there & so make an easy transit to Verdopolis.

Such was the stage of mellow maturity at which her wise projects had arrived when, about ten o'clock one morning, a servant came into her breakfast-room & laid down on the table beside her coffee-cup a letter—the first, the only one she had received since her arrival at Eden-Cottage. She took it up. She looked at the seal, the direction, the post-mark—the seal was only a wafer-stamp*—the direction, a scarcely legible scrawl—the post-mark Freetown. Here was mystery. Miss Caroline was at fault. She could not divine who the letter came from. She looked at it long. She could not bear to break the seal—while there was doubt there was hope. Certainty might crush that hope so rudely. At last she summoned courage, broke it, opened the missive & read.

Woodhouse-Cliffe—Freetown Nov^{br} 29th

My dear little Caroline,

Miss Vernon read so far & she let the letter fall on her knee & her head drop forward on to the table & fairly burst into a flood of tears. This was odd, but romantic young ladies are said to be often unaccountable. Hastily wiping away the tears from her eyes, she snatched the letter up again—looked at it—cryed once more—smiled in the midst of her weeping—rose—walked fast about the room—stopped by the window—&, while the letter trembled in the hand that held it, read with dim eyes that still flowed over the singular epistle that follows.*

My dear little Caroline,

Business has called me for a few days to Woodhouse-Cliffe, a place of Mr Warner's in the neighbourhood of Freetown. Freetown is a hundred miles nearer to Fidena than Verdopolis & the circumstance of closer proximity has reminded me of a certain letter left some weeks ago on the library-table at Wellesley-House. I have not that letter now at hand for as I recollect I locked it up in the drawer of a cabinet in my dressing-room intending to answer it speedily, but the tide changed & all remembrance of the letter was swept away as it receded. Now, however, that same fickle tide is flowing back again & bringing the lost scroll with it.

No great injury has been done by this neglect on my part—because I could not fulfil the end for which your letter was written—you wished me to act as intercessor with your father & persuade him if possible to change his mind as to your place of residence, for it seems Eden-Cottage is not to your taste. On this point I have no influence with him. Your father & I never converse about you Caroline. It would not do at all. It was very well to consult him now & then about your lessons & your masters when you were a little girl—we did not disagree much on those subjects. But since you have begun to think yourself a woman, he & I have started on a different tack in our notions concerning you. You know your father's plan—you must have had sufficient experience of it lately at Paris & now at Fidena. You don't know much about mine, & in fact it is as yet in a very unfinished state, scarcely fully comprehended even by its originator. I rather think, however, your own mind has anticipated something of its outline. There were moments now & then at Hawkscliffe when I could perceive that my ward would have been a constituent of her guardian's, in case the two schemes had been put to the decision of a vote, & her late letter bears evidence that the preference has not quite faded away. I must not omit to notice a saucy line or two concerning my character, indicating that you have either been hearing or reading some foolish nonsense on that head. Caroline, find no fault with it until experience gives you reason so to do. Foolish little girl! What have you to complain of? Not much I think.

And you wish to see your guardian again, do you? You would like another walk with him in the garden at Hawkscliffe? You wish to know if I have forgotten you? Partly. I remember something of a rather round face with a dimpled childish little chin & something of a head very much embarassed by its unreasonable quantity of black curls, seldom arranged in anything like Christian order—but that is all. The picture grows very dim. I suppose when I see you again there will be a change—you tell me you are grown more of a woman. Very likely. I wish you good-bye. If you are still unhappy at Eden-Cottage write and tell me so—

Yours &c.   Zamorna

People in a state of great excitement sometimes take sudden resolves & execute them successfully on the spur of the moment, which, in their calmer & more sane moments, they would neither have the phrenzy to conceive, nor the courage & promptitude to put in practice—as somnambulists are said in sleep to cross broken bridges unhurt & walk on the leads of houses in safety, where awake, the consciousness of all the horrors round them would occasion instant & inevitable destruction.

Miss Vernon, having read this letter, folded it up & committed it to the bosom of her frock. She then, without standing more than half a minute to deliberate, left the room—walked quickly & quietly up-stairs—took out a plain straw bonnet and a large shawl, put them on—changed her thin satin slippers for a pair of walking shoes—unlocked a small drawer in her bureau—took therefrom a few sovereigns, slipped them in to a little velvet bag—drew on her gloves—walked down stairs very lightly, very nimbly—crossed the hall—opened the front-door—shut it quickly after her—passed up a plantation out at a wicket gate—entered the high road—set her face towards Fidena with an intrepid, cheerful, unagitated air—kept the crown of the causeway and in about an hour was at the door of the General Coach Office asking at what time a coach would start for Freetown. The answer was that there were conveyances in that direction almost every hour of the day & that the Verdopolitan Mail was just going out. She took her place, paid her fare, entered the vehicle & before any one at Eden-Cottage was aware of her absence was already a good stage on the road to Woodhouse-Cliff.

Here was something more than the devil to pay*—a voluntary elopement without a companion, alone, entirely of her own free-will—on the deliberation of a single moment! That letter had so crowded her brain with thoughts, with hopes, with recollections & anticipations—had so fired her heart with an unconquerable desire to reach & see the absent writer—that she could not have lived through another day of passive captivity. There was nothing for it but flight. The bird saw its cage open—beheld a free sky—remembered its own remote isle & grove & nest—heard in spirit a voice call it to come—felt its pinion nerved with impatient energy—launched into air & was gone. Miss Vernon did not reflect, did not repent, did not fear. Through the whole day & night her journey lasted she had no moment of misgiving. Some would have trembled from the novelty of their situation, some would have quailed under the reproaches of prudence, some would have sickened at the dread of a cold or displeased reception at their journey's end. None of these feelings daunted Caroline a whit. She had only one thought, one wish, one aim, one object—to leave Fidena, to reach Freetown. That done, hell was escaped & heaven attained. She could not see the blind folly of her undertaking. She had no sense of the erroneous nature of

the step. Her will urged it. Her will was her predominant quality &
must be obeyed.

CHAP V

Mrs Warner, a quiet, nice little woman as every-body knows, had just
retired from the dinner-table to her own drawing-room, about six o'clock
one winter's evening. It was nearly dark—very still. The first snow had
begun to fall that afternoon & the quiet walks about Woodhouse-Cliffe
were seen from the long, low windows all white & wildered. Mrs Warner
was without a companion. She had left her husband & her husband's
prodigious guest in the dining room, seated each with a glass before
him & decanters & fruit on the table. She walked to the window, looked
out a minute, saw that all was cold and cheerless, then came to the fireside, her silk dress rustling as she moved over the soft carpet, sank into
a bergère* (as the French call it) & sat alone & calm—her earings only
glittering & trembling, her even brow relieved with smooth, braided
hair—the very seat of serene good temper.

Mrs Warner did not ring for candles. She expected her footman
would bring them soon, & it was her custom to let him choose his own
time for doing his work—an easier mistress never existed than she is. A
tap was heard at the door.

'Come in,' said the lady, turning round. She thought the candles
were come. She was mistaken: Hartley her footman indeed appeared,
with his silk stockings & his shoulder knots,* but he bore no shining
emblems of the seven churches which are in Asia.* The least thing
out of the ordinary routine is a subject of gentle wonderment to M^{rs}
Warner, so she said, 'What is the matter Hartley?'

'Nothing, madam, only a post-chaise has just driven up to the
door.'

'Well, what for?'

'Some one has arrived madam.'

'Who is it, Hartley?'

'Indeed, madam, I don't know.'

'Have you shewn them into the dining-room?'

'No.'

'Where then?'

'The young person is in the hall, madam.'

'Is it some one wanting Mr Warner do you think?'

'No, ma'am. It is a young lady who asked if the Duke of Zamorna were here.'

Mrs Warner opened her blue eyes a trifle wider. 'Indeed, Hartley! What must we do?'

'Why, I thought you had better see her first, madam. You might recognize her. I should think from her air she is a person of rank.'

'Well—but Hartley, I have no business with it. His Grace might be displeased. It may be the Duchess or some of those other ladies.' What Mrs Warner meant by the term 'other ladies' I leave it to herself to explain. However, she looked vastly puzzled & put about.

'What had we best do?' she inquired again, appealing to Hartley for advice.

'I really think, madam, I had better shew her up here. You can then speak to her yourself & inform His Grace of her arrival afterwards.'

'Well, Hartley, do as you please. I hope it's not the Duchess, that's all. If she's angry about anything it will be very awkward. But she would never come in a post-chaise, that's one comfort.'

Hartley retired. Mrs Warner remained fidgetting from her arm-chair to her work-table—putting on her gold thimble, taking it off—drawing her foot-stool to her feet—pushing it away. In spite of the post-chaise she still entertained a lurking dread that the new-comer might be her mistress the Duchess, & the Duchess was in Mrs Warner's idea a very awful, haughty, formidable little personage. There was something in the high, melancholy look of the royal lady's eyes which, when Mrs Warner met it, always made her feel uncomfortable & inspired a wish to be anywhere rather than in her presence. Not that they had ever quarrelled—nothing of the kind—& Her Grace was usually rather conspicuously civil to the lady of one of the most powerful men in Angria. Still, the feeling of restraint did exist & nothing could remove it.

Steps were heard upon the stair-case. Hartley threw open the pannelled folding-door of the drawing room, ushered in the visitor & closed it—first, however, depositing four thick & tall tapers of wax upon the table. Mrs Warner rose from her arm-chair, her heart fluttering a little & her nice face & modest countenance exhibiting a trivial discomposure. The first glance at the stranger almost confirmed her worst fears. She saw a figure bearing a singular resemblance to the Duchess of Zamorna in air, size & general outline. A bonnet shaded the face & a large shawl partially concealed the shape.

'I suppose you are Mrs Warner,' said a subdued voice and the stranger came slowly forward.

'I am,' said that lady, quite reassured by the rather bashful tone in which those few words were spoken, & then, as a hesitating silence followed, she continued in her kind way, 'Can I do anything for you? Will you sit down?'

The young person took the seat which was offered her. It was opposite Mʳˢ Warner & the brilliant wax-lights shone full in her face. All remains of apprehension were instantly dissipated—here was nothing of the delicate, fair & pensive aspect characteristic of Mary Henrietta. Instead of the light shading of pale brown hair, there was a profusion of dark tresses crowded under the bonnet. Instead of the thoughtful poetic hazel eye gazing rather than glancing, there was a full black orb, charged with fire, fitful, quick & restless. For the rest, the face had little bloom, but was youthful & interesting.

'You will be surprised to see me here,' said the stranger after a pause, 'but I am come to see the Duke of Zamorna.'

This was said quite frankly. Mʳˢ Warner was again relieved. She hoped there was nothing wrong as the young lady seemed so little embarrassed in her announcement.

'You are acquainted with His Grace are you?' she inquired.

'O yes,' was the answer. 'I have known him for a great many years. But you will wonder who I am, Mʳˢ Warner. My name is Caroline Vernon. I came by the coach to Freetown this afternoon. I was travelling all night.'

'Miss Vernon!' exclaimed Mʳˢ Warner. 'What, the Earl of Northangerland's daughter! O I am sorry I did not know you! You are quite welcome here. You should have sent up your name—I am afraid Hartley was cold & distant to you.'

'No, not at all. Besides that does not much signify—I have got here at last. I hope the Duke of Zamorna is not gone away.'

'No, he is in the dining-room.'

'May I go to him directly? Do let me Mʳˢ Warner!'

Mʳˢ Warner, however, perceiving that she had nothing to fear from the hauteur of the stranger & experiencing likewise an inclination to exert a sort of motherly or elder sisterly kindness & protection to so young & artless a girl, thought proper to check this extreme impatience. 'No,' said she. 'You shall go upstairs first & arrange your dress. You look harrassed with travelling all night.'

Caroline glanced at a mirror over the mantlepiece. She saw that her hair was dishevelled, her face pale & her dress disarranged.

'You are right, Mʳˢ Warner, I will do as you wish me. May I have the help of your maid for five minutes?'

A ready assent was given to this request. Mrs Warner herself shewed Miss Vernon to an appartment up stairs, & placed at her command every requisite for enabling her to appear in somewhat more creditable style. She then returned to her drawing-room, sat down again in her arm-chair, put her little round foot upon the foot-stool, & with her finger on her lip began to reflect more at leisure upon this new occurrence. Not very quick in apprehension,* she now began to perceive for the first time that there was something very odd in such a very young girl as Miss Vernon coming alone—unattended—in a hired conveyance to a strange house, to ask after the Duke of Zamorna. What could be the reason of it? Had she run away unknown to her present protectors? It looked very like it. But what would the Duke say when he knew? She wished Howard would come in; she would speak to him about it. But she didn't like to go into the dining-room & call him out. Besides she did not think there was the least harm in the matter—Miss Vernon was quite open & free, she made no mystery about the business. The Duke had been her guardian—it was natural she should come to see him. Only the oddity was that she should be without carriage or servants. She said she had come by the coach. Northangerland's daughter by the coach! Mrs Warner's thinking faculties were suspended in amazement.

The necessity of pursuing this puzzling train of reflections was precluded by Miss Vernon coming down. She entered the room as cheerfully & easily as if Mrs Warner had been her old friend and she an invited guest at a house perfectly familiar.

'Am I neat now?' were the first words as she walked up to her hostess.

Mrs Warner could only answer in the affirmative, for indeed there was nothing of the traveller's negligence now remaining in the grey silk dress, the smooth curled hair, the delicate silk stockings & slippers. Besides, now that the shawl & bonnet were removed a certain fine turn of form was visible, which gave a peculiarly distinguished air to the young stranger. A neck & shoulders elegantly designed, & arms round, white & taper, fine ancles & small feet imparted something classic, picturesque & highly patrician to her whole mien & aspect. In fact Caroline looked extremely lady-like—& it was well she had that quality, for her stature & the proportions of her size were on too limited a scale to admit of more superb & imposing charms.

She sat down. 'Now I do want to see the Duke,' said she smiling at Mrs Warner.

'He will be here presently,' was the answer. 'He never sits very long at table after dinner.'

'Don't tell him who I am when he comes in,' continued Caroline. 'Let us see if he will know me. I don't think he will.'

'Then he does not at all expect you?' asked the hostess.

'O no! It was quite a thought of my own coming here—I told nobody. You must know, Mrs Warner, Papa objected to my staying in Verdopolis this season, because, I suppose, he thought I had had enough gaiety in Paris where he & I spent the autumn & part of the summer. Well, as soon as ever town began to fill, he sent me up beyond Fidena to Eden-Cottage. You've heard of the place I daresay—a dismal, solitary house at the very foot of the Highlands. I have lived there about a month, & you know how stormy & wet it has been all the time. Well, I got utterly tired at last, for I was determined not to care anything about the misty-hills—thought they looked strange enough sometimes. Yesterday-morning I thought I'd make a bold push for a change. Directly after breakfast, I set off for Fidena with only my bonnet & shawl on, as if I were going to walk in the grounds. When I got there I took the coach & here I am.'

Caroline laughed. Mrs Warner laughed too. The nonchalant, off-hand way in which this story had been told her completely removed any little traces of suspicion that might still have been lurking in her usually credulous mind.

The reader will by this have discerned that Miss Vernon was not quite so simple & communicative as she seemed. She knew how to give her own colouring to a statement without telling any absolute lies. The very warm sentiments which she indulged towards her guardian were, she flattered herself, known to no living thing but the heart that conceived & contained them. As she sat on a sofa near the fire, leaning her head against the wall so that the shade of a projecting mantle-piece almost concealed her face, she did not tell Mrs Warner that, while she talked so lightly to her, her ear was on the stretch to catch an approaching foot-step—her heart fluttering at every sound—her whole mind in a state of fluttering & throbbing excitement—longing, dreading for the door to open—eagerly anticipating the expected advent, yet fearfully shrinking from it with a contradictory mixture of feelings.

The time approached. A faint sound of folding doors unclosing was heard below. The grand stair-case ascending to the drawing-room was again trodden—& the sound of voices echoed through the lobby & hall.

'They are here,' said Mrs Warner.

'Now don't tell who I am,' returned Miss Vernon, shrinking closer into her dim corner.

'I will introduce you as my niece, as Lucy Grenville,' was the reply & the young matron seemed beginning to enter into the spirit of the young maid's espièglerie.*

'Your Grace is perfectly mistaken,' said a gentleman opening the drawing-room door & permitting a taller man to pass. 'It is singular that reason does not convince Your Grace of the erroneous nature of your opinion. Those houses, my lord Duke, will last for fifty years to come with the expenditure of a mere trifle on repairs.'

'With the expenditure of two hundred pounds on the erection [of] new walls & roofs, plaster, painting & wood-work they will last a few years longer, I make no doubt,' was the reply.

'Your Grace speaks ignorantly,' rejoined Warner Howard Warner Esqre. 'I tell you those houses have stood in their present state for the last twenty years. I recollect them perfectly when I was only twelve years old & they looked neither better nor worse than they do now.'

'They could not well look worse,' returned the taller man, walking up to the hearth & pushing away an ottoman with his foot to make room for himself to stand on the rug.

'Are you talking about the Cliffe-Cottages still?' asked Mrs Warner, looking up.

'Yes, Mistress. They have been the sole subject of conversation since you left the room. Your master has increased his estimate of their value every five minutes & now at last he describes the rotten, roofless hovels as capital well-built mansion-houses, with convenient out-houses—to wit a pig-stye each, & large gardens, id est* a patch of dunghill two yards square—suitable for the residence of a genteel family. And he tells me if I would only buy them, I should be sure to make a rental of twenty pounds per annum from each. That won't wash,* will it Mistress?'

'What won't wash please Your Grace? The rug?'

'No, Mr Ferguson's pocket-handkerchief.'

'I don't know. Who is Mr Ferguson* & what kind of handkerchiefs does he wear?'

'Very shewy ones—manufactured at Blarney-Mills.* Your Master always buys of him.'

'Now Your Grace is jesting. Howard does nothing of the kind! His pocket-handkerchiefs are all of cambric.'

A half-smothered laugh, excited no doubt by Mrs Warner's simplicity, was heard from the obscure sofa-corner. The Duke of Zamorna, whose back had been to the mantle-piece & whose elbow had been supported by the projecting slab thereof, quickly turned. So did

Mʳ Warner. Both gentlemen saw a figure seated & reclining back, the face half hid by the shade & half by a slim & snowy hand, raised as if to screen the eyes from the flickering & dazzling fire-light.

The first notion that struck His Majesty of Angria was the striking similarity of that grey silk dress, that pretty form & tiny slender foot to something that ought to be a hundred miles off at Wellesley House—in fact, a vivid though vague recollection of his own Duchess was suggested to his mind by what he saw. In the surprise & conviction of the moment he thought himself privileged to advance a good step nearer—& was about to stoop down to remove the screening hand & make himself certain of the unknown's identity when the sudden & confused recoil, the half-uttered interjection of alarm with which his advances were received, compelled him to pause. At the same time Mʳˢ Warner said hurri[e]dly, 'My neice, Lucy Grenville.'

Mʳ Warner looked at his wife with astonishment. He knew she was not speaking the truth. She looked at him imploringly.

The Duke of Zamorna laughed. 'I had almost made an awkward mistake,' said he. 'Upon my word, I took Miss Lucy Grenville for some one I had a right to come within a yard of without being reproved for impertinence. If the young lady had sat still half a minute longer I believe I should have inflicted a kiss. Now I look better though, I don't know, there's a considerable difference—as much as between a dark dahlia & a lily—' His Grace paused, stood with his head turned fixedly towards Miss Grenville, scrutinized her features with royal bluntness—threw a transfixing glance at Mʳˢ Warner—abruptly veered round, turning his back on both in a movement of much more singularity than politeness—erelong dropped into a chair &, crossing one leg over the other, turned to Mʳ Warner & asked him if he saw day-light. Mʳ Warner did not answer, for he was busily engaged in perusing a newspaper. The Duke then inclined his head towards Mʳˢ Warner &, leaning half across her work-table, inquired in a tone of anxious interest whether she thought <u>This</u> would wash?

Mʳˢ Warner was too much puzzled to make a reply, but the young lady laughed again, fitfully & almost hysterically—as if there was some internal struggle between tears & laughter. Again she was honoured with a sharp, hasty survey from the King of Angria, to which succeeded a considerable interval of silence, broken at length by His Majesty remarking that he should like some coffee. Hartley was summoned & His Majesty was gratified. He took about six cups, observing when he had finished that he had much better have taken as many eight penn'orths of brandy & water & that if he had thought of it before he would have asked for it. Mrs Warner offered to ring the bell & order a case-bottle & a tumbler then, but the Duke answered that he thought on the whole he had better go to bed, as it was about half-past eight o'clock—a healthy primitive hour which he should like to stick to. He took his candle, nodded to Mr Warner, shook hands with Mrs Warner, & without looking at the neice, said in a measured, slow manner as he walked out of the room, 'Good-night, Miss Lucy Grenville.'

CHAP VI

How Miss Vernon passed the night which succeeded this interview the reader may amuse himself by conjecturing—I cannot tell him. I can only say that when she went up-stairs she placed her candle on a dressing-table, sat down at the foot of the bed where she was to sleep, & there remained, perfectly mute & perfectly motionless, till her light was burnt out. She did not soliloquize, so what her thoughts were it would be difficult to say. Sometimes she sighed—sometimes tears gathered in her eyes, hung a little while on her long eye-lashes & then dropped to her lap, but there was no sobbing, no strong emotion of any kind. I should say, judging from her aspect, that her thoughts ran all on doubt, disappointment & suspense, but not on desperation or despair. After the candle had flickered a long time, it at last sank into darkness. Miss Vernon lifted up her head, which had been bent all the while, saw the vital spark dying on the table before her, rose & slowly undressed. She might have had a peculiar penchant for going to bed in the dark when anything happened to disturb her. If you recollect, reader, she did so before, the night her father announced his resolution to send her to Eden-Cottage.

The next morning she woke late, for she had not fallen asleep before the dawn began to break. When she came down she found that the Duke & Mr Warner were gone out to take a survey of the disputed Cliffe-Cottages—two superannuated old hovels, by the bye, fit habitations for neither man nor beast. They had taken with them a stone-mason & an architect—also a brace of guns, two brace of pointers & a game-keeper. The probability, therefore, was that they would not be back before night fall. When Miss Vernon heard that, her heart was so bitter that she could have laid her head on her hand & fairly cryed like a child. If the Duke had recognized her—& she believed he had—what contemptuous negligence, or cold displeasure his conduct evinced!

However, on second thoughts she scorned to cry—she'd bear it all. At the worst, she could take the coach again & return to that dungeon at Fidena. And what could Zamorna have to be displeased at? He did not know that she had wished her sister dead & herself his wife. He did not know the restless, devouring feeling she had when she thought of him. Who could guess that she loved that powerful & austere Zamorna when, as she flattered herself, neither look nor word nor gesture had ever betrayed that frantic dream? Could he be aware of it when she had not fully learnt it herself till she was parted from him by mountain, valley & wave? Impossible! And since he was so cold, so regardless, she would crush the feeling & never tell that it had existed. She did not want him to love her in return—no, no, that would be wicked—she only wanted him to be kind—to think well of her, to like to have her with him—nothing more. Unless, indeed, the Duchess of Zamorna were to happen to die & then—, but she would drop this foolery—master it entirely—pretend to being in excellent spirits. And if the Duke should really find her out, affect to treat the whole transaction as a joke, a sort of eccentric adventure undertaken for the fun of the thing.

Miss Vernon kept her resolution. She drest her face in smiles & spent the whole day merrily & sociably with Mrs Warner. Its hours passed slowly to her & she still, in spite of herself, kept looking at the window & listening to every movement in the hall. As evening and darkness drew on she waxed restless & impatient. When it was time to dress, she arranged her hair & selected her ornaments with a care she could hardly account for herself.

Let us now suppose it to be eight o'clock. The absentees returned an hour since & are now in the drawing-room. But Caroline is not with them; she has not yet seen them. For some cause or other she has preferred retiring to this large library in another wing of the house. She is sitting moping by the hearth like Cinderella. She has rung for no candles; the large fire alone gives a red gleam & quivering shadows upon the books, the ceiling, the carpet. Caroline is so still that a little mouse, mistaking her no doubt for an image, is gliding unstartled over the rug & around her feet. On a sudden the creature takes alarm, makes a dart & vanishes under the brass fender. Has it heard a noise? There is nothing stirring. Yes, something moves somewhere in the wing which was before so perfectly still.

While Miss Vernon listened—yet doubtful whether she had really heard or only fancied the remote sound of a step—the door of her retreat was actually opened & a second person entered its precincts. The Duke of Zamorna came straying listlessly in as if he had found his way there by chance. Miss Vernon looked up, recognized the tall figure & overbearing build, & felt that now at last the crisis was come. Her feelings were instantly wound to their highest pitch, but the first word brought them down to a more ordinary tone.

'Well, Miss Grenville, good evening.'

Caroline, quivering in every nerve rose from her seat & answered, 'Good evening, my lord Duke.'

'Sit down,' said he, '& allow me to take a chair near you.'

She sat down. She felt very queer when Zamorna drew a seat close to hers & coolly installed himself beside her. Mʳ Wellesley was attired in evening-dress with something more of brilliancy & shew than has been usual with him of late. He wore a star on his left breast & diamonds on his fingers. His complexion was coloured with exercise, & his hair curled round his forehead with a gloss & profusion highly characteristic of the most consummate coxcomb going.

'You & I,' continued His Sublimity, 'seemed disposed to form a separate party of ourselves to-night I think Miss Lucy. We have levanted from the drawing-room & taken up our quarters elsewhere—I hope, by the bye, my presence is no restraint. You don't feel shy & strange with me do you?'

'I don't feel strange,' answered Miss Vernon.

'But rather shy just at the first I presume. Well use & better acquaintance will wear that off. In the meantime, if you have no objection, I will stir the fire & then we shall see each other better.'

His Grace stooped, took the poker, woke up the red & glowing mass & elicited a broad blaze which flashed full on his companion's face & figure. He looked first with a smile, but gradually with a more earnest expression. He turned away & was silent. Caroline waited, anxious, trembling, with difficulty holding in the feelings which swelled her heart. Again the Duke looked at her & drew a little nearer.

'He is not angry,' thought Miss Vernon. 'When will he speak & call me Caroline?' She looked up at him. He smiled. She approached, still seeking in his eye for a welcome. Her hand was near his; he took it, pressed it a little. 'Are you angry?' asked Miss Vernon in a low, sweet voice. She looked beautiful, her eye bright & glowing, her cheek flushed & her dark wavy hair resting lightly upon it like a cloud. Expectant, impatient, she still approached the silent Duke till her face almost touched his.

This passive stoicism on his part could not last long—it must bring a reaction. It did. Before she could catch the lightning change in face & eye, the rush of blood to the cheek, she found herself in his arms.

He strained her to his heart a moment, kissed her forehead & instantly released her.

'I thought I would not do that,' said Zamorna, rising & walking through the room. 'But where's the use of resolution? A man is not exactly a statue.' Three turns through the appartment restored him to his self-command. He came back to the hearth.

'Caroline! Caroline!' said he, shaking his head as he bent over her. 'How is this? What am I to say about it?'

'You really know me, do you?' answered Miss Vernon, evading her guardian's words.

'I think I do,' said he. 'But what brought you from Fidena? Have you run away?'

'Yes,' was the reply.

'And where are you running to?'

'Nowhere,' said Caroline. 'I have got as far as I wished to go. Didn't you tell me in your letter that if I was still unhappy at Eden-Cottage I was to write & tell you so? I thought I had better come.'

'But I am not going to stay at Woodhouse-Cliffe, Caroline. I must leave to-morrow.'

'And will you leave me behind you?'

'God bless me!' ejaculated Mr Wellesley, hastily raising himself from his stooping attitude & starting back as if a wasp had stung his lip. He stood a yard off, looking at Miss Vernon, with his whole face fixed by the same expression that had flashed over it before. 'Where must I take you Caroline?' he asked.

'Anywhere.'

'But I am to return to Verdopolis—to Wellesley-House—it would not do to take you there. You would hardly meet with a welcome.'

'The Duchess would not be glad to see me, I suppose,' said Miss Vernon.

'No, she would not,' answered the Duke, with a kind of brief laugh.

'And why should she not?' enquired the young lady. 'I am her sister. Papa is as much my father as he is hers. But I believe she would be jealous of any-body liking Your Grace besides herself.'

'Aye, & of My Grace liking anybody too, Caroline.'

This was a hint which Miss Vernon could not understand. These words & the pointed emphasis with which they were uttered broke down the guard of her simplicity & discomfited her self-possession. They told her that Zamorna had ceased to regard her as a child. They intimated that he looked upon her with different eyes to what he had done, & considered her attachment to him as liable to another interpretation than the mere fondness of a ward for her guardian—her secret seemed to be discovered. She was struck with an agony of shame—her face burned—her eyes fell—she dared look at Zamorna no more.

And now the genuine character of Arthur Augustus Adrian Wellesley began to work. In this crisis Lord Douro stood true to his old name & nature. Zamorna did not deny by one noble & moral act the character he has earned by a hundred infamous ones. Hitherto we have seen him rather as restraining his passions than yielding to them—he has stood before us rather as a mentor than a misleader—but he is going to lay down the last garment of light* & be himself entirely. In Miss Vernon's present mood—burning & trembling with confusion, remorse, apprehension—he might by a single word have persuaded her to go back to Eden-Cottage. She did not yet know that he reciprocated her wild, frantic attachment. He might have buryed that secret—have treated her with an austere gentleness he well knew how to assume—& crushed in time the poison flowers of a passion whose fruit, if it reached maturity, would be crime & anguish. Such a line of conduct might be trodden by the noble & faithful Fidena—it lies in his ordinary path of life—he seldom sacrifices another human being's life & fame on the altar of his own vices. But the selfish Zamorna cannot emulate such a deed—he has too little of the moral great-heart* in his nature. It is his creed that all things bright & fair live for him—by him they are to be gathered & worn as the flowers of his laurel crown. The green leaves are victory in battle; they never fade. The roses are conquests in love; they decay & drop off. Fresh ones blow round him, are plucked & woven with the withered stems of their predecessors. Such a wreath he deems a glory about his temples. He may in the end find it rather like the snaky fillet which compressed Calchas's brows, steeped in blue venom.*

The Duke reseated himself at Miss Vernon's side. 'Caroline,' said he, desiring by that word to recall her attention, which was wandering wide in the distressful paroxysm of shame that over-whelmed her. He knew how to give a tone, an accent to that single sound which should produce ample effect. It expressed a kind of pity. There was something protecting & sheltering about it as if he were calling her home. She turned. The acute pang which tortured her heart & tightened her breath dissolved into sorrow. A gush of tears relieved her.

'Now then,' said Zamorna when he had allowed her to weep a while in silence. 'The shower is over. Smile at me again my little dove. What was the reason of that distress? Do you think I don't care for you Caroline?'

'You despise me. You know I am a fool.'

'Do I?' said he quietly. Then after a pause, he went on. 'I like to look at your dark eyes & pretty face.'

Miss Vernon started & deeply couloured—never before had Zamorna called her face pretty. 'Yes,' said he, 'it is exquisitely pretty, & those soft features & dusky curls are beyond the imitation of a pencil. You blush because I praise you. Did you never guess before that I took a pleasure in watching you—in holding your little hand, & in playing with your simplicity, which has sported many a time, Caroline, on the brink of an abyss you never thought of.'

Miss Vernon sat speechless. She darkly saw or rather felt the end to which all this tended, but all was fever & delirium round her. The Duke spoke again—in a single blunt & almost coarse sentence compressing what yet remained to be said.

'If I were a bearded Turk, Caroline, I would take you to my harem.'

His deep voice, as he uttered this, his high-featured face & dark large eye, beaming bright with a spark from the depths of Gehenna,* struck Caroline Vernon with a thrill of nameless dread. Here he was—the man that Montmorency had described to her! All at once she knew him. Her guardian was gone—something terrible sat in his place. The fire in the grate was sunk down without a blaze, the silent, lonely library, so far away from the inhabited part of the house, was gathering a deeper shade in all its Gothic recesses. She grew faint with dread. She dared not stir—from a vague fear of being arrested by the powerful arm flung over the back of her chair.

At last, through the long & profound silence a low whisper stole from her lips. 'May I go away?'

No answer. She attempted to rise. This movement produced the effect she had feared, the arm closed round her. Miss Vernon could not resist its strength; a piteous upward look was her only appeal. He, Satan's eldest son, smiled at the mute prayer.

'She trembles with terror,' said he, speaking to himself. 'Her face has turned pale as marble within the last minute or two. How did I alarm her? Caroline, do you know me? You look as if your mind wandered.'

'You are Zamorna,' replied Caroline. 'But let me go.'

'Not for a diadem. Not for a Krooman's head. Not for every inch of land the Joliba waters.'*

'Oh, what must I do!' exclaimed Miss Vernon.

'Crede Zamorna!'* was the answer. 'Trust me, Caroline, you shall never want a refuge. I said I could not take you to Wellesley-House, but I can take you elsewhere. I have a little retreat, my fairy, somewhere near the heart of my own kingdom, Angria, sheltered by Ingleside & hidden in a wood. It is a plain, old house outside, but it has rooms within as splendid as any saloon in Victoria-Square. You shall live there. Nobody will ever reach it to disturb you. It lies on the verge of moors; there are only a few scattered cottages & a little church for many miles round. It is not known to be my property. I call it my treasure-house & what I deposit there has always hitherto been safe—at least,' he added in a lower tone, 'from human vigilance & living force. There are some things that even I cannot defy. I thought so that summer afternoon when I came to Scar House & found a King & Conqueror had been before me, to whom I was no rival, but a trampled slave.'*

The gloom of Zamorna's look as he uttered these words told a tale of what was passing in his heart. What vision had arisen before him which suggested such a sentence at such a moment it matters little to know. However dark it might have been, it did not linger long. He smiled as Caroline looked at him with mixed wonder & fear. His face changed to an expression of tenderness more dangerous than the fiery excitement which had startled her before. He caressed her fondly & lifted with his fingers the heavy curls which were lying on her neck. Caroline began to feel a new impression. She no longer wished to leave him, she clung to his side—infatuation was stealing over her. The thought of separation or a return to Eden was dreadful.* The man beside her was her guardian again, but he was also Mr Montmorency's Duke of Zamorna. She feared, she loved. Passion tempted. Conscience warned her.* But in a mind like Miss Vernon's conscience was feeble opposed to passion. Its whispers grew faint & were at last silenced. And when Zamorna kissed her & said in that voice of fatal sweetness which has instilled venom into many a heart, 'Will you go with me to-morrow, Caroline?', she looked up in his face with a kind of wild devoted enthusiasm & answered, 'Yes.'*

The Duke of Zamorna left Woodhouse-Cliffe on Friday,* the next morning, & was precisely seven days in performing the distance between that place & Verdopolis. At least, seven days had elapsed between his departure from Mr Warner's & his arrival at Wellesley-House. It was a cold day when he came & that might possibly be the reason that he looked pale & stern as he got out of his cariage, mounted the kingly steps of his mansion & entered under its roof. He was necessitated to meet his wife after so long a separation, & it was a sight to see their interview. He took little pains to look at her kindly. His manner was sour & impatient, & the Duchess, after the first look, solicited no fonder embrace. She receded even from the frozen kiss he offered her, dropped her hand, &, after searching his face & reading the meaning of that pallid, harrassed aspect, told him not by words but by a bitter smile that he did not deceive her, & turned away with a quivering lip, & with all the indignation, the burning pride, the heart struck anguish stamped on her face that those beautiful features could express. She left him & went to her room, which she did not leave for many a day afterwards.

The Duke of Zamorna seemed to have returned in a business mood. He had a smile for no one. When Lord Richton called to pay his respects, the Duke glanced at the card which he sent up, threw it on the table & growled like a tiger, 'not at home'. He received only his ministers; he discussed only matters of state. When their business was done he dismissed them; no hour of relaxation followed the hour of labour. He was as scowling at the end of the council as he was at the beginning.

Enara was with him one night & in his blunt way had just been telling him a piece of his mind, & intimating that he was sure all that blackening & sulking was not for nothing & that he had as certainly been in some hideous mess as he now wore a head.* The answer to this was a recommendation to Enara to go to hell. Henri was tasting a glass of spirits & water preparatory to making a reply, when a third person walked in to the appartment &, advancing up to him, said, 'I'll thank you to leave the room, sir.'

The Colonel of Blood-hounds looked up fierce at this address, but having discerned from whom it proceeded, he merely replied, 'Very well, my lord, but with your leave I'll empty this tumbler of brandy & water first. Here's to the king's health & better temper.' He drained his glass, set it down & marched away.

The new-comer, judging from his look, seemed likely to give the Duke of Zamorna his match in the matter of temper. One remarkable thing about his appearance was that, though in the presence of a crowned king, he wore a hat upon his head which he never lifted a hand to remove. The face under that hat was like a sheet it was so white & like a hanged malefactor's it was so livid. He could not be said to frown—his features were quiet but his eye was petrifying—it had that in its light irid which passes shew.*

This gentleman took his station facing the Duke of Zamorna & when Lord Etrei* had left the room, he said in a voice such as people use when they are coming instantly to the point & will not soften their demand a jot, 'Tell me what you have done with her.'

The Duke of Zamorna's conscience, a vessel of a thousand tons bur-then, brought up a cargo of blood to his face. His nostrils opened. His head was as high & his chest as full & his attitude standing by the table as bold as if from the ramparts of Gazemba he was watching Arundel's horsemen scouring the wilderness.*

'What do you mean?' he asked.

'Where is Caroline Vernon?' said the same voice of fury.

'I have not got her.'

'And you have never had her, I suppose? And you will dare to tell me that lie?'

'I have never had her—'

'She is not in your hands now?'

'She is not.'

'By G—d I know differently, sir. I know you lie.'

'You know nothing about it.'

'Give her up, Zamorna.'

'I cannot give up what I have not got.'

'Say that again.'

'I do.'

'Repeat the lie.'

'I will.'

'Take that, miscreant!'

Lord Northangerland snatched something from his breast. It was a pistol. He did not draw the trigger, but he dashed the but end viciously at his Son-in-law's mouth. In an instant his lips were crimson with gore. If his teeth had not been fastened into their sockets like soldered iron, he would have been forced to spit them out with the blood with which his mouth filled & ran over. He said nothing at all to this com-pliment, but only leaned his head over the fire & spat into the ashes, & then wiped his mouth with a white handkerchief which in five minutes was one red stain. I suppose this moderation resulted from the deep conviction that the punishment he got was only a millionth part of what he deserved.

'Where is she?' resumed the excited Percy.

'I'll <u>never</u> tell you.'

'Will you keep her from me?'

'I'll do my best.'

'Will you dare to visit her?'

'As often as I can snatch a moment from the world to give to her.'

'You say that to my face?'

'I'd say it to the D—l's face.'

A little pause intervened, in which Northangerland surveyed the Duke & the Duke went on wiping his bloody mouth.

'I came here to know where you have taken that girl,' resumed Percy. 'I mean to be satisfied. I mean to have her back. You shall not keep her. The last thing I had in the world is not to be yielded to you—you brutal, insatiable villain!'

'Am I worse than you Percy?'

'Do you taunt me? You are worse—I never was a callous brute.'

'And who says I am a brute? Does Caroline? Does Mary?'

'How dare you join those names together! How dare you utter them in the same breath—as if both my daughters were your purchased slaves! You coarse voluptuary, filthier than that filthy Jordan.'*

'I am glad it is you who give me this character & not Miss Vernon, or her sister.'

'Arthur Wellesley, you had better not unite those two names again. If you do, neither of them shall ever see you more—except dead.'

'Will you shoot me?'

'I will.'

Another pause followed which Percy again broke. 'In what part of Angria have you put Caroline Vernon? For I know you took her to Angria.'

'I placed her where she is safe & happy. I should say no more if my hand were thrust into that fire, & you had better leave the matter where it is, for you cannot undo what is done.'

Northangerland's wild blue eye dilated into wilder hatred & fury. He said, raising his hand & striking it on the table, 'I wish there was a hell for your sake! I wish—' The sentence broke off & was resumed as if his agitation shortened his breath too much to allow him to proceed far without drawing it afresh. 'I wish you might be withered hand & foot & struck into a paralytic heap—' again it broke.

'What are you? You have pressed this hand & said you cared for me. You have listened to all I had to tell you. What I am, how I have lived & what I have suffered. You have assumed enthusiasm—blushed almost like a woman & even wearied me out with your boyish ardour. I let you have Mary—& you know what a curse you have been to her—disquieting her life with your constant treacheries & your alternations of frost & fire. I have let you go on with little interference, though I have wished you dead many a time when I have seen her pale, harrassed look, knowing how different she was before she knew you & was subjected to all your monstrous tyrannies & tantalizations—your desertions that broke her spirit, & your returns that kept her lingering on with just the shadow of a hope to look to.'

'Gross exaggeration!' exclaimed Zamorna with vehemence. 'When did I ever tyrannize over Mary? Ask herself. Ask her at this moment when she is as much exasperated against me as ever she was in her life. Tell her to leave me. She will not speak to me or look at me—but see what her answer would be to that.'

'Will you be silent & hear me out?' returned Percy. 'I have not finished the detail of your friendship. That Hebrew imposter Nathan tells David, the man after God's own heart—a certain parable of an ewe lamb & applies it to his own righteous deeds.* You have learnt the chapter by heart, I think, & fructified by it. I gave you everything but Caroline. You knew my feelings to her. You knew how I reckoned on her as my last & only comfort. And what have you done? She is destroyed; she can never hold her head up again. She is nothing to me, but she shall not be left in your hands.'

'You cannot take her from me, & if you could—how would you prevent her return? She would either die or come back to me now. And remember, Sir, if I had been a Percy instead of a Wellesley, I should not have carried her away & given her a home to hide her from scorn & shelter her from insult. I should have left her forsaken at Fidena to die there, delirious in an inn as Harriet O'Connor did.'*

'I have my last word to give you now,' said Percy. 'You shall be brought into the courts of law for this very deed—I care nothing for exposure. I will hire Hector Montmorency to be my counsel. I will furnish him with ample evidence of all the atrocities of your character which, handled as he will delight to handle it, will make the flesh quiver on your bones with agony. I will hire half the press & fill the newspapers with libels on you & your court, which shall transform all your fools of followers into jealous enemies. I will not stick at a lie. Montmorency shall indite the paragraphs in order that they may be pungent enough. He will not scruple at involving a few dozens of court ladies in the ruin that is to be hurled on you. He shall be directed to spare none. Your cabinet shall be a herd of horned cattle.* The public mind shall be poisoned against you. A glorious triumph shall be given to your political enemies. Before you die you shall curse the day that you robbed me of my daughter.'

So spoke Northangerland. His son answered with a smile, 'The ship is worthless that will not live through a storm.'

'Storm!' rejoined the Earl. 'This is no storm, but fire in the hold—a lighted candle hurled into your magazine! See if it will fall like a rain-drop!'

The Duke was still unquelled. He answered as he turned & walked slowly through the room, 'In nature there is no such thing as annihilation. Blow me up & I shall live again.'

'You need not talk this bombast to me!' said Percy. 'Keep it to meet Montmorency with when he makes you the target of his shafts. Keep it to answer Warner & Thornton & Castlereagh when their challenges come pouring on you like chain-shot!'

His Grace pursued his walk & said in an undertone,

> 'Moored in the rifted rock,
> Proof to the tempest shock,
> Firmer he roots him the ruder it blow.'*

Farewell to Angria

I have now written a great many books, & for a long time I have dwelt on the same characters & scenes & subjects. I have shewn my landscapes in every variety of shade & light which morning, noon & evening—the rising, the meridian & the setting sun—can bestow upon them. Sometimes I have filled the air with the whitened tempest of winter—snow has embossed the dark arms of the beech & oak & filled with drifts the parks of the lowlands or the mountain-pass of wilder districts. Again the same mansion with its woods, the same moor with its glens, has been softly coloured with the tints of moonlight in summer, & in the warmest June night the trees have clustered their full-plumed heads over glades flushed with flowers. So it is with persons—my readers have been habituated to one set of features, which they have seen now in profile now in full-face, now in outline & again in finished painting, varied but by the change of feeling or temper or age—lit with love, flushed with passion, shaded with grief, kindled with ecstacy, in medi-tation & mirth, in sorrow & scorn & rapture, with the round outline of childhood, the beauty & fullness of youth, the strength of manhood & the furrow of thoughtful decline. But we must change, for the eye is tired of the picture so oft recurring & now so familiar.

Yet do not urge me too fast reader—it is no easy thing to dismiss from my imagination the images which have filled it so long. They were my friends & my intimate acquaintance & I could with little labour describe to you the faces, the voices, the actions, of those who peopled my thoughts by day & not seldom stole strangely even into my dreams by night. When I depart from these I feel almost as if I stood on the threshold of a home & were bidding farewell to its inmates. When I but strive to conjure up new inmates, I feel as if I had got into a dis-tant country where every face was unknown & the character of all the population an enigma which it would take much study to comprehend & much talent to expound. Still, I long to quit for a while that burning clime where we have sojourned too long. Its skies flame—the glow of sunset is always upon it. The mind would cease from excitement & turn now to a cooler region, where the dawn breaks grey and sober & the coming day for a time at least is subdued in clouds.

BRANWELL BRONTË

THE:

LIAR DETECTED

BY:

CAPTAN JOHN BUD

I VOL QUAR^{TO}

The Liar Unmasked—by Capt Bud
June 19/ 1830

CHAP I

It has always been the fortune of eminent men in all ages and every
country to have their lives, their actions and their works traduced by
a set of unprincipled wretches who, having no caracter of their own
to support and being too indolent to work, vilely employ their days in
spitting their venom on every author of reputation within their reach.
Homer had his Zoilus, Virgil his Maevius*—and CAPTAIN TREE
his Wellesly.* All these were & are alike contemptible in character and
influence, and like vipers can do no more than bite the heels of their
enimies.* Of Wellesly, this new recruit in their troops, I shall give a
small account, as many of my reader[s] have probably not before heard
of him.

He was born in England or Ireland—I know not which—sometime
in the year 1815, and while yet a bantling* was remarkable for remarking on and spitting at the visitors to his father's house and for which
he was often severely reprimanded. But this would not do, so I believe
he was sent in the 10th year of his age to th[e] college of Eton.* From
this place he was soon after removed to Africa, his father having gone
there.* It was then he heard of CAPT Tree. And though but 15 years
of age pushed himself in to all company, presumed to put forth his
"I thinks" and his "I believes" upon him and others for a year or

so—rather pitied & despised than otherwise—till some tim[e] lately, when he put forth a small book of verses.* This offer—delighting the ladies of fashion, being quoted in the young misses' letters, and so forth—was swept into oblivion. Another and another followed, they sharing the like fate till, quoth he, "Forsooth I'm the greatest man in the world and these ladies the best judges." And so he stuck up a little magazine to instruct them. It was now considered high time to quash him. Therefore Tree put forth a small tract for that purpose. Instantly the magazine was stopped. The poems ceased to be quoted, and the little stock of reputation [w]ithered before the breath of that [g]reat man, though still the little author strutted about, skelped* and barked round the feet of his destroyer like a puppy dog with its tail cut off. And to complete the sum of his petty villany, he vomited forth a dose of scandal and selfimportance in the shape of an octavo volumn. This was published June 18, 1830.* It is this work that I am about to confute, for however mean and paltry it be, the lies it contains are too daring to pass unnoticed. The little reptile has stung or endeavoured to sting no less than 15 individuals:*

Brock	1	Magrass	8
Bobadill	2	Bady	9
Bud	3	Douro	10
Naughty	4	Lofty	11
Laury	5	Rouge*	12
Tree	6	Y Rouge	13
S Bud	7	S Tree	14
		S Rouge	15

CHAP. II

The accomplished and noble author begins his work by stating that there are no men in the universe with whom he is so familiar as grooms, valets & footmen. This he states in a manner which might lead one to suppose that they were ministers of state, noblemen and soldiers. Now we all know that these persons are proverbial for their lying propensities. Therefore is not this a firm foundation to begin his fabric of truth and candour? But it is now time to see what his accusations are.

The footman who told him this budget* of information begins with the interview of Capt Tree and Lieut Brock and, in process of the narrative, states that while he was in the avenue he slipped over a hed[ge]. How could this be? A hedge in a covered avenue! Is not this sufficient to set the book and its author down as a lie and a liar? But to proceed again, he mentions the librarian being dressed in a cloak and a mask, and he (the footman) directly knew who it was. But stop young boy! How could a footman know one dressed in a cloak and mask that go in the dark? Impossible! But not content with this, our author proceeds into the same over the very next page. Not yet satisfied, the young lad mentions that Magrass opened the gate of the cemetery to them. Now we can prove that Magrass was then in Stumps Island, wither he went to attend at the opening of a will and is not yet returned. In a few pages after mention-ing their 2d visit to the cemetery, he states that Sir A. H. Bady, Edward Laury and Young Man Naughty slided down a perpendicular wall of smooth marble 100 feet high. This is indeed beyond the bounds of prob-ability, unless he could prove that they, like flies, were possessed of feet with which they could slide down marble or even glass. He says Tree was a great coward. How could that man be a coward who has fought in 8 battles, and in all was covered with wounds, blood and glory?

8th error. He makes Hume know th[e] books buried in the cemetery at a glance. Now we conceive Hume no great reader, and few could tell not only what the books were but to whom they belonged in deep midnight.

9th. He presumes to represent the Marquis of Douro as being in company with a monkey, an insolven[t], a sickly lawyer, a sour old gentleman, a coxcomb, an idiot. What company for good Marquis, the son of a king!

10. This learned author says that racking leaves one whole as before, but a little stretched. We deny this, for it puts one's bones out of joint and frequently kills.

11. He impudently (and we suppose to highten his own dignity) represents the Marquis of Douro as being a great freind of his—even calling him Charles love.

12. He now proceeds to a scene whi[ch] no doubt he thinks no poet or prose writer can equal for sublimity and grandeur. The ocean roar-ing, the trees and streams of the vale which were in all concience far enough of murmering, &c., &c. O how I fancy I can see the yong author, brimfull of himself after having finished this passage, rise up, take the manuscript in his greasy hand, rub his head, stick out his shirt frill, give a few hems, peep into Pope's Homer* to see if there was a passage there equal to it, then sit down, his self esteem no way abated, and fag away like one on a wager.

But we have now dispatched the little shop boy's volumn in blue morroco*—back with gilt edges—in truth a fit present for Miss M. H—me,* or any of her hysterical and delicate crew. Therefore we must proceed to see the crimes for which this Jupiter* has fulminated his thunders at us. They are as follows:

Brock	Felony & treason
Bobadill	An ugly countnance
Bud	Connivance at theft
Bady	Body snatching
Douro	Keeping bad company
Laury	Body snatching
Lofty	Puppyism*
Magrass	Connivance at theft
Naughty	Body snatching
Rouge	Extravagance
S Bud	Folly
S Rouge	Idiotism
S Tree	Felony and treason
Tree	Felony and treason
Y Rouge	Coxcombry

CHAP. III

One day lately as I was sitting in my study I recieved a note to be present at a dinner given by Lord L—d that day to several of the nobility, gentry &c. in the Glasstown. I accordingly made my appointment and came at the time perfixed. When I arrived I found a large company, among whom were the little puppy* C. Wellesly, fine furniture, an exellent dinner, &c.

After the dinner was done, we set to our bottles and [?the men] talked about politics, the state of France, poachers, Parry's goverment &c; the women, about the fashion, town news, &c. We enjoyed our selves for some time till the ladies and, amongst other[s], this Wellesly withdrew. And shortly after he was off, the master of the house remarked what a foolish lad he was to have so many monkeys about him.*

Young R—. answered: But I believe he is delighted with as a baby with its doll. I suppose it does not, indeed cannot, give him the return of affection.

Capt T—. Well enough for him, well enough for him! It diverts him from deluging the world with his paltry tracts.

Young S—t. What do you think of Lord Charles's 'VISION'?* Is not it a capital performance?

Young R—e. Very so, so I believe.

Capt T—. It is no more than a repetition of a former work of his—I [f]orget the name—which indeed was not worthy of remembring. But his whole works are of the same stamp: light, trifling, foolish & giddy, without the redeeming excellence to rescue them from that oblivion into which they must inevitably fall.

Old R—. Yet he seems to consider himself an admirable writer.

Capt T—. He does. As do many other[s]. I mean not to include Young S— and the Marquis of D—ro.* Their writings show mind, thought and poetry. His is but empty bombast.

Young S—. Gentlemen you seem too hard upon him! I must beg leave to differ from you in all respects as it regards him.

Young B—. Why you, Young S—, are patronised by his father and brother. Therefore, in the first place, you—

Young R—. Oh sir, do grant us a respite from your first, second and third places!

Young B—. I conceive, sir, that there is no article in law which authorizes you to stop my conversation. Therefore—

Lord L—. Come, come! Don't quarrel.

Capt T—. What do you think of his general character?

Lord L—. A rather silly but amiable young man.

Young R—. Amiable! Indeed! Does he not fight and attend rows every day of his life? Have I not seen—

Ned L—. Go to the palace and request him to attend a battle between two factions and did he not with the greatest alacrity join him?

Young S—. I beleive, sir, you have a little overcharged the picture.

Capt. T—. Not at all. I my self have seen him do these things and more also but—. What think you, Capt Bud, of his caracter?

Myself. I am sorry to say I entertain no very favourable opinion of him. On the contrary he is, I think, a boy uterly destitute of all common understanding, foolish and inconsiderate in the extreme, but with a few small marks of some sort of a genius.

Capt. T—. I myself do think that he is a child utterly without talent or genius of any sort, spitful to the greatest excess, presumptous, lying and vain. Add to these foolish, fanciful and ridiculous, & then I think you have his caracter.

The party now seperated, for it was near midnight, and I went home to think on the, I may say, public voice given as to the character of Charles Wellesly.

CHAP IV

Now, Charles Wellesly, I have given you the voice of the public and of myself praising and dispraising of you. I have reviewed faithfullly and candidly your last publication. I have corrected your errors. I have discovered your falshoods. And without malice or spleen I shall now give you my advice—attend to it and profit by it!

You have hitherto been fanciful and giddy to excess, and no one, not even your father, has ventured to stop the torrent of impetuousity which you are, I hope [?unmeanly], bringing on your future prospects in life. If you, Charles, conduct yourself in life with a caution and dignity worthy of you, you may rise to eminence, and flourish in greatness and prosperity. On the other hand, if you continue in your present course, poverty, shame, defeat and their attendant evils will over take you shortly.* And tossed on the ocean of human existence without one anchor or compass, you will at last be consigned to a prison or brought to the block, or die an outcast from all human society.

s || CAPTAIN. J. BUD,—

WORKS BY .BUD

A treatise on political Economy
in 3 vols quarto—3£3^S.

Discourses on the 4 Elements*
10 vols quarto—10£10^S.

IIId. ODE.
on the
Celebration of the Great
AFRICAN GAMES

177. Lines.

Once again bright Summer now
Shines on Afric's scorched brow*
Once again the vales appear
In the new glories of the year
Once again! yet once again!
Sunlike towering o'er the plain
Rises in light the Immense Olympian hall*
Back casting from its front grey twilight's dusky pall
Then rise ye thousand Nations rise
Lift to the east your joyful eyes
Lo o'er the desert drear and grim,
Floats widely sounding the triumphal hymn
Its parched and barren sands rejoice
In the sound of human voice
Let the heavens and earth and seas
Hail with joy the coming morn
On the widely wafting breeze
Let the tidings round be borne
Let every Nation now rejoice
While mighty Genii with an answering voice
Reecho back the Song
While you ye woods and Mountains grey—
And thou O everlasting sea
The joyful notes prolong
Come thou stern Monarch Lord of war*
Come from thy chosen land afar,
That land where Forests huge and hoar
Stretch their black shadows to the western shore
While Gambia's stream with glittering pride
Pours through those vales her winding tide

And on her rocky margin sees
Halls towers and towns of men rise o'er the shady trees*
   King of the North* arise and come!
   Down from thy wild and mountain home
   Where Casepurh huge and Dimdim grey
   Frown beetling o'er the Genii's sea*
   Where hills o'er hills rise black and high
   Eternal clouds! they shade the sky
   Their serried peaks by thunder riven
   And standing gainst the vault of heaven
      With an eternal frown
   While from their summits bleak and hoar
   O'er craggy rocks the torrents pour
   And onward with unceasing roar
      Rush hoarsely thundering down.
Thy freeborn sons O King attend thee now
From Morven's* snowy heights and Dimdim's cloudy brow
   And thou O sunny smiling plain
      Where Ardrah's* stream unfettered glides
   Sloping from vast Nevada's sides*
      Toward the glassy main
   Like Niger's waves your thousands pour
   From every hill and every shore
   Haste on ward haste your coming feet
While brightest joy appears your footsteps here to greet
   As when the sailor on the sea
   Tossed by the force of storms away
      Beholds the Heavens all hushed in gloom
   While the black Ocean stretching round
   In long dull waves without a bound
   With a drear melancholy sound
      Seems destined for his tomb
   Slowly the vessel labours on
   As slow the black waves glide along
   Her streamers drooping hang on high
   Still sleep the clouds in the iron sky
      Nature seems turned to stone
   When sudden bursts upon their sight
   A little Island shining bright
      Girt by the foaming sea
   All fair and green and broad it lies

In mist the blue hills stately rise
Their tall tops piercing through the skies
   With aspect bold and free.
A sudden breeze sweeps o'er the main
Up start the waves to sight again
From their high tops they shake the spray
And whiten with surf the merry sea
The stately Vessel mid sheets of foam
Glides swiftly through her watery home
Shrill scream the winds in her sailyards high
   And her streamers long and gay
Wave proudly in the summer sky
   As she ploughs upon her way
All Heaven bursts forth in sight again
Bright shine the clouds and bright the main
Even thus time silent passed along
   Nor left one flash to mark the circling year
     Nature herself seemed turned to stone
And the great world rolled round, a ruin dark and drear
   When as if sent from Heaven the Olympian Hall
     Sudden erects its pillared wall
     It dawned upon the eyes of men
     And gave them Light and Life again
     All thought dead Greece restored once more
     Afric seemed the Achaian shore*
     Mid sandy plains, and burning skies
     A greater Athens seemed to rise
     Again Olympus towered above the plain
   But looked not on the sunny Grecian sea
Where mid a thousand isles the light waves sported free
   No round it roared the immense Atlantic main
   Cradle of tempests and the whirlwind's reign
   Not awful Jove not golden Juno* here
     With bursting splendour fill the air
     Not here does Great Athena* shine
     Nor Phoebus* spread his beams divine
     No here dim forms involved in gloom
   Like spectres rising from a midnight tomb
     With winds and tempests fill the air
       I see I see appear.

Awful Brannii gloomy giant
    Shaking o'er earth his blazing air,*
Brooding on blood with drear and vengeful soul
He sits enthroned in clouds to hear his thunders roll
    Dread Tallii next like a dire Eagle flies
    And on our mortal miseries feasts her bloody eyes
Emii and Annii last with boding cry*
Famine and war foretell and mortal misery
    All these the blighters of the varied year
All these and more than these before my eyes appear
      Yes more far more a horrid train
      Rising like clouds above the main
        Meagre and black and thin
      Round their huge jaws the red foam churning
      Their souls for blood and battle burning
      And though from conflict still returning
        Yet still again impatient to begin
These not the golden deities of Greece
    These are the powers that rule our land
Nor can we hope their fetters to release.
    Or quench their scorching brand
    Then where oh where must Mortals turn their eyes
Not to the Genii-throning hills or tempest giving skies
No to the Twelves.* O Fathers of our fame
    O Fathers founders of our glorious name
    To you we look our latest hope
Our Great Defenders and our common prop
    Led on by you we force our way
    O'er every land through every sea
    Yes the vast Atlantic main
    Shall oppose her waves in vain
    With all the loudest winds of Heaven
    Full against its surface driven
    Let its billows rage and rave
    We will dare the stormiest wave
      If you upon us shine
    Let it be our common grave
      If you hide your Light divine
    But why thus cloud one glorious day
    With these sad thoughts O pass away
    Away ye tempests of the north

Let the Sun of hope shine forth
Bursting bright on earth and sea
Gilding the Olympian hall with splendour gay
And you our Fathers now descending
Glorious in your chariot's ride
While your children round attending
Hail in you their country's pride
Let us hasten onward all
To the vast Olympian hall
Now let the trumpets loud and shrill
Awake the Falcon on the rocky hill
Let the Heavens all tremble now
While the majestic organs blow
While you[r] assembled thousands raise
One universal song of praise
Haste Oh haste your coming feet
Joy appears your steps to greet
Haste upon this day of gladness
Drive away the voice of sadness
And of grim Despair
To the Olympian Hall arising
Your bewildered eyes surprising
Or all cares of Life despising
Haste Oh haste rejoicing there

P. B. Bronte.
June 26th
AD 1832

THE PIRATE
A TALE.

By Captain John Flower*

I. Vol.

P B Brontē. February 1833.

═══════════

THE PIRATE.
A Tale by
The Author of 'Letters from an
Englishman'.*
Great Glass Town   printed by Seargt Tree
P B Bronte Feb 8. 1833

CHAP. Ist.

P B Brontē
January
30, 1833

Alexander Rougue has just returned from no one knows where.* He
has bought a fine house in Georges Street, where he lives in the utmost
style of magnificence. But what are his *means*, or from whence he draws
his evidently princely income no one can guess. This is well known:
that every acre of his paternal possessions has long, long ago bid adieu
to him.*

Having several times in the course of my life been brought in to
collision, though much against my will, with this singular and mysterious character, I fancied I might without offence pay him a visit of
congratulation upon his arrival in the city. Ordering therefore my carriage, I drove off for Georges Street and alighted at the door of his
splendid mansion. Upon delivering my card I was ushered by a foreign

servant through many noble passages and up a grand staircase to his study. I entered with the usual compliments. He was seated alone on his sopha.

But before I describe the master, let me glance round the apartment. It was spacious as most drawing rooms; the ceiling painted in arabesque and the walls lined with books. 2 fine bay windows curtained with velvet lighted the apartment and opened a gorgeous view of the vast Glasstown harbour, with its endless shipping, crowded quays and mighty expanse of blue water stretching away till one might fancy they beheld, towering over its horizon, the hills of Stumps Land and the towering heights of Monkey's Isle. Over the rich Persian carpet were scattered a vast number of naval maps, plans and charts. The table groaned beneath a profusion of atlases and treatises on navigation, while round the room in rosewood stands and cases were placed the rarest and most valuable curiosities from every shore and ocean.

In the midst of this princely confusion sat Rougue upon his sofa, intently perusing a folio of maps and sipping incessantly from a bottle of the most fiery liquers. The moment I entered he started hastily, but recovering himself arose and welcomed me forward with his usual insidious and serpentlike smile. How much was I shocked to behold the ravages which I know not what had made upon him since I last saw him. True, his tall and statly form still stood as erect as ever, but his hair once a bright auburn, now looked thin and even grey. His eagle eye gleamed dully and glassily under his pale, high forehead, now covered with scars and wrinkles. His cheeks were hollow and bloodless, while as he shook my hand his felt cold and clammy. He trembled constantly and started at the slightest sound or motion. He bade me sit down and, himself taking a seat, began as follows in his usual careless scoffing manner.

'Well freind, I have taken, you see, to the navy since you last saw me. Why man, I've been on my voyages! Ha! I've turned merchant, you see. No, not so, I am Admiral. But I've not hit it yet. I'm more—I'm Rougue. I am all three. I'm three in one,* you know! Ha! Don't you? Look, my man, if you've money and want it in safe hands (here he took a long pull from a flagon of claret)—I say, if you've money and love it, let me have an hand on it and it'll stick to you for ever. Yes, I tell you, I'm not one of your pitiful land louping merchants who, when they send out their vessels, can never make sure of being able to send them back again. No, no! Bankruptcies and tempests and losses can never hurt Rougue. Ha! Nor *piracies* neither, ha? (Here he drank again and, turning suddenly round, he fixed his eyes upon me—I feared he would fall into some fit, but he continued.)

'Sir, Sir, I say! Did you ever know of a man whose wealth was in danger of being lessened by the very means he uses to get wealth? You don't understand me. How should you? (He paused.) It's all long of this (laying his hand on his forehead). I say, sir, I'm as near founder-ing as life can be. Be I say, I'm a perfect wreck. Why (drinking again largly), why, I couldn't keep body and soul together if it wasn't for this. Body and soul did I say? Fool! Who in the name of nonsense ever heard of two things seperating that were never together?* Ha! Now, sir, I'll lay 10 to 1 that I cannot walk without help from this fire to the door. (He tried but stopt at the window, where he stood ernestly gazing on the sea and, apparently forgetful of my presence, began soliloquizing to himself in such words as these.) Oh how I wish they would heave in sight! Surely with him on board they could never either founder, strike! No. He promised me a dozen prizes and (pulling out his watch) this is the hour in which he vowed to bring their goods in. Let me see. There's Grenville's 2, Luckyman's 2, Macadam 2, Bellingham and Co. 4, Cotterel* 3. In all, 13. Oh, how I wish they would heave in sight! If he deceives me!'

The reader may guess how I was surprised to hear him mention the name of my firm and myself in these suspicious transactions. I started involuntarily, at which he, recollecting himself, turned hastily round and looked at me keenly, but with evident embarrassment, as if to see whether I guessed his meaning or heard his words. I feigned a careless inattention and appeared to gaze upon Warder's Atlas.

At this moment several vessels bore up the harbour. He lighted up and took a vast draught from a bottle of raw brandy then, going again to the window, stood silently watching them unload. In about a quater of an hour the study door opened without notice being given or servant appearing. A little old man entered of decrepid figure and, wearing a vast slouched hat over his brow, a much worn great coat on his back and a stout stick in his hand. Without any salutation he began, first fixing his little keen grey eyes upon me as if he would read my inmost soul.

'Rogue Rogue do you doubt me now?'

'Oh,' he answered, 'I can't tell yet! You are an eternal deceiver. I'll wait till I see and handle the—the—you guess what.'

'Why don't you name them?' returned the old man.

'Why don't I name you?' asked Rogue.

'You dare not!' he replied.

'Why,' answered Rogue again, 'an' you begin your impudence I'll blow your brain out. If you take me and light me like a match just after—. Sit down and here's the waters of life.* Drink, drink!'

The old man drew a chair to the table and commenced drinking glass after glass of raw brandy with utmost indifference as if it had been cold water. Rougue stood against the mantel peice. Eyeing him with looks of mingled scorn, hatred, contempt and slavish obedience, the old man, shutting his eyes, continued drinking with an unearthly smile upon his haggard features.

At this moment the ponderous knocker rung below and some one was announced by a servent. He was ordered to be admitted. There accordingly entered the study a stout little old man wrapped in a military surtout and wearing a cocked hat on his head. He bowed politely to the company and, with his hands placed behind his back, began to pace rapidly round the apartment. He seemed agitated. Rougue smiled, but put on a behaviour of the utmost politeness. The stout little man stopping suddenly short, looked Rougue full in the face and, with much grimace, broke out as follows.

'What, in the name of wonder, is he about? What does he mean? Why is *he* to be insulted and defied by such a robber as him? Is the name of L'Empereur, the terror of Europe, to be set at naught and scorned by him? He tells him that Talleyrand* has informed of the loss of 3 ships of the French nation, which were reported to be taken by a pirate carrying scarlet colours, which he is informed are those carried by the ships belonging to the firm of Rougue and—and—he knows not what. But it does not matter! The circumstance is reported to your government, and he shall see what will follow.'

The Emperor Napoleon—for him it was here—turned round and, without speaking another word, left the apartment. Shortly we heard his carriage depart from the yard.

When he had shut the door behind him, Rougue burst out in to a loud laugh and, taking a full glass of spirits, said, turning to the little old man,

'Well Mr Sdeath* what now think you?'

'Why,' returned Mr Sdeath, if such was his title, 'I think him a bigger fool than yourself.'

At this moment the knocker rung again, and another visitor was announced. He entered: a tall military looking man, plainly dressed, with eagle eyes and aquiline nose. The moment Rougue beheld him, his face turned as black as death but preserved its usual effrontery. It was the Duke of Wellington! His Grace, bowing to me and biting his lip at Mr Sdeath adressed Rougue thus.

'Sir, I have this morning received information from several persons that a number of armed vessels carrying scarlet colours have been recently infesting these seas and comitting the most violent and wanton aggressions upon the vessels carrying the flags of this nation, as also upon those of France, Parry's, Ross's and my own. Now I have also learned that the ships employed by the concern of Rougue Sdeath and Co., of which you are a member, carry a scarlet flag, and report avers these to have been the identical vessels which comitted the piracies. Now, I am not qualified to judge upon this business, but, sir, you must know that your character does not stand perfectly free from reproach in the opinion of most. Therefore it is incumbent upon you to free yourself, if possible, from this new stain laid upon it. Sergeant Bud (here a sharp, thin lawyer like looking young ma[n] entered), I request you to make out a writ calling upon Alexander Rougue to present himself to morrow before the court of Admiralty to clear up some aspersion which at present rest[s] upon his character.'

The writ was executed in a twinkling and ready for Rougue's signature who, as he took up the pen said, 'I am sensible, Your Grace, that I have many enimies and it is these who have raised and propagated this infamous slander upon my own character and the honour of my firm. However, to morrow I shall not fail to clear them both in the eyes of the world and to my own content.'

His Grace then saying 'Very well, sir,' bowed to me, touched his hat to Rougue, and departed. I also took my leave, having more calls to make and much business to do.

CHAPTER. II.d.

That night, as I was sitting in my study looking over our clerk's accounts and musing upon the strange news I had gathered that morning relating to Rougue and his proceeding—news both strange and unpleasant to me—[I] liked not the mention of four of our vessels among the number of those he mentioned to himself as having taken, there suddenly burst in to my apartment 6 tall stout men wearing black cloaks, swords and visors. Without a word being spoken on either side, they seized & bound me. Then, taking me upon their shoulders, they hurried out of the house and plunged into a set of dark, narrow alleys or lanes. After rapidly threading these for some time, they stopped before the back door of a large house, where they gave a peculiar whistle, thrice repeated. The door was opened and they hurried me up a flight of stairs—breathless and unable to speak—into a large lighted apartment,

which I was astonished to find was that identical Rougue's study, which
I had left that morning. He himself I saw walking with hasty strides
through the apartment, his hat and gloves on, with a sword under his
arm. Around him were 9 or 10 tall dark looking men, armed and like
himself equipped for a journey. The old dwarf Mr Sdeath was seated at
a sideboard taking a long drink of his favorite liquors.

The moment I entered the reason for my forcible capture flashed
across my mind. I cried out in a fit of terror. 'Oh Rougue let me go, and
I will never divulge what I have heard this morning! I never will!'

Rougue answered, drinking off a glass of brandy, 'Well, sir, it's all as
one. Divulge or not divulge, I have you! Come gentlemen, follow me.
Our time is almost out.'

They all prepared to move, taking me with them, but Mr Sdeath
cried out in a passionate, screech owl voice, 'Dogs, stop till I've finished! Fools! What are ye so slippery for?'

They waited with great deference till he had drained off the contents
of a stone bottle of distilled waters. Then they, forcing me along with
them, moved down the steps. Mr Sdeath following—reeling along and
muttering curses to himself—we plunged at a running pace down a
narrow lane till we arrived at the great quay of the harbour. Here lay a
long, suspicious looking vessel with unfurled sails and grinning port-
holes. We all, Rougue and Sdeath taking the lead, mounted on to the
deck, where the crew received us in the utmost silence. At a signal given
by Rougue, the cables were loosed, the anchor drawn up and the vessel
pushed off from shore, gliding swiftly down the harbour into the open
sea. All this was the work of a minute and done almost ere I was aware
of being on board.

The moment I found the vessel was at sail, I flung myself on a heap
of cables and gave vent to my greif in a fit of groans and weeping. I
could scarcely credit my senses to think that I, in the space of a few
minutes, had been dragged from my quiet home thro[ugh] half the city
at the command of a merciless and cruel man and, without the slightest
show of reason, thrown bound on board of this unknown and suspicious
vessel—probably a pirate or privateer—there perhaps [to] die a violent
death or be carried and sold in foreign lands. My second thought was
to inquire of my self what could possibly be the reason why I was thus
treated. In a little while the result of my cogitations left me no doubt
that this was the truth of this cruel transaction.

Rougue had probably for some time past been in the habit of scouring
the Glasstown seas with vessels armed and manned by his dependant
desperadoes, and with these assaulting and capturing all the unarmed

and laden merchant vessels he could meet with. By this means, he had amassed those riches and obtained that splendid house which I had just left. When he had gained money enough by this illegal system to procure that palace, he resided in it and, under the title of the firm of Rougue Sdeath and Co., continued to send out these armed vessels as if for the purpose of peaceful trading and on their return sell the goods taken by them as if they were those lawfully bought by the ships of his company. This practice he had continued till it got wind and was rumored in all the Glasstowns. This morning when I visited him he was in suspense, expecting the arrival of the ship I was now in, and while gazing for it in a fit of abstraction had uttered some sentences in my hearing which were too plain for me not to guess their meaning. This, joined with my being present at the conference between him, the Duke of Wellington and the Emperor, both of whom had heard of his conduct, determined him at once to take me prisoner and stop me from reporting what I had heard by violent means. The circumstance of the Duke's commanding him to prove his innocence to morrow at the Admiralty, where Rougue knew well he could never prove it, determined him upon decamping that very night on board one of his vessels and conveying me along with [him] too, probably to sell as a slave in a foreign country* while he commenced anew his acts as a pirate.

While employed in these conjectures and lamentations, I took no notice of anything, but lay down upon the cables on the deck unheeding and unheeded. When, therefore, I lifted up my eyes again, what was my anguish to find myself far out upon the rolling sea! No trace of the Glass Town remaining, save the great Tower of Nations* standing black and huge against the long red lines of light which, stretched in the west, betokened the early dawn. The fast receding shores looked dark and gloomy in the twilight, while a cold raw breeze swept over the ocean, raising long undulating ridges of waves and howling with a mournful cadence amid the lofty masts and cordage of the gallant ship. The crew were all asleep and only the solitary watch remained pacing the deck with monotonous footsteps. With a mind and body exhausted by the events of the day and my eyesight lulled by the dead calm of nature, I at length fell into a deep sleep.

When I awoke it was mid day. The tropical sun glared hotly from a blazing sky, shooting his beams perpendicularly down upon the dancing and glancing waves. A thousand fish of the brightest and most varied dyes were playing and wallowing [around] the bows of the glowing vessel. The crew, tall, stern, dark looking fellows from the Northern Mountains, were all either lolling under the shade of the oil cloth awnings [or], leaning over the bows of the ship, were basking in the sunlight. But all this was as nothing to me. I continued groaning on the deck incapable of exertion and wishing myself packed in mine own grave, a 1000 fathom below the keel of the pirate vessel. I passed the day in execrating Rougue and his ruthless crew and heaving heavy groans, as I saw one point of land after another sink beneath the horizon, untill at sunset Africa had vanished, and I beheld one melancholy waste of waters* heaving and rolling all round the sky. 3 days I passed in this miserable state. On the fourth Rougue came up and commanded my fetters to be knocked off and assigned me a hammock in the steerage, giving me liberty to roam where I would about the ship. This was no act of charity—he saw that I could neither escape or do harm without a freind or succor for 300 miles round, for we were now within an equal distance from the Glasstown and Monkey Island, toward which we were evidently tending.

This day toward evening the man from the mast had cried out that he saw a strange sail standing to westward. Rougue took his telescope, but it was too distant to decide with certainty its identity. He however affirmed it to be a large vessel from the Glass Town. It was gradually coming toward us, but the darkness soon wrapt it from sight. Rougue, Sdeath and Carey* were up all night consulting with each other. When the morning again revealed the vessel, it was seen coming up with a great press of sail, while its sides, bristling with cannon and its crimson colours showed it to be a fine Glass Town frigate of the first class.

Mr Sdeath came upon deck in a captain's uniform and winked to the men, who evidently understood what he ment. They all went below, stripped their daggers & cutlasses, coming up again transformed into plain merchant seamen with blue jackets and seal skin caps instead of their red pirate handkerchiefs on their heads. I observed that the scarlet flags had been taken down in the darkness, while the green colours of Wellington were waving aloft in their stead. Rougue appeared not as usual on deck, but old Sdeath often went into his cabin and, after communing with him som[e] time, came out with a malignant grin adorning his withered features. It was evident some infernal plot was on foot against the ill fated vessel.

When she had bore up within speaking distance, an officer appeared upon her deck and commanded us to shorten sail. Our sailors obeyed with the utmost alacrity and stood to. The ship then lowered her boat and, placing about 20 men with an officer in it, came on our deck. Showing a warrant, signed Wellington and Grenville, for the apprehension of Alexander Rougue to answer for high crime and misdemeanours,

and authorising those bearing that warrant to search any or every vessel
for his body or information conserning him, the officer accordingly
demanded to see our captain. Mr Sdeath came up. He showed him his
document. After glancing over it our sham captain, making a profound
bow, said he was most happy to inform him tha[t] he was at present in
possession of the person he sought for, disiring him at the same time to
step down into the cabin where he would both see the prisoner and learn
how he had been captured. The officer, suspecting nothing, expressed
the utmost joy and, accompanied by his men, proceeded toward the
cabin. I sighed involuntarily to see these poor fellows going to certain
destruction, but Sdeath turning roun[d] gave me a horrid look, touching at the same time the hilt of his knife. They disappeared into the
room. 20 of the pirates were beconed in after them by the new captain.
In a few minutes I beheld with the utmost horror our sailors come out
one after the other, each with the head of one of these devoted victims
in his bloody hand. Rougue, in a genteel suit of black and with a smile
of satisfaction on his countenance, led them up the ladder and, placing
them in a row on the deck before the unhappy vessel, his crew raised a
tremendous shout of 'Rougue and victory'.

When their ill fated comrades beheld this spectacle, they for a
moment stood in mute consternation, and then all ran to their guns.
Before they could fire old Sdeath, snatching up his musket, took aim
at their captain. The ball whizzed true to its mark and that officer fell
dead from his deck into the sea. Rougue cried out, 'To your guns & the
pirates gave a tremendous broadside. This was returned with vigour,
and many on each side rolled on the decks wounded and dying. Our
vessel gave another broadside—with fatal effect. Every ball told. The
contending ship was nearly dismasted and, being struck between wind
and water, appeared rapidly sinking. Still her crew fought with determination, but Rougue, commanding his men to form with their pikes in
hand, run his vessel straight under the prow of the enemy and, placing
himself at their head, the[y] leapt on to its deck. A scene of dreadful
confusion followed, and the sinking vessel be[c]ame the scene of a most
bloody conflict. The superior skill and ferocity of the pirates soon prevailed. Their enemies lay dying round them and they, each man seizing
his prisoner, lept again on board their own vessel. They had scarcely
done this when the magazine* of the Glasstowner blew up with a horrid
row and the ill fated vessel went to the bottom, almost drawing us along
with her in the whirlpool occasioned by her sinking. This was followed
by one loud yell from the dying wretches, and all for a moment was
silent again. For a while the pirate crew stood on deck, astonished at the

speedy and decisive nature of their victory. This astonishment at length
vented itself in rude jests and bursts of savage laughter. As for Rougue,
he continued a while pacing the deck in silent abstraction. And Sdeath
betook himself with vast zeal and fervor to the keg of rum, untill he fell
grovelling and cursing on the floor like a crushed worm.

In the space of half an hour Rougue ordered the deck to be cleared
and the prisoners brought onto it. They were led up bound and pin-
ioned, 30 in number, all, fine, stout, heavy fellows. My very soul groaned
for them. They shook hands with each other as they were placed in a
square by themselves; they knew what would follow. A select number of
the pirates were placed before them with loaded muskets. Rougue, with
his usual stern, sneering look, commanded them to fire. They obeyed.
The thirty prisoners all fell dead or dying on the deck. At this moment
old Sdeath rushed forward with a large knife in his hand. Advancing to
the bloody heap he plunged it into hearts of all those yet alive and then,
wiping his nose with the cuff of his coat, looked round with a screech
owl laugh. I saw all the crew at this action cast upon the old wretch a look
of detestation. Even Rougue, hardened as his heart is to compassion,
giving him a glance of scorn and hatred cried, 'Get down below you
ugly brute! I did not tell you to do this!' Old Sdeath, gnashing at him
his toothless jaws and muttering curses to himself, obeyed his leader,
and retired in to the cabin. The dead bodies of these unhappy men were
now taken up one by one and thrown into the hungry ocean without a
groan or tear. The scarlet coulours were replaced on the mast head; the
sails unfurled to the breeze and off flew the conquering vessel, with its
ferocious crew, over the foamy billows towards its far off bourne.

: CHAPTER. IIId.

PBB
Febr^y.
8th 1833

Two days we continued sailing after this dreadful event. On the morning of the 3d another strange sail hove in to sight. The pirates, by their
leader's command, again played the old tricks, transforming their ship
into a peaceful Glass Town merchant man, but I observed that this time
our sham captain was Carey and not old Sdeath, who since the hateful part he had played in the last bloody tragedy and the reproof he

received from Rougue had continued sulky and intoxicated, muttering to himself all manner of curses and execrations.

The strange vessel on heaving to was observed to be a small ship carrying the Glasstown flag and bearing on board the Earl of Elrington and his family* on a visit to Stumps Island. When Rougue knew this he swallowed a vast bumper of claret and ordered the long boat to be launched. In it he placed Carey with 30 armed men bearing a warrant forged from the one brought by the unhappy crew of the former vessel, stated to be for the apprehension of Rougue. With this the 30 men hailed Elrington's vessel and, having all stepped on its deck, Carey proceeded to show his warrant, and while the master and the Earl were assuring him they had no such person on board, his pirate followers rushed forward, seized the guns and disarmed the crew, whose scanty numbers could offer no defence.

In spite of their offered resistance, the groans of the Earl, the cries of the young Elringtons and the remonstrances of Lady Zenobia, they were all led, but with the utmost civility and respect, from their own ship into ours. Rougue received them with an elegant dress and his best looks and, bowing to the Earl and young ones, he offered his hand to Zenobia. Leading them all into the best cabin, here they remained for some time when he appeared again and, calling for the captain of the captured vessel, held a long conference with him garnished with a seasonable bottle of wine, the result of which was that the Elringtons appeared again on deck with by no means that same expression with which they first trod it. I thought that Lady Zenobia especially seemed changed in her thoughts for the better. Rougue, with that winning, easy gentility which he well knows how to assume when he thinks it worth his while, conducted them all on board their own vessel. As they passed I heard Lord Aleana remark 'Sister, what a courtship!'

I and our crew were amazed to see the two vessels both tack round and sail back to the Glass Town side by side. The matter was soon guessed at, and ere night by their frequent interchanges of compliments and 'substantilities' the crews of both vessels were roaring drunk and merry. As for myself, I soon had an inkling of the matter, but how it was brough[t] a-bout I knew less of. I had often heard Rougue declare that of all the women in the world he most admired Zenobia Elrington. Her too I had not less often heard say that she thought Alexander Rougue in her mind, in spite of his conduct, had the form & spirit of a Roman hero.

I must now for a moment turn to another incident. My cabin lay between those of Rougue and Sdeath. That night, as I lay awake musing on the incidents of the day, I heard an unusual stumbling and muttering in the passage between the beforementioned rooms. Suspecting I knew not what, I jumped up, opened the door silently, and peeped out. I there beheld old Sdeath, with his great knife between his teeth (the way he usually carried it) stealing softly toward Rougue's room muttering, 'I'll be up with him for what he did to me.' He opened the door and, clenching his weapon in his hand as he saw Rougue before him, sprung on him with a feindish yell.

I ran in after him. The old dwarf was striving to strike his knife into Rougue's heart, who was grappling with him. They were both on the floor. In my hurry I seized a poker and, running up, dashed it at the head of Sdeath. This stunned him. Rougue, then snatchin' a pistol from the table, clapt it to his head and fired. The skull was blown in peices and the brains scattered round the room. Rougue, without speaking, motioned me to take hold of his feet and, himself seizing his shoulders, we proceeded silently up the steps to the deck. Here Rougue, crying, 'I have done with thee, thou wretch,' took the ugly heap of mortality and hurled it into the sea. When it touched the water a bright flash of fire darted from it. It changed into a vast GENIUS of immesurable and indefinable height and size, and seizing hold of a huge cloud with his hand, he vaulted into it crying, 'and I've done with thee, thou fool!' [and] disappeared among the passing vapours. Ere he departed, 3 vast flashes of fire came bursting a round. They were the Cheif Genii TALLI, EMII & ANNII. He that [was] ere this little hideous bloody old man was the Cheif Genius BRANNII.* I stood petrified with fear and astonishment.

But Rougue, who all the time knew well who he was, laughing said, 'Well, I've settled this business, however. Now Bellingham, for your generous assistance of me, I'll set you free on the spot. Why man, I'm going to settle down and become Alexander Rougue, Viscount Elrington and husband of the Lady Zenobia Elrington, the bonniest lass in the Glass Town.'

I fell on my knees and thanked him fervently for his generosity, and we both returned to our rooms, no one save ourselves knowing what had happened.

When morning arose both vessels were ploughing their course back to the Glass Town, where we arrived in two days. Rougue instantly proceeded to the residence of the Duke of Wellington where, in the presence of the Marquis of Wellesly, Captain Sir E. Parry, Lord Lofty, Col. Grenville and myself, he offered full recompense to all parties for the damage he had done as a pirate, on condition of being that moment pardoned his offences. This was immediatly agreed to and settled. He then stating his approaching marriage, invited all present to attend. They gave him their warmest congratulations. This morning I attended the wedding of Lady Zenobia Elrington with Alexander Rougue, now Viscount Elrington. I must break off, for I have to attend this evening at a grand feast given at Elrington Place by the old Earl in honour of the occasion where will attend all the nobility and gentry of the Glass Town.

P B Brontë February
the 8th, AD 1833.

Haworth—

THE. POLITICS. OF. VERDOPOLIS.
A Tale By. Captain John Flower MP.
In I. Vol.

CHAP. 1st.

From the title I have chosen one would expect the first chapter of this tale to place its scenes in Verdopolis, the seat of politics, in the House of Parliament, amid steam, noise and turbulence; in the Jacobin Club,* amid its darkness, muttering and treachery; or in the Cabinet council, amid flattery, scheming and discord. But, reader, I shall not so place my scene. I wish you to look to a spot different indeed from any of those just mentioned, a spot than which none could be more removed from the turmoils of political life: the Woodlands, 20 miles east of Wellington's Glass Town.*

The afternoon of the 1st September in this present year shone brightly over the noble parks of a majestic residence of ancient date, seated amid the forest grounds of Wellington's land. The sun, amid a blue and golden sky, was hanging over the western horizon, his bright beams shedding a splendid light upon the low fleecy clouds collecting round his resting place, the lower rays glancing and blazing among the leaves and boughs of the noble oaks which feathered over the smooth shaven lawns. These forest trees began to spread long shadows over the park, and amid the intervals of shade the ground seemed covered with broad lines of golden and glowing light. Above the great groups of trees, which at the upper end of the park stood dark against the sun, rose the several black stacks of chimneys and the many pointed gables of an ancient and noble old hall, with its well known accompanyments of curling smoke and weather cock above, walks, verdure, and sportive deer below. This was altogether a most serene and delightful sight, and it filled the beholder with soothing pleasure to turn his eyes toward the sun and follow up that golden lawn, those deep shadows, those mighty trees, up even to the grey hills appearing behind the alleys and the bright glorious heavens beyond. Little breeze could be felt in the balmy air, but over all things was diffused the calm spirit of evening, and though all this was in the wild burning land of Africa,* yet nothing gave sign of its being any other than a venerable English hall in a fair English evening.

But what I cheifly want to introduce to my reader is a small retired spot surrounded by vast leafy elms, save on one side where the scene look[ed] down on [an] ivy mantled little church and its undulating church yard. This small spot seemed from its perfect serenity and seclusion the gem of the whole scene. In the middle of the grassy turf was placed a simple elevated tablet and urn of white glistening marble which bore on its side this simple inscription.

This stone is raised.
Over the grave of.
MARY HENRIETTA.
PERCY*
Who died May. 1st.
AD. 1815.
Aged. twenty one years
By Her Husband.
Alexander R Percy.

The wild flowers twining round this unstained monument, the one beam of bright light which fell on it through two parting trees, its simple unflattering inscription, offered to the eye and mind the most calm and pleasing ideas, and the evident extreme care taken to preserve it from all encroachments of time and weather told more for the unchanged affection and unforgetting memory of the survivor than could have done the most pompous monument and elaborate eulogium. Yet had he who, then present, made these reflections, he would have been disposed to hesitate did he know who was that survivor.

At this time on the day before named, while all round lay thus under the bright beams of an evening sun, the wicket leading from the country to this secluded spot was opened and there entered a tall man dressed in black. He walked up to the monument and stood silent before it. The appearance of this stranger was extremely striking. He was, I have said, very tall, thin and statly, about 40 years of age, his countenance dark, stern and of a peculiar aspect. He seemed not melancholy, but thoughtful, deep, and his finely formed lips were curled into a cold sarcastic smile. He laid his gloved hand on the monument and looked round with an expression boding nothing good to whoever might chance to be loitering nigh. Seeing no one he turned again to the monument and, taking off his hat, laid it on the ground, uncovering a head of curled auburn hair and a forehead of aristocratic loftiness, ill agreeing with the dissipated sneering character of his face.

'Well,' he said to himself, 'I am here again. I dare say changed even since last year. I am sure, changed since I first stood before this grave. Ah, Mary, if you saw me now, you could no more know me than I you if you stood here. You are now earth in earth, ashes to ashes.* Well, Mary, I have walked through a weary world but have never seen one like thee—I think I never shall. I wonder what you would think of your Alexander should you see him now, worn, wasted, flying his country for ban of the law,* immersed in a fire of—hem—hem—ranting with his mouth of Methodism, Calvinism and such stuff;* thinking in his mind of things as contrary to that as thy tomb to this stone; speaking of republics, of democracy, freedom; thinking of aristocracy, titles, tyranny. Ha well, I'll shall drive on. My eye is fixed on something which I will join even should I find it not gold, but fire. This is a glorious evening, man. Times may change the sky—Nature, never. When I was here 18 years since, standing over the new covered grave, the mourners being all departed, the sky—the scene—was just as it is now,* and the same beam of light fell here, but not on this marble urn, no, on the raw black heaped up earth.' He stopped here and stood bending over the grave. With [a] strange smile, one of an expression yet more singular than the one he usualy seemed to wear it was partly mournful, bitter and sarcastic, he took from a black box a small portrait set with brilliants.* It was the countenance of a young woman of fair, mild aspect, and her large hazel eyes seemed to have a slight touch of sorrow about them which gave to the face, evidently young and beautiful, a soft melancholy expression, it seemed, looking at the stern dark man in whose hand it was held. He noticed this and went on: 'Ah, just so you often looked at me when you saw a glimpse of my nature, Mary. You never stopped me, but you always calmed me. It's twilight now. I must leave you here, Mary, in your cold damp house and go forward to mine. I wonder how time passes over you, Mary.' He had turned his head and with that bitter smile was about to leave the tomb when the gate leading from the park opened and a young lady entered the enclosure. A spectator would at once have been struck with the resemblance she bore to the portrait just mentioned and the man before her. She was about 17 or 18 years old, slight and slender in stature and figure. Her small hands and feet and slender waist united well with a head of curled auburn hair, a fair open forehead and large hazel eyes shining with a mild sad lustre.

Her smile was of soft, winning character, her dress fashionable, dark in colour and aristocratic in material. Indeed her whole air, though full of the sweet sadness suitable to the old hall, the old grove and ancient prospects round her, was strongly tinged with the pride and distance of him who stood before her. To this person, as soon as she observed him, she hastily ran forward.

'My father!'

'Well, Mary, how are you, child? I am here you see. But we will speak of that. Let us return to the house. How is it? Ah, Percy Hall!' he said as, taking his daughter's arm, he walked from the enclosure to the open lawn in view of the mansion. 'Mary, love, has all past well since I was last here? I hope that servants and all about the Hall have attended your word.'

'Oh yes. Had they not, I should have written.'

'You would?'

'Certainly.'

'Like some one.'

'Well, Father, I am suprised to see you here, but indeed agreeably so. I had begun to wish heartily, or to give over wishing, for your arrival. Are all you have left well? How is my Lady Elrington? Above all, how are you, Father, yourself? For the others I care little.'

'Oh, Mary! Well, my lady is tolerable. I am as you may guess how. I should not have come so soon, but—. It's a delightful evening. Child have you been visiting that you have got that beaver hat* on? For I suppose you still keep the whole plan of walking through the park without [a] bonnet.'

'Oh, I never visit. I am not so fond of it as to spend in so doing such a fair evening. I have been taking my usual walk with Roland here.' As she spoke a huge dog came bounding toward her but, observing her father, it gave a yell of joyful recognition, leapt round him, licked his hands, jumped into his face, and then set off at once around park at full chase, scattering the stags round in all directions.

'Dear Father! I wonder you will not oftner delight in this place, since all here so joyfully welcome you,' said his daughter, smiling as she looked up in his face.

'Silence, Mary! I care for no one's welcome but thine.'*

CHAPTER IId

Oct. 23.
1833.
PBB.

Next morning rose over Percy Hall as fair as the evening had sank, and every feild, park, wood and tower of this English like country was white with dew and golden with the beams of the morning sun. The Honourable Miss Percy, according to her usual unsophisticated custom, had arisen early to walk through the park and up the sequestered lanes of this pastoral region. Her usual guard, Roland, a huge deer hound, followed gaily the steps of his young mistress, and under his protection she walked slowly along. A large hat shaded the sun from her face and well set off her brown hair, expressive eyes and sunny smile. From the mild cordial manner and sweet voice with [which] she addressed the country 'apes' and 'rare lads'* who crossed the path, and the joyful hearty deference with which they obsequiously saluted her could directly be seen the admiration she was held in by her father's numerous tenantry. In our lands a young lady cannot find a simple opportunity for alms giving, distribution of tracts, soup or blankets and such condescending of cotters,* and the only way to secure the favour of the surrounding people is by a free cheerful look and kind sentence spoken in passing. Farther than this they neither wish nor need. And thus by her fairy shape, gentle voice and perfect cheerfulness the young lady of 'the Hall' gained the warmest affection in these fairer, rough, Irish like gentry. Should a shower come on in her walk, twenty bullet headed lads were off like lightning for the carriage from the Hall. Among her father's servants also, from the housekeeper to the mere servant wench, from the steward to the gardeners, just the same feeling reigned.

But among the gentry, the opulent people and the inhabitants of Wellington's Glass Town she showed a different character. Her high station, her rank and her father's wealth, power and vast consequence raised her above those who are considered the principal persons of the country Glass Towns, for be it remembered that the kings, their families and the great nobility all reside in the mighty Verdopolis. Here she was looked up to, paid deference to, invited as the queen of their parties, and considered the standard of taste for the youth of the city. But all these attentions were in vain. If she chose to be present at a party (which choice was seldom indeed) she was here altogether unapproachable by a cold distant pride, not shown in haughtiness, arrogance, or in an offensive manner but by her short, shy silence, quiet assumption of the principal place, and cold bows to those [who] would fain be thought most intimate acquaintances. The splendour of her carriage and equipage was equalled by many, but the unrecognising manner with which she passed through a crowd of silks and satins to enter it, and the air with which her chariot drove off could by none be approached. And what added to all was that, while she took leave of all entertainers with a single word and a silent nod, she perhaps turned from them to step in to the carriage with a kind cheerful familiar sentence to her coach man or foot man and a display of smiles and an alacrity on their part most laughably contrasting with the silent deference and eager assumption of the slightest shake of the hand by their superiors. Now all her conduct in these cases, though so cold and distant, was, I have said, preserved from being disagreeable by her unsophisticated looks and a manner perfectly free from haughtiness. When any one entered a party who was or wished to be considered of vast consequence, any lady blazing in satin and jewels, of course the hostess would introduce to her the Honourable Mary Percy, but while that fashionable lady sailed to her and greeted her with perfect appearance of equality, perhaps of superiority, this said Honourable Mary Percy would look at her with an unobservant turn of her hazel eyes, hold out her hand, and after a single sentence, retire back as if she had not seen her. Now, reader, this manner was about the same to the untitled as to the titled, and she affected not in the least to give one more word to a velvet robe than to a silk gown though she would give twenty to ruddy cheeks and a russet stuff. We all know that her father, filled as he is with the most restless contempt and hatred of mankind, extends not these sentiments to women, yet he swears that if he sees any woman exercising airs, striving to sit in the place of man, swaggering a fancied superiority, affecting contempt of her lord's, by the heart of Scylla,* he would cut off her head with his own hand. Now, his daughter possessed the sentim[ent.]*

Now though Lord Elrington stood aloof from freindship with any one, though he could look with a smile on no one, though he drove from his house his two sons* and threatened the most tremendous vengeance should they dare to molest him or look on his face again, yet, save the uncertain gleams of sunshine bestowed now and then on his lady, all the light of his favour was bestowed on this child of nature and aristocracy. She must want nothing. All her wishes must be gratified, and woe be to the man, woman or child who should dare to slight her, to the servant who should dare to neglect her word. Our readers must not suppose that he often, when absent, delighted to think of her or that he ever dropt a tear on thinking of her, or that he ever frequently wrote to her or saw her. But when he did think of, write, or visit his daughter, it was with a pleasant feeling and a relaxation of his cynical smile. She in fact was the only creature on whom he with pleasure bestowed a smile, favour, or kindly word, and in whom he felt pleasure and pride. Now, though by him she was thus petted and indulged, yet had she dared to contradict him or thwart him in any thing, the severest punishment, if he were present, an unsparing blow, would have been the instant effect of her disobedience. But she never did or would disobey him. Her father was with Mary Percy all in all, and the slightest word said in her presence against him would make her eyes flash and her glow with instant anger. Never more might that person hope to regain her favour. She was aware of the life of Elrington—his tremendous character, his ferocious and unrelenting disposition, his constant endeavour to light the flame of discord and to plunge his country in the convulsions of revolution and war, his dissipation and recklessness were all or partially known to her, but in her mind it mattered little what he said or did: it was, if not right, at least half justifiable by circumstances. At all events it was great, showed his vast power and ability. It was done by her father, he to whom she looked up with mingled fear, affection and awe.

I have digressed much concerning the Honb^le Miss M. Percy. But it is right my readers should understand her character. We left her walking with her dog through the parks of her father's Hall in a delightful autumn morning. Lord Elrington soon joined her. He had his gloves on his hands. 'Mary, I intend to ride [to] the city, this morning. The carriage is ready. You may accompany me. Get ready, child.'

'I am ready, I believe, Father.'

'What! You don't spend an hour or 2 in dressing, then, when you go out?'

'No, I go exactly as I happen to be. It is not worth while to dress.'

'Say, rather, child, for I detest cant,* that you think yourself always fine enough.'

'Yes, I do. Go home, Roland. Now, Father, I am ready. Ned (speaking to a stout ape who was going by) take Roland back to the Hall—here's something to drink my father's return with.' She dropt into his hand a sovereign, smiling.

The sturdy youth scratched his head. 'As how I'se—I'se drink it, my lady, and yours, too, as long as it lasts, I will.'

The carriage now drove up. They both mounted, and the aristocratic vehicle rolled away with well oiled wheels along the smooth road to the city. Miss Percy broke a short silence with, 'Father, from the works

lately published which I have received from the Great Glass Town, I
have taken the strongest desire to visit it. When will you take me?'

'Do you really wish to see it?'

'Yes, I do indeed.'

'Well, you shall go then, when I return.'

'I would like to thank you, Father, only it is needless.'

'I guess you will be pleased. But remember, Mary, you must behave
civilly to your step mother. You have not seen her. She will behave
coldly, but I've cautioned her against disrespect or haughtiness to you
in terms she will not forget. But, child, if you go, I must buy you a new
carriage and poneys and augment your cash accounts.'

'No, I—'

'Silence! I know very well what you must have. You now receive from
me 500 £ per ann. I shall augment it to 5000 £ so long as you continue in the city. You would not like to be behind the other ladies of the
capital.'

'But surely, Father, none of them possess that sum yearly. I shall
scarcely know what to do. I shall indeed feel the incumbrance of riches.'

'Oh, never fear, it will melt. But come, we're in the city, and a handsome one it seems to be. Yet how far below the great Verdopolis! Why,
it's not above one 20th of its size.'

They soon entered the great street stretching through the city, and
as they rolled along in their sumptuous chariot, attracting the instant
attention of all passengers, for, not to mention the young lady herself,
Lord Elrington was no common or uninteresting object in this western
capital. He alighted at a splendid hotel and, there leaving his carriage
and servants, crossed the street with his daughter on his arm and a
footman behind them. This attendant stepped up before them to the
door of a majestic mansion and knocked authoritatively, announcing to
the porter Lord Elrington and Miss Percy, who without further notice
walked into a splendid apartment. And while she was carelessly adjust-
ing her hat at a vast mirror (not taking it off) the master of the house
entered with evident marks of suprise on his countenance. He was a
thin, anxious looking man of middle age and gentlemanly manners. In
one hand he held a newspaper, with the other he shook that of Elrington
who, looking at him with a direful squint, cried 'Ha, Caversham.* Well,
what do you stare for? I am here, flying from the furys of that infernal
ministry, sir. My lord, I must relax a little, you know, at my country
seat.'

'Yes, my lord,' replied this noted nobleman, 'but have you seen this
morning's papers?'

'No. What in the name of earth is stirring?'

'Here's one of them, The Verdopolitan Intelligencer, published 5 days since, arrived here, this morning.'

Elrington seized the paper, threw himself onto the sopha, and wandered with searching glance through its columns. Caversham stood over him, leaning on the back of the sofa, twisting his keen eye towards him and smiling at the black expression of his countenance. Miss Percy looked at her father with fear and hesitation, for she saw that no little thing discomposed him. On a sudden, 2 splendid chariots, but splashed up to the windows, thundered up to the front door, the gallant horses as they were reined in snorting, tossing and curvetting back on their very haunches. Rougue hastily glanced to the window and cried, 'In the name of Belial,* these are Great Glass Towners!' Then turning to his daughter, 'Mary, love, you must ride back to the Hall. Come, I'll hand you to the chariot. I shall return perhaps to night. Good morning, child.' His daughter bowed to Lord Caversham, mounted the chariot, and it rolled off, wheeled round the corner and was out of sight. The folding doors of the parlour of this mansion flew back. The new visitors, 4 or 5 in number, dismounted and entered, one behind another in to the room. The first was a tall dark man, the second not so tall but still darker looking, the third was [a] gentleman of lofty stature and noble deportment, who wore his hat pulled firmly down over his forehead, leaving only seen beneath a fine crop of curled whiskers and black moustachios. Behind him followed 2 or 3 gentry of grim and forbidding aspect, emissaries seemingly of the very bearers of darkness.

'Hah, Connor and Gordon!'* cried Elrington stepping forward, for Caversham, before his master thought that, assumed a lower place. 'What in the name of wonder are you here for? Sit down gentlemen. Caversham, order the bottles. Stay, I'll ring. Here, Butler, out with your best. Now who is this? My noble freind, my dear aborigine, take your place and rehearse to me your reasons for this flight from the city.'

The third gentleman, to whom the latter portion of this speech was adressed, took his hat off and displayed a countenance of the darkest copper. He was a perfect Othello,* seemed nearly 30 years of age, and poss[ess]ed a majestic deportment, noble forehead and an eye like a young eagle. 'Reasons enough of them,' he muttered and sat down in silence.

'Come, gentlemen,' cried Rougue, 'we must speak of this business, sir. Hang it you know that those infernal ministers,* knowing us to be at present scattered lambs, have at once, hoping to find us unprepared, seized this opportunity to dissolve parliament and to order a new election. Now, please fate, they shall not find us unprepared. We must arm, sirs, and be doing. Of course I shall find means to return a host of gentry for other places, but at present we have most to do with this city, the strong hold of the constitution, sir. (Rising with animation) I will defeat them. By the bones of Scylla, I'll bring forward two members for this Wellington's Glass Town and I'll carry them through. Quashia, I have made up my mind and you shall stand for one, sir, you know.'

The African interrupted Elrington with, 'My lord, no one can command me, and—'

'Stuff! Silence! I say that since you are the Duke's adopted son, my heart, but you're best representative of his adopted city, Quashia. Quashia, funds are in my purse—draw, sir, at your need and draw freely.'

'I consent, Elrington, but rouse and commence operations. Who shall be collegue?'

'Volo.* Come to the Hall, all of you, to morrow to breakfast, and I'll tell you.' He stopt a moment. The others were about to speak. 'No words,' he interrupted. 'No voice, sirs. Ho, Caversham, give me yon desk, and while I write be silent.' He strode to the desk and, sitting down, began to write vehemently for [a] quarter of an hour, and then rising re commenced, 'Now, sirs, I have given you—stop, hand me that glass of claret. Hah—good. Well, I have given you at once the draught of a handbill for circulation, the plan for a comittee and a note or two on the subject. Now, first:

'To the freinds of freedom, to all Glasstowners, to the electors of the metropolis of Wellington's Land:

Freinds and fellow country men! A great crisis has arrived and a vast struggle will now ensue. Tyranny, corruption, and the ancient wish to retain. Freedom, justice, and the present wish to partake. Upon yourselves, my freinds, lies the option either to groan and pine, the slaves of despotism, or to rise and flourish, the lords of Africa. Undoubtedly you wish for nothing save the last, but your chains are on you and you see no hope of release. You are placed in the strong hold of the 12, governed by their laws, through their minions, bridled by your monarch and threatened by his vengeance. No people possess more sense than you, none than you are farther into the folly of our present government, none more wish to reform it. But, you say, our chains lie heavy round us and we dare not stir. Well, then, here I stand. Glasstowners, I am free, and my arms shall be employed to release you. I understand that the 12, frightened at the aspect of their affairs, have dissolved parliament and have proclaimed a new election. Undoubtedly, they will strive again to saddle you with members. But if our strength and justice avail us,* they shall not!

Electors of Wellington's Glass Town, we offer to you two men to represent your noble city in our common parliament on the broad basis of justice to yourselves, justice to all. At present I shall not say any further save to tell you that, on the afternoon of Monday, 4 September, they will occupy the front of the Western Hotel, there to show you their persons, their principles, the plan for your welfare. Meet them then, my freinds, and there judge them. Till then I remain your ardent well-wisher, A. Elrington.

—dated, Caversham House, Sept. 2d.

'Now for my second affair.

It being determined that M^r......... and M^r .... (blank for the names to be filled up) shall stand for the representations of Wellington's Glass Town in parliament on the principle of thorough reformation,* it is agreed that a committee be immediatly formed for the purpose of watching over and promoting their return. This comittee to hold its meetings every evening (beginning with Sept. 3d at 6 p.m. in the Western Hotel untill the conclusion of the election.

A. Elrington.

'Paper third.

The following noblemen and gentlemen are requested to form the comittee for promoting the return to parliament for Wellington's Glass Town of —— and ——.

> Alexander Viscount Elrington, M.P.
> Arthur O'Connor, Esqr M.P.
> George Charles Gordon, Esqr M P.
> Frederic Viscount Caversham, M.P.
> Captain John MacArthur
> Richard Wareham, Esqr
> Colonel James Fitzherbert
> Thorncliffe Eversham Gordon, Esqr
> Captain Julius Gordon
> St John Richard Streithton, Esqr*

A. Elrington.

'Paper fourth.

Copy of a circular to be adressed to the principal newspapers of the city:

Sir, not doubting that you will instantly take up the side of justice, the comittee for the return of two Liberal members for this city request you to accept of the enclosed bill of 1000 £ to meet your expenses in the cause of civil & religious freedom. Should you return a note stating your determination to advance that cause to the uttermost, you will, on directing it to the comittee's rooms, Western Hotel, have your bill doubled in amount.

                                                                    A. Elrington.

'Paper fifth.

Copy of a circular to be addressed to all the inns and public houses and places of entertainment in the city.

Sir, upon sending a note to the committee for the return of two Liberal members for Wellington's Glass Town, stating your cordial determination to support any reforming candidate, you will be requested to throw your house open to all persons for what they may demand, and at the conclusion of the election, you will direct your account to the comittee, which account will be punctually paid. Meanwhile, as a surety of their honourable dealing, they beg your acceptance of the enclosed note of 100 £.

                                                                    A. Elrington

'Paper sixth: a letter.

Enclosing the above 5 papers and addressed to Seargeant W. J. Despard,* Bookseller, Wellington's Street, Wellington's Glass Town:

Sir, the committee for the return of 2 Liberal candidates for this city request you to print off instantly of the first numbered paper herein enclosed 5000 copies; of the second, 500 copies; of the third, 500 copies; of the fourth 20 copies; and of the fifth, 500 copies. After printing, you must instantly forward them to Elrington Hall. Your bill you will please to place to the account of the comittee. Enclosed you will find a note of 1000 £ pounds for trouble & requesting your ardent support in the regeneration of your country. I remain,

                                                                    A. Elrington.'

'Now gentlemen,' continued Rougue with energy, after he had read these papers and folded them in a sealed wrapper, 'what think you of my speed and animation? Go on like me and rest assured you'll gain. Here, footman, take this parcel this moment to the bookseller Despard, and here's a guinea for your pains. Now go quickly.

'Well sirs, now to speak of money matters. Vast sums will be ready to carry our candidates through, but courage! We will speak of that to morrow, when you must, gentlemen, meet me at the Great Western Hotel. Good morning. I must go and call on the other members of the unborn committee to make them enter on the work.'*

Elrington bowed to his friends and, ordering his carriage, strode from the apartment. His companions, when the door was shut, gazed at each other in mute suprise.

Caversham first broke silence with, 'On my soul, he's energy! Why, he'll carry all before him.* Did any one ever hear of anything so audacious? Elect Democrats here, beard the lion in his den,* oppose to the Duke! You, my rare prince! On my soul, it beats any thing ever before done! Well, we shall gain. To your glasses gents. Connor, that corkscrew.'

They drew their chairs to the table, and at the bottles we shall leave them.

CHAPTER. III

—PBB. Nov. 5th 1833.

On the evening of this day the Hon. Miss Percy, in the noble supper room of Percy Hall, sat on a sofa in perfect ease amid the gorgeous splendour of all around her. She seemed a very picture of indulged aristocracy, on the splendid ottoman,* reclining before the glow of chandeliers and fire, with books, drawings and a hundred et ceteras strewed round her, and the huge dog Roland lying gazing up at her face and licking the small hand so condescendingly held out to him. Yet in spite of this, Africa held not a heart so freed from sophistry [as] that of the daughter of Lord Elrington. A footman entered.

'John, here, do place those books in order. I have thrown them round me most wickedly.'

'Yes, my lady, I will. There's an old gentleman in the hall who wishes to see my lord. I said he was not at home, but he won't go. He wished to see you.'

'Who is he? What is he like?'

'I can't say just for that, but as how he's stuck on the topp of as decent a prick of hog flesh* as a body could see.'

'Well, John, shew him in, but mind you stop here behind my sofa. Stay. Thomas, you shew the gentleman in here.'

A lad ran to obey his mistress's command. The visitor appeared at the door. The moment the young lady saw him she turned to her footman and whispered: 'Oh, John, I am glad I told you to stay.'

'I,* for that matter, I am.'

The visitor, a little withered old man, covered with a brown great coat and slouched hat which he did not take off, tramped readily from door to fire place, which, as he stood before the fire, spit in and then poked with his stick. Then scratching his head he began, turning to his offended hostess, 'I can't but zay, ma'am, bud I'm as how I'se come fro the Glasstown to speake to Rougue on a business or so, as how Sdeath's a cold.'* He continued rubbing his withered palms over the fire and then, elegantly blowing his nose with them, 'As how, ma'am, iv you're my Lord's—hum, haw, daugh—, I mean, Honb^le Miss Percy. You'd happen tell 'un when he'd be in, haw?' squirting into the fire a quid of tobbacco.

Miss Percy first stared, then looked frightened, then tried to look grave, and lastly laughed out right at the conclusion of this doughty* speech. 'John, John, take him in to the hall. Give him beer and refreshment. My father will be here shortly. You shall then see him. Take him in, John, and give him—'

'Aye, aye, I'se go, I'm agoing. You'll do as she tells you and get me somut. Haw, Sdeath's a hungry.' So saying he spit out a third quid and, taking his staff, followed the servant out of the room. He being gone, Miss Percy had not time to recover from her suprise when a carriage was heard driving up. The door opened and her father entered.

'Oh, Father, I am glad you're here. I suppose from the newspapers this morning there has been a dissolution of parliament, and have you been all day astir respecting it?'

'Yes, Mary, I have, but I am both cold and thirsty.'

'You look so.'

'I dare say, seeing I haven't eaten to day. But, here, is not supper nearly ready?'

'Yes, it is. But Father, there has just been here the strangest old man I ever saw. He wanted you. I could not make any—'

'Is he—. No, child, show him in. Sdeath, by my life! Show him in, child. Leave the room.'

'But you will take supper?'

'Stuff? No! In with him. Good night, Mary.'

'Good night, Father.' She departed and Sdeath entered.

'Well you scoundrel,' cried Elrington, 'what now?'

'The carriage is waiting,' answered Sdeath.

'Volo, another word on that subject and I'll cleave your scull to the chin.'

'Will you? So now we've had grand doings in our town, Rougue, and the Governmenters think they'll smash all before 'em, the dogs—haw, hem—but as how we'd a meeting of th'club and Mont an t'others* ha sent me to you, sixteen hundred mile and better, to speak on how we must fill the house and pile the courats with the slain as how—I means, the reforming members.'

'Stop, villain, I'll write a list of the principals. Sit down.'

'I, there's a bottle here.'

Elrington took pen and paper, wrote hastily and shortly delivered to Sdeath the following paper.

'Sweet Mont: Gordon for <u>Denard</u>; Connor, <u>Selden</u>; Carey, <u>Siladen</u>; Dorn, <u>Fidena</u>; Quashia and some other fellow, this city; Sdeath!!!!!!, <u>Sneakys Town</u>; Caversham, <u>Ross Town</u>, Thyself, <u>Parrystown</u>; Myself, <u>Glass Town</u>; Mc Carthy, <u>Harlaw</u>.* So much for principals. Secondaries: 13 to my 13 boroughs; 23 to their own private ones; 4 to thy 4 boroughs or seats; 2 to Caversham's couple of seats; 1 to Carey's; 3 to Dorn's; 50 or 60 to try where they can best hit and at the old sure places, 16. Total, 134, or perhaps 150 in the mainland. For Stumps, 11; for Monkeys, 21. Grand total, 166. Make up, if possible, 200 or 250 members in all. For cash from 150 to 200,000 £ of my own is at comand. Our struggles, Monty, must be violent, tremendous. Good day.

A. Elrington.

'Here, Sdeath, I am cracked up* with writing. How was Mont when you left and what did the city look like?'

'Mont was as mich astir as you are. The city was like in a bit of a confusion, the ministers as aye rapping from one another's offices like mad an' I could a wished to stick one or two I could.' Here this worthy, wiping his mouth with the sleeve of his coat, gave a deep sigh. 'Rougue, Rougue, I zay, if you are at a loss for a second member here, I can show you one.'

'Can you—where?'

'I, az I was a trotting here, I foregathered about 9 miles off with like a gentleman on horsback. He seemed rather fresh in our ways, but we began to talk a bit and I found him to be a bright 'un, a real leader, disposed, Rougue, to take any way to gain a name.' Here Sdeath got up. Rougue's eyes were bent on him with an eagle look. He continued vehemently. 'Rougue Elrington, take my word, sir. He's one who will rise, I could see that directly. Why though as raw as blood in these countries of ours, he did show sich eagerness in every thing about 'un, sich cautiousness in talking that, by Sdeath's heart, I felt him a stiff 'un.* Rougue, think no more on't but take him at once.'

Rougue looked for a minute thoughtfully on the fire and then, turning to the desk, drew out a sheet of paper, upon which writing he then read as follows:

'Sir,

I earnestly request the honour of your company at Percy Hall, about 6 or 7 o'clock to morrow morning. Apologising for the abruptness on the score of haste, I remain your &c.

A. Elrington.

'Sdeath, Sdeath, what's his name?'

'It's—I got it out on him though he was sharp—Sir Robert Weever Pelham,* of English Hotel in this city. He is building a house called Tamworth Hall,* a few miles off.'

Rougue wrote the direction, sealed it and rung the bell. A servant appeared. 'James, take a horse and carry this instantly to the place mentioned on the direction. Off, man!' The servant disappeared and they soon heard him clattering down the avenue. But now a second servant entered with a very large parcel, which he laid beside his lordship, stating it to have come from the bookseller Despard.

'Ha, well, give the bearer his skinfull.* Go.'

Rougue then, cutting open the parcel, took out a specimen from each printed paper and, handing them to Sdeath, said, 'Here, hound, fold in the letter to Mont these 5. It will show him how to get on. Now, go to the Hall, there rumble thy bellyful, spit fire.* Begone. I must write all night. Next morning thou must receive some more letters which I must write and then to thy ain het hame again.'* Sdeath chuckled a laugh and departed. Elrington walked to a cupboard concealed in the wall and from thence taking forth a bottle of brandy and glass, placed it by him. Then giving vent to a few oaths and curses, wound his watch and sat down to write the whole night through. First, he took the hand bills and filled up the blanks for the members' names with the names of the two whom he wished to be members, Zerayda Quamina Quashia and Robert Weever Pelham, but ere he had done he violently rung the bell. A servant appeared. 'Ho! Call in my secretary. Go.' This person soon appeared. 'Shut the door, Mr Seaton.* Take your implements, fill up these blanks with those two names. Indorse the papers of this pile with the names of the editors of our newspapers, those of this with the different inns. Then fold and seal them all, and afterward tell me.'

The man sat down to his work in silence. Elrington then set to writing hasty letters to his different tools and fellow labourers through our country, directing their motions, offering money, adjuring to exertion, and dilating on the tremendous crisis approaching. All this occupied his lordship till 5 o'clock in the morning, when he flung his pile of work to his secretary, and after telling him to direct and seal, he threw himself onto the sofa and fell into a feverish sleep. An hour had not elapsed ere his secretary awoke him by stating that he had finished his work. Elrington told him then to leave the room, and he being gone, the nobleman got up, extinguished the sickly and fading candles, and undrew the curtains of the ample window. He looked out with a weary smile. The sun had arisen. All the park and the distant hills were rolling away the dew and seemed filled with life and song. His daughter was walking in the lawn. He strode to the table, emptied the half finished bottle and, raising the window sash, stepped out into the grass.

Miss Percy advanced to him. 'Oh, Father, have you not slept to night? I see you have not. Now, take a walk through the country.'

'I can't, Mary, I can't. I must sleep still less for a while yet.'

They were stopped by a horseman who rode up, and, as he drew near, he dismounted. He seemed a tall gentlemanly person about 30 years of age, with light hair and handsome features composed into an expression of the most stern and guarded solemnity. He advanced to Rougue and, after bowing politely to Miss Percy, spoke.

'Lord Elrington, I believe.'

'I am, and I hope I may address you as Sir R. Pelham.'

'Certainly, my lord.'

'Oh, come then, sir, into my library. I wish to speak to you.'

The gentleman followed his lordship into the room where, he being seated, Elrington stood opposite, his pale countenance and fierce eye gleaming with light.

'Sir, you know, though perhaps you are a new comer, the state of our nation. You see what a convulsion is arriving. Oh, Sir Robert, he who wishes to rise must strive now, and since I hear of your talent and ability from sure sources, I do offer you the post of candidate for this city. Sir Robert, we must have little speech upon it. You know my principles. Profess them, sir, if only for a time, and then be sure of success. Look at these papers just printed, see my movements.' He stood looking anxiously on the Baronet, who, with a composed but peircing glance, first surveyed his host, then the papers.

'My lord, I realy profess liberal opinions. I see nothing to object to here but, of course, should I stand for the representation of this city, you will leave [me] my own course?'

'Yes, sir.'

'Before and after?'

'We will.'

'I stand, then.'

'Right, Sir Robert.'

They now began to talk together of the political affairs of our nation. Elrington bent his powers to extract the weight of his visitor's ability, who, though he showed a vast fund of cold cautious calculation, yet exhibited as much cool clear judgment, taste and fluency both of thought and language. He seemed well learned in the mysterys of politics. There was a strange, sinister expression and a deceitful smile in his otherwise fine countenance, which, though it would repulse most men, yet gave Elrington a still better opinion of him. He seemed during the conversation also to be measuring the character of that wonderful nobleman. They parted on mutual terms of seeming satisfaction, mutual agreement and internal cautiousness of each other. Rougue adjuring Pelham to be present two hours hence at the Western Hotel, and Pelham, consenting, wished Elrington good morning and rode off. This gentleman had scarcely gone when a carriage drove up to the door, out of which leaped Connor, Gordon and Quashia.

They walked into Rougue's study, and after the usual allowances of mutual cursing Connor exclaimed, 'Elrington, we have not only arrived to accompany you to the meeting, but to tell you a disagreeable piece of news. That cursed villain Capt Flower, with another gentleman called, I think, Morley,* accompanied by the Duke's agent and steward, Me^{ssrs} Maxwell and Evans, have arrived in the city, hot from the Glass Town, and what's worse, Earl St Clair, the feind incarnate,* is on his way here behind them. They affirmed that he will arrive toward noon. Volo, Elrington, we shall have hot work of it. But you've got energy, my heart. They say that the two first, Morley and Flower, will be proposed as candidates.'

'Well, Connor, and who's Morley?'

'Why, he is, they say, a young fellow stuffed with reading and politics—a dab at speaking too. Volo, my—'

'Well, I shall match him!'

'Rougue,' interrupted Gordon, 'we met a hound riding down from the avenue whom we did not like, now, a rum stiff 'un.* He bowed coldly to us and stared at Quashia's black phiz—'

'Hold your toungue, brute!'

'Yes, he did, but I'll have his blood! I—,' exclaimed the ireful African.

'Fool!' cried Elrington. 'Why, he is your colleague, sir. He is Sir Robert Weever Pelham.'

Quashia stood silent, but scarcely appeased he broke out, 'I hate him.'

'Stuff, Quashia! But, sir, I want to register your promise made to me before I consented to open a seat for you: Zoreyda Quamina Quashia promises to Alex, Viscount Elrington that upon his gaining him a seat in parliament, he will, should Elrington's party, on any great convulsion, need his assistance, bring down from the interior of Africa any number of native troops, commanded by himself, not exceeding 30,000 men, as witness our hands. Now, I've put my name. Then, Quashia, put your name. And you two scoundrels as witnesses, add yours.' The three did as commanded. Rougue muttered to Quashia, 'Now remember,' and taking first a glass each of brandy and next their hats, they sallied out, mounted their carriage and drove off. Rougue followed them in his chariot, and ere long they alighted in the very heart of the city at the Grand Western Hotel.

———————
———————

CHAPTER. IV.

Novr. 6.th
A D 1833
P B B—te

———————

Sir Robert Weever Pelham was by birth an Englishman. The fact of his not being educated in the Philosopher's Island* debarred him from the privileges of a thorough Glasstowner. He was born in Lancashire,* England, where his father, originally poor and of no note, had raised himself by ingenuity and perseverance to vast wealth and a baronet's title, which, on his death, he bequeathed to his son. Sir Robert, who finding himself unfettered and aware of his own great ability and knowledge, looked about for some place, some method by which to signalize himself, exert his ambition and employ his mind. But alas! England affords no feild for such. He saw that and determined to embark for the widely celebrated and magnificent regions of Africa, where he felt that his talent would find its way. He therefore instantly converted a property of 1,100,000 £ into ready money and set sail for Wellington's Glass Town, where so soon as he had arrived he bought a splendid estate and mansion called Tamworth Hall. Now he applied himself most ardently to the study of the history and politics of our strange and mighty country, in secret perfecting himself so that, could he contrive to emerge from his situation, it might [be] as the newly freed butterfly. The age of this gentleman was about 30. His person we have termed handsome, but extremely cold and proud. His character was like it, cautious, plausible, and even at times deceitful, always alert for politics and well versed in their labyrinths. Just now, after settling in this country, we see that the parliament was dissolved and the elections commenced. Sir Robert was looking round for a borough when he came in contact with Elrington, whose keen searching glance saw in a moment his vast ability. He fixed him, he thought, to his side and showed him the road to power. We left Sir Robert parting with Elrington. He turned his horse's head toward the city and mused for a while in silence. At last, soliloquizing to himself thus, 'Well, I have seen the great Elrington so soon after my landing—truely an unexpected acquaintance. I certainly could wish my step to parliament had been on the other side, but I shall be content as it is. It shall not hurt me. He is a great man and cannot sink.' While thus musing, a carriage dashed up from behind. It was the one containing Elrington, Quashia and the two others who, from the slow pace at which Pelham moved, had overtaken him.

Elrington called out: 'Well, Sir Robert, we are all bound on the same destination. Let me introduce to you, first your colleague, Z.Q. Quashia, son of the former monarch of Africa; next, to my worthy and excellent freinds, M^{essrs} Connor and Gordon.'

The first, Quashia, bowed to Pelham stiffly, the other two, eagerly and greedily. Pelham returned it gentlemanly, and all rode on together. On alighting at the hotel they found there assembled all those gentlemen mentioned before as to compose the comittee. After mutual introductions wine was called for. Elrington took the chair and business was entered on. 'Money makes the mare to go.'* This was therefore the first thing debated on. Quashia offered 40,000 £, Pelham, 50,000 £, the rest 20,000 £. Elrington at once offered 80,000 £, these making a total of 190,000 £, an immense sum which, Elrington remarked, must carry weight. The formid[ab]le nature of the opposition likely to be met with was talked over. Schemes were promptly formed for, by bribing, &c., getting over as large a number as possible of rare apes &c., who were to have arms placed in their hands, and [be] placed at the meetings to awe and overpower honest voters. A large sum was voted for bribes to electors, and every means, however unjust, were laid hold of to ensure success. Pelham sat amazed at the reckless and iniquitous nature of the proceedings, but he wisely looked on, winked and said nothing. After arranging matters for the speechifying and showing forth of the candidates to morrow, the meeting separated, Elrington inviting them all to dinner that evening at Elrington Hall.

In the meantime the handbills during the night had been posted up in all parts of this great metropolis. The morning newspapers appeared with long commentaries and speculations on the approaching struggle and its probable consequence, too many of them evincing palpable appearance of the ass laden with gold* having viol[at]ed their editors. All the inns were open. The scarlet flag was every where flying, and shoals of rascals about the streets were shouting 'Elrington and liberty, Democrats for ever!'* Public feeling was wound up very high, and this scene only presented an image of what was just now going on through the whole kingdoms. True, the master spirit worked here, but his agents were active everywhere. In the mean time the opposite and hitherto reigning party were far from being idle. The government of the Great Glass Town, to secure this city, had prepared means for instantly seizing the representation, and, as we have said, on this morning there arrived 2 or 3 carraiges containing the intended government candidates, Mr Morley, myself (ie, Capt Flower), and the Duke's two agents, with 3 or 4 other gentlemen, to forward the election. We saw at once on arriving that the most energetic measures must be had recourse to to keep pace with our formidable though new sprung antagonists. Placards, letters, handbills prepared at Verdopolis were instantly promulgated stating our arrival, motives for action and day of presentation. To bribery we disdained to have recourse. We knew that our party was strong enough without this aid.

Sir Robert Pelham, having left the hotel after the conclusion of the meeting, took his horse and proceeded along the noble banks of the Gambia toward Percy Hall, musing within himself upon the strange and awkward situation he was thrown into, for his politics and private opinions, it could easily be seen, were scarce so extreme as those of [the] strange men among whom he had pitched for a time his tent.* But, however, he at least, however raw in actual politics, was no novice in them. No man easily daunted his cool and searching intellect. [He] saw paths for escape where to others all seem[ed] thick rock and prison-wall, and his sly, wily, accomodating temper enabled him to worm through them with ease peculiar to himself.

Sir Robert, after riding 2 or 3 miles, entered the splendid avenue leading to Percy Hall. He gave his horse to a porter and stepped into the park, desirous to see it before entering the mansion—or rather to have an opportunity of finishing his speculations on his political prospects. But the beauty of the scenery around him often diverted his attention from these weightier matters. He was standing upon an eminence admiring the noble trees which stood above him, the green lawn spread far below him, the old Hall lifting its grey chimneys over the dark foliage before him, and the aerial peaks of Africa stretching in the sunlight in the clear calm heaven beyond him. While thus gazing, but with a mind perhaps rather occupied with other feeling than those of pure scenic admiration, a young lady, whom Sir Robert instantly recognised as Miss M. Percy, turning round a corner, appeared before him. She knew not of the vicinity of any one and happened to be reading. She looked up, but bowed without any confusion.

Sir Robert could not use his usual stiffness toward one so young and fair. He returned her morning salute, or rather (for he had made his first) after mentioning the reasons for his arrival, remarked, 'I have several times, madam, been mistaken in my notions of this country. I had supposed Africa to afford no prospect so fair and English as the one I here see. And give me leave to remark that I did not suppose the poet whose works you hold in your hand had been so much as heard of here.'

'Sir, in the latter case I believe you are right, or nearly so. Eastward of these mountains this work is scarcely known. Will you not give me credit for superior knowledge? I have lived nearer to your island and on looking over this book have scarcely found it so mean as England ought to produce. What does your nation think of Lord Byron?'

'My nation, madam, are frightened at him. They could not understand him. He was too much of a d—d Glasstowner for our comprehension.* For my self, I knew him and could appreciate him.'

Miss Percy's eye lighted up rather when she found Sir Robert had been personally acquainted with one whose works she admired. 'Did you know him, sir? My father has once or twice, on looking at his works, affirmed that he was born for our country and died because he could not stand in his natural soil. You are too proud of your poet, sir. Look at this one.' Miss Percy gave to him an exquisitely bound little duodecimo printed in a superlative stile upon paper like ivory.* The fly leaf bore: 'June—1824. A. Percy R. to his daughter, M. H. Percy.' It was a volumn of the poems of Arthur, Marquis of Douro.*

'Hah, madam, I know we must bow to this one. He is above us. Byron himself—'

'Must fail before him you would say.'

'Yes, they are like each other.'

'But, sir, you must walk forward to the Hall. My father expects you soon. Good morning, or evening.' She stepped into a side walk and disappeared among the trees. Sir Robert took his road to the Hall, where he stepped into the saloon and introduced himself with his usual staid formality. There soon entered his worthy fellow candidate, Quashia, and their supporters and committee men, to the number of a couple of dozens. Dinner was served up as usual in splendid style. Miss Percy presided at the head of the table and, in spite of her general shyness of manner, with the greatest ease and elegance. Elrington opened his vast store of brilliant language and varied information. He strove to please all, and his endeavour was not in vain. All his guests, though men of in general the most dark and treacherous character—for not one save Pelham was present who would have scrupled to the most infamous means to gain an end—were yet gentlemen and knew much. The cloth being drawn,* bottles and glasses were brought forth. The chairs were drawn closer. Eyes looked brighter, and with glass upon glass, tumbler over tumbler, bottle on bottle, there came out the full tide of Glass Town language, Glass Town politics and the momentous affair upon which they were then met. Pelham, who wished to preserve an unspotted character, took care, though he took a decent quantity, not to exceed the bounds of moderation, and his smooth, ready flow of gliding language kept his hearers from noticing his slower circuit of the bottle. Elrington poured down a bottle of spirits as a matter of every day occurrence; Quashia, half a dozen of wine as a thing of extremist pleasure. Ere 10 or 11 at night the company separated, many in a state of intoxication, all pleasantly exhilarated, all, too, intending to meet again on the morrow on the hustings* of Wellington's Glass Town.

CHAPTER. Vth.

Nov.ʳ—
the 14th
A D 1833.
P B B—te

The morning for the presentation of the 4 candidates on the hustings at length arose, and even ere the first reddening of the horizon thousands were astir through the city upon this all important business. A grand husting, capable of holding two or three hundred persons, had been erected in the great square in front of the City Hall. Two companys of cavalry were drawn up on each side, armed to prevent if possible the almost certain riots.* Every street of the city flamed with placards and handbills of brilliant red (the Democratic) and green (the Constitutional) colours. Innumerable flags and banners of the same hues preceded the different bodies of electors pouring into the city from every point, while bands of music, absurd clashing of bells, and peals of shouting, roaring and sounding at the same time, all tended to exhilarate and to heighten the scene.

I shall pass over the constant rows and fighting of this morning, the drinking and bribing and threating and extortion. These things every body can picture, but not so easily can my readers conceive, when the sun hung in his meridian over this noble city, all that vast Wellington Square crammed close with 200,000 men, every house and building bearing to one their roof windows and chimnies their countless numbers. The crowd was wedged to suffocation all round the hustings, then hung round thickly through the extremities of the square, and at every opening and vista of a receding street still appearing, still pouring forward with band and banner for each favourite candidate. Green and red, red and green, waved from spire, window and flagstaff with out ceasing. The hustings as yet was empty, but about noon a loud and over whelming shout from a distant street, taken up, continued and increased to a tremendous roar up to the very Town Hall, announced the arrival of the candidates. The storm of music rose higher, the banners floated thicker forwards and the crowds opened a long lane to admit the 2 splendid lines of noble carriages which dashed, dust and foam spattered, up to the hustings. The noble horses were reined in. First Mr Maxwell stepped out and took his station in the middle on an elevated seat, as the representative of the Duke absent, and high sheriff of the meeting. Then alighted from their row of chariots, amid the exclamation of their friends, the 2 Constitutional candidates, Mr Babbicombe Morley, myself (Capt Flower), with our supporters and backers in this arduous struggle. These took station on the sheriff's right hand. Then like wise amid the cries of their favourers, came up the tall form of Viscount Elrington, who, though no candidate, was considered by all of course prime mover of the opposition followed by his candidates, Sir R. Pelham, Q. Quamina, and the hosts of Cavershams, Gordons, Streightons, Connors and that dark revolutionary fry.* A small degree of silence having been obtained, the sheriff in a short speech explained the reasons for their being called together, the motives on which they ought to act, and in conclusion called upon the Constitutional candidates to appear and show themselves. His Highness, TRACKY, Duke of Nevada,* stood forward, and the assembled multitude took off hat and cap in reverence, save the dark looking group on the sheriff's left. He in a short and most condescending speech introduced to their notice myself as candidate for the office of representing in parliament this vast and mighty city. I advanced amid tremendous cheering and still greater opposition. In fact between the one and the other, I could not through my whole speech be heard beyond the platform in the crowd below. Many were the blows given and taken, many the broken heads and legs to be laid to my account on that day. It was long before silence could be restored, and not yet then without military force. The Right Honb^le Thomas Beresford Bobbadil, major general of the army of W[ellington]'s Land,* advanced and in a very short and scarcely gracious speech introduced the pekin* Thomas Babbicombe Morley. This young gentleman came forth amid the same wild and uproarious tumult as myself. But his loud and trumpet toned voice soon commanded attention, kept up by his short squat figure and broad glimmering countenance. But however unprepossessing in look, his overpouring voice, his readiness in speaking, the distinct arrangement of his ideas, and the eloquence, the weight, the sparkling antithesis of every sentence carried on in spite of every other hindrance. Elrington bent his keen eye on him, following him out through his speech with unmiked* intrest, and when he concluded with, 'and now, gentlemen, though placed in this strange dilemma of right and bigotry opposed to wrong and liberty, yet let us not at all despair. There is to man a body and soul. The first soon, in the lapse perhaps of a few seasons, must wear out, decay and pass in to annihilation; the last shall survive the loss of this companion, shall rise up to endure in unending, in eternal existence. So, though now in all our arguments and contest wrong is so strangely opposed to wrong, right opposed to right, so all mixed and warring in vain confusion, yet wait the time when that wrong shall rot off and vanish and leave the right to join its once seperate parts and endure in an existence which neither the force of man can extinguish or the lapse of ages destroy'*—then, with this last sentence, Elrington joined his powerful voice to the roar of applause that ranged from hustings to the horizon, mingled through at length with hissing, riot and fighting.

Frederic, Viscount Caversham in an elegant speech introduced Quashia Quamina. This strange and furious gentleman came forward,

bowed to the meeting and with lighted eye stepped back without speaking, affirming to his astonished freinds, 'Will I fawn on the descendants
of my father's murderers?* They shall die!' Viscount Elrington stepped
forward and, taking off his hat, prepared to introduce the last candidate.
The disapprobation which ran through the crowded square on his first
appearance soon subsided into undisguised interest and attention. He
began with his well known thrilling voice and unapproached majesty
of language. He spoke of the tyranny of the 12, of their unjustifiable
oppression of the people, he reprobated the disgraceful listlessness of
that people in so long enduring their iron yoke,* but described the feeling, the wish now abroad to throw it off; spoke of his own efforts and
losses in the cause of liberty; showed the means for the nation now soon
to gain it; introduced Sir R. Pelham as one grand step up the ladder;*
spoke of him in the highest terms as the only fit person to represent
their noble city; and thus concluded, 'On the death of Louis XIV,* the
great monarch of France, the Archbishop Fenelon* was appointed to
preach his funeral sermon. He mounted the pulpit and cast his eyes
first on the huge cathedral, whose pillars, windows and roof rose high
above him, then on the mixed and mighty multitude which filled choir
and nave and transept beneath him. He saw that building lighted with
the flame of a thousand torches, that assembly shining with the lustre of
their highest splendour. There were the mightiest nobles of the mightiest court of Europe gathered in full blown pomp and solemnity round
that coffin resting under its palls and canopies of velvet. And what did
Fenelon think that coffin contained. The body of a king? No, he knew
it held a dead and corrupting carcase, offensive to every sense, close
shut from human sight, fast festering to decay! It was that this mighty
building was open to admit this vast multitude assembled to deplore.
Fenelon lifted his hands over his hearers and cried out: "O my freinds,
God only is great!" Now, Glass Towners, apply this case to your own
circumstances and tell me: may I not say, when I see that old rotten
withered heap termed majesty, royalty, loyalty, constitution, and so forth
lying enshrined in the most pompous state, revered and worshipped by
the greatest nation on earth, and though in its life it had trampled on,
abused and sacrificed them, and in its death left them only fetters, bondage and misery, yet they still feared the corrupting maze, still held their
chains and slavery, and when one should come and tell them their time
of servitude was expired, should offer to strike the fetters from their feet
and give them a long unknown happiness—I say, would not you say to
such people: "Infatuated wretches! O wretched effects of despotism!"

Will you not let me cry, "My friends, life only alone is great!" Now then is not this case your own? Yes it is! Here (pointing to himself) stands Fenelon; there (pointing to the Constitutional candidates) there lies the rotten royalty. Here too, in the person of Sir Robert Pelham, stands your freedom, your salvation.' A roar of applause burst from the mighty audience. Sir R. Pelham came forth. His fine figure, gentlemanly adress and finely toned voice recieved its due attention. He entered on his speech without hesitation, but with an affectation of modesty, in calm, dignified, well-balanced language, finely glossed, smoothly reasoned argument, unmoved features and statuelike attitude. The consequence was that, on his speech being finished, though every man present stood convinced of his hollowness, insincerity and political trickery, yet charmed by his plausibility, gentlemanliness and ability. The sense of the meeting did most certainly run toward him. Now the high sheriff, after a few words in conclusion, ordered the poll to be opened. The hustings was cleared and that momentous part of the business was begun upon with the wildest and most outrageous uproar, fighting and even bloodshed.

CHAPTER. VI.

Nov 14
1833.
P B B.

On the evening of the day following that described in our last chapter, while Miss Percy was cross questioning her attendants on the probable fate of the election, the well known carraige dashed up and Lord Elrington entered the room. He looked quite exhausted.

'Oh, child, I am quite knocked up. I have never slept or rested since I left this house.' He threw himself on the sopha. 'Do order tea or supper—or what else it may be, Mary. Do you want to know the end of the election? It's over. Look at this paper.' His daughter took it and read:

For Pelham	_ _ _ _	4958.		
For Morley	_ _ _ _	3132.		D—7059.
For Flower	_ _ _ _	3011.		C—6143.
For Quashia	_ _ _ _	2101. (Total votes. 13,202)		

Returned: Sir Robert Weever Pelham (Democrat), and Thomas Babbicombe Morley (Constitutionalist). His daughter was about to speak when a thundering knock was heard at the door. Elrington motioned her to leave the room. Quashia entered. He seemed the picture of rage and stood before [?them all].*

'I'll never stand again! So is this the way in which I am to be made a fool of? Speak!'

'Why, my dear Q, what has come over you?'

'Why, I'll go back to Africa and you may find your 40,000 men just where you can.'

'Quashia, think! Are there not a hundred places besides to try at, for instance, Northtown?'

Quashia sat down for a while in moody silence. Soon he started up. 'Elrington, give me your daughter in marriage* and I'll promise you to return an MP and empowered to bring down 70,000.'

Elrington looked as if he did not know whether to knock his brains out. However, he directly put on an obliging smile and said, 'I promise, on those conditions.'

'Hah! But I'll have papers written out.'

'Well, here, ring the bell.' 2 servants entered. Elrington wrote down the promise. He and Qu — signed, and the servants put their names as witnesses.

Qu snatched it up, put it into his memorandum book, and after saying, 'Rougue, now you're safe. I intend to go to Northtown. The member is returned for this place, but (touching a pistol) this and Sdeath—hah! You understand. I shall set off to day. Good evening, Elrington.' He turned, strode from the room, and his carriage was soon heard whirling off from the Hall. He had scarcely gone when Elrington burst into a loud laugh.

'I, give Mary Percy to such a wildfire scoundrel! I, throw her away on an outlawed blackamoor?* Never! Hah! In spite of his promises, I've got him killing a member to obtain his seat! He and his promise shall smoke for it.'*

A servant here announced Sir R. W. Pelham, MP. As that gentleman entered Elrington rose up, shook him warmly by the hands, congratulated him most affectionately upon his success and rung the bell for his daughter. On her appearing he introduced Sir Robert to her as an MP for her native city, and her to him as mistress of Percy Hall.

'For,' said he, 'I must set off at daybreak to morrow morning for my own affairs. Not that I shall go to the great city—my oval* there is so secure that I shall hold it by proxy—but to other stations and elections, to aid my minions, as I have done here. And now, Sir R., your Tamworth Hall is, you know, only now rebuilding. I swear by the bones of Scylla that you shall make this Hall your home till I come back, which will be in 8 or 10 days. Not another word on it! Curse your pride and stiffness! Good night to you both. I shall not see you again to morrow. Sir Robert, here are your instructions and advice written out and sealed for you till I come back.' Elrington bowed to the Baronet and left the room before he could answer a single word. Sir Robert was about to remonstrate on this arrangement, but Miss Percy rose and said that it could not harm him. Her father wished it. She must request it. The Baronet bowed politely and they sat down to supper.

Elrington set off next morning. Sir Robert remained, shut up all day in the library. On the day following he appeared at breakfast, [?&] dinner, but during the remainder of the time was off in the city. On the third morning he relaxed his ungracious conduct, ordered his carriage, and entreated Miss Percy to accompany him to visit Tamworth Hall. She was as proud as himself, but when she knew that on one of his character [so] unbending it was time enough for her to do so too she gladly consented. He as gladly accepted. They drove off in a glorious exhilarating sunrise along a pleasant rural road for several miles, spent in delightful conversation, for the highly informed minds of both could well afford means of supply. Sir Robert spoke much of England, Europe, of literature, scenery. She supplied him with knowledge of our own noble country. Tamworth Hall soon appeared in sight, an unfinished but extensive and majestic edifice, surrounded by grounds laid out upon such a scale of taste and magnificence as could not but impress the beholder with the most exalted idea of Pelham's wealth, fine taste and judgment. They returned to Percy Hall through the fair lawn like woodland district, and the courteous manner, fine voice, flowing language and varied information of the titled MP made time fly on cheerily with his yong and beautiful hostess. As to his person—but it didn't matter.

Next morning, while [the] Honb^le Miss Percy's maid was arranging the [?ingaloreable]* curls of her mistress's auburn hair, the confidant, as usual, was in on the general chat of those privileged gentlewomen of her station. 'They say that Sir Robert Weever Pelham—I love to give folk the right name—they say he is a fine man and a proud man and a rich man, and I'm sure he is a handsome man. To be certain he is a little bit high, seldom speaks to one, but when he does, he's got such a voice! Oh, his lordship's was never like it, I think, though his was not the tone

one can always hear. Have you seen his new house that he is building? Young Ned Havealem took me and one or two besides, the day before yesterday, to see it, and it's as fine as this, almost, I'm sure.'

'Come, Jane, have done,' said her mistress.

But this corageous confidant was not to be silenced thus. She ran on upon Sir Robert, his house and the election, untill a late breakfast waited for her indulgent mistress. For a week Sir Robert continued to reside at the Hall. His pride and haughtiness was only exercised on those most used to it: the grooms, footmen and other such divinities. He continued himself to admire his position and his hostess more and more. Let not the reader suppose him taken by suprise in this matter. The moment Pelham entered the Hall his cool searching mind had foreseen that his admiration of Miss Percy, on further acquaintance, would certainly increase to fair love and devotion, but he prepared for all this. As for Mary Henrietta Percy, she was completly taken by suprise. She could not help admiring one of his character at first sight and appearance. Appearance—that goes for much. A tall gentlemanly figure, fine, statly, handsome countenance, proud reserved eye, and a slight but expressive smile go as far on the one hand as a small slender form, fairy hands and feet, bright curled auburn ringlets, large hazel eyes, little finely shaped nose and a mouth with an inimitable smile, with manners so unsophisticated, so natural, yet so curiously capricious and reserved and proud to her realy equals, or to those who wished to be thought so. And what, strange to say, made every one like her the more was the great similitude she bore in features to her tremendous and awful father: the same hand, the same nose, the same hair, when angry a look and flash of the eye by no means dissimilar. This, I say, went far enough with Sir R. W. Pelham. But enough of this. Let it be enough to say that, on the middle of the second week of Sir Robert's stay at Percy Hall, when through the boles and foliage of vast umbrageous elms the sinking sun scattered a dazzling and golden light upon the grassy summer lawn, Miss Percy stood beside the tomb of her mother, and Pelham there, with his usual calm, distinct and melliflous voice declared his feeling respecting her [and] made an offer of himself, possessions, and heart and hand. He concluded by saying that he did not wish to trifle or be trifled with. Miss Percy, first turning red then white, said that she dared not speak till her father returned. This was enough for both.

Next morning Elrington arrived from his long and harassing journey, as usual exhausted in body but vigourous in mind. Sir Robert had a long conversation with him in private, after which, when they had entered the breakfast room, Elrington called his daughter to him and said, 'Mary, you know that when I hated every thing living, that hatred never extended to you, and that I have not left you without any thing you wished that I could supply. You are aware that though I expelled— hem—let it pass. You know, however, that you have been and are now the creature on which I spend my sympathy. I have been made aware of the feeling you have entertained to each other during my absence. I am pleased. My words shall be few. Sir Robert, will you take Mary's hand?'

'I will, my lord,' was the prompt reply.

'Mary, will you accept Sir R. Pelham's hand?'

'I will, Father,' was the as decisive answer.

'Very well. In the Great Glasstown, a month hence—'

Lord Elrington was going to say more, but the door unfolded and Quashia entered in a travelling dress. A glance at the two figures of Sir R. & Miss P. standing in such confusion opposite, their hands clasped in each other and the stern countenance of Rougue, with a smile struggling in his own dark treacherous expression, convinced the quick thoughted African how the case stood.

'Villain!' he roared. 'Elrington, by the bones of my fathers—'

'Ho, Quashia, glad to see you. Step this way with me.' Elrington, frowning dreadfully, drew the ci devant* prince into the next room. There he made out his resolution to keep his promise and averred the scene with Pelham only a farce 'to keep him to him, you know.' Quashia left the house half dissatisfied, not withstanding his lordship's persuasion. Elrington then drew Pelham aside and explained to him his promise with Quashia, the reasons for it, &c. He then said, 'Now, should he turn restive, I have got him by the nose.* He has just attained a seat in parliament by causing to be assasinated the representative of a certain town. Now I have an excellent witness, Mr Sdeath, who was present, to prove the fact. I shall deliver him up to government, who will indeed be glad to have him.'

Next morning Elrington signified his intention of leaving Percy Hall for the G[reat] Glasstown with his daughter and retinue. Sir R. Pelham also intended to set off on the same route with him. Quashia, Caversham and many other leaders of the Democrats who had been getting elected to seats in the country would directly follow.

In two or 3 days they all set off.

CHAPTER. VII.

Nov 15.
1 8 3 3.
P B B.

This scene is to be laid in that vast emporium of all the universe, the Great Glasstown. In a splendid apartment of Elrington Hall, gorgeously fitted up and lighted with noble chandeliers, sat one evening on [a] sopha on one side of the fire, a magnificent looking young man in a half military costume. Opposite to him on the other sopha a tall, statly, majestic lady, with fine Italian features and robed in splendid velvet, the Viscountess Elrington, wife of the awful nobleman, as this was his Verdopolitan residence.

'So, Zenobia,' said the young officer, 'you expect his lordship to day. I'll certainly stop to see him. Fine work he's made for government, this sessions! I am positively dying to behold him and Miss Percy. By the bye, did you see the young lady?'

'No, my lord Marquis, I have not.'

'Do you expect with him that gentleman who has so fearlessly seized hold of a seat in my father's city? We have heard much of him.'

'I believe he will be here, and I should like to see him. Elrington in his letters mentions his ability and information. He is rich and proud.'

'Eh, Zenobia, what did I hear—Hem! There they are.'

As he spoke they heard the sound of many carriages dashing up and stopping [?at] the grand steps of the great entrance. Lady Zenobia was going to go out to meet her husband, but as she and her visitors arose the doors flew open and the well known form of Lord Elrington entered, a beautiful girl, splendidly dressed, leaning on his arm. From under her large gipsy hat* beamed the highly envied auburn hair, large bright eyes and aristocratic countenance of Miss Percy. Elrington directly introduced her to his lady with a look well understood by Zenobia, who received her step daughter with the utmost courtesy and kindness, mingled with the pride and distance which Miss Percy was not slow to return. Then Lord Elrington turned to the splendid looking person before mentioned.

'Ha! Well done! Good! And [?their] you here to welcome me! I've settled you well, Marquis. Here's my daughter, Mary Henrietta, and child, here is the Marquis of Douro.' Miss Percy had read this young nobleman's glorious works until he himself, though she had never seen him, [was] fixed as firmly in her mind as her own father. Her admiration of him was unbounded, and being quite unsophisticated and unused to disguise her feelings, kindly or unkindly, she warmly took his offered hand and, with lighted eye and enthusiastic smile was, ere three minutes, firmly acquainted with him. He admired her enthusiasm, language and appearance; said he was determining on a splendid party at Wellesly House, to morrow evening; and warmly invited Elrington, his lady, Miss Percy, and also, he begged leave to add, Sir R. Pelham to it. They assented willingly.

Next day, after dinner, the Marchioness of Douro, in her sitting room in Wellesly House, sat with her three intimate friends, Lady Julia Sydney, Lady Castlereagh, and Lady M. Sneachy,* who, as invited by her, had arrived several hours before the usual time to the great fete that night to be given.

'Well, Marian,' said the sprightly Lady Sydney to the Marchioness, 'I'm burning to see this new comer—a daughter of Lord Elrington forsooth, not an ordinary creature, you know. From what I have heard she must be a little, petted, proud, conceited thing who will speak to no body, or—but I'll tame her, Marian.'

'Oh, Julia, how you rattle!* But the Marquis saw her yesterday evening.'

'Did he? Did he!' exclaimed the ladies, all in a breath.

'Yes,' replied the Marchioness, 'and he quite admired her. She is enthusiastic, warm hearted, polished, as much as you, Julia, and 10 times as natural.'

'Stuff, Marian! We shall see. The Marquis's conceit leads him to believe that every body admires him. We shall hate her. But then there's Sir Robert—Robert—what—oh, Sir Robert Weever Pelham, too. Another wonder. I dare say he will be something decent now.'

'I,' said Lady Castlereagh, 'saw him, this morning, at my father's.' The ladies lighted up anew. 'He is quite a gentleman, looks like a born and bred Glasstowner, is tall and handsome, but, oh, I could not trust him.'

'Eh, a theif?' cried Lady Sydney.

'No—no, but he looks so insincere, so smooth, and his eye—'

'Ah—eye. You know he's a Rogueite and they must have eyes.'

'Come now,' cried the Marchioness, I believe the company are arriving. Cease your slandering do, and come into the saloons.'

Her three fashionable freinds arose and, in their splendid and dazzling attire, followed the elegant little Marchioness into the gorgeous saloon where the company were fast assembling. Ladies Sydney,

Sneachy, Castlereagh, and 1 or 2 others of high rank, beauty and fashion seated themselves apart to reconnoitre and make observation on the fast entering visitors, Julia using her eye glass with vast effect.

'Eh, look at Edward (Mr Sydney). He's been just so ever since the elections commenced. Do condole with me. I cannot tell what to do with him. There he is, hands stuck in his pockets, and I veryly believe he holds his eyesight in them, for his eyes are staring about as if they saw nothing. He is quite blue and white and sucks in his cheeks like a dried bladder.'*

'Julia, have the decency to spare—'

'To spare who, pray? Ha, there's the Duke, my uncle. How pleasant he looks. I admire him, so nicely dressed in black, with such keen eyes and such a ravishing smile. Eh, there's my father too.' The lively lady dropt her glass and sat down with an expression so inimitably demure that her friends and fellow criticisers could not help bursting into unsuppressed laughter. The Marquis of Wellesly who, supported on his cane, wrapt in 5 several* coats, splendidly decked out, and looking blue with cold, had entered the room, noticed their laughing and, seeing his daughter among the laughers, fidgetted up the room, turned bluer than indigo and adressed those about him in a voice so snappish as to startle all round.

'And there's my father!' exclaimed Lady M. Sneachy, as a very tall statly old gentleman (or king, rather) stalked up the apartment, bowed coldly to those round him, and after adressing a few words to the Duke of Wellington, again left the rooms.

'Come,' said Julia. 'We can see nothing here. Do come to the windows and see the carriages draw up.'

The other ladies followed her as she sailed majestically across the room, throwing killing glances to every side round her.

'Eh, whisht! Who's that, now?' she said, as a loud familiar voice was heard on the stair. Directly among the entering throng appeared a firm set, red haired, frank, arrogant looking young gentleman, handsomely attired in uncoxcomical black, with white gloves, and leading by the hand a well known little fellow, 8 years old perhaps, with a curly head and a roguish smile who, dressed in handsome black satin, swung from the hand of his conductor, stopping instead of going forward, twisting round, talking and laughing with all he met, and occasioning considerable inconvenience to the dashing gentleman who led him.

'Eh,' cried Julia, 'Thornton,* I declare, and got up again too. Old Girnington dead. Look how Charlie troubles him. Ah, my old friend Thornton, how d'ye do?'

This well known personage stepped fearlessly up to the ladies. 'Well, and how are you all? You, my Lady Julia? You my lady Castlereagh? You, sister? And you and you? Ha, I am well. Girnington's kicked the bucket.* 70,000 £ a year, a decent personable figure. If any lady would think it would suit, I can't say but I'm ready. I've quite got over my reumatism, d'ye know. Naught but a slight hold. Going to fit out Thornton Hotel in such style. Dash away! Come, have you seen my new coach? Here, look at it.' He drew them to the window where, amid the crowd of carriages he pointed out his own, a splendid new mourning coach* of the finest appearance.

Lady Julia cried, 'Ah, now look, they are coming.'

Three or 4 noble carriages were seen dashing up, emblazoned with the arms of Elrington, but as they drew up the crowd prevented them from seeing those who alighted. Julia and her accompanying freinds turned their heads to the door and waited patiently. Soon there entered Viscount Elrington, his lady, and the observed of all observers, his daughter, who was attired in plain unornamented but fashionable dark coloured satin, not a jewel, not an adornment in her hair. The strange Elrington cast of her countenance, yet so sweet, and animated by such unaffected grace, interested at once the company in her favour. Quite otherwise than many, Julia and her freinds among the number, instead of looking hurried, out of place and ignorant among so vast, new and splendid a company, [she] stood by her father, quite composed, without a smile on her face, but with a silent observant glance at the company round. She bore her introductions with such reserve and shyness and yet with such grace as was quite new and agreeable. The Marchioness of Douro introduced her to Lady Julia Sydney and the ladies about her. Julia began to rattle, tried to bring her to talk, laughed, ridiculed the company, pointed out characters to her, but it would scarce do. She was so cautious in coming out that at length Julia whispered to Lady Sneachy, 'Is her tongue cut out?' Miss Percy heard her. Her eyes lighted up with all the fire of her father's. War and bloodshed might have been the consequence had not the Marquis of Douro stepped up with Young Soult.

'Well, Miss Percy,' he said, glancing at the same time a frown to Lady Julia, 'I am glad, indeed, to see you here. From your expressions, yesterday evening, I believe you will be pleased to have an opportunity of forming acquaintance with my old freind Alexander Soult. Soult, Honble Miss Percy.'

Miss Percy, instead of behaving with the shyness Lady Julia was looking for, instantly entered into animated conversation with Young Soult, which that agreeable and eloquent young man returned with his banal enthusiasms. She shewed Lady Julia here that her tongue was not cut out, and the Marquis seemed quite pleased with her fine taste, quick fancy and highly informed mind. They moved off to where the Duke of Wellington was conversing with Sir R. W. Pelham, who had just entered with Lord Caversham.

'Well,' said Julia, 'the thing has got a tongue, but, oh, I detest—'

'Nay, stop, Julia,' said Lady Castlereagh. 'You are far too severe. She is proud and shy, but it looks pleasant with her, and she is very pretty. See how well she looks. But who's that gentleman standing by her talking so to the Duke and Marquis? Julia, lift your glass.'

Lady Julia obeyed like lightning. 'Lord, Harriet! It is Sir R. Pelham. Well, he is a fine looking man. Look how he smiles. What an abortive attempt! It is, indeed, a wooden smile. The Duke and the Marquis seem pleased with him. And now there is a broad, short, coarse, ill dressed, plebeian, sandy haired young fellow with great glimmering grey eyes come up to them with poor Edward, who looks for the world like a drowned rat.'

'Julia, spare your own—'

'Oh, Harriet, don't advise me. Why, look at yours! See, he has just spit into the fire. How he swashes about in his dandyish dress and with his coxcombical hairs! Oh, Castlereagh!'

The young nobleman came up. 'Well, my lady, I am glad indeed to see you. We've quite a new turn out to day.'

'Well, and what do you think of our heroine?'

'Pretty, very pretty—beautiful, shy as winter moorcock.* But she conversed with the Marquis and me till we forced her to smile.'

'I dare say,' said Julia.

'There's Sir Robert Pelham, my Lady Julia. Never saw such a man. He's as smooth as oil and as hollow as a gun barrel.'

'Very [?personal] Castlereagh. Proceed.'

'His Grace has taken [to] him mightily and the Marquis quite admires him. They say he's quite a lover of Miss Percy.'

'Who? The Marquis?'

'Ah, Marian—'

'No, no. Sir Robert. Ha, ha, ha! But have you seen Thornton? He's come out in such style. But I see Abercorn and Lofty* there. Good evening.' Castlereagh skipped away with the ease of a noble dandy.

'The coxcomb!' said Julia.

The company were now ushered into the ball room and matters were soon arranged for dancing. The orchestra was filled and the first couples led out. Miss Percy's hand was asked by a dozen. She refused all till the Marquis of Douro asked her. She looked at Sir R. Pelham. He nodded and the Marquis led her out with his usual perfect ease and gracefulness, while she, on hers, shewed the same to a degree that left not a shadow for envy to rest on. Sir R. Pelham advanced to Lady Julia and completely won her favour by leading her for[th] to waltz. Lord Elrington took Marchioness Fidena, and when Thornton swaggered up and asked her afterward, he received such a sly and well given hit from the Marquis Fidena that he retired back, clapping his hands to his side and groaning.* Mr Sydney took Lady Castlereagh. The Marquis of Fidena took Marchioness of Douro. Myself had the honour of leading out Lady Z. Elrington. As for Miss Percy, she had found a treasure. On sitting down on a sofa to rest, she observed a little wild looking creature with curly [hair], pale wild blue eyes and a ludicrous expression on its round laughing face, creeping about the sopha, chairs and tables, dreadfully annoying a little dapper gentleman in blue and white. She called this strange creature to her. It came forward. A thought struck her.

She hastily asked it, 'Are you Lord Charles Wellesly?'

'I have that supreme honour. And who may you be?'

'Mary Percy.'

'Mary Percy. And who's Mary Percy?' the little monkey* went on.

Miss Percy was quite delighted. She had read the works of this exquisite author 20 times. She admired them inexpressibly, and now she found the thing itself who had written them. In speaking to him, of course, she intirely laid aside her shy, distant manner, and assumed her natural cheerful, gay, laughing temper [which] she rarely exercised. She took the small monster up, lifted him onto the sofa, where he twisted about chattering, laughing, talking to her and, as he expressed it, 'not over and above ill pleased with her manners, considering.' She kept him in a good temper, but found it utterly impossible to control his wilful movements. She asked him how he liked his noble brother.

He exclaimed, 'Brother! The stuck pig ninny!* No brother of mine! Thornton says and Emii* too, says that I am to make away with him by a neckerchief tightly twisted round his craig.'*

This language Miss Percy could scarcely understand, but not withstanding she and Charlie scraped a handsome acquaintance.* Many ladies and some of the gentlemen had gathered round the back of her sofa and heard her gay cheerful conversation with the Whelp of Sin, as the Marquis of Douro had termed him during the evening. But when she saw herself beginning to be observed, she gradually relapsed into, first, plain staid speaking, and then silence. Nor could the imp's winding about, laying hold of her hands, looking into her face, sharp criticisms on the company, laughable observations regarding herself, antics or any other of his movements extract from her more than a smile, stroke of the hand (at which it was wildly indignant) or perhaps a single word or two spoken to it. The Duke of Wellington came up and entered into conversation with her. His Grace Miss Percy admired above all men almost, and in speaking to him all her reserve vanished in an instant. She was one too whom His Grace liked, and the special smile and voice which he can so well assume then ornamented his stern but kindly countenance. But morning had now begun to rise and the company was breaking up. Carriages were put in requisition, and the square before Wellesly House again became a scene of bustle and tumult. Almost every one in departing bowed and took their farewells of Miss Percy, and she received innumerable invitations. All these salutations she returned by a bow or single word, save those of the persons she liked, to whom she bid warm adieu, or at once accepted their invitations. And when her father and Lady Elrington departed, the Marquis of Douro led her to the door, and the Duke of Wellington himself handed her into the carriage.

CHAPTER. VIII

Nov^r –
15 –
1833
P B B–

Next morning the Duke of Wellington, his noble son, the Marquis of Douro, and M^r. Secretary Sydney were seated together in the room of the Home Office, talking on the aspect of politics, or on the fete of last night.

'Well,' said the Duke, 'Rougue has gained a real accession to his party. But I question that, too, for I fancy, it is a very insecure one. Sir R. Pelham is certainly a man of most extensive abilities, but as slippery, as diving a statesman as I have ever been able to see.'

'His information,' said the Marquis Douro, 'is remarkably extensive and his language is so extremely melliflous. I admire him, Father, but what do you think of the Honourable Mary Henrietta Percy, Elrington's daughter?'

'Why, Arthur, I don't think I've often seen a young lady whom I liked better. She is, I see, at times uncommonly shy, though.'

'Not to Your Grace, I'm sure. But my wife, alias, Lady Julia, is taken with such fits about her of hatred and then forced to like, I'm sure—'

'Now, Sydney. But she will be admired in our city. They say she is about to be married to Sir Robert Weever Pelham, and if so, as I believe is the case, it will join him strongly to Elrington's party.'

'Never fear, Arthur. She I can see will always go with her father, as she adores him, but in our country I am glad to say, however our ladies take a wholesome and healthful intrest in politics, they do not think of intermeddling or trying to stay the course of that wild and stormy current. And moreover, Pelham, I can see, is not one to be tied to any one. You will see—he can run, creep, walk, swim, fly, dive, or remain still, just as suits his ambition or intrests. These lie with the Constitutionalists, and to us, ere long, he will cast an eye.'

Here conversation was stopped by a clerk's announcing Lord Elrington and Mr Sdeath. The Duke and the others smiled with suprise, but they were introduced. Elrington, after nodding to all present, began at once, with a suitable oath and execration, to affirm he was wearied of that African traitor Q. Quamina; that he was injuring him sadly; and that he had made a resolution to deliver him up to government, for that scoundrel had killed Col. Ashton, MP for Northtown (whose death had excited, from its sudden and singular nature, such rumors in the papers) that by doing so he could mount to the seat, which he did; that Mr Sdeath there, worthy man, was present at the assassination—he was not prepared to state in what capacity and that he could prove anything requisite. The Duke stared and winked with wonder, but willingly consented to seize the dangerous African who, Elrington affirmed, was at present in a gambling house he named. Officers were immediatly sent off to apprehend him, and Elrington departed. The Marquis of Douro stept out after him to gain a true account of what seemed, on Elrington's part, so strange an action. Elrington at once told him that Quashia had refused him what he immensely stood in need of, unless he gave him Miss Percy in marriage; that he, to keep him to him, promised her; that upon Pelham declaring his attachment to her and hers to him, he, without hesitation agreed to their marriage, since he considered Pelham so, a lofty, wealthy, able man; and since he was certain that Miss Percy both wished the union and would find it the best she could ever have; upon knowing this, Quashia made a vast uproar, produced Elrington's written promise to him, and determined to strive by law to obtain fulfilment; that he (Elrington), of course, upon this, considered how he might put the black rascal out of the way; that he fixed upon this as the most just and defensible (for the assassination &c was a fact). As he and the Marquis were speaking together, Quashia was seen brought past to the prisons, in chains, foaming, swearing by his gods in the height of anger. He was safely lodged in stone walls.

Miss Percy has been eagerly received into all the great [?introube-mante]. All the city speak of her, admire her for her beauty, nature, pride, reserve, cheerfulness, gaity, freedom from sophistication and elegant mind. Sir Robert Weever Pelham, by the sheer force of his ability, has at once seated himself as a principal Glasstowner. His approaching marriage with Mary Henrietta Percy is publicly known, and vast preparations are making to celebrate it in a style of splendour worthy of himself and her great father. The Marquis of Douro will give the bride away. And two souls more fully framed to unite together were never formed than these of Robert Weever Pelham and Mary Henrietta Percy. NB highly important. Lord Charles Wellesly has condescended to say: 'she is one whom I can say I am pleased.'*

————End. P B Bronte Nov 15th AD—1833.

An Angrian Battle Song
composed by H Hastings

———

Storms are waking to inspire us
  Storms upon our morning sky
Wildly wailing Tempests fire us
  With their loud and God given cry
Winds our trumpets howling come
Thundering waves our deeper drum
    Wild woods o'er us
    Swell the chorus
Bursting through the stormy gloom
What's their Omen? whence its doom?

Loud those voices stern their pealing
  Yet what is't those voices say?
Well we feel, when, God revealing,
  All his wrath their powers display
  Trembles every child of clay
    Still we know
    That blow on blow
  O'er bursting day by day
  Shews that wrath as well as they

But 'tis not a common call
  That wakes such mighty melody
Crowns and kingdoms rise or fall
  Man and nation's chained or free
  Living death or liberty
  Such their terrible decree
    And yonder skies
    Whose voices rise
  In that unearthly harmony
    Through Angria round
    Shall wake a sound
  A voice of victory
  A thundering o'er the sea

Whose swelling waves
And howling caves
Shall hear the prohecy

Storms are waking
Earth is shaking
Banners wave and bugles wail
    While beneath the tempest breaking
Some must quench and some must quail
Hark the artillery's iron hail
Rattles through the ranks of war*
    Who beneath its force shall fail
    Must the Sun of Angria* pale
        Upon the Calabar?
        Or yonder bloody star
        O'er Afric's main
        With fiery train
        That wanders from afar

No O God! our Sun its brightness
    Draws from thine eternal throne
And come what will through good or ill
    We know that thou wilt guard thine own!
    'Tis not gainst us that thunders tone
        But, risen from hell
        With radiance fell
'Tis the wanderer of the west* whose power shall be o'erthrown!

Tempest blow thy mightiest blast
    Wildwind wail thy wildest strain
        From God's right hand
        O'er his chosen land
    Your music shall waken its fires again
And over the earth now and over the ocean
    Where ever shall shadow these storm covered skies

The louder through battle may burst your commotion
Twill only sound stronger <u>O Angria Arise!</u>

———————

P B Brontë.

Written January—1836—
Transcribed May 26. 1837.
67 lines

═══════

Haworth. Yorkshire.

Percy's Musing's
upon the Battle of Edwardston
June 1836

Through the hoarse howlings of the storm
    I saw—but did I truely see
One glimpse of that unearthly form
    Whose very name <u>was</u>—<u>VICTORY</u>
'Twas but a glimpse—and all seems past
    For cares like clouds again return
And I'll forget him till the blast
    For ever from the soul has born
That vision of a Mighty Man*
    Crushed into dust!—

Forget him!—Lo the cannon's smoke
    How dense it thickens till on high
By the wild stormblast roughly broke
    It parts in volumes through the sky
    With dying thunder drifting by
Till the dread burst breaks forth once more
    And loud and louder peals the cry
Sent up with that tremendous roar
    Where—as it lightens broad before
    The thick of battle rends in twain
With roughened ranks of bristling steel
    Flashing afar while armed men
In mighty masses bend and reel
    Like the wild waters of the main
    Lashed into foam!—Where, there again
Behold him! as with sudden wheel
At bay against a thousand foes
He turns upon their serried rows
All heedless round him though they close
    With such a bloodhound glare
That eye with inward fires so bright

Peirces the tempest of the flight
And lightens with the Joyless light
   Of terrible despair!
He sees his soldiers round him falling
In vain to heaven for vengeance calling
He sees those noble freinds whom he
   Had called from happy—happy Home
For a vain prise of victory
   Over the eastern world to roam
He sees them lie with glaring eye
   Turned up to him that wandering star
Who led them still from good to ill
   In hopes of power to meet with war
And fall from noontide dreams of glory
To this strange rest so grim and gory!—
When rolling on those freinds o'er thrown
War's wildest wrack breaks thudering down
Zamorna's pale and ghastly brow
Darkens with anguish—all in vain
To stem the tide of battle now
   For every rood of that wide plain
Is heaped with thousands of his dead
Or shakes beneath the approaching tread
   Of foes who conquer o'er the slain
   No! never must he hope again
Though still abroad that banner stream's
On whose proud folds the Sun of glory beams
   Though still, unslaughtered, round their lord
His chosen cheifs may grasp the unvanquished sword
Still, all is Hopeless!—and he knows it so
   Else would not anguish cloud his brow
   Else would not such a withering smile
   Break oer his hueless face—the while
   Some freind of years falls hopelessly
   And yet up-on that Eagle eye
   Gazing with dying extacy!
   That Eagle eye! the beacon light
   Through all the changes of the fight
   Whose glorious glance spoke victory
   And fired his men to do or die
   On the red roar of battle bent

As if it[s] own wild element
And glancing o'er each thundering gun
As he were wars unconquered Son
That Eye! Oh I Have seen it shine
    Mid scenes that differed far from these
As Gambias woods* and skies divine
    From Greenlands icy seas*
I've seen its lustre bent on me
    In old adventure gone
With beam as bright and glance as free
    As His own Angria's sun
When o'er those mighty wastes of Heath
    Around Elymbos' brow*
As side by side we used to ride
    I smiled to mark its glow
I smiled to see him how he threw
    His feelings into mine
Till my cold spirit almost grew
    Like his a thing divine
I saw him in his beauty's pride
    With manhood on his brow
The falcon eyed with heart of pride
    And spirit stern as now
Almost as stern—for many a shade
    Had crossed his youthful way
And clouds of care began to mar
    The dawning of his day*
I knew him and I marked him then
    For one remote as far
From Earth's surrounding crowds of men
    As Heaven's remotest star
I saw him in the battles hour
    And conquered by his side
I was with him in his height of power
    And truimph of his pride

'Tis past!— but I am with him now
    Where he spurs fiercely through the fight
His pride and power and crown laid low
    His glorious future wrapped from sight
Mid clouds like those which frown on high

Over the plains in purpled gloom
With rain and thunder driving by
  To shroud a nations bloody tomb
  And in the cannons ceaseless boom
The Toll which wafts the parting soul
  While Heavens bright flashes serve to illume
Like torches its funeral stole
Its Horrid funeral—Far and wide
  I see them—falling in the storm
Mid ranks of Horse that wildly ride
  Above each gashed and trampled form
His charger shot Zamorna down
Mid foes and freinds alike oerthrown!
Yet never may that desperate soul
Betray the thoughts which o'er it roll
Teeth clenched cheeks blenched and eyes that dart
A Lion fierceness from his heart.
As all the world were nought beside
The saving of his iron pride
For every one on earth might die
And not a tear should stain that eye
Or force a single sob or sigh
     From him who cannot yeild
Yet stay—one moment —'tis but one
A Single glance to heaven is thrown
One frenzied burst of greif —!—'Tis gone
    Again that Heart is steeled!
That was a burst of anguish—there
Blazed all the fierceness of despair
It said—Oh all is lost for ever!
  All he loves to him is dead
  All his hopes of glory fled
  All the past is vanished
    Save what nought can sever
  Ever living memories
  That shall haunt him till he dies
  With what he can realise
    Never Never Never!

I said I saw his anguished glance
  Say did it fall on me?

Incendiary of rebel France
　　Parrot of Liberty!
The wretched Traitor who let in
　　On Afric's opened Land
Deceit and craft and hate and sin
　　In an united band
Who raised the Standard of Reform
　　And shouted Earth be free
To whelm his country 'neath the storm
　　Of rebel Tyranny
Who called himself the good right hand
　　And Father of our King*
Only on his adopted Land
　　A Double curse to bring
Aye and it was I and only I
　　That hurled Zamorna down
From power and glory placed on high
　　This day to be o'erthrown
I barbed the arrow which has sped
　　To peirce my sovereign's breast
And only on my guilty head
　　May all his sufferings rest!

　　　　P B Brontē

　　　　　　　　Written June 22ᵈ 1836.*
　　　　　　　　Transcribed May 30ᵗʰ 1837.
　　　　　　　　　175 lines.

Mary's Prayer.

Remember Me when Death's dark wing
  Has born me far from Thee;
When, Freed from all this suffering
  My Grave shall cover me.

Remember me, and, if I die
  To perish utterly
Yet shrined within thy memory
  Thy Heart my Heaven shall be!*

'Twas all I wished when first I gave
  This hand unstained and free
That I from thence might ever have
  A place my Lord with thee

So if from off my dying bed
  Thou'dst banish misery
O say that when I'm* cold and dead
  Thou wilt Remember Me!

      ————   P B B. June 16 1837. 16 lines

EMILY BRONTË

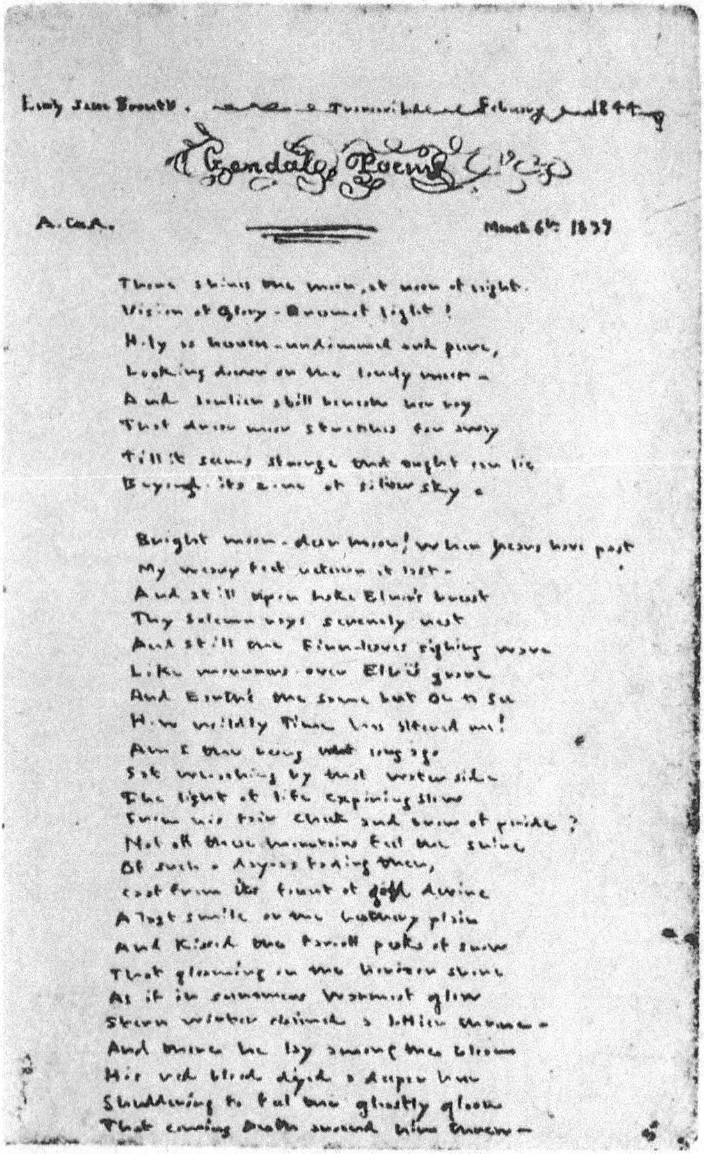

Plate 2: The first page of the 'Gondal Poems' Notebook, including the poem headed 'A.G.A.', beginning 'There shines the moon' (courtesy of the British Library).

I

High waving heather 'neath stormy blasts bending
Midnight and moonlight and bright shining stars
Darkness and glory rejoicingly blending
Earth rising to heaven and heaven descending
Man's spirit away from its drear dungeon* sending
Bursting the fetters and breaking the bars

All down the mountain sides wild forests lending
One mighty voice to the life giving wind*
Rivers their banks in the jubilee* rending
Fast through the vallys a reckless course wending
Wider and deeper their waters extending
Leaving a desolate desert behind

Shining and lowering and swelling and dying
Changeing forever from midnight to noon
Roaring like thunder like soft music sighing
Shadows on shadows advancing and flying
Lightening bright flashes the deep gloom defying
Coming as swiftly and fading as soon

2

A.G.A.   March 6th 1837

There shines the moon, at noon of night*—
Vision of Glory—Dream of light!
Holy as heaven—undimmed and pure,
Looking down on the lonely moor*—
And lonelier still beneath her ray
That drear moor stretches far away
Till it seems strange that aught can lie
Beyond its zone of silver sky—

Bright moon—dear moon! when years have past
My weary feet return at last—

And still upon Lake Elnor's* breast
Thy solemn rays serenely rest
And still the Fern-leaves sighing wave
Like mourners over Elbë's grave*
And Earth's the same but Oh to see
How wildly Time has altered me!
Am I the being who long ago
Sat watching by that water side
The light of life expiring slow
From his fair cheek and brow of pride?*
Not oft these mountains feel the shine
Of such a day—as fading then,
Cast from its fount of gold devine
A last smile on the heathery plain
And kissed the far-off peaks of snow
That gleaming on the horizon shone
As if in summer's warmest glow
Stern winter claimed a loftier throne—
And there he lay among the bloom
His red blood dyed a deeper hue
Shuddering to feel the ghastly gloom
That coming Death around him threw—
Sickening to think one hour would sever
The sweet, sweet world and him forever
To think that twilight gathering dim
Would never pass away to him—
No—never more! That aweful thought
A thousand dreary feelings brought
And memory all her powers combined
And rushed upon his fainting mind.
Wide, swelling woodlands seemed to rise
Beneath soft, sunny, southern skies*—
Old Elbë Hall his noble home
Tower'd mid its trees, whose foliage green
Rustled with the kind airs that come
From summer Heavens when most serene—
And bursting through the leafy shade
A gush of golden sunshine played;
Bathing the walls in amber light
And sparkling in the water clear

That stretched below—reflected bright
The whole wide world of cloudless air—
And still before his spirit's eye
Such wellknown scenes would rise and fly
Till, maddening with dispair and pain
He turned his dying face to me
And wildly cried, 'Oh once again
Might I my native country see!
But once again—one single day!
And must it—can it <u>never</u> be?
To die—and die so far away
When life has hardly smiled for me—
Augusta*—you will soon return
Back to that land in health and bloom*
And then the heath alone will mourn
Above my unremembered tomb*
For you'll forget the lonely grave
And mouldering corpse by Elnor's wave—'

3

A.G.A. to A.E.*   E August 19th 1837

Lord of Elbë, on Elbë hill
The mist is thick and the wind is chill
And the heart of thy freind from the dawn of day
Has sighed for sorrow that thou went away—

Lord of Elbë, how pleasant to me
The sound of thy blithesome step would be
Rustling the heath that, only now
Waves as the night-gusts over it blow

Bright are the fires in thy lonely home
I see them far off, and as deepens the gloom
Gleaming like stars through the high forest-boughs
Gladder they glow in the park's repose—

O Alexander! when I return,
Warm as those hearths my heart would burn,

Light as thine own, my foot would fall
If I might hear thy voice in the hall—

But thou art now on a desolate sea—
Parted from Gondal and parted from me—
All my repining is hopeless and vain,
Death never yeilds back his victims again—

4

August 1837

Alone I sat the summer day
Had died in smiling light away
I saw it die I watched it fade
From misty hill and breezeless glade

And thoughts in my soul were rushing
And my heart bowed beneath their power—
And tears within my eyes were gushing*
Because I could not speak the feeling
The solemn joy around me stealing
In that devine untroubled hour*

I asked my self O why has heaven
Denied the precious gift to me
The glorious gift to many given
To speak their thoughts in poetry

Dreams have encircled me I said
From careless childhood's sunny time
Visions by ardent Fancy fed
Since life was in its morning prime

But now when I had hoped to sing
My fingers strike a tuneless string
And still the burden of the strain
Is strive no more 'tis all in vain

5

November 1837

The night is darkening round me
The wild winds coldly blow
But a tyrant spell* has bound me
And I cannot cannot go

The giant trees are bending
Their bare boughs weighed with snow
And the storm is fast descending
And yet I cannot go

Clouds beyond clouds above me
Wastes beyond wastes below
But nothing drear can move me
I will not cannot go

6

I'll come when thou art saddest
Laid alone in the darkn'd room
When the mad day's mirth has vanish'd
And the smile of joy is banished
From evening's chilly gloom

I'll come when the heart's real feeling
Has entire unbiassed sway
And my influence o'er thee stealing
Greif deepening joy congealing
Shall bear thy soul away

Listen 'tis just the hour
The awful time for thee
Dost thou not feel upon thy soul
A Flood of strange sensations roll
Forerunners of a sterner power
Heralds of me

7

A.G.A. to A.S.*   E. May 20th 1838

O wander not so far away!
O love, forgive this selfish tear.
It may be sad for thee to stay
But how can I live lonely here?

The still may morn is warm and bright
Young flowers look fresh and grass is green
And in the haze of glorious light
Our long low hills are scarcely seen—

The woods—even now their small leaves hide
The blackbird and the stockdove* well
And high in heaven so blue and wide
A thousand strains of music swell—

He looks on all with eyes that speak
So deep, so drear a woe to me!
There is a faint red on his cheek
Not like the bloom I used to see.

Can Death—yes, Death, he is thine own!
The grave must close those limbs around
And hush, for ever hush the tone
I loved above all earthly sound.

Well, pass away with the other flowers
Too dark for them, too dark for thee
Are the hours to come, the joyless hours
That Time is treasuring up for me.

If thou hast sinned in this world of care
'Twas but the dust of thy drear abode—
Thy soul was pure when it entered here*
And pure it will go again to God—

8

Arthur Ex[ina] To Marcius*

In dungeons dark I cannot sing
In sorrow's thrawl 'tis hard to smile
What bird can soar with broken wing
What heart can bleed and joy the while

9

Song by J. Brenzaida to G.S.*   October 17th 1838—

I knew not 't was so dire a crime
To say the word, Adieu:
But, this shall be the only time
My slighted heart shall sue.

The wild moorside, the winter morn
The gnarled and ancient tree—
If in your breast they waken scorn
Shall wake the same in me

I can forget black eyes and brows
And lips of rosey charm
If you forget the sacred vows
Those faithless lips could form—

If hard commands can tame your love,
Or prison walls can hold
I would not wish to grieve above
A thing so false and cold—

And there are bosoms bound to mine*
With links both tried and strong;
And there are eyes, whose lightening shine
Has warmed and blessed me long:

Those eyes shall make my only day,
Shall set my spirit free
And chase the foolish thoughts away
That mourn your memory!

10

F. De Samara to A.G.A.*   E. November 1st 1838.

Light up thy halls! 'Tis closing day;
I'm drear and lone and far away—
Cold blows on my breast, the northwind's bitter sigh
And Oh, my couch is bleak beneath the rainy sky!

Light up thy halls—and think not of me;
That face is absent now, thou has hated so to see—
Bright be thine eyes, undimmed their dazzling shine,
For never, never more shall they encounter mine!

The desert* moor is dark; there is tempest in the air;
I have breathed my only wish in one last, one burning prayer—
A prayer that would come forth although it lingered long;
That set on fire my heart, but froze upon my tongue—

And now, it shall be done* before the morning rise;
I will not watch the sun ascend in yonder skies.
One task alone remains—thy pictured face to view
And then I go to prove if God, at least, be true!

Do I not see thee now? Thy black resplendant hair;
Thy glory-beaming brow, and smile how heavenly fair!
Thine eyes are turned away—those eyes I would not see;
Their dark, their deadly ray would more than madden me

There, go, Deceiver, go! My hand is streaming wet,*
My heart's blood flows to buy the blessing—To forget!
Oh could that lost heart give back, back again to thine
One tenth part of the pain that clouds my dark decline!

Oh could I see thy lids weighed down in cheerless woe;
Too full to hide their tears, too stern to overflow;
Oh could I know thy soul with equal greif was torn—
This fate might be endured—this anguish might be borne!

How gloomy grows the Night! 'Tis Gondal's wind that blows
I shall not tread again the deep glens where it rose—
I feel it on my face—where, wild Blast, dost thou roam?
What do we, wanderer, here? So far away from home?

I do not need thy breath to cool my death-cold brow
But go to that far land where She is shining now;
Tell Her my latest wish, tell Her my dreary doom;
Say, that my pangs are past, but Hers are yet to come*—

Vain words—vain, frenzied thoughts! No ear can hear me call—
Lost in the vacant air my frantic curses fall—
And could she see me now, perchance her lip would smile
Would smile in careless pride and utter scorn the while!

And yet, for all Her hate, each parting glance would tell
A stronger passion breathed,* burned in this last farewell—
Unconquered in my soul the Tyrant rules me still
Life bows to my control, but, Love I cannot kill!

I I

December 4ᵗʰ 1838

A little while, a little while
The noisy crowd* are barred away;
And I can sing and I can smile—
A little while I've holyday!*

Where wilt thou go my harassed heart?
Full many a land invites thee now;
And places near, and far apart
Have rest for thee, my weary brow—

There is a spot mid barren hills*
Where winter howls and driving rain
But if the dreary tempest chills
There is a light that warms again

The house is old, the trees are bare
And moonless bends the misty dome
But what on earth is half so dear—
So longed for as the hearth of home?

The mute bird sitting on the stone,
The dank moss dripping from the wall,
The garden-walk with weeds o'er-grown*
I love them—how I love them all!

Shall I go there? or shall I seek
Another clime, another sky.
Where tongues familiar music speak
In accents dear to memory?

Yes, as I mused, the naked room,
The flickering firelight died away
And from the midst of cheerless gloom
I passed to bright, unclouded day—

A little and a lone green lane
That opened on a common wide—
A distant, dreamy, dim blue chain
Of mountains circling every side—

A heaven so clear, an earth so calm,
So sweet, so soft, so hushed an air
And, deepening still the dreamlike charm,
Wild moor-sheep feeding everywhere—

That was the scene—I knew it well
I knew the path-ways far and near
That winding o'er each billowy swell
Marked out the tracks of wandering deer*

Could I have lingered but an hour
It well had paid a week of toil
But truth has banished fancy's power*
I hear my dungeon bars* recoil—

Even as I stood with raptured eye
Absorbed in bliss so deep and dear
My hour of rest had fleeted by
And given me back to weary care*—

12

E. April 17ᵗʰ 1839—

By R. Gleneden*—

From our evening fireside now,
Merry laugh and cheerful tone,
Smiling eye and cloudless brow,
Mirth and music all are flown:

Yet the grass before the door
Grows as green in April rain;
And as blithely as of yore
Larks have poured their day-long strain.

Is it fear, or is it sorrow
Checks the stagnant stream of joy?
Do we tremble that tomorrow
May our present peace destroy?

For past misery are we weeping?
What is past can hurt no more;
And the gracious Heavens are keeping
Aid for that which lies before—

One is absent,* and for one
Cheerless, chill is our hearthstone—
One is absent, and for him
Cheeks are pale and eyes are dim—

Arthur, brother, Gondal's shore
Rested from the battle's roar—
Arthur, brother, we returned
Back to Desmond lost and mourned:

Thou didst purchase by thy fall
Home for us and peace for all;
Yet, how darkly dawned that day—
Dreadful was the price to pay!*

Just as once, through sun and mist
I have climbed the mountain's breast
Still my gun with certain aim
Brought to earth the fluttering game:

But the very dogs repined,
Though I called with whistle shrill
Listlessly they lagged behind,
Looking backward o'er the hill*—

Sorrow was not vocal there;
Mute their pain and my dispair
But the joy of life was flown
He was gone, and we were lone—

So it is by morn and eve—
So it is in field and hall—
For the absent one we grieve,
One being absent, saddens All—

13

A.G.A.   To the bluebell*—   E. May 9th 1839.

Sacred watcher, wave thy bells!
Fair hill flower and woodland child!
Dear to me in deep green dells—
Dearest on the mountains wild—

Blue bell, even as all devine
I have seen my darling* shine—
Bluebell, even as wan and frail
I have seen my darling fail—
Thou hast found a voice for me—
And soothing words are breathed by thee—

Thus they murmer, 'Summer's Sun
Warms me till my life is done—
Would I rather choose to die
Under winter's ruthless sky?

'Glad I bloom—and calm I fade
Weeping twilight dews my bed
Mourner, mourner dry thy tears.
Sorrow comes with lengthened years!'

14
May 19 1839*

I am the only being whose doom
No tongue would ask no eye would mourn
I've never caused a thought of gloom
A smile of joy since I was born

In secret pleasure—secret tears
This changeful life has slipped away
As freindless after 18 years
As lone as on my natal day

There have been times I cannot hide
There have been times when this was drear
When my sad soul forgot its pride
And longed for one to love me here

But those were in the early glow
Of feelings not subdued by care
And they have died so long ago
I hardly now beleive they were

First melted off the hope of youth
Then Fancy's rainbow fast withdrew
And then experience told me truth
In mortal bosoms never grew

'Twas greif enough to think mankind
All servile insincere—*
But worse to trust to my own mind
And find the same corruption there

15

E J Brontë   July 12th
1839

And now the housedog streched once more
His limbs upon the glowing floor
The children half resumed their play
Though from the warm hearth scared away
The goodwife left her spinning wheel
And spread with smiles the evening meal
The Shepherd placed a seat and pressed
To their poor fare his unknown guest*
And he unclasped his mantle now
And raised the covering from his brow
Said, voyagers by land and sea
Were seldom feasted daintily
And checked his host by adding stern
He'd no refinement to unlearn
A silence settled on the room
The cheerful welcome sank to gloom
But not those words though cold and high
So froze their hospitable joy
No—there was something in his face
Some nameless thing they could not trace
And something in his voice's tone
Which turned their blood as chill as stone
The ringlets of his long black hair
Fell o'er a cheek most ghastly fair
Youthful he seemed—but worn as they

Who spend too soon their youthful day
When his glance drooped 'twas hard to quell
Unbidden feelings sudden swell
And pity scarce her tears could hide
So sweet that brow with all its pride
But when upraised his eye would dart
An icey shudder through the heart
Compassion changed to horror then
And fear to meet that gaze again
It was not hatred's tiger-glare
Nor the wild anguish of dispair
It was not artless misery
Which mocks at friendship's sympathy
No—lightening all unearthly shone
Deep in that dark eye's circling zone
Such withering* lightening as we deem
None but a spectre's look may beam
And glad they were when he turned away
And wrapt him in his mantle grey*
Leant down his head upon his arm
And veiled from view their basilisk charm*

16

14 November 1839 [*Poems* 1846]

'Well, some may hate and some may scorn
And some may quite forget thy name
But my sad heart must ever mourn
Thy ruined hopes, thy blighted fame'—

'Twas thus I thought an hour ago
Even weeping o'er that wretch's woe—
One word* turned back my gushing tears
And lit my altered eye with sneers—
'Then bless the friendly dust,' I said,
'That hides thy unlamented head
Vain* as thou wert, and weak as vain
The slave of Falsehood, pride and pain—
My heart has nought akin to thine—
Thy soul is powerless over mine'

But these were thoughts that vanished too
Unwise, unholy and untrue—
Do I despise the timid deer
Because his limbs are fleet with fear?
Or would I mock the wolf's death-howl
Because his form is gaunt and foul?*
Or hear with joy the leveret's* cry
Because it cannot bravely die?
No—then above his memory
Let pity's heart* as tender be
Say 'Earth, lie lightly on that breast,*
And kind Heaven, grant that spirit rest!'

17

May 18 1840—

If greif for greif can touch thee,
If answering woe for woe,
If any ruth can melt thee
Come to me now!

I cannot be more lonely,
More drear I cannot be!
My worn heart throbs so wildly
'Twill break for thee—

And when the world despises—
When Heaven repells my prayer—
Will not mine angel comfort?
Mine idol* hear?

Yes by the tears I've poured,
By all my hours of pain
O I shall surely win thee
Beloved,* again!

18

1 March 1841 [*Poems* 1846]

Riches I hold in light esteem
And Love I laugh to scorn
And lust of Fame was but a dream
That vanished with the morn—

And if I pray—the only prayer
That moves my lips for me
Is—'Leave the heart that now I bear
And give me liberty'—

Yes—as my swift days near their goal
'Tis all that I implore—
Through Life and death, a chainless soul*
With courage to endure!—

19

May 16th 1841

Shall Earth no more inspire thee,
Thou lonely dreamer now?
Since passion may not fire thee
Shall Nature cease to bow?

Thy mind is ever moving
In regions dark to thee;
Recall its useless roving—
Come back and dwell with me—

I know my mountain breezes
Enchant and soothe thee still—
I know my sunshine pleases
Despite thy wayward will—

When day with evening blending
Sinks from the summer sky,

I've seen thy spirit bending
In fond idolatry*—

I've watched thee every hour—
I know my mighty sway—
I know my magic power
To drive thy greifs away—

Few hearts to mortals given
On earth so wildly pine
Yet none would ask a Heaven
More like the Earth than thine*—

Then let my winds caress thee—
Thy comrade let me be—
Since nought beside can bless thee
Return and dwell with me—

20

Geraldine*   E. August 17th 1841.

'Twas night, her comrades gathered all
Within their city's rocky wall;
When flowers were closed and day was o'er
Their joyous hearts awoke the more

But lonely, in her distant cave
She heard the river's restless wave
Chafing its banks with dreamy flow;
Music for mirth, and wail for woe—

Palmtrees and cedars towering high*
Deepened the gloom of evening's sky
And thick did raven ringlets veil
Her forehead, drooped like lily pale

Yet I could hear my lady sing;
I knew she did not mourn,

For never yet from sorrow's spring
Such witching* notes were born

Thus poured she in that cavern wild
The voice of feelings warm
As, bending o'er her beauteous child
She clasped its sleeping form—

   'Why sank so soon the summer sun
   From our Zedora's* skies?
   I was not tired, my darling one,
   Of gazing in thine eyes—

   'Methought the heaven whence thou hast come
   Was lingering there awhile
   And Earth seemed such an alien home
   They did not dare to smile.

   'Methought each moment, something strange
   Within their circles shone
   And yet, through every magic change
   They were Brenzaida's own.

   'Methought—What thought I not, sweet love?
   My whole heart centred there;
   I breathed not but to send above
   One gush of ardent prayer.

   'Bless it, my gracious God! I cried,
   Preserve thy mortal shrine
   For thine own sake, be thou its guide
   And keep it still devine!

   'Say, sin shall never blanche that cheek
   Nor suffering charge that brow
   Speak, in thy mercy maker, speak
   And seal it safe from woe!

   'Why did I doubt? In God's control
   Our mutual fates remain

And pure as now, my angel's soul
<u>Must</u> go to heaven again!'*

The revellers in the city slept,
My lady, in her woodland bed;
I, watching o'er her slumbers wept
As one who mourns the dead!

21

September 1st 1841–

E.   Rosina

Weeks of wild delirium past—
Weeks of fevered pain,
Rest from suffering comes at last—
Reason dawns again—

It was a pleasant April day
Declining to the afternoon
Sunshine upon her pillow lay
As warm as middle June.

It told her how unconsciously
Early spring had hurried by
'Ah Time has not delayed for me!'
She murmured with a sigh.

'Angora's hills have heard their tread
The crimson flag is planted there*—
Elderno's waves* are rolling red,
While *I* lie fettered here?

'—Nay, rather, Gondal's shaken throne
Is now secure and free;
And my King Julius reigns alone,
Debtless, alas, to me!'

Loud was the sudden gush of woe
From those who watched around;
Rosina turned and sought to know
Why burst that boding sound.

'What then, my dreams are false,' she said
'Come maidens, answer me.
Has Almedore* in battle fled?
Have slaves subdued the free?

'I know it all, he could not bear
To leave me dying far away—
He fondly, madly lingered here
And we have lost the day!

'But check those coward sobs, and bring
My robes and smooth my tangled hair:
A noble victory you shall sing
For every hour's dispair!

'When will he come? 'T will soon be night—
He'll come when evening falls—
Oh I shall weary for the light
To leave my lonely halls!'

She turned her pallid face aside
As she would seek repose;
But dark Ambition's thwarted pride
Forbade her lids to close—

And still on all who waited by
Oppressive mystery hung;
And swollen with greif was every eye
And chained was every tongue.

They whispered nought, but, 'Lady, sleep,
Dear Lady, slumber now!
Had we not bitter cause to weep
While you were laid so low?

'And Hope can hardly deck the cheek
With sudden signs of cheer
When it has worn through many a week
The stamp of anguish drear'—

Fierce grew Rosina's gloomy gaze;
She cried, 'Dissemblers, own
Exina's* arms in victory blaze
Brenzaida's crest is down'

'Well, since it must be told, Lady
Brenzaida's crest *is* down
Brenzaida's sun is set, Lady,
His empire overthrown!

'He died beneath this palace dome—
True hearts on every side—
Among his guards, within his home
Our glorious monarch died

'I saw him fall, I saw the gore
From his heart's fountain swell
And, mingling on the marble floor
His murderer's life-blood fell—

'And now, mid northern mountains lone
His desert grave is made;
And, Lady, of your love, alone
Remains a mortal shade!'*

22

Yes holy be thy resting place*
Wherever thou may'st lie
The sweetest winds breathe on thy face
The softest of the sky

And will not guardian Angels send
Kind dreams and thoughts of love

Though I no more may watchful bend
Thy [?loved] repose above?

And will not heaven itself bestow
A beam of glory there
That summer's grass more green may grow
And summer's flowers more fair

Farewell Farewell 'tis hard to part
Yet loved one it must be
I would not rend another heart
Not even by blessing thee

Go we must break affection's chain
Forget the hopes of years
Nay [?linger] not wouldst thou remain
To waken wilder tears

This herald breeze with thee and me
Roved in the dawning day
And thou shouldest be where it shall be
Ere evening far away

23

M G – For the U.S.*   December 19th 1843

'Twas yesterday at early dawn
I watched the falling snow;
A drearier scene on winter morn
Was never streched below—

I could not see the mountains round
But I knew by the wind's wild roar
How every drift in their glens profound
Was deepening ever more—

And then I thought of Ula's bowers
Beyond the Southern Sea

Her tropic prairies bright with flowers
And rivers wandering free—

I thought of many a happy day
Spent in her Eden isle
With my dear comrades young and gay
All scattered now so far away*
But not forgot the while!

Who that has breathed that heavenly air
To northern climes would come
To Gondal's mists and moorlands drear
And sleet and frozen gloom?

Spring brings the swallow and the lark
But what will winter bring?
Its twilight noons and evenings dark
To match the gifts of Spring?

No, look with me o'er that sullen main
If thy spirit's eye can see
There are brave ships floating back again
That no calm southern port could chain
From Gondal's stormy sea

O how the hearts of the voyagers beat
To feel the frost-wind blow!
What flower in Ula's gardens sweet
Is worth one flake of snow?

The blast which almost rends their sail
Is welcome as a friend;
It brings them home, that thundering gale
Home to their journy's end;

Home to our souls whose wearying sighs
Lament their absence drear
And feel how bright even winter skies
Would shine if they were here!

24

E.W. to A.G.A.*   March 11ᵗʰ 1844

How few, of all the hearts that loved,
Are grieving for thee now!
And why should mine, to night, be moved
With such a sense of woe?

Too often, thus, when left alone
Where none my thoughts can see,
Comes back a word, a passing tone
From thy strange history—

Sometimes I seem to see thee rise
A glorious child again—
All virtues beaming from thine eyes
That ever honoured men—

Courage and Truth, a generous breast
where Love and Gladness lay;
A being whose very Memory blest
And made the mourner gay—

O, fairly spread thy early sail
And fresh and pure and free
Was the first impulse of the gale
That urged life's wave for thee!

Why did the pilot, too confiding
Dream o'er that Ocean's foam?
And trust in Pleasure's careless guiding
To bring his vessel home?

For, well, he knew what dangers frowned,
What mists would gather dim,
What rocks and shelves and sands lay round
Between his port and him—

The very brightness of the sun,
The splendour of the main,

The wind that bore him wildly on
Should not have warned in vain

An anxious gazer from the shore,
I marked the whitening wave
And wept above thy fate the more
Because I could not save—

It recks not now, when all is over,
But, yet my heart will be
A mourner still, though freind and lover
Have both forgotten thee!

25

May 1ˢᵗ 1844 [*Poems* 1846]

The linnet in the rocky dells,*
The moorlark* in the air,
The bee among the heather bells
That hide my lady fair—

The wilddeer browse above her breast;*
The wildbirds raise their brood,
And they, her smiles of love carest,
Have left her solitude!

I ween,* that when the grave's dark wall
Did first her form retain
They thought their hearts could ne'er recall
The light of joy again—

They thought the tide of greif would flow
Unchecked through future years
But where is all their anguish now,
And where are all their tears?

Well, let them fight for Honour's breath
Or Pleasure's shade* pursue—

The Dweller in the land of Death,
Is changed and careless too—

And if their eyes should watch and weep
Till sorrows' source were dry
She would not in her tranquil sleep
Return a single sigh—

Blow, west wind, by the lonely mound
And murmer, summer streams,
There is no need of other sound*
To soothe my Lady's dreams—
                                        EW*

26

3 September 1844 [*Poems* 1846]

To Imagination

When weary with the long day's care
And earthly change from pain to pain
And lost and ready to dispair
Thy kind voice calls me back again—
O my true friend,* I am not lone
While thou canst speak with such a tone!

So hopeless is the world without
The world within I doubly prize
Thy world, where guile and hate and doubt
And cold suspicion never rise—
Where thou and I and Liberty
Have undisputed sovereignty.

What matters it that all around
Danger and greif and darkness lie
If but within our bosom's bound
We hold a bright unsullied sky
Warm with ten thousand mingled rays
Of suns that know no winter days—

Reason indeed may oft complain
For Nature's sad reality
And tell the suffering heart how vain
Its cherished dreams must always be
And Truth may rudely trample down
The flowers of fancy newly blown

But thou art ever there to bring
The hovering visions back and breathe
New glories o'er the blighted spring
And call a lovelier life from death
And whisper with a voice divine
Of real worlds as bright as thine.*

I trust not to thy phantom bliss*
Yet still, in evening's quiet hour
With Never failing thankfulness
I welcome thee benignant power
Sure solacer of human cares
And brighter hope when hope dispairs—

27

EJB. Nov 11th 1844
From a Dungeon Wall in the Southern College*—JB. Sept. 1825*—

'Listen! when your hair like mine
Takes a tint of silver grey,
When your eyes, with dimmer shine,
Watch life's bubbles float away,

'When you, young man, have borne like me*
The weary weight of sixty three
Then shall penance sore be paid
For these hours so wildly squandered
And the words that now fall dead
On your ears be deeply pondered
Pondered and approved at last
But their virtue will be past!

'Glorious is the prize of Duty
Though she be a serious power
Treacherous all the lures of Beauty
Thorny bud and poisonous flower!

'Mirth is but a mad beguiling
Of the golden gifted Time—
Love—a demon meteor wiling
Heedless feet to gulfs of crime.

'Those who follow earthly pleasure
Heavenly knowledge will not lead
Wisdom hides from them her treasure,
Virtue bids them evil speed!

'Vainly may their hearts, repenting,
Seek for aid in future years—
Wisdom scorned knows no relenting—
Virtue is not won by tears

'Fain would we your steps reclaim
Waken fear and holy shame
And to this end, our council well
And kindly doomed you to a cell
Whose darkness, may perchance, disclose
A beacon-guide from sterner woes—'

So spake my Judge—then seized his lamp
And left me in the dungeon damp,
A vault-like place whose stagnant air
Suggests and nourishes dispair!

Rosina, this had never been
Except for you, my despot queen!
Except for you the billowy sea
Would now be tossing under me
The wind's wild voice my bosom thrill
And my glad heart bound wilder still

Flying before the rapid gale
Those wondrous southern isles* to hail

Which wait for my companions free
But thank your passion—not for me!

You know too well—and so do I
Your haughty beauty's sovereignty
Yet have I read those falcon eyes*—
Have dived into their mysteries—
Have studied long their glance and feel
It is not love those eyes reveal—

They Flash—they burn with lightening shine
But not with such fond fire as mine;
The tender star fades faint and wan
Before Ambition's scorching sun—
So deem I now—and Time will prove
If I have wronged Rosina's love—

28

3 March 1845 [*Poems* 1846]

R Alcona to J Brenzaida*

Cold in the earth* and the deep snow piled above thee!
Far, far removed cold in the dreary grave!
Have I forgot, my Only Love, to love thee,
Severed at last by Time's allwearing wave?

Now, when alone, do my thoughts no longer hover
Over the mountains on Angora's shore:
Resting their wings where heath and fern-leaves cover
That noble heart for ever, ever more?*

Cold in the earth, and fifteen wild Decembers*
From those brown hills have melted into spring—
Faithful indeed is the spirit that remembers
After such years of change and suffering!

Sweet Love of youth, forgive if I forget thee
While the world's tide is bearing me along

Sterner desires and darker Hopes beset me
Hopes which obscure but cannot do thee wrong—

No other sun has lightened up my heaven;
No other star has ever shone for me
All my life's bliss from thy dear life was given—
All my life's bliss is in the grave with thee

But when the days of golden dreams had perished
And even Dispair was powerless to destroy
Then did I learn how existence could be cherished
Strengthened and fed without the aid of joy

Then did I check the tears of useless passion,
Weaned my young soul from yearning after thine;
Sternly denied its burning wish to hasten
Down to that tomb already more than mine!

And even yet, I dare not let it languish,
Dare not indulge in memory's rapturous pain
Once drinking deep of that devinest anguish
How could I seek the empty world again?

29

May 28th 1845.

A.E. and R.C.*

Heavy hangs the raindrop
From the burdened spray;
Heavy broods the damp mist
On Uplands far away;

Heavy looms the dull sky,
Heavy rolls the sea—
And heavy beats the young heart
Beneath that lonely Tree—

Never has a blue streak
Cleft the clouds since morn—

Never has his grim Fate
Smiled since he was born—

Frowning on the infant,
Shadowing childhood's joy;
Guardian angel knows not
That melancholy boy.

Day is passing swiftly
Its sad and sombre prime;
Youth is fast invading
Sterner manhood's time—

All the flowers are praying
For sun before they close
And he prays too, unknowing,
That sunless human rose!

Blossems, that the westwind
Has never wooed to blow
Scentless are your petals,
Your dew as cold as snow.

Soul, where kindred kindness
No early promise woke
Barren is your beauty
As weed upon the rock—

Wither, Brothers, wither,
You were vainly given—
Earth reserves no blessing
For the unblessed of Heaven!*

Child of Delight! with sunbright hair*
And seablue, sea-deep eyes
Spirit of Bliss, what brings thee here
Beneath these sullen skies?

Thou shouldest live in eternal spring
Where endless day is never dim
Why, seraph, has thy erring wing
Borne thee down to weep with him?

'Ah, not from heaven am I descended
And I do not come to mingle tears
But sweet is day though with shadows blended
And though clouded, sweet are youthful years—

'I, the image of light and gladness
Saw and pitied that mournful boy
I swore to take his gloomy sadness
And give to him my beamy joy—

'Heavy and dark the night is closing
Heavy and dark may its biding be
Better for all from greif reposing
And better for all who watch like me—

'Guardian angel, he lacks no longer;
Evil fortune he need not fear;
Fate is strong but Love is stronger
And more unsleeping than angel's care—'

30

October 9th 1845 [*Poems* 1846; part only]

Julian. M. and A.G. Rochelle*—

Silent is the House—all are laid asleep;
One, alone, looks out o'er the snow-wreaths* deep;
Watching every cloud, dreading every breeze
That whirls the wildering drifts and bends the groaning trees—

Cheerful is the hearth, soft the matted floor
Not one shivering gust creeps through pane or door
The little lamp burns straight; its rays shoot strong and far
I trim it well to be the Wanderer's guiding star—

Frown my haughty sire, chide my angry Dame;
Set your slaves to spy, threaten me with shame;
But neither sire nor dame, nor prying serf shall know
What angel nightly tracks that waste of winter snow—

In the dungeon crypts idly did I stray
Reckless of the lives wasting there away;
'Draw the ponderous bars, open Warder stern!'
He dare not say me nay—the hinges harshly turn—

'Our guests are darkly lodged' I whispered gazing through
The vault whose grated eye showed heaven more grey than blue;
(This was when glad Spring laughed in awaking pride.)
'Aye, darkly lodged enough!' returned my sullen guide.

Then, God forgive my youth, forgive my careless tongue!
I scoffed as the chill chains on the damp flagstones rung;
'Confined in triple walls, art thou so much to fear,
That we must bind thee down and clench thy fetters here?'

The captive raised her face; it was as soft and mild
As sculptured marble saint or slumbering, unweaned child*
It was so soft and mild, it was so sweet and fair
Pain could not trace a line nor greif a shadow there!

The captive raised her hand and pressed it to her brow
'I have been struck,' she said, 'and I am suffering now
Yet these are little worth, your bolts and irons strong
And were they forged in steel they could not hold me long—'

Hoarse laughed the jailor grim, 'Shall I be won to hear
Dost think fond, dreaming wretch that I shall grant thy prayer?
Or better still, wilt melt my master's heart with groans?
Ah sooner might the sun thaw down these granite stones!—

'My master's voice is low, his aspect bland and kind
But hard as hardest flint the soul that lurks behind:
And I am rough and rude, yet, not more rough to see
Than is the hidden ghost which has its home in me!'

About her lips there played a smile of almost scorn
'My friend,' she gently said, 'you have not heard me mourn
When you, my parents' lives—my lost life, can restore
Then may I weep and sue, but, never, Friend, before!'

Her head sank on her hands, its fair curls swept the ground
The Dungeon seemed to swim in strange confusion round—
'Is she so near to death?' I murmured half aloud
And kneeling, parted back the floating golden cloud

Alas, how former days upon my heart were borne
How memory mirrored then the prisoner's joyous morn—
Too blithe, too loving Child, too warmly, wildly gay!
Was that the wintry close of thy celestial May?

She knew me and she sighed 'Lord Julian, can it be,
Of all my playmates, you, alone, remember me?
Nay start not at my words, unless you deem it shame
To own from conquered foe, a once familiar name—

'I can not wonder now at aught the world will do
And insult and contempt I lightly brook from you,
Since those who vowed away their souls to win my love
Around this living grave like utter strangers move!

'Nor has one voice been raised to plead that I might die
Not buried under earth but in the open sky;
By ball or speedy knife or headsman's* skillful blow—
A quick and welcome pang instead of lingering woe!

'Yet, tell them, Julian, all, I am not doomed to wear
Year after year in gloom and desolate despair;
A messenger of Hope comes every night to me
And offers, for short life, eternal liberty—*

'He comes with western winds, with evening's wandering airs,
With that clear dusk of heaven that brings the thickest stars;
Winds take a pensive tone and stars a tender fire
And visions rise and change which kill me with desire—

'Desire for nothing known in my maturer years
When joy grew mad with awe at counting future tears;
When, if my spirit's sky was full of flashes warm,
I knew not whence they came from sun or thunder storm;

'But first a hush of peace, a soundless calm descends;
The struggle of distress and fierce impatience ends;
Mute music soothes my breast—unuttered harmony*
That I could never dream till earth was lost to me.

'Then dawns the Invisible, the Unseen its truth reveals;
My outward sense is gone, my inward essence feels—
Its wings are almost free, its home, its harbour found;
Measuring the gulf it stoops and dares the final bound!

'Oh, dreadful is the check—intense the agony
When the ear begins to hear and the eye begins to see;
When the pulse begins to throb, the brain to think again,
The soul to feel the flesh and the flesh to feel the chain!*

'Yet I would lose no sting, would wish no torture less;
The more that anguish racks the earlier it will bless:
And robed in fires of Hell, or bright with heavenly shine
If it but herald Death, the vision is divine—'*

She ceased to speak and I, unanswering watched her there
Not daring now to touch one lock of silken hair—
As I had knelt in scorn, on the dank floor I knelt still,
My fingers on the links of that iron hard and chill—

I heard and yet heard not the surly keeper growl;
I saw, yet did not see, the flagstones damp and foul;
The keeper, to and fro, paced by the bolted door
And shivered as he walked and as he shivered, swore—

While my cheek glowed in flame, I marked that he did rave
Of air that froze his blood and moisture like the grave—
'We have been Two hours good!' he muttered peevishly,
Then, loosing off his belt the rusty dungeon key,

He said, 'you may be pleased, Lord Julian, still to stay
But duty will not let me linger here all day;
If I might go, I'd leave this badge of mine with you
Not doubting that you'd prove a jailor stern and true'

I took the proffered charge; the captive's drooping lid
Beneath its shady lash a sudden lightening hid
Earth's hope was not so dead heaven's home was not so dear
I read it in that flash of longing quelled by fear

Then like a tender child whose hand did just enfold
Safe in its eager grasp a bird it wept to hold
When pierced with one wild glance from the troubled hazle eye
It gushes into tears and lets its treasure fly

Thus ruth and selfish love together striving tore
The heart all newly taught to pity and adore;
If I should break the chain I felt my bird would go
Yet I must break the chain or seal the prisoner's woe.

Short strife what rest could soothe—what peace could visit me
While she lay pining there for Death to set her free?
'Rochelle, the dungeons teem with foes to gorge our hate—
Thou art too young to die by such a bitter fate!'

With hurried blow on blow I struck the fetters through
Regardless how that deed my after hours might rue
Oh, I was over-blest by the warm unasked embrace—
By the smile of grateful joy that lit her angel face!

And I was overblest—aye, more than I could dream
When, faint, she turned aside from noon's unwonted beam;
When though the cage was wide—the heaven around it lay—
Its pinion would not waft my wounded dove away—

Through thirteen anxious weeks of terror-blent delight
I guarded her by day and guarded her by night
While foes were prowling near and Death gazed greedily
And only Hope remained a faithful friend to me—

Then oft with taunting smile, I heard my kindred tell
'How Julian loved his hearth and sheltering rooftree well;
How the trumpet's voice might call the battle-standard wave
But Julian had no heart to fill a patriot's grave—'

And I, who am so quick to answer sneer with sneer;
So ready to condemn to scorn a coward's fear—
I held my peace like one whose conscience keeps him dumb
And saw my kinsmen go—and lingered still at home.

Another hand than mine, my rightful banner held
And gathered my renown on Freedom's crimson field
Yet I had no desire the glorious prize to gain—
It needed braver nerve to face the world's disdain—

And by the patient strength that could that world defy;
By suffering with calm mind, contempt and calumny;
By never-doubting love, unswerving constancy,
Rochelle, I earned at last an equal love from thee!

31

14 September 1846

Why ask to know the date—the clime?*
More than mere words they cannot be:
Men knelt to God and worshipped crime,
And crushed the helpless even as we—

But, they had learnt from length of strife—
Of civil war and anarchy
To laugh at death and look on life
With somewhat lighter sympathy.

It was the autumn of the year;
The time to labouring peasants, dear:
Week after week, from noon to noon,
September shone as bright as June—
Still, never hand a sickle held;
The crops were garnered in the field—
Trod out, and ground by horses' feet
While every ear was milky sweet;
And kneaded on the threshing-floor
With mire of tears and human gore.

Some said they thought that heaven's pure rain
Would hardly bless those fields again.
Not so—the all-benignant skies
Rebuked that fear of famished eyes—
July passed on with showers and dew,
And August glowed in showerless blue;
No harvest time could be more fair
Had harvest fruits but ripened there.

And I confess that hate of rest,
And thirst for things abandoned now,
Had weaned me from my country's breast
And brought me to that land of woe.

Enthusiast—in a name delighting,*
My alien sword I drew to free
One race, beneath two standards fighting,
For Loyalty, and Liberty—
When kindred strive, God help the weak!
A brother's ruth 'tis vain to seek:
At first, it hurt my chivalry
To join them in their cruelty;*
But I grew hard—I learnt to wear
An iron front to terror's prayer;
I learnt to turn my ears away
From torture's groans, as well as they.
By force I learnt—what power had I
To say the conquered should not die?
What heart, one trembling foe to save
When hundreds daily filled the grave?
Yet, there *were* faces that could move
A moment's flash of human love;
And there were fates that made me feel
I was not to the centre, steel—
I've often witnessed wise men fear
To meet distress which they foresaw;
And seeming cowards nobly bear
A doom that thrilled the brave with awe;

Strange proofs I've seen, how hearts could hide
Their secret with a life-long pride,

And then, reveal it as they died—
Strange courage, and strange weakness too,
In that last hour when most are true,
And timid natures strangely nerved
To deeds from which the desperate swerved.
These I may tell, but leave them now.
Go with me where my thoughts would go;
Now all today, and all last night
I've had one scene before my sight—

Wood-shadowed dales; a harvest moon
Unclouded in its glorious noon;
A solemn landscape, wide and still;
A red fire on a distant hill—
A line of fires, and deep below,
Another dusker, drearier glow—
Charred beams, and lime, and blackened stones
Self-piled in cairns* o'er burning bones
And lurid flames that licked the wood
Then quenched their glare in pools of blood—
But yestereve—No! never care;
Let street and suburb smoulder there—
Smoke-hidden, in the winding glen,
They lay too far to vex my ken.*
Four score shot down—all veterans strong—
One prisoner spared, their leader young—
And he within his house was laid,
Wounded, and weak and nearly dead.
We gave him life against his will;
For he entreated us to kill—
But statue-like we saw his tears—
And harshly fell our captain's sneers!

'Now heaven forbid!' with scorn he said
'That noble gore our hands should shed
Like common blood—retain thy breath
Or scheme, if thou canst purchase death—
When men are poor we sometimes hear
And pitying grant that dastard prayer;
When men are rich, we make them buy
The pleasant privilege, to die—

O, we have castles reared for kings
Embattled towers and buttressed wings
Thrice three feet thick, and guarded well
With chain, and bolt, and sentinel!
We build our despots' dwellings sure;
Knowing they love to live secure—
And our respect for royalty
Extends to thy estate and thee!'

The suppliant groaned; his moistened eye
Swam wild and dim with agony—
The gentle blood could ill sustain
Degrading taunts, unhonoured pain.
Bold had he shown himself to lead;
Eager to smite and proud to bleed—
A man, amid the battle's storm;
An infant in the after calm.

Beyond the town his mansion stood
Girt round with pasture-land and wood;
And there our wounded soldiers lying
Enjoyed the ease of wealth in dying:

For him, no mortal more than he
Had softened life with luxury;
And truly did our priest declare
'Of good things he had had his share.'

We lodged him in an empty place,
The full moon beaming on his face
Through shivered glass, and ruins, made
Where shell and ball the fiercest played.
I watched his ghastly couch beside
Regardless if he lived or died—
Nay, muttering curses on the breast
Whose ceaseless moans denied me rest:

'Twas hard, I know, 'twas harsh to say,
'Hell snatch thy worthless soul away!'
But then 'twas hard my lids to keep
Night following night,* estranged from sleep.

Captive and keeper, both outworn,
Each in his misery yearned for morn;
Even though returning morn should bring
Intenser toil and suffering.

Slow, slow it came! Our dreary room
Grew drearier with departing gloom;
Yet, as the west wind warmly blew
I felt my pulses bound anew,
And turned to him—nor breeze, nor ray
Revived that mould of shattered clay,
Scarce conscious of his pain he lay—
Scarce conscious that my hands removed
The glittering toys his lightness loved;
The jewelled rings, and locket fair
Where rival curls of silken hair,
Sable and brown revealed to me
A tale of doubtful constancy.

'Forsake the world without regret;'
I murmured in contemptuous tone;
'The world, poor wretch, will soon forget
Thy noble name, when thou art gone!
Happy, if years of slothful shame
Could perish like a noble name—
If God did no account require
And being with breathing might expire!'*
And words of such contempt I said
Cold insults o'er a dying bed
Which as they darken memory now
Disturb my pulse and flush my brow;
I know that Justice holds in store,
Reprisals for those days of gore—
Not for the blood, but for the sin
Of stifling mercy's voice within.
The blood spilt gives no pang at all;
It is my conscience haunting me,
Telling how oft my lips shed gall
On many a thing too weak to be,
Even in thought, at enmity—
And whispering ever, when I pray,

'God will repay—God will repay!'
He does repay and soon and well
The deeds that turn this earth to hell
The wrongs that aim a venomed dart
Through nature at the Eternal Heart—
Surely my cruel tongue was cursed
I know my prisoner heard me speak
A transient gleam of feeling burst
And wandered o'er his haggard cheek
And from his quivering lids there stole
A look to melt a demon's soul
A silent prayer more powerful far
Than any breathed petitions are
Pleading in mortal agony
To mercy's Source but not to me—
Now I recall that glance and groan
And wring my hands in vain distress
Then I was adamantine stone
Nor felt one touch of tenderness*
My plunder ta'en I left him there
To struggle with his last despair*
Regardless of the wildered cry
Which wailed for death yet wailed to die
I left him there unwatched alone
And eager sought the court below
Where o'er a trough of chiselled stone
An ice cold well did gurgling flow
The water in its basin shed
A stranger tinge of fiery red.
I drank and scarcely marked the hue
My food was dyed with crimson too
As I went out a wretched child
With wasted cheek and ringlets wild
A shape of fear and misery
Raised up her [?helpless] hands to me
And begged her father's face to see
I spurned the piteous wretch away
Thy father's [face] is lifeless clay
As thine mayst be ere fall of day
Unless the truth be quickly told
Where thou hast hid thy father's gold

Yet in the intervals of pain
He heard my taunts and moaned again
And mocking moans did I reply
And asked him why he would not die
In noble silent agony—uncomplaining
Was it not foul disgrace and shame
To thus disgrace his ancient name?
Just then a comrade came hurrying in
Alas he cried sin genders sin
For every soldier slain they've sworn
To hang up five come morn.
They've ta'en of stranglers* sixty three
Full thirty from one company
And all my father's family
And comrade thou hadst only one
They've ta'en thy all thy little son
Down at my captive's feet I fell
I had no option in despair
As thou wouldst save thy soul from hell
My heart's own darling bid them spare
Or human hate and hate divine
Blight every orphan flower of thine
He raised his head—from death beguiled
He wakened up he almost smiled
I lost last night my only child
Twice in my arms twice on my knee
You stabbed my child and laughed at me
And so, with choking voice he said
I trust I hope in God she's dead
Yet not to thee not even to thee
Would I return such misery
[?Such is] that fearful grief I know
I will not cause thee equal woe
Write that they harm no infant there
Write that it is my latest prayer
I wrote—he signed and thus did save
My treasure from the gory grave
And O my soul longed wildly then
To give his saviour life again.*
But heedless of my gratitude
The silent corpse before me lay*

And still methinks in gloomy mood
I see it fresh as yesterday
The sad face raised imploringly
To mercy's God and not to me—*
The last look of that glazing eye
I could not rescue him his child
I found alive and tended well
But she was full of anguish wild
And hated me like we hate hell
And weary with her savage woe
One moonless night I let her go

32

May 13th 1848

Why ask to know what date what clime
There dwelt our own humanity*
Power-worshipers from earliest time
Foot-kissers of triumphant crime
Crushers of helpless misery
Crushing down Justice honouring Wrong
If that be feeble this be strong

Shedders of blood shedders of tears
Self-cursers avid of distress
Yet mocking heaven with senseless prayers
For mercy on the merciless

It was the autumn of the year
When grain grows yellow in the ear
Day after day from noon to noon,
That August's sun blazed bright as June

But we with unregarding eyes
Saw panting earth and glowing skies
No hand the reaper's sickle held
Nor bound the ripe sheaves in the field

Our corn was garnered months before
Threshed out and kneaded-up with gore*
Ground when the ears were milky sweet
With furious toil of hoofs and feet
I doubly cursed on foreign sod
Fought neither for my home nor God

ANNE BRONTË

Verses by Lady Geralda

Why when I hear the stormy breath,
Of the wild winter wind,*
Rushing o'er the mountain heath,
Does sadness fill my mind?

For long ago I loved to lie
Upon the pathless moor,
To hear the wild wind rushing by
With never ceasing roar;

Its sound was music then to me
Its wild and lofty voice
Made my heart beat exultingly
And my whole soul rejoice

But now, how different is the sound?
It takes another tone
And howls along the barren ground
With melancholy moan.

Why does the warm light of the sun
No longer cheer my eyes?
And why, is all the beauty gone,
From rosey morning skies?

Beneath this lone and dreary hill
There is a lovely vale
The purling of a crystal rill,
The sighing of the gale,

The sweet voice of the singing bird,
The wind among the trees,
Are ever in that valley heard;
While every passing breeze

Is loaded with the pleasant scent,
Of wild and lovely flowers.

To yonder vales I often went,
To pass my evening hours.

Last evening when I wander'd there
To soothe my weary heart
Why did the unexpected tear
From my sad eyelid start?

Why did the trees the buds the stream
Sing forth so joylessly?
And why did all the vally seem
So sadly changed to me?

I plucked a primrose* young and pale,
That grew beneath a tree
And then I hasten'd from the vale
Silent and thoughtfully.

Soon I was near my lofty home,
But when I cast my eye
Upon that flower so fair and lone
Why did I heave a sigh?

I thought of taking it again
To the vally where it grew
But soon I spurn'd that thought as vain
And weak and childish too.

And then I cast that flower away
To die and wither there;
But when I found it dead to-day
Why did I shed a tear?

O why are things so changed to me?
What gave me joy before
Now fills my heart with misery,
And nature smiles no more.

And why are all the beauties gone
From this my native hill?

Alas! my heart is changed alone,
Nature is constant still.

For when the heart is free from care,
What-ever meets the eye —
Is bright, and every sound we hear
Is full of melody.

The sweetest strain the wildest wind
The murmur of a stream
To the sad and weary mind
Like doleful death knells seem.

Father! thou hast long been dead
Mother! thou art gone
Brother! thou art far away
And I am left alone!*

Long before my mother died,
I was sad and lone
And when she departed too
Every joy was flown.

But the world's before me now
Why should I despair?
I will not spend my days in vain,
I will not linger here!

There is still a cherished hope
To cheer me on my way,
It is burning in my heart
With a feeble ray.

I will cheer the dying spark
And raise it to a flame
And it shall light me through the world,
And lead me on to fame.

I leave thee then my childhood's home
For all thy joys are gone

I leave thee through the world to roam
In search of fair renown.

From such a hopeless home to part
Is happiness to me
For nought can charm my weary heart
Except activity.

Anne Brontë
December—1836

100 lines*

2

Alexander and Zenobia

Fair was the evening and brightly the sun
Was shining on desart and grove,
Sweet were the breezes and balmy the flowers
And cloudless the heavens above.

It was Arabia's distant land
And peaceful was the hour
Two youthful figures lay reclined*
Deep in a shady bower.

One was a boy of just fourteen
Bold beautiful and bright
Soft raven curls hung clustering round
A brow of marble white.

The fair brow and the ruddy cheek
Spoke of less burning skies
Words cannot paint the look that beamed
In his dark lustrous eyes.

The other was a slender girl,
Blooming and young and fair,
The snowy neck was shaded with
The long bright sunny hair

And those deep eyes of watery blue
So sweetly sad they seem'd
And every feature in her face
With pensive sorrow teem'd

The youth beheld her saddened air
And smiling cheerfully
He said 'How pleasant is the land
Of sunny Araby!*

'Zenobia I never saw
A lovelier eve than this
I never felt my spirit raised
With more unbroken bliss!

'So deep the shades, so calm the hour,
So soft the breezes sigh,
So sweetly Philomel* begins
Her heavenly melody;

'So pleasant are the scents that rise
From flowers of loveliest hue
And more than all—Zenobia
I am alone with you!

'Are we not happy here alone
In such a heavenly spot?'
He looked to her with joyful smile
But she return'd it not

'Why are you sorrowful' he ask'd
And heav'd a bitter sigh
'O tell me why those drops of woe
Are gathering in your eye!'

'Gladly would I rejoice' she said
'But grief weighs down my heart.
Can I be happy when I know
To-morrow we must part?

'Yes Alexander I must see,
This happy land no more
At break of day I must return
To distant Gondal's shore.

'At morning we must bid farewell,
And at the close of day
You will be wandering alone
And I shall be away

'I shall be sorrowing for you
On the wide weltering sea
And you will perhaps have wander'd here
To sit and think of me.'

'And shall we part so <u>soon</u>' he cried
'<u>Must</u> we be torn away
<u>Shall</u> I be left to mourn alone
Will you no <u>longer</u> stay?

'And shall we never meet again—
Hearts that have grown together?
Must they at once be rent away
And kept apart for ever?'

'Yes Alexander we must part,
But we may meet again
For when I left my native land
I wept in anguish then.

'Never shall I forget the day,
I left its rocky shore
We thought that we had bid adieu
To meet on earth no more

'When we had parted how I wept
To see the mountains blue
Grow dimmer and more distant—till
They faded from my view.

'And you too wept—we little thought
After so long a time,
To meet again so suddenly
In such a distant clime.

'We met on Graecia's classic plains,
We part in Araby
And let us hope to meet again
Beneath our Gondal's sky.'

'Zenobia do you remember
A little lonely spring
Among Exina's woody hills*
Where blackbirds used to sing

'And when they ceased as day light faded
From the dusky sky
The pensive nightingale began
Her matchless melody.

'Sweet bluebells* used to flourish there,
And tall trees waved on high,
And through their ever sounding leaves
The soft wind used to sigh.

'At morning we have often played,
Beside that lonely well
At evening we have lingered there
Till dewy twilight fell.

'And when your fifteenth birthday comes,
Remember me my love
And think of what I said to you
In this sweet spicy grove

'At evening wander to that spring
And sit and wait for me
And ere the sun has ceased to shine
I will return to thee.

'Two years is a weary time
But it will soon be fled
And if you do not meet me—know
I am not false—but dead.'

     x   x   x   x   x

Sweetly the summer day declines
On forest, plain, and hill
And in that spacious palace hall*
So lonely wide and still.

Beside a window's open arch,
In the calm evening air,
All lonely sits a stately girl,
Graceful and young and fair;

The snowy lid and lashes long
Conceal her downcast eye,
She's reading—and till now the hours
Have passed unnoticed by.

But see she cannot fix her thoughts,
They are wandering away,
She looks towards a distant dell
Where sunny waters play;

And yet her spirit is not with
The scene she looks upon,
She muses with a mournful smile
On pleasures that are gone;

She looks upon the book again,
That chained her thoughts before,
And for a moment strives in vain
To fix her mind once more.

Then gently drops it on her knee
And looks into the sky,
While trembling drops are shining in
Her dark celestial eye

And thus alone and still she sits
Musing on years gone by.

Till with a sad and sudden smile
She rises up to go
And from the open window springs
On to the grass below.

Why does she fly so swiftly now
Adown the meadow green
And o'er the gently swelling hill
And the vale that lies between?

She passes under giant trees
That lift their arms on high
And slowly wave their mighty boughs
In the clear evening sky,

And now she threads a path that winds
Through deeply shaded groves
Where nought is heard but sighing gales
And murmuring turtle doves

She hastens on through sunless gloom
To a vista opening wide
A marble fountain sparkles there
With sweet flowers by its side

At intervals in the velvit grass
A few old Elm trees rise
While a warm flood of yellow light
Streams from the western skies

Is this her resting place? Ah no
She hastens onward still,
The startled deer before her fly
As she ascends the hill,

She does not rest till she has gained
A lonely purling spring,

Where zephyrs* wave the verdant trees
And birds in concert sing.

And there she stands and gazes round
With bright and searching eye
Then sadly sighing turns away
And looks upon the sky.

She sits down on the flowery turf
Her head droops on her hand
Her soft luxuriant golden curls
Are by the breezes fanned.

A sweet sad smile plays on her lips
Her heart is far away,
And thus she sits till twilight comes
To take the place of day,

But when she looks towards the west
And sees the sun is gone
And hears that every bird but one
To its nightly rest is flown

And sees that over Nature's face
A sombre veil is cast
With mournful voice and tearful eye
She says—'the time is past'

'He will not come! I might have known
It was a foolish hope;
But it was so sweet to cherish
I could not yeild it up.

'It may be foolish thus to weep
But I can not check my tears
To see in one short hour destroyed
The darling hope of years,

'He is not false but he was young
And time rolls fast away

Has he forgotten the vow he made
To meet me here to day?

'No if he lives he loves me still
And still remembers me
If he is dead—my joys are sunk
In utter misery.

'We parted in the spicy groves
Beneath Arabia's sky
How could I hope to meet him now
Where Gondal's breezes sigh?

'He was a shining meteor light
That faded from the skies,
But I mistook him for a star
That only set to rise.

'And with a firm yet trembling hand
I've clung to this false hope
I dared not surely trust in it
Yet would not yeild it up.

'And day and night I've thought of him,
And loved him constantly
And prayed that Heaven would prosper him
Where ever he may be—

'—He will not come he's wandering now
On some far distant shore
Or else he sleeps the sleep of death
And can-not see me more!

'O Alexander is it thus
Did we but meet to part
Long as I love thy name will be
Engraven on my heart

'I shall not cease to think of thee
While life and thought remain

For well I know that I can never
See thy like again!'

She ceases now and dries her tears
But still she lingers there
In silent thought till night is come
And silver stars appear.

But lo! a tall and stately youth
Ascends the grassy slope
His bright dark eyes are glancing round
His heart beats high with hope.

He has journeyed on unweariedly
From dawn of day till now,
The warm blood kindles in his cheek
The sweat is on his brow.

But he has gained the green hill top
Where lies that lonely spring
And lo! he pauses when he hears
Its gentle murmuring.

He dares not enter through the trees
That veil it from his eye
He listens for some other sound
In deep anxiety.

But vainly—all is calm and still;
Are his bright day dreams o'er
Has he thus hoped and longed in vain,
And must they meet no more?

One moment more of sad suspense
And those dark trees are past
The lonely well bursts on his sight
And they are met at last!

Anne Brontë   July 1 1837-

274 lines

3

A Voice from the Dungeon

I'm buried now I've done with life
I've done with hate revenge and strife
I've done with joy and hope & love
And all the bustling world above

Long have I dwelt forgotten here
In pining woe and dull despair;
This place of solitude and gloom
Must be my dungeon and my tomb;

No hope no pleasure can I find
I am grown weary of my mind
Often in balmy sleep I try,
To gain a rest from misery,

And in one hour of calm repose
To find a respite from my woes
But dreamless sleep is not for me
And I am still in misery.

I dream of liberty 'tis true,
But then I dream of sorrow too,
Of blood and guilt and horrid woes,
Of tortured friends and happy foes;

I dream about the world but then
I dream of fiends instead of men
Each smiling hope so quickly fades,
And such a lurid gloom pervades

That world—that when I wake and see
Those dreary phantoms fade and flee,
Even in my dungeon I can smile,
And taste of joy a little while.

And yet it is not always so
I dreamt a little while ago

That all was as it used to be
A fresh free wind passed over me

It was a pleasant summer's day
The sun shone forth with cheering ray
Methought a little lovely child
Looked up into my face and smiled.

My heart was full I wept for joy,
It was my own my darling boy
I clasped him to my breast and he
Kissed me and laughed in childish glee.

Just then I heard in whisper sweet
A well known voice my name repeat
His father stood before my eyes
I gazed at him in mute surprise

I thought he smiled and spoke to me
But still in silent extasy
I gazed at him I could not speak
I uttered one long piercing shriek*

Alas! Alas that cursed scream
Aroused me from my heavenly dream,
I looked around in wild despare
I called them but they were not there,
The Father and the child are gone
And I must live and die—alone!

                              Marina Sabia*

        Anne Brontë *October 6 1837**
54 lines

4

The Captive's Dream

Methought I saw him but I knew him not;
He was so changed from what he used to be,

There was no redness on his woe-worn cheek,*
No sunny smile upon his ashy lips,
His hollow wandering eyes looked wild and fierce,
And grief was printed on his marble brow,
And O I thought he clasped his wasted hands,
And raised his haggard eyes to Heaven, and prayed
That he might die—I had no power to speak,
I thought I was allowed to see him thus,
And yet I might not speak one single word;
I might not even tell him that I lived
And that it might be possible if search were made,
To find out where I was and set me free,
O how I longed to clasp him to my heart,
Or but to hold his trembling hand in mine,
And speak one word of comfort to his mind,
I struggled wildly but it was in vain,
I could not rise from my dark dungeon floor,
And the dear name I vainly strove to speak,
Died in a voiceless whisper on my tongue.
Then I awoke, and lo it was a dream!
A dream? Alas it was reality!
For well I know where ever he may be
He mourns me thus—O Heaven I could bear
My deadly fate with calmness if there were
No kindred hearts to bleed and break for me!

———————

27 lines   Alexandrina Zenobia   *Anne Brontë Written Jan.*
24 1838

5

The North Wind —*

———————

That wind is from the North I know it well.
No other breeze could have so wild a swell.
Now deep and loud it thunders round my cell,
   Then faintly dies,
   And softly sighs,

And moans and murmurs mournfully.
I know its language; thus it speaks to me—*

'I have passed over thy own mountains dear,
Thy northern mountains—and they still are free,
Still lonely, wild, majestic, bleak, and drear,
And stern, and lovely, as they used to be

'When thou a young enthusiast,
As wild and free as they,
O'er rocks and glens and snowy heights,
Didst often love to stray.

'I've blown the pure untrodden snows
In whirling eddies from their brows,
And I have howled in caverns wild,
Where thou a joyous mountain child,
Didst dearly love to be.
The sweet world is not changed but thou
Art pining in a dungeon now,
Where thou must ever be;
No voice but mine can reach thine ear,
And Heaven has kindly sent me here,
To mourn and sigh with thee,
And tell thee of the cherished land
Of thy nativity.'

Blow on wild wind, thy solemn voice,
However sad and drear,
Is nothing to the gloomy silence,
I have had to bear;

Hot tears are streaming from my eyes,
But these are better far,
Than that dull gnawing tearless [time]*
The stupor of despair.

Confined and hopeless as I am,
O speak of liberty,

O tell me of my mountain home,
And I will welcome thee.

———————

Alexandrina Zenobia

40 lines   Anne Brontë Jan 26 1838

6

The Parting —

1*

The chesnut steed stood by the gate,
His noble master's will to wait,
The woody park so green and bright,
Was glowing in the morning light,
The young leaves of the aspen trees
Were dancing in the morning breeze.
The palace door was open wide,
Its lord was standing there,
And his sweet lady by his side,
With soft dark eyes and raven hair,
He smiling took her ivory hand,
And said 'No longer here I stand,
My charger shakes his flowing mane
And calls me with impatient neigh
Adieu then till we meet again,
Sweet love I must no longer stay.'

2

'You must not go so soon,' she said
'I will not say fare well,
The sun has not dispelled the shade,
    In yonder dewy dell;
Dark shadows of gigantic length,
    Are sleeping on the lawn;
And scarcely have the birds begun,
    To hail the summer morn;

Then stay with me a little while.'
She said with soft and sunny smile.

3

He smiled again, and did not speak,
But lightly kissed her rosey cheek,
And fondly clasped her in his arms,
Then vaulted on his steed.
And down the park's smooth winding road,
He urged its flying speed,
Still by the door his lady stood,
And watched his rapid flight,
Until he came to a distant wood,
That hid him from her sight,
But ere he vanished from her view—
He waved to her a last adieu,
Then onward hastily he steered,
And in the forest disappeared.

4

The lady smiled a pensive smile,
    And heaved a gentle sigh,
But her cheek was all unblanched the while
And tearless was her eye,
'A thousand lovely flowers,' she said
'Are smiling on the plain,
And ere one half of them are dead,
My lord will come again,
The leaves are waving fresh and green
On every statly tree,
And long before they die away
He will return to me!'—
Alas! fair Lady say not so,
Thou canst not tell the weight of woe,
That lies in store for thee.

5

Those flowers will fade, those leaves will fall,
Winter will darken yonder hall,

Sweet Spring will smile o'er hill and plain,
And trees and flowers will bloom again,
And years will still keep rolling on,
But thy beloved lord is gone.
His absence thou shalt deeply mourn,
And never smile on his return.

———————

63 lines   *July 9 1838*

7

1

The lady of Alzerno's hall,
Is waiting for her lord,
The black-bird's song the cuckoo's call,
No joy to her afford,
She smiles not at the summer's sun,
Nor at the winter's blast,
She mourns that she is still alone,
Though three long years have passed.

2

I knew her when her eye was bright,
I knew her when her step was light,
And blithesome as a mountain doe's,
And when her cheek was like the rose,
And when her voice was full and free,
And when her smile was sweet to see.

3

But now the luster of her eye,
So dimmed with many a tear;
Her footstep's elasticity,
Is tamed with grief and fear;

The rose has left her hollow cheeks,
In low and mournful tones she speaks,
And when she smiles 'tis but a gleam,
Of sunshine on a winter's day,
That faintly beams through dreary clouds,
And in a moment dies away.
It does not warm, it does not cheer,
It makes us sigh for summer days,
When fields are green, and skies are clear,
And when the sun has kinder rays.

4

For three years she has waited there,
Still hoping for her lord's return,
But vainly she may hope and fear,
And vainly watch and weep and mourn,
She may wait him till her hairs are grey,
And she may wear her life away,
But to his Lady and his home,
Her noble Lord will never come.

5

'I wish I knew the worst,' she said
'I wish I could dispair,
These fruitless hopes this constant dread,
Are more than I can bear!'—
'Then do not hope and do not weep,
He loved thee faithfully,
And nothing short of death could keep
So true a heart from thee;
Eliza he would never go,
And leave thee thus to mourn,
He must be dead, for death alone
Could hinder his return.'

6

'Twas thus I spoke* because I felt,
As if my heart would break,
To see her thus so slowly pining
For Alzerno's sake;

But more than that I would not tell,
Though all the while I knew so well,
The time and nature of his death;
For when he drew his parting breath
His head was pillowed on my knee,
And his dark eyes were turned to me,
With an agonised heart breaking glance,
Until they saw me not—
O the look of a dying man,
Can never be forgot—!

62 lines   Alexandrina Zenobia
Anne Brontë   1837*
July 10 1838

8

Verses to a Child

1

O raise those eyes to me again
And smile again so joyously,*
And fear not love, it was not pain
Nor grief that drew these tears from me;
Beloved child thou canst not tell,
The thoughts that in my bosome swell
    When e'er I look on thee!

2

Thou knowst not that a glance of thine,
Can bring back long departed years
And that thy blue eyes' magic shine
Can overflow my own with tears,
And that each feature soft and fair

And every curl of golden hair,
   Some sweet remembrance bears.

3

Just then thou didst recall to me
A distant long forgotten scene;
One smile and one sweet word from thee
Dispelled the years that rolled between,
I was a little child again,
And every after joy and pain,
   Seemed never to have been.

4

Tall forest trees waved over me,
To hide me from the heat of day,
And by my side a child like thee,
Among the summer flowerets lay.
He was thy sire: thou merry child.
Like thee he spoke, like thee he smiled,
   Like thee he used to play.

5

O those were calm and happy days,
We loved each other fondly then
But human love too soon decays,
And ours can never bloom again.
I never thought to see the day,
When Florian's* friendship would decay,
   Like those of colder men.

6

Now Flora thou hast but begun
To sail on life's deceitful sea,
O do not err as I have done,
For I have trusted foolishly,
The faith of every friend I loved,
I never doubted till I proved
   Their heart's inconstancy.

7

'Tis mournful to look back upon
Those long departed joys and cares,
And I <u>will</u> weep since thou alone
Art witness to my streaming tears.
This lingering love will not depart,
I cannot banish from my heart,
    The friend of childish years.

8

But though thy Father loves me not,
Yet I shall still be loved by thee,
And though I am by him forgot,
Say wilt not thou remember me?
I will not cause <u>thy</u> heart to ache,
For thy regretted Father's sake,
    I'll love and cherish thee.

Alexandrina Zenobia
56 lines   *Anne Brontë August 21 1838.*

9

A Fragment   [*Poems* 1846]

'Maiden thou wert thoughtless once
    Of beauty or of grace
Simple and homely in attire,
    Careless of form and face
Then whence this change? and why so oft—
    Dost smooth thy hazel hair
And wherefore deck thy youthful form
    With such unwearied care?

Tell us—and cease to tire our ears
    With yonder hackneyed strain

Why wilt thou play those simple tunes
   So often o'er again?'
'Nay gentle friends I can but say
   That childhood's thoughts are gone
Each year its own new feelings brings
   And years move swiftly on

And for those little simple airs—
   I love to play them o'er—
So much I dare not promise now
   To play them never more.'
I answered and it was enough
   They turned them to depart
They could not read my secret thoughts
   Nor see my throbbing heart.

I've noticed many a youthful form
   Upon whose changeful face
The inmost workings of the soul
   The gazer's eye might trace
The speaking eye the changing lip
   The ready blushing cheek
The smiling or beclouded brow
   Their different feelings speak

But thank God! you might gaze on mine
   For hours and never know
The secret changes of my soul
   From joy to bitter woe
Last night as we sat round the fire
   Conversing merrily
We heard without approaching steps
   Of one well known to me.

There was no trembling in my voice
   No blush upon my cheek
No lustrous sparkle in my eyes
   Of hope or joy to speak
But O my spirit burned within
   My heart beat thick and fast

He came not nigh—he went away
   And then my joy was past

And yet my comrades marked it not
   My voice was still the same
They saw me smile and o'er my face—
   No signs of sadness came
They little knew my hidden thoughts
   And they will never know
The anguish of my drooping heart
   The bitter aching woe!

———————

56 lines   Olivia Vernon
written January 1st 1840
    Anne Brontë

10

Lines written at Thorp Green*
August 28th 1840   [*Poems* 1846]

O! I am very weary
   Though tears no longer flow
My eyes are tired of weeping
   My heart is sick of woe

My life is very lonely
   My days pass heavily
I'm weary of repining
   Wilt thou not come to me?

Oh didst thou know my longings
   For thee from day to day
My hopes so often blighted
   Thou wouldst not thus delay

                                   A. B.

11

The Consolation   [*Poems* 1846]

Though bleak these woods and damp the ground
With fallen leaves so thickly strewn
And cold the wind that wanders round
With wild and melancholy moan

There is a friendly roof I know
Might shield me from the wintry blast
There is a fire whose ruddy glow
Will cheer me for my wanderings past

And so though still where'er I roam
Cold stranger glances meet my eye
Though when my spirit sinks in woe
Unheeded swells the unbidden sigh

Though solitude endured too long
Bids youthful joys too soon decay
Makes mirth a stranger to my tongue
And overclouds my noon of day

When kindly thoughts that would have way
Flow back discouraged to my breast
I know there is though far away
A home where heart and soul may rest

Warm hands are there that clasped in mine
The warmer heart will not belie
While mirth and truth and friendship shine
In smiling lip and earnest eye

The ice that gathers round my heart
May there be thawed; and sweetly then
The joys of youth that now depart
Will come to cheer my soul again

Though far I roam* this thought shall be
My hope, my comfort everywhere

While such a home remains to me
My heart shall never know despair

———————

Hespera Caverndel   Anne Brontë Nov. 7ᵗʰ
                                              1843

12

Memory   [*Poems* 1846]

Brightly the sun of summer shone,
Green fields and waving woods upon,
    And soft winds wandered by.
Above, a sky of purest blue
Around, bright flowers of loveliest hue
    Allured the gazer's eye.

But what were all these charms to me
When one sweet breath of memory
    Came gently wafting by?*
I closed my eyes against the day,
And called my willing soul away,
    From earth and air and sky;

That I might simply fancy there,
One little flower—a primrose* fair
    Just opening into sight.
As in the days of infancy,
An opening primrose seemed to me
    A source of strange delight.

Sweet memory ever smile on me;
Nature's chief beauties spring from thee;
    O still thy tribute bring.
Still make the golden crocus shine
Among the flowers the most divine,
    The glory of the spring.

Still in the wallflower's fragrance dwell,
And hover round the slight bluebell,
    My childhood's darling flower.
Smile on the little daisy still,
The buttercup's bright goblet fill,
    With all thy former power.

Forever hang thy dreamy spell,
Round golden star and heatherbell;
    And do not pass away
From sparkling frost, or wreathed snow,
And whisper when the wild winds blow,
    Or rippling waters play.

Is childhood then so all divine?
Or memory is the glory thine
    That haloes thus the past?
Not all divine, its pangs of grief
Although perchance their stay is brief,
    Are bitter while they last.

Nor is the glory all thine own,
For on our earliest joys alone
    That holy light is cast.
With such a ray no spell of thine
Can make our later pleasures shine
    Though long ago they past.

Anne Brontë May 29th
48 lines   1844

13

Lines inscribed on
the wall of a dungeon in the southern P of I*
by A.H.*

Though not a breath can enter here,
I know the wind blows fresh and free,
I know the sun is shining clear,
Though not a gleam can visit me.

They thought while I in darkness lay,
'Twere pity that I should not know,
How all the earth is smiling gay;
How fresh the vernal breezes blow.

They knew, such tidings to impart,
Would pierce my weary spirit through
And could they better read my heart,
They'd tell me, <u>she</u> was smiling too.

They need not, for I know it well;
Methinks I see her even now;
No sigh disturbs her bosome's swell,
No shade o'ercasts her angel brow.

Unmarred by grief her matchless voice,
Whence sparkling wit, and wisdom flow:
And others in its sound rejoice,
And taste the joys, I must not know.

Drink rapture from her soft dark eye,
And sunshine from her heavenly smile;
On wings of bliss their moments fly
And I am pining here the while!

Oh! tell me does she never give—
To my distress a single sigh?
She smiles on them, but does she grieve
One moment, when they are not bye?

When she beholds the sunny skies,
And feels the wind of heaven blow;
Has she no tear for him that lies
In dungeon gloom, so far below?

While others gladly round her press
And at her side their hours beguile,
Has she no sigh for his distress
Who can not see a single smile

Nor hear one word nor read a line
That her beloved hand might write
Who banished from her face must pine
Each day a long, a lonely night?

Anne Brontë   Alexander April
Dec 16th 1844   1826

14

'Call me away'

Call me away; there's nothing here,
    That wins my soul to stay;
Then let me leave this prospect drear,
    And hasten far away.

To our belovèd land I'll flee,
    Our land of thought and soul,
Where I have roved so oft with thee
    Beyond the World's controll.

I'll sit and watch those ancient trees,
    Those Scotch firs dark and high:
I'll listen to the eerie breeze,
    Among their branches sigh.

The glorious moon shines far above,
    How soft her radiance falls,

On snowy heights, and rock, and grove
　　And yonder palace walls!

Who stands beneath yon fir trees high?
　　A youth both slight and fair,
Whose bright, and restless azure eye,
　　Proclaims him known to care,
Though fair that brow, it is not smooth.
Though small those features yet in sooth
　　Stern passion has been there.

Now on the peaceful moon are fixed,
　　Those eyes so glistening bright,
But trembling tear-drops hang betwixt,
　　And dim the blessed light.

Though late the hour, and keen the blast,
　　That whistles round him now,
Those raven locks are backward cast
　　To cool his burning brow.

His hands above his heaving breast,
　　Are clasped in agony—
'O Father! Father! let me rest!
　　And call my soul to thee!

'I know 'tis weakness thus to pray;
　　But all this cankering care—
This doubt tormenting night and day
　　Is more than I can bear!

'With none to comfort, none to guide
　　And none to strengthen me.
Since thou my only friend hast died—
　　I've pined to follow thee!
Since thou hast died!—And did he live—
What comfort could his counsel give—
　　To one forlorn like me?

'Would <u>he</u> my Idol's form adore—
　　Her soul, her glance, her tone?

And say, "Forget for ever more,
 Her kindred and thine own,
Let dreams of her thy peace destroy,
Leave every other hope and joy
 And live for her alone?" '

He starts, he smiles, and dries the tears,
 Still glistening on his cheek,
The lady of his soul appears,
 And hark! I hear her speak—

'Aye dry thy tears; thou wilt not weep—
While I am by thy side—
Our foes all day their watch may keep
But cannot thus divide
Such hearts as ours; and we tonight
Together in the clear moon's light,
 Their malice will deride.

'No fear our present bliss shall blast
 And Sorrow we'll defy
Do thou forget the dreary past
 The dreadful future I.'

Forget it? Yes, while thou art by
 I think of nought but thee,
'Tis only when thou art not nigh
 Remembrance tortures me.

But such a lofty soul to find,
 And such a heart as thine,
In such a glorious form enshrined
 And still to call thee mine—
Would be for earth too great a bliss,
Without a taint of woe like this,
 Then why should I repine?

       A.B. Jan^ry 24th 1845.

15

Song

We know where deepest lies the snow,
And where the frost-winds keenest blow,
  On every mountain's brow.
We long have known and learnt to bear,
The wandering outlaw's toil and care,
But where we late were hunted, there
Our foes are hunted now.

We have their princely homes,* and they,
To our wild haunts are chased away,
Dark woods, and desert caves,
And we can range from hill to hill,
And chase our vanquished victors still,
Small respite will they find, until
They slumber in their graves.

But I would rather be the hare,
That crouching in its sheltered lair,
Must start at every sound;
That forced from cornfields waving wide
Is driven to seek the bare hillside,
Or in the tangled copse to hide,
Than be the hunter's hound.

————————

Sept 3rd 1845

16

Song—

Come to the banquet—triumph in your songs!
Strike up the chords—and sing of Victory!
The oppressed have risen to redress their wrongs;

The Tyrants are o'erthrown; the Land is free!
The Land is free! Aye shout it forth once more;
Is she not red with her oppressors' gore?

We are her champions—shall we not rejoice?
Are not the tyrants' broad domains our own?
Then wherefore triumph with a faltering voice;
And talk of freedom in a doubtful tone?
Have we not longed through life the reign to see
Of Justice, linked with Glorious Liberty?

Shout you that will, and you that can rejoice
To revel in the riches of your foes.
In praise of deadly vengeance lift your voice,
Gloat o'er your tyrants' blood, your victims' woes.
I'd rather listen to the skylarks' songs,
And think on Gondal's, and my Father's wrongs.

It may be pleasant, to recall the death
Of those beneath whose sheltering roof you lie;
But I would rather press the mountain heath,
With naught to sheild me from the starry sky,
And dream of yet untasted victory—
A distant hope—and feel that I am free!

O happy life! To range the mountains wild,
The waving woods—or Ocean's heaving breast,
With limbs unfettered, conscience undefiled,
And choosing where to wander, where to rest!
Hunted, opposed, but ever strong to cope—
With toils, and perils—ever full of hope!*

'Our flower is budding'—When that word was heard
On desart shore, or breezy mountain's brow
Wherever said—what glorious thoughts it stirred!
'Twas budding then—Say has it blossomed now?
Is this the end we struggled to obtain?—
O for the wandering Outlaw's life again!

A.B. Sept 4th 1845

17

July 15ᵗʰ 1846

Mirth and Mourning

'O cast away your sorrow;—
   A while, at least, be gay!
If grief must come tomorrow,
   At least, be glad today!

'How can you still be sighing
   When smiles are everywhere?
The little birds are flying
   So blithely through the air;

'The sunshine glows so brightly
   O'er all the blooming earth;
And every heart beats lightly,—
   Each face is full of mirth.'

'I always feel the deepest gloom
   When day most brightly shines:
When Nature shows the fairest bloom,
   My spirit most repines;

'For, in the brightest noontide glow,
   The dungeon's light is dim;
Though freshest winds around us blow,
   No breath can visit <u>him</u>.

'If he must sit in twilight gloom,
   Can I enjoy the sight
Of mountains clad in purple bloom,
   And rocks in sunshine bright?—

'My heart may well be desolate,—
   These tears may well arise
While prison wall and iron grate
   Oppress his weary eyes.'

'But think of him tomorrow,
    And join your comrades now;—
That constant cloud of sorrow
    Ill suits so young a brow

'Hark, how their merry voices
    Are sounding far and near!
While all the world rejoices
    Can you sit moping here?'

'When others' hearts most lightly bound
    Mine feels the most oppressed;
When smiling faces greet me round
    My sorrow will not rest.

'I think of him whose faintest smile
    Was sunshine to my heart,
Whose lightest word could care beguile
    And blissful thoughts impart;

'I think how he would bless that sun,
    And love this glorious scene;
I think of all that has been done,
    And all that might have been.

'Those sparkling eyes, that blessed me so,
    Are dim with weeping now;
And blighted hope and burning woe
    Have ploughed that marble brow.

'What waste of youth, what hopes destroyed,
    What days of pining care,
What weary nights of comfort void
    Art thou condemned to bear!

'O! if my love must suffer so—
    And wholly for my sake—
What marvel that my tears should flow,—
    Or that my heart should break!'

———————

Zerona—

18

July 28th 1846

Weep not too much, my darling;
   Sigh not too oft for me;
Say not the face of Nature
   Has lost its charm for thee.
I have enough of anguish
   In my own breast alone;
Thou canst not ease the burden, Love,
   By adding still thine own.

I know the faith and fervour
   Of that true heart of thine;
But I would have it hopeful
   As thou wouldst render mine.
At night, when I lie waking,
   More soothing it will be
To say—'She slumbers calmly now,'
   Than say—'She weeps for me.'

When through the prison grating
   The holy moonbeams shine,
And I am wildly longing
   To see the orb divine
Not crossed, deformed, and sullied
   By those relentless bars
That will not show the cres-cent moon,
   And scarce the twinkling stars,

It is my only comfort
   To think, that unto thee
The sight is not forbidden—
   The face of heaven is free;—
If I could think Zerona
   Is gazing upward now—
Is gazing with a tearless eye,
   A calm unruffled brow;

That moon upon her spirit
   Sheds sweet, celestial balm,—
The thought, like Angel's whisper,
   My misery would calm.
And when, at early morning,
   A faint flush comes to me,
Reflected from those glowing skies
   I almost weep to see;—

Or when I catch the murmur
   Of gently swaying trees,
Or hear the louder swelling
   Of the soul-inspiring breeze,
And pant to feel its freshness
   Upon my burning brow,
Or sigh to see the twinkling leaf,
   And watch the waving bough;

If, from these fruitless yearnings,
   Thou wouldst deliver me,
Say that the charms of Nature
   Are lovely still to thee;
While I am thus repining,
   O! let me but believe,
'These pleasures are not lost to her,'
   And I will cease to grieve.

O, scorn not Nature's bounties!
   My soul partakes with thee.
Drink bliss from all her fountains;
   Drink for thyself and me!
Say not,—'My soul is buried
   In dungeon gloom with thine;'
But say,—'His heart is here with me;
   His spirit drinks with mine.'

A-E-

19

Z——'s Dream

Sept 14th 1846

I dreamt last night; and in that dream
My boyhood's heart was mine again;
These latter years did nothing seem
With all their mingled joy and pain,
Their thousand deeds of good and ill,
Their hopes which time did not fulfil,
Their glorious moments of success,
Their love that closed in bitterness,
Their hate that grew with growing strength,
Their darling projects—dropped at length,
And higher aims that still prevail,—
For I must perish ere they fail,—
That crowning object of my life,
The end of all my toil and strife,
Source of my virtues and my crimes,
For which I've toiled and striven in vain,—
But, if I fail a thousand times,
Still I will toil and strive again:—
Yet even this was then forgot;
My present heart and soul were not:
All the rough lessons Life has taught,
That are become a part of me,
A moment's sleep to nothing brought
And made me what I used to be.

And I was roaming, light and gay,
Upon a breezy, sunny day,
    A bold and careless youth:
No guilty stain was on my mind;
And, if not over soft or kind,
    My heart was full of truth.
It was a well-known mountain scene;—
Wild steeps, with rugged glens between
I should have thirsted to explore,
Had I not trod them oft before.

A younger boy was with me there.
His hand upon my shoulder leant;
His heart, like mine, was free from care,

His breath, with sportive toil, was spent;
For my rough pastimes he would share,
And equal dangers loved to dare,
(Though seldom I would care to vie
In learning's keen pursuit with him;
I loved free air and open sky
Better than books and tutors grim,)
And we had wandered far that day
O'er that forbidden ground away—
Ground, to our rebel feet how dear;
Danger and freedom both were there!—
Had climbed the steep and coursed the dale
Until his strength began to fail.

He bade me pause and breathe a while,
But spoke it with a happy smile.
His lips were parted to inhale
The breeze that swept the ferny dale,
And chased the clouds across the sky,
And waved his locks in passing by,
And fanned my cheek; (so real did seem
This strange, untrue, but truthlike dream;)
And, as we stood, I laughed to see
His fair young cheek so brightly glow.
He turned his sparkling eyes to me
With looks no painter's art could show,
Nor words portray;—but earnest mirth
And truthful love I there descried;
And, while I thought upon his worth,
My bosom glowed with joy and pride.

I could have kissed his forehead fair;
I could have clasped him to my heart;
But tenderness with me was rare,
And I must take a rougher part:
I seized him in my boisterous mirth;
I bore him struggling to the earth

And grappling, strength for strength we strove,—
He half in wrath,—I all for love;
But I gave o'er the strife at length,
Ashamed of my superior strength,—
The rather that I marked his eye
Kindle as if a change were nigh.

We paused to breath a little space,
Reclining on the heather brae;
But still I gazed upon his face
To watch the shadow pass away.
I grasped his hand, and it <u>was</u> fled;—
A smile—a laugh—and all was well:—
Upon my breast he leant his head,
And into graver talk we fell,—
More serious—yet so blest did seem
   That calm communion then,
That, when I found it but a dream,
I longed to sleep again.

At first, remembrance slowly woke.
Surprise—regret, successive rose,
That Love's strong cords should thus be broke,
And dearest friends turn deadliest foes.
Then, like a cold, o'erwhelming flood
   Upon my soul it burst—
This heart had thirsted for his blood;
   This hand alayed that thirst!
These eyes had watched, without a tear,
   His dying agony;
These ears, unmoved, had heard his prayer;
This tongue had cursed him suff'ring there,
And mocked him bitterly!

Unwonted weakness o'er me crept;
I sighed—nay, weaker still—I <u>wept</u>!
Wept, like a woman o'er the deed
I had been proud to do:—
As I had made his bosom bleed;
My own was bleeding too.

Back foolish tears!—the man I slew
Was not the boy I cherished so;
And that young arm that clasped the friend
Was not the same that stabbed the foe:
By time and adverse thoughts estranged,
And wrongs and vengeance, both were changed.
Repentance, now, were worse than vain:
Time's current cannot backward run;
And, be the action wrong or right,
    It is for ever done.

Then reap the fruits—I've said his death
Should be my Country's gain:—
If not—then, I have spent my breath,
    And spilt his blood in vain:
And I have laboured hard and long,
    But little good obtained;
My foes are many, yet, and strong,
    Not half the battle's gained;
For, still, the greater deeds I've done,
The more I have to do,
The faster I can journey on,
    The farther I must go.
If Fortune favoured for a while,
I could not rest beneath her smile,
    Nor triumph in success:
When I have gained one river's shore
A wilder torrent, stretched before,
Defies me with its deafening roar;
    And onward I must press.

And, much I doubt, this work of strife,
    In blood and death begun,
Will call for many a victim more
    Before the cause is won.—
Well! my own life, I'd freely give
    Ere I would fail in my design;—
The cause must prosper if I live,
And I will die if it decline;
Advanced thus far, I'll not recede;—

Whether to vanquish or to bleed,
Onward, unchecked, I must proceed.
    Be Death, or Victory mine!

150 lines   E Z—

20

October 1846

Gloomily the clouds are sailing*
    O'er the dimly moonlit sky;
Dolefully the wind is wailing;
    Not another sound is nigh;

Only I can hear it sweeping
    Heathclad hill and woodland dale,
And at times the night's sad weeping
    Sounds above its dying wail.

Now the struggling moonbeams glimmer;
    Now the shadows deeper fall,
Till the dim light, waxing dimmer,
    Scarce reveals yon stately hall.

All beneath its roof are sleeping;
    Such a silence reigns around
I can hear the cold rain steeping
    Dripping roof and plashy ground.

No; not all are wrapped in slumber;
    At yon chamber window stands
One whose years can scarce outnumber
    The tears that dew his claspéd hands.

From the open casement bending,
    He surveys the murky skies,
Dreary sighs his bosom rending,
    Hot tears gushing from his eyes.

Now that Autumn's charms are dying,
   Summer's glories long since gone,
Faded leaves on damp earth lying,
   Hoary Winter striding on, —

'Tis no marvel skies are lowering,
   Winds are moaning thus around,
And cold rain, with ceaseless pouring,
   Swells the streams and swamps the ground;

But such wild, such bitter grieving
   Fits not slender boys like thee;
Such deep sighs should not be heaving
   Breasts so young as thine must be.

Life with thee is only springing;
   Summer in thy pathway lies;
Every day is nearer bringing
   June's bright flowers and glowing skies.

Ah, he see no brighter morrow!
   He is not too young to prove
All the pain and all the sorrow
   That attend the steps of love.

APPENDIX A
DIARY PAPERS

Six diary papers were written by Emily and Anne Brontë with a view to recording events in their lives and reviewing them four years later. They give a graphic picture of parsonage life interspersed with tantalizing glimpses of the sisters' imaginary world of Gondal.

The papers of 1834 and 1837 were written jointly, whereas each of the sisters wrote her own paper on 30 July 1841 and 30 [31] July 1845, marking the date of Emily's birthday. Exact transcriptions of these hastily written, poorly spelt, personal manuscripts are presented in the following text , including all errors (in one case a facsimile has been used where the manuscript was unavailable). See the *Oxford Companion*, 163–6, for further discussion of the Diary Papers.

*Emily and Anne Brontë, Diary Paper 24 November 1834**

November the 24
1834 Monday
Emily Jane Brontë
Anne Brontë

I fed Rainbow, Diamond, Snowflake Jasper pheasent (alias[)]* this morning Branwell went down to Mr Drivers* and brought news that Sir Robert peel* was going to be invited to stand for Leeds* Anne and I have been peeling Apples for Charlotte to make an apple pudding and for Aunts nuts and apples Charlotte said she made puddings perfectly and she was of a quick but limted intellect Taby* said just now Come Anne pilloputate (ie pill a potato[)] Aunt* has come into the kitchen just now and said where are your feet Anne Anne answered On the floor Aunt papa opened the parlour Door and gave Branwell a Letter saying here Branwell read this and show it to your Aunt and Charlotte—The Gondals are discovering the interior of Gaaldine Sally Mosley is washing in the back kitchin

It is past Twelve o'clock Anne and I have not tided ourselvs, done our bed work or done our lessons and we want to go out to play we are going to have for Dinner Boiled Beef Turnips, potato's and applepudding the kitchin is in avery untidy state Anne and I have not Done

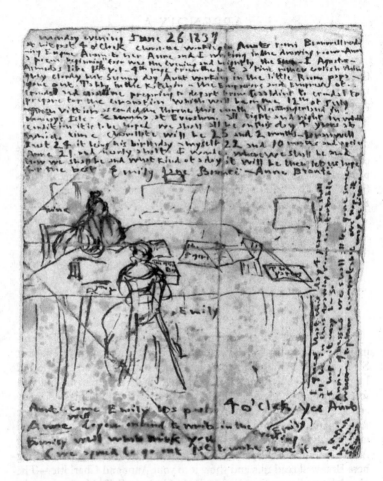

Plate 3: Emily Brontë's Diary Paper for 26 June 1837 (courtesy of the Brontë Parsonage Museum).

our music exercise which consists of b major Taby said on my putting a pen in her face Ya pitter pottering there instead of pilling a potate I answered O Dear, O Dear, O Dear I will directly with that I get up, take a knife and begin pilling (finished pilling the potatoes[)] papa going to walk Mr Sunderland* expected

Anne and I say I wonder what we shall be like and what we shall be and where we shall be if all goes on well in the year 1874—in which year I shall be in my 57th year Anne will be going in her 55th year Branwell will be going in his 58th year And Charlotte in her 59th year hoping we shall all be well at that time we close our paper

Emily and Anne
November the 24 1834

Emily and Anne Brontë, Diary Paper 26 June 1837*

Monday evening June 26 1837
A bit past 4 o'clock Charlotte working in Aunts room Branwell reading Eugene Aram* to her Anne and I writing in the drawing room—Anne a poem beginning 'fair was the evening and brightly the sun'*—I Agustus—Almedas life 1st vol—4th page from the last a fine rather coolish thin grey cloudy but sunny day Aunt working in the little Room papa—gone out. Tabby in the kitchin—the Emprerors and Empresses of Gondal and Gaalddine preparing to depart from Gaaldine to Gondal to prepare for the coranation which will be on the 12th of July Queen Victiora ascended the throne this month* Northangerland in Monceys Isle—Zamorna at Eversham.* all tight and right in which condition it is to be hoped we shall all be on this day 4 years at which time Charlotte will be 25 and 2 months—Branwell just 24 it being his birthday—myself 22 and 10 months and a peice Anne 21 and nearly a half I wonder where we shall be and how we shall be and what kind of a day it will be then let us hope for the best

Emily Jane Brontë—Anne Brontë

Aunt. come Emily its past 4 o'clock. Emily, Yes Aunt Anne well do you intend to write in the evening Emily well what think you (we agreed to go out 1st to make sure if we Get into a humor we may stay [?out)]*
I guess that this day 4 years we shall all be in this drawing room comfortable I hope it may be so Anne guesses we shall all be gone somewhere together comfortable We hope it may be either

Emily Brontë, Diary Paper 30 July 1841*

A Paper to be opened
when Anne is
25 years old
or my next birthday after—
if
—all be well—

Emily Jane Brontë   July the 30th 1841. .

It is Friday evening—near 9 o'clock—wild rainy weather I am seated in the dining room alone having just concluded tidying our desk-boxes—writing this document. Papa is in the parlour. Aunt upstairs in her room—she has been reading Blackwood's Magazine to papa—Victoria and Adelaide* are ensconced in the peat-house—Keeper* is in the kitchen—Nero* in his cage—We are all stout and hearty as I hope is the case with Charlotte, Branwell, and Anne, of whom the first is at John White Esqre upperwood House, Rawdon The second is at Luddenden foot and the third is I beleive at Scarborough*—editing* perhaps a paper corresponding to this—

A scheme is at present in agitation for setting us up in a school of our own as yet nothing is determined but I hope and trust it may go on and prosper and answer our highest expectations. This day 4-years I wonder whether we shall still be dragging on in our present condition or established to our heart's content Time will show—

I guess that at the time appointed for the opening of this paper—we (i e) Charlotte, Anne and I—shall be all merrily seated in our own sitting-room in some pleasant and flourishing seminary* having just gathered in for the midsummer holydays Our debts will be paid off and we shall have cash in hand to a considerable amount. papa Aunt and Branwell will either have been, or be coming—to visit us—it will be a fine warm summery evening. very different from this bleak look-out. Anne and I will perchance slip out into the garden [?for] a few minutes to peruse our papers. I hope either this or something better will be the case—

The Gondalians are at present in a threatening state but there is no open rupture as yet—all the princes and princesses of the royal royaltys are at the palace of Instruction*—I have a good many books on hand—but I am sorry to say that as usual I make small progress with any—however I have just made a new regularity paper! and I mean verb sap—to do great things—and now I close sending from far an exhortation of courage! to exiled and harassed Anne wishing she was here

Anne Brontë, Diary Paper 30 July 1841*

July the 30ᵗʰ AD. 1841

This is Emily's birthday she has now completed her 23ʳᵈ year and is I believe at home Charlotte is a Governess in the family of Mʳ White Branwell is a clerk in the railroad station at Luddenden foot and I am a governess in the family of Mʳ Robinson* I dislike the situation and wish to change it for another I am now at Scarborough my pupils are gone to bed and I am hastening to finish this before I follow them.

We are thinking of setting up a school of our own but nothing definite is settled about it yet and we do not know whether we shall be able to or not—I hope we shall—and I wonder what will be our condition and how or where we shall all be on this day four years hence at which time if all be well I shall be 25 years and six months old Emily will be 27 years old Branwell 28 years and 1 month and Charlotte 29 years and a quarter. We are now all separate and not likely to meet again for many a weary week but we are none of us ill that I know of and are all doing something for our own livelihood* except Emily who however is as busy as any of us and in reality earns her food and raiment as much as we do.

> How little know we what we are
> How less what we may be!*

Four years ago I was at school since then I have been a Governess at Blake hall,* left it, come to Thorp Green and seen the sea and york minster Emily has been a teacher at miss patchet's school* and left it charlotte has left Miss Wooler's* been a Governess at Mrs Sidgwick's* left her and gone to Mrs White's Branwell has given up painting been a tutor in cumberland left it and become a clerk on the railroad* Tabby has left us Martha brown has come in her place We have got Keeper* got a sweet little cat and lost it and also got a hawk got a wild goose which has flown away and 3 tame ones one of which has been killed—All these diversities with many others are things we did not expect or foresee in the July of 1837—What will the next 4 years bring forth? Providence only knows. But we ourselves have sustained very little alteration since that time. I have the same faults that I had then only I have more wisdom and experience and a little more self possession than I then enjoyed—How will it be when we open this paper and the one Emily has written—? I wonder whether the Gondaliand will still be flourishing and what will be their condition—I am now engaged writing the 4th volume of Sofala* Vernon's life—

For some time I have looked upon 25 as a sort of era in my existence it may prove a true presentiment or it may be only a superstitious fancy the latter seems most likely but time will show.

Anne Brontë —

Emily Brontë, Diary Paper 30[31] July 1845*

Haworth—Thursday—July 30th 1845.

My birthday—showery—breezy coo[l]—I am twenty seven years old to day—this morning Anne and I opened the papers we wrote 4 years since on my twenty third birthday—this paper we intend, if all be well, to open on my 30th three years hence in 1848—since the 1841 paper, the following events have taken place

Our school-scheme has been abandoned and [instead] Charlotte and I went to Brussels* on the 8th of Febrary 1842 Branwell left his place at Luddenden Foot* C and I returned from Brussels November 8th 1842 in consequence of Aunt's death—Branwell went to Thorpgreen as a tutor where Anne still continued—January 1843 Charlotte returned to Brussels the same month and after staying a year came back again on new years day 1844 Anne left her situation at Thorp Green of her own accord—June 1845 Branwell [?left]—July 1845* Anne and I went [on] our first long Journey by ourselves together—leaving Home on the 30th of June—monday sleeping at York—returning to Keighley Tuesday evening sleeping there and walking home on Wednesday morning—though the weather was broken, we enjoyed ourselves very much except during a few hours at Bradford and during our excursion we were Ronald Macelgin, Henry Angora, Juliet Angusteena, Rosabelle [?Esmaldan], Ella and Julian Egramon[t] Catharine Navarre and Cordelia Fitzaphnold escaping from the palaces of Instruction to join the Royalists who are hard driven at present by the victorious Republicans—The Gondals still flo[u]rish bright as ever I am at present writing a work on the First Wars—Anne has been writing some articles on this and a book by Henry Sophona—We intend sticking firm by the rascals as long as they delight us which I am glad to say they do at present—I should have mentioned that last summer the school scheme was revived in full vigor—We had prospectuses printed.* despatched letters to all acquaintances imparting our plans and did our little all—but it was found no go—now I dont desire a school at all and none of us have any great longing for it. We have cash enough for our present wants with a prospect of accumolation*—we are all in decent health—only that papa has a complaint in his eyes and with the exception of B who I hope will be better and do better, hereafter. I am quite contented for myself—not as idle as formerly, altogether as hearty and having learnt to make the most of the present and hope for the future with less fidget[i]ness that I cannot do all I wish—seldom or ever troubled with nothing to ie and merely desiring that every body could be as comfortable as myself and as undesponding and then we should have a very tolerable world of it—

By mistake I find we have opened the paper on the 31st instead of the 30th Yesterday was much such a day as this but the morning was devine—

Tabby who was gone in our last paper is come back and has lived with us—two years and a half and is in good health—Martha who also departed is here too. We have got Flossey,* got and lost Tiger*—lost the Hawk. Nero which with the geese was given away and is doubtless dead for when I came back from Brussels I enquired on all hands and could hear nothing of him—Tiger died early last year—Keeper and Flossey are well also the canary acquired 4 years since

We are now all at home and likely to be there some time—Branwell went to Liverpool on Tuesday to stay a week. Tabby has just been teasing me to [?turn] as formerly to—pilloputate. Anne and I should have picked the black currants if it had been fine and sunshiny. I must hurry off now to my turning* and ironing I have plenty of work* on hands and writing and am altogether full of buis[ness] with best wishes for the whole House till 1848 July 30th and as much longer as may be I conclude

E J Brontë

Anne Brontë, Diary Paper 31 July 1845*

Thursday July the 31st 1845

Yesterday was Emily's birthday and the time when we should have opened our 1845 [1841] paper but by mistake we opened it to day instead. How many things have happened since it was written—some pleasant some far otherwise—Yet I was then at Thorp Green and now I am only j[us]t escaped from it.* I was wishing to leave [?it] then and if I had known that I had four years longer to stay how wretched I should have been—[?then] too. <I was writing the fourth volume of Sophala>* but during my stay I have had some very unpleasant and undreamt of experience of human nature—* Others have seen more changes Charlotte has left Mr White's and been twice to Brussels where she stayed each time nearly a year—Emily has been there too and stayed nearly a year—Branwell has left Luddendenfoot and been a Tutor at Thorp Green and had much tribulation and ill health he was very ill on Tuesday but he went with John Brown to Liverpool where he now is I suppose and we hope he will be better and do better in future—This is a dismal cloudy wet evening we have had so far a very cold wet summer—Charlotte has lately been to Hathersage in Derbyshire on a visit of three weeks to Ellen Nussy—she is now sitting sewing in the Dining-Room Emily is ironing upstairs I am sitting in the Dining Room in the Rocking chair before the fire with my feet on the fender Papa is in the parlour Tabby and Martha are I think in the Kitchen Keeper and Flossy are I do not know where little Dick* is hopping in his cage—When the last paper was written we were thinking of setting up a school—the scheem has been dropt and long after taken up again and dropt again because we could not get pupils—Charlotte is thinking about getting another situation—she wishes to go to Paris—Will she go? she has let Flossy in by the bye and he is now lying on the sopha—Emily is engaged in writing the Emperor Julius's life* she has read some of it and I want very much to hear the rest—she is writing some poetry too I wonder what it is about*—I have begun the third volume of passages in the life of an Individual.* I wish I had finished it—This afternoon I began to set about making my grey figured silk frock that was dyed at Keighley—What sort of a hand shall I make of it? E. and I have a great deal of work* to do—when shall we sensibly diminish it? I want to get a habit of early rising shall I succeed? We have not yet finished our Gondal chronicles that we began three years and a half ago when will they be done?—The Gondals are at present in a sad state the Republicans are uppermost but the Royalists are not quite overcome—the young sovereigns with their brothers and sisters are still at the palace of Instruction—The Unique Society above half a year ago were wrecked on a dezart Island as they were returning from [?Gaaldin]*—they are still there but we have not played at them much yet—The Gondals in general are not in first rate playing condition—will they improve? I wonder how we shall all be and where

and how situated on the thirtyeth of July 1848 when if we are all alive
Emily will be just 30 I shall be in my 29th year Charlotte in her 33rd and
Branwell in his 32nd and what changes shall we have seen and known
and shall we be much chan[g]ed ourselves? I hope not—for the worse
[a]t least—I for my part cannot well b[e] <u>flatter</u> or older in mind than I
am n[o]w—Hoping for the best I conclude Anne Brontë

APPENDIX B

GONDAL NOTES

(a) *List of place names noted by Anne in* A Grammar of General Geography, *by Revd J. Goldsmith (1823, MS in BPM)*

Alexandia, A kingdom in Gaaldine.
Almedore, a kingdom in Gaaldine.
Elseraden, a kingdom in Gaaldine.
Gaaldine, a large Island newly di[s]covered in the South Pacific,
Gondal, a large Island in the North Pacific.
Regina, the capital of Gondal.
Ula, a kingdom in Gaaldine, governed by 4 Sovereigns.
Zelona, a kingdom in Gaaldine.
Zedora, a large Provence in Gaaldine Governed by a Viceroy.

(b) *List of twenty-six names recorded by Anne on a scrap of paper (MS in the Ransom Humanities Research Center at Austin, Texas)*

Arthur Exina

Gerald Exina

Edward Hybernia

Gerald ——
Alexander——
Halbert Clifford
Julius Al
Archibald MacRay
Gerald F
Henry Sophona
Eustace Sophona
Adolphus St Albert
Albert Vernon
Alexander D

Alexandria Zenobia Hybernia
Isabella Senland
Xirilla Senland

Lucia Angora
Catharina T G Angusteena
Isabella Abrantez
Eliza Hybernia
Harriet Eagle
Isidora Montara
Helen Douglas
Cornelia Alzerno
Rosalind Fizheron

(c) *List of sixteen names recorded by Anne on a sheet of paper, together
with the rough draft of a poem beginning 'A prisoner in a dungeon deep'
(see* The Poems of Anne Brontë: A New Text and Commentary, *ed.
Edward Chitham (London: Macmillan, 1972), 126–8. MS in BPM)*

'Busy'
John Mertleheath
Gerald Exina [erased]
Gerald Hybernia [erased]

Exina
Eustacce
Eustace Sophona
Albert Vernon [erased]

Edward Hybernia
John Mertleheath [erased]
John Mertleheath [erased]
Alexander Hybernia

'pompous'
Isabella Abrantez
Isabella Senland
Una Campbell

Flora Alzerno
Emily Vernon [erased]
Lucia MacElgin [erased]
Angora

(d) *List by Anne of personal features of five characters on a poetry MS*

Ronald Stwart—28 June 8th E—6—Brown H—Grey E—EN—R
and W—7—— 1 ——
      *   *

Regina 24 April 29th—C—57—Dark brown H—Grey E—GN—
F—7 —— 1 ——
     *

Marcellus Stwart 21 August 3d B—511—light brown H—Grey
E—RN—F—7—#—1 —
Flora
* 17 June 18th B—56—Chesnut H—brown E—GN—R and
W—#—#—1—8—
Francesca 18 July 20th—V—56—light brown H—Grey E—RN—
P and W—7—1 ————
      21 aug

EXPLANATORY NOTES

Abbreviations have been used in the notes to refer to frequently occurring books and manuscript sources, as listed below. Full bibliographical details of relevant Brontë books and articles cited less frequently are listed in the Select Bibliography. Page references to novels by the Brontës are to the Clarendon editions published by Oxford University Press under the general editorship of Ian Jack. Details of all other printed sources are given in the relevant note.

Notes on the meanings and derivations of words have been derived chiefly from the *Oxford English Dictionary* (*OED*), Brewer's *Dictionary of Phrase and Fable* (Brewer), *1811 Dictionary of the Vulgar Tongue* (*DVT*), Joseph Wright's *The English Dialect Dictionary* (Wright), and Partridge's *Dictionary of Slang and Unconventional English* (Partridge).

ABBREVIATIONS

Alexander *EW*	Christine Alexander, *The Early Writings of Charlotte Brontë* (Oxford: Basil Blackwell, 1983).
Alexander *EEW*	*An Edition of the Early Writings of Charlotte Bontë*, ed. Christine Alexander (Oxford: Basil Blackwell for the Shakespeare Head Press), vol. 1 (1987); vol. 2, parts 1 and 2 (1991); vol. 3 (forthcoming).
Alexander and Sellars	Christine Alexander and Jane Sellars, *The Art of the Brontës* (Cambridge: Cambridge University Press, 1995).
BL	British Library
BPM	Brontë Parsonage Museum
Chitham *ABP*	*The Poems of Anne Brontë: A New Text and Commentary*, ed. Edward Chitham (London: Macmillan, 1972).
Gezari *EBP*	*Emily Brontë: The Complete Poems*, ed. Jane Gezari (Harmondsworth: Penguin, 1992).
Neufeldt *BBP*	*The Poems of Patrick Branwell Brontë: A New Text and Commentary*, ed. Victor A. Neufeldt (New York and London: Garland, 1990).
Neufeldt *BBWorks*	*The Works of Branwell Brontë*, ed. Victor A. Neufeldt, 3 vols. (New York and London: Garland, 1997, 1999).
Oxford Companion	Christine Alexander and Margaret Smith, *The Oxford Companion to the Brontës* (Oxford: Oxford University Press, 2003).
Poems 1846	*Poems* by Currer, Ellis and Acton Bell (London: Aylott & Jones, 1846).
Roper *EBP*	*The Poems of Emily Brontë*, ed. Derek Roper with Edward Chitham (Oxford: Oxford University Press, 1995).

Smith *Letters*   *The Letters of Charlotte Brontë with a Selection of Letters by Family and Friends*, ed. Margaret Smith, vol. 1 (Oxford: Clarendon Press, 1995).

CHARLOTTE BRONTË

3 THE HISTORY OF THE YEAR. Charlotte Brontë's second earliest surviving manuscript: 4 pages (10 × 6 cm) in BPM: B80(11). The text, continued by the following two fragments, explains how the children's 'plays' were formed. This description of the Brontës' initial encounter with the toy soldiers is later recast by Charlotte in fictional form in chapter 3 of the following story, 'The Twelve Adventurers'.

my sister Maria: eldest of the six Brontë children, who at the age of 7 assumed much of the responsibility for the younger children after their mother's death in 1821. It was Maria who first taught the children to act their own little plays, and records exist of her precocious knowledge of current political events. Both Maria and her next sister Elizabeth fell seriously ill with pulmonary TB at the Clergy Daughters' School at Cowan Bridge and returned home to die within a month of each other in 1825.

Tabby the servant: Tabitha Aykroyd (spelt 'Taby' in MS), Methodist, widow, and loyal servant at the Brontë parsonage from 1824 until just before her death almost thirty years later. She was much loved by the children, who gleaned from her most of their knowledge of fairy tales and local lore.

gone: the date 'March 12 1829' appears here at the end of the first MS page.

Aunt: Miss Elizabeth Branwell of Penzance, who stayed to help the Brontë family after the death of her sister Mrs Maria Brontë; she remained with them for the rest of her life.

Leeds Intelligencer . . . Mr Hernaman: John Hernaman and Joseph Ogle Robinson (replaced 1829 by Robert Perring) were proprietors of the *Leeds Intelligencer* (established 1754); they were joined in late 1829 by Edward Wood who had been on the staff since 1824 but was never the editor.

Leeds Mercury: the aggressive Whig politics of the *Leeds Mercury* (founded 1719) and its rivalry with the Tory *Leeds Intelligencer* inspired the young Brontës to emulate its lively, belligerent style in their early writings. The editor Edward Baines and his three sons are ridiculed by Charlotte in 'Tales of the Islanders', vol. 1 (see Alexander *EEW*, 1. 25–8).

Mr Driver: probably the Revd Jonas Driver (d. Dec. 1831 and buried by Mr Brontë), who lent the Brontës periodicals, but who had discontinued *Blackwood's Magazine* by May 1832, when Elizabeth Branwell decided to subscribe to *Fraser's Magazine* for her nephew and nieces (see Smith, *Letters*, 1. 112).

Mr Christopher North: pseudonym of John Wilson, editor of *Blackwood's Edinburgh Magazine* (founded 1817) and author with John Gibson Lockhart and Dr William Maginn of the famous 'Noctes Ambrosianae', a series of boisterous imaginary conversations which appeared in *Blackwood's* from 1822 to 1835 and were imitated by the Brontës in their own magazines. Timothy Tickler, Ensign O'Doherty (Maginn), Peter Macrabin, Mordecai Mullion, and the 'Ettrick Shepherd' (James Hogg) are interlocutors in the 'Noctes Ambrosianae'.

Hogg: the date 'March 12' appears here in the MS.

Aesop's Fables: a collection of moral tales about animals attributed to a Greek slave 'Aesop' in about 600 BC, although they are probably the work of many authors.

Young Men's: this heading occurs at the top of MS p. 4, the remainder of which is cancelled, and the description continues on the next page.

Papa bought Branwell some soldiers at Leeds: Branwell gives a detailed account of this event in 'The History Of The Young Men From Their First Settlement To The Present Time', 15 December 1830–7 May 1831, in Neufeldt *BBWorks*, 1. 137.

mine!: the misspelt words 'Arther' and 'Athur' appear above and below; Arthur was the Duke of Wellington's Christian name.

4 *Gravey . . . Waiting Boy . . . Bonaparte*: the names of Emily's and Anne's favourite soldiers were soon changed to 'Parry' and 'Ross', two famous explorers who feature in articles in *Blackwood's* (Nov. 1820 and June 1821). Gravey (later Gravii) survived in the saga as the Glass Town's Metropolitan Archbishop. Napoleon Bonaparte, Wellington's great adversary, had recently died as a prisoner on St Helena in May 1827, but his legendary fame was still equal to that of Charlotte's hero Wellington. Bonaparte continues to play a background role in the saga, although Branwell changed his original soldier's name to 'Sneaky', whom he described as 'Injenous artful deceitful but courageous' (Neufeldt *BBWorks*, 1. 142).

'THE ORIGIN OF THE O'DEARS'. This one page fragment (9.5 × 6.2 cm) in BPM: B80(11) continues the description of the early 'plays'.

O'Dears: transcription of this name is difficult because of the final letter, which could be either 'n' or 'r'. Since Branwell also refers to the name as 'O Deay' or 'O Dear', it seems likely that Charlotte wrote 'O Dear' and not 'O Deay', as suggested by Winifred Gérin (*Charlotte Brontë: The Evolution of Genius*, 25), or 'O'Dean' as I originally suggested in Alexander *EEW* 1. 6.

Hay Man . . . Boaster . . . Hunter . . . Clown: only Boaster and Clown can be found in the titles of *Aesop's Fables*; Hay Man and Hunter are not mentioned in the 1825 edition, translated by Samuel Croxall, which Gérin suggests the young Brontës used (*Charlotte Brontë*, 25). Branwell Brontë signed several of his early tales 'Boaster' but the other names are not found elsewhere in the juvenilia.

'THE ORIGIN OF THE ISLANDERS'. Single page fragment (9.5 × 6.2 cm; in BPM: B80(11)) that continues the description of the formation of the 'plays'. A retelling of this account can be found at the beginning of the first volume of Charlotte Brontë's 'Tales of the Islanders' (see Alexander *EEW*, vol. 1).

4 *Isle of Man . . . Isle of Wight*: islands off the coast of Britain, each reflecting the children's interests: the Isle of Man is in the Irish Sea, Arran and Bute are off the west coast of Scotland, Jersey is part of the Channel Islands, and the Isle of Wight is just off the south English coast.

John Bull . . . Mr Abernethy, &c, &c: the Brontës' chief men were almost all famous men of the time: John Abernethy and Sir Astley Paston Cooper were noted surgeons, the latter being surgeon to George IV and the Duke of Wellington's neurologist; Sir Henry Halford was a well-known physician and doctor to Mrs Charles Arbuthnot, a close friend of the Duke of Wellington; Michael Thomas Sadler and Lord George Bentick were Members of Parliament, the former a social reformer and the latter a supporter of Catholic Emancipation and the Reform Bill and later leader of the Opposition; James Henry Leigh Hunt, Sir Walter Scott, John Gibson Lockhart, and John Wilson (the 'Christopher North' of *Blackwood's Magazine*, listed by Charlotte in 'The History of the Year') were all well-known poets, writers, and critics. Lockhart married Scott's daughter and their eldest son was Emily's favourite, Johnny Lockhart, the suffering 'Hugh Littlejohn' for whom Scott wrote *Tales of a Grandfather*, owned by the Brontë children. John Bull was a popular name for England, personifying the bluff frankness and solidity of the English character.

5 TWO ROMANTIC TALES: THE TWELVE ADVENTURERS AND AN ADVENTURE IN IRELAND. The title appears on the brown-paper cover of the MS, which is a hand-sewn booklet formerly in the Law Collection (private). The present text of 'The Twelve Adventurers', Charlotte's first story of the Young Men, is based on the Shakespeare Head edition (referred to below as *SHCBM*), ed. Wise and Symington, *The Miscellaneous and Unpublished Writings of Charlotte and Patrick Branwell Brontë*, 1. 3–13; and the most significant variant readings from a typed transcript formerly owned by C. W. Hatfield and now in the BPM are recorded below. In the case of 'An Adventure in Ireland', however, the present text is based on the Hatfield Transcript (subsequently referred to as HT). Both texts have been amended in accordance with the editorial policy for this volume.

The Twelve Adventurers: this title and the following chapter headings do not appear in the MS; they were listed by Charlotte in her 'Catalogue of my Books, 3 August 1830', and used by Clement Shorter and C. W. Hatfield, in their edition, *The Twelve Adventurers and Other Stories* (1925). The original title in the MS is 'A ROMANTIC TALE'.

Gaul: ancient name for France.

the country of the Genii: Charlotte is establishing here a mythology and traditional European connection with the land her adventurers are about to colonize. See Introduction for the role of the four Chief Genii, the Brontë children themselves.

land: 'sand' in HT.

'*The Travels of Captain Parnell*', *out of which the following is an extract*: the following narrative appears to be a composite of typical descriptions of deserts in the late eighteenth and early nineteenth centuries, such as those found in Goldsmith's *Animated Nature* and in *The Percy Anecdotes*. The book title is probably imaginary, perhaps inspired by Goldsmith's *Life of Parnell*.

6 '*About four in the afternoon I saw a dark red cloud arise in the east . . . where the bones had lain*': the mixture of biblical resonance and interest in ancient bones in this extract is strikingly representative of the period. The Brontës keenly followed current debates in geology and palaeontology; and church and science maintained a comfortable partnership in these pre-Darwinian days, before the implications of Lyell's *Principles of Geology* (1830–3) were worked out in Darwin's *Origin of Species* (1859).

Maimoune: a fairy, daughter of Damriel, king of a legion of genii in 'The Story of the Amours of Camaralzaman', *Arabian Nights Entertainments*.

Marcus O'Donell . . . Frederick Brunswick, and Arthur Wellesley: only the last two characters survive to play a dominant role in the Glass Town saga; others remain as minor characters and several are replaced by characters in Branwell's alternative list of the 'Twelves', recorded a year and a half later in his version of the founding of Glass Town, 'The History of the Young Men' (Neufeldt *BBWorks*, 1. 137–69). As in history, Frederick Brunswick became the Duke of York and Arthur Wellesley was made Duke of Wellington after the battle of Waterloo; both characters assume these titles later in the story.

Henry Clinton: Sir Henry Clinton, a British general under Wellington at the battle of Waterloo, was aide-de-camp to the Duke of York in 1793, the date of this story.

Oxeye: sailor's name for a cloudy speck indicating the approach of a storm.

7 *bawled*: 'shouted' in HT.

even the chief doctor was afraid: quoted in Branwell, 'History of the Young Men', in Neufeldt *BBWorks*, 1. 141; Branwell was fond of displaying documentary evidence (however imaginary) and announced that his quotation was from 'the *Author of The Romantic Tale*'.

1793: 1791 in manuscript, an obvious error.

palm-trees: the word 'jessamine' follows in HT.

8 *fierce*: 'fine' in HT.

'*Ashantee*': modelled on Ashantee, a kingdom on the west coast of Africa in what is now Ghana. The Brontës read of the Ashantee Wars of the 1820s in old newspapers and magazines. Branwell records in detail the children's imaginary wars between the 'Twelves' and the Ashantees in 'The History of the Young Men'.

8   *The situation . . . evil deserts*: the actual location of Glass Town and
     its surroundings was probably inspired by an article in *Blackwood's
     Magazine* (June 1826), entitled 'Geography of Central Africa. Denham
     and Clapperton's Journals', which included a detailed map of the Niger
     River delta, showing the Mountains of the Moon (or Jibbel Kumri) to the
     east and Ashantee to the west. An earlier article in *Blackwood's* describes
     the country and customs of Ashantee ('Mission from Cape Coast Castle
     to Ashantee', May and June 1819). The region is also described in
     Goldsmith's *A Grammar of General Geography* (London, 1823), used by
     the young Brontës (BPM: B45).

9   *'The Genius of the Storm'*: Branwell, also referred to as 'Chief Genius
     Bany Lightning', the most tyrannical of the four Chief Genii.

     a figure: possibly Charlotte asserting her authority over the 'play'; she and
     her sisters, as Chief Genii, assume a protective role towards the Young
     Men in the face of Branwell's more violent activities.

     Great Tower: the Tower of All Nations, inspired by the biblical Tower of
     Babel that was a dominant feature in the iconography of John Martin's
     engravings, known to the young Brontës: see Alexander, ' "The Burning
     Clime" '.

11   *mist*: reading from HT; *SHCBM* has 'light [*sic*]' which may indicate an
     error in the MS.

     too bright to look upon: the blinding light and fabulous palaces of the Genii
     owe much to Charlotte's fondness for the book of Revelation and other
     biblical references to human encounters with supernatural beings.

     till it vanished: not in HT.

12   *gave us leg bail*: a sporting term used by extension to mean 'to run away';
     not in HT.

     inconceivable: 'amazing' in HT.

13   *ordered*: 'asked' in HT.

     English: 'Englishmen' in HT.

     who: replaced by 'None of us doubted, they' in HT.

     Hill: modelled on General Sir Roland Hill, whom the Duke of Wellington
     served with in Copenhagen (1807) and again in the Peninsular Wars, and
     who was commander-in-chief of the British Army while Wellington was
     prime minister.

     Beresford: modelled on General William Carr Beresford, friend of
     Wellington and Marshal of the Portuguese Army. His reorganization of
     this army led to its victories under Wellington in the Peninsular Wars.

14   *Murray*: variously spelt 'Muray' and 'Murray' in *SHCBM*; 'Murry' in
     HT and in Charlotte's poem, 'A Wretch in Prison, by Murry' (1 February
     1830). Based on General Sir George Murray, an old Peninsular officer of
     the Duke of Wellington, who also served in the Duke's Cabinet 1828–30.

     but our most noble general is: 'but he is one of our most noble generals', in HT.

superior: reading incorporated from HT; marked in *SHCBM* as illegible.

despot: Napoleon Bonaparte, defeated finally and decisively at the battle of Waterloo, 18 June 1815, by the allied British, Netherlands, Hanoverian, Brunswick, and Prussian forces.

15 *Duke!' Wellington now rose. Immediately*: 'Duke of Wellington!" and almost immediately' in HT.

pervaded: 'prevailed in' in HT.

as follows, 'Soldiers: 'Fellow-soldiers' in HT.

Cahir: 'Cahin' in HT and *SHCBM*, but this is probably a mistranscription for 'Cahir', a town in Tipperary, Ireland. The following mountains of Killala are in Co. Mayo, Ireland.

17 *the roar of mighty waters . . . giant's cauldron*: cf. *Sadak in Search of the Waters of Oblivion*, a painting by John Martin, whose cataclysmic landscapes had a profound influence on the Brontës' writings: see note to p. 9: 'Great Tower'.

whose: recorded then deleted in HT.

18 SECOND VOL OF TALES OF THE ISLANDERS. The four little manuscript volumes of 'Tales of the Islanders' (12 March 1829–30 July 1830) are based on a Brontë 'play' begun in December 1827. In volume 1 and volume 2 (chapters 1 and 2 only), Charlotte describes past events; and the remaining tales of volumes 2, 3, and 4 appear to be Charlotte's own inventions, involving political allegory and fairytale adventure. The four volumes were originally hand-sewn booklets of twenty pages (9.9 × 6.3 cm); these have since been separated and bound together as a single volume, in the New York Public Library: Berg Collection.

The School Rebellion: the chapter titles are those given by Charlotte in her 'Catalogue of my Books' (Alexander *EEW* 1. 212); they are not in the MS. The title 'SECOND VOL OF TALES OF THE ISLANDERS' appears on the original brown paper cover of volume 2.

the subject of the school . . . &c.: the Palace School, established for young nobles on Vision Island, is governed by the Marquis of Douro and Lord Charles Wellesley in the absence of their father the Duke of Wellington, who is the Chief Governor. The Brontës themselves, as 'Little King and Queens', form the highest authority on Vision Island, controlling events and actively participating in the discipline of the children.

seeing how well it: Charlotte originally wrote 'seeing how well things were conducted'; when she deleted 'things' and substituted 'it' above the deletion, she forgot to also alter the verb to its singular form, so this slip should not be seen as indicative of poor grammar.

the great Catholic Question: when Wellington formed a Cabinet in January 1828 with Peel as home secretary, Roman Catholics could not sit in Parliament. By June, when O'Connell, a Catholic, defeated Vesey Fitzgerald (a Protestant Irish landlord who favoured Catholic relief and was Wellington's choice for a ministerial position) in his Clare re-election, Wellington and Peel realized that if they did not now support Catholic Emancipation they might be faced with an Irish revolt. In April 1829, a Catholic Emancipation Bill finally passed both houses, thus averting the danger of civil war in Ireland and giving Catholics the right to sit in parliament, hold civil office and vote, providing they met the required property qualifications.

18 *M* *Peel*: later Sir Robert Peel (1788–1850), born in Lancashire, son of a wealthy cotton manufacturer, entered Parliament as a Tory, under-secretary for the colonies (1811), secretary for Ireland (1812–18), home secretary (1822–7) and under Wellington (1828–30), PM (1834–5). Peel is the model for the Glass Town character Sir Robert Weaver Pelham.

19 *Catholics [could] do no harm with such good security*: Catholics, like Dissenters, were to have civil rights, providing the Protestant establishment was secured and Catholics could be removed when necessary. This was a primary concern of Mr Brontë (and hence of his family) and a prerequisite for his support of Catholic Emancipation. Although he had little trust in Catholic oaths of loyalty to the state (because this would be compromised by their loyalty to the Pope), he wrote three letters to the *Leeds Intelligencer* (1829) advocating emancipation as just and pragmatic in view of 'the manifest danger of a general convulsion'. His risk in espousing a view so unpopular with his Tory and evangelical friends helps to account for the passionate debate and excitement about the issue in the Brontë household.

O'S[haughnesy] and his nephew: according to the first volume of 'Tales of the Islanders', these are 'the guards for thrashing the children'.

20 *Doctor Hume*: Dr Alexander Hume Badey; based on the historical Duke's surgeon, Dr John Robert Hume, who attended him from the time of the Peninsular Wars (1808).

'*Blood an 'ounds*': abbreviated form of the old blasphemous oath 'God's blood and wounds!'; used collectively to refer to Wellington's blood-hounds that feature in the Young Men's Play.

P[rince] Polignac, P[rince] George & Johnny Lockhart & the Princess Vittoria: Prince Jules de Polignac, French ambassador in London and later chief minister of Charles X; George IV, reigned 29 January 1820–26 June 1830; Johnny Lockhart, son of John Gibson Lockhart and grandson of Sir Walter Scott; and Princess Victoria, who became queen on 20 June 1837 on the death of her uncle William IV, previously Duke of Clarence. The various factions in the school rebellion probably refer to the different alliances preceding Catholic Emancipation. George IV vacillated between his brother Cumberland, who opposed the bill, and Wellington, who now supported it; Polignac, a leader of the 'Cottage Clique' of foreign ambassadors, often caused difficulties for Wellington in his relationship with George IV.

21 *aerie*: spelling trials for this word appear at the foot of MS page 1: 'erie', 'eire', 'aerie'.

hardihearted: a word probably coined by Charlotte Brontë.

22 *Old Man Cockney*: former veteran of the fictitious Duke of Wellington; now supervisor of his household at Strathfieldsay.

23 *a giant clothed in the sun with a crown of 12 stars on his head*: cf. Revelation 12: 1.

24 *William Pitt*: William Pitt, 'The Younger', English statesman and prime minister (1783–1801) during the outbreak of the French Revolution and again from 1804 to 1806.

in India or Spain: Wellington served in India with his regiment from 1796 to 1803, gaining rapid promotion through his ability and the influence of his brother Lord Mornington, later Marquis Wellesley, governor-general of India. In 1808, Wellington was promoted lieutenant general and placed in command of troops destined to fight against the French in Spain and Portugal in the Peninsular Wars.

Battle [of] Salamanca: Salamanca, the famous Spanish university city situated on the River Tormes, was the site of one of Wellington's great victories on 22 July 1812.

25 *daring robbers & organized banditti*: gangs of outlaws were a prerequisite of picturesque descriptions and prints of Mediterranean scenery in the eighteenth and nineteenth century, encouraged especially by Gothic novels and the paintings of Salvator Rosa.

Victory: the personification of Victory here heralds the following political allegory of the relationship between England and Ireland, the latter crippled by the bigotry of the Roman Catholic church, a view passionately held by Mr Brontë despite his support for Catholic Emancipation and expressed in his novella, *The Maid of Killarney*. The iconographic descriptions of the battle and the two islands, with their traditional symbols (England, the rose and the oak; Ireland, the 'emerald isle' of the shamrock and the harp), appear to be drawn from the popular political cartoons of the period.

26 *dark cypress*: coniferous tree with dense dark foliage, a symbol of mourning.

a warrior: the Duke of Wellington, whose support of the Catholic Emancipation Bill of 1829 is clearly seen as a victory by the Brontë family (see note to p. 18: 'the great Catholic question').

27 *amaranths interwove[n] with laurel*: symbolic of everlasting (amaranth) and victorious (laurel) peace.

sung: throughout the manuscripts of 1826 to 1839, Charlotte uses 'sung' as the past tense of 'to sing', a practice common in the seventeenth, eighteenth, and early nineteenth centuries but now rare.

Anno Domini 1829: common Latin tag meaning 'in the year of (our) Lord'; usually written AD. Following this on the next line are the words 'Monieu L [?Cos]' in large longhand.

Oberon & Titania: King and Queen of the Fairies in Shakespeare's *A Midsummer Night's Dream*.

28 *on the face of the earth*: 'on the face of the earth' is added above the line with no clear indication where it should be inserted. The sentence could also read '& Night walks on the face of the earth in awful majesty', although this is less likely in view of the following quotation.

Night walks in awful majesty: as in many of Charlotte's phrases, there are Byronic echoes here: cf. the Hebrew Melody 'She Walks In Beauty', 1. 1 ('She walks in beauty, like the night'); and *Bride of Abydos*, 1. 175 ('The night, the majesty of Loveliness').

29 *Roman Catholics . . . necromancy*: Charlotte is reflecting popular Protestant prejudice of the time, fuelled by Gothic novels that associated Roman Catholic priests with the dark arts of the necromancer, who communicated with the dead and practised sorcery. Catholics were seen as imposed on by sinister priests, subject to the confessional and to idolatrous foreign rituals, and ignorant of the Bible.

30 *Seringpatan, Old Man Cockney, Game-keeper, Jack of all Trades & Orderly Man*: veterans of the fictitious Duke's early campaigns, now his retainers. Apart from Old Man Cockney, who resides at the Hall, they live in soldiers' cottages on the estate of Strathfieldsay and frequent the Horse Guards in London.

31 AN INTERESTING PASSAGE. The title page appears on the blue paper cover of the MS, which is a hand-sewn booklet of sixteen pages (5.3 × 3.7 cm), in the Houghton Library, Harvard University (Lowell 1(1)). Charlotte gives this manuscript a variant title in her *Catalogue of my Books*: 'An Interesting Incident in the Lives of Some of the Most Eminent Persons of the Age'.

  Although the tale is based on a theft at the local Keighley Mechanics' Institute Library, it is presented as a typical fabrication of Lord Charles Wellesley (Charlotte), written to discredit the prominent members of Glass Town's literary society, in particular his rival Captain Tree (another of Charlotte's narrators). Captain Bud (Branwell) hits back at Lord Charles's 'dirty work' in his manuscript 'The Liar Detected', written the following day (see p. 317).

waded so far or deep in the slough of criminality: compare *Macbeth*, III.iv. 136; and 'the slough of despond' in John Bunyan's *The Pilgrim's Progress*.

32 *my monkey*: Lord Charles's pet monkey Tringia, which features— together with his pet kitten, nightingale, and parrot—in many manuscripts of 1829–30.

Babylon the great: the Great Glass Town, often associated with the ancient city of Babylon, luxurious capital of the Chaldee Empire and model for the mystical Babylon of the Apocalypse. A number of writers, including Byron, likened the corruption of London to that of Babylon, an association also used by Charlotte and extended to her African 'London'.

Golconda: an ancient kingdom and city in India, famous for its great wealth, especially for the diamonds that were cut and polished there.

33 *valet de chambre*: personal attendant.

Captain T——: Captain Tree. Charlotte's use of capitals for proper names is usually a shorthand device but, in this MS she has adopted the nineteenth-century practice of using initial capital letters and a dash for people's names when referring to scandalous material. This is part of her narrator Lord Charles Wellesley's disingenuous pose as reporter of public corruption, pretending not to reveal the identity of his victims.

Lieutenant B——: Lieutenant Brock.

34 *Fetish Inn*: a name based on the Brontës' knowledge of Africa gleaned from the pages of *Blackwood's*. The word 'fetish' originally referred to objects used by the Ashantees and others of the Guinea coast as amulets with inherent magical powers. T. E. Bowdich's *Mission from Cape Coast to Ashantee* (1819), reviewed at length in *Blackwood's*, describes fetish-gold, cast into various shapes, worn as ornament and, after death, deposited with the bones of the wearer in a fetish-house.

Sergeant T—— & Sergeant B——, . . . *bookseller*: Sergeant Tree and Sergeant Bud.

General Bobadill: General Bobadill is based on the boasting, cowardly soldier Bobadilla in Ben Jonson's play *Every Man in His Humour* (1598).

35 *Captain B——*: Captain John Bud.

Doctor H—— B——, the other Young Man N—— & the third Ned L——: Doctor Hume Badey, Young Man Naughty, and Ned Laury, Glass Town compatriots in bodysnatching and dissection. The following incident clearly shows that Charlotte was aware of the famous case of the murderers Hare and Burke, who sold bodies to the surgeon Dr Knox for dissection (1829).

36 *macerating tub*: comical Glass Town device for resurrecting characters by steeping them in liquid to dissolve excess fat and presumably reduce their egos, as in the case of Captain Tree, the narrator's rival.

Young Rouge: the spelling here indicates Young Rogue and his father are Branwell's characters at this stage in the Glass Town saga; Charlotte later amends his name to 'Rogue' but Branwell retains his earlier spellings 'Rouge' and 'Rougue'.

Lord Lofty, a buck: probably Lord Frederic Lofty, rather than his younger brother Lord Macara Lofty. A 'buck' was slang for a dashing fellow, 'a gay debauchee' (*DVT*).

37 *That instrument*: the rack was an instrument of torture, usually consisting of a frame with two rollers at each end, to which the victim was fastened by wrist and ankles and his joints stretched; used in Roman times and in the Middle Ages, especially popular during the Spanish Inquisition.

38 SECOND SERIES OF THE YOUNG MEN'S MAGAZINE. The *Young Men's Magazine* was begun by Branwell in January 1829, under the title

Branwell's Blackwood's Magazine, clearly indicating the source of its inspiration in *Blackwood's Edinburgh Magazine*. Charlotte contributed to this journal as part of the Young Men's Play, and after six months she took over as 'editor' in August 1829, changing the name first to *Blackwood's Young Men's Magazine* and then to *Young Men's Magazine* in August 1830 when she began a second series.

The contents of this October issue of the second series, with its title page, editorial note, and contents listed at the front and 'Advertisments' at the end, are typical: a short story relating to the Glass Town saga, poetry by an eminent Glass Town poet, and a dramatic piece modelled on the conversations of *Blackwood's* 'Noctes Ambrosianae', which discuss relevant cultural or political issues (see note to p. 3: 'Mr Christopher North'). In each item Charlotte boldly establishes her own literary taste and style in contrast to that of her siblings, first by scorning Emily and Anne's mundane provincial creations and then by ridiculing the poetic effusions of Branwell's character Young Soult. The MS (BPM: B85) is a hand-sewn booklet of twenty pages (5.4 × 3.3 cm), written in minuscule print, and has a brown paper cover dated on the front at the top 'OCTOBER 1830'.

38 *SERGEANT TREE*: spelt 'Seargeant' (an archaic form) here and twice more in this MS, but 'sergeant' is the dominant form used by Charlotte.

40 *William Edward's country*: Parry's Land. Lord Charles Wellesley's disparagement of Parry's Land reflects Charlotte's scorn for the unromantic, realistic characters and setting of her sister's early writings.

41 *'on I travelled many a mile'*: cf. Wordsworth, 'The Sailor's Mother', l. 23.

   maun and waman: 'man and woman' in the original Young Men's language, invented by Branwell and spoken with fingers 'applied to' the nose; an early attempt to reproduce the local Yorkshire dialect (see Alexander *EW*, 35). The earlier description of the inhabitants of Parry's Land, in blue jackets and white aprons, corresponds to the inhabitants of 'Mons and Wamons Islands' described in *Branwell's Blackwood's Magazines* for January and June 1829 (in Neufeldt *BB Works*, 1. 9 and 14).

   Lady Aumly: Parry's dialect pronunciation of 'Emily'; 'Emily' is cancelled in the manuscript and replaced by 'Aumly'.

42 *his self*: dialect, in general use throughout England, Scotland, and Ireland.

   The solemn hush . . . around: unidentified; a common image in Gothic writing, such as the poems of Anne Radcliffe and her novel *The Mysteries of Udolpho*.

43 *Genius Emily . . . & vanished*: although Ross is usually protected by 'Chief Genius Annii' (Anne), Emily clearly assumes control of events in her kingdom.

   MORNING BY MARQUIS DOURO: a typical poem of the Marquis of Douro, who has a penchant for classical allusion and melancholy subjects. Sunrise and sunset are favourite topics; later, as King of Angria, Douro chooses the rising sun as his emblem and he himself is constantly compared to Apollo, who is often identified with Helios the Greek god of the sun. Apollo's other attributes are also applied to Douro: musicianship, eloquence, skill in fine arts, poetry, and science, and expert marksmanship; he is represented by Charlotte as the perfection of youthful manhood.

Aurora in crimson robes glowing | For the horses of fire doth unfold: Aurora, Roman goddess of the dawn, heralds the passage of Apollo at sunrise, as he drives his chariot of fiery horses from the east across the sky.

44 *Philomela*: nightingale, from the Greek myth of Philomela (lover of song) who was changed into a nightingale by the Gods after her brother-in-law raped her; hence the name of Lord Charles Wellesley's pet nightingale, 'Philomel'.

Luna: the moon, from the Roman goddess of the moon and months.

45 *De Lisle*: the distinguished Glass Town artist is a guest of the other regular members of 'Conversations'. His presence is used as a springboard for discussion on the Sister Arts of painting and poetry, modelled on similar debates in *Blackwood's*.

Bravey's Inn: owned by Bravey, one of the original twelve Young Men listed in Branwell's version of the founding of Glass Town. Like 'Gravey', he is revered for his authority but his role is reduced to that of a highly respected, corpulent landlord and master of ceremony of the Glass Town equivalent of *Blackwood's* 'Noctes Ambrosianae'.

Tower of all Nations: see 'A Romantic Tale', note to p. 9: 'Great Tower'.

Chimborazo or Teneriffe: mountains in Ecuador and the Canary Islands respectively; celebrated for their height in the Brontës' copy of J. Goldsmith's *Grammar of General Geography* (see *Oxford Companion*, 206–7).

46 *Ochone!*: Scottish and Irish exclamation of lamentation (*OED*).

M[arian] H[ume]: based on Elizabeth Hume, eldest daughter of the historical Duke's surgeon, who (like her counterpart in the Glass Town saga) is involved in a secret romance with the Duke's 14-year-old son Douro. In the saga, Marian Hume eventually marries Douro, but during the courtship Lord Charles Wellesley cannot resist teasing his elder brother about the romance, as his fabrication of her death in the following story, 'Albion and Marina', demonstrates.

the dark hills of Jibbel Kumri . . . the lone traveller's hath seen: the isolated landscape north of the Glass Town, home of the Genii; described in the early manuscripts (see 'The Twelve Adventurers').

tout à la coup: 'all of a sudden' (French: *tout à coup*).

47 *I veil my eyes with a holy fear*: cf. Coleridge's 'Kubla Khan', l. 53 ('And close your eyes with holy dread'). Unlike Coleridge's vision of paradise, 'Art had not yet built a palace' in Young Soult's Eden where benign and 'wrothful' spirits (the Genii) dwell.

47 *hartshorn, cold water, vinegar, salvolatic, [?salzaikaling] and sal everything else*: popular restoratives in the Victorian period. The shavings of hartshorn, served as a jelly, were thought particularly nourishing; vinegar was used (among other things) as a cooling medicine in fevers; sal volatile or 'spirit of amonia' was used as a stimulant in fainting; and various other salts ('sal') were commonly used. Mr Brontë was considered something of a hypochondriac and his children were familiar with the various medicines listed in his annotated book of remedies, *Modern Domestic Medicine* (London: Simpkin & Marshall et al. 1826), by Thomas John Graham, MD, whose name may have suggested that of Dr Graham in *Villette*.

The poet has fallen into an inspiration dream! . . . save his life!: Charlotte is mocking the romantic excesses and posturing of Branwell by ridiculing his character (and pseudonym) Young Soult.

48 *'all of heaven and not of earth'*: Young Soult is quoting himself here (line 31 of the poem he has just recited)—a further example of Charlotte's satire of Branwell's poetic extravagance.

49 *tout le monde:* everybody (French).

50 *Exeunt omnes*: all go out (Latin); stage direction for all to retire.

The Elements of LYING: Lord Charles Wellesley prides himself on deception and subterfuge, his chief method of gathering material for his stories. His *An Interesting Passage in the Lives of Some Eminent Men of the Present Time* was fabricated to humiliate his literary rival Captain Tree, and *Albion and Marina* is likewise written 'out of malignity': he boldly states in the preface, 'The conclusion is wholly destitute of any foundation in truth.'

51 *Orion & Arcturus*: two hunters who, in Greek mythology, were transported to heaven to become constellations. Orion was a giant and hunter of Boeotia. Arcas, son of Zeus, mistakenly pursued his mother Callisto while hunting; she had been changed into a bear by the jealous Hera. To prevent the crime of matricide, Zeus transformed his son into a bear and transported both bears to heaven: Callisto as the Great Bear and Arcas as the little Bear (Ursa Minor). According to some, Arcas was identified with Bootes and became Arcturus (bear's tail; spelt 'Arturus' by Charlotte), the brightest star at the end of the constellation Bootes (Gertrude Jobes, *Dictionary of Mythology, Folklore and Symbolism* (New York: Scarecros, 1961)).

52 *bragadocio*: empty boaster, swaggerer; from the Spenserian character personifying 'vainglory' (*OED*, modern spelling 'braggadocio').

53 *fisty-cuffs*: boxing, fighting with gloved and often ungloved fists, a fashionable sport for which Branwell had a particular enthusiasm (see *Oxford Companion*, 114).

54 ALBION AND MARINA. This is Charlotte's first love story, written by Lord Charles Wellesley as a spoof to annoy his older brother Arthur, Marquis of Douro (Albion), who is courting Marian Hume (Marina), daughter of his father's doctor. The characters are those of Glass Town, thinly

disguised by altered names and possibly influenced by a recent reading by Charlotte of her father's didactic love story, *The Maid of Killarney, or Albion and Flora*. The manuscript of 'Albion and Marina', now in the Wellesley College Library, Mass., is a hand-sewn booklet of sixteen pages (5.6 × 3.9 cm) in a cover of blue recycled paper, which is labelled on the reverse: 'Purified Epsom Salts, SOLD BY WEST, CHEMIST & DRUGGIST, Keighley.' The cover is titled: 'ALBION AND MARINA/A TALE BY/LORD Charles Wellesley/October 12 1830'.

Paris, &c.: end of title page.

55 *Lady Zelzia Elrington*: Lady Zenobia Ellrington (spelt 'Elrington' here, as in Branwell's manuscripts). This is the first appearance of this prominent character in the Glass Town saga: her frenzied, unrequited love for the Marquis of Douro is a constant theme from now on in the early juvenilia, and in latter manuscripts she becomes the Countess of Northangerland.

miller, jockey, talker, blue stocking, charioteer & beldam: abusive slang words, found also in Scott's novels and *Blackwood's*. A 'miller' is slang for 'pugilist' or 'murderer' (Zenobia was noted for her violent actions); a 'jockey' was a cheat or caird; a 'bluestocking' is a literary woman (an abusive term here but later used in a laudatory sense by Charlotte in *Shirley*, vol. 3, ch. 4); and 'beldam' means a 'hag' or 'virago', in this context. Zenobia was also known as a great conversationalist and an accomplished rider and driver of horses (*DVT*, Partridge, *OED*).

Albion & Marina are both alive & well for ought I know: the marriage of Arthur, Lord Douro, and Marian Hume (Albion and Marina) is recorded by Charlotte in *The Bridal*, written two months later in October 1830 (Alexander *EEW* 1. 335–48). In subsequent manuscripts, Marian's name is expanded to Florence Marian Hume.

Tree: Lord Charles has just tried to discredit his rival in 'An Interesting Passage'.

romantic grandeur . . . pretensions: Charlotte's primary model for novel-writing was Sir Walter Scott ('all novels after his are worthless', she told Ellen Nussey in 1834), whose works are generally set in the grand romantic scenery of the Scottish highlands. She follows the conventions of Scott and others here in her depiction of the South of England as picturesque rather than sublime and romantic: see *Oxford Companion*, 444–6.

'nae sheepshank': Charlotte wrote 'na sheepshanks', imitating this Scots dialect reference to a person of no small importance.

56 *'Duke of Strathelleraye'*: modelled on the historical Duke of Wellington and his estate of Strathfield Saye in Hampshire, England.

Of her I can only say . . . ever more: Kitty Pakenham, the real Duchess of Wellington, was known for her charitable works, her simple dress, and lack of ornamentation. As mistress of Strathfield Saye, her chief concern was for her servants and the poor.

56   *Lord Corneilius*: Lord Charles Wellesley, a comically incorrect self-portrait in which he attributes many of his brother's characteristics to himself.

   black as the hoody's wing: a variation of 'black as a crow'; the hoody is a hooded or Royston crow.

   Marquis of Tagus: Marquis of Douro, named here after the River Tagus, which (like the River Duero) flows through Portugal and Spain and which was associated with Wellington's Peninsular Campaign.

   Apollo Belvedere: an ancient statue of Apollo in the Belvedere Gallery in the Vatican and renowned as a model of ideal male beauty. See notes to p. 43.

57   *Sir Alured Angus*: Sir Alexander Hume Badey.

   querelous: an obsolete, rare form of 'querulous', meaning complaining or peevish (*OED*).

   Quaker-like in its simplicity: simplicity was one of the four codes of the Quakers, members of the Religious Society of Friends, founded by George Fox in the mid-seventeenth century. In the nineteenth century they were particularly noted for their opposition to fashion and for their plainness in dress and speech. Charlotte's heroine Jane Eyre describes herself as a 'plain, Quakerish governess' (*Jane Eyre*, vol. 2, ch. 9).

   one row of pearls round her neck: in Western traditions pearls are associated with love and marriage. Marina's single strand of pearls indicates her purity and taste; in later Glass Town stories, a single strand of pearls denotes a married woman.

58   *Oak-wood House*: a name probably suggested by Oakwell House, home of the Walkers, near Birstall, which Charlotte visited about this time with her new schoolfriend Ellen Nussey. Oakwell Hall, said to be the original of Fieldhead in *Shirley*, stood opposite the Walkers' house.

   both are yet too young: the real Duke of Wellington was not amused to discover the secret romance between his 14-year-old son Douro and his surgeon's daughter Elizabeth Hume. Although it had been supported for several years by his wife, the Duke abruptly curtailed the affair (see *Oxford Companion*, 535).

59   *It seemed as the cities of old Nineveh or Babylon . . . Semele*: Glass Town is often likened to Babylon, once the magnificent capital of the Assyrian Empire on the banks of the Euphrates. Its mystical nature in the Apocalypse would also have made it attractive to Charlotte as a model, as would the Old Testament associations of the ancient city of Nineveh. She was also familiar with visual images of both in the paintings of John Martin (see Alexander, '"The Burning Clime"').

   Belus, the most sacred god of the Assyrians, was often identified with the Greek Zeus or Latin Jupiter, hence 'Jupiter Belus'. His son Ninus, King of Assyria, was the husband of the legendary queen Semiramis and the reputed builder of Nineveh; and another son, Babylon, is said to have founded the city that bears his name. Astarte, goddess of fertility and reproduction, was called Ishtar (Venus) by the Babylonians and so also considered a moon goddess. Semele is the mother, by Zeus, of the god Dionysus; her request to see Zeus in all his splendour, armed with thunder and lightning, caused her death, but her son later made her a goddess.

Salamanca Palace: known as Waterloo Palace elsewhere in the Glass Town saga.

60 *Sophocles the majestic*: one of the three great Greek tragedians and favourite poet of the Athenians. His tragedies are known to be more human, less heroic, than those of Aeschylus; and more dramatically effective than those of Euripides.

Parnassus: mountain near Delphi, Greece, one of whose summits was consecrated to Apollo and the muses; and hence regarded as the seat of poetry and music.

like Milton, 'to write somewhat that the gracious Muses should not willingly die': Milton, *Reason of Church Government*, bk. II: 'I might perhaps leave something so written to aftertimes, as they should not willingly let it die.'

Necropolis . . . the mysteries of ancient Egyptian worship: in Egyptian myth, the West was the realm of the dead, since this is where the sun sets. Douro is from the West of the Glass Town Federation and thus associated with the setting sun.

Amalthea: a nymph in Greek mythology, the nurse of Zeus; presumably Douro's choice here is indicative of his expectations in a wife.

titles of his various works . . . Marina: Douro's poetic career is represented by the Glass Town manuscript 'The Violet, A Poem With Several Smaller Pieces, By The Marquis of Douro', written by Charlotte the following month (14 November 1830). It includes seven poems which display Douro's Classical learning and his longing for Marina (see for example 'Matin' in Neufeldt, Victor A. (ed.), *The Poems of Charlotte Brontë* (New York: Garland, 1985), 106).

61 *Creachan*: spelt 'Cruachan' here but standardized to previous spelling.

Madame de Stael: Anne Louise Germaine Necker, Baronne de Staël-Holstein (1766–1817), referred to by Byron as the greatest mind of her times; a noted intellectual who received in her Paris salon, on the eve of the Revolution, the most progressive elements in French society. She emigrated to England in 1793, returned to Paris 1795, and was exiled by Napoleon first from Paris and then from France. She first met Wellington, whom she regarded as a heroic liberator, in 1814 in her reconstituted Parisian salon (he was then ambassador to the reinstated French court of Louis XVIII), and they subsequently became friends and correspondents. Charlotte Brontë often refers to Lady Zenobia Ellrington as the Verdopolitan de Stael.

62 *this extraordinary incident*: cf. *Jane Eyre*, vol. 3, ch. 9, in which Jane hears Rochester's voice crying out to her although he is many miles away.

62 *the 18 of June 1815, 12 o'clock at night*: the date of the battle of Waterloo, which probably influenced Charlotte's choice of a significant date here.

63 *1817*: 1815 in MS; an obvious error.

66 THE SPELL. 'The Spell' is another fabrication of Lord Charles Wellesley, woven in revenge against his elder brother the Duke of Zamorna and newly created King of Angria (Arthur Wellesley, Marquis of Douro). The story is essentially an imaginary excursion from the central Glass Town plot: Lord Charles invents a twin brother for Zamorna (named Ernest) to account for the multiplicity of his interests and increasingly complex relationships; but it is also a rewriting of Zamorna's early life (his affair/ marriage to Lady Helen Victorine, Baroness Gordon) and an exploration of the Gothic mode.

The size of Charlotte's hand-sewn manuscripts has increased since 'Albion and Marina', written four years earlier; the title pages are now more elaborate and the narratives longer despite Charlotte's continuing use of her minuscule script. The MS of 'The Spell', now in the British Library (Add. MS. 34255), comprises twenty-four pages, each measuring 11 × 18.5 cm.

VERDOPOLIS: at the end of 1830, to mark the growing sophistication of the Great Glass Town, the Brontës renamed the city 'Verreopolis', which Lord Charles Wellesley notes was 'compounded of a Greek and French word to that effect' (Alexander *EEW* 1. 298); by the following year the name had been corrupted to 'Verdopolis'. The Glass Town Federation likewise is now the Verdopolitan Union or Federation.

Coomassie Square: a central square in Verdopolis, named after the battle of Coomassie, won by the original twelve Young Men against the Ashantee tribes. Like many of the early Glass Town names, Coomassie is a town that can be found on the map of Africa in the Brontës' early geography books: see Alexander, 'Imagining Africa'.

67 *exclusion*: Lord Charles Wellesley has recently been placed under the guardianship of General Thornton, since Zamorna could no longer tolerate his younger brother's watchful eye and the subsequent literary reports on his behaviour. Nevertheless Lord Charles still has his apartments in Wellesley House.

sister-in-law: Mary Henrietta Percy, Zamorna's new bride (and third wife), introduced into the saga the previous year by Branwell (in his story 'The Politics of Verdopolis', 23 October 1833) and adopted by Charlotte the following January 1834 when she took a future glance at her characters in 'A Leaf from an Unopened Volume' and made Mary her central heroine in March 1834, in 'High Life in Verdopolis' (Alexander *EEW* 2(1). 321, and 2(2). 3). Florence Marian Hume, the heroine of 'Albion and Marina', was increasingly neglected by her husband Zamorna and died of a broken heart soon after the birth of her son. In 'The Spell', however, Lord Charles suggests that both mother and son died from consumption.

Angria: the new kingdom of Angria.

68 *young Marquis of Almeida*: Arthur Julius Wellesley, Lord Almeida. The title 'Almeida' is derived from the frontier fortress town of Almeida in north-east Portugal, situated on a tributary of the River Douro. During the Peninsular War, Almeida was taken by the French in 1810 but relieved by Wellington the following year.

his first-born: Lord Almeida is actually Zamorna's second son. His first son is Ernest Edward Gordon Wellesley, known as 'Fitzarthur' ('Fitz Arthur' or 'Fitz-Arthur') as an indication of his position as a morganatic son of Zamorna by his first wife Lady Helen Victorine, Baroness Gordon, who died in childbirth; the narrator Lord Charles weaves this aspect of Zamorna's past into 'The Spell'. The name Gordon originated from Byron's Gordon relatives on his mother's side.

Mina Laury . . . the father: Mina saved Zamorna's life when he was a youth (see 'Something about Arthur', Alexander *EEW* 2(1)). Her name possibly derives from Minna, lover of the pirate Cleveland in Scott's *The Pirate*, a work well known to the Brontës.

manor house: Grassmere Manor, a name derived from 'Grasmere' in the English Lake District, is Zamorna's secluded estate in Wellingtonsland where Mina Laury cares for his children.

69 *upas-tree*: A Javanese tree with poisonous juice used for tipping arrows; legend tells of a putrid steam rising from it, hence its figurative use for a corrupting or pernicious influence (Brewer). Brontë uses it again in *Jane Eyre*, vol. 3, ch. 1.

when respiration begins to rattle . . . but bones: the gruesome details of the progress of consumption (or TB as it is now called) were all too familiar to the young Brontës and their contemporaries. They had seen their two eldest sisters die of consumption in 1825; and Charlotte was later to watch Emily and Anne die of the same fatal disease.

70 *Adrianopolis*: the capital of the new kingdom of Angria is still under construction on the banks of the River Calabar; envisaged as a city of grand palaces and vast colonnades inspired by John Martin's paintings of Babylon and Nineveh: see Alexander, '"The Burning Clime"').

71 *Tadmor in the wilderness*: cf. 2 Chronicles 8: 4; Tadmor, the ancient city of Palmyra, is referred to again in *Villette*, vol. 3, ch. 34. For connections between its queen, Zenobia, and the Angrian character of the same name, see Alexander *EW*, 23.

voiceless as Tyre on the forsaken sea: cf. Isaiah 23: 11 and 15.

72 *Ernest & Emily*: Ernest Julius Mornington Wellesley, Duke of Valdacella, Marquis of Alhama, twin brother of Zamorna, and his wife, Emily Inez, Duchess of Valdacella, who appear only in 'The Spell'.

Free-Town: city in the south of Sneachiesland, 150 miles north of Verdopolis, named after Freetown, capital of Sierra Leone on the West African coast, then a British colony and so-named because it was settled by liberated slaves from 1787.

73 *bedral's*: an inferior church officer in Scotland, who combined the duties of clerk, beadle, sexton, gravedigger, and bellringer (Wright).

74 *dree her weird*: to suffer her destiny, to endure her fate (archaic).

76 *Douro Villa*: Florence Marian Hume's former retreat, a Palladian country house belonging to Zamorna, in the Verdopolitan Valley.

Countess Seymour: formerly Lady Isabella Wellesley, dowager Countess of Mornington, sister of the Duke of Wellington. She has one son, Lord Fitzroy, and six daughters, who all fall under Zamorna's influence and form part of his Angrian 'harem' in later manuscripts.

78 *craped hat*: the customary band of black crêpe material worn round the hat in token of mourning.

St Michael's: the Verdopolitan cathedral, which (like Westminster Abbey) is the site of coronation and contains the royal vaults. The name was probably derived from Haworth parish church of St Michael's and All Angels, of which Mr Brontë was perpetual curate.

Mr Sumner . . . Dr Alford: Sumner is the doctor who attended Lord Almeida at Grassmere Manor and who continues to attend Zamorna's other son by a previous marriage (see note to p. 68: 'his first-born'); and Alford is physician to Zamorna (see note to p. 4: 'John Bull,' for source).

79 *Ernest Fitz-Arthur*: see note to p. 68: 'his first–born'. In 'The Spell', however, he is called Ernest Edward Fitz-Arthur (or Fitzarthur) Ravenswood Wellesley, son of Zamorna's twin brother (see note to p. 72: 'Ernest & Emily').

80 *Lord Rossendale*: John Augustus Sheachi.

earth to earth, ashes to ashes: from 'Burial of the Dead', the Book of Common Prayer for the Church of England.

'I know that my Redeemer liveth': from Handel's *Messiah*, based on Job 19: 25; an anthem heard recently by the Brontës at the opening of the new organ for St Michael's church, Haworth, in May 1834.

83 *stun one with your larums*: startle or bewilder with an uproar (Yorkshire dialect).

cold meat: contemporary slang: cf. 'A dead wife is the best cold meat in a man's house' (*DVT*).

84 *ingle nook*: chimney corner; 'ingle' is Scottish dialect for 'flame' (Wright).

the assassin in Uwins's picture: Thomas Uwins, who exhibited at the Royal Academy from 1803 to 1807, painted *The Confessional of the Black Crucifix*, in which the face of the husband/assassin is covered with a cloak; since this was not exhibited until 1836, however, Charlotte may have read a review of a similar earlier painting.

85 *Edward & William*: disowned by their father, Edward and William Percy have had little relationship with their sister Mary. Edward's rise in society has been rapid and he is now Angrian Minister of Trade, married

to Princess Maria Sneachie. William, who dislikes factories and the wool trade, has quarrelled with his brother and purchased a commission in the army, becoming Colonel Sir William Percy. The two brothers are proto-types for Edward and William Crimsworth (*The Professor*), and Robert and Louis Moore (*Shirley*).

Ithuriel: in Milton's *Paradise Lost* (4. 788 ff.), one of the angels charged by Gabriel to search for Satan in Paradise; Charlotte has marked this page in her copy of the book.

86 *Roland & Roswal couched amicably on the rug*: an allusion to the Duke's intention to marry her. Roland is Mary Percy's Newfoundland guard dog, owned by her before her marriage and named after the most famous of Charlemagne's paladins, the flower of French chivalry and subject of romance. Roswal is Zamorna's favourite stag-hound. Large dogs commonly accompany Charlotte's heroes and heroines, in imitation of Scott's and Byron's similar dogs: cf. Rochester's dog, Pilot, in *Jane Eyre*, and Shirley Keeldar's dog, Tartar, in *Shirley*.

88 *Niger*: the Glass Town River Niger. Throughout the 1820s, the Brontës followed the controversy about the course and termination of the Niger in *Blackwood's*: see Alexander, 'Imagining Africa'.

89 *Oedipus*: the Theban hero who, according to ancient Greek legend, solved the riddle propounded by the Sphinx.

90 *M.L.*: Mina Laury.

Narcissus of Chantrey's: Henry Chantrey, a young Verdopolitan sculptor patronized (and later knighted) by Zamorna; named after Sir Francis Chantry, a celebrated contemporary sculptor of portrait statues and busts and a friend of Byron. A statue of Narcissus, the beautiful youth of Greek legend who was so enamoured of his reflection in the water that he jumped in to embrace it and drowned, is a particularly appropriate embellishment for Douro Villa, retreat of the dying Marian who suffered because of Zamorna's concern for his own proud image.

93 *Mary Stuart*: Mary, Queen of Scots (1542–87), married to Francis II of France, to Lord Darnley and then to Bothwell. She was the Roman Catholic cousin of Elizabeth I who imprisoned and finally beheaded this Queen of Scotland. Mary Stuart (whose name and character probably suggested those of Mary Henrietta, Queen of Angria) figures in Scott's *The Abbot*; and the young Brontës would certainly have been familiar with her tragic history described in detail in Scott's *Tales of a Grandfather*, given to them by their Aunt Branwell in 1828 (BPM: 4). Emily Inez Wellesley, the woman referred to in this passage, is from a Scottish Catholic family and is clearly based on Mary, Queen of Scots. As mother of Ernest Edward 'Fitzarthur' Wellesley, she is probably the late Lady Helen Victorine Gordon, the 'Lily of Loch Sunart', re-created for 'The Spell': see note to p. 68: 'his first-born'.

Edward: Ernest Edward Fitzarthur: see note to p. 68: 'his first-born'. Only in 'The Spell' does he have a sister, Lady Emily Augusta Wellesley.

93 *Castle Oronsay*: named after the Island of Oronsay, part of the Inner Hebrides of Scotland.

Keswick: like Grassmere, Keswick is derived from the English Lake District town of the same name, associated with Wordsworth and Coleridge.

Lady Millicent Hume, & Euphemia Lindsay: the former is the blind sister of the late Marian Hume. Neglected by her family and left out of her father's will, she falls under the 'protection' of Zamorna and earns her living as a governess to Euphemia (Effie) Lindsay, first in the lodge at Grassmere Manor and later at Alderwood, former estate of the Humes in Wellingtonsland, later inherited by Zamorna on the death of Sir Alexander Hume Badey.

94 *Mornington-Court*: where Mina first worked for Zamorna's mother the Duchess of Wellington; derived from the Wellesley family title, inherited by the real Duke of Wellington's eldest brother Lord Mornington.

97 *large Venetian windows*: windows which each have three openings, the central one arched and wider than the others. The style, also called Serliana, is one of the hallmarks of Palladianism in eighteenth-century England.

98 *Edward*: Edward Percy.

99 *rare apes*: 'rare lads' or 'rare apes' are Verdopolitan equivalents of modern gangs. The term is used chiefly by the early Glass Town 'heavies' to refer both to themselves and to others, usually those destined to be victims of their midnight bodysnatching raids, as in 'An Interesting Passage'.

distaff: the staff used in hand-spinning, hence a reference to female authority as opposed to the male 'sceptre'.

Hector: 'A bully, a swaggering coward. To hector; to bully, probably from such persons affecting the valour of Hector, the Trojan hero' in Homer's *Iliad* (*DVT*).

owls on earth should croak his doom & scream his epitaph: owls are proverbial not only for their judge-like solemnity but also for their association with imminent death and (as nocturnal birds) with the Kingdom of Sleep.

100 *'rings & plumes & pearls'*: cf. Byron, *Don Juan*, canto 11, stanza 52, l. 548: 'Of gems and plumes and pearls and silks'.

101 *field . . . my reapers*: cf. Revelation 14: 15.

102 *Kamschatka*: now Kamchatka; defined in the Brontës' copy of Goldsmith's *Grammar of General Geography* (BPM: B45) as 'a large peninsula, on the east of Asiatic Russia'.

103 *jessamine*: an unusual use, probably meaning delicate and fragrant, from a perfume derived from jasmine flowers.

105 *Atropos*: in Greek mythology, the eldest of the three Fates and the one who severs the thread of life.

Messalina-like given him poison: Messalina was the wife of the Emperor Claudius of Rome, known for her sexual profligacy and executed by order of her husband. Although she was responsible for the deaths of many, it was Claudius' second wife Agrippina who poisoned him. In *Jane Eyre* (vol. 3, ch. 1) Rochester refers to his mad wife, Bertha, as 'my Indian Messalina'.

Queen of Scots: see note to p. 93: 'Mary Stuart'; Mary, Queen of Scots was suspected of being complicit in the murder of her second husband Lord Darnley.

a cup, drugged like the one Socrates drank: Socrates (469–399 BC), the great Greek philosopher, was sentenced to death by drinking hemlock.

Mary Stuart: Emily Inez Wellesley, see note to p. 93: 'Mary Stuart'.

106 *poniard*: dagger.

107 *Elimbos*: a mountain in the Branni Hills, the immense chain of unexplored mountains stretching hundreds of miles beyond the most northern city of the Verdopolitan Federation and named after Chief Genius Branni (Branwell). Since these and the nearby mountain chain, Dimdims Throne, are the seat of the Chief Genii, 'Elimbos' may reflect Mt. Olympus, mythical home of the Greek gods.

108 *suttee*: Hindu custom of burning the widow on the funeral pyre of her deceased husband.

the setting, not the rising, sun: the new emblem of Angria is the rising sun; it is emblazoned in gold on the scarlet flag, on Zamorna's carriage, and on all similar accoutrements.

Pelham: Sir Robert Pelham, Mary's disappointed suitor, a landowner from Wellingtonsland and political protégé of her father.

110 *Mr Abercrombie & Sir Astley Coleridge*: Verdopolitan doctors, whose names were suggested by contemporary medical men and the poet Coleridge: cf. Sir Astley Paston Cooper, the Duke of Wellington's neurologist (see 'Origin of the Islanders') and John Abercrombie, one of the chief consulting physicians in Scotland during the Brontës' lifetime.

113 *St Augustine's*: the second Verdopolitan cathedral, modelled on St Paul's in London; cf. St Michael's, note to p. 78.

114 *Egyptian bondage*: biblical reference to the captivity of the Israelites in Egypt. Mina's self-sacrificing slavery for Zamorna, which prefigures Jane Eyre's initial idolization of Rochester, is examined in detail in 'Mina Laury'.

115 *waur*: a possible dialect rendering of 'worse'.

in my bit of a hut: Ned Laury sheltered the 15-year-old Zamorna (then Douro) in his cottage in Wellingtonsland after he was wounded in an attack on a rival's property: see Alexander *EW* 88–9.

home-close: yard or enclosure around the house.

Battle of Velino: a decisive battle in the 'War of Encroachment' (*c.* November 1833).

his own camp bed: reminiscent of the behaviour of the Duke of Wellington, and of Alexander the Great, whom the Brontës also used as a model.

115 *He screened me . . . Lord Richton*: an incident recorded in one of Branwell Brontë's manuscripts. Flower was the author of 'An Historical Narrative of the "War of Encroachment"' (Newfeldt *BBWorks*, 1. 365).

   the west: Wellingtonsland, home of Ned Laury and the Wellesley family.

116 *Mr Maxwell*: William Maxwell, Jr, Zamorna's steward.

   Scylla: spelt 'Sylla' in MS; a favourite saying of Northangerland. In Greek legend, Scylla was a hideous sea monster who was the terror of ships and sailors in the Straits of Messina. Originally a beautiful nymph, she was changed by the jealous Circe into a hideous creature with twelve feet, six heads, and a body made up of monsters like dogs which barked unceasingly.

120 *C'est fait de moi!*: 'I'm done for!' (French).

121 *Temple*: the housekeeper; a name used again by Charlotte in *Jane Eyre*.

123 *'the water stood in her eyes'*: a phrase used several times in Bunyan's *The Pilgrim's Progress* (ed. Roger Sharrock (London: Oxford University Press, 1966), 177 and 255). Cf. also *Villette*, vol. 2, ch. 21.

   piangendo: weeping, crying, plangent (Italian).

125 *was once like a girl*: Zamorna's early effeminate appearance is often recalled by characters who wish to taunt him. Henry Bramham Lindsay, for example, calls him 'Augusta' (Alexander *EEW*, 2(2). 123).

   the young satrap of Angria: a satrap is the governor of a province under the ancient Persian monarchy; an image suggestive of Zamorna's growing tyranny and ostentatious splendour.

   Quashia: Quashia apparently thrashed Zamorna as a boy and Zamorna's irrational pursuit of Quashia in the later Angrian wars is said to have originated in this incident. Their relationship is explored in Alexander, 'Imagining Africa'.

126 *Candahar & Ispahan*: now Kandahar in Afganistan and Isfahan in Iran, respectively. Goldsmith's *Grammar of General Geography*, used by the Brontës, gives the following definitions: 'Cairo; capital of Egypt'; 'Candahar; a province of Cabul'; 'Cabul; a kingdom of northern Hindoostan, including part of Persia'; and 'Ispahan; a former capital of Persia'. Verdopolis, the Queen of Nations, is modelled not only on London but also on the exotic capitals of the ancient world.

   the jarvie: a hackney-coachman (*OED*).

   Girnington-Hall: rambling Gothic country house of General Thornton, situated at the upper end of the Valley of Verdopolis; acquired from 'Old Girnington', whose fortune Thornton has recently inherited.

   quick-set: living plants or cuttings, especially of white hawthorn, set to form a hedge (colloquial).

128 *I hate that confession . . . than tell him*: cf. *Villette*, vol. 1, ch. 15, and Charlotte's own experience of confession (see Herbert Rosengarten and Margaret Smith (eds.), *Villette* (Oxford: Clarendon Press, 1984), 729).

She may have heard of the Blessed Gonsalvi of Amaranth (1187–1259), a Portuguese who lived a life of solitary contemplation; but Gonsalvi (usually Gundisalvus, and spelt Gonsalvo later in this manuscript) is a common Portuguese religious name.

129 *Castle Oronsay*: see note to p. 93: 'Castle Oronsay'. Many of the following names mentioned by Fitzarthur as part of his 'Highland' home (such as Loch Sunart, Ben Carnach, and Glen Avon) are based on Scottish place-names, found chiefly in the Western Highlands.

130 *faint heart never won fair lady*: cf. Burns, 'To Dr Blacklock': 'And let us mind, faint heart ne'er wan | A lady fair'.

Sirius! Condor!: two of Zamorna's stag-hounds: named after Sirius, the Dog-Star, and the Condor, a huge South American vulture. See also note to p. 86 .

132 *Mary Stuart*: see note to p. 93: 'Mary Stuart'.

Gazelle . . . such a wild, flashing eastern loveliness: cf. Byron's *Don Juan*, canto 2, stanza 202, l. 1612: 'Of his gazelle-eyed daughters, she was one'.

133 *Lucifer*: the demon of 'Sinful Pride', *Paradise Lost* (10. 425–6); often synonymous with Satan.

Solons: Solon was an Athenian statesman and sage (*c*.638–*c*.558 BC), a great lawgiver and one of the Seven Sages of Greece (Brewer).

134 *Princess Florence, the Princess Henrietta or the Princess Inez*: the late Florence Marian Wellesley; Mary Henrietta, Queen of Angria; and Emily Inez Wellesley.

You have brewed a bitter cup. Now, go, & drink it to the very dregs: cf. Psalm 75: 8.

Rhadamanthus: in Greek mythology, Rhadamanthus was one of the three judges of hell.

Joachim: Joachim Murat, the flower of French chivalry, who assisted Zamorna in fighting the Ashantees and was rewarded by being made an Angrian minister. Named after Napoleon's French cavalry commander of the same name.

Draco: an Athenian of the seventh century BC who drew up a code of laws noted for their severity, hence the adjective 'Draconian'.

Jupiter: also Jupiter Tonans, the thundering Jupiter. Supreme god of Roman mythology, who determined the course of human affairs; corresponding to the Greek Zeus, who held court on Mt. Olympus and who punished the Titan Prometheus for stealing fire from heaven and giving it to men by chaining him to Mt. Caucasus, where his liver was preyed upon by an eagle by day and renewed every night.

135 *Tartarus*: the infernal regions in classical mythology, often equivalent to Hades although Homer placed it beneath Hades.

The Furies: merciless goddesses of vengeance who punished all transgressors, especially those who, like Zamorna, neglected filial duty or claims of kinship.

135 *Hebe, perform thine office!*: cupbearer to the gods, she administers nectar
and ambrosia, drink and food that conferred immortality on them; Mina
Laury is also called Hebë by Zamorna.

137 *The trials of Job . . . progress*: Thornton's guardianship of Lord Charles
compared to the trials of Job: although Satan (with God's permission)
smote Job with boils, reduced him to poverty, and destroyed his family,
Job suffered with patience and refused to curse God (Book of Job).

138 *And young Rogue's imposing & fiery beauty, overbearing demeanour . . .
fiercer man than William*: the physical and temperamental contrast,
and resulting rivalry, between the Percy brothers, William and Edward
('young Rogue' here after his father), prefigures the rivalry between the
Crimsworth brothers in *The Professor* and between the Moore brothers in
Shirley (see Alexander *EW*, ch. 29).

at the going down of the sun: cf. Exodus 17: 12, and Deuteronomy 11: 30,
16: 6.

139 *Lady Frances Millicent Hume*: see note to p. 93.

140 *like an index*: the style of a sundial, cf. Peacock, *Melincourt*, ch. 32, 'There
was a sun-dial in the centre of the court; the sun shone on the brazen
plate, and the shadow of the index fell on the line of noon.'

141 *Marquis of Alhama*: probably after the Alhama River and the Sierra de
Alhama in Spain.

142 *Gemini*: twins (Latin), a constellation and one of the signs of the Zodiac,
after Castor and Pollux, twins of classical mythology.

On this day, precisely twenty two years ago: it was customary for Charlotte
to set events in her stories exactly at the time of writing. Thus, 'The
Spell' was begun on 21 June and finished on 21 July 1834, and the passage
referred to here was written on 18 July, as the following text makes clear.

143 *Like an Esau . . . willing supplanter*: Esau sold Jacob his birthright; and
Jacob, with his mother Rebecca's assistance, deceived the blind Isaac and
received his father's blessing in place of his elder brother: see Genesis 25
and 27.

144 *Harry*: Henry Bramham Lindsay, an early playmate of Zamorna.

gaberlunzie: Scottish term for a mendicant or one of the king's beadsmen;
like so many of the archaisms used in the juvenilia, it is a word revived by
Scott.

without plack or boddle: without a farthing (Scots and northern dialect).

clishma-claver: foolish talk, gossip (Scots).

Hibernian: the Laurys (like the Wellesleys) are natives of Wellingtonsland,
the 'Ireland' of the Verdopolitan Union. 'Hibernia', from the Latin for
Ireland ('iuberna, iuverna, iverna'), is a variant of the old Celtic Erin
(Brewer).

Sampson-like: see Judges 15 and 16. The spelling and context also
indicate a possible reference to Domine Sampson, a character in Scott's

Guy Mannering: a humble, irascible, very old-fashioned, and pedantic scholar.

145 *red-wud*: stark mad, completely mad, furious, distracted (Scots).

rottens: probably a variant of 'ratton' (Scots and northern dialect) meaning 'rat'. Usually spelt 'ratton', 'raton', or 'rattan' by Charlotte Brontë, but she was probably attempting to imitate a Scots accent here.

trapple: windpipe, throat, neck (Scots dialect); used by Burns.

146 *shyed*: a quick jerking throw (colloquial).

Lady Isidore Hume: wife of Sir Alexander Hume Badey and mother of Florence Marian (Zamorna's second wife) and the blind Frances Millicent Hume (see note to p. 93).

Mr Maxwell: steward to the Duke of Wellington, father of Zamorna's steward William Maxwell.

147 *Henri Nicolai*: suggestive of Old Nick, the devil. His profession as butcher (flesher) and spirit merchant refers to the devil's trade in bodies and souls. His address refers to Hades, the abode of departed spirits, which is often confused with hell; and to the River Styx of classical mythology, 'the flood of deadly hate' (*Paradise Lost*, 2. 577) that flowed round the infernal regions.

148 *Kinrira*: after the village of Kinrira on the River Spey, Inverness-shire, Scotland. Adjacent to the village is Tor of Alvie, which is crowned by Waterloo cairn and the Duke of Gordon monument, both names associated with Zamorna.

Lily Hart: the tale of how John, Duke of Fidena, secretly wooed the humble Lily Hart with the help of Zamorna is told in 'Lily Hart' (Alexander *EEW* 2(1). 301).

Oramare is certainly Zamorna's and so is Alderwood: Zamorna inherited Oramare on the death of his wife Lady Florence Marian Hume in trust for their son Arthur Julius Wellesley, Lord Almedia. With the castle of Oramare he 'acquired' Lady Frances Millicent Hume.

Ilderim: a term often applied to the Zamorna; probably derived from the name of the mysterious Saracen in Scott's *The Talisman*. It is also possible that Charlotte read Henry Gally Knight's poem *Ilderim. A Syrian Tale*, about the robber-hero Ilderim, which was published by Byron's publisher John Murray in 1816 and referred to by Byron in 'To Mr Murray', l. 6; and 'Versicles', l. 5. Knight notes that 'Ilderim, in Turkish, means lightning' (p. 72).

149 *not a stiver more*: a stiver is a small coin of the Netherlands, used (like a penny) to denote a coin of small value or 'a bit' of anything. For Edward Percy's (Young Rogue) hostility towards his brother see note to p. 85.

150 *'All earth a dreary void to him, All heaven a cloud of gloom.'*: cf. Byron, *The Giaour* l. 958, and *Don Juan*, canto 14, stanza 79).

thy sun their exalting standard: see note to p. 107: 'the setting, not the rising, sun'.

151 'WE WOVE A WEB IN CHILDHOOD'. Written at home during her first Christmas holidays as a teacher at Miss Wooler's school, Charlotte reassesses the significance of her imaginary saga and traces a series of fragmentary Angrian visions that she experienced in the previous term at school. Like the following Roe Head papers, the six-page manuscript (11 × 18 cm) is untitled and written in a loose minuscule script; now located in the Huntington Library. The poem was previously published under the title 'Retrospection'.

mustard seed: Matthew 13: 31–2; Mark 4: 31–2; Luke 13: 19.

almond rod: Numbers 17: 2–8.

a mighty tree: see note to 'mustard seed' above.

152 *The dry unbudding almond-wand . . . as on Aaron's sceptre fell*: see note to 'almond rod' above.

grave-mound: here at the foot of the first MS page, Charlotte numbered the lines she had written to this point, viz. '38'. She did the same thing after line 68 and in two other places, although these last two numbers are incorrect.

Sirius: the Dog-Star, from the Greek adjective *seirios*, meaning hot and scorching.

roof-tree: literally, the main beam of a roof, but used allusively in Scotland and northern England to refer to one's fireside or family.

153 *demi-god*: Zamorna, King of Angria.

Scythian crown: the rulers of Scythia, the ancient name for much of European and Asiatic Russia, were known for their fierceness and defiance.

154 *Georgian mantle*: short, loose, sleeveless cape with a high collar, worn especially during the Georgian era in England; the Duke of Wellington is often portrayed in such a cloak.

satrap: see note to p. 125: 'the young satrap'.

155 *boded doom*: probably Arthur Julius Wellesley, Lord Almeida. The child's complexion suggests that of his mother Marian Hume, who died of consumption, a fate Zamorna fears his son will share.

dust to its own dust might return: cf. Genesis 3: 19.

bent: bent grass; also used to refer to various grass-like reeds and rushes.

156 *Camalia's ancient field*: the bloody battle of Camalia, fought on the plains at the foot of the Jibbel Kumri, between the Glass Town Federation (as it was called then) under the Duke of Wellington and the Ashantee rebels under Quashia, supported by Moorish and Abyssinian forces: see 'The Green Dwarf' (Alexander *EEW* 2(1). 188).

It was . . . did his duty well: possibly an imitation of the later sections of Scott's *Marmion*: cf. especially the end of stanza 37, canto 6, which Charlotte's verse echoes in both content and metre.

Free-Town: usually 'Freetown', capital of Sneachiesland.

Edward, here's my kinsman's tomb: Macarthy appears to be related to 'the dark malignant scowling Gordons', Scottish relatives of Zamorna.

157 *'Oh Grave where is thy sting; | Oh Death where is thy victory'*: Corinthians 15: 55.

Miss Lister: probably Harriet Lister, a 'clever—but refractory' pupil, sister of Mrs Ingham of Blake Hall, Mirfield, where Anne was governess from April to December 1839 (see Smith *Letters*, 1. 158 n. 3).

158 THE ROE HEAD JOURNAL.: 1–6. The following fragmentary manuscripts (numbered in this edition for clarity in referencing) form a distinct group of semi-autobiographical prose papers, written while Charlotte Brontë was a teacher at Miss Margaret Wooler's school for three and a half years from 29 July 1835. They were composed while the school was situated at Roe Head, Mirfield, about 20 miles south-east of Haworth, near Hartshead, which is 7 miles south of Leeds in Yorkshire. In early 1838, the school moved to nearby Heald's House, Dewsbury Moor. On 23 May, Charlotte left in a depressed state, but returned to teach for a further term until December 1838.

The 'Journal' content of these fragments, which we find usually at the beginning and end of an Angrian vignette, constitutes the most important evidence surviving of Charlotte's difficult years as a teacher. Her biblical allusions, as in 'I'm just going to write', to Psalm 22 (which begins 'My God, my God, why hast thou forsaken me?'), indicate the depth of her depression. The previous poem, 'We wove a web in childhood', should also be read in relation to these manuscripts since it records events of Charlotte's first school term as a teacher. 'Well, here I am at Roe Head' was written near the beginning of her second term, on 4 February 1836.

1. 'WELL, HERE I AM AT ROE HEAD'. Three-page diary manuscript (11.5 × 18.6 cm) in minuscule script, in the Bonnell Collection, Pierpont Morgan Library. This fragment and the following one are written on a single sheet of paper, folded to form four pages. 'Well, here I am at Roe Head' was written on pages 2, 3, and 4; 'Now as I have a little bit of time' begins halfway down page 4 and continues over to page 1. The dating (see the following fragment) suggests that the two fragments were not written on the same day.

the ark . . . boundless deluge: Genesis 7: 17–18.

as God . . . the still small voice: 1 Kings 19: 11–12.

a far & bright continent: Central West Africa, where the Glass Town Federation (now referred to as the Verdopolitan Union) and kingdom of Angria are situated.

like heath in the wilderness: Jeremiah 48: 6.

verily this foot trod . . . Adrianopolis: while Charlotte was at school, Branwell had initiated a series of wars (collectively known as the Second Angrian War, late 1835–7), which threatened the existence of Angria and plunged the Verdopolitan Union into civil war. By early 1836, when this manuscript was written, Angria has been expelled from the Union,

Zamorna has been declared an outlaw and has retreated to his country estate of Hawkscliffe. Adrianopolis has been invaded by neighbouring Ashantee tribes under the leadership of Quashia Quamina, at present an ally of the central Verdopolitan government now ruled by Zamorna's enemy Ardrah and his Reform Ministry.

158 *was not darkened*: Ecclesiastes 12: 3.

159 *a young man*: Arthur, Marquis of Douro, Duke of Zamorna and King of Angria.

coron[al]: relating to a crown or coronet; 'coron' is an obscure word for 'crown', but since the word runs off the page at the end of a line in the manuscript Charlotte may have intended to write 'coronal'.

a young lady: Mary Henrietta, Queen of Angria, has been deserted by her husband Zamorna as part of his strategy to punish her father, the Earl of Northangerland, who has threatened Zamorna and his Angrian kingdom with civil war at a time when it is also at war with the Ashantees. She has taken refuge at Alnwick Castle, where she pines away and comes close to death.

160 *a swarth & sinewy moor . . . solitary revelling*: Quashia has always envied and fought against Zamorna, and, since his wife Mary's first appearance, Quashia has lusted after her. Branwell describes his bid to marry her in 'The Politics of Verdopolis'. See also note to p. 228: 'You promised me another'.

sable hair . . . savagely exulting: Quashia's 'savage' image reflects nineteenth-century European stereotypes: initially fascinating, even noble, in early Brontë stories, he is also passionate and ultimately treacherous. *Blackwood's* reported on 'African ignorance and superstition, and barbarity, and indolence'; and the Brontës' copy of Goldsmith's *Grammar of General Geography* announced that 'Even man, in this quarter of the world, exists in a state of the lowest barbarism' (quoted in Alexander, 'Imagining Africa', 203 and 208).

Miss W[ooler]: headmistress of the private girls' school at Roe Head that Charlotte attended. For information on Margaret Wooler, see *Oxford Companion*, 548–9.

2. 'NOW AS I HAVE A LITTLE BIT OF TIME'. Two-page manuscript (11.5 × 18.6 cm) in minuscule script, in the Bonnell Collection, Pierpont Morgan Library; written on the same sheet of paper (folded to form four pages) as the previous fragment. The final section, beginning 'Two gentlemen in earnest conversation' (p. 1), continues in further detail Charlotte's vivid realization of her scene at Hawkscliffe (p. 4). This section was formerly thought to be a separate manuscript fragment because of the way the pages were folded: see Christine Alexander, 'Some New Findings in Brontë Bibliography', *Notes and Queries* (June, 1983), 236.

Friday afternoon: this date appears immediately above 'Now as I have a little bit of time' and apparently on the same line as Charlotte's date immediately below the final words of the previous fragment ('*Feby the 4th* 1836');

yet the style of the two longhand dates is rather different (particularly the upper-case 'F'), suggesting that they were written on different days and belong to different manuscript fragments. Working with unlined paper, Charlotte seldom managed to keep her lines straight in these hastily written fragments. Moreover, 4 February 1836 was a Thursday, further suggesting that 'Now as I have a little bit of time' was written the next day on Friday afternoon, 5 February. See note to p. 161: '29th of June', for further discussion on dating.

161 *Hawkscliffe Forest*: on Zamorna's remote country estate in provincial Angria, through which flows the River Arno (named after the Italian river of the same name).

war was over: see note to p. 158: 'verily this foot trod'. This is wishful thinking by Charlotte: Branwell had only just begun to wreak havoc with the political and domestic stability of Angria.

Italian articulation: Charlotte began learning Italian at Roe Head as a pupil; her teacher Margaret Wooler, now her employer and companion, was 'a fine Italian scholar' (Smith *Letters*, 1. 269 n.). Charlotte was fascinated by the warmth of Italy and her early writings include a number of Italian words (see Christine Alexander, 'Imagining Italy: Charlotte Brontë's "pictured thoughts" of "the sweet south" ', in Michael Holington, John Jordan, and Cathy Waters (eds.), *Imagining Italy: Victorian Travellers and Writers* (Cambridge: Cambridge Scholars Press, 2010).

'Henrico' . . . 'Monsignore': Henri Fernando di Enara, an Italian known as 'The Tiger', Commander-in-Chief of the Angrian forces; and the Duke of Zamorna, King of Angria, the younger of the two men.

the fire-dyed banner: the Angrian flag bore the symbol of the rising sun against a red background.

29th of June: Heather Glen suggests that this intriguing date may indicate Charlotte's present writing date (a common feature in her writing); this would mean that Charlotte was at home, writing this manuscript page (p. 1, beginning 'Two gentlemen') at a much later date when events in the Angrian saga were at a low ebb for Zamorna, following the battle of Edwardston on 27 June 1836 (*Tales of Angria*, 551–2). By this date, Zamorna was on the run, hiding in the Warner Hills, and the province of Angria (and Hawkscliffe, where this scene is set) had been occupied by the Reform Army (and later Provisional Government forces) since May 1836. When she was at home with Branwell (as she was on 29 June), Charlotte's writing usually kept pace with Angrian events, so if she was writing this page on 29 June, then her visualization of an earlier scene at Hawkscliffe is very different to the actual Angrian events of the time, despite suggestions of 'gathering darkness'.

the rays of the setting sun . . . Memnon's wondrous statue: the rising sun, rather than the setting sun, caused Memnon's statue to 'sing'. According to tradition, the great statue of Amenophobis near Thebes was supposed to represent Memnon, the handsomest of mortals slain by Archilles in the

Trojan War. When struck by the rays of the rising sun (Eos, the Dawn, mother of Memnon), it is said to have acknowledged the greeting with a musical note.

162   3. 'ALL THIS DAY I HAVE BEEN IN A DREAM'. Four-page manuscript (11.3 × 18.6 cm) in minuscule script, in the Bonnell Collection, BPM. Page 1 is dated 11 August and appears to have been written two months earlier than the other three pages, dated 14 October 1836, although page 2 (beginning 'In the afternoon, Miss E—— L——') reads as a possible continuation of page 1.

Friday Aug^{st} 11th: 11 August 1836 was a Thursday. Juliet Barker suggests that the confusion may have arisen because Charlotte wrote on the Friday about the Angrian visions she had experienced the day before (*The Brontës*, 886 n. 100).

the infernal world: the imaginary African dreamworld, referred to by both Charlotte and Branwell as the 'infernal world' or the 'world below', suggesting that it was in some way sinful.

Miss Lister, Miss Marriott & Ellen Cook: cf. Charlotte's letter of October 1836, written about the same time: 'Weary with a day's hard work— during which an unusual degree of Stupidity has been displayed by my promising pupils I am sitting down to write a few hurried lines'. Again, in December, she complains of her work and her irritation with the same pupils: 'Ever since last Friday I have been as busy as I could be in finishing up the half-year's lessons which concluded with a terrible fag in Geographical Problems: (think of explaining that to Misses M[arriot] and L[ister])'. For Miss Harriet Lister see note to p. 157. Miss Marriott was possibly the daughter of George Marriott, former owner of Roe Head; and 8-year-old Ellen Cook was the daughter of Thomas Cook, a banker and merchant in Dewsbury (Smith *Letters*, 1. 152–3, 157, 158 n.).

parsing lesson: analysis of the syntax of a sentence, basic grammar probably taught from Charlotte's copy of W. Pinnock's *A Comprehensive Grammar of the English Language* (1830) (BPM).

Huddersfield . . . Calder: Roe Head, on the north outskirts of Mirfield, had extensive views over the Calder Valley towards the wealthy market town of Huddersfield in West Yorkshire, where Charlotte and Anne stayed with Mr and Mrs Franks in June 1836, during the school holidays. The River Calder formed the southern boundary of the five parishes of Birstall, Batley, Mirfield, Dewsbury, and Hartshead, all of which have Brontë associations. Hopton was a village in the parish of Mirfield; and Heaton Lodge was the next town on the main road and railway from Mirfield to Bradford.

163   *The spirit of all Verdopolis . . . the river-watered East*: Charlotte is referring not to the federal capital here but to the whole Verdopolitan Union, which has distinct geographical regions, including the kingdom of Angria, originally a province in the 'river-watered East'.

Miss E—— L——: Ellen Lister, apparently no relation to Miss Harriet Lister cited above (note to p. 162).

trigonometrically œcumenical: Charlotte probably means her pupil wandered vaguely at a tangent from the point of the lessons. 'Œcumenical' means universal or general; 'trigonometry' relates to the measurement of triangles, a branch of mathematics Charlotte had to teach at a rudimentary level at Roe Head.

abymé: eighteenth- and nineteenth-century form of *abîmé*, meaning overwhelmed, profoundly depressed.

164 *Dr Charles Brandon and another William Locksley Esqr*: none of the imaginary characters in this manuscript appears elsewhere in Charlotte's juvenilia.

revolved in misty panorama: Charlotte would have read about, if not seen, the huge revolving panoramas of the time that produced the illusion of moving scenes and historical events for popular entertainment; a precursor to the cinema.

reminded me of one who might . . . be dead & buried under the newly plotted sod: Lucy's 'faded bloom' reminds Charlotte of her heroine Mary Percy's predicament. When Charlotte left Haworth for Roe Head, Mary was declining because of Zamorna's neglect; Charlotte fears that Branwell may already have recorded her death in their joint saga.

165 *A thousand things . . . subverted & reinstated*: the Angrian Wars Branwell had set in motion throughout 1836. Ryder appears to have been wounded as a result of insurgency against the rapacious forces of the new Revolutionary Government under Northangerland: see Neufeldt *BBWorks*, 2. 605.

the lady's erect & symmetrical figure, of her spirited & handsome face: this brave mysterious beauty strongly suggests Mina Laury.

The weight pressed me as if some huge animal had flung itself across me: cf. Henry Fuseli's image of nightmare, with a grotesque animal pressed as a weight on the sleeping woman's chest, representing current ideas about dreams. Charlotte may have seen a reproduction of this popular image, since she copied one of his other illustrations. She would also have read in her father's *Modern Domestic Medicine* by Thomas J. Graham (1826) of nightmare as 'a nervous affection, in which there is a violent struggle and tremor, with a severe pressure on the chest' (BPM).

4. 'I'M JUST GOING TO WRITE BECAUSE I CANNOT HELP IT'. Two-page manuscript (11.3 × 18.6 cm) in minuscule script, dated about October 1836, in the Bonnell Collection, BPM; previously thought to include the prose fragment 'My compliments to the weather'.

Wiggins . . . scriblomania: Patrick Benjamin Wiggins, a caricature of Patrick Branwell Brontë; introduced into the Glass Town and Angrian saga by Branwell himself but then taken up by Charlotte to mock not only her brother's extravagances but also her own (see *Oxford Companion*, 540).

Here she ridicules her compulsive writing, which she calls 'scriblomania', a term used by other nineteenth-century writers (as 'scribblemania' or 'scribbleomania' in *OED*).

165 *bulls ... of Bashan*: in Psalm 22: 12–13, enemies 'compassed' and 'gaped' upon the speaker like the fierce 'strong bulls of Bashan', a kingdom beyond the River Jordan conquered by the Israelites under Moses.

A. C——k ... E. L——r ... and Miss W——r: Ann Cook, a friend of fellow-pupil Anne Brontë and elder sister of Ellen Cook (mentioned in 'All this day I have been in a dream'), was born in 1825; the daughter of Thomas Cook, a Dewsbury banker and merchant, she died tragically early in 1840. Despite Charlotte's comments here, she appears to have been fond of Ann Cook, describing her in a letter as 'a young, beautiful, and happy girl ... a warm-hearted, affectionate being, and I cared for her' (Smith *Letters*, 1. 208–9 n. 1). Ellen Lister is also mentioned in *Roe Head Journal* 3; and for Miss Wooler, see note to p. 160.

Stupidity ... asses the society: reference to the ass is proverbial for stupidity or foolishness, as in the rabbinical expression, 'Till the ass ascends the ladder', i.e. never.

166 *There is a voice*: the 'still small voice', referred to in note to p. 158: 'as God'.

That wind, pouring in impetuous current through the air ... with a rapid gathering stormy swell: very high winds were a feature of October 1836. Charlotte's letter, also written that month, describes 'a Stormy evening and the wind is uttering a continual moaning sound that makes me feel very melancholy'. Margaret Smith cites a report in *The Times* from Harwich dated 1 October: 'It has blown tremendously heavy all day from S.S.W., thick, with heavy squalls and rain', and ships blown off course in gales (*Letters*, 1. 153–4 n. 2). The present weather and Charlotte's accompanying mood are habitually transferred to her imaginative writing; here we see the method clearly illustrated.

me & Anne: when Charlotte was employed as assistant teacher at Roe Head in July 1835, her wages were in exchange for her sister Emily's schooling. The following October, Anne replaced Emily, who was extremely homesick and unable to endure even the relatively relaxed routine of Miss Wooler's school.

Northangerland: since June 1836, Northangerland has been in control of the new French-style Provisional Government of the Grand Republican Union (formerly the Verdopolitan Union), which includes direct control of Angria where his allies (Ashantee, French, and Bedouin forces) wreck a reign of terror. His victory is short-lived, however: he is shattered by the news of his daughter's death in September (see note to p. 166: 'the Duchess'); his self-seeking mistresses in Verdopolis offer him no support; and he must soon head an army against the Constitutional troops of the former Verdopolitan government under Wellington and Fidena.

Hohenlinden! ... The burial of Moore: heroic events celebrated in poetry that Charlotte had read by this time. All record death in battle: Thomas

Campbell's *Battle of Hohenlinden* (1802); Byron's *Childe Harold's Pilgrimage* (1812–18); Scott's *Marmion, A Tale of Flodden Field* (1808); and Charles Wolfe's *The Burial of Sir John Moore* (1817). She recommends the works of these authors in a letter to Ellen Nussey dated 4 July 1834 (Smith *Letters*, 1. 30–1).

hand: 'head' mistakenly written in manuscript.

the Duchess: Mary Henrietta Percy, Duchess of Zamorna and Queen of Angria, has been wasting away since her separation from her husband, Zamorna. While Charlotte is still at school, Branwell does indeed 'kill' the Duchess in one of his stories (19 September 1836; Neufeldt *BB Works*, 2. 613), but during the following Christmas holidays Charlotte 'revives' her favourite heroine (see Alexander *EW*, 156).

like the quenching of the last spark that averted utter darkness: throughout the juvenilia there are implications that Northangerland, like Faust, has sold his soul to the devil.

Zenobia's: Lady Zenobia Ellrington has been separated from her husband (because of his infidelities and confrontation with Zamorna) since the start of the Angrian war, living alone at Ennerdale, an Ellrington country estate in Wellingtonsland.

Paulina: Paulina Lousiada, the Castilian beauty who married Lord Henry Ellrington. Her daughter Zenobia has inherited both her pride and violent temper.

167 *power of* ——: fragment ends abruptly here; Charlotte's writing was probably again interrupted by a pupil or by Miss Wooler demanding her attention. Charlotte was about to describe Northangerland's power over Zenobia: although she has been humiliated by his recent behaviour, his accumulation of mistresses, and his disloyalty to her aristocratic coterie, she is still caught in the thrall of his magnetic personality.

The remainder of the page is filled by a rough draft of the following poem (exact transcription), written in different ink at another time and describing Charlotte's frustration at not being able to access her visions.

> Look into thought & say what dost thou see
> Dive, be not fearful how dark the waves flow
> Sink through the surge & bring pearls up to me
> Deeper aye deeper, the fairest lie low
>
> I have dived I have sought them but none have I found
> In the gloom that closed o'er me no [?form] flowed by
> As I sunk through the void depths so black & profound
> How dim died the sun & how far hung the sky
>
> What had I given to hear the soft sweep
> Of a breeze bearing life through that vast realm of death
> Thoughts wear untroubled & dreams were asleep
> The spirit lay dreadless & hopeless beneath

167 5. 'MY COMPLIMENTS TO THE WEATHER.' Seven-page manuscript (11.2 × 18.6 cm) in minuscule script, except for the first line as indicated; in the Bonnell Collection, BPM.

calling up spirits from the vasty deep: cf. *Henry IV Part 1*, III. i. 53–5.

surtout & jane trowsers: a surtout was a man's great-coat or overcoat; jane trowsers were made of twilled cotton cloth; also 'jean' trowsers (OED).

John of the Highlands: Charlotte's larger print here in the manuscript denotes this character's importance and royal status in the Glass Town and Angrian saga, a characteristic typical of Branwell's early manuscripts where such names appear in capital letters.

Mr Saunderson: in the MS, 'Sneachie' has been cancelled and 'Saunderson' inserted instead, perhaps to disguise his relationship to the Angrian saga. Saunderson is, however, John Sneachie, Duke of Fidena, since he is referred to as 'John of the Highlands' (the Glass Town equivalent of the Scottish Highlands in Sneachiesland) and his closest ally is the fictitious Duke of Wellington ('Mr Wellesley Senr'), who with Fidena, Warner, and Zamorna has recently led the Constitutional Army to victory, overthrowing Northangerland's Republican Government in Verdopolis and leaving the way clear for Zamorna and his Angrian army to drive their enemies out of Angria.

mull . . . black rappee: 'mull' is a Scottish term for a snuffbox, originally one that could ground coarse snuff like 'black rappee' (made from the darker and ranker tobacco leaves) into a powder (*OED*).

'Only March has left the Angrians madder than ever': referring to the saying 'Mad as a March Hare', hares being unusually wild in March, their rutting season (Brewer). Although both Mr Sanderson and the narrator appear scornful of Zamorna's war-weary Angrian forces in the East, they have now gained the upper hand after defeating the Revolutionary troops at the Battles of Leyden and Westwood, and are soon to win the last major battle of the Angrian wars at Evesham on 30 June 1837.

168 *sworn by his hilts*: an oath sworn on the handles of swords or daggers.

Mr Wellesley Senr: see note to p. 167: 'Mr Saunderson'.

I: the 'I' is no longer that of Charlotte but of her Angrian narrator Charles Townshend, who continues to the end of this interview in his typically irreverent style (eg. the use of the contemporary slang word 'soaking' for 'drinking').

again—: as is made clear in the following text, Charlotte's vision has been interrupted and there is a lapse of a fortnight in the writing here.

that little room . . . twenty miles away: the small bedroom, only 9 × 5 feet, shared by Charlotte and Emily, in the Haworth parsonage.

169 *the rack*: usually 'the rack of clouds', a mass of storm clouds moving quickly.

Annesley Estate: in the 'West' (Wellingtonsland), where most of the older Verdopolitan aristocracy hail from. The younger generation of 'High Society' have moved to Angria and its imperial capital Adrianopolis.

170 *I scarce dare think of them*: Charlotte's favourite heroines (such as Mary Henrietta Percy) who originally came from Wellingtonsland (also called Senegambia) and are imbued with all the values of 'the West': viz, sensitivity, elegance, and poise; as opposed to the unsophisticated and rather crass beauties of the Angrian 'East' (such as Jane Moore in the following text).

171 *Anne's quiet image . . . opposite side of the table*: see note to p. 165: 'me & Anne'. In the manuscript Charlotte has spelt her sister's name without the 'e'; although 'Ann' could also refer to Ann Cook: see note to p. 165: 'A. C——k'.

her father's handsome new mansion: Kirkham Lodge, situated in Kirkham Wood on the country estate of Lord Hartford, Arundel Province, Angria.

forests of Kentucky: Kentucky was famous for its forests, especially hardwood production of white and red oak and yellow popular.

Doverham: southern port of the Verdopolitan Union, situated on the coast of Angria, south-east of Verdopolis; modelled on the English port of Dover and its relationship to London. Doverham is the last port of call before sailing for Calais in Branwell's Frenchyland.

prairies: usually referring to the temperate grasslands of North America; together with her earlier reference to the forests of Kentucky, this suggests that Charlotte was thinking of the landscape of the Angrian province of Arundel in terms of the fertile inland farming areas of the United States.

an Angrian coronet too: Jane Moore, known as 'The Rose of Zamorna' (i.e. Zamorna Province and city), intends to marry Lord Hartford.

Edwardston: like its leading citizen and founder, Edward Percy, this Angrian manufacturing city exhibits the characteristics of the Yorkshire woollen trade.

172 *that Harriet had left them for ever*: the only occasion in the juvenilia where Charlotte explicitly recalls the death of a revered eldest sister. Branwell, however, often refers to the death of his eldest sister Maria, whom he refers to as 'Harriet'. It is interesting to compare this description with Jane Eyre's reaction to Helen Burns's fatal illness and death, since Helen Burns was modelled on Maria Brontë.

M^r & Mrs Kirkwall & Sir Frederic & Lady Fala: minor Angrian aristocracy.

173 *scarlet*: the colour of Angria, whose emblem is the rising sun.

illustrissima: Charlotte has femininized the Italian *illustrissimo* (pl. *illustrissimi*), a term also used in English to refer to the most illustrious or distinguished, usually of the Italian nobility. See note to p. 161: 'Italian articulation'.

'Sound the Loud Timbrel!': 'Sound the loud Trumpet o'er Afric's bright sea', national anthem composed by Henry Hastings (pseudonym for Branwell); see Neufeldt *BBP*, 151–2.

173   6. 'ABOUT A WEEK SINCE I GOT A LETTER FROM BRANWELL.' Although
      this single-page fragment (Bonnell Collection, BPM) is undated, inter-
      nal evidence points to *c*.October 1837, rather than 1835 as suggested by
      Barker (*The Brontës*, 884 n. 46). Branwell (as Lord Richton) had reported
      the death of Mary, Queen of Angria on 19 September 1836; however,
      the following December Charlotte (as Charles Townshend) refuted this
      report and explained that it was a political ploy to rouse the Angrians
      against their invaders (see Alexander *EW*, 156). Mary's shattered health
      is soon restored by a letter from her estranged husband Zamorna. His
      victory at the battle of Evesham, 30 June 1837, brings peace again to
      Angria; but it also brings exile for his ex-prime minister Northangerland,
      Mary's father, who had fled Verdopolis as Zamorna and his allies, the
      Constitutional forces, took over the city (December 1836). By October
      1837, Mary is back in Zamorna Palace, the official royal residence in
      Adrianopolis. Northanger is in self-exile in Monkey's Isle, 'wasting
      out that life which decay and sorrow and disappointed Ambition is fast
      undermining' (Neufeldt *BBWorks*, 3. 113); but—as Branwell's letter to
      Charlotte describes—he is now about to return to Angria.

174   *tomorrow commit himself in that steamer*: Northangerland has written to his
      daughter, Mary, announcing his return from exile after 'lingering out 3
      quarters of a year in utter solitude' (Neufeldt *BBWorks*, 3. 168).

175   MINA LAURY. Despite the difficulty of writing at Roe Head, Charlotte
      continued to write long Angrian narratives at home during her mid-year
      and Christmas holidays. During 1836–7 she completed 'Passing Events',
      'It is all up!', 'Julia, and 'Four Years Ago'; then in January 1838, when she
      was 21, she wrote 'Mina Laury', a novelette that demonstrates a new con-
      fidence in her skill as a writer. Instead of a medley of unrelated episodes
      that mark the previous four works, 'Mina Laury' is centred on the theme
      of Mina's devotion for the unworthy Zamorna, King of Angria, and his
      related duplicity and continued neglect of his wife Mary. The story is
      set in the aftermath of the disastrous Angrian civil war, caused chiefly
      by Northangerland's treachery against Zamorna despite the continuing
      allegiance between them. Zamorna is back in power but the situation in
      Angria is still politically precarious.

      The plot divides naturally into two parts (Charlotte clearly marks part
      'II' in the MS); and the narrator is either Charlotte herself or possibly
      Charles Townshend, author of her last four 'books' and later version of the
      mischievous Lord Charles Wellesley who wrote 'The Spell'. Townshend,
      however, is typically cynical and dismissive of Angrian affairs, whereas
      the narrator of 'Mina Laury' is an alert observer who empathizes with the
      emotional predicaments of the two heroines.

      The untitled manuscript of thirty-five pages (11.2 × 18.3 cm), located
      in the Robert H. Taylor Collection of the Princeton University Library,
      is written in clearly printed minuscule script in straight lines (unlike the
      hasty rough lines of the Roe Head Journal) and signed 'C Brontë Jan[y]
      17th Haworth 1838'. It was given the title 'Mina Laury' by Fannie E.
      Ratchford, in *Legends of Angria* (New Haven: Yale University Press, 1933),

following Hatfield's earlier publication of part 2 under this title in Clement Shorter and C. W. Hatfield (eds.), *The Twelve Adventurers and Other Stories* (London: Hodder and Stoughton, 1925).

my last book . . . Alnwick House: There are no surviving manuscripts by Charlotte that conclude at Alnwick House, formerly Alnwick Castle where the neglected Mary, Queen of Angria, took refuge and nearly died (see note to p. 159: 'a young lady').

dreary, wildered look of all without: Charlotte habitually sets her Angrian scenes in the same climatic conditions as those she is experiencing at the time of writing. The wild frozen landscape of Haworth in January 1838 (one of the coldest months in England on record) is transferred to the Angrian situation.

damask: a rich silk fabric woven with elaborate designs (originally produced in Damascus); by the nineteenth century the term also referred to materials made out of wool, silk, and cotton, or simply twilled linen with woven designs that show up as they are reflected in the light.

176 *Harlaw*: in Charlotte's 'The Scrap Book: From the *Verdopolitan Intelligencer*', Zamorna accuses Northangerland of allowing Harlaw and Ardrah to publish 'vile and detestable falsehoods' in his 'hired press' (Alexander *EWW* 2(2). 374).

man mountain: giant; a phrase derived from Swift's *Gulliver's Travels* (1726) where Gulliver is referred to as 'man mountain' by the Lilliputians.

177 *baleful . . . North Star*: this is the star closest to the North Celestial Pole and therefore a reliable guide for navigation, in Greek mythology thought to have been created by Zeus, King of the Gods; thus, the term is an ironic allusion to Zamorna's perverse support of Northangerland, his former mentor and prime minister of Angria, and Northangerland's continuing unreliable and corrupt influence on Zamorna.

Hector . . . Paris . . . Sampson & Delilah, Hercules & the distaff: unflattering references to weakness in Zamorna's relationship with Northangerland. In Homer's *Iliad*, both Hector and Paris were sons of Priam, King of Troy; but whereas Hector was a respected and powerful military leader, Paris's judgement is influenced by his weakness for women, and his abduction of Helen famously led to the destruction of Troy. In Judges 16: 4–21, Samson is betrayed to the Philistines by his wife, Delilah, who destroys his superior strength by cutting off his hair. In one of his many trials, the Greek hero Hercules, a man of super-human strength, was humiliated by being forced to wear women's clothes and to do the women's work of spinning (the distaff is the staff of a hand spinning-wheel).

Bunyan's Giant Pope: in John Bunyan's *Pilgrim's Progress*, there are two elderly giants, Pope and Pagan, who are too weak and senile to trap pilgrims; a satire on the papacy and, here, on Zamorna's feeble state.

"Much cry & little wool": proverbial equivalent of 'much ado about nothing'; the original proverb was 'Great cry and little wool, as the Devil said when he sheared the hogs'. A favourite with the Brontës, the proverb was

used by Charlotte as the motto at the head of her story 'High Life In Verdopolis' (Alexander *EEW* 2(2). 3) and in *Villette*, ch. 40.

181 *'Ma belle! . . . cruse-là!'*: My beauty! Let me carry that jug! (French).

183 *Stancliffe's Hotel in Zamorna*: the premier inn in the Angrian city of Zamorna and the setting for the opening of Charlotte's next novelette 'Stancliffe's Hotel', written in June 1838 during her next school holidays (Heather Glen (ed.), *Tales of Angria*, 65–123).

184 *raking*: living like a rake; dissolute, debauched behaviour (*OED*).

187 *sent to Coventry*: excluded from society because of objectionable behaviour; particularly appropriate here since the punishment was originally inflicted by officers of the army on other officers for improper behaviour (*DVT*).

188 *banks of the Cirhala*: Zamorna's victorious battle at Evesham on the banks of the River Cirhala, on 30 June 1837, ended the Campaign of the West and concluded the last of the Angrian Wars.

that western dandy knows the genius of our land: Zamorna, like Mina Laury, hails from Senegambia in the west—the 'Ireland' of the Verdopolitan Union; yet he is familiar with the distinctive character or spirit ('genius') of Angria.

"Take the bull by the horns": attack a threatened danger fearlessly, like a Matador who grasps the horns of a bull about to toss him (Brewer).

the end is not yet: from Matthew 24: 6; see also Mark 13: 6 and Luke 21: 9.

golden wine . . . Guanache: Charlotte may mean 'Grenache' or 'Garnacha', an ancient and still widely planted variety of red-wine grape from Spain and southern France; it is also used to produce a sweet fortified wine, like muscat, in the Languedoc-Rousillon area of south-west France.

190 *Rivaulx*: an Angrian village on the edge of Hawkscliffe Forest (see note to p. 160), halfway between the city of Angria and the Sydenham Hills in the province of Angria; named after Rivaulx Abbey and village in north Yorkshire.

191 *Lodge of Rivaulx*: also known as the 'Cross of Rivaulx', after a nearby obelisk with a sculptured cross; the home of Mina Laury, on the border of Zamorna's Hawkscliffe estate, just outside the village of Rivaulx. The name was inspired by an engraving, 'Cross of Rivaulx', copied by Charlotte on 23 June 1836 (Alexander and Sellars, 244–5).

193 *The Duchess . . . Catherine Pakenham*: like her husband, the Duke of Wellington, the Angrian Duchess is based on her historical counterpart Catherine (or Kitty) Pakenham, known for her generosity to young people. At the end of Charlotte's tale 'Something About Arthur' (1833), she befriends the heartbroken Mina Laury after Zamorna's first romantic encounter with her and trains her as a lady's maid. Mina then nurses the Duchess before her death.

a common soldier: Sergeant Ned Laury.

194 *when Lord Northangerland resigned the seals*: Charlotte's 'The Scrap Book' reports Zamorna's denunciation of Northangerland's treachery, his threat to harm Northangerland's daughter Mary (also Zamorna's own wife), and his demand that Northangerland give up 'the seals of office' as premier of Angria (Alexander *EEW* 2(2). 376).

triumph of: triumph over (obsolete usage, *OED*).

Restoration: in December 1836, Zamorna returned from exile to re-establish his kingdom in a series of victorious battles and by the end of June 1837 his position as king was fully restored: see note to p. 188: 'banks of the Cirhala'.

captivity in the hands of Jordan: after Zamorna's defeat at the battle of Edwardston (26 June 1836), Angria was occupied by marauding troops of Ashantees, Arabs, and the Provisional Army of Northangerland. In fleeing from Lord Jordan with her young charge, Ernest Edward Fitz-arthur, Mina was attacked by Quashia and his Ashantees, who brutally murder the young boy because he is Zamorna's son.

196 *Platonist*: referring here to Platonic love, the idea of spiritual love between men and women without any sexual implications; from a misunderstanding of Plato's praise, in his *Symposium*, for Socrates' non-sexual admiration of young men (Brewer).

warm & western heart: Mina Laury, despite her peasant origins, has the same revered characteristics as Charlotte's other 'Irish' beauties from the western kingdom of Wellingtonsland: see note to p. 170: 'I scarce dare think'.

before I left Ellibank & forgot the St Cyprian & dishonoured my father: before Mina left home to follow Zamorna as his mistress, she lived with her father Ned Laury beside the St Cyprian River, on the Duke of Wellington's estate of Mornington, in the hills of Ellibank, Wellingtonsland. The reference to St Cyprian of Carthage (a third-century Christian martyr known for his self-denial and chastity) underscores Mina's early innocence; but Charlotte may also have chosen 'Cyprian' as an ironical reference to Mina's 'dishonoured' status: because Cyprians were famous for their worship of Aphrodite (Venus), goddess of love, the name 'Cyprian' became synonymous with 'prostitute' in the early nineteenth century.

199 *dashing his spurs . . . up to the rowels*: cf. Scott's *Marmion* (1808): 'Lord Marmion turn'd . . . And dash'd the rowels of his spurs' (VI. x. iv). The rowels are the small rotating wheels with sharp points at the end of the riding spurs.

surtouts, with a water-proof white beaver hat, an immense mackintosh cape & beaver gloves: men's greatcoats or overcoats (surtouts) and the waterproof protection of the 1830s. Garments made of beaver fur were particularly fashionable, as was the newly patented mackintosh cloth, waterproofed with rubber and made by Charles Mackintosh in 1823.

200 *worshippers of Juggernaut*: the belief that fanatical pilgrims of the Hindu god Juggernaut threw themselves under the wheels of the huge decorated

car with his image, to be crushed to death on the last day of their main festival.

201 *wine of Cyprus or Cythera*: referring to their status in Greek mythology as the islands of Aphrodite, goddess of love, since both islands claim her birth: see note to p. 196: 'before I left Ellibank'.

202 *fighting a duel . . . detachment of police . . . under safe ward*: duelling was illegal by the nineteenth century and the newly established Metropolitan police force (1829) was designed to handle such disputes; Lord Richton echoes the modern views of Sir Robert Peel (home secretary who helped created the police force and later prime minister of Britain) on this issue. However, until the 1840s, duels with strict codes of conduct (including the presence of a doctor) by 'honourable' gentlemen were tolerated though frowned on. Duels such as those between George Canning and Lord Castlereagh, and the Duke of Wellington and Lord Winchelsea were common knowledge for newspaper readers like the young Brontës.

205 *Dr Cooper*: named after Sir Astley Paston Cooper (1768–1841), eminent surgeon to George IV, William IV, Queen Victoria, and the Duke of Wellington: see note to p. 4: 'John Bull'.

206 *Her desk*: a portable ladies' desk that could be used either on one's lap or on a table, as in this case. The Brontë sisters each had one of these small writing boxes, with sloping lids and storage inside for ink, pens, and papers.

207 *practice*: in mathematics, a way of performing multiplication where qualities are expressed in more than one unit (such as pounds, shillings, and pence).

Necessity has no law: a phrase common to many languages, probably first used in English by Langland in *Piers Plowman* in the fourteenth century.

208 *driving of Jehu the son of Nimshi*: 2 Kings 9: 20: Jehu 'driveth furiously'. Despite the Biblical reference, Jehu, King of Israel, was actually the grandson of Nimshi.

209 *presently*: meaning 'immediately', 'without delay'; now rarely used.

210 *Pakenhams*: family name of the historical Duke of Wellington's wife: see note to p. 193. Zamorna uses the name 'Mr Pakenham' when he wishes to travel incognito in Angria.

royal liberties: the king's domain or property.

211 *Mrs Irving . . . a minister in the Northern Kirk*: the Brontës would have known of the controversial Scottish preacher Edward Irving (1792–1834), under whose influence the Catholic Apostolic Church was founded and who was a contributor to the early issues of *Fraser's Magazine* which the Brontës read.

214 *Come, Esther . . . it shall be granted*: Esther 7: 2; the answer given by King Ahasueus to his Jewish wife Queen Esther when she is about to plead with him to spare her people from massacre. Branwell made a watercolour

copy of a print by John Martin of the same subject (Alexander and Sellars, 298).

215 *Milesian*: Irish; the name given to the ancient Irish because of the legend that two sons of Milesius, a fabulous king of Spain, conquered and settled in Ireland.

218 *dated 'Mornington—1829'*: the poem appears to have been written in Zamorna's youth, when he was an accomplished poet and soon after his boyish affair with his first love, Mina Laury: a story recorded in Charlotte's 'Something about Arthur' (Alexander *EEW* 2(1). 31–40).

219 *left hand cousin*: a cousin whose parents 'married with the left hand', i.e. contracted a morganatic marriage, and whose child is therefore illegitimate.

the wicked is caught in his own net. . . . "yet shall I withal escape": cf. Psalm 141: 10: 'Let the wicked fall into their own nets, whilst that I withall escape.'

220 *Apollo*: an ironic reference to Zamorna's early character as Marquis of Douro, noble and talented and frequently likened to Apollo, a model of manly beauty and god of music, poetry, archery, prophecy, and healing art in Greek mythology.

His passion is neither weakened . . . by absence: Lord Hartford's despair is expressed in Charlotte's poem ' "O! let me be alone" he said', written at this time, in January 1838 (Neufeldt (ed.), *The Poems of Charlotte Brontë*, 258).

For a long space of time: Charlotte is about to return to school where it is impossible to find the time or creative energy to write a sustained narrative, as the *Roe Head Journal* fragments demonstrate.

221 CAROLINE VERNON. In this last Byronic escapade, Charlotte Brontë traces the beginning of a teenage infatuation for the now middle-aged but still rapacious Zamorna. The narrator is the cynical Charles Townshend, who has disguised his regal identity in order to gain access to a greater variety of situations and to pursue his favourite hobby, eavesdropping.

The untitled manuscript is divided into two parts, both located in the Widener Collection, Harvard College Library (sixty-seven pages, each 12.8 × 20.3 cm, incorrectly numbered by an unknown hand). Neither part is signed or dated, but from internal dating (Charlotte habitually set her stories at the time of composition) and from biographical evidence, it is possible to suggest that the two parts were written late July/early August and late November/early December 1839 (see Alexander *EW*, 198; and note to p. 271: 'It is now November'). The manuscript is carelessly written: there are no title pages or prefaces, and the text includes two versions of a particular episode (see note to p. 264: 'He had never been so stern') and the first draft of a letter that has not been cancelled (see note to p. 292: 'epistle that follows'). The surviving text of 'Caroline Vernon' is, strictly speaking, a draft; and the title was first used by Fannie Ratchford in *The Brontës' Web of Childhood* (1941).

221 *Scarce three moons have waxed & waned*: from May to 19 July 1839, Charlotte was governess to the Sidgwick family of Stonegappe, Lothersdale. 'Caroline Vernon', begun on her return home, was interrupted the following September when she spent five weeks' holiday with Ellen Nussey at Easton and Bridlington, on the east coast of Yorkshire. This break in composition probably accounts for the two parts of the manuscript, the second part not being completed until about December 1839.

'the creature's at his dirty work again': Alexander Pope's 'Epistle to Dr Arbuthnot' (1735), l. 91; suggesting the tenaciousness of the satirical writer.

fire-flaught: like a meteor or a flash of lightning, Scots and northern dialect; cf. Scott, *Old Mortality*, ch. 38, 'He passed by me like a fire-flaught' (*OED*).

Zamorna: a thriving industrial and commercial city in the west of Angria, halfway between the old capital of the Union, Verdopolis, and the new capital of Angria, Adrianopolis, situated on the Calabar River.

flags & . . . sedge: both generic names for coarse, reed or rush-like plants that grow in moist places.

Doverham: see note to p. 171.

Alnwick: in the far north-west of the Verdopolitan Union; site of Mary, Queen of Angria's recent ordeal at the Percy family estate: see note to p. 159: 'a young lady'. Zamorna has now won back his kingdom, Mary is queen again, and an uneasy relationship has been re-established with Northangerland.

under a willow: the weeping willow is anciently associated with sorrow, as in Psalm 137 that laments the captivity of Babylon. Townshend's cavalier attitude towards the genius of the place here is typical of his anti-romanticism.

female of the house of Wharton who had died twenty years ago: Lady Maria Henrietta Wharton, second wife of Northangerland (then Alexander Percy) and mother of Edward, William, Henry, and Mary Percy. Percy was idyllically happy in this marriage but Lady Maria died of consumption, aggravated by the distressful loss of her three sons who were banished from her at birth because of her husband's unnatural aversion to male offspring.

rhodomontade: ranting, blustering, bragging speech (now spelt 'rodomontade').

222 *Howsumdiver*: Charlotte's dialect version of 'howsumdivver' (East Yorkshire), meaning 'whatever the case may be'.

notes of a tourist, may sell when committed to paper: from about 1780, which the *OED* cites as the date of the first use of the word 'tourist', engravings and descriptions of picturesque tours and various tour journals and guides increased in popularity, especially in the first half of the nineteenth century. The Brontës copied engravings from travel books on the Lake District and the Rhine, for example, and read reviews of travel books in *Blackwood's* and *Fraser's* (Alexander and Sellars, 55).

Gentleman Squire . . . with his blackguards & boors: reference to Warner Howard Warner's guerilla activities in the Warner Hills (the 'Yorkshire' part of Angria) during the recent invasion of Angria, while the Duke of Zamorna (then in exile) and Lord Northangerland either create alliances or fight each other and the Union, as intimated in the following lines.

iligant: Irishism for 'elegant', used chiefly in the nineteenth century.

A Shopkeeper militant . . . Like a man of his hands: this verse refers satirically to the 'unholy' alliance in the late war between the former linen-draper and banker Jeremiah Simpson (viz. Sir Jehu Macterrorglen, the leader of disorderly Scots troops), and the Ashantee tribes under King Boy, King Jack, and the often-drunk African prince, Quashia Quamina Kashna, who (together with Jordon, the Sheik Medina) execute Northangerland's occupation of Angria. The Holy Alliance was formed by Russia, Austria, and Prussia in 1815, ostensibly to promote peace in European politics but was used to shore up monarchy against revolutionary influence (especially following the French Revolution).

A Death & a Marriage . . . 'Cause the Earl hadn't rather: refers to events in Zamorna's life over the last few years, including the death of his wife Marian, his marriage to Mary Percy, suggestions of bigamy (in 'The Spell'), his tyrannical behaviour towards the Verdopolitan Union, his exile from Angria, and his ambiguous relationship with his father-in-law Lord Northangerland.

Leyden . . . Evesham . . . Cirhala . . . Westwood: sites of recent bloodshed in the Angrian War (see note to p. 158: 'Verily this foot trod'). The Revolutionary troops that invaded Angria are routed at the battle of Leyden, near Alnwick, and at Westwood, before being finally defeated by Zamorna's Angrian forces at the battle of Evesham on the Cirhala River (June 1837). Townshend's flippant attitude to the recent dramatic events in Angria, masterminded by Branwell while Charlotte was away from Haworth, reflect her impatience with her brother's detailed cataloguing of political events in Angria; although even Branwell is keen to acknowledge the need to renew and restore Angria to a more civilized state of affairs. In his chronicle 'Angria and the Angrians V', he states that 'the removal of Old things though Violent has given more room for the vigorous springing of the New' (Neufeldt *BBWorks*, 3. 247).

223 *Does Love fold his wings when Victory lowers her pennons*: Cupid, the Roman god of love, is always represented as a winged boy; and Victory in classical sculpture as a woman with large wings (poetically, pennons or pinions), as in the famous (and headless) Winged Victory of Samothrace.

nobleman: the Duke of Zamorna.

Mesdames Greville, Lalande & St James: Northangerland's mistresses, dating from his early days as a political revolutionary.

shrivelling 'like a parched scroll': cf. Scott, *The Lay of the Last Minstrel*, canto 6, stanza 31, ll. 5–8; and Byron, *The Giaour*, l. 1255.

223 *great ex-president*: cynical reference to Northangerland's former office of prime minister of Angria and, more recently during the civil war, of Lord President of the republican Provisional Government in Verdopolis.

exies: northern Scots word probably meaning 'the hysterics'. Used by Scott, e.g. *The Antiquiry*, ch. 35, 'Jenny Rintherout has ta'en the exies, and done naething but laugh and greet' (*OED*).

224 *en déshabillé*: in a state of undress (French).

225 *hysterical*: the entry 'Of Hysterics' in the Brontës' much-used medical guide, Graham's *Modern Domestic Medicine* (1826), characterizes the disease as one of 'wild and irregular actions . . . alternate fits of laughter, crying, and screaming, incoherent expressions' and more prevalent in unmarried women, between puberty and 35 years, at the time of menstruation. Compare also Charlotte's references to hysteria in *Jane Eyre*, ch. 7 and *Villette*, ch. 39.

Miss Delph: 'the Great Heiress' Victoria Delph, whose name is legendary in Angria for her wealth; she is generally caricatured in society for her plump, diminutive figure and 'petted caprice', though even Northangerland has been tempted by her fortune (see Neufeldt *BBWorks*, 3. 263–4; and *Oxford Companion*, 157).

'The Furies, I believe, had hair of live snakes': not the Furies (goddesses of vengeance) but the three Gorgons of classical mythology, who had serpents instead of hair.

226 *we all love them that love us*: a perversion of Scripture typical of Northangerland: from Matthew 5: 46: 'For if ye love them which love you, what reward have ye?'

seventy & seven times: again, a facetious allusion to the number of times a Christian should forgive a sinner: 'Jesus saith unto him, I say not unto thee, Until seven times: but, Until seventy times seven' (Matthew 18: 22).

Mr Steaton: also 'Steighton' and 'Seaton' in the saga MSS.

hay-tenters: unskilled haymakers; the word 'tenters' is usually applied to people who attend machinery or who are assistants to a weaver (*OED*).

cock: part of a plough, now obsolete.

"at the close of the day when the hamlet is still": first line of James Beattie, 'The Hermit', from *Poems on Several Occasions* (1776).

ad libitum: at one's pleasure, as much as one desires (Latin).

227 *defy all hands—mercantile, genteel & juvenile—that ever existed*: like the new 'science' of phrenology, handwriting also became an indicator of character and status in the early nineteenth century, as Charlotte confirms in *The Professor* when Crimsworth says: 'They talk of affinities between the autograph and the character' (ch. 21). Quashia's bold scrawl suggests his chaotic, unreliable, and violent character, which the content of his letter affirms.

Daddy Long-legs: a popular name for the cranefly and for spiders with slender long legs; the reference suggests Northangerland's dangerous character and ability to hurt. Quashia's use of 'daddy' throughout his letter is familiar contemporary slang for 'old boy'. His jumbled allusions indicate that he is anything but sober.

sitting on my right hand and on my left: cf. Matthew 20: 21.

Sai Too-Too: King of the Ashantees, father of Quashia.

Sambo Mungo Anamaboo: a mishmash of contemporary references to Africa. 'Sambo' was a nickname for an African. Mungo refers to Mungo Park, British explorer of the Niger basin (1797), whose popular travels the Brontës read about in *Blackwood's Magazine*. The King of Anamaboo, on the coast of Ghana, also features in *Blackwood's* which was their chief source on Africa: see *Oxford Companion*, 4.

daddles!: hands; late eighteenth-century slang (*DVT*).

the earth reels, the heavens stagger: cf. Joel 2: 10.

old Ocean himself trembles: cf. James Macpherson, *The Poems of Ossian*, ll. 318–19; a book owned by the Brontës.

child of perdition: destined to damnation.

a cab of dove's dung: 2 Kings 6: 25.

hoyle: room (dialect); used later by Charlotte in *Shirley*, ch. 12.

228 *the play's nearly played out*: cf. *Henry IV, part 1*, II. iv. 478; and Byron, *Don Juan* (11: 676). Charlotte uses this again in *Jane Eyre*, ch. 19, and *Villette*, ch. 39.

foxes & holes . . . neither: confused version of Matthew 8: 20.

toil & spin . . . one of these: a distortion of Luke 12: 27.

Scaramouch: a stock character in Italian farce, a cowardly and foolish boaster (*OED*).

Queen of Heaven: probably referring to Mary Percy, a blasphemous association by Quashia with the Virgin Mary, who is referred to by this title in Roman Catholicism; in ancient times, various goddesses (such as Astarte and Diana) were also referred to by this title.

Loved lady . . . prison house: the object of Quashia's desire is now Caroline Vernon.

heaven opens & thy bridegroom waits: images associated with the Messiah; Quashia's mixed biblical references throughout his letter are intended to align him with the Messiah, the chosen one.

You promised me another, but she, 'like a lily drooping, bowed her head & died': Quashia tried to woo Mary Percy before her marriage to Zamorna; Northangerland initially supported this in return for military assistance but reneged on his promise (see Branwell's 'Politics of Verdopolis', ch. 4). The quoted lines are from a well-known ballad by John Gay, 'What D'Ye Call It' (1715). Byron also echoes this in Haidée's death scene, *Don Juan* (4. 467–8).

A better lot is thine, fair maid: paraphrase of lines from Sir Walter Scott's *Rokeby*, given to Charlotte on her departure from Roe Head, 23 May 1838: 'A weary lot is thine, fair maid' (3. 28.8).

228 *Eden's bowers*: Caroline lives at Eden Cottage, so-called because it was where Louisa Vernon first entertained Northangerland when she became his mistress; referring to a place of pleasure or garden of Eden (Genesis 2: 15).

229 *Q in the corner*: referring to Quashia. 'Q in a corner' is an old children's game, perhaps similar to our 'Puss in the corner'; the expression also refers to something not seen at first but subsequently brought to notice (Brewer).

fine Roman hand: ironic comment on Quashia's bold handwriting, the opposite of the Italian cursive style popular amongst women at the time (see note to p. 227: 'defy all hands'). Cf. also *Twelfth Night*, III. iv. 29, with reference to Malvolio: 'I think we do know the sweet Roman hand'.

230 *varry*: in the following conversation, the man in black (General Thornton) speaks in a regular Yorkshire dialect (see Wright).

croft: a piece of enclosed arable land used by a tenant farmer, usually adjacent to his house.

beck: a stream usually in rugged country (northern dialect).

tight: a commendatory dialect word, suggesting the girl is capable, smart, and lively; also well formed and shapely.

231 *fairing*: a present given at or brought from a fair (*OED*).

jilt: a woman who encourages a lover and then capriciously abandons or deceives him.

232 *It's nought to me 'at I know on.*: a third of a page has been left here at the bottom of the manuscript page, suggesting that Charlotte intended to continue the conversation at a later date.

object of filial attention: Northangerland, Edward Percy's estranged father; Northangerland's lack of popularity in Angria also stems from his responsibility for the recent civil war and the abuse of his position as prime minister.

233 *deep-mouthed bark of welcome*: cf. Byron, *Don Juan* (1818), canto 1, ll. 977–8: ''Tis sweet to hear the watch-dog's honest bark | Bay deep-mouth'd welcome.'

put up his repeater: put away his repeating watch in its case.

234 *vade-mecum*: manual or handbook (Latin).

235 *croft . . . bigging*: enclosed arable land ('croft'), adjacent to a dwelling place, usually an outbuilding ('bigging', northern dialect).

house: kitchen living room of a farmhouse.

sprung: tipsy, intoxicated (Wright).

in a rope: in a halter made of rope.

237 *We dine early, seldom later than three*: an unfashionably early dining time, typical of the north of England (and of Zamorna's Angrian country life).

Mr Kashna: Quashia.

238 *Society for the Diffusion of Genuine Vitality*: mocking reference to the pop-ular Society for the Diffusion of Useful Knowledge, begun in England in 1826 to provide inexpensive texts for the rapidly expanding reading public, especially the working class; and to the failure of Northangerland's political philosophy to harness and implement the 'Vitality' of the nation (see Charlotte's 'The Scrap Book', Alexander *EEW*, 2(2). 305–6).

Arthur Wellesley would stick the bills: the young Zamorna (then Arthur Wellesley, Marquis of Douro) would put up posters or petitions announ-cing their joint concerns at the time.

stick the whole concern: Zamorna is punning on the verb 'to stick', here meaning to kill or end.

239 *Musical talent she ought to inherit*: Caroline's mother Louisa Vernon was the former opera star Louisa Allen, and Northangerland was known for his 'extraordinary musical genius' in his youth (Neufeldt *BBWorks*, 2. 124).

writing . . . with a silver pencil-case: in the nineteenth century, pencil lead was encased in a holder or pencil case, usually made of metal and often highly ornamented.

240 *Selden-House or Eden-Hall*: residences belonging to Northangerland, safely located well away from Verdopolis (in Rossesland and Sneachiesland respectively); Charlotte continues to play on the name Eden as Caroline's last abode of innocence before her 'fall'.

241 *very*: incorrectly used here as an adverb but, as with its use as an adjective, meaning 'really' or 'truly', an emphatic affirmation of a statement, chiefly used as an echo of biblical usage.

243 *Donna Julias, your Signora Cecillias*: the older, married woman Donna Julia seduced the young Don Juan in Byron's *Don Juan* (1918), canto 1. 'Signora' is the Spanish equivalent of 'Mrs', suggesting Northangerland's penchant for married women.

eat: see Note on the Text.

244 *'where ignorance is bliss 'tis folly to be wise'*: Thomas Gray, *Ode on a Distant Prospect of Eton College* (1742), ll. 99–100.

245 *'Has sorrow thy young days shaded'*: Thomas Moore, *Irish Melodies* (1808–34), vol. 6; Moore's poetry and biography of his friend Byron were favourites with the Brontës (*Oxford Companion*, 328).

shog: go away, begone; used in this sense by Shakespeare, *Henry V*, II. i. 43.

wild-fire: will-o'-the-whisp, *ignis fatuus*; a phosphorescence common on marshy moorland that often misleads travellers, thus referring to an illu-sion or figment of the imagination.

246 *ree*: Scottish dialect for excited, especially with drink; elevated; crazy, delirous (*OED*).

vapours: nervous disorder such as depression of spirits, hypochondria, or hysteria.

246 *Attendez . . . folie*: Wait a little—Monsieur loves you madly (French).

'*Non, avec tendresse, avec ivresse*': No, with tenderness and rapture (French).

247 *C'est trop modest'*: He's too modest (French).

Ecoutez la fille! . . . mon preux Percy: 'Listen to the girl! He's a hard man. As for love he hardly knows what it is. He looks upon women as mere slaves—he enjoys their beauty momentarily and then he abandons them. Such a man must be hated and avoided. As for me I hate him—very much—yes, I detest him. Goodness knows how much! He is different from my Alexander. Elise, do you remember my Alexander—the handsome Northangerland!'

'He was very nice,' responded Elise.

'Nice!' ejaculated her ladyship. 'Elise, he was an angel. It seems to me that I can see him—in this same room—with his blue eyes, with such a sweet expression on his face—and his marble brow framed with chestnut locks.' [Charlotte uses the noun *châtaignes* in the MS, instead of the adjectival form.]

'But the Duke has chestnut hair too,' interposed Elise.

'Not like that of my gallant Percy,' (French.)

il sut apprécier mes talents: he knew how to appreciate my attributes (French).

Newmarket coat: a close-fitting coat for men, originally worn for riding.

248 *Drover*: Alexander Percy (Northangerland); one of the many careers of his profligate early days.

Lord George . . . Vernon: Louisa Vernon's first husband.

249 *as M*r *Ambler used to smother me when he had the part of Othello & I had that of Desdemona*: Shakespeare's *Othello* was well known to the young Brontës, who read various reviews of contemporary performances. *Blackwood's Edinburgh Magazine*, 18 (1925), 299, refers to a Parisian production of *Othello* in French; special note is made of the death of Desdemona and the effect it had upon the audience, eliciting swooning and fainting fits.

Miss Gordon: Lady Helen Victorine, Baroness Gordon, the Scottish heiress Zamorna married in his youth.

Julia Corelli's, who was the first figurante at the Verdopolitan Opera: probably inspired by the French dancer and choreographer Jean Corelli (1779–1854), whose interpretation of *Le Diable Borteux* (1836), *La Tarantule* (1839), and *Giselle* (1843) were part of the standard repertoire.

250 *"Jim Crow"*: a popular African-American plantation song first introduced as a 'nigger ministrel' song and dance in Louisville by Thomas D. Rice in 1828 and brought to the Surrey Theatre, London, in 1836 (Brewer).

251 *mauvaise honte*: literally false shame (French), but also terrible shyness; cf. Charlotte's own 'miserable mauvaise honte which torments & constrains me' (Smith *Letters*, 1. 198).

worked trousers: pantaloons worn by young girls, frilled and embroidered (worked) at the bottom where they were on display.

256 *Aladdin's lamp*: a magic lamp whose genie could grant any wish of the holder; from the story of *Aladdin, or the Wonderful Lamp*, in *The Arabian Nights' Entertainments*, a book that had a profound influence on the early juvenilia of the Brontës: see *Oxford Companion*, 16.

Lord Edward Fitzgerald: the Brontës, who had read Thomas Moore's *Life of Byron* (1830), were also familiar with his *Life of Lord Edward Fitzgerald* (1831), as the following conversation indicates. Fitzgerald (1763–98) was an Irish aristocrat and revolutionary who fought in the American War of Independence, explored the Canadian forests, and sympathized with the doctrines of the French Revolution, staying with and being inspired by Thomas Paine in Paris. After renouncing his title he joined the United Irishmen, engaging in revolutionary activities to secure an independent Irish republic, until he was captured on the eve of the rebellion in 1798 and died of his wounds in Newgate Prison, Dublin.

257 *Miss Martineau*: Harriet Martineau (1802–76), novelist and writer of essays designed chiefly to popularize economic subjects and advocate social reform. She visited America in the 1830s and published *Society in America* (1838), reviewed in *Fraser's Magazine* (May 1839). Brontë greatly admired Martineau's novel *Deerbrook* (1839), and was later to become a friend of the atheistic Martineau, staying with her at her home at Ambleside but later quarrelling with her, after Martineau's adverse review of *Villette* and her criticism of Brontë's obsession with love in her novels.

republic . . . an Athenian: the Athenians had a democracy not a republic. Brontë's deliberate confusion of facts here and in the following conversation indicates Caroline's haphazard learning, her immaturity, and 'enthusiasm'.

Alcibiades: Athenian general and statesman (450–404 BC); the stock type of the sophisticated aristocrat, endowed with all possible advantages as well as personal ambition, outstanding both in his vices and in his virtues.

Alexander the Great: (356–323 BC), general and ruler of Macedonia and king of Persia, who, with the army inherited from his father Philip II of Macedon, conquered the Mediterranean world and built a powerful empire extending through Asia Minor.

they never dared mutiny against him, though he made them suffer hardships: there was an unsuccessful mutiny at Opis in 324 when Alexander disbanded Macedonian veterans for Iranian troops.

Hephæstion: (356–324 BC) Macedonian general, boyhood friend and lover of Alexander the Great. Although not universally popular with the Macedonians, because of his self-importance, his sudden death from fever caused Alexander excessive grief; an extravagant tomb was erected and he was given heroic honours.

Lord Arundel . . . Lord Castlereagh & General Thornton, & General Henri Fernando di Enara: leaders, together with Warner, of the Angrian faction under the Duke of Zamorna; also Lord Lieutenants of Angrian provinces.

257 *I saw a picture . . . he was so handsome*: cf. Jacques-Louis David's painting of Napoleon crossing the Alps (1800).

258 *And you're a pirate*: see Branwell's 'The Pirate' for Northangerland's early career and his first encounter with Zenobia Ellrington.

those ancient doddered kings up at Verdopolis . . . old fellow Alexander: the elderly and decayed (doddered) kings of the original Verdopolitan Union, who still reign and hold thrones in the Verdopolitan Parliament in Verdopolis. The word 'doddered' is usually an attribute of old oaks that have lost their tops or branches; cf. Charlotte's *Villette*: 'Nasturtiums clustered beautifully about the doddered orchard giants' (ch. 12).

send all those doting constitutionalists to Jericho: send them 'anywhere out of the way'; 'Jericho' is used in various phrases to suggest an indefinite place. Cf. also 'Go to Jericho!' meaning 'Go to Hell!'

259 *thread-paper & may-pole style*: slender tall figure; resembling the long narrow strips of paper that were used to separate different embroidery threads, or the decorated pole used in May celebrations.

260 *Ferdinand Alonzo FitzAdolphus*: a whimsical conflation of heroic names used by Shakespeare, Byron, and others. Brontë may have known the story of Alonzo of Aquilar, the subject of a number of ballads, who, during an attack from the Moors in 1501, was killed while planting the banner of Ferdinand, King of Aragon, on the heights of Granada. When his body was exposed in the wood, Moorish damsels, struck by its beauty, buried it near the brook of Alpuxarra.

Charles Seymour or Edward Clifford: Zamorna has various Seymour and Clifford cousins whose names he assumes as disguises. Both are aristocratic English names, belonging to people associated with the Duke of Wellington. See Alexander *EW*, 118.

Harold, Aurelius Rinaldo Duke of Montmorency di Valdacella: again, a medley of heroic names. Harold suggests Byron's Childe Harold and his namesake, King Harold II, last of the Saxon monarchs killed at the battle of Hastings in 1066. Marcus Aurelius (121–80) was an intelligent, well-educated Roman emperor with a penchant for philosophy (he wrote twelve books of *Meditations* despite a reign dominated by war). Rinaldo was one of the heroes of medieval romance, a paladin of Charlemagne, cousin and rival of Orlando; and subject of Tasso's romantic epic *Rinaldo* (1562) in which he featured as the Achilles of the Christian army. The Montmorencys were French dukes, prominent in the sixteenth and seventeenth centuries; the Angrian Lord Montmorency bears their name if not their invidious characters. Duke of Valdacella is the name used by Brontë for the fictitious twin brother of Zamorna in 'The Spell'.

Babylon: the magnificent city, once the capital of the Chaldee Empire; also, the mystical Babylon of the Apocalypse and hence used rhetorically to refer to any great and luxurious city. The Brontës, following Byron, John Martin, and others who refer to London as Babylon, use the epithet to characterize their own luxurious capitals of Verdopolis and Adrianopolis.

Alhambra: palace of the Moorish kings (caliphs or sultans) built at Granada, Spain, in the thirteenth century.

261 *laudanum & prussic acid*: in the nineteenth century laudanum referred to various preparations in which opium was the main ingredient; now it is usually an alcoholic tincture of opium. The villains of the early Glass Town saga often use the poison prussic acid (hydrocyanic acid), so called because it was derived from prussian blue (ferric ferrocyanide used in painting and dyeing).

262 *houri*: a nymph of the Muslim paradise; used especially by Byron, Scott, and other contemporary writers to refer to seductively beautiful dark-eyed women.

inexpugnables: possibly a Brontë coinage, based on an analogy with 'inexpressibles', a nineteenth-century euphemism for trousers. The adjective 'inexpugnable' (impregnable, invincible), coupled with the following 'stiff black stock' (necktie), suggests a dig at Zamorna's profligacy.

263 *wae*: obscure dialect form of 'woe' (*OED*).

Victoria-Square: location of Wellesley House.

Paris, or Fidena or Rossland: old haunts of Northangerland. Paris is the captial of Branwell's southern Frenchyland; Fidena is the capital of Sneachiesland to the north of the Verdopolitan Union.

264 *Fontainebleau*: modelled on the French equivalent, a town south of Paris and castle and forest of the same name.

He had never been so stern & didactic before: the text following these words (until the end of section I) constitutes a second, rewritten ending to the first part of 'Caroline Vernon'. Brontë appears to have been dissatisfied with her first attempt that is uncancelled in the manuscript and reads as follows:

> She wanted to change the conversation and so by way of giving it another turn she asked the Duke whether he would be so kind as to write to her sometimes when she was gone. He said he did not know, he could not promise—his time was very much occupied. Caroline was again silent. She thought the answer scarcely kind.
> 'Would he never write to her,' she said after a pause.
> 'Perhaps he might sometimes—there was no impossibility in the case.'
> Again Miss Vernon was disappointed & saddened. His Grace was certainly displeased with her—he was not accustomed to speak so coldly, & instead of holding her hand as he generally did when she walked with him he had allowed her arm to drop & barely suffered her to keep by his side.
> 'And won't you even think of me, my lord,' she said at last.

'I shall think of you when I hear your name I suppose,' replied the Duke.

Caroline slackened her pace & dropped behind. This was too bad: she had always thought herself a favourite. She found she was mistaken. Her guardian cared nothing about parting with her. The last night, when she had thought he would be kinder & fonder than ever, to treat her so coolly, so austerely! Her heart swelled, & a tear to two was forced into her eye.

'Now child, where are you?' said the Duke, turning abruptly. She was only a pace or two behind him & her handkerchief was at her eyes. 'What ails you?' continued His Grace, taking her hand from her face. 'A little touch of sentimentalism about leaving Hawkscliffe, eh? Come, come, all will be right to-morrow.'

'You don't know me,' said Miss Vernon. 'You think I'm pleased with all kinds of novelties, but I'm not.'

'Stuff! This little fit will go off soon.'

His Grace stood in the moonlight & looked at Miss Vernon & laughed. She turned away, feeling about as bitter a pang at that moment as she had ever known in her life—it was the anguish of discovering that her strongest & most genuine feelings were not appreciated, that a person whom she was disposed to care for intensely would not condescend to let her tell him how much she regarded him, would not stoop to understand her emotions, to enter into them or in the least degree return them. Stifling her sobs & dashing away her tears as well as she could, she would have hurried away to the house, but His Grace said, 'Caroline!'

She did not stop for the first call, nor answer it.

He repeated, 'Caroline!'

The tone was not one to be disobeyed. Besides, she felt that if she parted from her guardian so without a reconciliation she would not sleep that night, so she returned to him. They were near a little bower with a seat in it. He took her there &, having sat himself down, he placed his ward beside him. He divided her hair from her forehead &, as he smoothed away her curls, said in a far different tone from what he had hitherto used, a tone that changed the whole idea of his character, 'What is all this little flutter about Caroline? Tell me now.'

Miss Vernon's answer was plain truth at least. 'I'm sorry,' said she, 'that I'm going to part with you, & still more sorry that you don't care for parting with me.'

'Who told you that I did not care?' asked His Grace.

'You're so cold,' said she. 'You call me child, & look as if you despised me.'

It is probable that the Duke smiled at these words, though it was almost too dusk to see for the moon penetrated but faintly into the little bower.

'Come Caroline,' he said after a pause. 'You & I can't afford to quarrel, so we'll be friends again. Now is all right.'

'I'm afraid you don't care for me,' persisted Miss Vernon distrustfully.

'Hush, no more misunderstanding,' said the Duke. 'What is there to make you doubt whether I care for you now? Can you be nearer to me?'

All at once Miss Vernon's fears were removed. She was satisfied. It was not the Duke's words but his voice that produced this happy change—there was something in its tone that assured her he did not now, at least, regard her as a mere child.

'Are you cold, Caroline?' he asked. 'Does the air feel damp?'

'No.'

'What are you looking at so earnestly, my little girl?'

'Only the sky— it seems so full of stars. I shall always remember this night. Oh I can't bear to go away to-morrow! But I won't think of to-morrow.'

Just then a voice was heard in the Garden crying, 'Miss Caroline! Miss Caroline!' It was Mademoiselle Touquet who had been sent in search of the young lady.

I am grateful to Heather Glen for correcting my earlier assumption that the manuscript pages were numbered correctly; by examining the way Brontë gathered her sheets into a single quire to form a 'book', Glen shows conclusively that MS p. 67 (that includes Brontë's first version above) follows p. 62, which ends 'He had never been so stern & didactic before' (*Tales of Angria*, 534 n. 95). I argued in *EW* (p. 198) that the first version of this intimate conversation between Zamorna and his young ward preserves their ostensibly innocent friendship, so that Caroline's later pursuit of Zamorna in Part 2 still maintains an element of naivety; but it appears Charlotte was not so concerned about this as she was in developing her ironic examination of Zamorna's behaviour and Caroline's embryonic sexuality, or the clever debunking of sentimental romance that occurs in her rewritten version.

264 *Lalande . . . S*^t *James*: see note to p. 223.

267 *the hours—those 'wild-eyed charioteers' as Shelley calls them*: in *Prometheus Unbound* (1820), 2. 4. 129 ff.: 'through the purple night | I see cars drawn by rainbow-wingèd steeds | Which trample the dim winds: in each there stands | A wild-eyed charioteer urging their flight. | . . . These are the immortal Hours'.

vineyard of experience . . . picture: the vineyard is a common biblical symbol of the world. Ruth gleaned corn in a field belonging to Boas, hoping she would find favour in his sight (see Ruth 2).

light both broad & burning: cf. Shelley, 'The broad and burning moon' ('The Sunset', l. 18).

268 *clay in the hands of the potter*: Jeremiah 18: 6: 'Behold, as the clay in the potter's hand, so ye in mine hand, O house of Israel.' A common biblical image used frequently by Byron and the Brontës.

268 *just as if she mistook him for Endymion*: in Greek mythology, the Moon goddess Selene loved the shepherd Endymion and came down nightly to embrace him; story used by Keats in his *Endymion* (1818).

the noiseless tenor of his way: cf. Thomas Gray, *Elegy in a Country Churchyard* (1751): 'Along the cool sequestered vale of life | They kept the noiseless tenor of their way.'

270 *Lucifer-match*: matches were a new invention in the Brontës' day. First called a 'friction light' (1826), they were sold as 'Lucifers' in the Strand *c.*1829 by Samuel Jones.

whether his mother knew he was out?: 'Does your mother know you're out?' was a fashionable jeering remark addressed to a presumptuous youth or to a simpleton; first used in a comic poem in 1838, it became a catchphrase in England and America (Brewer).

271 *It is now November . . . about four months has lapsed in the interim*: since Brontë usually sets her early tales at the time of writing, this allows us to date the composition of the second half of the manuscript to November/ December 1839. See note to p. 221: 'Scarce three moons'.

in statu quo: in the same state (Latin).

as merry as a grig: a common phrase for an extravagantly lively person, referring either to a little eel, cricket, or grasshopper (grig) or to a corruption of 'merry as a Greek' (*OED*).

persons in paper-caps who seemed to gather about the lamp-posts: Branwell's Paris in Frenchyland is modelled on France of the French Revolutionary period. In the streets of Paris, revolutionists wore paper caps with 'Revolution de Paris' printed on them and 'A la lanterne!' ('Hang him from the lamp-post!') was a common cry.

272 *ton*: fashionable style.

éclat: glamour, renown; a French word more frequently used in English in the early nineteenth century than nowadays.

273 *their faction—the Dupins, the Barrases & the Bernadottes*: Northangerland's faction is a kind of anti-royalist, Jacobin Club whose members are loosely derived from people associated with the French Revolution and with Napoleon. André Marie Jean Jacques Dupin (1783–1865), a French advocate, president of the Chamber of Deputies and of the Legislative Assembly, supported the restoration but also worked under Napoleon and was one of those chiefly responsible for the codification of the laws of the empire. The Viscomte de Barras (1775–1829) was an early member of the Jacobin Club, a successful military leader and one of the most powerful members of the Directory (a factor which brought him into rivalry with Napoleon and led to his fall from power). Jean Baptiste Jules Bernadotte (1763–1844) was a celebrated marshal under Napoleon, who engineered Bernadotte's election to the Swedish throne.

jeunes gens: young men (French).

mauvais sujets: bad lots (French); Brontë's Anglocentric prejudice towards the French always emerges in her early references to Frenchyland.

men-monkeys: 'man-monkey', meaning 'apelike person', was a common derogatory term; used here for French aristocrats, like those who had taken refuge in London during the French Revolution and who had returned to Paris after Waterloo.

cette jolie petite fille à cheveux noirs: that pretty little girl with black hair (French).

274 *It's a bit in Augusta's way*: Caroline's style reminds Montmorency of the young Zamorna ('Augusta'), who was known for his early 'femininity'.

gentleman of the west: of Irish temperament; the western kingdom of the Verdopolitan Union (Wellingtonsland, now Senegambia) is based on Ireland.

the Lord's Prayer written within the compass of a sixpence: there was a nineteenth-century fashion to write the Lord's prayer in miniature script within the circumference of the shape of a coin. Brontë's own such exercise, written in the shape and size of an old 3*d.* coin, is preserved in the Huntington Library, California.

275 *the Simon Pure*: the upright person, the genuine article; from a Quaker in Susannah Centlivre's comedy *A Bold Stroke for a Wife* (1717), who is impersonated by another character.

276 *'the stoic of the woods, the man without a tear'*: Thomas Campbell, *Gertrude of Wyoming or the Pennsylvanian Cottage* (1809), part 1, l. 207; referring to the character of the American Indian, especially one particular chief.

278 *Eden-Cottage*: see note to p. 228.

dour & drumly: sullen and gloomy; words common in dialect usage and often used by Scott.

no partiality to the Scotch: Eden cottage is in Sneachiesland, the 'Scotland' of the Glass Town Federation.

279 *badger*: a pedlar (Irish English used in the north of England); probably from Mr Brontë's usage.

280 *a considerable organ*: a derisive reference to phrenology, the pseudo-science that analysed character by reading the size and shape of 'bumps' on the skull, thus referring to 'the benevolent organ' or the 'organ of wonder' (see *Shirley*, ch. 1).

reverieing: the *OED* cites 'Nochtes Ambrosianae' in *Blackwood's*, Oct. 694, for this rare usage.

284 *a bob & two joeys*: a shilling and two fourpenny pieces (obsolete slang).

285 *jest was given for earnest & earnest for jest*: cf. Shakespeare, *Richard III*, V. i. 24.

286 *agacerie*: allurement, coquetry, pestering (French).

287 *rounded her periods like a blue*: able to complete ('rounded') grammatically balanced sentences ('periods'), like a 'bluestocking' or clever woman.

mountains . . . crowning them 'with the wandering star': quoting the national anthem of Angria, Branwell's 'Sound the loud Trumpet' (Neufeldt *BBWorks*, 1. 204): 'All ye proud mountains that shadowing afar | Crown your blue brows with the wandering star.' 'The wandering star' is a phrase common to a number of Romantic poets, including Byron, Wordsworth and Thomas Moore; also in Isaac Watts's 'A Morning Hymn'.

288 *camarade de voyage & also her camarade de vie*: travel companion and lifelong companion (French).

her Siberia & not her Eden: place of exile and imprisonment rather than pleasure and paradise (see note to p. 228).

rencontres: encounters (French).

tournure: bearing (French).

irreproachables: trousers; a euphemism coined by Charlotte (possibly from the French 'irreprochable' meaning 'impeccable') to mock Zamorna's sexual proclivities; cf. Charlotte's similar satirical use of 'inexpugnables', note to p. 262.

tower looking towards Lebanon: cf. Song of Solomon 7: 4: 'thy nose as the tower of Lebanon which looketh toward Damascus'.

289 *dickey with all these dreams*: slang for 'all up' or 'all over with' these dreams.

In deep meditation—in the watches of the night: cf. Psalm 63: 'and meditate on thee in the night watches'; Psalm 119 is similar, and both Isaac Watts and John and Charles Wesley transpose the phrase 'night watches' into 'watches of the night' in their hymns, which Charlotte would also have known.

290 *little Flowers*: children of Sir John Flower, Lord Richton.

292 *only a wafer-stamp*: an impression made by a hand-stamp on a small round wafer seal (made of flour and gum), used for sealing letters or envelopes. It is thought rather common and crude by those who can afford the time and money to use sealing wax and an embossed heraldic seal.

epistle that follows: The following undeleted draft of the letter appears here first in the manuscript. A change of pen and ink may indicate a lapse of time between the two versions.

My dear little Caroline

You trusted to an unsafe plan when you left your letter at Wellesley-House to wait for me till my coming there. The chances were ten to one that I might never have received it, & indeed it was not put into my hands till many days after my arrival. Even then I had no leisure to answer as the first week or two of my stay in town brought continual & pressing calls on my attention. I am at present a little more disengaged, having contrived to get away from Verdopolis in order to complete a small business transaction relative to an affair of some old houses which has for many years been pending between myself & Mr Warner. The matter is not one likely ever to be settled because it only relates to a rental of some ten pounds per annum arising from a brace of tenements whose roofs are nearly off. However, it gives Mr Warner pretext in demanding my presence at his place Woodhouse-Cliffe about twice a year in order to survey the buildings & discuss afresh the disputed point of their value. Mr Warner, my little Caroline, wishes me to take them off his hands without requiring any repairs and I am considerably too much a man of business to consent to any such arrangement. My young ward will wonder what all this has to do with her.

294   *Here was something more than the devil to pay*: a variation of 'Here's the very Devil to pay' meaning 'I'm in a pretty mess' (Brewer).

295   *bergère*: an easy armchair with cane arms and back, fashionable in the eighteenth century.

shoulder knots: knotted ribbons of the family colours, part of a servant's livery.

shining emblems of the seven churches which are in Asia: seven golden candlesticks: see Revelation 1: 11 and 20.

298   *Not very quick in apprehension*: this is a very different Mrs Warner from the lively intelligent young bluestocking Warner woos in 'High Life in Verdopolis' (Alexander *EEW* 2(2). 21 ff.).

300   *espièglerie*: mischievousness (French).

id est: that is (Latin).

won't wash: stand the test, prove to be genuine (colloquial).

Who is Mᵣ Ferguson: early nineteenth-century fictional character, used to replace the real name of a culprit.

Blarney–Mills: Blarney Castle in Ireland was the legendary scene of soft cajolery to gain an end, hence the colloquial use of 'blarney' as 'the art of flattery or of telling lies with unblushing effrontery' (Lewis, *Topographical Dictionary of Ireland*; quoted by *OED*).

306   *garment of light*: cf. Psalm 104: 2: 'Who coverest thyself with light as with a garment'.

the moral great-heart: Great Heart was the escort of Christiana and her children on their way to the Celestial City in Bunyan's *The Pilgrim's Progress*.

like the snaky fillet which compressed Calchas's brows, steeped in blue venom: Charlotte has confused Calchas, the Greek soothsayer, with Laocoön, the Trojan priest of Apollo, who was crushed to death by sea-serpents when he rushed to the defence of his sons. The story is told in Virgil's *Aeneid*, and it is Dryden's translation that Charlotte's vocabulary echoes: cf. 2. 290–1: 'With both his hands he labours at the knots; | His holy fillets the blue venom blots'.

307   *depths of Gehenna*: a place of eternal torment and unquenchable fire: see Jeremiah 19: 1–6 for its biblical origins, and Milton, *Paradise Lost*, 1. 403.

Not for a diadem. Not for a Krooman's head. Not for every inch of land the Joliba waters: in ancient times a diadem was a headband worn by kings as a badge of royalty; when it was eventually made of gold it became inseparable from a crown. Kroomen were a seafaring black tribe on the coast of Liberia, but the reference here may be to any slave's head, since the *OED* cites an 1884 usage of 'Kru-men' as 'indigenous slaves of the country . . . men, for instance, of the lower Congo tribes, that are sold by their chiefs to European merchants'. Joliba is the local Mali name for the River Niger in Africa, not named as such on the maps owned by the Brontës but mentioned in *Blackwood's* and in Edward Quillinan's 'The Retort Courteous' (1821), in which he mocks Lockhart's and Wilson's *Peter's Letters to his Kinsfolk*, published by Blackwood.

307 *'Crede Zamorna!'*: trust Zamorna (Latin); cf. Byron's motto 'Trust Byron!' Thomas Moore, *Letters and Journals of Lord Byron: with notices of his Life* (Paris, 1837), 5.

308 *There are some things that even I cannot defy . . . a trampled slave*: reference to the fate of Rosamund Wellesley, former mistress and cousin of Zamorna (see Alexander *EW*, 196).

     a return to Eden was dreadful: Zamorna has become the serpent in the garden of Eden precipitating Caroline's willing temptation and fall.

     Passion tempted. Conscience warned her: Jane Eyre suffers the same conflict: 'conscience, turned tyrant, held passion by the throat' (*Jane Eyre*, ch. 27).

     answered, 'Yes.': gap in manuscript here; possibly intended as a chapter break.

     on Friday: the date '7th of Dec^br' is deleted here, but probably indicates Charlotte's time of writing.

309 *as he now wore a head*: possibly a version of 'to have a head', to experience the after-effects of heavy drinking (Partridge).

     it had that in its light irid which passes shew: cf. *Hamlet* I. ii. 85–6: 'But I have that within which passes show, | These but the trappings and the suits of woe.'

     Lord Etrei: Henry Fernando di Enara.

310 *as if from the ramparts of Gazemba he was watching Arundel's horsemen scouring the wilderness*: Fort Gazemba in Angria was one of the strongholds of Zamorna's army in the Angrian wars; Lord Arundel, Zamorna's trusted friend, is an expert horseman and 'the Darling of the Army'.

311 *that filthy Jordan*: Lord Jordon, Northangerland's brother-in-law by his first wife; he and his troops prove unreliable to Northangerland in the Angrian Wars.

312 *Hebrew imposter Nathan tells David, the man after God's own heart—a certain parable of an ewe lamb & applies it to his own righteous deeds*: see 1 Samuel 13: 14, and 2 Samuel 12: 1–15; Nathan is an 'imposter' possibly because he tricked David by the parable into condemning himself.

     as Harriet O'Connor did: Harriet is seduced by Northangerland, friend of her profligate brother Arthur O'Connor.

     herd of horned cattle: cuckolds, traditionally represented with horns on their brows.

313 *'Moored . . . the ruder it blow'*: from ''Boat Song' in Walter Scott's *The Lady of the Lake* (1810), canto 2, v. 19.

314 FAREWELL TO ANGRIA. Untitled single-page manuscript fragment (12.5 × 20 cm), written about 1839; in the Bonnell Collection, BPM. The last of the early manuscripts relating directly to the Glass Town and Angrian saga, it is commonly known as 'Farewell to Angria', an autobiographical statement in which Charlotte draws on her experience in the visual arts as she characterizes her saga in terms of a lurid and familiar painting.

The generally accepted composition date of 1839 has been disputed by Keith C. Odom ('Dating Charlotte Brontë's *Villette*: A Reappraisal', *Papers of the Bibliographical Society of America*, 82/3 (1998), 341–7); however the present editor believes that the content, handwriting, and information on the reverse of the fragment confirm an approximate date of 1839 rather than 1850 as Odom suggests.

BRANWELL BRONTË

317 THE LIAR DETECTED. 'The Liar Detected' or 'The Liar Unmasked' (both titles appear in the MS) is a small hand-sewn booklet of thirteen manuscript pages (5.3 × 3.7 cm), enclosed in a titled grey paper cover, in the BPM. Written the day after Charlotte's 'An Interesting Passage in the Lives of Some Eminent Men of the Present Time' by Lord Charles Wellesley (see p. 31), it is typical of the narrative rivalry between the young Brontës. Captain Bud, Branwell's pseudonym when writing prose and Glass Town's 'ablest political writer', was implicated by Wellesley in a library theft, and is determined to refute the scandalmongering of his young rival. Bud's systematic debunking of 'An Interesting Passage' is representative of the legalistic, debating style in much of Branwell's writing, especially when his characters are recording parliamentary debates, recounting battles or reviewing books. Lord Charles retaliates to 'The Liar Detected' a month later in 'The Poetaster', by satirizing the romantic posturing of Young Soult, Branwell's poetic persona (see Alexander *EEW*, vol. 1).

Homer had his Zoilus, Virgil his Maevius: Zoilus, a Greek rhetorician of the fourth century BC, was known as 'Homer's scourge' because he mercilessly attacked the epics of Homer; his name became proverbial as that of a witty but spiteful, carping critic. The later minor Roman poet Maevius (first century BC) was lampooned by Virgil in his *Eclogues*, and also by Horace. Although these allusions underline Branwell's interest in the classics, it is likely he encountered Maevius through William Gifford's satire on the Della Cruscan school of poets, 'The Maeviad' (1795).

and CAPTAIN TREE his Wellesly: rivalry exists not only between the authors of the Glass Town saga and their respective personas, but also between the different personas of the author. Wellesley (usually spelt 'Wellesly' by Branwell) eventually ousts his rival Tree as the leading Glass Town prose writer; both are pseudonyms of Charlotte.

and like vipers can do no more than bite the heels of their enimies: cf. Genesis 3: 15.

317 *bantling*: a young child, a brat; often used deprecatingly as a synonym for bastard.

college of Eton: Eton College, near Windsor in England, was the preparatory school of the historical Duke of Wellington and his two sons, Arthur and Charles Wellesley.

Africa, his father having gone there: see Charlotte's 'Albion and Marina' for an account of the fictitious Wellesley family's removal to Africa.

318 *small book of verses*: 'Miscellaneous Poems', a hand-sewn MS booklet by Charlotte, dated 31 May 1830, including 'The Vision A Short Poem' referred to later in 'The Liar Detected'.

skelped: skipped, incorrectly spelt 'skleped' in manuscript; northern and Scots dialect, frequently used by Burns and Scott.

published June 18, 1830: Charlotte's 'An Interesting Passage in the Lives of Some Eminent Men of the Present Time'.

15 individuals: Magrass is the gatekeeper of the Glass Town cemetery: see 'An Interesting Passage'; for other characters, several of whose names are spelt differently by Branwell, see Glossary of the Glass Town and Angrian Saga.

Rouge: Branwell's consistent spelling of 'Rouge' in this manuscript and 'Rougue' in his other manuscripts has been preserved (see Note on the Text).

budget: bundle or collection of news; a bag or pouch in dialect.

319 *Pope's Homer*: Alexander Pope's translation of Homer's *Iliad* (1715–20), though not an accurate version of the original, was considered one of the great poems of the age. Branwell would have used it in his classical studies as an example of free poetic translation.

320 *volumn in blue morroco*: Charlotte's manuscript is also in blue covers.

Miss M. H——me: Miss Marian Hume.

Jupiter: also Jove, supreme god of Roman mythology and special protector of Rome, who determined the course of human affairs. Branwell's sarcasm here is interesting since he himself assumed the role of 'Jupiter tonans' or 'thundering Jupiter' in the early Glass Town saga.

Puppyism: impertinent conceit or affectation, Lofty's chief characteristic throughout the Brontë manuscripts. *DVT* defines 'Puppy' as 'an affected or conceited coxcomb'.

the little puppy: see note above.

so many monkeys about him: see note to p. 31: 'my monkey'.

321 *Lord Charles's 'VISION'*: see note to p. 318: 'small book of verses'.

Young S—— and the Marquis of D—ro: Young Soult and the Marquis of Douro.

322 *if you continue in your present course . . . attendant evils will over take you shortly*: a sadly ironic comment in the light of Branwell's own later

incautious behaviour and dependence on drink and drugs that contributed to his early death.

Discourses on the 4 Elements: a title possibly modelled on the Greek theory
of matter that saw the four elements, earth, air, fire, and water, as the
basic constituents of matter. Early occurrences of this theory occur in
Empedocles (492–432 BC) and in Plato's *Timaeus* (*c*.360 BC). Aristotle's
development of the theory of the four elements greatly influenced the
thought of the alchemical philosophers in Europe in the sixteenth and
seventeenth centuries and the concept has continued to be significant in
metaphysical systems into the twentieth century.

323 IIID. ODE. ON THE CELEBRATION OF THE GREAT AFRICAN GAMES.
The composition date of the poem (26 June 1832) was a day of personal
celebration for Branwell: his fifteenth birthday. Real life events were often
marked by similar occasions in the imaginary Brontë sagas, in this case
the Glass Town equivalent of the Olympic Games. Branwell also made a
habit of assuming the role of poet laureate and, usually in the persona of
Young Soult, commemorating Glass Town events in poetry. This poem is
typical of Branwell's early songs and dirges invoking the conflict between
the warring, vengeful Genii and the Glasstowners, led by the Twelves. It
represents one of his last attempts to preserve a tyrannical role for the
Genii against the opposition of Charlotte, and the disinterest of Emily
and Anne who were busy establishing Gondal at this time. Branwell's
frustration with his sisters' response is recorded at the beginning of his
next manuscript, 'The Monthly Intelligencer' (Neufeldt *BBWorks*, vol.
1). The following year, however, Charlotte takes up Branwell's idea of the
African Olympic Games and transforms it into a Medieval Tournament
(see 'The Green Dwarf', Alexander *EEW* 2(1)).

'Ode on the Celebration of the Great African Games' also gives an
excellent picture of the classical origins and the geography of the Glass
Town Federation, or Verdopolitan Federation (later 'Union') as it is
now called. The manuscript is written in longhand, 176 lines (Branwell
miscounted the total as 177) on five pages of a hand-sewn notebook containing fair copies of five poems, in the BPM.

Once again . . . Shines on Afric's scorched brow: the collaboration between
the four Chief Genii on their Glass Town saga was temporarily destroyed
when Charlotte went to school at Roe Head (January 1831–May 1832).
Emily and Anne abandoned it for Gondal, and Branwell enthusiastically
reverted to bloody battles and rebellions led by his new character Rogue
(see 'The Pirate'). On Charlotte's return home, however, peace is re-
established and she and Branwell begin a fruitful literary partnership.

Olympian hall: originally built by the supernatural power of the Genii
(see Charlotte's 'The Twelve Adventurers', ch. 3) and now resurrected by
them.

stern Monarch Lord of war: Duke of Wellington, King Wellington's Land
in the west of the Glass Town Federation. As in the original Senegambia

(now Senegal and Gambia), the River Gambia flows through Wellington's Land.

324 *And on her rocky margin . . . rise o'er the shady trees*: Wellington's Glass Town is situated on the River Gambia.

King of the North: Alexander Sneaky, King of Sneaky's Land.

Casepurh huge and Dimdim . . . Genii's sea: Casepurh and Dimdim are part of the Dimdims Throne, a vast chain of mountains or 'Highlands' that surround the Lake of the Genii; the whole area (in particular Mt. Aornos, the Glass Town equivalent of Mt. Olympus, home of the Greek gods), is the mythical home of the Chief Genii.

Morven's: mountain named after a mythical kingdom in James Macpherson's *Poems of Ossian* (1819), owned by the Brontës.

Ardrah's: Arthur Parry, Marquis of Ardrah, son of the King of Parry's Land in the south of the Federation.

Nevada's sides: huge mountain situated in the north of Parry's Land; named after the Spanish Nevadas.

325 *Achaian shore*: also Achaean; a name used by Homer to refer to Greece. Also referred to by Pope in his translation of the *Iliad* (1817), 2. 834, which Branwell used.

awful Jove . . . golden Juno: Jove or Jupiter, supreme god in Roman mythology (equivalent of the Greek Zeus), and his wife Juno.

Great Athena: Athene (spelt 'Athenia' by Branwell), goddess of wisdom and patron goddess of Athens, and of arts and crafts.

Phoebus: also Apollo, Greek god of the sun.

326 *Awful Branii . . . blazing air*: Chief Genius Brannii, also known as 'Genius of the Storm', is evoked in an untitled poem by Young Soult beginning 'O Mars who shakest thy Fiery hair'; thus, Branwell may have intended 'hair' instead of 'air' in this line.

Dread Tallii . . . boding cry: wishful thinking by Branwell: none of his sisters supported his bloodthirsty Genii antics in the saga, and Emily and Anne were tired of being 'last'.

Twelves: here the founders of Glass Town are equated with Classical heroes, pitted against the vengeance of the gods.

328 THE PIRATE. While Charlotte was at school (January 1831–May 1832), Branwell had been creating his new hero, the demagogue Rogue (or 'Rougue' as Branwell usually calls him), formerly only 'Old Rogue's youngest son, a promising youth'. Modelled chiefly on Napoleon at this stage, Rogue leads a rebellion ending in a French Revolutionary 'terror' and provisional government in Verdopolis, which is finally overthrown by the four Kings and Crashie, their Patriarch. After organizing a second rebellion in Sneaky's Land, Rogue is captured and shot; but Branwell 'resurrects' him in 'The Pirate' and thus begins Rogue's upwardly mobile career under the successive titles of Alexander Percy, Lord Ellrington, Earl of Northangerland, and Prime Minister of Angria. Influenced by

Scott's novel *The Pirate* (1812) and by Byron's poem *The Corsair* (1814), Branwell provides the requisite love affair for his pirate, but with a difference: Rogue/Percy assumes his wife's title and enters Verdopolitan society as a foil to the man who rejected his new wife (see Charlotte's 'Albion and Marina' in which Zenobia Ellrington is rejected by the Marquis of Douro). The story also introduces the symbiotic relationship between Rogue and Robert Patrick S'death, who is Rogue's evil genius and the new impersonation of the mischievous Chief Genius Brannii. The manuscript of 'The Pirate' consists of fifteen pages in minuscule script, in a hand-sewn booklet of larger format than earlier volumes (11.4 × 13.5 cm), in grey paper cover; in the BPM.

Captain John Flower: the author or 'editor' of 'The Pirate' may be Flower (i.e. Branwell), but the narrator is obviously James Bellingham   (see below).

Author of 'Letters from an Englishman': the English merchant James Bellingham. 'Letters from an Englishman' are 'edited' by Captain John Flower, in six miniature hand-sewn volumes, now in the Brotherton Library, University of Leeds. They were written between 6 September 1830 and 2 August 1832, and focus on Glass Town's villains (in particular the most accomplished, 'Rogue'), recording the recent Great Rebellion of 1831 and the rebellion in Sneaky's Land (both prompted by the contemporary threat of revolution in England with the possible rejection by Parliament of the Reform Bill and the recent 1830 revolutions in Europe).

returned from no one knows where: Charlotte records in 'The Green Dwarf. A Tale of the Perfect Tense' (2 September 1833) the downfall of the once brilliant soldier Colonel Augustus Percy, his abduction of Lady Emily Charlesworth and treachery against Lord St Clair which earned him sixteen years' exile, wandering 'through the world, sometimes a pirate, sometimes a leader of banditti, and ever the companion of the most dissolute and profligate of mankind' (Alexander *EEW*, 2(1). 205).

every acre of his paternal possessions . . . bid adieu to him: facts about Percy's early life only emerge gradually as Branwell and Charlotte continually create and rewrite them. In manuscripts as late as 1837–8, we learn that Edward Percy Senior ('Old Rogue') was murdered by Percy's first wife, the wicked Italian aristocrat Lady Augusta Romana di Segovia, in order to secure his fortune, but the plot miscarried after she was herself poisoned by her accomplices for withholding their payment. Percy then married Mary Henrietta Wharton and was a reformed man until her consumptive death, exacerbated by the 'unnatural barbarity' of Percy's removal and disowning of his three sons (see Alexander *EW*, 181–2).

329 *I'm three in one*: an example of Rogue's atheistic manipulation of theological ideas which increases in later manuscripts; here he scorns the idea of the Trinity.

330 *Body and soul . . . were never together*: Rogue's increasing association with atheism reflects not only Branwell's efforts to flesh out his character but

also Branwell's increasing interest in the complex, satanic personalities of Milton's Lucifer, Byron's Manfred, Scott's Varney, Hogg's Robert Wringhim, and the atheistic writing of Shelley.

330 *Grenville's . . . Cotterel*: Colonel John Bramham Grenville, referred to again later in this story, is a wealthy mill owner, who fought with Wellington during Rogue's rebellion. The other characters are wealthy merchants and bankers, whose ships Rogue has plundered.

waters of life: referring to brandy or whiskey, a phrase Branwell would have encountered in *Blackwood's* and also in John Wilson's *Lights and Shadows of Scottish Life* (1822).

331 *L'Empereur . . . Talleyrand*: Emperor Napoleon and Talleyrand, from Frenchyland (see note to p. 4: 'Gravey'). Talleyrand (1754–1838), the powerful French statesman who survived the Revolution, was instrumental in consolidating Napoleon's power until 1814, when he changed sides and supported the restoration of the monarchy. (Although this paragraph is reported speech, Branwell's speech marks have been retained.)

Sdeath: spelt 'Sdeath' here in MS, reflecting the origin of the word 'S'death' as a euphemistic abbreviation of the oath 'God's death'. Branwell subsequently drops the apostrophe but Charlotte invariably spells the name 'S'death'. See also note to p. 339.

334 *to sell as a slave in a foreign country*: Branwell's interest in the slave trade can be noted throughout his writing, culminating in his rewriting of the character Quashia, in his 1845 novel *And The Weary Are At Rest* (ed. C. W. Hatfield, London: privately printed, 1924), in which Quashia assumes Percy's pirate past.

Tower of Nations: see note to p. 9: 'Great Tower'.

335 *waste of waters*: cf. Byron's *Don Juan*, 2. l. 386; and *The Corsair*, 1. l. 170.

Carey: Captain Lucius Carey, one of Rogue's earliest minions who also supported his recent rebellions against the Federation.

336 *magazine*: the powder magazine, where arms, ammunition, and explosives are stored.

338 *Earl of Elrington and his family*: Lord Ellrington (always spelt 'Elrington' by Branwell), an Irish emigrant, established himself as a nobleman in Wellingtonsland, with a palace in Verdopolis (purchased by Rogue). His wife, Paulina Louisiada Ellrington, a Spanish beauty of dubious morality, has died and he lives with his daughter Zenobia and three young sons. The origin of the name 'Elrington' is reflected in Branwell's spelling. It seems likely that he knew of or used Thomas Elrington's edition of Euclid and possibly his edition of Juvenal. Thomas Elrington (1760–1835), professor of mathematics at Dublin University and an Irish bishop, would have been known to Patrick Brontë.

339 *this little hideous bloody old man was the Cheif Genius BRANNII*: Branwell has found a way of retaining an interventionist role in his narratives by subsuming the Chief Genius Brannii into the character of Sdeath, alter ego and motivator of Percy's sardonic behaviour.

341 THE POLITICS OF VERDOPOLIS. This manuscript is important for its introduction of the heroine Mary Percy, who was to become a crucial player in the fluctuating relationship between the Marquis of Douro and Lord Ellrington (Alexander Percy/Rogue). Mary is the beautiful but proud 17-year-old daughter of Ellrington and his second wife Maria Henrietta Wharton; she is destined to become Douro's third and last wife, the Duchess of Zamorna and Queen of Angria, but also an unhappy pawn in the power-play between her husband and her father. In 'Politics of Verdopolis', Ellrington is already using his daughter as bait to secure political support in his election campaign for seats in the Verdopolitan Parliament, events inspired by the American elections of 1828 (see note to p. 361: 'Elrington and liberty') and by the electioneering leading up to the British Reform Bill of 1832, which passed against a background of widespread unrest and fierce Tory opposition. Branwell and Charlotte disagreed with their father who supported the Bill against his own Tory party. The historical Wellington and Sir Robert Peel were central players, and the newly introduced Glass Town character Sir Robert Weaver Pelham (spelt 'Weever' by Branwell) reflects the Brontës' ambiguous attitude towards the socially awkward and cold but clever statesman Peel. Branwell translates the agitation and excitement of the British and American political situations into his 'African' context, which is becoming increasingly English in landscape and culture. The following notes detail his familiarity with both political and evangelical rhetoric of the time.

The MS is a hand-sewn booklet of eighteen pages (11.5×18.5 cm), with a grey paper cover; in the BPM. At the bottom of manuscript p. 4, the text is written closely around a detailed pen-and-ink sketch of a European-style cityscape with tall buildings and a bridge (see Alexander and Sellars, 305). Inside the front cover Branwell has written: 'by Red Rover/ Lynn Coach./ Thursday night./ March 6. 1834./ To be delivered as/ soon as possible/ Carriage Paid/ $1/0^d$' (originally 2^d, changed to 0^d). The later date suggests that Branwell may have sewn his text into the cover several months after it was written (23 October – 15 November 1833), using paper that had already been used for another purpose. Long-distance coaches were customarily given names such as 'Red Rover' (the origin of the name of Alexander Percy's pirate ship); there were at least four 'Red Rovers' operating in England in 1834. This particular 'Red Rover' is probably the London to Manchester coach which stopped at Lichfield; the package delivered may have come by local coach from Lynn, 4 miles south-west of Lichfield, and then transferred to the 'Red Rover'.

Jacobin Club: famous French Revolutionary society; founded at Versailles in 1789 but moved to Paris and met in a former Jacobin convent, hence the name. Its aim was to propagate principles of extreme democracy and absolute equality and its badge was the Phrygian Cap of Liberty. Branwell was aware that eminent members included Mirabeau, Robespierre, and Marat (models for his Glass Town revolutionaries), and he imitates their success, in his tales, in controlling the country through their many branch societies in the provinces.

341 *Wellington's Glass Town*: capital city of Wellington's Land in the far west of the Glass Town Federation. Wellington's Land was modelled originally on Ireland, where the historical Duke of Wellington was born, but it becomes increasingly English in its landscape.

burning land of Africa: cf. Richard Blackmore, 'The Nature of Man', in *A Collection of Poems on Various Subjects* (1718), bk. 1, ll. 60–1.

342 *MARY HENRIETTA. PERCY*: née Wharton, second wife of Alexander Percy, and mother of his three sons (Edward, William, and Henry Percy) and daughter (Mary Henrietta). Percy is idyllically happy with her, living at Percy Hall in Wellington's Land; his grief at her death by consumption, exacerbated by his unnatural aversion to his sons whom he banishes at birth, confirms his atheistic beliefs and causes him to return to his former wild and dissipated life.

343 *earth to earth, ashes to ashes*: paraphrase from the English burial service, 'ashes to ashes, dust to dust', denoting finality.

flying his country for ban of the law: Ellrington (Percy) is on the run from the government, having been involved in a series of robberies as the secret leader of criminal gangs (see Alexander *EW*, 104–5; and 'Real Life in Verdopolis: A Tale', in R. G. Collins (ed.), *The Hand of the Arch-Sinner: Two Angrian Chronicles of Branwell Brontë* (Oxford and New York: Clarendon Press, 1993).

Methodism, Calvinism and such stuff: meaning extreme Protestantism here. Methodism is based on the Christian teachings of John and Charles Wesley; the name was given in 1729 to members of their Holy Club at Oxford, because of the methodical way in which they observed their principles, and later also applied to the Nonconformist church that grew out of the evangelical movement started by the Wesleys in the late 1740s. Originally members of the Church of England, the separate Methodist church was not established until after John Wesley's death in 1791 and then underwent numerous schisms over the following fifty years. Calvinism was a more extreme form of Nonconformism, based on the strict teachings of Jean Calvin (1509–64) who emphasized the doctrines of original sin, predestination, and election, and the sole authority of Scripture and the Holy Spirit. John Wesley espoused Arminian views of predestination, opposing the 'Calvinistic Methodists' (under Whitefield) who held that God was responsible for evil. The young Brontës, though opposed to such exclusive doctrines, were not untouched by Calvinist strictures at crucial times in their lives; yet at all times they found Nonconformist forms of worship amusing, in particular the open-air preaching of the Primitive Methodists who were commonly known as 'Ranters'. Politically, Nonconformity was closely linked with the Liberals (they campaigned for disestablishment)—hence Ellrington's Reform Movement is referred to as 'Liberal' and uses Methodist cant (see note to p. 352: 'the work').

Satire against Methodists becomes more extreme in the later Brontë juvenilia (Ellrington/Percy frequently adopts the role of the hypocrital Methodist preacher 'Mr Ashworth'), which is curious since the children's mother and aunt had both been raised Wesleyan Methodists and Patrick Brontë had always been supported by the Methodists in disputes with local Baptists and stricter sects. The equation between Methodism and hypocrisy for the Brontës continues in their novels: in *Shirley* the leader of the Luddite rioters is a drunken Methodist lay preacher, and in *Wuthering Heights* Methodism is caricatured in the figure of Jabes Branderham and his sermon.

When I was here 18 years since . . . now: Charlotte quoted this passage as the epithet to her poem 'Captain Flower's Last [?Novel]', written on 20 November, five days after Branwell finished his story (see Alexander *EEW* 2(1). 262). Her quotation is not exact, but it is so close as to suggest that Branwell has just read this scene to her, inspiring her poem. Charlotte was so taken by this scene that she recreated it in her story 'High Life in Verdopolis' (20 February–20 March 1833), where she describes 'Flower's lovely heroine' and the wicket-gate of that churchyard 'so sweetly described' at the beginning of 'The Politics of Verdopolis' (Alexander *EEW*, 2(2). 35–7). Here we find an excellent example of the close literary cooperation between brother and sister.

brilliants: diamonds of the finest cut and brilliancy (*OED*).

344 *beaver hat*: hats and bonnets made of beaver skin were prized in the Brontës' day; worn particularly by men.

thine: following text deleted in MS: 'We need not speak of the manner in which Lord Elrington for he it was was received by his ancient servant in the halls of his fathers. We will next view him seated with his daughter at supper in this splendid parlours of his Aristocratic mansion. "Do you visit the city often child?" asked his lordship. "No—seldom they think me far high for them."'

345 *'apes' and 'rare lads'*: see note to p. 99: 'rare apes'.

cotters: peasants who occupy a cottage belonging to an estate and rent a small plot of land under a form of tenure; a term used especially in Ireland and Scotland.

346 *by the heart of Scylla*: see note to p. 116: 'Scylla'.

sentim[ent.]: illegible deletion of 4 lines follows in manuscript.

he drove from his house his two sons: see note to p. 342: 'MARY HENRIETTA. PERCY'.

347 *cant*: insincere or hypocrital speech, jargon peculiar to a social class, profession, or sect; here the word may simply mean 'hackneyed expression', as used in Irish dialect (Wright).

348 *Caversham*: Viscount Colonel George Frederic Caversham, heavy-drinking card-playing long-time crony of Ellrington. The ink sketch of tall buildings and bridge (mentioned above in note to p. 341) begins here and fills the bottom right corner of the page.

349 *Belial*: spirit of evil personified; often synonymous with the Devil, and used by Milton in *Paradise Lost* as the name of one of the fallen angels.

349 *Connor and Gordon!*: Arthur O'Connor and Captain Julian Gordon, profligate associates of Ellrington. Gordon is brother of Lady Helen Victorine
Gordon.

a perfect Othello: in Shakespeare's tragedy, Othello, a moor employed
as general in the Venetian army, is duped by his ensign Iago—just as
Ellrington is about to dupe Quashia. Othello's jealous love for Desdemona
and his irrational behaviour are evoked in the character of the black
Quashia and his pursuit of Mary Percy. See also *Roe Head Journal* 1; and
'Caroline Vernon', ch. 1.

those infernal ministers: the 'Tory' Verdopolitan Government, under the
Earl St Clair as prime minister.

350 *Volo*: 'I am willing' (Latin); Branwell often uses the slang sense of 'Let's
go!', 'Let's do it!'. Latin phrases were common in political speeches
reported in contemporary newspapers or in *Blackwood's*, eg. *sic volo, sic
jubeo* appears in 'A Conversation on the Reform Bill', *Blackwood's* (August
1831), 300 (which Branwell would have read).

351 *our strength and justice avail us*: Ellrington's Movement Party, referred to
as 'Liberals' or 'Democrats'.

thorough reformation: see Ellrington's conditions for reform reported
in his speech 'House of Commons', 25 April 1833, in 'The Monthly
Intelligencer' (Neufeldt *BBWorks*, 1. 255).

Alexander Viscount Elrington . . . Richard Streithton, Esqʳ: Ellrington's
coterie; for Caversham and Gordon see notes to pp. 348 and 349.

352 *Seargeant W. J. Despard*: name probably suggested by that of the Irish
conspirator Edward Marcus Despard (1751–1803) who, after a successful
career as an ensign in the West Indies and false imprisonment, became
involved in a hair-brained plot to assassinate the King and seize the Tower
and Bank of England.

the work: evangelical diction; a possible pun is intended here with the
slang meaning of 'work' as 'criminal activity'. Ellrington's references
to his party as 'scattered lambs', his pretence of support for 'religious
freedom', and his apocalyptic and evangelical diction with its often apostolic connotations, suggest his increasingly hypocritical use of religion
for political ends: he becomes a master of Calvinistic Methodist cant (see
note to p. 343: 'Methodism').

353 *he'll carry all before him*: carry off all the prizes, be highly successful in the
contest.

beard the lion in his den: to defy personally, to have it out face to face; also
a probable play on the lion as a symbol of royalty: cf. Shakespeare's *King
John*, v. i. 57–8.

ottoman: cushioned seat like a sofa, but without back or arms, for sitting
or reclining.

a prick of hog flesh: 'prick' is a vulgar term of abuse for a man (from the
slang for 'penis'); 'pig flesh' (and presumably 'hog flesh') is slang for
'human flesh' (Partridge).

354 *I*: 'Aye'; Branwell often uses this spelling for the archaic 'aye' (meaning 'yes'), common still in dialectal and parliamentary usage.

Sdeath's a cold: one of Sdeath's habitual phrases, cf. Edgar's repeated lament in Act III, scene xi of Shakespeare's *King Lear* (Quarto 1608): 'Poor Tom's a-cold'.

doughty: worthy, valiant (archaic, humorous use by the nineteenth century).

355 *th'club and Mont an t'others*: the Paradise of Souls or Elysium Club, a private gaming and drinking club in Verdopolis, led by Ellrington; originally a secret society based on the Masonic Lodge of the Three Graces in Haworth, which Branwell later joined. For Montmorency ('Mont') see Glossary of the Glass Town and Angrian Saga.

Gordon for _Denard_ . . . _Harlaw_: major towns (underlined) of the Verdopolitan Federation with Ellrington's cronies contesting the seats. Denard and Fidena are in Sneaky's Land; Harlaw and Selden are in Ross's Land; Sneakys Town, Ross Town, and Parry's Town are the original Glass Towns of Sneaky's, Ross's, and Parry's Lands respectively.

cracked up: ruined, crazy (colloquial).

a stiff 'un: sturdy, resolute, also obstinate (Yorkshire dialect).

356 *Sir Robert Weever Pelham*: newly arrived from Lancashire in England (see Glossary for his career); modelled on Sir Robert Peel (1788–1850) and Henry Pelham (1811–60), both English statesmen with north-of-England associations. Peel (also from Lancashire) opposed the Reform Bill (carried by the Whig ministry under Earl Grey in 1832) and was vigilant in his criticism against the too rapid strides of Liberalism (hence Branwell's Sir Robert soon becomes a conservative); see 'Tales of the Islanders', note to p. 18. Pelham, later 5th Duke of Newcastle (1851), was MP for South Nottinghamshire 1832–46 (when he was ousted for supporting Peel's Free Trade measures) and again 1852–4, 1859–64; held various offices including lord of the Treasury (1834–5), Irish secretary, and colonial secretary.

Tamworth Hall: Branwell's knowledge of British politics is up-to-date: Sir Robert Peel was elected to the seat of Tamworth in 1833 (the date of this MS) and held it till his death.

his skinfull: as much as he can drink (from wine once kept in skin vessels).

rumble thy bellyful, spit fire: cf. *King Lear*, III. ix. 14: 'Rumble thy bellyful! Spit, fire! spout, rain!' (Quarto, 1608).

thy ain het hame again: 'Your own hot home again' (Scots dialect). S'death's 'hot home' refers to his association with the devil.

Mr Seaton: 'Steaton' or 'Steighton' in later MSS; steward of Ellrington's estates and his minion in various crimes, including the murder of his youngest son. Steighton's son Timothy, a lawyer, becomes clerk to Ellrington's eldest son Edward Percy.

358 *Morley*: Thomas Babbicombe Morley, pompous but knowledgeable speaker who becomes one of the Angrian coterie.

358 *Earl St Clair, the fiend incarnate*: current Verdopolitan prime minister, opposed to Ellrington; modelled on James St Clair, Lord Rosslyn, a member of Wellington's cabinet and colleague of Peel.

   rum stiff 'un: 'rum' meaning 'strange, queer, bad' (slang); for 'stiff 'un' see note to p. 355.

359 *Philosopher's Island*: site of the university (also called College of Philosophers) where Glass Town nobles were educated, under the instruction of Manfred the magician (cf. Byron's *Manfred*), in the mysteries of life and death (and sworn not to misuse their knowledge); graduates formed a secret society which becomes associated with the Elysium Club (see note to p. 355: 'th' club'). Branwell is employing the word 'philosopher' in a common seventeenth-century usage, meaning an adept in the occult, an alchemist, magician (*OED*). The island of the philosophers is the place where the alchemists were said to seek the magical philosophical tree, a symbol for both the philosopher's stone, and for the *prima materia* from which the stone was produced (see Lyndy Abraham, *Marvell and Alchemy* (Aldershot: Scolar Press, 1990), 139–40).

   Lancashire: cf. Peel, note to p. 356.

360 *'Money makes the mare to go'*: you can do anything with money; from the old song:

> 'Will you lend me your mare to go a mile?'
> 'No, she is lame leaping over a stile.'
> 'But if you will her to me spare,
> You shall have money for your mare.'
> 'Oh ho! say you so?
> Money will make the mare to go.'

361 *ass laden with gold*: cf. Shakespeare's *Julius Caesar*, IV. i. 21: 'He shall but bear them, as the ass bears gold'. The donkey or ass was the emblem of the American Democratic Party (see note below).

   'Elrington and liberty, Democrats for ever!': 'Democrats' was the name given to the American President Andrew Jackson's party in the 1830s. The political tactics and use of flags in Branwell's narration suggests his knowledge of the Jackson election of 1828, popularly renowned as a milestone in 'the Rise of the Common Man' against the aristocracy. A lawyer, senator, and judge, Jackson fought against the British in the 1812 War of Independence and was made a major general. When he was finally elected president (he had previously had the highest popular vote but not a majority), he swept out great numbers of minor officials to fill their places with his partisans. The Brontës followed these events with interest: in one of Branwell's earliest magazines (June 1829), Andrew Jackson proposes a toast to 'American Liberty!' (C. Alexander and V. Benson (eds.), *Branwell's Blackwood's Magazine* (Edmonton: Juvenilia Press, 1995), 18), and Jackson features again in Charlotte's 'An American Tale' of the same year (Alexander *EEW* 1. 84).

had pitched for a time his tent: common biblical phrase (eg. Genesis 13: 12) used figuratively. The text is saturated with similar biblical echoes.

362 *too much of a d——d Glasstowner for our comprehension*: the Brontës delighted in Byron's risqué reputation, appropriating the stories of his adultery, exile, poetic fortunes, political escapades, and personal disillusion into the fabric of their own heroes.

little duodecimo printed in a superlative stile upon paper like ivory: Branwell's bibliographic knowledge was impressive; he both appreciated and mocked the jargon of the bibliophile in his writing. Duodecimo denotes the small size of the book in which each leaf is one-twelfth of a whole sheet.

volumn of the poems of Arthur, Marquis of Douro: most of Charlotte's early poems were signed with the pseudonym of her Glass Town hero the Marquis of Douro, including the miniature hand-sewn volume 'The Violet A Poem With Several Smaller Peices By The Marquis of Douro'.

363 *The cloth being drawn*: tablecloth removed after dinner.

hustings: temporary platform from which, previous to the Ballot Act of 1872, the nomination of candidates for Parliament was made, and on which these stood while addressing the electors (*OED*).

364 *almost certain riots*: popular unrest in the north of England and increasingly violent agitation for political reform was routinely and often harshly dealt with by soldiers, many of whom had fought at Waterloo. Parallels for riotous incidents in the Glass Town saga can be found, for example, in the recent reform riots of 1831 (inspired by the 1830 July Revolution in France), especially those in Bristol that were likened to the Gordon Riots of 1780, and in the 1819 'Peterloo' massacre in Manchester, when cavalry charged a reform meeting of Lancashire weavers—an event described by Byron as 'a yeoman's holiday' for a lot of 'bloody Neros'. For Charlotte's use of such events see Alexander *EW*, 177–8.

dark revolutionary fry: sinister revolutionary clique; used contemptuously in Scottish dialect, 'fry' means a set or swarm of people.

365 *His Highness, TRACKY, Duke of Nevada*: one of Branwell's original 'Twelves', contemporary of Cracky, Stumps, and Monkey and, like them, now considered elder venerable statesmen of the Glass Town Federation. For 'Nevada' see note to p. 324.

Thomas Beresford Bobbadil, major general of the army of W[ellington]'s Land: for Beresford, friend and marshal under the real Wellington, see note to p. 13; for the origins of 'Bobbadil' see note to p. 34.

pekin: In his biography *Napoleon* (1827), read by the Brontës, Scott defines 'pekin' as 'a word of contempt, used by soldiers to those who did not belong to their profession'; the Brontës also encountered the word in *Blackwood's* and used it in other stories.

unmiked: attentive; 'to mike' is Yorkshire dialect for 'to idle'.

365 *So . . . lapse of ages destroy*: see note to p. 352: 'the work', on evangelical cant; other phrases too, like 'the lapse of ages', were commonly used by Romantic poets like Wordsworth, Byron, Shelley, and Southey.

366 *my father's murderers?*: Quashia's father, the warlike King Sai Too Too, was killed at the battle of Coomassie which decided the defeat of the Ashantee kingdom and the superiority of the Glasstowners.

iron yoke: severe restraint. A phrase commonly occurring in John and Charles Wesley's hymns; also frequently used by Edmund Burke in his famous political speeches of the 1770s–1790s, which Branwell may have known about. Among other vital causes, Burke fought for the emancipation of the House of Commons from the control of King and 'the King's friends', and supported Wilberforce in the abolition of slavery—issues echoed in Ellrington's speeches.

one grand step up the ladder: Branwell was aware of the predominant image of the ladder as a symbol for ambition in Shakespeare's history plays, as for example in *Richard II*, v. i. 55–6: 'Northumberland, thou ladder wherewithal | The mounting Bolingbroke ascends my throne'. The Earl of Northumberland and his son Henry Percy contributed in part to the names and character of Alexander Percy (Ellrington and later Duke of Northangerland).

Louis XIV: King of France (1643–1714), famous for his palatial residence at Versailles from where he ruled without a prime minister, thus becoming the archetypal absolute monarch.

Archbishop Fenelon: Fénelon (1651–1715), French archbishop, theologian, and man of letters; tutor to Louis IV's grandson for whom he wrote *Les Adventures de Télémaque* (1699), expressing his liberal political ideas and seen by the King as a satire on his court.

368 *[?them all]*: half a line of illegible text has been squeezed in above the line here.

give me your daughter in marriage: the first hint in the saga of Quashia's fixation on Mary Percy which culminates several years later in his 'savagely exulting' in her empty boudoir after his battle victory (see *Roe Head Journal* 1). See also 'Caroline Vernon' (ch. 1), where Quashia transfers his feelings to Mary's younger half-sister.

blackamoor: dark-skinned African.

smoke for it: suffer for it (obscure).

oval: possibly referring to the elliptical shape of his sphere of influence.

369 *[?ingaloreable]*: this difficult word to decipher ('ingalroeable' in MS) may be a Branwell coinage deriving from the Gaelicism 'in galore' meaning 'in abundance'.

371 *ci devant*: former.

got him by the nose: he is tamed, like a wild animal led by a ring in the nose, ready to be betrayed and delivered up to government; cf. Shakespeare's

Iago who comments that the betrayal of Othello will be easy: he 'will as tenderly be led by th' nose | As asses are' (I. iii. 393–4).

372 *gipsy hat*: woman's hat or bonnet with large side-flaps.

373 *Lady Julia Sydney, Lady Castlereagh, and Lady M. Sneachy*: Lady Julia is the thoughtless, flirtatious cousin of the Marquis of Douro, newly married to Edward Sydney but already disillusioned by his serious attitude to life; Lady Harriet Castlereagh, wife of Douro's friend Lord Castlereagh; and Princess Maria Sneaky, wife of Ellrington's eldest disowned son Edward Percy.

rattle: talk without consideration, chatter.

374 *dried bladder*: prepared animal bladders were much in use in the Brontës' day as receptacles for liquids like lard or paint, and also for floats and bagpipes.

several: distinct, separate.

Thornton: Thornton Wilkin Sneaky (who eventually becomes Lady Julia's second husband) has recently inherited Girnington's estate and taken on the guardianship of Lord Charles Wellesley.

375 *kicked the bucket*: died (slang).

mourning coach: black coach formerly used during the whole period of mourning.

376 *winter moorcock*: the plumage of the male red grouse (moorcock) is particularly vibrant in winter (the hunting season and hence the bird is 'shy') before the spring courting season; Castlereagh's sexual innuendo is intentional here.

Abercorn and Lofty: Lord Abercorn and Viscount Frederick Lofty, both fops like Castlereagh, who improve once they assume the responsibility of military command under Douro.

377 *when Thornton . . . groaning*: coolness is still maintained between Thornton and his proud siblings.

little monkey: despite Lord Charles's youth, his mischief-making is notorious; his publications are seen as scandalmongering (see 'The Liar Detected') and his brother Douro has expelled him from his house because of his 'spying' (thus Thornton has become his guardian, see note to p. 375).

stuck pig ninny!: a double insult, 'ninny' being a 'fool' or 'simpleton', and a 'stuck pig' meaning a pig that has had its throat cut, hence the slang 'to stare like a stuck pig'.

Emii: formerly Chief Genius Emii, Emily Brontë who by now has withdrawn from the Glass Town saga; a rare reference to her continuing knowledge of the saga despite her own preoccupation with Gondal and to her obvious disapproval of Charlotte's hero.

craig: neck or throat (Yorkshire dialect).

scraped a handsome acquaintance: curried favour with each other and insinuated themselves into each other's company.

380 *NB highly important ... pleased'*: Lord Charles's and therefore Charlotte's approval and ready adoption of Branwell's new heroine paves the way for her increasingly central position in the saga. Her marriage to Pelham never takes place; by February 1834 Charlotte is recording Mary's marriage to Douro, the new Duke of Zamorna and King of Angria (see Alexander *EW*, 112–13).

381 AN ANGRIAN BATTLE SONG. Soon after finishing 'The Politics of Verdopolis', Branwell launches the 'War of Encroachment', an invasion by Napoleon with his army from Frenchyland and Ashantee allies. The defence of the Glass Town Federation (or 'Verdopolitan Union' as it now is) is fought in the east around the city of Angria and provinces of Zamorna and Northangerland. Both Ellrington and Douro are appointed leaders of the Verdopolitan army but they form an alliance for mutual aggrandizement and effect a military coup which gives them temporary control of both the government and the army. They achieve a victory in the east which 'decided the fate of all Africa' and the focus of the saga itself. Ellrington and Douro win new titles from the land they conquer: Earl of Northangerland and Duke of Zamorna respectively; and, on 4 February 1834, they force the Verdopolitan government to bestow on Zamorna the new kingdom of Angria. The action of the saga now moves with Zamorna, his new bride Mary Percy, and Prime Minister Northangerland to Adrianopolis, his new capital on the River Calabar.

The uneasy coalition between Zamorna and Northangerland, however, does not last long. Northangerland's old role as leader of the Democratic Party reasserts itself and he launches into another series of speeches and alliances with his old cronies against the kingdom of Angria and its ministers. While Charlotte is away at school (see the *Roe Head Journal*), Branwell embarks on the Second Angrian War (late 1835–1837), which threatens the existence of Angria and plunges the Verdopolitan Union into civil war. The Verdopolitan Reform Party (with the Machiavellian Northangerland inciting it) expels Angria from the Union, declares its ministers outlaws, and sends in an army supported by French, Ashantee, and Arab troops (all of whom are now allies of this Verdopolitan faction). The Verdopolitan Constitutionalists (under Wellington, Sneaky, and his son Fidena) enter the war on Zamorna's side.

Captain John Flower (now Lord Richton) retires as Branwell's pseudonym, and the chronicler of these new events is the rising young author Captain Henry Hastings. Hastings responds immediately to Zamorna's proclamation urging all Angrians to rise in revolt and composes 'An Angrian Battle Song'; he becomes the unofficial poet laureate of Angria.

The manuscript is written in longhand on three pages, transcribed on 26 May 1837 into one of Branwell's poetry notebooks (BPM: BS 125), from an earlier fragmentary version dated 6 January 1836 (see Neufeldt *BBP*, 431–3).

382 *Hark the artillery's iron hail | Rattles through the ranks of war*: the phrase 'hail rattles' occurs frequently in James Macpherson's *Poems of Ossian*

(1819), which the Brontës owned; cf. also Samuel Rogers, 'The Campagna of Rome' in *Italy* (1822–8) for the phrase 'iron-hail of war'.

Sun of Angria: Angria's emblem is the rising sun, its banner is scarlet and its battle cry is 'Arise!'.

the wanderer of the west: Earl of Northangerland.

384 PERCY'S MUSING'S UPON THE BATTLE OF EDWARDSTON. While Angria and the Verdopolitan Union struggle with civil war, Northangerland manipulates events for his own gain, forming and breaking alliances with Zamorna and others at will. His aim is to create revolution in Verdopolis, an obsession since his early Glass Town days as 'Rogue', and on 26 June 1836 he is successful: the city rises and overthrows the Reform Ministry. Northangerland declares a Republic and establishes a Provisional Government on the French Model, a repeat of his early career. Meanwhile Zamorna, in a desperate attempt to reach Verdopolis and join Northangerland against the Reform Ministry, is defeated at the battle of Edwardston and escapes into the Warner Hills. In this poem, Northangerland—always ambiguous about his love-hate relationship with Zamorna—muses on Zamorna's fortunes, his own role in them and the significance of his influence over his son-in-law.

The manuscript, written in longhand, occupies three-and-a-half pages of the same poetry notebook that includes 'An Angrian Battle Song' and 'Mary's Prayer' (BPM: BS 125). Two early versions of this poem also exist, one dated 22 July [*sic*] 1836 (see Neufeldt *BBP*, 435–9). Numerous phrases in the poem, such as 'inward fires', 'In vain to heaven', 'That wandering star', 'sun of glory', and 'from good to ill', echo the hymns and sacred poems of John and Charles Wesley and the hymns of Isaac Watts.

Mighty Man: Zamorna.

386 *Gambias woods*: in Wellington's Land, where Zamorna and Northangerland spent their youth.

From Greenlands icy seas: cf. Heber's 'Missionary Hymn', 'From Greenland's icy mountains', copied by Charlotte on 13 February 1835 into a notebook belonging to her schoolfriend Ellen Nussey (BPM: 14).

Around Elymbos' brow: Mt. Elymbos (or Elimbos) in the highlands of Sneachiesland, where Zamorna lived for a time with the Gordons and married Lady Helen Victorine Gordon, who died in childbirth.

clouds of care began to mar . . . day: Zamorna was affected by fits after the death of Lady Helen Gordon, whom he deserted to go to the college on Philosophers' Island.

388 *Who called himself the good right hand | And Father of our King*: Northangerland, father-in-law of Zamorna, has again become prime minister of Angria against the wishes of Zamorna's other ministers and friends.

June 22^d 1836: an early version of the poem is dated 'July 22 1836' (see Neufeldt *BBP*, 435), which suggests that Branwell may have meant to write 'July' instead of 'June' here. This is supported by the fact that, in the Angrian saga, the battle of Edwardston took place on 26 June and Percy's musings obviously occurred after the event.

389 MARY'S PRAYER. Mary Percy becomes a pawn in the power struggle between her husband Zamorna and her father Northangerland. Northangerland's machinations have caused Zamorna to lose his kingdom of Angria. The only way Zamorna can wreak vengeance is to destroy the one thing Northangerland loves: his daughter Mary, who is also Zamorna's beloved wife. When she takes refuge at Alnwick in Wellingtonsland during the civil war, Zamorna begins a campaign of neglect and she pines away without word from him. Lord Richton records her death on 19 September 1836, but Charlotte's narrator Charles Townshend refutes this report and reunites her with Zamorna, thus preserving the central Angrian heroine. See also Charlotte's *Roe Head Journal*, which records her anxiety about Mary's fate and Angrian events left in the hands of the action-loving Branwell.

Thy Heart my Heaven shall be!: interesting parallel with the wish of Catherine in *Wuthering Heights* (ch. 9) that her heaven should be to remain on earth with Heathcliff.

I'm: 'thou art' cancelled here in MS and 'my' (intended to be deleted) written above, then 'I'm'.

EMILY BRONTË

Initials and names of Gondal speakers at the head of poems are treated as titles, followed by the first line of the poem; untitled poems are referred to by their first line.

Where relevant, changes made by Emily for *Poems* 'by Currer, Ellis and Acton Bell' (Aylott & Jones, May 1846) follow the notes for each poem and are keyed to line references.

The 'E.J.B.' Notebook, so-called because the MS is headed 'E.J.B. Transcribed February 1844', is referred to as 'in the Law Collection (private)'; however a facsimile is available in the Shakespeare Head Brontë: Wise and Symington (eds.), *The Poems of Emily Jane Brontë and Anne Brontë*.

393 1. 'HIGH WAVING HEATHER'. MS on single leaf in BPM. This poem celebrates the power and excitement of the wind, one of Emily's favourite themes. The mountains, wild forests, and heather suggest the 'Scottish' landscape of Gondal, although Emily's personal experience of the wind is also clearly manifest in this poem. The regular inexorable dactylic rhythm, not unlike a hymn metre, suggests the onslaught of natural forces and the excitement of the storm. Like Shelley, Emily often used the wind to symbolize freedom or change. In later poems the liberating force of the wind heralds or is likened to the poet's imagination freeing her from the constrictions of mortal life (see poem 30).

dungeon: prisons, dungeons, and confinement are constant themes in Emily's poetry: see Introduction. MS spelling is 'dongoen': Gezari suggests Emily has misspelt the archaic 'dongeon', but since Emily frequently uses the modern word 'dungeon' elsewhere in poems in this edition, it seems more likely that this is a simple spelling error.

life giving wind: cf. Shelley's 'Ode to the West Wind', and the New Testament association of the wind with the Holy Spirit.

jubilee: the biblical meaning of 'an exultant shout', signifying a time of release or emancipation proclaimed by a blast of trumpets, echoes the 'one mighty voice' of the preceding line.

2. A.G.A. 'THERE SHINES THE MOON'. This is the first poem that Emily copied into the 'Gondal Poems' Notebook in the BL: see illustration, p. 392. The initials at the head of the poem denote the speaker, Augusta Geraldine Almeda, Queen of Gondal. In this poem written while she is in prison, Augusta imagines herself returning to the grave of Alexander, Lord of Elbë, by Lake Elnor where she recalls and mourns his death.

at noon of night: cf. Byron, *Childe Harold's Pilgrimage*, canto 3, stanza 26.

lonely moor: cf. Wordsworth's 'Leech-gatherer on the lonely moor', final line of 'Resolution and Independence'.

394 *Lake Elnor's*: Lake Elnor ('Elmor' in some MSS) is in Gaaldine where Lord Elbë is buried, far from his Gondal home.

Elbë's grave: Alexander, Lord of Elbë, died in the arms of A.G.A.

brow of pride?: cf. Scott, *Lord of the Isles*, canto 2, stanza 9. Emily's enthusiasm for the work of Scott and for the scenery of Scotland is evident in the earliest Brontë games where she chose Scott for her 'chief man', and Arran, off the coast of Scotland, as her island for 'Tales of the Islanders'; see also Charlotte's 'Origin of the Islanders'.

sunny, southern skies: in Gaaldine, the site of Lord Elbë's dying vision of home, viz. Elbë Hall in northern Gondal.

395 *Augusta*: the first time Emily's Gondal heroine A.G.A. is mentioned by name in the manuscripts.

bloom: 'joy' cancelled and 'bloom' inserted in MS.

tomb: the following two cancelled lines are undecipherable.

3. A.G.A. TO A.E. 'LORD OF ELBË, ON ELBË HILL'. MS in 'Gondal Poems' Notebook in BL; signed 'E' just before the date at head of poem, a practice Emily continued on twenty-seven of the poems in this Notebook. Two early versions of this poem exist: one in cancelled MS in the BPM and a later one in the Ashley MS in the BL, which has only the last five lines. Both these early versions suggest that Alexander is not dead but 'on the desolate sea | Thinking of Gondal, and grieving for' Augusta. In the Ashley MS version 'on the desolate sea' is changed to 'on a desolate sea', indicating that this is the second version that was copied into the 'Gondal Poems' Notebook.

A.G.A. to A.E: Augusta Geraldine Almeda addresses her dead lover/husband Alexander, Lord of Elbë; see poem 2.

396 4. 'ALONE I SAT THE SUMMER DAY'. MS in BPM (Bonnell 127); initial
'O' at top right indicates Emily's code for inclusion in the 'Gondal Poems'
Notebook. Whether or not this poem is spoken by a Gondal narrator, it
expresses the same memories of childhood visions and their association
with poetic inspiration as those found in Charlotte's poem 'We wove a
web in childhood' (see p. 151). Since wind is the harbinger of poetic inspiration (cf. poem 1), the 'breezeless glade' here signifies the failure of the
speaker's imagination. The signs of 'writer's block', despite the evident
thoughts and feelings of her vision, resemble Coleridge's 'Dejection: An
Ode': cf. stanza 2 and Coleridge's 'I see them all so excellently fair, | I see,
not feel, how beautiful they are!' (ll. 37–8). Thus the poem is seen as the
first datable poem referring to Emily's own experiences as a poet (Roper
EBP, 226).

gushing: this word and 'rushing' (two lines above) were originally 'rushing'
and 'gushing' respectively in the MS but subsequently reversed by Emily.

In that devine untroubled hour: like the speaker, Emily was habitually
inspired to write in the calm of the evening when she was alone.

397 5. 'THE NIGHT IS DARKENING ROUND ME'. MS in BPM (Bonnell 127).
The imprisoning stasis that prevents the protagonist from fleeing the
impending violence of the storm in the first stanza metamorphoses by the
end of the poem into a strength of will that enables her to stand firm in
the face of danger. Although critics warn that reading autobiography into
Emily's poetry can be misleading, it is hard not to link this poem (probably spoken by a Gondal character) with the author herself. Charlotte
describes Emily's extraordinary will during her final sickness: 'Stronger
than a man, simpler than a child, her nature stood alone. The awful point
was, that, while full of ruth for others, on herself she had no pity; the
spirit was inexorable to the flesh; from the trembling hand, the unnerved
limbs, the faded eyes, the same service was exacted as they had rendered
in health' ('Biographical Notice of Ellis and Acton Bell', in Charlotte
Brontë's 1850 edition of *Wuthering Heights* and *Agnes Grey*).

a tyrant spell: Barker suggests that this may be the speaker's 'maternal
emotions', related to an incident when one of the Gondal heroines
'exposes her child to die on the mountains in the depths of winter'
(*Selected Poems*, 121).

6. 'I'LL COME WHEN THOU ART SADDEST'. Undated and unsigned,
except for an initial 'O' at the top right, Emily's code for inclusion in the
'Gondal Poems' Notebook. The poem is written immediately below poem
5 (dated November 1837) on the same MS leaf in the BPM (Bonnell 127).
The two poems appear to be companions, with the visionary speaker in
this poem promising release to the speaker of poem 5. On this basis,
Gezari considers the two poems, and a third unfinished fragment of
seven lines, as 'a single poetic utterance' despite differences in metre and
rhyme (Gezari *EBP*, 56–7, 246; and *Last Things*, 91). The theme of visit-
ation by some eagerly anticipated mysterious creative power has overtones
of Wordsworth's 'Tintern Abbey' and Shelley's 'Hymn to Intellectual

Beauty'. Although intensely personal, the Imaginative experience in this poem involves an external power inhabiting and controlling a passive recipient.

398 7. A.G.A. TO A.S. 'O WANDER NOT SO FAR AWAY!' MS in 'Gondal Poems' Notebook in BL; signed 'E' just before the date at head of poem. An early version survives in the Ashley MS in the BL. Gondal love poems characteristically involve death: here A.G.A. tries to persuade her lover Lord Alfred Sidonia of Aspin Castle not to leave her, though his appearance suggests he is dying.

A.G.A. to A.S.: Augusta Geraldine Almeda to Alfred Sidonia. After a passionate affair, Augusta left him; presumably pining for her, he died (Roper *EBP*, 230).

stockdove: European wild pigeon (*OED*).

Thy soul was pure when it entered here: rejection of the doctrine of original sin; similar idea to Wordsworth in 'Immortality Ode': it is not the child who is tainted but the world that corrupts the innocent. Cf. poem 20 where Geraldine would prefer death for her child rather than let it be corrupted by life.

An earlier draft version with all but the first stanza cancelled survives in the Ashley MS in the BL. It has the following variants:

A.G.A. to A.S.] Lines by A.G.A. to A.S.

Young flowers look fresh] Sweet flowers are fresh

The woods] Our woods

small] young. In the Gondal Notebook, 'small' is written above 'thick'.

stockdove] throstle

must] shall

399 8. ARTHUR EX[INA] TO MARCIUS 'IN DUNGEONS DARK I CANNOT SING'. MS in New York Public Library, Berg Collection; undated but the poem immediately below on the same MS leaf is dated 'September 23 1838' and two other poems on the same leaf are also dated 1838. The poem was probably written soon after Emily went to Law Hill, near Halifax, as a teacher at the end of September 1838. She remained there until March 1839 when ill health due to overwork forced her to return home. The large number of poems she wrote during her first three months at Law Hill indicates that despite her exhaustion and loneliness she was able to take refuge in Gondal. The following three poems suggest that the personal misery and exile of her fictitious characters provided an analogue for her own condition.

Arthur Ex[ina] To Marcius: the title 'Arthur Ex To ——' appears on the top left of the poem and the name 'Marcius' is written in pencil below in Emily's hand. Arthur Exina, son or brother of King Gerald of Exina, was imprisoned when Julius Brenzaida overthrew Gerald and claimed the throne of Gondal (Roper *EBP*, 12). Marcius is not mentioned elsewhere in extant poems of the Brontës.

399 9. SONG BY J. BRENZAIDA TO G.S. 'I KNEW NOT 'T WAS SO DIRE A
CRIME'. MS follows another song by Julius Brenzaida to 'Geraldine', in
'Gondal Poems' Notebook in BL; also written at Law Hill (see note to
poem 8.). Following the title Charlotte has written in pencil the words
'Loves Farewell', though she titled the poem 'Last Words' in her 1850
edition. Charlotte also changed a number of words in pencil on the
MS for her edition, removing any clues to the source of the poem (e.g.,
'moorside' changed to 'hill side'). The poem has been seen as a 'sketch'
for the central relationships in *Wuthering Heights* and a possible parallel
with Heathcliff's reproach to Catherine for deserting him (Visick, *Genesis
of Wuthering Heights*, 31–2, 84).

J. Brenzaida to G.S.: Julius Brenzaida addresses Geraldine S., his lover
and probably his wife. Here we find him repudiating Geraldine (also
identified as A.G.A.) because she has become 'false' and 'cold' (stanza 4).
The name Geraldine suggests Emily was influenced by the heroines in
Coleridge's 'Christabel' and Scott's 'Lay of the Last Minstrel'.

And there are bosoms bound to mine: Brenzaida was previously involved
with Rosina Alcona, an ambitious woman who encourages him to become
ruler of Angora and eventually to seize the Gondal throne from Gerald
Exina. If these lines suggest he intends to return to her (Roper *EBP*, 234)
then Rosina and Geraldine cannot be the same person (see Ratchford,
Gondal's Queen, 26–7).

400 10. F. DE SAMARA TO A.G.A. 'LIGHT UP THY HALLS! 'TIS CLOSING DAY'.
MS in 'Gondal Poems' Notebook in BL; signed 'E' just before the date
at head of poem, and an initial 'O' beneath title. Written at Law Hill
(see note to p. 399). Emotions expressed here in Fernando's love-hate
relationship with Augusta prefigure those in *Wuthering Heights*, especially
in the destructive love of Catherine and Heathcliff.

F. De Samara to A.G.A.: Fernando De Samara to Augusta Geraldine
Almeda; Fernando was once Augusta's lover but she imprisoned him and
then forced him into exile. In this poem his loneliness and despair drive
him to suicide.

desert: uninhabited, desolate.

And now, it shall be done: i.e. the act of taking his own life.

streaming wet: wet with blood.

401 *But go to that far land . . . yet to come*: De Samara exhorts the imagined
Gondal wind to take news of his death back to Augusta.

breathed: written over 'lived' in MS.

11. 'A LITTLE WHILE, A LITTLE WHILE'. MS in E.J.B. Notebook,
Law Collection (private). This poem is seen as 'the most clearly autobiographical' of the poems Emily wrote at Law Hill (Barker, *The Brontës*, 295).
Certainly it communicates a sense of fatigue and homesickness related to
an imaginary world, as in the case of Charlotte's *Roe Head Journal*. It is
significant that the speaker should prefer to spend her precious moments
of reverie conjuring up visions of Gondal rather than Haworth. Whether

this is a Gondal character or not, the speaker explores the nature and effect of her visionary experience.

   Charlotte made a number of changes in pencil on the MS in preparation for publication in 1850 when she called this poem 'Stanzas' and left out stanza 6 that leads from memories of home to thoughts of 'Another clime'. Her removal of possible Gondal references is clear in her handling of this poem where she removes 'deer' and 'dungeon bars'.

noisy crowd: in a biographical reading, these would be Emily's students at Law Hill.

holyday: holiday, the spelling possibly signifying both a time of leisure and the sanctity of a peaceful time alone.

402 *There is a spot mid barren hills*: the next three stanzas could relate either to Haworth parsonage and its environs, or to the north of Gondal.

The garden-walk with weeds o'er-grown: although Charlotte removes this undignified reference to home in her publication of the poem, Anne also recalls the unkempt garden with affection: 'Where knotted grass neglected lies, | And weeds usurp the ground' ('Home', Chitham *ABP*, 100).

A little . . . wandering deer: Emily's description of Gondal with its lush landscape, encircling Highland mountains, moorland sheep and deer, recalls not only her love of Scotland but her kingdom of Parry's Land in the Glass Town saga, suggesting a close relation between the two visionary lands. Apart from the deer, the vision also suggests her Haworth home.

403 *truth has banished fancy's power*: yet fancy has won out in the end: it has produced this poem. Irony lies in the fact that in human history it is truth, not poetry, that proves to be ephemeral. Compare Charlotte's similarly painful interruption of 'fancy's power' in the *Roe Head Journal*, p. 163.

my dungeon bars: here Emily likens her own teaching position to that of her imprisoned Gondal characters.

And given me back to weary care: in the MS Charlotte altered Emily's final line to 'And brought back labour, task & tear' (having first changed 'weary care' to 'pain & fear'); then in the 1850 version she altered it to 'And brought back labour, bondage, care'.

12. BY R. GLENEDEN 'FROM OUR EVENING FIRESIDE NOW'. MS in 'Gondal Poems' Notebook in BL; signed 'E' just before the date at head of poem. An early cancelled version of lines 1–3 and 34–44 survives in the Ashley MS in the BL. The poem is another example of the blending of personal and Gondal material.

By R. Gleneden: since the poem is presented as written by R. Gleneden it seems logical to see Gleneden as the protagonist mourning the death of someone fallen in battle. It is not clear who has died and to whom Gleneden is speaking—Arthur or possibly Desmond. If Arthur has died, as seems likely, then the name Desmond could refer to the family seat. R. Gleneden's place in the Gondal saga is problematic. Ratchford identifies 'R. Gleneden' as E. R. Gleneden, a woman whose brother Arthur

Gleneden was killed or imprisoned, although the hunting in this poem
suggests R. Gleneden is a male (see Gezari *EBP*, 256).

403 *One is absent*: Anne had left Haworth just over a week before to take up
a post as governess with the Ingham family at Blake Hall, near Mirfield.
Her absence may have generated the mournful mood of the poem.

404 *Dreadful was the price to pay!*: the theme of self-sacrifice for others echoes
the motive underlying Anne's departure, to relieve the economic burden
at home.

the very dogs repined . . . o'er the hill: Emily had an affinity for dogs and
was a keen observer of their behaviour, as shown by this image of the dogs
expectantly awaiting their dead master to accompany them. After her own
death, Emily's faithful dog Keeper followed her coffin to the grave and
moaned for nights outside her bedroom door (Barker, *The Brontës*, 578).
A watercolour of Keeper (reproduced in Alexander and Sellars, plate III)
was found amongst Emily's papers; and Charlotte recorded her sister's
devotion to the dog in *Shirley*, where Keeper is the model for Shirley's
dog Tartar.

13. 'A.G.A.: TO THE BLUEBELL—'. MS in 'Gondal Poems' Notebook in
BL; signed 'E' just before the date at head of poem. A cancelled version
survives in the Ashley MS in the BL. As in this poem, the bluebell is
associated with grief: in Greek mythology the classical hyacinth sprang
from the blood of the dying prince Hyacinthus. The bluebell Emily is
referring to, however, is probably the bluebell of Scotland and northern
England (a species of Campanula that grows in summer and autumn
and is found on the Yorkshire moors), rather than the wild hyacinth,
commonly known as bluebell in England and elsewhere and found mainly
in woodland in spring. See also note to p. 447.

bluebell: MS spelling varies between 'bluebell' and 'blue bell'; *OED* gives
'blue bell' and 'blue-bell', but this edition preserves Emily's word division
(see Note on the Text).

405 *my darling*: A.G.A. is probably referring to Alfred Sidonia (Roper *EBP*,
256), one of her lovers who pined to death when she left him (see poem 7).

14. 'I AM THE ONLY BEING WHOSE DOOM'. MS in Princeton University
Library; the date is centred above the poem and written in cursive script,
an unusual practice for Emily who writes all dates in minuscule script
on the right above her poems. The recurrent themes of isolation and
exile in Emily's poetry are particularly prevalent here. This poem and
others written during 1839, such as poem 15, reveal her growing interest
in doomed Byronic characters that was to culminate in Heathcliff. The
characteristically terse style aptly conveys the speaker's bitter cynicism,
prevents him from lapsing into self-pity, and creates a powerful sense of
intimacy. The poem is seen as 'one of her grimmest poems' in which she
assimilates victims to victimizers (Gezari, *Last Things*, 65–6).

May 19 1839: The date is significant since it repudiates the idea that this
piece is solely autobiographical as once thought: Emily would have been
20 at the time of its composition, not 18 like the 'I' in the poem.

406 *to think mankind | All servile insincere*: this Byronic speaker reflects Emily's own misanthropy. A pupil at Law Hill school, for example, recalled Emily's telling them that the house-dog 'was dearer to her than they were' (Mrs Ellis H. (Esther Alice) Chadwick, *In the Footsteps of the Brontës* (1914), 123–4). In the MS Emily originally wrote 'All hollow lying insincere', then replaced the two adjectives with 'servile'; she also considered 'Deceitful' (written in margin but cancelled).

15. 'AND NOW THE HOUSEDOG STRETCHED ONCE MORE'. MS in Princeton University Library; signed above poem 'E J Brontë' in cursive script. Written only two months after poem 14, this poem features the same Gothic character that prefigures Heathcliff.

unknown guest: an obvious Byronic character, possibly the outlaw Douglas; cf. Byron's *The Giaour*: 'Dark and unearthly is the scowl | That glares beneath his dusky cowl' (ll. 832–3). The following six lines accord with Scott's description of the arrival of Bertram at Oswald's castle in *Rokeby* (1. 6), owned by the Brontës, since there is the same disregard for the courtesies of his host (Roper *EBP*, 242).

407 *withering*: the shepherd's guest has the Byronic hero's disdain for humanity and the latent power to 'wither at a glance'; see note below: 'basilisk charm'.

And wrapt him in his mantle grey: cf. Shelley: 'Wrap thy form in a mantle grey' ('To Night', l. 8).

basilisk charm: both an oxymoron and a play on the word charm in the sense of 'spell': the Basilisk was the fabulous king of serpents, possessed of a fatal charm; a glance from his eyes could kill (Brewer). Emily employs a mythical analogy to place her stranger outside the human pale, just as Byron does by associating his Giaour with the Gorgon (ll. 890–8). Both Basilisk and Gorgon were fatal to look upon. Keats's snake-woman in *Lamia* may have been another influence; her evil power eventually destroys her gullible lover. In *Wuthering Heights* Heathcliff is described as having the eyes of a basilisk and the appearance of 'a ghoul or a vampire' (*Wuthering Heights*, ch. 34). Charlotte's hero Zamorna is also likened to a basilisk because of the way he charms women (Alexander *EEW* 2(2). 17.

16. 'WELL, SOME MAY HATE AND SOME MAY SCORN' (*Poems* 1846 title: 'Stanzas to ——'). MS in E.J.B. Notebook, Law Collection (private). We are immediately thrust into a Gondal monologue that traces a change in attitude towards an unfaithful or worthless lover who has died. Despite the initial temptation to moralize and scorn, the speaker affirms Emily's own belief that all creatures are destined to act according to their inherent natures—a belief that governs the behaviour of Gondal characters. Who these stanzas are addressed to is not known; both Branwell and Shelley have been suggested although the poem is ostensibly part of the Gondal saga. It was written nine years before Branwell's death, but his downward decline commenced around this time (he had begun taking opium in May 1839). The Gondal narrative has been seen as providing a means for

Emily to distance herself and anticipate not only Branwell's ignominious
death but also her feelings of contempt for his behaviour (Miles, 71–2).
Shelley has also been seen as an addressee, since Emily would have read
of him and seen his portrait in Moore's *Life of Byron* and may have known
his poetry by this time (Chitham, 'Emily Brontë and Shelley', 59; and
Life of Emily Brontë, 72). Apart from the addition of a title, Emily made
no changes for publication in 1846.

407   *One word*: it is assumed that if the wretch refers to Branwell, then the 'one
word' would have been opium (Roper *EBP*, 247); if to Shelley, 'atheist'
(Chitham, 'Emily Brontë and Shelley', 69–70).

Vain: foolish or idle (*OED*).

408   *Do I despise . . . foul?*: the direct address, usually in the form of a question
or exclamation, is typical of Emily's dramatic technique by which she
involves the reader. Here the speaker persists in involving the listener in
a series of questions.

leveret: young hare. Cf. *Wuthering Heights* where Heathcliff tells Edgar:
'Your type is not a lamb, it's a sucking leveret' (ch. 11). See *Oxford
Companion*, 13, for the Brontës' use of animals in their writing.

heart: 'eye' cancelled in MS and 'heart' written above.

Earth, lie lightly on that breast: echoes Pope's 'Elegy to the Memory of an
Unfortunate Lady', l. 64: 'And the green turf lie lightly on thy breast'.

17. 'IF GREIF FOR GREIF CAN TOUCH THEE'. MS in E.J.B. Notebook,
Law Collection (private). A passionate Gondal love poem of betrayal
and haunting, similar to that of Catherine and Heathcliff in *Wuthering
Heights*. The 'beloved' has also been interpreted as Emily's 'God of
Visions' (Gérin, *Emily Brontë*, 111); see note below: 'Beloved'. This has
been called 'a perfect illustration of her Gondal manner . . . inescap-
ably, a cry from the soul—but whose?', demonstrating the paradoxical
way Emily's dramatic poetry projects the intensity and energy of her own
mind rather than that of her characters (Miles, 'A Baby God', 76). The
poem was given the title 'The Appeal' in 1923.

mine angel . . . Mine idol: the juxtaposition of 'mine angel . . . mine idol'
suggests the speaker is invoking something illicit, worshipped against
the wishes of heaven: 'heaven repells my prayer'. The term idol suggests
someone or something pagan that supplants the Christian God; cf. *Jane
Eyre*, ch. 24: 'I could not, in those days, see God for His creature: of
whom I had made an idol.'

Beloved: it is suggested that this poem 'describes its speaker's longing
for imaginative release' (Gezari *EBP*, 264). Homans reads the poem as
an appeal to the imagination (*Woman Writers and Poetic Identity*). Thus
the 'beloved' the speaker hopes to win again is the ability to write poetry.
Poem 4 contains a similar but more direct appeal for 'the glorious gift'
to be given.

409   18. 'RICHES I HOLD IN LIGHT ESTEEM' (*Poems* 1846 title: 'The Old Stoic').
MS in E.J.B. Notebook, Law Collection (private). Although spoken

by a Gondal character nearing death, the poem expresses Emily's attraction to stoicism. Emily may have read Elizabeth Carter's *The Discourses of Epictetus*, a collection of the principles of the Stoic philosopher Epictetus compiled by his disciple Arrian (see Margaret Maison, 'Emily Brontë and Epictetus', *Notes and Queries*, NS 25 (June 1978), 230–1). The Stoic aim of living according to nature reflects Emily's attitude, especially in relation to her death when in the final stages of tuberculosis she chose to die without medical intervention. Compare also Byron's 'The Prisoner of Chillon' as a possible source; and his 'Sonnet on Chillon' that uses Epictetus's idea of the chainless soul (see below and poem 30).

chainless soul: The idea of the bound body and the unbound soul is a recurrent theme in Emily's poetry. Cf. Epictetus: 'Fortune is an evil chain to the body, and vice to the soul. For he whose body is unbound, and whose soul is chained, is a slave. On the contrary, he whose body is chained, and his soul unbound, is free' (*Fragments* vii; cited in Roper *EBP*, 252).

Changes for Poems *1846 edition:*

11. Through Life] In life

19. 'SHALL EARTH NO MORE INSPIRE THEE'. MS in E.J.B. Notebook, Law Collection (private). The cajoling voice of Nature with its caressing winds is wooing the listener, promising to free her (through imaginative association) from the miseries of mortal life. Charlotte provided the following comment on this poem when she published it in 1850: 'The following little piece has no title; but in it the Genius of a solitary region seems to address its wandering and wayward votary, and to recall within his influence the proud mind which rebelled at times against what it most loved.' The suggested Gondal context reveals feelings that again agree with those of Emily herself; her pantheism is radically manifest here. Emily has marked '2' above this poem and '1' above another poem in the MS, suggesting that the poems might be paired: in '1' ('The Night Wind', Gezari *EBP*, 126), the wind is personified as a liberating force of nature wooing the listener.

410 *idolatry*: worship, carrying connotations of anti-Christian paganism; see poem 17 for a similar idea.

Yet none would ask a Heaven | More like the Earth than thine: these lines epitomize the tension at the heart of Emily's poetry: her longing to escape the misery of her earthly life, but loving earth and its beauty so much she is loathe to forsake it. Cf. Catherine Earnshaw's dream of being in heaven and breaking her heart with weeping to come back to earth (*Wuthering Heights*, ch. 9).

20. GERALDINE ''TWAS NIGHT, HER COMRADES GATHERED ALL'. MS in 'Gondal Poems' Notebook in BL; signed 'E' just before the date at head of poem. The last stanza seems to have been added later in the MS.

Geraldine: probably Augusta Geraldine Almeda (A.G.A.). In this poem we learn that she has a child by Julius Brenzaida, but she has been discarded by him because she scorned him and now lives apart. See poem 9, addressed to Geraldine by Brenzaida.

410 *Palmtrees and cedars towering high*: poem set in the subtropical South Pacific island of Gaaldine.

411 *witching*: bewitching, enchanting.

Zedora's: a province in Gaaldine.

412 *my angel's soul | Must go to heaven again!*: Geradine ends her song on an unsettling note. What happens to the baby she is already referring to in the past tense? In the final stanza the observing narrator who opened the poem weeps 'as one who mourns the dead'.

21. ROSINA 'WEEKS OF WILD DELIRIUM PAST'. MS in 'Gondal Poems' Notebook in BL. The title refers to the central character in the narrative, Rosina Alcona, whose direct speech and reactions are recorded by an unidentified observer. Rosina has been ill for some time; as she gains consciousness we experience her immediate reactions as she assesses her situation and responds to the news of the death of her husband Julius Brenzaida, whom she mourns fifteen years later in poem 28.

Angora's hills . . . crimson flag is planted there: Julius Brenzaida's flag flies in his homeland, the kingdom of Angora in northern Gondal.

Elderno's waves: Lake Elderno, on which is situated Regina, the capital of Gondal.

413 *Almedore*: Julius Brenzaida; named here for the kingdom he conquered in Gaaldine.

414 *Exina's*: Gerald Exina, ruler of Exina province in southern Gondal, is Julius's opponent.

shade: a ghost or memory.

22. 'YES HOLY BE THY RESTING PLACE'. Undated MS in BPM; poems on verso are dated 26 July 1843. Gondal scholars agree that in this poem A.G.A. farewells one of her husbands but conjecture as to which one, either Lord Alfred Sidonia (poem 7) or Alexander of Elbë (poems 2 and 3). The final lines echo the beginning of another poem dated 2 March 1844 and headed 'A.G.A. to A.S.', suggesting Alfred Sidona is the wronged husband, sent by A.G.A. into exile on the orders of Julius Brenzaida, who is now her lover.

holy be thy resting place: A.G.A.'s words are ironic since Sidona commits suicide; his spirit is unable to rest and he returns to haunt Aspin Castle, his ancestral home.

415 23. M G – FOR THE U.S. ''TWAS YESTERDAY AT EARLY DAWN'. MS in 'Gondal Poems' Notebook in BL. The speaker contrasts the warm southern island of Gaaldine with the cold northern island of Gondal, reassuring herself that she and her comrades of the Unique Society are happy to return to the freezing north.

M G – For the U.S.: probably stands for 'Mary Gleneden – For the Unique Society'.

416 *comrades . . . scattered now so far away*: some of the Unique Society were shipwrecked on a desert island while returning from Gaaldine: see Anne's Diary Paper, 31 July 1845 (Appendix A).

417 24. E.W. TO A.G.A. 'HOW FEW, OF ALL THE HEARTS THAT LOVED'. MS in 'Gondal Poems' Notebook in BL; the words 'On a life perverted' inserted below the Gondal heading by Charlotte. The speaker is reflecting on the life of the Gondal heroine Augusta Geraldine Almeda, who has been assassinated. In her 1850 publication of the poems, Charlotte added the title 'The Wanderer from the Fold' possibly with Branwell Brontë in mind; he died in 1848. C. Day Lewis commented on the 'Cowperish thought and tone' of the poem ('The Poetry of Emily Brontë', *BST* 13/67 (1957), 86).

E.W. to A.G.A.: Lord Eldred W to Augusta Geraldine Almeda; Lord Eldred, Augusta's faithful retainer, is identified on the grounds of a similar speech, using sailing metaphors, that he gives in a long poem on her death (see Gezari *EBP*, 148–68).

418 25. 'THE LINNET IN THE ROCKY DELLS' (*Poems* 1846 title: 'Song'). MS in 'Gondal Poems' Notebook in BL; Emily made no changes for her 1846 publication. In this poignant lament, Lord Eldred W is once again faithfully remembering his queen, A.G.A., who was murdered and has now been buried on the moor for a considerable time. The natural imagery and quiet slumber of the dead, now immune to the noise and frenzy of human life, is echoed in Lockwood's description of the graves at the end of *Wuthering Heights*.

linnet in the rocky dells: the linnet is a common grey/brown moorland finch, whose breast and crown turn crimson in summer; dells are fairly small deep natural valleys, with sides usually clothed with rocks, small trees, or foliage.

moorlark: probably the skylark that appears elsewhere in Emily's poems and is common on the Yorkshire moors. It sings hovering high in the air and is almost invisible.

The wilddeer browse above her breast: cf. *Fingal*, 3, final sentences that include 'The wild roes feed upon the green tomb', from James Macpherson, *Poems of Ossian* (Edinburgh, 1792), a book owned and much used by the Brontës in childhood (*Oxford Companion*, 53).

ween: think or surmise (archaic).

shade: deliberately ambiguous word here, referring to obscurity and retirement but also possibly death or a spectre.

419 *There is no need of other sound*: Augusta is sealed off from the clamour of human life; she has become one with nature and only hears its sounds. Cf. Wordsworth's 'A Slumber Did My Spirit Seal'.

EW: these initials identify the speaker as Lord Eldred W, and link the poem with the preceding poem, spoken by the same character.

26. TO IMAGINATION (*Poems* 1846 title: 'To Imagination'). MS in E.J.B. Notebook, Law Collection (private); title added later in MS, probably

just before Emily published it in 1846. Although the poem may have originated in a Gondal context, it provides a clear statement of the central importance in Emily's life of imagination—what she referred to a month later as her 'God of Visions' ('Plead for me', in Gezari *EBP*, 22). The speaker praises imagination, while still acknowledging its limitations. Here Emily's characteristic dialogue format is between Reason and Imagination rather than two Gondal characters.

419 *O my true friend*: Emily apostrophizes Imagination. In the MS, this poem immediately follows 'How clear she shines', a poem that apostrophizes Fancy as 'my Fairy love'; Gezari suggests that Emily may have been thinking of Coleridge's distinction between Imagination and Fancy (Gezari *EBP*, 234).

420 *worlds as bright as thine*: cf. 'The Gondal's still flourish as bright as ever' (Diary Paper, 30 July 1845 (Appendix A)). The 'hovering visions' may refer to other worlds associated with Gondal although, as Roper notes (*EBP*, 262), Gondal is hardly free from grief and darkness.

I trust not to thy phantom bliss: the speaker welcomes the imagination but is resigned to the fact that it can only provide brief solace from reality.

Changes for Poems *1846 edition*:

5. O] Oh,

14. greif] guilt

16. unsullied] untroubled

26. visions] vision

36. brighter] sweeter

27. 'FROM A DUNGEON WALL IN THE SOUTHERN COLLEGE — JB'. MS in 'Gondal Poems' Notebook in BL. A dramatic monologue by Julius Brenzaida, who has been imprisoned because of his involvement with the ambitious Rosina Alcona, possibly to prevent him sailing to Gaaldine with his companions (stanza 10) because she suspects him of disloyalty. Julius begins by quoting the moralizing jailer and then addresses the absent Rosina when the jailer leaves.

The poem illustrates Emily's method of randomly composing poems relating to various stages of the Gondal saga, which had its own strict timeline of events. Here Emily is returning to events early in the saga when Julius was a young man. Later he and Rosina became reconciled and marry; see following poem written only a year later yet recording Rosina's lament for Julius, cut down in later life by an assassin in his palace.

Southern College: the concept of a school for young noblemen, complete with stone dungeons, appears very early in the Brontë juvenilia: see entries 'Tales of the Islanders' and 'Palace School' in *Oxford Companion*. Imprisonment for young nobles was not uncommon in Gondal: several of Emily's poems purport to have been written on the walls of the Northern College and one of Anne's is titled 'Lines inscribed on the wall of a dungeon in the southern P[alace] of I[nstruction]' (see her poem 13).

JB. Sept. 1825: Julius Brenzaida and the Gondal date.

me: refers to the jailer.

421 *Those wondrous southern isles*: Gaaldine.

422 *falcon eyes*: cf. Scott, *Lady of the Lake*: 'Bent o'er the fall'n, with falcon eye' (canto 4, stanza 26).

28. R ALCONA TO J BRENZAIDA 'COLD IN THE EARTH AND THE DEEP SNOW PILED ABOVE THEE!' (*Poems* 1846 title: 'Remembrance'). MS in 'Gondal Poems' Notebook in BL. Emily's most anthologized poem and the culmination of her poems on loss and mourning. Hailed by F. R. Leavis as 'the finest poem in the nineteenth-century part of *The Oxford Book of English Verse*' (*Revaluation: Tradition and Development in English Poetry* (London, 1936) 13). The speaker expresses a doubleness of feeling: the strong appeal of the divine world beyond the grave is at the same time sternly denied. 'The growth of feeling seems to rely on the powerful syntax which checks, permits, drives, and shapes sharp feeling' (Barbara Hardy, in Anne Smith (ed.), *Art of Emily Brontë*, 117–18): for a summary on the poem's effective musical metre and rhyme see Gezari *EBP*, 228–9). The most thorough discussion of the poem can be found in Gezari's *Last Things* (41–58), in which she places the concept of Remembrance in its nineteenth-century context and points out that, like Freud, Emily (and the speaker in the poem) is 'alert to how memory threatens that survival' of remembrance.

R Alcona to J Brenzaida: Rosina Alcona mourns the death and lonely moorland grave of her great love and husband Julius Brenzaida after fifteen years of separation.

Cold in the earth: the Irish poet Thomas Moore, friend of Byron and Shelley, used this phrase twice in *Irish Melodies*, several of which were copied by Anne into her music manuscript book. Charlotte and Emily also knew his poetry well and the family probably owned Moore's *Life of Byron* (see notes to p. 245: 'Has sorrow', and 256: 'Lord Edward Fitzgerald'). Anne also echoes this phrase in 'Night', written about the same time as Emily's poem (Chitham *ABP*, 110).

Resting . . . heath and fern-leaves cover | Thy noble heart . . . ever more?: Rosina likens her thoughts to exhausted birds resting their wings on the heath above Brenzaida's grave; cf. A.G.A.'s resting place beneath the moor in poem 25 where the 'wilddeer browse above her breast; | The wildbirds raise their brood'. In his elegy to A.G.A., Lord Eldred's view of death as a reconciliation with nature contrasts with the passionate sense of loss reflected in Rosina's bitter outcry in this poem.

fifteen wild Decembers: 'this has struck many readers as prefiguring the eighteen years of Heathcliff's mourning for Catherine' (Visick, *Genesis of Wuthering Heights*, 15).

Changes for Poems *1846 edition:*

4. allwearing] all-severing

6. Angora's] that northern

8. That] Thy

15. Sterner desires and darker Hopes] Other desires and other hopes

17. other sun] later light

18. other star] second morn

423   29. A.E. AND R.C. 'HEAVY HANGS THE RAINDROP' (includes 'Child of Delight'). MS in 'Gondal Poems' Notebook in BL. Includes two discrete poems that function as 'companion poems, composed and imagined in relation to each other' (Gezari, *Last Things*, 91). Charlotte first printed the poems as a pair in 1850, under the title 'The Two Children', with an added stanza and revisions. The contrasted children prefigure Heathcliff and Catherine, and Hareton and Cathy in *Wuthering Heights*, although the gender of the fair-haired child who plays a redemptive role in the second part is not obvious.

A.E. and R.C.: A.E. usually stands for Alexander Elbë, or possibly Alexander Exina. R.C. does not appear in any other poems.

424   *the unblessed of Heaven*: like Heathcliff, the desolate child is as unregenerate as the landscape he inhabits; without 'kindred kindness' he is destined to a grim fate.

sunbright hair: cf. Thomas Moore, 'Maids from the West with sun-bright hair' (*Lalla Rookh*, canto 7, stanza 42).

425   30. JULIAN. M. AND A.G. ROCHELLE 'SILENT IS THE HOUSE — ALL ARE LAID ASLEEP' (sections published in *Poems* 1846 under the title 'The Prisoner'). MS in 'Gondal Poems' Notebook in BL. A powerful Gondal love poem set during the Gondal civil war between Royalists and Republicans. The speaker (Lord Julian) waits for a secret visit from his lover (A.G. Rochelle, 'the Wanderer'), whom he has released from prison, hidden and nursed for thirteen weeks. Former childhood playmates, the lovers are now caught in a family feud, reminiscent of *Romeo and Juliet*; the dramatic interpolated story tells of their first meeting in prison. Replete with Romantic and Gothic images, the poem graphically describes a mystic experience thought to reflect that of Emily herself. It also contains Emily's most comprehensive statement of the theme of freedom in death, again echoing Epictetus: 'We will allow those only to be free who do not endure captivity; but, as soon as they are taken, die, and escape' (quoted in Roper *EBP*, 269).

Charlotte's chance discovery of the Gondal notebook was made around the time of composition (9 October 1845) in the autumn of 1845 and it is possible that this was the first of the poems she read, since Emily would either have just finished composition or still be working on it. Lines 13–44 and 65–92 (with modifications and a new final stanza) were published as 'The Prisoner' (1846), and Charlotte published lines 1–12 (with eight lines appended by her) as 'The Visionary' (1850), changing the gender of the speaker to suggest a personal poem; the alterations in these published versions change the meaning to such an extent that it can be argued that they represent separate poems.

Julian. M. and A.G. Rochelle: these names do not appear elsewhere in the poems.

snow-wreaths: banks or drifts of snow, chiefly Scottish.

426 *slumbering, unweaned child*: cf. Byron 'And ocean slumbered like an unweaned child' (*Don Juan*, 2. 70. 2).

427 *headsman's*: executioner's.

A messenger of Hope . . . eternal liberty: the powerful metaphor in the following six stanzas, in which the captivity of the prisoner represents the confinement of the soul in the body, has attracted much critical debate (see *Oxford Companion*, 275–6). C. Day Lewis hailed this passage of visional experience as 'the greatest passage of poetry Emily Brontë wrote' (*BST* 13/67 (1957), 92).

428 *Mute music . . . unuttered harmony*: paradox is used to express a state of mystical possession.

The soul . . . to feel the chain!: see note to p. 409: poem 18, on the Stoic idea of the chainless soul, also used by Byron in his 'Sonnet on Chillon' (ll. 1–8).

And robed in fires of Hell, or bright with heavenly shine | If it but herald Death, the vision is divine—: the speaker appears indifferent to the theological implications of her vision or the type of death it might herald.

Changes for Poems *1846 edition:*

28. which] that

31. parents'] kindred's

33. Yet, tell them, Julian, all] Still, let my tyrants know

40. which] that

60. After this, Emily concludes the 1846 version as follows:

> She ceased to speak, and we, unanswering, turned to go—
> We had no further power to work the captive woe:
> Her cheek, her gleaming eye, declared that man had given
> A sentence, unapproved, and overruled by Heaven.

430 31. 'WHY ASK TO KNOW THE DATE — THE CLIME?' MS in 'Gondal Poems' Notebook in BL; a revision of the first twenty-six lines constitutes the following and last poem in the notebook (see poem 32). Although a draft, poem 31 is praised as a 'superbly vivid narrative' (Jonathan Wordsworth, 'Wordsworth and Emily Brontë', 85). It is a dramatic monologue that recounts not only the horrors of civil war, but reveals the speaker's own decline into inhumanity and his inability to atone for his crime. He idealistically enlisted with the Gondal Republicans but, having inured himself to the brutality of war, his callous treatment of a dying nobleman prevents him from ever achieving redemption; cf. Anne's poem 'Z——'s Dream', written on the same date. The potentially melodramatic events are contained by the fluent speaking rhythms and by the convincing emotional fluctuations of the speaker.

The second half of the manuscript is heavily revised and it is clear that Emily is now using her 'Gondal Poems' Notebook for composition. Two large sections are cancelled (lines 149–56 and 172–89), but I follow Gezari and Roper in restoring them in the text since Emily gives no alternative lines.

430 *Why ask to know the date—the clime?*: the unwillingness of the speaker to specify time and place suggests his story is a tale for all times.

431 *Enthusiast—in a name delighting*: the speaker scorns himself as a self-deluding zealot of Republicanism; ironically the violence of war has led him and others to betray the ideals they fought for.

their cruelty: Emily was familiar with Scott's descriptions of the 'fero-cious cruelty' of the civil wars in sixteenth-century Scotland, described in his *Tales of a Grandfather* that the Brontës owned, and also similar descriptions in Byron's oriental tales. Shelley's *Prometheus Unbound* (ll. 574–8) also records the betrayal of revolutionary ideals in the Terror of the French Revolution and the way 'kindred murder kin' in a struggle which only 'slaves and tyrants win' (Stevie Davies, *Emily Brontë: Heretic* (London: Women's Press, 1994), 241).

432 *cairns*: monuments of rough stones piled high.

ken: sight; cf. the common saying 'beyond my ken', beyond my sight and, by implication, beyond my concern.

433 *Night following night*: Emily may have meant to cancel 'Night following' and replace it with 'Through this long', which is written below.

434 *'Forsake the world . . . might expire!'*: these lines are cancelled with a cross in the MS, but have always been considered part of this poem, which now becomes more carelessly written and difficult to read. There are many deletions and a number of alternative words, the most significant listed below.

435 *He does repay . . . one touch of tenderness*: lines cancelled with a cross in MS.

struggle with his last despair: above this are the alternative words 'draw breath in the morning air'.

436 *stranglers*: a possible mistake for 'stragglers'.

And O my soul . . . life again: two alternative lines follow: 'And I would freely, gladly then | Have given his saviour life again'.

The silent corpse before me lay: cf. Byron's *The Giaour*, in which 'that sullen corse' also thwarts the hero (ll. 1078–94).

437 *To mercy's God and not to me*: an incomplete alternative line follows: 'And mercy's God'.

32. 'WHY ASK TO KNOW WHAT DATE WHAT CLIME'. The last poem in 'Gondal Poems' Notebook in BL; immediately before is a much longer draft of this poem (composed 14 September 1846, at least six months after *Wuthering Heights* was completed), suggesting the revised poem is unfin-ished. This is also the last of Emily's surviving poems, demonstrating that

'so far from growing out of Gondal during the composition of *Wuthering Heights*, she returned to it to write some of her most impressive verse' (Jonathan Wordsworth, 'Wordsworth and Emily Brontë', 88). As in the draft, the speaker is a foreigner who has joined the Republicans in the civil war; he comments on personal and national anarchy that results from remorseless crimes of bloodshed. This poem and the previous one are both 'apocalyptic, like Lockward's dream of the battle in the Chapel of Gimmerden Sough in *Wuthering Heights* (ch. 3), where every man's hand is against his neighbour' (Gezari, *Last Things*, 65).

humanity: added in this revised version to stress the central theme of the disintegration of humanity in civil war. Emily sees us all as bearing a heart of darkness and potentially capable of ruthless acts at such times (poem 31: 'even as we').

438 *Our corn was garnered . . . with gore*: the crops were men's lives (just as the hands held swords rather than sickles). The horror and violence of war is vividly conveyed in the distortion of normal life that habitually follows the seasons.

ANNE BRONTË

Where relevant, changes made by Anne for *Poems* 'by Currer, Ellis and Acton Bell' (Aylott & Jones, May 1846) follow the notes and are keyed to line references.

Several of Anne's poems are referred to as 'in the Law Collection (private)'; they have been transcribed with kind permission of the owner. The manuscripts are reproduced in facsimile in the Shakespeare Head Brontë: T. J. Wise and J. A. Symington (eds.), *The Poems of Emily Jane Brontë and Anne Brontë* (1934).

441 1. VERSES BY LADY GERALDA. MS in Princeton University Library. This is Anne Brontë's first extant poem, written when she was home on holiday from Miss Wooler's school at Roe Head. As in many of Anne's poems, the metre draws on traditional ballads and the more recent literary ballads by Wordsworth, Coleridge, and others, who appropriated the form. The Gondal speaker, Lady Geralda, appears only in this poem, though the similarity of her name to Emily's character 'Geraldine' suggests they may be related. Lady Geralda questions the change in her familiar natural environment that no longer brings her joy; and she comes to the realization that, following the death of her parents, it is she who has changed and not the natural surroundings.

wild winter wind: cf. Emily's first poem and the significance of the wind in her subsequent poetry. Both Emily and Anne commonly begin their poems with an actual feature of the weather associated with an emotion that they transfer into a Gondal situation.

442 *a primrose*: herald of Spring and traditionally linked with youth and innocence. The association here with home and childhood memories is also mentioned in 'Memory', poem 12 below, and in Anne's novel *Agnes Grey*, ch. 13, entitled 'The Primroses'; in all these references a preference for

wild flowers over cultivated ones is recorded. The primrose would not normally be blooming in December in the blast of the 'wild winter wind' (Chitham *ABP*, 166). Elsewhere, however, Anne uses it in the appropriate growing season.

443 *Father! . . . left alone!*: themes of loneliness and abandonment recur throughout Anne's Gondal poetry.

444 *100 lines*: this is followed by a decorative line of leaves in MS. Unlike Emily, Anne records the number of lines at the end of most of her poems.

2. ALEXANDER AND ZENOBIA. MS in Princeton University Library; punctuation added after 'together', stanza 18. Beneath the title is a tiny pencil sketch of a desert with the setting sun and a grove of trees in the foreground. The unidentified speaker of this two-part poem tells a story of young lovers, parted several times and finally reunited. In the first part, Alexander and Zenobia savour the warmth and happiness of Gaaldine, but must face Zenobia's departure the next day for northern Gondal. Alexander promises that in two years' time, on Zenobia's fifteenth birthday, he will return to their favourite childhood meeting place. Part two records Zenobia's thoughts as she waits in suspense by the lonely spring in 'Exina's woody hills' for the return of Alexander. This 'Zenobia' is probably identical to Alexandrina Zenobia, Gondal speaker of four of Anne's poems ('The Captive's Dream', 'The North Wind', 'The Parting', and 'Verses to a Child'), and the same character as 'Alexandria Zenobia Hybernia' listed in Appendix B, although the name may have derived from the earlier Zenobia in the Glass Town and Angrian saga, who is also paired with an 'Alexander' (Alexander Percy, Duke of Northangerland). The name 'Alexander' appears several times in the Gondal saga, apparently referring to different characters. See also Emily Brontë's Diary Paper of 26 June 1837, in which she mentions that Anne is composing this poem (Appendix A).

Two youthful figures lay reclined: this image of the two young lovers is reminiscent of Eros and Psyche in Keats's 'Ode to Psyche': 'two fair creatures, couchéd side by side' (l. 9), while the Arabian setting recalls the Don Juan and Haidée episode in Byron's *Don Juan*, canto 2, stanzas 128–52.

445 *Araby*: romanticized poetic rendering of Arabia or the Arab world, suggesting its exotic and mysterious nature.

Philomel: poetic name for the nightingale, 'lover of song'; from the Greek myth about Philomela, sister of Procne wife of King Tereus of Thrace. Tereus, infatuated with Philomela's beauty, raped and imprisoned her after cutting out her tongue to prevent her revealing her fate. Tereus told his wife Philomela was dead, but Philomela managed to tell Procne her story by weaving it into a robe. Procne, in revenge, cut up her own son and served it to Tereus in a stew. As Tereus pursues the sisters in fury, the Gods transform all three into birds: Tereus becomes a hawk, his wife a swallow, and Philomela, a nightingale (Brewer).

447 *Exina's woody hills*: Exina is a province in the south of Gondal, home to several of Anne's Gondal characters.

bluebells: the bluebell was one of Anne's favourite flowers, although it is unclear whether she is referring here to the wild hyacinth, known in England as 'bluebell', or the harebell, also called 'bluebell' in Scotland and northern England. The relationship of Gondal with Scotland, and Anne's and Emily's familiarity with the poetry of Scott, suggest the latter. In her autobiographical poem 'The Bluebell' (1840), the flower inspires recollections of home and childhood, as it does in this Gondal poem; see also *Agnes Grey*, ch. 12: 'He had not forgotten bluebells were numbered among my favourite flowers.' See also Emily's poem 13.

448 *palace hall*: suggestive of Zenobia's noble birth.

450 *zephyrs*: mild, gentle breezes.

453 3. A VOICE FROM THE DUNGEON. MS in Princeton University Library. Written while Anne was at Roe Head (late October 1835–December 1837), about the time when she was seriously ill and in need of physical and psychological help. Despite its clear Gondal context, the speaker's misery and nightmare may reflect Anne's own desperate situation. Marina Sabia's 'darling boy' and Anne's fondness for drawing babies at this time has been seen as reflecting her subconscious preoccupation with motherhood (Chitham *ABP*, 53).

454 *piercing shriek*: cf. Emily's 'the shrieking wind' in a poem composed 14 October 1837 (Gezari *EBP*, 51). Anne's use of words like shriek, scream, and ecstasy relate quite specifically to poems composed by Emily about the same time. An annotation on the transcript of Anne's poem held at the Harry Ransom Center, University of Texas at Austin, notes that 'this poem is signed by Anne but it is more like Emily's work in the period Oct 1837/March 1838'. The dungeon motif also strongly suggests Emily's influence.

Marina Sabia: the only appearance of this character in surviving Gondal manuscripts.

October 6 1837: date and following '54 lines' recorded in minuscule print in MS (distinguished here and in Anne's signatures in the following poems by italics); the remainder of the poem is in Anne's usual cursive script. Anne uses minuscule print chiefly to distinguish her signature and date of composition from Gondal signatures and dates.

4. THE CAPTIVE'S DREAM. MS in Pierpont Morgan Library (Bonnell Collection). Together with the previous poem, 'The Captive's Dream' represents the Gondal preoccupation with separation and imprisonment. Again, Emily's influence can be detected, but the speaker's empathy for another's suffering—despite her own dire situation—is a particular characteristic of Anne's poetry.

no redness on his woe-worn cheek: cf. Augusta's lament on the death of her lover Alfred Sidonia in Emily's 'A.G.A. to A.S.' composed a few months later (20 May 1838): 'There is a faint red on his cheek | Not like the bloom I used to see' (stanza 4).

455   5. THE NORTH WIND. MS in Pierpont Morgan Library (Bonnell Collection); punctuation added after 'language', stanza 1. Written at home soon after leaving Roe Head and while Anne was recovering from her illness. The mood is still one of melancholy, as the imprisoned Alexandrina Zenobia grieves for her beloved country. Yet, as painful as it is, the vision of her mountain homeland suggested by the wind and its attendant freedom is superior to the hopeless despair she is experiencing. A month earlier, Emily wrote a similar poem, 'To a Wreath of Snow', where a drift of snow reminds the captive of the snow-capped mountains of her native country (Gezari *EBP*, 57).

455   *The North Wind*—: cf. Emily's watercolour illustration titled 'The North Wind', copied from William Finden's engraving of Richard Westall's 'Ianthe', used as the frontispiece to volume 2 of Thomas Moore's *Life of Byron* (1839), owned by the Brontës (see. Alexander and Sellars, 114).

456   *thus it speaks to me*—: the imprisoned Alexandrina Zenobia hears the sympathetic language of the wind; compare Emily's poems where the wind speaks or is a messenger (see note to Emily's poem 1).

Than that dull gnawing tearless [time]: the final word was cut off the end of this line, probably when T. J. Wise had the poems bound, since this line appeared at the top of a manuscript page. The word 'time' was then written above the word 'tearless'. The editions of C. K. Shorter and others retain 'time', apart from Chitham, who also indicates by square brackets that it is not clear whether 'time' is an accurate transcription of the missing word.

457   6 & 7. THE PARTING (including 'The lady of Alzerno's hall'). MS in Pierpont Morgan Library (Bonnell Collection); punctuation added at the end of stanza 4, poem 7. Although they appear to be separate in the manuscript and are printed thus in subsequent editions, these two poems of parting and loss are essentially one, grouped under a single title at the head of the first poem and a single Gondal signature at the end of the second poem. The speaker is Alexandrina Zenobia, who tells first of the parting of Lord Alzerno and his wife Eliza, and then, in the second section (poem 7) beginning 'The lady of Alzerno's hall', continues the story three years hence. Eliza is probably Eliza Hybernia, the sister of Alexandrina Zenobia (see Appendix B). The influence of Scott is reflected in both the subject and form of this ballad; and there is also a suggestion of Tennyson's 'Lady of Shalott', first published in 1833.

1: unlike Emily, Anne numbers the verses in several of her poems.

460   *'Twas thus I spoke*: Alexandrina Zenobia has known all along that Alzerno was dead. There seems to be some mystery here. Why can't she tell his wife about his death? Was Alexandrina his lover?

461   *1837*: the 'fictional' date of composition. The Gondal situation, like Glass Town and Angria, generally coincides with the time of Anne's writing;

here, she clearly distinguishes between events in Gondal and her actual date of composition, 10 July 1838.

8. VERSES TO A CHILD. MS in Pierpont Morgan Library (Bonnell Collection); comma altered to semicolon after 'from me' in stanza 1. The poem reveals Alexandrina Zenobia's desertion by the father of her child, once her early playmate, lover, and (presumably) husband. The poem may have been occasioned by the same Gondal situation of a deserted mother of an illegitimate child as Emily's poem 'A Farewell to Alexandria', in which Alexandria (who may be identical with Alexandrina Zenobia) exposes her baby to death in mountain snows (Gezari *EBP*, 106).

And smile again so joyously: the healing effect of memory triggered by the smile of this child suggests the influence of Wordsworth.

462 *Florian's*: in the manuscript the name 'Mary' was erased and replaced by 'Florian' here and 'Flora' in stanza 6. Chitham sees this, and the fact that the ascription to Alexandrina Zenobia was added in smaller script possibly after the poem had been transcribed, as evidence that Anne had not specifically composed it for a Gondal context but had fitted it into the Gondal saga afterwards (Chitham *ABP*, 168); however, the names 'Mary' and 'Flora' also appear together in Emily's Gondal poems (see for example Gezari *EBP*, 128).

463 9. A FRAGMENT (*Poems* 1846 title: 'Self-Congratulation'). MS in Pierpont Morgan Library (Bonnell Collection). Despite the Gondal signature 'Olivia Vernon', the subject also suggests Anne's personal experience. The title she chose for the 1846 version carries a bitter irony since the protagonist is congratulating herself on being able to stifle her true feelings. She spurns all the conventional literary tropes of love—'the speaking eye, the changing lip, | The ready blushing cheek'—for a mask of complacency. It is usually accepted by commentators that the poem is describing Anne's bitter disappointment at William Weightman's failure to recognize her love for him; but Anne would have known Weightman (her father's curate from August 1839 until his death from cholera in 1842) for only a few weeks since her return home from the Inghams at Blake Hall, where she had been a governess since April. Anne's habit of assuming a calm and meek exterior is blamed for depreciating her in the eyes of others, including her siblings. Yet, had she recognized this as self-possession, Charlotte would have admired Anne for this trait that she herself struggled so hard to achieve.

The poem is the earliest of Anne's verses to be included in the 1846 edition and is a good example of how she 'deGondalized' her poems for publication. The archaic diction of the MS version conveys a sense of timelessness and age, despite the very Victorian subject matter; the 1846 version, with its opening on the typically nineteenth-century name 'Ellen', is a more unambiguously contemporary poem. Compare the similar name of Anne's heroine 'Helen' in her novel *The Tenant of Wildfell Hall*; and the name of Charlotte's friend, Ellen Nussey, who was also the friend of Anne.

Changes for Poems *1846 edition:*

1. 'Maiden thou wert] Ellen, you were

5. why so oft—] wherefore now

6. Dost smooth thy hazel hair] So often smooth your hair?

7. thy] your

10. yonder hackneyed strain] that familiar strain—

11. wilt thou] will you

13. 'Nay gentle friends] 'Indeed, dear friends,

17. those] these

28. gazer's eye] gazer well

36. bitter] keenest

45. O] oh!

46. thick] full

55. The anguish of my drooping heart] The aching anguish of my heart,

56. aching] burning

465   10. LINES WRITTEN AT THORP GREEN (*Poems* 1846 title: 'Appeal'). MS in the Law Collection (private). Compared to Anne's earlier poetry, this heartfelt, poignant appeal is notable for its terse, economic style. The twin themes of exile and longing are typically Gondal, yet the poem could also reflect the unhappiness and homesickness of its young author. When she wrote this poem, Anne was living away from home at Thorp Green as governess to the Robinson children. Three months earlier, Emily, who was living happily at home, wrote a poem with similar themes (see her poem 17), a salutary warning of presuming too readily that real life and Gondal overlapped for the Brontës (see Barker, *The Brontës*, 343–4).

Lines Written at Thorp Green: Anne wrote another poem with this title a year later, 19 August 1841, which again expresses a sense of loneliness (see Chitham *ABP*, 79). Thus she renamed this first poem 'Appeal' for *Poems* 1846.

Changes for Poems *1846 edition:*

1. O!] Oh,

466   11. THE CONSOLATION (*Poems* 1846 title: 'The Consolation'). MS in Pierpont Morgan Library (Bonnell Collection). An example of an apparently quite personal poem given a Gondal context by its ascription to 'Hespera Caverndel', an unidentifiable Gondal character; although, again, the feelings expressed are reminiscent of earlier Gondal poems. The autumnal setting accords with the November date of the poem's composition, and the speaker's isolation and longing for her understanding companions at home suggest Anne's own desolate situation as governess at Thorp Green.

Though far I roam: cf. Thomas Moore's 'As down in the Sunless retreats':

> So, dark as I roam, in this wintry world shrouded,
> The hope of my spirit turns trembling to Thee.

Anne copied this and five other poems by Moore into her music manuscript book in 1843 (Akiko Higuchi, *The Brontës and Music*, 2nd ed., Tokyo: Yushodo, 2008, vol. 2, p. 78).

Changes for Poems *1846 edition:*

2. strewn] strown

9. stranger glances] stranger-glances

10. roam] go,

467   12. MEMORY (*Poems* 1846 title: 'Memory'). MS in the Law Collection (private). The poem expresses Anne's witness to the power of memory to transform nature and recall the joy and security of childhood in which her Gondal partnership with Emily flourished. Wordsworth's influence is strongly felt in the imaginative recollection of the past and the emphasis on childhood experience. The 'dreamy spell' is similar to Charlotte's and Emily's memories of childhood visions and their association with poetic inspiration: see note to p. 396: poem 4. See also Anne's poem 19, 'Z——'s Dream', for an example of the way the memory of childhood influences present action.

As usual, Anne's punctuation is surprisingly heavy; in line with my policy in Note on the Text, I have made only a few punctuation changes: in stanza 2, comma changed to question mark; in stanza 3, comma removed at end of line 5; stanza 6, full stop removed at line 3; stanza 8, comma removed at line 2.

When one sweet breath of memory | Came gently wafting by?: example of the power of the wind to initiate memory and trigger the imaginative faculty; a common motif in Romantic poetry and especially prevalent in Emily's poetry.

primrose: see note to p. 442.

Changes for Poems *1846 edition:*

21. O] Oh,

25. wallflower's] wall-flower's

31. forever] For ever

32. golden] mountain

38. memory] Memory

40. all] *all* (italicized)

41. is] be

48. past] passed

469   13. LINES INSCRIBED ON THE WALL OF A DUNGEON IN THE SOUTHERN P OF I. MS in the Law Collection (private); comma inserted in final line. Anne is again home for the Christmas holidays and influenced by Emily's continuing enthusiasm for Gondal: compare Emily's poem 27 with a similar prison title and theme, written only a month earlier and probably

read to Anne on her return home. The speaker is Alexander Hybernia, who appears to be the brother (or husband) of Alexandrina Zenobia and brother of Eliza Hybernia (see Anne's list of characters, Appendix B). The early Gondal date of '1826' indicates that Anne and Emily's intention to chronicle events in Gondal has now provided a firm chronology for their imaginative writing: see Anne's 1845 Diary Paper, Appendix A.

469   *southern P of I*: Palace of Instruction in the south of Gondal; see note to Emily's poem 27, p. 420: 'Southern College'.

   A.H.: Alexander Hybernia, also the narrator of 'An Orphan's Lament' (see Chitham *ABP*, 78–9).

470   14. 'CALL ME AWAY'. MS in the Law Collection (private); full stop removed at end of line 4, stanza 13. This is the first of a series of bleak works written by Anne early in 1845. Anne wrote the poem a few days after she and Branwell returned to their teaching posts at Thorp Green following the Christmas break, and it is seen as reflecting in a Gondal setting the alleged affair between Branwell and Mrs Robinson (Chitham *ABP*, 182). Yet it is not clear how much Anne knew of Branwell's relationship with Mrs Robinson in January 1845, or indeed how involved with Mrs Robinson he actually was at this stage. It also seems unlikely that the sensitive and moral Anne would identify so closely with Branwell's precarious position and resolve, as the speaker of this poem does, to continue his illicit liaison despite its 'taint of woe'. The early verses may well reflect Anne's wish to 'hasten far away' to the Scottish setting of Gondal (stanza 3) where she imagines the passionate outburst of the speaker and his tormenting conflict. The poem is complex because of the continued use of the subjunctive: the opening speaker desires a return to Gondal in which he anticipates seeing a hero lamenting the death of a friend and longing for continued relationship with a female lover.

473   15. SONG 'WE KNOW WHERE DEEPEST LIES THE SNOW'. MS in the Huntington Library, San Marino (HM 2576). Anne left Thorp Green for good on 11 June 1845 and, apart from a brief trip to York with Emily at the end of the month (see 1845 Diary Papers, Appendix A), she began a period of intense writing activity in the company of Emily that indicates renewed interest in Gondal and the draft of her first novel. The subject and vocabulary are typical of early Gondal poems, although the final verse sounds a more personal note than might be expected of Anne. The speaker of this and the following song appear to be referring to the same Gondal situation.

   We have their princely homes: possibly indicates that the Royalists have been defeated by the Republicans.

   16. SONG 'COME TO THE BANQUET'. MS in the Huntington Library, San Marino (HM 2576). The Gondal speaker is cynical about the fruits of victory and, as in the previous song, would prefer the free, wandering life of the outlaw than the life of the victor won through vengeance and now burdened by conscience of wrongs committed. The adventurous life

of the outlaw is a reminder of the strong influence of Scott's novels, such as *Rob Roy*, in the Gondal saga.

474   *ever full of hope!*: the importance of the virtue of hope is a central theme of Anne's religious poetry. Cf. 1 Corinthians 13: 7.

475   17. MIRTH AND MOURNING. MS in the Huntington Library, San Marino (HM 2576). The poem, written in July 1846, carries the same title as chapter 18 of *Agnes Grey*, which was completed and ready for publication by April 1846, and probably composed during 1845–6. The juxtaposition in the title represents the dialogic form of the poem, with its contrasting happy and sad speakers, a favourite device of Anne. Zerona, the narrator, mourns her lover while another speaker urges her to postpone sorrow and rejoice, as nature around her rejoices in the summer weather.

477   18. 'WEEP NOT TOO MUCH, MY DARLING'. MS in the Huntington Library, San Marino (HM 2576). Written thirteen days later than 'Mirth and Mourning', the poem is a reply to Zerona from the lover she mourns. A.E. (Arthur Exina?) selflessly begs her not to suffer and lose her interest in nature for his sake; he would rather know that she is hopeful, free to enjoy the pleasures of nature that he so earnestly seeks from his dungeon cell. The moon 'crossed, deformed, and sullied' by the 'relentless bars' of the prison window is a powerful image of man barred from the beauty of the world. But the importance of a positive view in life is implied in the contrasting constructions of the two final sentences.

479   19. Z——'S DREAM. MS in BPM (135). For Anne, memory is reinforced by dreams that recall the joys of childhood. In this Gondal poem, the speaker's present moral predicament is complicated by a dream of his beloved boyhood companion whom, in adulthood, he pursued as his deadly enemy and murdered. The fate of both boys seems to have been determined by the political situation in their country: the speaker, one of Gondal's Republican heroes of the civil war, sees his former friend's death as furthering his cause but makes it clear that victory is still far off. The poem is interesting for its use of a male narrator and its masculine relationship, although friendship, betrayal, and murder are common concerns in Gondal: cf. Emily's last poem, 'Why ask to know the date—the clime?' (poem 31), written on the same date and also involving a remorseless act and the anarchy of war. The themes in Anne's poem of memory and youth, innocence and experience, combined with a fictional autobiographic tone, are suggestive of Wordsworth.

    The MS appears to be a rough draft. The erased title is difficult to decipher, and the speaker's initials in the signature 'EZ' do not match any of the Gondal names in Anne's lists. There are a number of deletions, the most significant lines being: 59 'And in my dream I laughed to see'; 63 'Nor words declare'; 88 'quiet confidence'; 93 'friendship's bands'.

483   20. 'GLOOMILY THE CLOUDS ARE SAILING'. MS in BPM (136). Anne's final Gondal poem; her last personal poem was written over two years later on 28 January 1849. The scene of a 'stately hall' amidst 'Heathclad hill and woodland dale' and the theme of grief in love suggest her fictional

world, but the speaker's emotion may be that of personal expression. The MS has a comma after 'Now' (line 25) and after 'lowering' (line 29).

483   *sailing*: 'above' follows this in MS, cancelled.

APPENDIX A

485   DIARY PAPER 24 NOVEMBER 1834: MS in BPM (Bonnell 131); a single scrap of paper (99 × 60 mm) with a tiny sketch in the left margin of a lock of hair, labelled 'A bit of Lady Julet's hair done by Anne': illustrated in Alexander and Sellars, p. 398. Written by Emily in a very untidy combination of longhand and minuscule script, with surprisingly poor spelling for a 16-year-old. A cancelled heading 'November the 24/ Emily Jane Brontë' appears upside down at the foot of the page where Emily made a false start.

(alias[)]: Emily uses only an opening parenthesis in this Diary Paper.

Mr Drivers: James Driver, grocer of Haworth; not to be confused with the Mr Driver who lent the Brontës periodicals (see Charlotte's 'History of the Year').

Sir Robert peel: see note to p. 18; and Branwell's 'Politics of Verdopolis' for his characterization of Peel as Sir Robert Weaver Pelham.

stand for Leeds: this news was incorrect: Peel's constituency was Tamworth, a seat he held until his death.

Taby: Tabitha Ackroyd (or Aykroyd), servant to the Brontë family from 1824; usually spelt Tabby.

Aunt: Elizabeth Branwell, elder sister of the Brontës' mother, who came to Haworth in 1821 to nurse her dying sister and stayed for the remainder of her life to care for her nephew and nieces.

487   *Mr Sunderland*: Abraham Stansfield Sunderland, the Keighley organist who taught the young Brontës music from about late 1833 until the end of 1834. He also gave Branwell flute and organ lessons, and conducted orchestral and choral concerts. He is satirized in the Glass Town and Angrian saga as Mr Sudbury Figgs, organist at Howard in Angria.

DIARY PAPER 26 JUNE 1837: MS in BPM (E9); heavy creases indicate where the paper has been folded to fit into a tin box about 2 inches long (still surviving in the BPM). The second paragraph is written at the foot of the page below a sketch and the final paragraph is written along the side on the right (see facsimile illustration, p. 486). The sketch represents Anne (top left) and Emily working on the Diary Paper, with 'The papers' and 'The tin box' on the table. Despite the joint signature, the MS is written by Emily on the evening of Branwell's twentieth birthday.

Eugene Aram: novel by Edward Bulwer Lytton, published in 1832.

'fair . . . sun': titled 'Alexander and Zenobia', dated 1 July 1837: see Anne's poem 2.

Queen Victoria ascended the throne this month: the 18-year-old Queen Victoria was the same age as Emily herself.

Northangerland . . . Eversham: evidence that Emily and Anne are still aware of ongoing events in the Glass Town and Angrian saga.

out): final word difficult to decipher; previously transcribed as 'in'.

488 EMILY BRONTË DIARY PAPER 30 JULY 1841: MS in the Law Collection (private); text transcribed with kind permission of the owner. Facsimile in Clement Shorter, *Charlotte Brontë and Her Circle* (London: Hodder and Stoughton, 1896), opp. p. 146. On either side of the heading are two tiny sketches of Emily writing at her 'desk-box' on a table and Emily standing at the window: illustrated in Alexander and Sellars, 383.

Victoria and Adelaide: pet geese named after Queen Victoria and her aunt, the widowed Queen Adelaide.

Keeper: Emily's dog: see note to p. 404: 'the very dogs', and her water-colour of Keeper in Alexander and Sellars, plate III.

Nero: Emily's hawk, probably the one referred to in Anne's Diary Paper; see also Emily's watercolour of a hawk, possibly Nero (Alexander and Sellars, plate VI).

Charlotte . . . Scarborough: Charlotte went as governess to the White family at Upperwood House, about 5 miles from Bradford, from end Feb./Mar. until 30 June 1841; Branwell gained a job on 1 April as clerk at Luddenden Foot, a small station on the Leeds–Manchester railway near Halifax; and Anne, governess to the Robinson family of Thorp Green, near York, spent time in the summer with them at an apartment on the sea front at Scarborough.

editing: spelt 'enditing' in MS.

we . . . seminary: Charlotte, Emily, and Anne first made plans at this time to establish their own school, financed by their aunt Elizabeth Branwell, but the idea was eventually relinquished in 1845 after unsuccessful attempts to secure pupils.

489 *palace of Instruction*: see note to p. 420: 'Southern College'.

ANNE BRONTË DIARY PAPER 30 JULY 1841: MS in the Law Collection (private); text transcribed with kind permission of the owner.

Charlotte . . . Mᴿ Robinson: for the situations of the Brontë siblings, see note to p. 488: 'Charlotte . . . Scarborough'.

livelihood: Spelt 'livlihood' in MS.

How little . . . bel!: cf. 1 John 3: 2, and also Byron, *Don Juan*, canto 15: 99; and Shakespeare's *Hamlet*, Act IV, scene v.

Blake hall: owned by Joshua and Mary Ingham in Mirfield, Yorkshire.

miss patchet's school: at Law Hill, near Halifax; see note to p. 399: poem 8.

charlotte has left Miss Wooler's: see note to p. 158: THE ROE HEAD JOURNAL.

489 *a Governess at Mrs Sidgwick's*: Charlotte was governess to the family of Mr and Mrs John Benson Sidgwick from May to July 1839.

a clerk on the railroad: Branwell tried unsuccessfully to make a living as a portrait painter in Bradford, then went as a tutor to the family of Robert Postlethwaite of Broughton-in-Furness, Cumberland, before becoming a railway clerk at Sowerby Bridge station and then at Luddenden Foot.

Keeper: for the Brontë animals, see notes to p. 488.

490 *Sofala*: incorrectly transcribed in previous publications as 'Solala'. Sofala Vernon does not appear elsewhere in extant Gondal manuscripts, although 'Olivia Vernon' is the speaker of Anne's poem 9. Both names are used for characters in the Glass Town and Angrian saga. Sofala was an early mistress of the Duke of Zamorna, and Louisa Vernon was a mistress of Alexander Percy and mother of Caroline Vernon.

EMILY BRONTË DIARY PAPER 30[31] JULY 1845: MS in private collection of William Self. Following the signature Emily has sketched her bedroom with herself in back view, seated on a stool and writing her Diary Paper on her 'desk-box'. Her dog Keeper lies on the floor near her and Anne's dog Flossy and a cat are on her bed. Emily actually wrote this paper on 31 July but dated it the day before (her birthday), when she had intended to open her previous paper and write this new one.

Charlotte and I went to Brussels: Charlotte and Emily had gone to Brussels to improve their qualifications for teaching, but on their return they were unsuccessful in attempts to establish a school at Bridlington, Dewsbury Moor, or even at Haworth where no pupils were forthcoming.

Branwell left his place at Luddenden Foot: he was dismissed at the end of March 1842 because his accounts were 'found deficient' due to the dishonesty of a porter under his supervision.

Branwell [left]—July 1845: dismissed from Thorp Green for 'proceedings . . . bad beyond expression' (Smith *Letters*, 1, 412).

491 *We had prospectuses printed*: published in Smith *Letters*, 1, 365.

We have cash enough . . . accumulation: Emily took charge of investing the sisters' small legacies from their Aunt in railway shares.

Flossey: Anne's King Charles spaniel given to her by her two pupils at Thorp Green.

Tiger: the parsonage cat.

turning: plain sewing: the turning of worn parts of garments to prolong wear, as in the case of collars and cuffs, and sheets that were turned 'sides to middle'.

I have plenty of work: probably referring to needlework here.

ANNE BRONTË DIARY PAPER 31 JULY 1845: MS in private collection of William Self.

492 *I was at Thorp Green . . . escaped from it*: Anne was at Thorp Green from about May 1840 until June 1845.

Sophala: spelt 'Sofala' in Emily's 1845 Diary Paper. Sentence in pointed brackets deleted in MS.

very unpleasant . . . experience of human nature: presumably a reference to the affair between Branwell and Mrs Robinson.

little Dick: the canary mentioned in Emily's 1845 Diary Paper.

Emperor Julius's life: Julius Brenzaida: see Glossary of the Gondal saga.

I wonder what it is about: despite composing in the same house, it is clear that the sisters did not read each other's poetry, which was considered more personal than the prose. See Emily's 1845 poems 'R Alcona to J Brenzaida' ('Cold in the Earth'), 'A.E. and R.C.' ('Heavy hangs the raindrop'), and 'Julian. M. and A.G. Rochelle' ('Silent is the House'), some of her best work written at this time.

the third volume . . . Individual: this may refer to the 'book by Henry Sophona' mentioned in Emily's 1845 Diary Paper, or to an early version of *Agnes Grey*, Anne's first novel.

I have a great deal of work: needlework that Emily also referred to.

[Gaaldin]: Gaaldine.

GLOSSARY OF MAIN CHARACTERS AND PLACES IN THE GLASS TOWN AND ANGRIAN SAGA

Characters are known by a variety of names and titles, as the saga becomes more sophisticated. Spelling often changes accordingly.

Adrianopolis imperial capital of Angria, situated on the banks of the River Calabar, 150 miles from Verdopolis. Considered grandiose and ostentatious compared to the old capital of Verdopolis.

Alnwick House (Alnwick Castle) ancestral home of the Percys in Sneaky's Land in the north-west of the Glass Town Federation.

Angria, King of *see* Zamorna, Duke of.

Angria province of the kingdom of Angria, governed by Warner Howard Warner. Based on Yorkshire, its inhabitants speak in dialect and its capital city, Angria, is surrounded by moors.

Angria, Kingdom of created for Zamorna by the Verdopolitan Parliament in February 1834, as recompense for his success in the War of Encroachment, which took place on the eastern borders of the Verdopolitan Union against the native Ashantees and their allies the Arabs and the French. It has seven provinces: Zamorna, Angria, Douro, Calabar, Northangerland, Arundel, and Etrei.

Ardrah, Arthur, Marquis of son of the King of Parry's Land. Leader of the Reformers in Verdopolis and Commander of the Verdopolitan Navy; opposed to Zamorna and the creation of Angria.

Arundel province in Angria, known for its fertile pastures and woods; governed by the Earl of Arundel.

Arundel, Earl of *see* Lofty, Lord Frederic.

Ashantees originally wooden ninepins, representing native Africans, enemies of the Young Men; later, under Quashia, allies of the Verdopolitan Reform Ministry and Northangerland against Angria.

Ashantee, Kingdom of the area of west Africa colonized by the Twelves, based on the Ashanti Empire of the eighteenth and nineteenth centuries.

Bady *see* Hume Bady.

Bobadill, Thomas Beresford, General an ugly, tall man, originally from the Young Men's Play; major general in Wellington's army but known as a boasting, cowardly soldier.

Branni, Chief Genius *see* Genii, Chief.

Brock, Lieutenant chief librarian of the Glass Town.

Bud, Captain John (pseudonym of Branwell) an eminent political writer, antiquarian, and historian; contemporary of Wellington. Friend of the young Lord Charles Wellesley and father of Sergeant Bud.

Bud, Sergeant son of Captain John Bud; he is an unscrupulous lawyer.

Calabar, River flows through Adrianopolis, Angria.

Castlereagh, Lord, Frederick Stuart a dandified early friend of Zamorna, who makes him Earl of Stuartville and an Angrian minister.

Cirhala, River Angrian river on which Evesham is situated; site of Zamorna's victorious battle that ended the last of the Angrian wars.

De Lisle, Frederick (or Sir Edward) a distinguished Verdopolitan portrait painter, patronized by Zamorna.

Douro, Marquis of (pseudonym of Charlotte) *see* Zamorna, Duke of.

Doverham port on the west coast of Angria, the closest point to Calais on the island of Frenchyland.

Edwardston chief manufacturing town of Zamorna province in Angria, on the banks of the Olympia River; site of Zamorna's defeat by Northangerland's Reformist forces during the Angrian civil war.

Ellrington (Elrington), Lady Zenobia, Countess of Northangerland bluestocking friend of Douro (Zamorna) and rival of Marian Hume for his love; becomes the third wife of Alexander Percy who adopts her name and title; elevated to Countess of Northangerland on the creation of Angria, but is neglected by her husband and retains her love for Zamorna.

Ellrington-House home of Northangerland and his wife, formerly Lady Zenobia Ellrington, in Verdopolis.

Ellrington, Lord *see* Northangerland, Earl of.

Enara, Henri Fernando di, Baron of Etrei one of Zamorna's generals whom he created baron and governor of the Angrian province of Etrei.

Fidena, Prince John Sneachi, Duke of the morally upright heir to the throne of Sneachiesland. Fidena is not a member of Zamorna's Angrian coterie; yet despite this and his antipathy to Zamorna's character, Fidena is Zamorna's most respected and trusted friend. He is leader of the Constitutionalists in Verdopolis.

Finic the Marquis of Douro's elusive mute dwarf servant, the offspring of a liaison between the young Douro and Sofala, a Negress who prayed on her deathbed that her son might bring shame to his false father.

Flower, Captain Sir John (pseudonym of Branwell) contemporary of the Duke of Wellington and eminent Glass Town scholar, chronicler of the Angrian Wars and the rise of the new kingdom of Angria; becomes Viscount Richton, Baron Flower, Verdopolitan ambassador to Angria.

Freetown capital of Sneaky's land.

Frenchyland island south of the Great Glass Town in the Gulf of Guinea; established by Branwell in the early saga to allow him to pursue his interest in French revolutionary politics and the fate of Napoleon. The capital is Paris.

Gambia, River the major river flowing through Wellingtonsland (Senegambia), on which Wellington's Glass Town is situated.

Genii, Chief (Tallii, Brannii, Emmii and Annii, variously spelt) representing the four Brontë children as supernatural guardians and players in the Glass Town and Angrian saga. The concept of four protectors, each with a Chief Man, derived from the Young Men's Play, but other plays had similar presiding beings, such as 'Little King and Queens' in the Islanders' Play. The Chief Genii and their minions live in the Jibbel Kumri or Mountains of the Moon. Branwell preferred a tyrannical role as 'Chief Genius Brany Lightening', mischievously subverting the Young Men and admonishing the other Chief Genii. As the Genii gradually disappear from the saga, Branii morphs into the evil character Sdeath. By the time Angria is founded, the concept of Chief Genii has become simply part of Glass Town's early history.

Girnington-Hall rambling Gothic country house of General Thornton, situated at the upper end of the Valley of Verdopolis; acquired from 'Old Girnington', whose fortune Thornton inherited.

Glass Town Federation (renamed Verdopolitan Union) carved out of the Kingdom of Ashantee by the Twelves, and united by the four kings of Wellington's Land, Sneaky's Land, Ross's Land, and Parry's Land. It is bounded by the Gulf of Guinea in the south, the mountains of the Jibbel Kumri in the north, and deserts in the east. The federal capital is the Great Glass Town. Later, the federal parliament reluctantly agrees to include Angria in the Federation.

Gordon, Lady Helen Victorine, Baroness Scottish heiress known as the 'Lily of Loch Sunart'; Zamorna's first wife who died giving birth to their first son, Ernest Edward Gordon Wellesley. Sister of the villainous Captain Julius Gordon, early associate of Northangerland.

Great Glass Town (Glasstown) *see* Verdopolis.

Hartford, General Lord Edward Angrian nobleman and victorious commander of Zamorna's troops at the battles of Westwood and Leyden.

Hawkscliffe Zamorna's remote country estate in Angria Province, the northern 'Yorkshire' region of Angria; includes Hawkscliffe Forest and his country residence Hawkscliffe House.

Hawlaw, Marquis of *see* Ross, Edward Tut.

Hume Bady, Dr Alexander (later Sir Alexander Hume, Duke of Badhi and Duke of Alderwood) originally 'Bady', the notorious surgeon of the early Glass Town, who dissects stolen bodies and resurrects people in his 'macerating tub'. He is the Duke of Wellington's physician and his daughter Marian becomes Zamorna's second wife.

Hume, Florence Marian daughter of Dr Alexander Hume Bady and devoted second wife of Zamorna. Mother of Arthur Julius Wellesley, she dies from a broken heart because of Zamorna's infidelities.

Jibbel Kumri known as the Mountains of the Moon where the Genii dwell. They form the northern borders of both the Glass Town and the historical kingdom of Ashantee.

Jordon, John Julian, Lord part-Italian brother of Alexander Percy's first wife Augusta (or Maria) di Segovia, who squandered Jordon's fortune on her husband. A flamboyant Roman Catholic, Jordon later becomes the Sheik Medina, dresses (like Byron) in Turkish costume, and (in league with Northangerland and the Ashantees) leads a ruthless army of Arab troops against Angria.

Kirkwall, Sir John an Angrian MP in the Verdopolitan Parliament, and general in the Angrian army.

Laury, Sergeant Edward (Ned) a soldier who turns bodysnatcher and poacher before mending his ways and becoming a loyal retainer of the Duke of Wellington. Father of Mina Laury, he later becomes chief ranger of Zamorna's Angrian estates.

Laury, Mina daughter of Edward Laury and maid to the Duchess of Wellington and then to Zamorna's wife Florence Marian Hume. When she dies, Mina becomes Zamorna's devoted mistress and 'mother' to his two eldest children.

Little King and Queens *see* Genii, Chief.

Lofty, Lord Frederic, Earl of Arundel appointed earl and 'Grand Chamberlain' by Zamorna when Angria is created; close early friend of Zamorna, accomplished horseman (nicknamed 'The Chevalier'), and popular field-marshal in the Angrian army. Brother to Marcara Lofty and married to Edith Sneachie.

Lofty, Lord Macara dissolute scoundrel who later becomes a leader of the Republican Rebellion; friend of Lord Charles Wellesley.

Monkey's Isle *see* Stumps Land.

Montmorency (Montmorenci), Hector Matthias Mirabeau wealthy Verdopolitan French émigré, who was actually born in Wellingtonsland where he has an estate; sinister friend of Northangerland. Later a banker and ally of Ardrah against Zamorna's campaigns; finally exiled to Paris.

Mornington-Court Wellesley family home in Wellingtonsland.

Napoleon Buonaparte ruler of Frenchyland and opponent of the Glass Town Federation and its leading ruler the Duke of Wellington. Originally Branwell's Chief Man, he is superseded first by Sneaky and then by Rogue, who retains Napoleon's courageous but deceitful characteristics.

Niger, River flows from the north in Sneaky's Land south to the Vale of Verdopolis and the Gulf of Guinea. Wellesley House and other palaces are built on the Niger in Verdopolis.

Northangerland, Earl of, Alexander Percy (Rogue), Lord Ellrington (Elrington) (principal pseudonym of Branwell) demagogue, revolutionary, and politician; corrupted early in life by his ally Montmorency. After a dissolute youth of gambling and drinking, including marriage to Maria di Segovia who is poisoned, he marries the innocent Maria Henrietta Wharton, mother of their daughter Mary Percy (Zamorna's third wife) and two sons, Edward and William Percy, whom Northangerland (then Percy) unnaturally disowns at birth. Maria dies young of consumption and grief at the loss of her sons; brokenhearted, Percy becomes an aggressive atheist, cattle-dealer (known as 'The Drover'), pirate, and seducer of numerous women, including the mother of his second daughter Caroline Vernon. Through his third wife Lady Zenobia Ellrington he re-enters society. His talented restless character is constitutionally incapable of loyalty or of supporting stability in government. His closest bond is with Zamorna, whom he corrupted as a youth and with whom he maintains a complex love-hate relationship. After helping Zamorna become king of Angria, he is made first prime minister of Angria, against which he soon conspires. He encourages Quashia and the Ashantees against Angria, helps Ardrah occupy Angria with troops, and tries to establish a republican government in Verdopolis, sending Zamorna into exile and almost causing the death of his own daughter Mary. When Zamorna finally regains Angria he allows Northangerland to live as a private individual rather than be exiled.

Northangerland, Countess of *see* Ellrington, Lady Zenobia.

O'Connor, Arthur a profligate associate of the young Northangerland.

Paris capital of Frenchyland.

Parry, Captain Sir William Edward, King of Parry's Land (later, Parrisland) Emily Brontë's chief man in the Young Men's Play.

Parry's Land (later, Parrisland) one of the four Glass Town kingdoms, ruled by Captain Sir William Edward Parry; considered provincial and old-fashioned (like Yorkshire itself) by sophisticated Glass Town society.

Pelham, Sir R. Weaver politician recruited by Northangerland on arrival from England and courts Mary Percy before Zamorna meets her; later deserts Northangerland and leads the moderates, supporting the Constitutionalists (Wellington and Fidena).

Percy, Alexander *see* Northangerland, Earl of.

Percy, Edward with his younger brother William, disowned at birth by his father Northangerland. Determined to work their way back into society, the two brothers work first in a sweat shop and then begin a wool-combing business. Mean and ruthless towards William, whom he employs as a clerk in his counting house, Edward soon acquires mills and factories along the Olympia River in Angria. Edwardston is named after him; he becomes Angrian minister of trade, and marries Princess Maria Sneachie.

Percy Hall country residence of the Percy family in Wellingtonsland, where both Northangerland and his daughter Mary were born, and where Lady Helen Percy still resides.

Percy, Lady Helen mother of Northangerland, grandmother and confidante of Mary Henrietta, Duchess of Zamorna. She lives at the Percy family homes, Alnwick House and Percy Hall.

Percy, Mary Henrietta, Duchess of Zamorna, Queen of Angria eldest daughter of Northangerland and his second wife Mary Henrietta Wharton.

Percy, Sir William youngest son of Northangerland and, like his brother Edward, rejected at birth; ill treated by Edward, he eventually goes his own way in society, becoming a lieutenant general in the Angrian army and a diplomat (*see* Percy, Edward).

Quashia Quamina Kashna leader of the Ashantees and enemy of Angria. On the death of his father (King Sai Too Too Quamina), he was adopted as a baby by the Duke Wellington and a bitter antagonism grew between him and his stepbrother Zamorna. He lusts after Northangerland's two daughters, and invades Angria with Northangerland, Ardrah and MacTerrorglen.

Richton, Viscount *see* Flower, Captain Sir John.

Rogue (Rouge, Rougue) in the early plays, 'Young Rogue' and 'Old Rogue' refer to Alexander Percy and his father; in the later Angrian stories, the names refer to Edward Percy and Northangerland respectively.

Rosier, Eugene Zamorna's favourite page.

Ross, Captain John, King of Ross's Land (Rossesland) friend and ally of Parry, father of Edward Tut Ross, Marquis of Harlaw; Anne's chief man in the Young Men's Play.

Ross, Edward Tut, Marquis of Harlaw son of Captain John Ross. His opposition to Zamorna and that of his close friend Ardrah, mirrors the antagonism of their parents towards the Duke of Wellington.

Ross's Land (later Rossesland) Kingdom of Captain John Ross, in the south-west of the Glass Town Federation.

Sdeath (S'death), Robert Patrick servant, alter ego, and evil motivator of Alexander Percy, whose father and wife he murders. His inability to be destroyed (he has a form of demonic immortality) reflects his origins as Chief Genius Branni; and his 'hideous' appearance (small stature, fiery red hair), quick temper, and cynicism reflect Branwell's caricature of himself, his own appearance, emotional behaviour, and increasing espousal of atheism.

Sneachi *see* Sneaky.

Sneaky (Sheachi), Alexander, King of Sneaky's Land replaces Napoleon as Branwell's Chief Man in the Young Men's Play. Father of the upright Fidena, the good-natured sometime-wayward Thornton, and Princesses Edith and Maria. Sneaky is a stern, conservative character and ally of Wellington.

Sneaky (Sneachi), John Augustus, Marquis of Rossendale eldest son of the Duke and Duchess of Fidena.

Sneaky (Sneachi), Prince John *see* Fidena, Prince John Sneachi.

Sneaky (Sneachi), Thornton Wilkin (Wilson), General Thornton brother to the Duke of Fidena, Princesses Edith and Maria Sneachi, and second son of the King of Sneachiesland; but disowned and disinherited by his family because of his wild youth. The good-natured Thornton is adopted by 'Old Girnington' and inherits his estate. Created general by his friend Zamorna, and made guardian of Lord Charles Wellesley.

Sneaky's Land (later Sneachiesland) kingdom of Alexander Sneaky, in the north of the Federation.

Soult, Alexander, Marquis of Marseilles, Duke of Dalmatia (pseudonym of Branwell) a poet with romantic inclinations, first known as

'Young Soult' and mocked by Charlotte as 'The Rhymer'; patronized by Zamorna and later made Angrian ambassador to Verdopolis.

St Clair, Earl noble Highland chief from Roslyn Castle, Sneaky's Land; Verdopolitan prime minister, friend of Wellington, and long-standing enemy of Northangerland.

Stumps Land (Stumps Island) and Monkey's Isle (Moncey's Island) islands south-west of Verdopolis; ruled by the former soldiers, Monkey and Stumps of the early Young Men's Play, they are considered a provincial backwater suitable only as a seaside resort for holidays and convalescence.

Thornton, General *see* Sneaky, Thornton.

Townshend, Charles (pseudonym of Charlotte) *see* Wellesley, Lord Charles Albert Florian.

Tree, Captain (pseudonym of Charlotte) famous Glass Town novelist, rival of Captain Bud and of Lord Charles Wellesley. Father of Sergeant Tree.

Tree, Sergeant John son of Captain Tree; Glass Town's chief bookseller and publisher.

Twelves the Twelve Young Men, original founders of Glass Town, including the four kings of the Federation.

Verdopolitan Union *see* Glass Town Federation.

Verdopolis (Great Glass Town) federal capital of the Glass Town Federation (later called Verdopolitan Union), situated in the Gulf of Guinea at the mouth of the Niger and opposite the island of Fernando Po. Distinguished by landmarks such as the Tower of All Nations, St Michael's Cathedral and Bravey's Inn. Its hinterland is the Verdopolitan Valley where the nobility own estates.

Vernon, Caroline teenage daughter of Northangerland and his former mistress Louisa Vernon. She lives in seclusion with her mother, who is a prisoner of Zamorna, at Eden Cottage near the city of Fidena, in the north of the Verdopolitan Union.

Warner, Howard Warner prime minister of Angria. Head of the oldest and most influential Angrian family; a contemporary and important ally of Zamorna, his relationship with his monarch is similar to that between the historical Duke of Wellington and Sir Robert Peel, on whom Warner is based.

Waterloo Palace residence of the Duke of Wellington in Verdopolis.

Wellesley, Arthur *see* Wellington, Duke of; and Zamorna, Duke of.

Wellesley, Arthur Julius, Lord Almeida infant son of Zamorna and his second wife, Marian Hume.

Wellesley, Ernest Edward Gordon, 'Fitz-Arthur' Zamorna's eldest child by his first wife Lady Helen Victorine, Baroness Gordon, who died in childbirth. Ernest is murdered by Quashia and his troops during the Angrian civil war.

Wellesley House home of the Duke of Zamorna in Verdopolis.

Wellesley, Lady *see* Wellington, Duchess of.

Wellesley, Lord Charles Albert Florian (principal pseudonym of Charlotte) younger son of the Duke of Wellington. A witty and cynical observer of Glass Town affairs, he plagues his older brother Zamorna by reporting (and elaborating) on his numerous love affairs and political intrigues. He gradually discards his royal lineage and as Charles Townshend, dandy and young man about town, he is responsible for most of Charlotte's Angrian novelettes.

Wellington, Arthur Wellesley, Duke of King of Wellington's Land and senior of the four Kings of the Glass Town Federation. Like his historical original, he is revered for his victory over Napoleon and military prowess. He presides over Glass Town events as Charlotte's chief man, but gradually adopts the role of elder statesman and stern father as his increasingly wayward eldest son Zamorna takes centre stage.

Wellington, Lady Catherine, Duchess of known for her kindness to young people, she dotes on her two sons, Arthur and Charles, and assists Marian Hume and Mina Laury. Like her original, she lives in retirement at the country estate of Mornington in Wellington's land.

Wellington's Land (later Wellingtonsland *or* Senegambia) ruled by the Duke of Wellington; the 'Irish' West of the Glass Town Federation, its geography resembles the English Lake District. Location of the family estates of many of the main characters, such as Mornington Court (Wellesley estate) and Percy Hall. It also has secluded estates such as Grassmere Manor.

Young Soult (pseudonym of Branwell) *see* Soult, Alexander.

Zamorna, Arthur Augustus Adrian Wellesley (Wellesly), Marquis of Douro, Duke of (early poetic pseudonym of Charlotte) eldest son of the Duke of Wellington; later King of Angria. As Marquis of Douro, he is noble and talented, an 'Apollo' in manly beauty, music, and poetry, and patron of the arts. As Zamorna and under the influence of Alexander Percy, his character develops into a cynical adulterer and ambitious political and military leader. His three wives (Helen Victorine Gordon, Marian Hume, and Mary Percy) all suffer as a consequence; and yet they and his long-suffering mistress Mina Laury remain loyal to him. After the War of Encroachment Zamorna is granted his own kingdom of Angria, where he builds his capital Adrianopolis and appoints Percy (now Northangerland) prime minister. When he is opposed by Ardrah and the Reformist Party from Verdopolis, Percy turns against him. Angria is invaded first by the Ashantees, then by Ardrah's army and by Arab troops under Jordan. Zamorna is captured and sent into exile by Northangerland. With the help of Fidena, Warner, and his loyal generals, Zamorna regains Angria.

Zamorna, Duchess of *see* Percy, Mary Henrietta.

Zamorna province in Angria, governed by Lord Castlereagh. The capital city, Zamorna, and Edwardston are both thriving industrial towns situated on the Olympian River.

GLOSSARY OF MAIN CHARACTERS AND PLACES IN THE GONDAL SAGA

The names of characters in Gondal are notoriously difficult to establish and almost as enigmatic as the plot. Several characters appear to have the same name or may be the same character at different stages in their life (see Alexander), and others may be referred to by several different names which are still subject to debate (see A.G.A.).

Alcona, Rosina an ambitious, haughty member of the Gondal aristocracy, possibly the same character as A.G.A. She is the cause of Julius Brenzaida's imprisonment in the 'Southern College' but later appears to have married him. She supports his campaigns for power in Gaaldine and mourns his death and burial in Angora in Gondal. She has been likened to Catherine Earnshaw in *Wuthering Heights*.

Alexander, Lord of Elbë lover and possibly husband of A.G.A. He dies in her arms on the shores of Lake Elmor, while recalling Elbë Hall in his distant sunny home in the south. A 14-year-old 'Alexander' appears in Emily's poem 'Fair was the evening and brightly the sun' (*see* Zenobia, Alexandrina); another 'Alexander' is in a dungeon in the Southern Palace of Instruction in April 1826; and Anne Brontë writes of an 'Alexander' whose surname is Hybernia.

A.G.A. Augusta [?Geraldine] Almeida (Almeda), Queen of Gondal; beautiful and ruthless in love and war. She is overthrown by rebellion, regains her crown but is assassinated. Her many lovers include Amedeus; Alexander, Lord Elbë; Alfred Sidonia (whom she marries and abandons); Julius Brenzaida (whom she probably married—see below); and Fernando De Samara. The 'G' in 'A.G.A.' has been read as 'Geraldine' and Geraldine S. and Rosina Alcona have been seen as the same person as A.G.A. (Ratchford, *Gondals Queen*, 26–7). If this is so, then A.G.A. married Brenziada after abandoning Sidonia. It has also been suggested that A.G.A. was 'reincarnated' after her death in May 1844 as A. G. Rochelle (Edward Chitham, *The Birth of Wuthering Heights* (London: Macmillan, 1998) 71).

Almedore (place) a kingdom in Gaaldine in the Gondal saga and name given to the Emperor Julius Brenzaida.

Almeida (Almeda), Augusta Geraldine, et al. *see* A.G.A.

Amedeus lover of A.G.A. and, with his previous lover Angelica, possibly the murderer of Julius Brenzaida.

Angelica raised as a child in the same house as A.G.A. in Gondal. She falls in love with a dark boy called Amedeus, who is lured away by the treacherous A.G.A. After A.G.A. tires of Amedeus, she sends both him and Angelica into exile where they live a life of crime, waiting to avenge themselves on

Gondal's Queen. Angelica later persuades Douglas, who has always loved her, to murder A.G.A.

Angora a kingdom in the north of Gondal, homeland of Julius Brenzaida, who is also referred to as 'Angora'. Another character in the Gondal saga is the Royalist Henry Angora.

Brenzaida, Emperor Julius sometimes called Julius Angora. A Gondal noble, he is imprisoned in 1825 for his involvement with the ambitious Rosina Alcona (whom he probably married), but later conquers Almedore and becomes King of Gaaldine. He then defeats Gerald Exina, after agreeing to an alliance, and becomes emperor of Gondal. Soon after, he is assassinated (possibly by Amedeus) in his palace, where Rosina lies ill. Other lovers include Geraldine Sidonia, whom he left grieving over their child in Zedora. *See also* A.G.A.

Douglas, M. lover of E. R. Gleneden and possibly the same man 'Douglas' who became a traitor and then, at the instigation of another lover Angelica, murderer of A.G.A.

Eldred W, Lord loyal retainer to A.G.A. and Captain of the Queen's Guard, he ruminates over her corpse and sends his followers after her murderer Douglas.

Exina a province in the south of Gondal, which has a sea-green standard. 'Exina' is the surname for several Gondal characters, including Arthur Exina, a noble who is imprisoned, and Gerald Exina, probably ruler of Exina province (*see* Brenzaida, Emperor Julius). Anne Brontë's characters, Eustace and Henry Sophona, also come from Exina.

Gaaldine a large island in the south Pacific, with a contrasting tropical landscape and climate to that of Gondal. Discovered by the Gondals, who divided the island into six kingdoms, held by constant warfare and revolution amongst themselves: Alexand(r)ia, Almedore, Esleraden, Ula, Zelona, and Zedora (the latter a province with a viceroy).

Geraldine black-haired, dark-eyed lover of Julius Brenzaida, whose child she bears. Persuaded by others, she no longer supports him politically, so he leaves her and returns to those who love him unreservedly. She is also referred to as 'Geraldine S.' and 'G.S.', possibly the same character as A.G.A.

Gleneden family name for a number of patriotic Gondal characters who helped restore peace in Gondal after a period of tyranny under Julius Brenzaida. References to them are cryptic. *See also* Unique Society.

Gondal a large island in the north Pacific, with Regina as its capital, possibly located on Lake Elderno. Gondal is divided into four parts: Gondal, Angora, Alcona, and Exina; its landscape and climate are similar to the Yorkshire moors. The country becomes torn by civil war between Royalists and Republicans.

Palace of Instruction place of education for the princes and princesses of Gondal. Beneath the Northern and Southern Colleges lie dungeons where the young nobility are often imprisoned and write poems on their prison walls. Even A.G.A., Gondal's Queen, suffers this fate at one time.

Rochelle, A.G. fair-haired girl, playmate of Julian M. Her parents are dead and she is imprisoned, tended by Julian. *See* A.G.A.

Samara, Fernando De a guitar player, different in temperament from the usual inhabitants of Gondal (yet similar to Heathcliff in *Wuthering Heights*). Although he pledges his love to the daughter of the family of Areon Hall in Exina, where he is raised, A.G.A. steals his heart; after an affair she sends him to a dungeon in the Gaaldine Caves. He escapes but, after looking at A.G.A.'s miniature, he commits suicide, his heart still ruled by 'the Tyrant'.

Sidonia, Lord Aspin, Alfred the fair-haired, blue-eyed lover of the dark A.G.A. He appears to have married her since their pictures hang side by side in his ancestral home. In his infatuation with A.G.A. who is disliked by his people, Sidona neglects his fair-haired daughter. He dies in England but his ghost haunts Aspin Castle.

Ula one of the five kingdoms of Gaaldine; ruled by four sovereigns.

Unique Society, the a group of Gondal characters who sail to 'Zedoras strand and Ula's Eden sky' in Gaaldine. Their names suggest they belong to the noble Gleneden family: R. Gleneden, Edmund, Mary, Flora, and possibly Arthur. Their loyalty and preference, however, are for Gondal's 'mists and moorlands drear', and while returning to Gondal they are shipwrecked on a desert island.

Zenobia, Alexandrina speaker of four of Anne Brontë's poems and possibly the same character as 'Alexandria Zenobia Hybernia'. She may be the girl Zenobia who, aged 13, promises to meet a boy 'Alexander' in Exina, Gondal, in two years' time (*see* Alexander, Lord of Elbë).

INDEX OF TITLES AND FIRST LINES

American Literature

British and Irish Literature

Children's Literature

Classics and Ancient Literature

Colonial Literature

Eastern Literature

European Literature

Gothic Literature

History

Medieval Literature

Oxford English Drama

Poetry

Philosophy

Politics

Religion

The Oxford Shakespeare

A complete list of Oxford World's Classics, including Authors in Context, Oxford English Drama, and the Oxford Shakespeare, is available in the UK from the Marketing Services Department, Oxford University Press, Great Clarendon Street, Oxford OX2 6DP, or visit the website at www.oup.com/uk/worldsclassics.

In the USA, visit www.oup.com/us/owc for a complete title list.

Oxford World's Classics are available from all good bookshops. In case of difficulty, customers in the UK should contact Oxford University Press Bookshop, 116 High Street, Oxford OX1 4BR.

Late Victorian Gothic Tales

JANE AUSTEN
Emma
Mansfield Park
Persuasion
Pride and Prejudice
Selected Letters
Sense and Sensibility

MRS BEETON
Book of Household Management

MARY ELIZABETH
BRADDON
Lady Audley's Secret

ANNE BRONTË
The Tenant of Wildfell Hall

CHARLOTTE BRONTË
Jane Eyre
Shirley
Villette

EMILY BRONTË
Wuthering Heights

ROBERT BROWNING
The Major Works

JOHN CLARE
The Major Works

SAMUEL TAYLOR
COLERIDGE
The Major Works

WILKIE COLLINS
The Moonstone
No Name
The Woman in White

CHARLES DARWIN
The Origin of Species

THOMAS DE QUINCEY
The Confessions of an English
    Opium-Eater
On Murder

CHARLES DICKENS
The Adventures of Oliver Twist
Barnaby Rudge
Bleak House
David Copperfield
Great Expectations
Nicholas Nickleby
The Old Curiosity Shop
Our Mutual Friend
The Pickwick Papers

ANTHONY TROLLOPE

The American Senator

An Autobiography

Barchester Towers

Can You Forgive Her?

The Claverings

Cousin Henry

The Duke's Children

The Eustace Diamonds

Framley Parsonage

He Knew He Was Right

Lady Anna

Orley Farm

Phineas Finn

Phineas Redux

The Prime Minister

Rachel Ray

The Small House at Allington

The Warden

The Way We Live Now

ANTON CHEKHOV

About Love and Other Stories
Early Stories
Five Plays
The Princess and Other Stories
The Russian Master and Other Stories
The Steppe and Other Stories
Twelve Plays
Ward Number Six and Other Stories

FYODOR DOSTOEVSKY

Crime and Punishment
Devils
A Gentle Creature and Other Stories
The Idiot
The Karamazov Brothers
Memoirs from the House of the Dead
Notes from the Underground and
   The Gambler

NIKOLAI GOGOL

Dead Souls
Plays and Petersburg Tales

ALEXANDER PUSHKIN

Eugene Onegin
The Queen of Spades and Other Stories

LEO TOLSTOY

Anna Karenina
The Kreutzer Sonata and Other Stories
The Raid and Other Stories
Resurrection
War and Peace

IVAN TURGENEV

Fathers and Sons
First Love and Other Stories
A Month in the Country